Researching and Writing in Law

Thomson Reuters (Professional) Australia Limited
100 Harris Street Pyrmont NSW 2009
Tel: (02) 8587 7000 Fax: (02) 8587 7100
LTA.Service@thomsonreuters.com
www.thomsonreuters.com.au
For all customer inquiries please ring 1300 304 195
(for calls within Australia only)

INTERNATIONAL AGENTS & DISTRIBUTORS

NORTH AMERICA
Thomson Reuters
Eagan
United States of America

ASIA PACIFIC
Thomson Reuters
Sydney
Australia

LATIN AMERICA
Thomson Reuters
São Paulo
Brazil

EUROPE
Thomson Reuters
London
United Kingdom

Researching and Writing in Law

by

TERRY HUTCHINSON

BA, LLB (Qld), DipLib (UNSW), MLP (QUT) PhD (Griffith)

Senior Lecturer, School of Law
Queensland University of Technology

Third Edition

LAWBOOK CO. 2010

Published in Sydney by

Thomson Reuters (Professional) Australia Limited ABN 64 058 914 668
    100 Harris Street, Pyrmont, NSW

First edition 2002
Second edition 2006

National Library of Australia
    Cataloguing-in-Publication entry

Hutchinson, Terry C. M.

Researching and writing in law/Terry Hutchinson.

3rd ed.

978 0 455 226781 (pbk.)

Includes index.

Legal research – Australia.
Legal research.
Academic writing.
Report writing.

340.072

Editor: Wendy Fitzhardinge
Senior Project Editor: Merilyn Shields
Product Developer: Jasmine Kemp
Publisher: Robert Wilson

Typeset in Legacy Serif and Legacy Sans, 9.5 on 11 point, by RE Typesetting, Woy Woy, NSW

Printed by Ligare Pty Ltd, Riverwood, NSW

This book has been printed on paper certified by the Programme for the Endorsement of Forest Certification (PEFC). PEFC is committed to sustainable forest management through third party forest certification of responsibly managed forests. For more info: www.pefc.org

PEFC™

PEFC/21-31-17

*I dedicate this third edition of my text
to the 'community of scholars' —
my colleagues and students who
have provided such support and inspiration*

Preface

This book is modelled on a postgraduate research unit that I have taught for several years within the Faculty of Law at the Queensland University of Technology. I was very much inspired and directed in establishing the postgraduate unit (and also the undergraduate research units developed in the early 1990s), by several main research texts, and I think it worthwhile to acknowledge this conceptual debt here. Foremost of these texts were the early editions of Enid Campbell's *Legal Research: Materials and Methods*,[1] Nick Moore's *How to Do Research*,[2] Ortrun Zuber-Skerritt's *Starting Research — Supervision and Training*[3] and Morris Cohen's *How to Find the Law*.[4] These and other writers have aided the development of my research skills, and for this reason I have added the "Further Reading" lists in each chapter. These lists provide readers with references to additional sources of expertise, innovative ideas and depth of knowledge in the many areas that are really only touched on in the text.

How to use the book and some presumptions

When I discuss the writing process in Chapter 8, I suggest that a writer needs to visualise their expected audience. In my mind's eye, the likely readers for this book are lawyers or law students who are involved in researching and writing whether it be for an undergraduate assignment, a masters by coursework paper, a journal article or a doctoral thesis. My expectation is that they will not necessarily read this book from cover-to-cover, but dip into it and use it when information and ideas are required quickly.

I should note a few self-imposed limitations on the scope of this undertaking. This is not an English grammar text, so any comments in that section are directly related to the legal framework, and stem from my experience in teaching and assessing legal work. Another obvious underlying assumption is that the reader has some familiarity with Australian sources of law, common law legal frameworks and precedent. Yet another assumption is that my readers will have had some exposure to legal theory.

---

1 Campbell E, Poh-York L and Tooher J, *Legal Research: Materials and Methods* (4 ed, Sydney: LBC Information Services, 1996)

2 Moore N, *How to Do Research* (3 ed, London: Library Association, 2000).

3 Zuber-Skerritt O, *Starting Research — Supervision and Training* (Brisbane: The Tertiary Education Institute, University of Queensland, 1992).

4 Cohen M, Berring R and Olsen K, *How to Find the Law* (9 ed, St Paul, Minn: West Publishing Company, 1989).

The Checklists cover all the Australian and the major overseas jurisdictions with a general segment at the beginning on research functions that are cross-jurisdictional.

1 Cross-jurisdictional reference sources

2 Commonwealth of Australia

3 Australian Capital Territory

4 New South Wales

5 Northern Territory

6 Queensland

7 South Australia

8 Tasmania

9 Victoria

10 Western Australia

11 England

12 Canada

13 United States

14 European Union Law

15 New Zealand

16 India

Aspects covered within each of the jurisdictions vary slightly depending on the local availability of materials. However, in the main, each includes the following information and in this order:

* an introduction to the jurisdiction
* a broad picture of law in the jurisdiction
* parliamentary publications
* Bills
* explanatory material about Bills
* subject index to legislation
* the commencement date of legislation
* egislation in full text
* updates for legislation
* subject index to delegated legislation
* full text of delegated legislation
* a subject index to cases
* full text of cases in the jurisdiction
* cases that have been judicially considered
* cases that have dealt with specific legislative sections

Within the Parliamentary Publications section, joint house publications are listed first followed by the Lower House and then the Upper House. Official or authorised publications are listed before unauthorised and commercial offerings. Paper versions are noted followed by the internet sites.

The emphasis is on current, not historical sources, and on free, internet-based sources in preference to those requiring a subscription, although these sources are listed selectively. For example, basic reference tools such as the encyclopaedias are included even though they are only available by subscription. Most of the United States sources are available on both Westlaw and LexisNexis. These subscription services have generally not been mentioned specifically for material in that jurisdiction. Both of these fee-based services also include an ever-expanding list of sources for Australia, England and Canada. These have not been noted directly.

I have dedicated this third edition to the 'community of scholars'. I am not quite sure who first coined this phrase but I first came across the term in John Gava's article, 'Scholarship and Community'.[5] In particular, 1 would like to express my gratitude to my research mentors, Professors David Gardiner, Michael A Adams, David Barker and Charles Sampford. In addition my thanks to Nigel Duncan, Professor Clive Bean, Alexandria McClintock, Natalie Cuffe and Joanna Fear for their helpful suggestions and for reviewing parts of the third edition prior to publication. I also wish to acknowledge and thank the research assistants who have worked with me on the Research Checklists over the years, including Mark Thomas, Tristan Sandon-Skousgaard, Harmony Adams, Pernilla Kvick, Karen Rutherford and Joshua Om Caeiro. My thanks also to those who worked on the manuscripts, particularly Margaret Hall, Suzanne Lewis and Safina Ahmed. I also want to express my gratitude to my family, my husband, John Leahy and my children, Patrick, Majella and Dominic for their support in my endeavours.

DR TERRY HUTCHINSON

Brisbane
January 2010

Acknowledgments

The following extracts attributed herein were reproduced with the kind permission of:

AGIS (Attorney-General's Information Service): www.ag.gov.au
- Sample entry from AGIS Record:
  http://www.ag.gov.au/agd/www/Agdhome.nsf/Page/RWP145A0CC6F5D96165CA256E
  EF001A1B7F?OpenDocument

Australian Government, Department of Education, Employment and Workplace Relations: www.dest.gov.au
- Council of Australian Law Deans (CALD), *Research Quality Framework: Responses to the Issues Paper* (2005).

Australianpolitics.com: www.australianpolitics.com
- Justices of the Australian High Court — Current

Carswell, a division of Thomson Canada Limited: www.carswell.com
- Jacqueline R Castel and Omeela K Latchman, *The Practical Guide to Canadian Legal Research* (2nd ed, 1996).

Commonwealth Copyright Administration, Intellectual Property Branch, Dept of Communications, Information Technology and the Arts
- D Pearce, E Campbell and D Harding, *Australian Law Schools: A Discipline Assessment for the Commonwealth Tertiary Education Commission, A Summary* (AGPS, Canberra, 1987).

Counselor Education and Supervision (CES) Journal (by the Ohio University): www.ohiou.edu/che/ces
- C Burnett, 'The supervision of doctoral dissertations using a collaborative cohort model' (1999) 39(1) *Counselor Education and Supervision* 46 as cited in F Zhao, 'Enhancing the Effectiveness of Research and Research Supervision Through Reflective Practice' UltiBASE.

Federation Press: www.federationpress.com.au
- M Kirby, 'Are We There Yet?' in B Opeskin and D Weisbrot (eds), *Promise of Law Reform* (2005).

FranklinCovey Co: www.franklincovey.com
- 'The Time Management Matrix' in S Covey, *The Seven Habits of Highly Effective People: Restoring The Character Ethic* (1989).

La Trobe University, School of Health Systems Sciences: www.latrobe.edu.au
- G Bammer, 'Multidisciplinary Policy Research — An Australian Experience' (1997) 15(1) *Prometheus* 27 (Paper presented at a symposium on strategies for facilitating multi-disciplinary public health policy research, School of Health Systems Sciences, La Trobe University, 23 May 1996).

Lawbook Co., part of Thomson Reuters (Professional) Australia Limited: www.thomsonreuters.com.au
- Commonwealth Law Reports (CLR).

LexisNexis Butterworths, Australia: www.lexisnexis.com.au

- D A Ipp, 'Judicial impartiality and judicial neutrality: Is there a difference?' (2000) 19 *Australian Bar Review* 212, quoting from Justice L'Heureux-Dube, 'Reflections on Judicial Independence, Impartiality and the Foundations of Equality', *CIJL Yearbook* vol vii 95.
- A Mason (then Chief Justice of the High Court of Australia), 'The use and abuse of precedent' (1998) 4 *Australian Bar Review* 93.

National Health and Medical Research Council: www.nhmrc.gov.au

- Australian Code for the Responsible Conduct of Research.

OECD Observer: www.oecdobserver.org

- J Caddy, 'Why citizens are central to good governance', *OECD Observer*, 31 October 2001, p 59.

Quality in Postgraduate Research (QPR): www.qpr.edu.au

- E Arthur, *The Commonwealth's role in assuring quality in postgraduate research education*, Quality in Postgraduate Research: Integrating Perspectives (Adelaide, University of Canberra, 2002), cited in M Kiley, *Quality in Postgraduate Research Overview* (2004): http://www.qpr.edu.au/overview.html.
- M Kiley, *Quality in Postgraduate Research Overview* (2004): http://www.qpr.edu.au/overview.html.
- H Pearse, *Encouraging timely doctoral completions: The implementation of the Research Training Scheme* (Research on Doctoral Education Forum, Deakin University, 2002), cited in M Kiley, *Quality in Postgraduate Research Overview* (2004): http://www.qpr.edu.au/overview.html.

Queensland University of Technology: www.qut.edu.au

- B Horrigan, 'Black holes in black letter law: Applying legal theory and fostering critical thinking in legal practice and teaching' (Unpublished Paper, 1999).
- *Master of Laws LWN048 Advanced Legal Research Study Guide*, Semester Two 2009.

Routledge & Kegan Paul, UK: www.routledge.co.uk

- L Scarman, *Law Reform: The New Pattern* (1968).

Southern Cross University Press, Lismore, New South Wales: www.scu.edu.au

- S Laske and O Zuber-Skerritt, 'Frameworks for postgraduate research and supervision: An overview' in O Zuber-Skerritt (ed), *Frameworks for Postgraduate Education* (1999).

University of Lagos, Faculty of Law: www.unilag.edu

- W Twining, *Taylor Lectures 1975 Academic Law and Legal Development* (1976).

University of New South Wales, Faculty of Law: www.unsw.edu.au

- G Mackenzie, 'A Question of Balance: A Study of Judicial Methodology, Perceptions and Attitudes in Sentencing' (PhD Thesis, 2001).

University of New South Wales Law Journal: www.unswlawjournal.unsw.edu.au

- A Lynch and G Williams, 'The High Court on Constitutional Law: The 2008 Statistics' (2009) UNSWLJ 181.

University of Queensland, Faculty of Law: www.uq.edu.au

- E Phillips, 'The PhD — Assessing quality at different states of its development' in O Zuber-Skerrit (ed), *Starting Research Supervision and Training* (Tertiary Education Institute, University of Queensland, 1992).

Merv Wilkinson

- M Wilkinson, 'Action Research: For People and Organisational Change' (Brisbane, 3rd ed, 1996).

Windsor Yearbook of Access to Justice (by the University of Windsor, Canada): www.uwindsor.ca

- C Boyle, and M MacCrimmon, 'To serve the cause of justice: disciplining fact determination' (2001) 20 *Windsor Yearbook of Access to Justice* 55.

Table of Contents

Preface vii

Acknowledgments xi

Part I — Formulating and Writing Your Legal Research Project. 1

1   Setting the Scene: Research and Writing in Context 5

2   Standard Doctrinal Research Methodologies. 35

3   Additional Legal Research Frameworks. 51

4   Basic Electronic Research Techniques. 79

5   Social Science Methodologies for Lawyers. 97

6   Formulating a Research Topic 137

7   Refining the Topic and Thesis 157

8   Legal Writing Basics. 195

Part II — Checklists for Locating and Validating the Law 221

1   General — *How Do You Find* 227

2   Australia — *How Do You Find* 261

3   Australian Capital Territory — *How Do You Find* 301

4   New South Wales — *How Do You Find* 309

5   Northern Territory — *How Do You Find*. 321

6   Queensland — *How Do You Find* 329

7   South Australia — *How Do You Find*. 347

8   Tasmania — *How Do You Find* 359

9   Victoria — *How Do You Find* 367

10   Western Australia — *How Do You Find* 379

11   England — *How Do You Find*. 387

12   Canada — *How Do You Find* 409

13   United States — *How Do You Find* 431

14   European Union Law — *How Do You Find*. 459

15   New Zealand — *How Do You Find* 483

16   India — *How Do You Find*. 497

Index 507

PART

I

Formulating and Writing
Your Legal Research Project

Part I — Table of Contents

1   Setting the Scene: Research and Writing in Context. 5
    1.1   What is Research? 5
            1.1.1   Pure basic research 6
            1.1.2   Strategic basic research. 6
            1.1.3   Applied research 6
            1.1.4   Experimental development 7
    1.2   What is Different About Legal Research? 7
    1.3   Changing Research Paradigms. 9
            1.3.1   Is doctrinal methodology part of the accepted legal
                    research paradigm?. 9
            1.3.2   What is a paradigm?. 10
            1.3.3   What facets form the current research paradigm for law?. 11
    1.4   Changing Contexts 12
            1.4.1   What legal forces have driven change?. 12
            1.4.2   The Australian higher education context 18
    1.5   Choosing a Methodology 21
    1.6   Expanded Legal Research Frameworks. 23
    1.7   Ethics in Research. 24
    1.8   Recording the Research Process. 27
    1.9   Reading and Critique 29
    1.10   Conclusion. 33

2   Standard Doctrinal Research Methodologies 35
    2.1   Standard Research Methods 39
    2.2   Doctrinal Research Model under a Positivist Tradition 40
            2.2.1   Sourcing Information 41
    2.3   Broad to Narrow 43
    2.4   Extending Existing Knowledge 43
            2.4.1   The case approach 44
            2.4.2   The legislative approach 44
            2.4.3   The keyword/fact approach. 44
            2.4.4   The legal words and phrases approach 45
            2.4.5   The looseleaf approach. 45
            2.4.6   The keyword/case/legislation approach 45
    2.5   Categorising Topics 46
    2.6   Using Checklists 46
    2.7   Using Flowcharts 47

2.8   Handy Research Hints. 48
2.9   How Much Research is Enough? 49
2.10   Conclusion. 49

3   **Additional Legal Research Frameworks** 51
3.1   Theoretical Research. 52
        3.1.1   Western legal tradition timeline. 53
        3.1.2   Jurisprudential method 61
3.2   Law Reform Research 63
        3.2.1   What is law reform and what topics are likely to be
                 covered by law reform bodies? 64
        3.2.2   In what form is law reform published?. 65
        3.2.3   How is this material used? 65
        3.2.4   What are the usual methods pursued by the law reform
                 commissions?. 66
3.3   Policy Research. 71
        3.3.1   Methodology for change 73
        3.3.2   Policy change cycle 75

4   **Basic Electronic Research Techniques.** 79
4.1   The Concept of Electronic Research and How It Works 79
4.2   Increasing Benefits 80
4.3   A Note on Formats. 82
        4.3.1   The internet 82
        4.3.2   Fee-based online services. 82
        4.3.3   Intranets. 82
        4.3.4   Bibliographic databases 82
        4.3.5   Full text databases 83
4.4   Overview of Australian Electronic Sources 83
4.5   International online services 84
4.6   Generic Search Techniques 86
        4.6.1   Overall structure of the databases. 86
        4.6.2   Choosing search terms 87
        4.6.3   Searching for your terms in specific fields. 90
        4.6.4   Use of logical operators and Boolean logic 91
        4.6.5   Use of positional operators. 93
        4.6.6   Use of truncation to include plurals and alternate endings
                 for search terms 93
        4.6.7   Provision for modification of searches 94
        4.6.8   Retrieval. 94
4.7   Planning Electronic Searches for Optimum Results. 95
4.8   Conclusion. 96

5   **Social Science Methodologies for Lawyers** 97
5.1   Why Should Lawyers Consider Using Social Science Methods and
        Empirical Data? 99
        5.1.1   In what areas can lawyers find social science methods useful? . . . 100
5.2   Reasons for Lawyers' Reluctance to Move Beyond the Doctrinal 100
5.3   The Role of Social Science in the Judicial Process. 102
5.4   An Overview of Quantitative v Qualitative Methodologies 106
        5.4.1   Quantitative research 107
        5.4.2   Qualitative research 107

5.5   The Quantitative Research Model and Methods. 107
    5.5.1   Surveys and questionnaire design 108
    5.5.2   A checklist for survey research in law 110
    5.5.2   Evaluating what you read and recognising error 112
5.6   Qualitative Research Models and Methods 112
5.7   Action Research 116
5.8   Lawyers Using Non-doctrinal Methods 117
    5.8.1   Comparative research 117
    5.8.2   Benchmarking. 123
    5.8.3   Citation analysis 124
    5.8.4   Content analysis 127
5.9   Triangulation 128
    5.9.1   Case studies of methodologies from theses 130
5.10 Conclusion. 133

6   Formulating a Research Topic 137
6.1   How Do You Choose a Topic and Formulate a Plan? 137
6.2   Brainstorming. 137
6.3   Heuristics. 139
6.4   De Bono's 'Thinking Hats' 143
6.5   Mind Mapping Your Project 144
6.6   Visual Demonstration of Ideas 147
    6.6.1   Fishbone diagrams 147
    6.6.2   Langrehr's designs. 148
    6.6.3   Using causes and effects mapping 150
    6.6.4   Using connections to map the scene 150
    6.6.5   If you need to go further 151
6.7   Horrigan's Project Analysis Matrix. 152
6.8   Conclusion. 155

7   Refining the Topic and Thesis 157
7.1   Developing and Refining the Topic 158
    7.1.1   Is the research area 'resource-rich'? 158
    7.1.2   Will the project 'work' given your stated parameters?. 159
    7.1.3   Will the project be achievable within your stipulated
           timeframe? 159
    7.1.4   Will the writing augment existing work? Is this a significant
           study in that the area requires further research? 159
    7.1.5   Does the area involve unresolved issues? 160
    7.1.6   Does the topic have enough scope (or too much scope) for
           your research goal?. 160
    7.1.7   Does your academic background fit the topic chosen? 160
    7.1.8   Have you read broadly enough 'around' the topic? 160
    7.1.9   Does your topic coincide with the research strengths of
           the faculty?. 161
    7.1.10 Do you have access to a supervisor with the knowledge of the
           area you want to work in and knowledge of what work has
           been done?. 161
    7.1.11 What are the likely outcomes?. 163
    7.1.12 Is the area likely to sustain your interest? 163
7.2   What About Originality?. 164

7.3   What Should You Include in the Research Proposal? 165
    7.3.1   What is your research background and what is the context
           in which you are situating your work? 166
    7.3.2   Research objectives? 167
    7.3.3   What about a hypothesis? 167
    7.3.4   What is the appropriate methodology and how do you plan
           to achieve your objectives? 168
    7.3.5   A meaningful title 168
    7.3.6   Publication of your research? 169
    7.3.7   Timelines or scheme of work? 170
    7.3.8   Budgeting. 173
7.4   Critiquing Your Own Proposal. 175
7.5   Writing a Summary or Abstract 177
7.6   Presenting Your Research to Your Peers 178
7.7   The Literature Review 181
7.8   Keeping a Research Diary 185
7.9   Conceptual Frameworks 186
7.10   Structuring the Final Paper 189
    7.10.1 But what of the actual layout of the chapters? 189
    7.10.11 Conclusion 191

8   Legal Writing Basics 195
8.1   What Are the Current Trends in Legal Writing? 195
8.2   Continual Development 196
8.3   What is Plain Legal Language? 197
8.4   How Do You Best Convey the Message? 198
    8.4.1   What is the purpose of your writing? 198
    8.4.2   Who is your intended audience? 198
    8.4.3   How do you organise your work? 201
    8.4.4   Legal essays 202
    8.4.5   Casenotes. 203
    8.4.6   Office research memos 204
8.5   How Do You Complete a First Draft? 205
8.6   Polishing, Rewriting and Revising the First Draft 208
8.7   Style and Grammar. 211
    8.7.1   Paragraph construction, punctuation, spelling and grammar 211
    8.7.2   Gender neutral language 213
    8.7.3   When to use quotes 213
    8.7.4   How do you acknowledge sources? 214
8.8   Conclusion. 217

1

Setting the Scene: Research and Writing in Context

The essential characteristic of research activity is that it leads to publicly verifiable outcomes which are open to peer appraisal.[1] Research and writing are interdependent activities. What is the point in uncovering new information without communicating it to others so that it can be read and used? How can the message be delivered successfully if the communication process is not effective and meaningful? These ideas form the basis for the material in this text.

This chapter overviews the expanding scope of legal research. The legal research banner is not one-dimensional. It includes both doctrinal and non-doctrinal methodologies, and covers the varied prisms of legal activity not encompassed in practice-oriented research conducted within traditional frameworks by solicitors and barristers. This text challenges the reader to broaden their view of possible research perspectives within the legal discipline area. This first chapter provides the groundwork for the topics covered later. The approach is based on a specific framework that includes:

* integrating the research and writing processes;
* looking at the research process rather than the research materials; and
* recognising the need for moving outside the narrow 'black letter' doctrinal research 'box'.

Legal research has progressed into a new era and, while the sources are more accessible, new skills and perspectives are required for the legal researcher to succeed in the new research environment.

1.1 What is research?

Legal research has become more sophisticated in the last decade. It is now a highly valued aspect of academic work. This change has occurred during a time when the number of university law schools has increased, and a new breed of career academics has replaced the practitioners who previously taught those entering the legal profession. As part of this change legal academics are required to compete and prove their worth within the academy — usually having to meet research criteria set down for those researching in the scientific fields. One result of this movement within legal education has been an increase in the number of lawyers holding post-graduate qualifications and, increasingly, doctoral

---

1   *2001 Higher Education, Research Data Collection-Specifications for Preparing Returns* (Higher Education Division, Department of Education, Training and Youth Affairs, Canberra, April 2001), 12. See also http://www.unisa.edu.au/res/data/HERDC.asp (5/11/2009).

qualifications. However, along the way there has been a need to establish that the type of research being carried out by legal academics is more than mere 'scholarship', that it is systematic, has an element of originality and will increase society's wellbeing — that the research has quality and real impact.

At this point, it is useful to take a step back and look at generally accepted definitions of research. The OECD definition of 'research and experimental development', for example, highlights the importance of creativity, originality, and systematic activity that increases the world's 'stock of knowledge'.[2] It applauds research that applies new knowledge in new ways. Largely in order to enhance statistical data collection on research and development, the Australian Standard Research Classification (ASRC)[3] has attempted to classify research undertaken in Australia. It has done this according to type of activity, research fields, courses and disciplines and socioeconomic objectives. The types of activity include the following:

* pure basic research;
* strategic basic research;
* applied research; and
* experimental development.

1.1.1 *Pure basic research*

Pure basic research is experimental or theoretical work undertaken primarily to acquire new knowledge without a specific application in view. It is carried out without looking for long-term economic or social benefits other than the advancement of knowledge and includes most humanities research.

1.1.2 *Strategic basic research*

Strategic basic research is experimental or theoretical work undertaken primarily to acquire new knowledge without a specific application in view, and is directed into specific broad areas in the expectation of useful discoveries. It provides the broad base of knowledge necessary for the solution of recognised practical problems.

1.1.3 *Applied research*

Applied research is original work undertaken to acquire new knowledge with a specific practical application in view. Its aim is to determine possible uses for the findings of basic research or to determine new methods or ways of achieving some specific and pre-determined objective.

---

2 OECD, *Frascati Manual: Proposed Standard Practice for Surveys on Research and Experimental Development* (Paris: OECD, 2002), 30.

3 See Australian Bureau of Statistics, *Australian Standard Research Classification* (ASRC 1998, 1297.0); http://www.abs.gov.au/ausstats/abs@.nsf/0/2d3b6b2b68a6834fca25697e0018 fb2d?OpenDocument (5/11/2009). For the current scheme, see Australian Bureau of Statistics, *Australian and New Zealand Standard Research Classification* (ANZSRC 2008, 1297.0); http://www.abs.gov.au/AUSSTATS/abs@.nsf/Latestproducts/809BF4F37565C37ECA25741 80004B6EA?opendocument (5/11/2009).

1.1.4 *Experimental development*

Experimental development is systematic work, using existing knowledge gained from research and/or practical experience, for creating new or improved materials, products, devices, processes or services. In the social sciences, experimental development may be defined as the process of transferring knowledge gained through research into operational programs.[4]

This classification aims to provide a national and international measure for the research being undertaken in all discipline areas, and also in government, universities and business within Australia and internationally. Much legal research 'fits' within the third category of applied research, being directed to specific problems and aiming for tangible outcomes for professional use. However, legal research can be difficult to classify because of its variable contexts and facets.

1.2 What is different about legal research?

Within the tertiary sector, various national review bodies have attempted to define the parameters of legal research. Foremost of these is the Pearce Committee, which reviewed Australian law schools and the legal research and publications emanating from the schools. They categorised research as encompassing:

1 Doctrinal research — 'Research which provides a systematic exposition of the rules governing a particular legal category, analyses the relationship between rules, explains areas of difficulty and, perhaps, predicts future developments.'

2 Reform-oriented research — 'Research which intensively evaluates the adequacy of existing rules and which recommends changes to any rules found wanting.'

3 Theoretical research — 'Research which fosters a more complete understanding of the conceptual bases of legal principles and of the combined effects of a range of rules and procedures that touch on a particular area of activity.'[5]

These categories reflect a conservative but realistic view of the limits within which legal writing had developed to this point. Doctrinal research is library-based, focusing on a reading and analysis of the primary and secondary materials. The primary materials are the actual sources of the law — the legislation and case law. The secondary materials include the commentary on the law found in textbooks and legal journals. Often, reference sources such as legal encyclopaedias, case digests and case citators are needed to index and access the primary sources.

Many doctrinal researchers tend to take a reformist approach but, traditionally, law reform-oriented research has been undertaken within law reform commissions. However, the reform process has become more open, with reform agendas being undertaken within individual government departments.

---

4 Australian Bureau of Statistics, *Australian and New Zealand Standard Research Classification* (ANZSRC 2008), Chapter 2; http://www.abs.gov.au/ausstats/abs@.nsf/Latestproducts/ 1297.0Main%20Features42008?opendocument&tabname=Summary&prodno=1297.0& issue=2008&num=&view= (5/11/2009).

5 Pearce D, Campbell E and Harding D ('Pearce Committee'), *Australian Law Schools: A Discipline Assessment for the Commonwealth Tertiary Education Commission* (1987), vol 3, 17.

Suggestions for reform aimed at the judiciary are now often included in articles in law reviews. A good example of this is the 'Before the High Court' segment in *The Sydney Law Review*, which provides an opportunity for legal academics and other commentators to provide their views on upcoming High Court decisions.

Theoretical, philosophical legal writing has usually formed a separate category — the province of jurisprudence. Recent theorists have endeavoured to bridge the gap between the practical and the theoretical by emphasising how underlying rationales are relevant to the real world. In fact, the unfolding critiques have accelerated this process as they are based in unpacking the assumptions lying behind law's objectivity and, in doing so, opening jurisprudence to a new era.

The 1982 landmark study on the state of legal research and scholarship in Canada, the *Arthurs Report*, includes a fourth category covering non-doctrinal methodologies:

4 Fundamental research — 'Research designed to secure a deeper understanding of law as a social phenomenon, including research on the historical, philosophical, linguistic, economic, social or political implications of law.'[6]

This type of research acknowledges the need for lawyers to understand the implications and effects of the law on society. In doing so, many of the social science methodologies have been used, either through collaboration with quantitative researchers or by law researchers using social science methodologies (such as survey work) to investigate issues. Sometimes lawyers have simply used statistics freely available from governmental organisations to enhance their views on the law's operational aspects.[7]

The Council of Australian Law Deans (CALD) in their Submission in Response to the Research Quality Framework Issues Paper tried to address some of the basic definitional issues raised in the earlier research reports and still considered fundamental to the main arguments. They stipulated that:

> The breadth of the idea of fundamental legal research illustrates the point about overlapping categories. Legal research today may be thought to be considerably broader than the tripartite classification of the Pearce Report, as it embraces *empirical* research (resonating with the social sciences), *historical* research (resonating with the humanities), *comparative* research (permeating all categories), research into the *institutions* and *processes* of the law, and *inter-disciplinary* research (especially, though by no means exclusively, research into *law and society*). The Pearce Report did not really capture these extended elements of legal research, yet in some ways they are not so much new categories as new or newly-emphasised perspectives or methodologies. They highlight law as an intellectual endeavour rather than as a professional pursuit, though the latter is undoubtedly enriched by the former.[8]

---

6 Social Sciences and Humanities Research Council of Canada, *Law and Learning: Report to the Social Sciences and the Humanities Research Council of Canada by the Consultative Group on Research and Education in Law* (1983), 66.

7 See, for example, the Australian National Data Service (ANDS) http://ands.org.au/ (5/11/2009).

8 Council of Australian Law Deans, *Research Quality Framework (RQF): Responses to the Issue Paper* (2005) http://www.dest.gov.au/NR/rdonlyres/62C38170-6F41-45F1-9180-D0065FB 33089/6011/RQF010117CALD.pdf (5/11/2009), 5. See also QUT Faculty of Law, *Legal Research Profile* (1992).

The Submission attempted to delineate the existing categories of legal research but admitted that this was too difficult, 'the flavour of the richness and diversity of legal research in Australia today may best be sampled by actually perusing collected outputs.'[9]

All attempts at categorisation in legal research have recognised the primacy of the doctrinal methodology. This stems from the intrinsic need for lawyers to have the ability to locate, analyse, synthesise and critique the primary materials of the law, as well as the historical connection between the profession and practice. It is an important requirement for law practitioners to have the ability to find and apply the law. These are basic doctrinal legal research skills.

1.3   Changing research paradigms

1.3.1   *Is doctrinal methodology part of the accepted legal research paradigm?*

The questions emerging from these changes are then firstly 'Does legal research have an accepted legal paradigm?' and, if so, 'Are the changes spurring a change in the paradigm?' It has been suggested in the past that one of the main difficulties facing legal scholars is the lack of a legal research paradigm.[10] Without a paradigm, Peter Ziegler warns that all factors may seem equally relevant. All research, including every exploration of case law or legislation, may be equally random and equally valid. This can lead to 'neological seduction' – the seduction of the new or the latest theoretical fashion.[11] Ziegler suggests that in the scientific world paradigms involve two criteria:

1   theories that are sufficiently unprecedented to attract an enduring group of adherents away from the existing/competing concepts; and

2   theories that are sufficiently open-ended to leave reconciliation of the rest of the discipline's domain to be resolved.

In the scientific (or social science) world, parsimonious research is then carried out to examine the implications of the new theory. Scientific method has traditionally retained its strict rules as a quality control mechanism. Theories tend to emanate from earlier research, and are then developed and tested under conditions that can be replicated to re-affirm their validity. Citation patterns can be used as a valid test of a cumulative research tradition. However, Ziegler warns that without a 'steering factor' or paradigm, there is no direction and guidance for research efforts, and no basis for selection of the right questions and data sources.[12]

---

9   Council of Australian Law Deans, *Research Quality Framework (RQF): Responses to the Issue Paper* (2005) http://www.dest.gov.au/NR/rdonlyres/62C38170-6F41-45F1-9180-D0065FB 33089/6011/RQF010117CALD.pdf (5/11/2009), 5.

10   Ziegler P, 'A general theory of law as a paradigm for legal research' (1988) 51 September *The Modern Law Review* 569.

11   Ziegler P, 'A general theory of law as a paradigm for legal research' (1988) 51 September *The Modern Law Review* 569 at 578.

12   Ziegler P, 'A general theory of law as a paradigm for legal research' (1988) 51 September *The Modern Law Review* 569 at 578.

1.3.2 *What is a paradigm?*

Some would refer to a paradigm as a 'unifying rationale'; that is, some thing or some idea giving direction within a discipline. Paradigms form a model or pattern 'based on a set of rules that defines boundaries and specifies how to be successful within those boundaries'.[13] Success within the profession among the adherents tends to be measured within these paradigm boundaries.

One of the main exponents of the idea of paradigms was Thomas Kuhn, who wrote of the overthrow of old systems of thought by new theories in scientific fields.[14] Kuhn viewed paradigms as a shared frame of reference among researchers that could be upset by new revelations leading to generational struggles between young and old researchers.[15] Thus, paradigms are shared worldviews, which determine what topics are 'suitable' to study, what methodologies are acceptable, and what criteria may be used to judge success.

There are other definitions of paradigms available as well. John Jones' description of paradigms as 'taken-for-granted mind sets' presents a more accessible and tangible view.[16] According to this view, socialisation into the discipline is instrumental in ensuring that the practitioners and academics take on these 'ways of knowing'.[17]

When paradigm shifts take place, either gradually or suddenly, those wedded to old paradigms are left behind. New ways are found to approach problems. This happened when the car replaced horses as transport. It happened when the keyboard replaced the fountain pen, photocopiers replaced roneo machines and emails replaced letters. The development of technology is continually presenting a changing paradigm throughout all disciplines and range of activities; none more so than in research, and legal research in particular.

Every research project is based on and developed within an underlying paradigm. It is the 'overarching framework of ideas' behind the project that will be used to 'define what the problem is and how it is to be addressed'.[18] Often, the research paradigm lies unacknowledged — it is not articulated. As a result, the research may become dysfunctional. Action researchers, for example, may be faced with a disparity between the paradigm of action research itself and academic discipline expectations. Action research incorporates a deep belief in

13 Scott Fogler H and Le Blanc SE, *Strategies for Creative Problem Solving* (New Jersey: Prentice Hall PTR, 1995), 15.

14 Kuhn T, *The Structure of Scientific Revolutions* (3 ed, Chicago: University of Chicago Press, 1996).

15 An incremental change in the scientific paradigm, for example, took place when Robin Warren and Barry Marshall proved their Nobel Prize winning theory that stomach ulcers are caused by bacteria and not stress.

16 Jones J, 'Undergraduate students and research' in Zuber-Skerritt O, *Starting Research — Supervision and Training* (Brisbane: The Tertiary Education Institute, University of Queensland, 1992), 54.

17 Jones J, 'Undergraduate students and research' in Zuber-Skerritt O, *Starting Research — Supervision and Training* (Brisbane: The Tertiary Education Institute, University of Queensland, 1992), 54.

18 Curtain R, 'The Australian Public Policy Research Network: Promoting New Approaches to Public Policy' (2001) December 102 *Canberra Bulletin of Public Administration* 5 at 6.

the researcher becoming part of the project, while not necessarily retaining power in determining the direction of the research cycles. This may conflict with the expectations of supervisors and examiners in regard to the proper development of a written thesis. Higher degree students may feel powerless to change the traditional research paradigm expectations in the short term. However, fashions and expectations can and do change, however slowly. This culture clash is evident in the disparity in general expectations of research undertaken for the professional doctorate (SJD) and for a PhD. Examiners and supervisors have needed to acknowledge the difference between the two, and tailor their expectations accordingly.

1.3.3 *What facets form the current research paradigm for law?*

Assuming these definitions are correct, a paradigm would need to encompass more than a mere methodology, such as doctrinal research. Certainly, in law, research success has tended to be measured within a doctrinal framework that is based on the tracing of common law precedent and legislative interpretation and change. This has been one aspect of the dominant 'paradigm'. It would also seem to encompass more than an underlying philosophy, such as liberalism, with its ideas of the primacy of the individual, individual self-determination, and rationalism. These all pervade the western legal tradition which has been inherited from Britain. The prevalent view of law as objective and neutral is also part of this paradigm. Positivism, with its view of law as being 'what is' rather than what 'could be' or 'should be' also forms part of the paradigm.

However, the dominant legal paradigm is changing. A more outward-looking focus is encompassing interdisciplinary approaches to methodology. Internationalisation, globalisation and economic rationalism promoting global market views are inspiring a less cloistered or chauvinistic approach to legal problems. These indicate changing paradigms that need to be acknowledged and incorporated into the way lawyers approach problem-solving. The traditional model of legal research has tended to embrace practice-oriented research. Increasingly, the extension of this paradigm includes reflection on knowledge-in-practice. This is a way of translating textbook knowledge combined with good old-fashioned 'know-how' or knowing-in-action, and the immediate reflecting-in-action which takes place when a practitioner is presented with a problem. This results in learning through reflection-on-action. A research process such as this is becoming an important link between practice and research.[19]

Thus, when choosing a legal research topic, it would seem appropriate to be mindful of existing paradigms and to try to adhere to the scholarly expectations of your chosen research paradigm. Of course, it is always necessary to acknowledge existing research endeavour and to structure your research so that it in some way references and builds on what has been done previously. In doing this, it may be possible to seek out new paradigms and new ways of 'seeing' within the legal environment. However, it is still vital to acknowledge the existing foundations before building new versions of the truth.

---

19 Schon D, *The Reflective Practitioner: How Professionals Think in Action* (US: Basic Books, 1983); Brockbank A and McGill I, *Facilitating Reflective Learning in Higher Education* (Philadelphia: SRHE and Open University Press, 1998), Chapter 5.

1.4 Changing contexts

The last twenty years has seen a myriad of changes in the overall context of Australian law. On top of this, there has been a series of transformations in the tertiary sector. These have all changed the face of legal research, and have been played out on a stage where the technological revolution forms the backdrop.

1.4.1 *What legal forces have driven change?*

Historically, England was our closest trading partner and this affected Australian law, particularly commercial law.[20] Gradually, trade directions shifted to Japan, China, the United States and the European Union, with closer economic ties being forged with our geographic neighbours, New Zealand and the Asian-Pacific, and more recently the Indian Rim nations. Other changes have pushed Australian law away from its predominantly British orientation. These include the abolition of appeals to the Privy Council and the corresponding change in attitude to the use of precedent from other foreign courts. One reason behind this change in direction has been Britain's decision to join the European Union.

Another reason for change lies in the less closed view of the law demonstrated by the High Court in the last decades of the twentieth century. No longer simply prepared to 'declare' the common law, the High Court began to be more open to policy considerations and more inclined to consider whether the law fitted modern Australian conditions. Thus, there has been a gradual trend away from an adherence to the traditional British-based common law, and an increasing recognition of the relevance of law from comparative common law jurisdictions, predominantly the United States, Canada, and New Zealand.

Australian common law was inherited from Britain, but often insufficient consideration was given by the courts to its suitability to Australian conditions.[21] Inadequate consideration was also given to the interaction and balance of the British-based common law and new Australian legislation. Australian legislation has never had a completely British basis. As early as the nineteenth century, the influence of European and North American ideas, such as universal suffrage, juvenile courts and industrial arbitration, were accepted and infused. Other legislation, such as the Torrens System of land tenure, was particularly devised for Australian conditions.

The 1970s saw the enactment of much new legislation, such as the *Family Law Act 1975* (Cth) and the *Trade Practices Act 1974* (Cth), which encroached into areas previously covered by derivative common law. Increasingly, legislative models of North American origin were also adopted. Trade practices, consumer protection, freedom of information, and recovery of the proceeds of crime, are but examples.[22] Other legislation, such as the *Racial Discrimination Act 1975* (Cth), was enacted to comply with international obligations.

20 Sutton KCT, *Sales and Consumer Law in Australia and New Zealand* (4 ed, Sydney: The Law Book Company Limited, 1995), 3.

21 See, for example, *State Government Insurance Commission v Trigwell* (1978) 142 CLR 617 and see generally, Finn P, 'Statutes and the common law' (1992) 22 *Western Australian Law Review* 7.

22 Although not a direct use of US legislation, the *Trade Practices Act 1974* (Cth) reflects the common approach to commercial problems; in this case, attempts to restrict competition. See *Sherman Act 1890* (US); *Clayton Act 1914* (US) and various amending Acts.

In any case, in 1973 the United Kingdom had joined the European Economic Community, and thus agreed to apply and be subject to the laws of the Communities, including the Treaty of Rome and the European Court of Justice. This led Chief Justice Mason (as he then was) to comment:

> The pervasive impact of European law and legal thinking on the courts of the United Kingdom will necessarily qualify and diminish the value which English case law has for us as we continue to develop the common law for Australia, and also to interpret our own statutes which are no longer closely modelled on United Kingdom statutes.[23]

Appeals to the Privy Council from all Australian courts including State courts ended with the passage of the *Australia Acts* in 1986.[24] Appeals from the High Court had stopped earlier with the enactment of the *Privy Council (Limitation of Appeals) Act 1968* and the *Privy Council (Appeals from the High Court) Act 1975*. However, a right of appeal to the Privy Council remained from State courts, in matters governed by State law, until 1986.

In *Cook v Cook*, in the joint judgments of Justices Mason, Wilson, Deane, and Dawson, the High Court commented:

> Subject, perhaps, to the special position of decisions of the House of Lords given in the period in which appeals lay from this country to the Privy Council, the precedents of other legal systems are not binding and are useful only to the degree of the persuasiveness of their reasoning.[25]

Therefore, foreign precedent is used for guidance in the drafting and interpretation of legislation and in legislative reform. Foreign case law is used to inform decisions in our courts.[26] The courts are identifying values that can be imported into our legal system from decisions in foreign countries. However, Australian courts are not simply accepting these legal ideas and decisions outright, but are screening acceptance by reference to their 'fit' with the domestic law.[27]

In addition, Australia has become party to hundreds of international agreements. Many of these agreements have their origin in the increasing focus on international rights, which became evident after the Second World War. These treaties and conventions have affected Australia's domestic law and, incidentally, brought Australia into the purview of the world. Some have been enacted directly by legislation. Until recently, the general rule had been that:

> Unless specifically incorporated by a valid federal law, international rules (whether of treaties or of customary law) are not, as such, part of Australian domestic law.[28]

---

23 Mason A, 'The use and abuse of precedent' (1988) 4 *Australian Bar Review* 93 at 108.

24 *Australia Act 1986* (Cth) and the *Australia Act 1986* (UK).

25 *Cook v Cook* (1986) 162 CLR 376 at 390.

26 See *Environment Protection Authority v Caltex Refining* (1993) 178 CLR 477, where the High Court examined US, UK, Canadian and New Zealand authorities in deciding whether an incorporated company was entitled to a privilege against self-incrimination in the Australian context.

27 *Renard Constructions v Minister for Public Works* (1992) 26 NSWLR 234.

28 Kirby M, 'The role of the judge in advancing human rights by reference to international human rights norms' (1988) 62 *Australian Law Journal* 514.

Some treaties have been found to conflict with existing legislation leading to an extension of the Federal Government's powers using the external affairs powers. Nick Toonen's application to the United Nations Human Rights Committee regarding the Tasmanian criminal sanctions for homosexuality was an example of this. Using the provisions of the First Optional Protocol of the International Covenant on Civil and Political Rights, Toonen was able to take a complaint to an international forum which culminated in the passing of federal legislation — the *Human Rights (Sexual Conduct) Act 1994* (Cth). In another example, the Commonwealth government has ratified the *United Nations Convention on the Rights of the Child*, but it has not been legislated into law in Australia. Despite this, there is a reporting mechanism associated with the *UN Convention on the Rights of the Child*. All States' parties are obliged to submit regular reports to the UN Committee on the Rights of the Child describing how the rights are being implemented. The Committee examines each report and addresses its concerns and recommendations to the State party in the form of 'concluding observations'. Recently it has voiced its concerns about an aberration in Queensland where children who are 17 years old are included in the adult justice system rather than dealt with under juvenile legislation as occurs in the other Australian States.[29]

Values from international agreements have been imported into the common law. Take for example, the *Mabo case*,[30] where reference was made to the *Racial Discrimination Act* (Cth) implementing the *Convention on the Elimination of All Forms of Racial Discrimination*. In the case of *Teoh v Minister for Immigration, Local Government and Ethnic Affairs*, the High Court held that the ratification of a convention, in this case the *United Nations Convention on the Rights of the Child*, was an adequate foundation for a legitimate expectation — that administrators in the government would act in conformity with that convention. Justices Mason and Deane commented that:

> The provisions of an international convention to which Australia is a party, especially one which declares universal fundamental human rights, may be used by the courts as a legitimate guide in developing the common law rights.[31]

Therefore, international and comparative law is affecting Australian law in many different ways. There are the conventions and treaties directly enacted into legislation, sometimes allowing the federal government to legislate in areas by rights belonging within State jurisdiction. There is the opportunity for Australian law to be judged in terms of its human rights status by international forums. There is the use of values identified from international agreements to inform the common law, and the use of universal fundamental rights as a guide in developing the common law.

---

29 UN Committee on the Rights of the Child Fortieth Session Consideration of Reports Submitted by States under Article 44 of the Convention Concluding observations: Australia (20/10/2005). CRC/C/15/Add.268, 16. http://www.unhchr.ch/tbs/doc.nsf/(Symbol)/CRC. C.15.Add.268.En?OpenDocument (5/11/2009). And see generally Hutchinson Terry C, 'Being Seventeen in Queensland' (2007) 32 (2) *Alternative Law Journal* 81.

30 *Mabo v The State of Queensland (No 2)* (1992) 175 CLR 1.

31 *Teoh v Minister for Immigration, Local Government and Ethnic Affairs* (1995) 183 CLR 273 at 288. But now see also the more conservative views expressed in *Re Minister for Immigration and Multicultural Affairs; Ex parte Lam* (2003) 214 CLR 1.

In 1991, in *Smith Kline & French Laboratories (Aust) Ltd v The Commonwealth*,[32] constitutional validity of the statute which substituted a special leave requirement for the previous monetary qualifications for appeal to the High Court was upheld, thus reserving to the High Court 'the power to affect the general direction of our law'.[33] The alternative would have been to simply raise the monetary criterion and would have meant the court's time would be totally taken up with large commercial and property law cases — what Justice Kirby has referred to as 'elaborate disputes about debt recovery'.[34] In *Nguyen v Nguyen*,[35] the High Court threw the onus back on the Supreme and Federal Courts to avoid a rigid adoption of outmoded principles where there was no right of appeal to the High Court.

> This court has never regarded itself as bound by its own decisions, which is all the more appropriate now that it is a court of last resort for all purposes. There is a point of view that different considerations should govern the situation of an intermediate court of appeal. But even if that view were correct, now that appeals to the High Court are by special leave only, the appeal courts of the Supreme Courts of the states and of the Federal Court are, in many instances, courts of last resort for all practical purposes. In these circumstances, it would seem inappropriate that the appeal courts of the Supreme Courts and of the Federal Court should regard themselves as strictly bound by their own decisions. In cases where an appeal is not available or is not taken to this court, rigid adherence to precedent is likely on occasions to perpetuate error without, as experience has shown, significantly increasing the corresponding advantage of certainty.

In the 1980s and 1990s, the High Court adopted a less formalist approach to its role — a legal 'Reformation'.[36] The High Court began to develop the law to reflect Australian society rather than merely following British approaches. This change of approach was tied to the changing composition of the High Court bench. 'Old Testament'[37] jurisprudence consisting of a conservative approach which treated the law as a closed logical system, where the correct answer was available to be 'found' via a process of induction or deduction, gradually changed to an approach that included considerations of policy, public interest, justice and equity. There was an acknowledgment of substance rather than form in the court's decisions. Equity and principles of natural justice were given more prominence. The tracking of the changing views of the members of this highest and most powerful court in the Australian system is a necessary tool in the legal research process. The same is true for other jurisdictions. It is always most useful to be aware of the composition and prevalent philosophy of the highest court in the legal system in which you are researching.

---

32 *Smith Kline & French Laboratories (Aust) Ltd v The Commonwealth* (1991) 173 CLR 194.

33 Kirby M, 'Changes seen, foreseen and unforeseen' (1993) 4 (2) *Legal Education Review* 299 at 309.

34 Kirby M, 'Changes seen, foreseen and unforeseen' (1993) 4 (2) *Legal Education Review* 299 at 310.

35 *Nguyen v Nguyen* (1990) 169 CLR 245 at 269.

36 Kirby M, 'Judicial activism? A riposte to the counter-reformation' (2004) 24 *Australian Bar Review* 1 at 8.

37 Kirby M, 'Judicial activism? A riposte to the counter-reformation' (2004) 24 *Australian Bar Review* 1 at 2.

The composition of the High Court has changed significantly in the last five years. There have been several retirements and new appointments. Justice Mary Gaudron, the first woman appointed to the Court, retired from the bench in 2003 and Justice Michael McHugh retired in November 2005. Justice Michael Kirby, who developed the reputation for being the most-published but also the most dissenting judge of the High Court in recent times, retired in February 2009.[38] Three new appointments were made to the Court by the Howard Liberal government within a short period, these being Justice Hayne (September 1997), Justice Callinan (February 1998) and Chief Justice Murray Gleeson (May 1998). John Howard's government appointed another three judges before losing office in 2008. The Labor government under the leadership of Kevin Rudd has made three appointments including the new Chief Justice Robert French. The most recent appointment is Justice Virginia Bell who brings the number of women on the current bench to three.

Justices of the Australian High Court — Current[39]

No	Name	Date Appointed	Prime Minister at time of appointment	Party in Govt at time of appointment
1	Robert French (Chief Justice)	Sep 01, 2008–	Kevin Rudd	ALP
2	William Gummow	1995–	Paul Keating	ALP
3	Kenneth Hayne	1997–	John Howard	Liberal
4	John Dyson Heydon	Feb 11, 2003–	John Howard	Liberal
5	Susan Crennan	Nov 08, 2005–	John Howard	Liberal
6	Susan Kiefel	Sept 03, 2007–	John Howard	Liberal
7	Virginia Bell	Feb 03, 2009–	Kevin Rudd	ALP

The High Court judges are able to take an individual course in their actions. Judgments are at times unanimous but there are often dissenting or concurring opinions provided. Andrew Lynch and George Williams in their latest study of the Court have commented that:

> Dissent remains rare for the majority of serving Justices. Justice Crennan has dissented just four times in her first three years of service. Justices Gummow and Hayne continue their long pattern of rarely speaking from the minority position and Heydon J has not repeated his 15 per cent of dissenting opinions of 2006. Justice Kiefel dissented six times which, while hardly a staggering amount, is, in this company, nevertheless notable — particularly in her first year on the Court. Even so, it hardly seems likely that she will assume the mantle of the recently-departed Kirby J as a regular outlier from the Court's opinion.[40]

Once a judge is on the bench, there is often no correlation between the conservatism or otherwise of the government appointing the judge and the judge's decisions.

---

38 Lynch A and Williams G, 'The High Court on Constitutional Law: The 2003 Statistics' (Paper Presented at the Constitutional Law Conference Art Gallery of New South Wales, Sydney, Friday 20 February 2004).

39 http://australianpolitics.com/constitution/highcourt/high-court-judges.shtml (5/11/2009).

40 Lynch A and Williams G, 'The High Court on Constitutional Law: The 2008 Statistics' (2009) 32 *University of New South Wales Law Journal* 181 at 188.

Such changes on the bench have had sometimes profound effects on the outcomes of litigation heard by the Court. The new century witnessed the Coalition appointed High Court taking a more formal and legalistic line in its judgments than its predecessors in the late 1980s. An example is the different decisions reached on similar issues by differently composed courts in the cases of *Gould v Brown* and *Re Wakim; Ex parte McNally*.[41] The general tenor of the decisions has been conservative and literal. In *Al-Kateb v Godwin*[42] the High Court upheld the validity of provisions of the *Migration Act 1958* providing for indefinite detention of people who had been denied asylum but were unable to be deported because no country would receive them. The Court also in *Fardon v Attorney-General for the State of Queensland*[43] upheld the validity of the *Dangerous Prisoners (Sexual Offenders) Act 2003* (Qld) which was an Act empowering Queensland courts to order continuing detention of persons convicted of serious sexual offences after expiry of their sentence where there is an 'unacceptable risk' of the prisoner committing a serious sexual offence in the future. Thus, there have been forces pushing for a 'Counter-Reformation'[44] by 'old style formalists' and a return to 'strict and complete legalism'.[45] However, it appears that this has not been entirely successful and instead we are witnessing what Justice Kirby has termed a 'Concordat' consisting of judicial creativity within constraints which other commentators have termed a 'new legalism'.[46] In this process, there has been a tendency towards individual reasons for judgments rather than one combined majority judgment and to comparative and cross-jurisdictional discussion and an increasing number of references to academic commentary.[47] Other commentators have been more critical of the 'cautious approach' of the court especially in relation to constitutional law.[48] They have suggested that 'the Gleeson Court is unlikely to be remembered as a leading era in the development of Australian constitutional jurisprudence' and that 'major opportunities' to develop principles and doctrine 'have not been fully grasped'.[49] It is too early to predict the direction the current court might take though the recent case of *CAL No 14 Pty Ltd v Motor Accidents Insurance Board; CAL No 14 Pty Ltd v Scott*[50] with its shift to personal responsibility in negligence cases suggests a stronger approach.

---

41 *Gould v Brown* (1998) 193 CLR 346 and *Re Wakim; Ex parte McNally* (1999) 198 CLR 511.

42 *Al-Kateb v Godwin* (2004) 208 ALR 124; (2004) 78 ALJR 1099.

43 *Fardon v Attorney-General for the State of Queensland* (2004) 210 ALR 50; (2004) 78 ALJR 1519.

44 Kirby M, 'Judicial activism? A riposte to the counter-reformation' (2004) 24 *Australian Bar Review* 1 at 8.

45 Kirby M, 'Judicial activism? A riposte to the counter-reformation' (2004) 24 *Australian Bar Review* 1 at 13.

46 Kirby M, 'Judicial activism? A riposte to the counter-reformation' (2004) 24 *Australian Bar Review* 1 at 13; Patapan H, 'High Court Review 2001: Politics, Legalism and the Gleeson Court' (2002) 37 (2) *Australian Journal of Political Science* 241 at 243.

47 Orr G, 'Comments: Verbosity and richness: current trends in the craft of the High Court' (1998) 6 *Torts Law Journal* 21.

48 Lynch A and Williams G, 'The High Court on Constitutional Law: The 2008 Statistics' (2009) 32 *University of New South Wales Law Journal* 181 at 193.

49 Lynch A and Williams G, 'The High Court on Constitutional Law: The 2008 Statistics' (2009) 32 *University of New South Wales Law Journal* 181 at 193.

50 [2009] HCA 47 (10 November 2009).

The Australian legal context therefore is not static. Legal researchers, while being mindful of the overriding importance of precedent and stability within the system, also need to be able to place their research agenda within a relevant context. This context consists of various factors including politics, society, prevalent economic and social theoretical forces as well as the dominant judicial reasoning perspectives within the High Court. The Timeline in Chapter Three will also assist you in determining your project's context.

1.4.2 *The Australian higher education context*

The Australian higher education sector is also undergoing change that affects research programming. General restructuring of Australian universities began with the Dawkins reforms in the 1980s. The Coalition Government's Green Paper *New knowledge, new opportunities: A discussion paper on higher education research and research training*[51] and then the White Paper *Knowledge and innovation: A policy statement on research and research training*[52] took this restructuring further. There was a growth in the number of university law faculties under the Dawkins reforms,[53] which led to more choice and competition in the market, and resources being allocated according to government-driven policy incentives. This led to increased subject specialisation through research centres in law faculties, and an instrumental view of research agendas. Researchers are encouraged to plan their projects and schedules to maximise financial rewards from central and government funded incentives schemes. Accountability and outcomes are the current catchcries. Refereed journal articles, external grants and PhD completions are the goals. There is more emphasis on interdisciplinary work (and a corresponding acceptance of the need for social science methodologies) along with the need for practical outcomes leading to strategic links being forged with industry.

There have been some other important changes in the higher degree research context in Australia, for example, recognition of the important link between research, knowledge, globalisation and a healthy economy.[54] This has affected the research training being offered by universities. Thus, the professional doctorate which is more aligned with applied research based on industry objectives is gaining some acceptance. However, the PhD, which was first introduced by the University of Oxford in 1917, is still considered the highest form of original research and research training.

---

51 Kemp DA, *New knowledge, new opportunities: A discussion paper on higher education research and research training* (Canberra: Ausinfo, 1999). http://www.dest.gov.au/archive/highered/otherpub/greenpaper/index.htm (5/11/2009).

52 Kemp DA, *Knowledge and innovation: A policy statement on research and research training* (Canberra: Ausinfo, 1999). http://www.dest.gov.au/archive/highered/whitepaper/report.pdf (5/11/2009).

53 Dawkins J, *Higher Education: A Policy Statement* (Canberra: AGPS, July 1988).

54 McWilliam E et al, *Research Training in Doctoral Programs: What can be learned from professional doctorates?* (Canberra: Cth Dept of Education Science and Training, 2002).

Recent Australian government reports have argued that an evaluation of the system indicated that:

> Australian government policy did not do enough to encourage diversity and excellence, universities were not sufficiently connected with national innovations in research and development, there was too little concentration by universities on areas of strength, graduates were not adequately trained for employment, and there was a wastage of private and public resources with long completion times and low completion rates.[55]

To address some of these issues the Australian federal government decided that, in future, it would provide performance-based funding for research student places, with this funding to include a significant factor for completion rates (rather than enrolments). In addition, time limits were placed on funding for postgraduate research students. The government also introduced additional requirements for universities, such as annual Research Training plans and reporting. These reports covered issues such as 'the research environment, proposed future directions, quality assurance arrangements, collaboration with other universities and industry, management of commercialisation, intellectual property rights, reviews of past performance, graduate outcomes/attributes and employment, and a tallying of "research active" members of academic staff, outputs and achievements'.[56] These measures were introduced to overcome some of the basic weaknesses in the postgraduate research training systems including 'poor environments associated with poor supervision, lack of departmental support and impoverished infrastructure, a mismatch between institutional research priorities and students' interests, and limited opportunities for students to gain experience in appropriate research environments, creating a gap between academic researchers and industry'.[57]

The main positive benefits, however, include 'support and development programs for supervisors with many universities implementing registration of supervisors and supervisory panels, support and education programs for students including short-term scholarships for students who have almost completed but need some financial assistance in the last few months, structured research programs, induction programs, the active and conscious attempts to develop a research culture and the provision for funds for conferences and seminars, the implementation of milestones, progress reviews and, what some universities are calling, "active progress management".'[58]

In March 2005, the release of the issues paper 'Research Quality Framework: Assessing the quality and impact of research in Australia' (RQF)

---

55 Kiley M, *Quality in Postgraduate Research Overview* http://www.qpr.edu.au/overview.html (5/11/2009).

56 Kiley M, *Quality in Postgraduate Research Overview* http://www.qpr.edu.au/overview.html (5/11/2009).

57 Arthur E, *The Commonwealth's role in assuring quality in postgraduate research education.* (Quality in Postgraduate Research: Integrating Perspectives, Adelaide, University of Canberra, 2002), cited in M_Kiley http://www.qpr.edu.au/overview.html (5/11/2009).

58 Pearse H, *Encouraging timely doctoral completions: The implementation of the Research Training Scheme.* (Research on Doctoral Education Forum, Deakin University, 2002), cited in M_Kiley http://www.qpr.edu.au/overview.html (5/11/2009).

heralded increased policy focus on the area.[59] The change of government that occurred in the Australian federal election in November 2007 resulted in the cancellation of this project. The new Innovation, Industry, Science and Research Minister Kim Carr announced another research quality review system — the Excellence for Research in Australia (ERA) scheme.[60]

Subsequently the tertiary education sector witnessed the release of the Bradley Report which underlined the urgent need for increased funding for Australia's universities.[61] In December 2008, the House of Representatives Standing Committee on Industry, Science and Innovation tabled its report on the inquiry into research training and research workforce issues in *Australian Universities: Building Australia's Research Capacity* which again pointed to the need for government nurturing of the higher education sector.[62] The report speaks about the 'years of neglect' of the sector and the 'inadequate funding' being a 'fundamental obstacle' to building Australia's full research capacity. In 2009, in *Powering Ideas: An Innovation Agenda for the 21st Century*, the government acknowledged that 'public research capacity is critical' even though 'the pay-off may be indirect and a long time coming': 'We depend so much on universities — that if their performance slips, the whole innovation system suffers' ... therefore 'they must be able to demonstrate genuine and consistent excellence'.[63]

In the last decade, the government has been directing any research funding towards certain priority areas. The National Research Priorities set in 2002, include An Environmentally Sustainable Australia, Promoting and Maintaining Good Health, Frontier Technologies for Building and Transforming Australian Industries and Safeguarding Australia. Understandably, it is often difficult for all legal researchers to bring themselves within these subject areas.

These developments raise a number of issues which directly affect legal researchers including:

* What is the nature and meaning of 'legal research'?
* What is 'different' about how lawyers research?[64]
* How are academic lawyers to measure impact when there are no dedicated citation indexes for law?

59 Australian Department of Education Science and Training, Expert Advisory Group for an RTF 'Research Quality Framework: Assessing the quality and impact of research in Australia' http://www.dest.gov.au/NR/rdonlyres/E32ECC65-05C0-4041-A2B8-75ADEC69E159/4467/rqf_issuespaper.pdf (5/11/2009).

60 Brennan A and Malpas J, 'Researchers drowning in sea of paper', *The Australian* (Sydney), 16 April 2008, 25.

61 Department of Education, Employment and Workplace Relations, *The Review of Australian Higher Education: Final Report* (Chair Prof Denise Bradley December 2008) http://www.deewr.gov.au/HigherEducation/Review/Pages/ReviewofAustralianHigherEducationReport.aspx (5/11/2009).

62 Parliament of Australia, House of Representatives, House Standing Committee on Industry, Science and Innovation, *Inquiry into research training and research workforce issues in Australian universities* http://www.aph.gov.au/House/committee/isi/research/report.htm (5/11/2009).

63 Department of Innovation, Industry, Science and Research, *Powering Ideas: An Innovation Agenda for the 21st Century*, 32. http://www.innovation.gov.au/innovationreview/Documents/PoweringIdeas_fullreport.pdf (5/11/2009).

64 QUT Faculty of Law, *Legal Research Profile* (1992).

* How are lawyers going to successfully argue that they have international recognition and their research has extensive impact when so much of legal work is based on individual jurisdictional issues?
* Do academic lawyers need to stop writing doctrinal based text books and instead place their efforts towards publishing in peer reviewed journals because student and practitioner texts hold little value within the framework?

This process of government examination of higher education and research agendas continues and will have an important effect on higher degree research students in law.

Because of these broader environmental factors, researchers need to position their endeavours within overarching government and institutional frameworks. Careful planning is needed to best take advantage of the current research funding contexts. There is still a small window for purely academic endeavour through, for example, the Australian Research Council Discovery Grant funding if the research is pushing the boundaries of current thinking and has clear social value. However, the pre-eminent focus is on applied research.

1.5   Choosing a methodology

Thus far, this chapter has considered definitions for research, research paradigms and the current contexts of Australian legal research. Another issue that needs to be addressed is research methodology. Broadly speaking, methodology can be defined in terms of what it is not. It is not a hypothesis or guiding argument of the paper. It is not the objective or overall aim in undertaking the research. The methodology is the means used to gather information and data, and achieve a valid outcome. Within the status-quo paradigms or structures of legal research, there are accepted ways of proving arguments. The methodology of any science 'involves its rules of interpretation and criteria for admissible explanation, as well as the research designs, data-collecting techniques, and data-processing routines that have been developed from these rules and criteria'. Therefore the methodology includes a valid and correct use of the discipline's 'preferred instrumentation and data-processing techniques', as well as the proper use of the discipline's 'rules of interpretation and the criteria for admissible explanation that exist independently of these instrumentations and routines'.[65]

Whenever legal research comes on the agenda, the assumption is that we are talking about a doctrinal or library-based research methodology. But even within this research category there are a variety of approaches to research depending on the role of the person undertaking the research, whether they are an academic, a postgraduate scholar, or a law librarian. The approach taken will be reflective of the purpose of the endeavour. Whereas a student or an academic might be intending in-depth research within a specific area, a practising lawyer may be focused on finding a precise answer to a legal problem or situation that has already occurred. This latter focus necessarily includes a very narrow view of the topic, which is often accompanied by strict time and cost limitations.

---

65   Holt R and Turner J, *The Methodology of Comparative Research* (NY: The Free Press, 1970), 2.

The process also varies. A distinction must be drawn between the processes involved in locating the source or finding information, and reading it, compared to the understanding and linking of that information to the problem being researched. Sometimes these links are inevitable and clear. Often, however, the conceptualisation of a solution requires hard thinking, and the gaps in the information only become apparent when the researcher tries either to verbally communicate the results of the search or attempts to write up the conclusions.

So, for the most part, law students and practising lawyers undertake doctrinal legal research. This results from the types of operational work in which the profession is engaged; for example, advising clients on what the law is, and where they stand in relation to the law. The knowledge and ability to carry out such research is a defining skill of a competent practitioner. There is a professional expectation that once students graduate from law school, they will be able to locate, read, understand and communicate the law. This is a 'tall order', especially in this era of technological change. The laws change, the legal sources change, computer software changes and, like all skills, researching ability can wane without regular practice. An increasing amount of legal research can now be done electronically. At the same time, most professionals would recognise that not all work places have access to the latest technology because of cost and size factors. For this reason, and also because many of the electronic sources are modelled on the traditional legal reference sources, it is of paramount importance they know how to find their way around the so-called 'hardcopy' sources.

However, this book does not aim to be a mechanistic tour through the various legal sources. Legal research is an intellectual process, and involves much more than this. Research requires conceptualisation, planning and communication, whether the outcome is an undergraduate assignment, or a PhD. It also requires a broad focus in keeping with the modern worldview. In the present political and cultural climate, unstated theoretical views are more likely to be recognised. The so-called 'objectivity' of the law has been attacked with some success.

In addition, there have been overwhelming criticisms made of the doctrinal methodology; for example, that it is too theoretical, too technical, uncritical, conservative, narrow in its choice and range of subjects, trivial, and without due consideration of the social and economic significance of the legal process. The central weakness of the expository tradition according to William Twining, 'is that typically it takes as its starting point and its main focus of attention rules of law, without systematic or regular reference to the context of problems they are supposed to resolve, the purposes they were intended to serve or the effects they in fact have'.[66]

Law has traditionally been viewed as a conservative and staid discipline, but this is being challenged in the modern context. We are living in a period of immense change, and while the legal profession and the law may not be at the forefront of this change it cannot but help reflect the pattern. The law today is at a volatile and fluid stage and thus legal research skills are of paramount

---

66 Twining W, *Taylor Lectures 1975 Academic Law and Legal Development* (Lagos: University of Lagos Faculty of Law, 1976), 20.

importance for lawyers. They cannot hope to simply learn the law once and for that body of principle to remain static during the rest of their working life. Most students find that there have been major changes in the law during their years of study, so that even when they graduate, they may find subjects and areas of law studied in first year have changed beyond recognition by final year.

Non-doctrinal research is characterised by a lesser emphasis on the primary and secondary sources of law. It is not based exclusively on analysing the written sources of law — law reports, particularly appeal cases, legislation, and the plethora of other traditional sources, such as parliamentary debates and government publications generally. Doctrinal research hypotheses tend to originate in impressionistic ideas and arguments, the so-called 'hunches', but the non-doctrinal research methodologies move beyond an analytical treatment of existing legal sources to actually testing hypotheses. The process frequently involves contextual aspects of social research and looking outside the written words for answers to legal questions. The methodologies used necessitate careful design and planning, often building on prior doctrinal and empirical studies. Non-doctrinal methodologies can be used effectively in the legal context in combination with doctrinal studies, or with a mixture of different techniques to produce a rounded vision of a topic. Social science or empirical methodologies are numerous. These will be explained in more detail in later chapters, but include both quantitative and qualitative research methodologies. Some methods, such as action research, may be outside an accepted legal research 'paradigm', but also hold a great challenge and reward for those legal researchers interested in a reform process, especially within the legal profession itself. Action research identifies those involved 'on the ground' as the repository of knowledge in any reform or change process. It involves an investigation of reality in order to initiate change. To date, it has been most prominent in the field of education.

The research methodology chosen needs to be directly tailored to the purpose of your research. Your choice of methodology is instrumental. Methodology is subsidiary to objectives and hypothesis. It is the means to your end.

1.6 Expanded legal research frameworks

Although doctrinal research may be recognised as 'the norm', there are some expanded legal research frameworks that are well-accepted extensions to the overall legal 'paradigm'. These are theoretical research, law reform research and policy research. Each of these categories makes use of a variety of methodologies and expands the legal process. These have tended to challenge the frontiers and boundaries of legal development.

Theoretical research examines the philosophies underlying law and the legal system, including questions of justice, criminological theory, liberalism, natural law, critical legal studies, feminism, and economic analysis to name but a few. The methodology examines the historical development of the theory of law itself and frequently it uses theory as a springboard to critique existing law, legal reform and practice.

A separate arm of government often conducts law reform research in order to provide advice on changes and reform of existing law. Usually the

Commissions are limited to those topics referred by the Attorney-General for consideration, but they can conduct wide public consultation within their briefs. At times, their role may extend to drafting new legislation.

Policy research is most often conducted within government departments. It is the process of conducting research on, or analysing, fundamental social problems in order to provide policy-makers with 'pragmatic, action-oriented recommendations for alleviating problems'.[67]

These extensions to the legal research framework are examined in more detail in Chapter Three.

1.7 Ethics in research

Three main ethical issues impinge on legal research. These are:

1 the necessity to observe set guidelines for responsible practice and, where necessary, obtain institutional ethical clearance prior to carrying out research affecting humans or animals;

2 the need to act ethically in relation to choice and practice in research methodology, and in the reporting of data so as to avoid fabrication and falsification of data; and

3 the obligation to act ethically in writing up your research, specifically in relation to plagiarism.[68]

In 2007, the National Health and Medical Research Council released its *National Statement of Ethical Conduct in Human Research*.[69] The principles espoused have generally been incorporated into university research control procedures.[70] Now any research involving a human subject requires some level of ethical scrutiny and may require an application to your institution's Research Ethics Committee. Sometimes multiple clearances will be required including a clearance from, for example, a specific faculty biosafety committee as well as other more general university committees. The institutions will ensure that the research being carried out under its banner will enhance its reputation and accord with accepted professional standards.

Ethical clearance requirements are generally directed at social science methodologies rather than doctrinal legal research, but even with empirical research, some projects will be exempt from full scrutiny. Exempt categories cover research conducted within universities to test the universities' own procedures; for example, the subject and teacher evaluations given to students to complete during their courses. Clearance will not normally be required for the gathering of data that is already publicly available, or for interviewing people where the

---

67 Majchrzak A, *Methods for Policy Research* (Beverley Hills: Sage Publications, 1984), 12.

68 Hutchinson A, 'Beyond black-letterism: Ethics in law and legal education' (1999) 33 (3) *Law Teacher* 301.

69 *National Statement of Ethical Conduct in Human Research* (Canberra: National Health and Medical Research Council, 2007), http://www.nhmrc.gov.au/publications/synopses/e72syn.htm (5/11/2009).

70 See, for example, the Queensland University of Technology's University Research Ethics Page, http://www.research.qut.edu.au/ (5/11/2009).

data will not be assessed by formal analysis. The normal procedure is to submit a brief ethics checklist to have each project assessed.

Ethical issues become most important when using social science research methodologies. Researchers must observe professional practice. This should happen right from the point of involvement of research subjects, so that the researcher ensures the subject has full capability to freely consent, along with full information being given of the objectives, nature, likely benefits and detriment that may arise as a result of the project.

The *Australian Code for the Responsible Conduct of Research* developed jointly by the National Health and Medical Research Council, the Australian Research Council and Universities Australia has now replaced the *Joint NHMRC/AV-CC Statement and Guidelines on Research Practice*.[71] This sets out a code of conduct for the responsible practice of research, and lays down procedures for dealing with allegations of research misconduct within Australian universities. Examples of misconduct falling under the Code include:

* fabrication of results
* falsification or misrepresentation of results
* plagiarism
* misleading ascription of authorship
* failure to declare and manage serious conflicts of interest
* falsification or misrepresentation to obtain funding
* conducting research without ethics approval as required by *the National Statement on Ethical Conduct in Research Involving Humans and the Australian Code of Practice for the Care and Use of Animals for Scientific Purposes*
* risking the safety of human participants, or the wellbeing of animals or the environment
* deviations from this Code that occur through gross or persistent negligence
* wilful concealment or facilitation of research misconduct by others.[72]

The Code notes that it does not include 'honest differences in judgment in management of the research project, and may not include honest errors that are minor or unintentional. However, breaches of this Code will require specific action by supervisors and responsible officers of the institution'.[73]

Plagiarism is perhaps the most difficult issue faced by legal researchers. Plagiarism is different from 'cheating'. Students can 'cheat' by paying for assignments to be written for them or copying other students' work. These infringe ethical research standards and would probably fall under the rule of

71 *Australian Code for the Responsible Conduct of Research* (Canberra: National Health and Medical Research Council, 2007) http://www.nhmrc.gov.au/publications/synopses/ r39syn.htm (5/11/2009).

72 *Australian Code for the Responsible Conduct of Research* (Canberra: National Health and Medical Research Council, 2007), 10.2. http://www.nhmrc.gov.au/publications/synopses/ r39syn.htm (5/11/2009).

73 *Australian Code for the Responsible Conduct of Research* (Canberra: National Health and Medical Research Council, 2007), 10.1. http://www.nhmrc.gov.au/publications/synopses/ r39syn.htm (5/11/2009).

'misleading ascription of authorship'.[74] In addition, electronic files and the wealth of material available on the internet have made inadvertent copying easier. Short timelines can lead to hasty preparation and submission of research papers. The busy scholar can overlook a cut and paste carried out without the inclusion of the source, or where the citation source has been separated from the quote. Sometimes prose can be so clear that it seeps into a writer's consciousness and the source is lost. Sensible record management should counter inadvertence, but ignorance is no excuse in relation to the rules of citation. In the undergraduate context, most universities have Policies on Academic Dishonesty which students are asked to read. Students are also called upon to sign declarations when they submit assessment attesting to the originality of their work. Such a declaration might take the following form:

1. I have not:
   - copied the work of another student; or
   - submitted this paper previously for a degree or diploma at any university or other institution of higher education.

2. I have not, without clear acknowledgment of the origin of the work:
   - directly copied any part of another person's work or a case report (this includes information which is in electronic form and/or available on the internet); or
   - summarised the work of another person (this includes articles and case reports in paper or electronic form); or
   - used or developed an idea or thesis derived from another person's work.

3. I have read and understand the Faculty Policy on Academic Dishonesty.[75]

The second part of this declaration pertains to plagiarism. Ten years ago, Anita Stuhmcke was one of the few scholars within the legal academic framework, who attempted to explain and define the concept of 'plagiarism' for legal researchers.[76] But there is now a growing body of literature on the issue spurred no doubt by some high profile cases where the courts have been asked to determine whether law students' referencing practices should be regarded as plagiarism in terms of the ethical standards required to be admitted to legal practice.[77]

---

74 *Australian Code for the Responsible Conduct of Research* (Canberra: National Health and Medical Research Council, 2007), 10.2. http://www.nhmrc.gov.au/publications/synopses/ r39syn.htm (5/11/2009).

75 QUT Faculty of Law, *Master of Laws LWN048 Advanced Legal Research Study Guide*, Semester Two 2009, 20. See also Zobel J and Hamilton M, 'Managing Student Plagiarism in Large Academic Departments' (2002) 45 (2) *Australian Universities Review* 23; Carroll J, 'Handling student plagiarism: moving to mainstream' (2005) 2 (1) *Brookes eJournal of Learning and Teaching* 1; McGowan U, 'Academic Integrity: An Awareness and Development Issue for Students and Staff' (2005) 2(3) *Journal of University Teaching and Learning Practice* Article 6.

76 Stuhmcke A, *Legal Referencing* (3 ed, Sydney: Butterworths, 2005), 20-25.

77 *Humzy-Hancock* [2007] QSC 34; *Re AJG* [2004] QCA 88 (Unreported, de Jersey CJ, Jerrard JA, and Philippedes J, 15 March 2004); Corbin L and Carter J, 'Is plagiarism indicative of prospective legal practice?' (2007) 17 (1&2) *Legal Education Review* 53; Cahock K, 'When students reference plagiarised material — what can we learn (and what can we do) about their understanding of attribution?' (2008) 4 (1) *International Journal for Educational Integrity* 3.

Professional ethics are intrinsic to the practice of law and research ethics are a small aspect of this.[78] In addition, the doctrinal legal research methodology can be broadly categorised within a qualitative research framework. This means that the value of the analysis inherent in doctrinal work is dependent on the individual researcher and author. It is important that this individual voice is authentic. This authenticity relates not only to the way for example the research is conducted as might be the case in scientific and social science contexts, but also to the way the doctrinal research results are analysed and communicated. This is the ethical crux of the plagiarism issue for legal scholars.

1.8 Recording the research process

Effective research requires a well planned and pertinent methodology. It also requires a literature review with accurate recording of searches and organisation of material located. There are four basic physical steps in this part of the research process, including:

1 gathering materials relevant to your topic;

2 storage and indexing;

3 note-taking; and

4 writing.

In the very early stages of the project, it might be worth considering if you will be collecting any particular types of materials; for example, survey forms, full text cases, or data analysis sheets, and how you plan to store these. Consider whether the materials you are collecting will be of use for other projects. What volume of materials are you likely to need? What are your main subject headings or keywords? These can be used to organise photocopies or electronic copies of items found. How long will you be required to store the data?

While you are researching you will need to record your process so that you are very clear in regard to the steps that have been done and those that are still to be completed. It is important with a lengthy project to date your searches and copies, and keep a research diary, so that current awareness and updating searches can be carried out towards the end of the process. It is also useful to keep a running bibliography, possibly under topic, so that you have a full cite of every piece of information you have seen, with a clear indication of those items not yet located and read. You may use a research database for this purpose. You may consider giving each item an individual code or number which is also noted on the hardcopy. If you are engaged in doctrinal research you should keep a record of the following:

1 any primary materials (case law and legislation) relevant to your topic, and what sources you used to find these;

2 whether you have updated these sources by checking for recent legislative changes or judicial consideration in unreported judgments;

3 a note of all keywords and subject headings used in electronic sources;

---

78 See generally Parker C and Evans A, *Inside Lawyers' Ethics* (Cambridge: Cambridge University Press, 2007).

4 the exact searches carried out on each database or with each internet search engine. It is very easy to sit down at a computer and simply try whatever searches come to mind (Chapter Four contains a discussion of the importance of careful planning of electronic research. Without planning you are certain to miss relevant information.);

5 the search terms used in the catalogues (your own and other libraries'), and whether you have carried out shelf checks;

6 the exact terms and the volumes you have checked when using hardcopy sources, for example journal indexes. (Often, one volume may be missing from the shelf — or a new issue may come in. This can be 'picked up' in your final check before completing your paper.); and

7 a track of your inter-library loan requests and reservations, so that if they do not turn up within a reasonable time, they can be queried or re-ordered.

Card files are an 'old-fashioned' but effective method for organising and recording research. The method consists of compiling two series of palm cards:

1 the bibliographic search cards; and

2 the bibliography cards.[79]

Additional sets of cards can be written out for law reports and legislation. Bibliography cards can be arranged alphabetically or in separate sets by topic.

Bibliographic search cards include the record of research and include the following information:

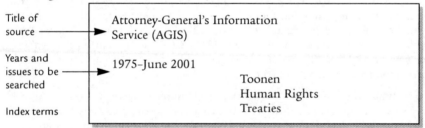

Title of source → Attorney-General's Information Service (AGIS)

Years and issues to be searched → 1975–June 2001

Toonen
Human Rights
Index terms → Treaties

The Bibliography card includes the correct cite for each item and other tracking information.

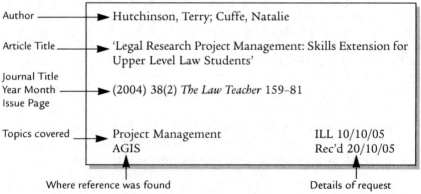

Author → Hutchinson, Terry; Cuffe, Natalie

Article Title → 'Legal Research Project Management: Skills Extension for Upper Level Law Students'

Journal Title
Year Month → (2004) 38(2) *The Law Teacher* 159–81
Issue Page

Topics covered → Project Management   ILL 10/10/05
AGIS   Rec'd 20/10/05

Where reference was found   Details of request

---

79 Clinch P, *Using a Law Library: A Student's Guide to Legal Research Skills* (2 ed, London: Blackstone Press, 2001), 289, and see generally 287–291.

Research database software, such as EndNote, offers an alternative method of attaining the same result. Systems such as AustLII will eventually expand their search services to include support for bibliographic databases (BDBs). BDB support allows users to import search results from the electronic journal indexes into their personal research databases for later reference and use. This makes correct footnoting and bibliographies simple. However, significant amounts of time must be expended in programming the software to accept Australian legal citation formats, whereas most social science citation formats are programmed into the software on purchase.

It is essential to develop a process for storing and locating sources. Manilla folders in a filing cabinet may be sufficient. Ringbinders may be tidier. Each article should be given a file number, and if this is noted on the bibliography card or electronic file, locating hardcopy items should be easy. Remember to back up your work and store duplicate copies of computer files at different sites. Renumber new versions of files. Be cautious about pertinent material located on websites. If it is relevant, print off a hardcopy. Take careful note of the web address and date. Include an author and title, not just an URL in your notes. Quite frequently, by the time your research is published, the item will have disappeared off the web or the address will have changed.[80] Whichever system you use, be aware of the necessity to be organised, and record your research progress throughout the project.

1.9 Reading and critique

Locating relevant material can be a time-consuming exercise — but sometimes not nearly as frustrating as wading through the fruits of your searches! At a very basic level you will be sifting and sorting the material according to the two standard criteria of currency and the authority or 'standing' of the author.[81] Always use the latest material first — recently published journal articles, the latest editions of texts, the most recent cases from the superior courts and updated legislation. Be aware of the source and authority of the author. If you are unsure of the ideas or veracity of an author's theories, try to find a book review or commentary on the research. Having used these basic tests to sift through the sources located, it is necessary to use some effective shortcuts in order to read the material you have located effectively.

Most students are forced to work out some 'active reading' strategies early in their law careers.[82] It is not efficient to begin by reading a scholarly work from beginning to end, paragraph by paragraph, taking copious notes. It saves time to browse the article or book first, looking at the contents pages, chapter or section headings. This identifies whether the whole document or only part of the document is relevant. Having done this, you should scan the introduction to gain an outline of the arguments about to be presented. A look at the conclusion or final chapter should provide you with a restatement and summary of these.

80 Internet archives are accessible since the launch of The Internet Archive http:// www.archive.org/index.php (5/11/2009).

81 Berry R, *The Research Project — How to Write It* (5 ed, Abingdon, Oxon: Routledge, 2004), 46-47.

82 Adler MJ and Van Doren C, *How to Read a Book: The Classic Guide to Intelligent Reading* (New York: Simon & Schuster, 2003), 4-6.

Once you decide that the article is worth reading, make sure you take down a correct citation, preferably in your chosen citation style. After this, you can go back and read the material more slowly and thoughtfully, summarising arguments according to section or chapter. Any direct quotes should be put in inverted commas and the correct page reference added.

Reading cases is a special skill.[83] By now, you will have read many cases, and most of you will have formulated a 'plan of attack' for efficient case reading. A law report, of course, is a story of legal reasoning, and normally when you read you are looking at it as a source of principle, precedent and overt or covert policy. Sometimes you may prefer to read a casenote, article or text which states the established principles of a case, so that when you come to read the case you can focus on the relevant aspects of the decision, rather than reading the case like a book or short story. You need to look for the shorthand pointers to lead you through the unfamiliar text.

When reading cases, you will be seeking the legal essence or the message in what is often a jungle of legal terminology. You usually only develop an easy facility in reading appeal cases with practice. When you read cases, look for the pointers and significant aspects flagged for you. 'Legal readers' do not normally read the case like a book or story, enjoying the trivial and the human interest. Nor do they always read the case from beginning to end. In addition, they are usually reading the case for a particular purpose, and often one case may be of use or relevance for more than one legal rule. It is not normal practice and certainly not efficient practice to read cases 'blind', without having some idea of what might be there.

The focused reader will scan the case and note the following:

* the year of the decision;
* the jurisdiction and court in which the decision was made;
* the parties — whether personal or corporate, and the judges sitting on the bench;
* whether there is a combined judgment from all the judges or whether some judges have wanted to give their own separate reasons for coming to a decision; and
* whether there is any dissenting judgment or whether the decision was tightly split and therefore liable to be changed if the issues come to be heard again before a different group of judges.

At that point, they might read the headnote for the material facts, the decision, and ostensible reasons for that decision, all the time bearing in mind that sometimes the barristers who write the headnotes get it wrong. A total reliance on the headnote can sometimes be fatal.

The focused legal reader examines the catchwords which categorise or keyword index the legally significant points of the decision. The headnote classifies the subject of the case. The headnote also points out any important cases or legislation referred to by the court in coming to its decision. If the

---

83 Christopher Enright has an interesting chapter on this topic for some further reading: Enright C, *Studying Law* (5 ed, Sydney: The Federation Press, 1995), Chapter 32.

headnote, for example, includes *Donoghue v Stevenson* as a case 'discussed' or 'followed', then the 'legal reader' knows automatically the legal history of the text before them.

Similarly, if the headnote has a reference to legislation, then that may suggest another line of thought in relation to theories of legislative interpretation. Most likely, the legal reasoning in the case is not such that it can be understood simply from a brief headnote. The reader must go to the text. There will often be paragraph guides in the headnotes to significant passages for each separate proposition or finding.

Usually, there is a pattern within each separate judgment — a generic structure. This is most useful to indicate the comparative outcomes according to each judge's reasoning. Many judges will review the pertinent facts, events and history of the case, or perhaps refer to another judge's reasons where this has already been covered adequately. The judgment usually deals with each issue in turn, discussing the law and facts in relation to it, the reasoning and conclusion including the principle or rule applicable, and a ruling.[84]

When you are reading other material also look for the guides or structure. These signposts may not be as obvious as they are for case law. Look for the main topic and the main message or thesis. The argument propounding this message will probably have a number of issues with discussion of each occurring sequentially.

Sometimes the issues are not set out logically. In that case, language is your clue to recognition of the key information. Connecting words and phrases are the keys to the progression of thought and important aspects of the message. Arguments in academic philosophical writing and legal theory can be difficult to 'deconstruct'. Just as you do with the law report, it is useful to first skim the material looking for the main conclusion. This conclusion may be in proximity to words, such as 'therefore', 'so', and 'thus'. One way of reconstructing the argument might be to actually insert the connecting words or argument indicators that are missing, for example, 'because', 'since' and 'that is why'. Complex literature provides another opportunity to use mindmaps to good advantage. Identify the reasons given and the relationship between the reasons — whether each must be read together as support for the conclusion or whether they support the conclusion independently.

Language is often the first indicator of bias. Look out for very descriptive and emotive words. Judge whether the writer is trying to arouse a sense of pity in the reader, and is perhaps using this as an argument to persuade others to their views. Scare tactics may be used for the same purpose. Often, these types of arguments are of the black/white variety with no compromise or allowance for other views.

The final step is to evaluate the message by judging whether the basic reasons given are acceptable and the inference steps are also acceptable. To do this, you need to assess the evidence being put forward (providing some reasons

---

84   Maley Y, 'The language of the law' in Gibbons J (ed), *Language and the Law* (London; New York: Longman, 1994), 44.

are included!). Is the information reliable, relevant and sufficient for the claims being based on it? How old is the material? When was it published? Who carried out the study? Is that person reputable in the area? Is the article putting forward both sides of any debate? Is there a balanced view taken of the issues?[85]

Glen Lewis and Christina Slade suggest three main steps in the process, beginning with analysis of the information being conveyed, followed by a process of drawing out the ramifications of what is being said, including identifying any underlying assumptions. Finally, they suggest the reader evaluates (or critiques) the whole message in light of these issues. Therefore, before you critique what you are reading, it is necessary to understand the main message through the process of analysis. This includes:

* identifying what is being said;
* distinguishing what is relevant from what is not;
* seeing connections between different strands of thought;
* recognising vagueness and ambiguity, then clarifying terms if necessary;
* identifying members of a class, in terms of likeness;
* identifying counter instances, as different in some respects; and
* identifying analogies.[86]

Thus, Mortimer Adler explains in *How to Read a Book: The Classic Guide to Intelligent Reading*, 'You must be able to say, with reasonable certainty "I understand", before you can say any one of the following things: "I agree", or "I disagree", or "I suspend judgment".'[87] Part of the deeper understanding of the text may include the process of drawing inferences from what has been written. This process includes:

* drawing out the consequences of what is said;
* identifying underlying assumptions;
* generalising from particular instances, ie abstracting;
* applying analogies to reach new conclusions; and
* recognising cause/effect relationships.[88]

Only at that point can you proceed to be critical of the message, and give reasons for not agreeing with the ideas conveyed. Lewis and Slade refer to this process as evaluation and include the following processes:

* giving reasons for beliefs and decisions and then choosing how to act;
* criticising ideas constructively; and
* modifying ideas in response to criticism.[89]

---

85 Petelin R and Durham M, *The Professional Writing Guide: Writing Well and Knowing Why* (Warriewood, NSW: Business & Professional Publishing, 1998), Chapter 4.

86 Lewis G and Slade C, *Critical Communication* (Sydney: Prentice Hall, 1994), 77.

87 Adler MJ and Van Doren C, *How to Read a Book: The Classic Guide to Intelligent Reading* (New York: Simon & Schuster, 2003), 143.

88 Lewis G and Slade C, *Critical Communication* (Sydney: Prentice Hall, 1994), 77.

89 Lewis G and Slade C, *Critical Communication* (Sydney: Prentice Hall, 1994), 77.

Critical reading has been defined as 'active thoughtful reading, as opposed to passive acceptance of whatever appears on the printed page'.[90] Evaluation is part of this process. Constructive criticism might include showing where the author is uninformed, misinformed, illogical in their argument, or perhaps where the account is incomplete.[91] Critical thinking is an important skill in terms of assessing your research sources. Critical thinking is easy to recognise when juxtaposed with non-critical thinking.[92] Luckily, there is a growing body of literature and even software packages now available to enhance critique abilities and to aid in the mapping of complex arguments.[93] You will need to apply these skills when you come to write your Literature Review. This Literature Review process is covered in Chapter Seven.

1.10 Conclusion

This chapter has been an attempt to map the focus points and context for this text. Legal research is unique, but in the context of evolving technology and dynamic change, new methodologies and ways of seeing need to be explored. However, in taking cognisance of the future, researchers also need to be comfortable with what has come before.

Further reading

Adler MJ and Van Doren C, *How to Read a Book: The Classic Guide to Intelligent Reading* (New York: Simon & Schuster, 2003).

Berry R, *The Research Project — How to Write It* (5 ed, Abingdon, Oxon: Routledge, 2004).

Clinch P, *Using a Law Library: A Student's Guide to Legal Research Skills* (2 ed, London: Blackstone Press, 2001).

Davies GL and Cowen MP, 'The persuasive force of the decisions of the United States courts in Australia' (1996–1997) 15 *Australian Bar Review* 51.

Davies M, 'Reading cases' (1987) 50(4) *The Modern Law Review* 409.

Dawson J and Peart N (eds), *The Law of Research: A Guide* (Dunedin: University of Otago Press, 2003).

Eisner C and Vicinus M (eds), *Originality, Imitation and Plagiarism: Teaching Writing in the Digital Age* (Ann Arbor: The University of Michigan Press and the University of Michigan Library, 2008).

Lewis G and Slade C, *Critical Communication* (Sydney: Prentice Hall, 1994).

Lewis HS, 'Integrity in research' (1992) 42 (4) *Journal of Legal Education* 607.

Nevile J (ed), *Ethics, Research and the University: A Select Bibliography* (Sydney: New

---

90 Ruggiero VR, *The Art of Thinking: A Guide to Critical and Creative Thought* (New York: Pearson Longman, 2007), 63.

91 Adler MJ and Van Doren C, *How to Read a Book: The Classic Guide to Intelligent Reading* (New York: Simon & Schuster, 2003), 164.

92 See a basic example in Sanson M, Worswick D and Thalia A, *Connecting with Law* (Melbourne: Oxford University Press, 2009), 16.

93 See http://www.austhink.org/ and http://www.aboutus.org/Debatemapper.com (5/11/2009).

College Institute for Values Research, University of New South Wales, 1995).

Petelin R and Durham M, *The Professional Writing Guide: Writing Well and Knowing Why* (Warriewood, NSW: Business & Professional Publishing, 1998).

Ruggiero VR, *The Art of Thinking: A Guide to Critical and Creative Thought* (New York: Pearson Longman, 2007).

Von Nessen P, 'The use of American precedents by the High Court of Australia, 1901-1987' (1992) 14 *Adelaide Law Review* 181.

Ziegler P, 'A general theory of law as a paradigm for legal research'(1988) 51 *The Modern Law Review* 569.

2

Standard Doctrinal Research Methodologies

Just as there are a variety of learning styles — auditory (hearing), visual (picture), tactile/kinaesthetic (physical) — so too there are any number of doctrinal legal research methodologies that cater for individual abilities and preferred work techniques.[1] Some people are visual learners, while others are more responsive to the spoken word.[2] Some are intuitive, while others are analytical. Just as with learning styles, it is useful to identify what research style and methodologies work best for you. However, to only adopt the doctrinal approaches that most appeal will mean you may be ignoring important resources. Although your preference may be for a particular mode of doctrinal research, one approach will not work in every instance. Nor is it sufficient to simply state that you are undertaking 'doctrinal research' and think that this is a sufficient methodological explanation.

This chapter aims to provide a number of standard techniques that encapsulate the legal researcher's tools of trade and which can be categorised under the doctrinal methodology banner. These techniques can be used, combined and re-used at different stages in the research process. Each project will have a number of steps and phases some of which will require doctrinal research and analysis and some of which will require the use of other methodologies.

Before examining the details of the doctrinal method, it is useful to look at some contextual issues. The first of these is to determine how law is situated in terms of the other disciplines. The Excellence in Research for Australia (ERA) Initiative has placed the discipline of law within the Humanities and Creative Arts (HCA) cluster. This cluster includes literature, history, philosophy, religion, language and literary studies. This cluster also includes architecture and regional planning. Sociology and criminology are categorised separately within the Social, Behavioural and Economic Sciences. This placement suggests a close connection between law and the humanities in terms of subject matter and methods.

Secondly, there is another issue that has not been fully examined and is broadly pertinent to this discussion. This question is 'Where does the doctrinal methodology "fit" within the spectrum of scientific and social research methodologies?' Where does legal research 'fit' in terms of the research undertaken in

---

1   Le Brun M and Johnstone R, *Quiet Revolution: Improving Student Learning in Law* (Sydney: The Law Book Company Limited, 1994), 79; See also Sarasin LC, *Learning Style Perspectives Impact in the Classroom* (Madison: Atwood Publishing, 1999).

2   The absence of illustration in law materials is notorious. See Wilson G, 'Comparative Legal Scholarship' in McConville M and Chui WH (eds), *Research Methods for Law* (Edinburgh: Edinburgh University Press, 2007), 99.

other disciplines? The doctrinal methodology has tended to be 'under-theorised'.[3] The practitioner lawyer of the past had little time to reflect on process, and in any case, other methods were not considered relevant. The doctrinal method was the core legal research method, and it was not thought to require explanation or classification within any broader research framework.

So what is doctrinal research? Doctrinal research is not a scientific methodology. Nor will you normally find the word 'doctrinal' in the index or table of contents of a social research methods text.

Richard Posner even suggested that law is 'not a field with a distinct methodology, but an amalgam of applied logic, rhetoric, economics and familiarity with a specialized vocabulary and a particular body of texts, practices, and institutions'.[4] The doctrinal methodology has aspects in common with hermeneutics in that there is sometimes an analysis of text but lawyers are not always interested in the broader or underlying historical context of the text which they are analysing.[5] It is aligned with discourse analysis which critically analyses language in text and other communications.[6] Unlike historical research which seeks to find the truth through considering the perspective and view of every actor, and examining every conceivable range of data, doctrinal research for the most part focuses on privileged voices.[7] As an example, these voices or versions of the truth are those of the judges in relation to case law and the parliament in terms of legislation.

Some commentators in discussing the issue of delineation of methodology have sought to draw a distinction between the 'internal method' used in doctrinal legal research reflecting the viewpoint of the participant in a legal system compared to the 'external method' reflecting 'the conceptual resources of extra-legal disciplines' and studying the law in practice.[8] The internal method includes the study of law 'using reason, logic and argument' and the 'primacy of critical reasoning based around authoritative texts'.[9] This internal approach includes the 'analysis of legal rules and principles taking the perspective of an insider in the system'.[10] Such an idea seems to encapsulate the pure doctrinal legal method. This internal aspect of law can be approached in a systematic fashion and the stages documented sufficiently to effect a separate doctrinal methodology. It is qualitative in part and it is unique. It uses arguments and forms of reasoning

---

3   Hutchinson T, 'Developing Legal Research Skills: Context, Framework and Practice' (2008) 32 (3) *Melbourne University Law Review* 1065 at 1081.

4   Posner, 'Conventionalism: The Key to Law as an Autonomous Discipline' (1988) 38 *University of Toronto Law Journal* 333 at 345 as quoted in Schwartz R, 'Internal and external method in the study of law' (1992) 11 (3) *Law and Philosophy* 179 at 199 iv.

5   Bryman A, *Social Research Methods* (3 ed, Oxford: Oxford University Press, 2008), 532-533.

6   Bryman A, *Social Research Methods* (3 ed, Oxford: Oxford University Press, 2008), 499-513.

7   Storey WK, *Writing History: A Guide for Students* (2 ed, New York: Oxford University Press, 2004).

8   Lucy W, 'Abstraction and the Rule of Law' (2009) 29 (3) *Oxford Journal of Legal Studies* 481.

9   McCrudden C, 'Legal Research and the Social Sciences' (2006) 122 (Oct) *Law Quarterly Review* 632.

10 McCrudden C, 'Legal Research and the Social Sciences' (2006) 122 (Oct) *Law Quarterly Review* 632 at 633.

such as induction, deduction and analogy. There are steps in each argument needing information and analysis. This is doctrinal research methodology.

Doctrinal legal research can be classified as qualitative research because it is 'a process of selecting and weighing materials taking into account hierarchy and authority as well as understanding social context and interpretation.'[11] The doctrinal methodology does take on aspects of a qualitative social research methodology in that the researcher in interpreting and analysing the law is undertaking a process that is not able to be readily replicated by another researcher. It is a subjective process personal to the individual researcher. Each legal researcher comes to the law with their own level of skills, their own theoretical stance, and individual level of judgment or ability. Even High Court judges can disagree amongst themselves about the interpretation of the law in 'hard cases'.

One of the few attempts to describe the doctrinal methodology compares it to a social science literature review and discovers many similarities but the doctrinal research methodology is much more than a literature review.[12] The literature review steps used for the comparison are derived from Fink's *Conducting Research Literature Review: From the Internet to Paper*.[13]

1. 'Selecting research questions
2. Selecting bibliographic or article databases
3. Choosing search terms
4. Applying practical screening criteria
5. Applying methodological screening criteria
6. Doing the review
7. Synthesising the results.'

This linear methodology breaks down in relation to Requirements 4 and 5 and again for 6 and 7. This is because of the differences between 'legal literature', that is, primary documents setting out the law, and regular 'literature'. The screening criteria are necessarily more rule bound and intricate for legal primary materials than for a regular literature review. The doctrinal research methodology is not simply a literature review. It is not simply 'scholarship'. It is the location and analysis of the primary documents in order to establish the nature and parameters of the law.

Doctrinal method is a two-part process because it involves both finding the law and interpreting and analysing the document or text. In the first step, the researcher is attempting to determine an 'objective' reality. The law is in part legislative fact. The law can be broadly categorised as primary data. Legislation in particular is written down. In that respect the law is concrete. However, many

---

11 Dobinson I and Johns F, 'Qualitative Legal Research' in McConville M and Chui WH (eds), *Research Methods for Law* (Edinburgh: Edinburgh University Press, 2007), 22.

12 Fink A, *Conducting Research Literature Review: From the Internet to Paper* (2 ed Sage: Thousand Oaks) in McConville M and Chui WH (eds), *Research Methods for Law* (Edinburgh: Edinburgh University Press, 2007), 22, 23.

13 Fink A, *Conducting Research Literature Review: From the Internet to Paper* (2 ed Sage: Thousand Oaks) in McConville M and Chui WH (eds), *Research Methods for Law* (Edinburgh: Edinburgh University Press, 2007), 22, 23.

aspects of the law are not clear and must be interpreted within the fact situations presented. The law is often contingent. Christopher McCrudden commented that 'If legal academic work shows anything, it shows that an applicable legal norm on anything but the most banal question is likely to be complex, nuanced and contested. Law is not a datum; it is in constant evolution, developing in ways that are sometimes startling and endlessly inventive'.[14]

No doubt there are similarities between a literature review and doctrinal legal research — both are largely dealing with the interpretation of text. But doctrinal research is different. It requires background research of secondary commentary and sources as a first step as do all research projects, and so in this respect it requires a literature review, that is, 'a critical analysis of the existing research literature, theoretical and empirical', related to the research topic. The literature review thus informs us of 'what is known and not known' about the topic.[15] But doctrinal research also requires a trained expert in legal doctrine to locate, read and analyse the law — the primary sources — the legislation and case law. A doctrinal research project can thus be categorised in this way —

1. Locating and analysing background commentary

2. Locating and analysing primary materials

So research does not simply consist of locating information. It includes those next steps of reading, analysing and linking the new information to that already established. This necessarily assumes a non-linear and eclectic approach because one source can suggest a totally different source follow-up. A journal article, for example, may lead you to consider a video that carries an interview discussing your issue from a different angle. So one source may suggest:

* different formats of similar topic information;

* totally different but parallel topics or lines of case law; and

* useful case studies that call on examples from diverse legal subject areas.

For this reason, it is very important to tabulate what sources you use, and what steps you have already taken in the research process. If you do this, you will not have to repeat searches or backtrack. It also means that you will be less likely to neglect to update. A useful footnote may lead to a pertinent case — but you need to ensure validation of your research, which may mean updating your case by checking the citators, the journal indexes and current updating sources.

While footnotes are important and useful sources of information, they can constitute a very hit and miss approach to research if they are the only research method used. Thoroughness is all! If there is insufficient opportunity to be thorough because of time constraints, then knowledge of the crucial research rules (such as updating) and a reflective approach to the information available to you is the next best thing.

Where does the methodology 'fit' within your research process? It is necessary for you firstly to identify the objectives of your project. Next you need

---

14 McCrudden C, 'Legal Research and the Social Sciences' (2006) 122 (Oct) *Law Quarterly Review* 632 at 648.

15 Walter M (ed), *Social Research Methods* (2 ed, South Melbourne: Oxford University Press, 2010), 485.

to formulate your hypothesis or main argument. At that point you should be able to isolate some specific aims that will help you in explaining and examining your hypothesis. It is only at that point that you need to think about the methodology for finding the information that you need in relation to each aim. There may be a different methodology for each step in the process because of the different type of data you require. Even if every aim that you articulate as a step required in proving your hypothesis can be achieved by using a doctrinal methodology, the doctrinal techniques used for each step may be different. There are a variety of doctrinal techniques to choose from in any situation.

2.1 Standard research methods

There are a variety of methods to approach 'library' research. Many of these approaches are predicated on finding the 'one right answer'.[16] Thus, the methods are directed to specific inquiries in order to locate particular pieces of information, such as:

* what legislation encompasses this fact situation (for example, criminal prosecution for child abuse);
* what specific section covers this; and
* has this section been changed or amended recently?

All of these types of questions have definite answers that can be found and verified.

However, some questions have more nebulous answers that may be buried in the internal workings of government departments and within ongoing policy formulation, and, in order to answer them, other methodologies may need to be used. Take for example, the following: 'Are there changes "in the pipeline" through new legislation, government inquiries or law reform agendas?'

After researching the hardcopy and electronic public sources, it may be necessary to 'tap into' the other sources. To do this, you may need to approach government departments and try to verify the stage reached in government deliberations, making use of your knowledge of policy research methodology. Some of this information may be limited in its circulation so, unless you can prove legitimate research intention, you may not have access to it. Ideally, you would attempt to infiltrate the internal information 'loop' by having your name placed on distribution lists for discussion papers and other documents. The answer to your question may still be the 'one right answer', but this answer itself may have many dimensions and quite frequently may be different according to whom you speak to within the policy formulation body.

At the next level, when you are setting your own overall research agenda, the issue may not be to locate the right answer, but to locate your own version of the 'truth' from the doctrinal certainties and possibilities. This 'truth' can be formulated from information collected by using a variety and combination of research methodologies, including doctrinal and non-doctrinal, and qualitative or quantitative.

---

16 Bettel Dawson T, 'Legal research in a social science setting: The problem of method' (1992) 14 (3) *Dalhousie Law Journal* 445 at 446.

This chapter deals mainly with a selection of specific legal research devices that can 'leap frog' you to a more complete understanding of an area. Research is not a linear process and requires an analytical and conceptual approach to the project, making use of various shortcuts along the way. The only important aspect of this is to retain a record of the 'zig-zag' research path so that any research gaps can be identified.

2.2 Doctrinal research model under a positivist tradition

The following table represents some suggested steps in formulating a research project. The preparation for a large project includes many of the issues canvassed in a formal Research Proposal. Steps one and two cover the stages required for all projects and are not methodology specific.

Step	Elements
1 Research preparation	• Selection of a general research topic after a review of relevant literature, reading and adequate reflection • Formulation of objectives, general 'hunch', research questions • Selection of doctrinal research as an appropriate methodology • Further exploration, reading and documentation of literature review • Consider jurisdictional aspect of topic • Consider comparative and international aspects of topic • Consider interdisciplinary aspects of topic • Reflect on timelines, budget, and grant options
2 Planning	• Review of the selected legal area using brainstorming techniques and Horrigan's matrix • Reflection on your conceptual framework — personal, legal, theoretical • Selection of more precise hypothesis • Plan research methodology using concept and issues mapping • Write research proposal and abstract to encapsulate ideas in specific inquiry • Check value of hypothesis using the 'So What' test
3 Gathering information/synthesis	• Finalise secondary literature review • Collect empirical data • Collect primary data • Data organisation using research databases, files or card systems • Grouping and presentation of data in note taking and writing
4 Communicating	• Re-editing and refinement of written argument • Publication of the findings[17].

17 See Sarantakos S, *Social Research* (2 ed, Melbourne: Macmillan, 1998), 100.

This chapter is referring to the processes that take place in step three where the decision has been made to follow a doctrinal methodology. Some very basic issues need to be addressed. Firstly, in a practical situation or problem-based exercise, any relevant facts need to be pulled together and connections determined. In a legal office, this step has much more importance and scope than where students are simply presented with a factual legal problem to solve. So the first step is to identify the material facts. Next, these facts are analysed with a view to determining what issues of law are being raised. Once the legal issues are identified, the relevant law may be ascertained. This is applied to the facts and a tentative conclusion is reached. This process has been worked and reworked and given several names with a variety of easily remembered acronyms being used. Many refer to the process as IRAC — a four step method of picking the Issues, determining the relevant Rule of law, and then Analysing the facts in terms of the law which then leads to the formation of a probable Conclusion.

2.2.1 *Sourcing information*

When you include research within the IRAC process, additional steps are infused. These steps include analysing and unpacking the legal issues in order to identify which issues need further research, then perhaps looking for background reading where necessary. This may be most relevant where the area of law is unfamiliar. Having located background commentary, the next step is to locate the primary sources of law — the legislation and case law. Once the requisite sources are ascertained, it is then possible to move on to the next step of synthesising the whole so as to come to a conclusion.

Here is a model of the traditional problem based doctrinal approach, highlighting the various sources of law. We can refer to this as the Bibliographic Approach to Problem Based Doctrinal Research. Obviously this methodology is not suitable in its entirety for academic projects where you are not working from a fact-based problem, but even then steps 4-7 are still pertinent.

1 Assemble facts
   When you are assembling the facts of your problem, it is useful to make a list of major subjects or terms as a precursor to beginning your search through the hardcopy indexes and electronic services.

2 Identify the legal issues
   This step often takes the form of jotting down a number of legal questions, and then deciding which of these questions is more important.

3 Analyse the issues with a view to searching for the law

4 Background reading

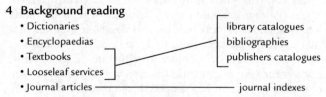

- Dictionaries
- Encyclopaedias
- Textbooks
- Looseleaf services
- Journal articles

library catalogues
bibliographies
publishers catalogues

journal indexes

5 Locate primary material

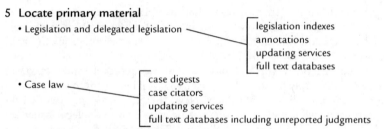

- Legislation and delegated legislation
  - legislation indexes
  - annotations
  - updating services
  - full text databases

- Case law
  - case digests
  - case citators
  - updating services
  - full text databases including unreported judgments

6 Synthesise all the issues in context

7 Come to a tentative conclusion

The items listed as background reading are those necessary to assemble an overall picture of the law. These include dictionaries for definitions of terms (and possibly a list of cases or legislation where they have been used) and encyclopaedias for a summary of the legal principles accompanied by footnoted sources. The pre-eminent reference sources are now available in electronic format. Major textbooks and treatises on the subject, and looseleaf services can be identified through the library catalogue. But do not neglect to check the catalogues of other libraries besides your own, and also current bibliographies listing books in print or publisher's catalogues for new titles not yet on the library shelves. Journal articles are best located through legal journal meta-indexes, but keep in mind that there is often quite a timelag in hardcopy publishing. Consider browsing the latest hardcopy issues of relevant journals.

In locating legislation, the table directs you to subject indexes of legislation to ascertain the correct titles, then legislation annotations to identify the latest reprint and references to case law discussing the legislation, and then finally to the updating services to verify that the legislation is still on foot, and that there are no recent amendments. The electronic full text databases can circumvent some of these steps if the jurisdiction you are working in has up-to-date reprints including every latest amendment. It is still worthwhile engaging in a general environmental scan to ensure there are no imminent changes, checking for Bills and Explanatory Notes, parliamentary discussion papers and the Debates, noting in particular the Second Reading Speech.

Case digests provide a summary of the main reported cases, and case citators include the subsequent judicial history of the case. These will inform you of the manner in which the judgments have been treated in subsequent decisions. Some case citators also refer you to journal articles discussing and critiquing the cases. These, together with the updating sources referring to recent unreported judgments on the topic, should provide a sufficient reporting scan. Of course, the electronic databases usually hold all this data — it is simply not edited and arranged in as accessible a fashion so that the researcher's electronic search skills become more crucial to achieve worthwhile results. Some unreported database scans for very current information will also provide you with confidence that nothing important has slipped through your net.

This chart has some drawbacks. It is an overall process rather than one driven by limited time or known information or the level of certainty required. It is an example of a linear 'umbrella' methodology, which might be most appropriate for a student researching an area where they have little or no prior knowledge. It is also book-based rather than electronic. However, as will become apparent, most of the main legal reference sources began their life as hardcopy. The same sources have been transferred to electronic formats. The legal publishers have now largely changed their electronic data presentation so that the data is accessible according to the information it contains rather than its old hardcopy presentation format. One example of this is Thomson's repackaging of the *Australian Digest* database. However, when the question is asked 'Have electronic sources restructured research methods?' the answer is still only a qualified 'Yes'.

2.3   Broad to narrow

The previous bibliographic methodology was based on a very fundamental premise, which is that the researcher will not be familiar with the topic and will need to begin the process with a scan for background commentary. There is one line of thought that it is imperative to form your own opinion of a primary source of law rather than relying on another commentator's views which would colour the issue from the outset. However, such an approach is dependent on the researcher's individual knowledge and level of expertise. It is often necessary to access basic interpretation and context before a newcomer to the area has any hope of understanding, let alone critiquing, the law. Students and researchers often need assistance in interpreting statutes and law reports until such time as they have gained sufficient familiarity with the area. Of course, the law exists within the primary authority and this should always be read carefully. While commentary is important to open the door, others cannot always be relied upon to 'get it right'. After completing some background research, find the pertinent primary materials. Locate the actual piece of legislation and read it. Likewise with all the relevant case law — and beware of simply relying on the headnote or summaries and annotations in the texts. These are frequently inaccurate and incomplete.

The next step in this process is validation. This term encompasses more than simply updating legislation or locating the most recent unreported judgment. It entails a more holistic approach, including reading the law and determining context. It is a check on what you have located through the background research and through the search for specific material on point. It completes the process which began with a broad scan of the law leading to a narrowing of focus.

2.4   Extending existing knowledge

Most researchers start the research process with some knowledge of their topic. The trick is being able to use what information is available to lead on to additional materials. To begin with, sort out what you know into categories. Enid Campbell suggested a stepped approach as another targeted methodology in this case. She identified several approaches to use as starting points — cases, legislation, key words, and 'words and phrases' judicially considered.[18] Once you have one piece of information it is easy to augment.

---

18   Campbell E, Glasson E, Poh-Yorke L and Sharpe J, *Legal Research: Materials and Methods* (3 ed, Sydney: The Law Book Company Limited, 1988), 276.

2.4.1 *The case approach*

If you have one case name in a subject area, you should be able to use this piece of information to locate:

* other cases, through the case digests and citators; and

* relevant legislation, through the encyclopaedias.

The scheme is to map your existing knowledge in order to access further relevant material. This is one key to expanding your information base.

2.4.2 *The legislative approach*

If you know the name of one Act, then you should be able to use this piece of information to locate:

* an updated version of the Act and any amendments through the annotations; and

* cases discussing the legislation through the annotations and encyclopaedias.

Once again, you will be using existing knowledge to link to further information relevant to your subject.

2.4.3 *The keyword/fact approach*

If you know a keyword, then that word can be used to search the indexes of texts, encyclopaedias, and electronic databases generally. Sometimes your knowledge may be limited to the facts of the situation; for example, a problem including cattle or kangaroos on the highway. However, it is best to attempt to include legal concepts in your keyword scan. If you are aware that, for example, concepts of fiduciary duties and professional liability are involved, then include these more analytical/legal concepts in your scan.

One keyword is generally insufficient. The next step is to brainstorm and increase your possible search terms. Take euthanasia as an example. Think about terms that might relate to:

* the type of activity or event under discussion (for example, death, assisted suicide);

* the relationship between the parties (for example, doctor/patient/family); and

* the place where the event takes place (for example, hospitals, hospice, palliative care units and also consider jurisdiction, whether State or federal).[19]

Consider the acronym TARP as a means of extending the possible keywords:

T thing (what things are involved in your situation);

A action (what legal action may be involved? Procedural or substantive matter? Defences);

R relief; and

P parties.[20]

---

19 Yogis J and Christie I, *Legal Writing and Research Manual* (4 ed, Toronto: Butterworths, 1994), 122.

20 Good CE, *Legal Research — Without Losing Your Mind* (Charlottesville: LEL Enterprises, 1993), 61–62. This is very similar to another method outlined in Chapter 4 called SCARP.

The euthanasia example is difficult to 'fit' within this formula. What about an action for compensation based on negligent driving?

T convicted offenders, victims;

A negligence, tort, contributory negligence;

R damages; and

P drivers, third parties.[21]

Another method for augmenting your search terms is the Cartwheel. Discussion of this is to be found in Chapter 4. Searching under keywords in the full text electronic databases can be an inefficient method of locating material.[22] It is preferable to isolate the subject terms that are used in the database and use these. Take a law report as an example. Most reported cases will include headnotes and these have catchwords. This means that a qualified editor has determined that the main principles of law in the case fall within specific legal terms or catchwords, roughly equivalent to those terms used in the reference tools, such as the digests and updating sources. While headnotes are not available for unreported judgments, there are often catchwords and your search will be much more likely to bring up relevant hits if you use those recognised subject terms. In a similar fashion, you will be more successful in identifying relevant journal articles in a journals index database or texts in a catalogue by searching under the assigned subject headings rather than a variety of keywords.

2.4.4 *The legal words and phrases approach*

If there is a particular legal term that is pertinent to your research, then it might be useful to look at sources where these particular terms have been discussed by using the words and phrases dictionaries. These will refer you to cases or legislation where the term has been discussed. In any case, it is always worthwhile to define terms when you are researching so that your discussion is precise.

2.4.5 *The looseleaf approach*

Looseleaf services can be excellent timesavers for basic information as they usually contain legislation, case law and commentary in a focused format. The new additions segment often also contains the latest material, such as government papers not easily accessible in other sources in such a timely fashion. Some subject areas are best accessed using this method because they change so often and are administrative in nature. Taxation is a very relevant example. For most purposes, tax law is not easily or usefully researched in the normal research sources.

2.4.6 *The keyword/case/legislation approach*

Any of these various approaches can be combined and the keyword, case and legislation combination makes good sense. This is a way of marshalling the various aspects of information at your command and using these as a base for further research. Thus, if you are searching for information on whether a

---

21 There are a number of variations on these techniques. See some further examples at 4.5.2.

22 Stein L, 'A methodology for computer-based retrieval of legal decisions' (1995) 69 *Australian Law Journal* 650.

mortgage over the family home might be enforceable against a guarantor wife, your search might take one of three approaches, taking into consideration your existing knowledge base:

Subject	Case	Legislation
domestic violence	*Lavalee*	Criminal
BWS	*Osland*	Crimes
battered wives syndrome		

Identify basic search terms and then choose the appropriate resources to enhance and extend that knowledge. This cannot be a purely linear process.

2.5 Categorising topics

In order to get started on any law library search for legal information, it is important to categorise as much as possible. Usually this is done initially and intuitively, and consists of deciding what area of law or subject matter your problem falls within. This step can be most important when you are using hardcopy material because of the necessity to look under subject areas. Of course, if you consult the general indexes or do a broad subject search in the electronic services, you will come out with a similar result. In the hardcopy, you may be referred to several different aspects of a topic under a variety of indexed topics. In the electronic services, such as journal indexes, when you do your broad search you will be able to identify the articles that closest meet your search objective and, at that point, you can check the article description to identify the correct indexed subject term. The same process needs to be pursued when using the catalogue. It may consist of carrying out a keyword search to access likely subject terms or using the subject heading lists, such as the Library of Congress Subject Headings, to ascertain the preferred subject heading. The way in which you approach research will depend on the subject matter of your problem. Criminal law problems are researched in a totally different manner to tax issues and a basic contract law issue on the postal rule will have a different starting point to a new legislative commercial provision.

So, in categorising topics, there are four basic steps:

1 Heading — Decide on a preferred subject heading.

2 Civil or criminal — Once you have decided on your subject heading you must decide whether the aspect you are concerned with is civil or criminal.

3 Legislative or common law based — Following this, you can usually call on your own general knowledge to categorise the area into legislative, whether Commonwealth or State, or a common law jurisdictional issue. It may be that you will need to look at subject indexes and updating services to ensure that new legislation has not been passed in the area.

4 Substantive or procedural — The next phase is to ask whether the particular aspect is substantive or procedural in nature.

2.6 Using checklists

Checklists can be great timesavers. Often, all you require is to know how to update basic legal information; for example, to locate the subsequent judicial history of cases, or to ascertain if there are any cases on specific sections of legislation. Such regular research functions are tabulated at the back of this volume and include checklists of reference sources as well as information on the sources and tips for using them. If you approach your research by function, once you are familiar with the basic steps involved in the updating process, all you really require are the pertinent sources for the jurisdiction. Most primary materials, including case reports and statutes, are now available through electronic subscription or on the internet. However, the basic legal reference tools, such as the legal encyclopaedias, are still very valuable for researchers as these provide the edited access to the bulk of information available. This means that the cases and legislation are edited by subject and summarised for easy accessibility.

The full list at the back of this volume contains headings, such as:

* locating texts on a particular topic;
* locating an encyclopaedic coverage of the law;
* locating journal articles on a particular topic;
* locating case law on a specific topic;
* locating cases judicially considered; that is, the subsequent history of cases;
* locating articles or notes about individual cases;
* locating cases on specific sections of legislation;
* locating Bills;
* locating discussion and explanatory notes or memoranda for legislation;
* locating legislation on a particular subject;
* establishing whether a particular Act has been amended or repealed;
* locating law reform publications;
* locating commencement dates for legislation;
* locating delegated legislation;
* locating meanings of citations and abbreviations;
* locating definitions of legal words and phrases;
* locating international treaties and conventions; and
* locating comparative law.

You will gradually become so familiar with the main sources in your own jurisdiction that, for the most part, you will not need a list. However, sometimes it is nice to be able to fall back on the less familiar options in the checklists when you are unsure.

2.7 Using flowcharts

If you are a visual learner, you will find flowcharts most helpful in determining each individual step in the intricate research process.

This is an example of an updating scheme for a legal topic. There are no sources indicated, so if these were not known the chart would need to be used in conjunction with the Checklists.

2.8 Handy research hints

There are some basic tips for using legal resources, whether published in hardcopy, online or on the web. Whenever you come to use a source, consider:

* whether the reference source covers the necessary geographical jurisdictions; for example, are materials from both the United Kingdom and the United States indexed;

* whether there is a more specific reference source for your jurisdiction; obviously, a looseleaf service on sentencing in Queensland is going to be more helpful than an entry in a legal encyclopaedia if you need any in-depth coverage of the issues;

* whether valuable older information might only be accessed using hardcopy sources;

* whether the reference source covers all the court jurisdictions; for example, are both District and Supreme Court cases digested;

* whether the period you are looking for is covered. Remember, for example, that there is a timelag in the production of journal indexes so they will not be most useful for journals issued in the last week!;

* whether you have double-checked the alternative sources available for your information, because one research source may include information overlooked by another. Thus it is important to consult a variety of updating sources, including both the Australian updating series, *Australian Legal Monthly Digest* and *Australian Current Law*, and all suscription services on similar topics from competing publishers; and

* whether the currency date of the resource or web page includes the currency of material covered as well as the date of last change made.

Timeliness is the major issue in legal research — making certain you have the correct section number, the latest wording of the legislation, the latest High Court decision. This is the area where most mistakes can be made.

2.9 How much research is enough?

This is a question often asked by novice researchers. The answer is not 'cut and dried'. Sometimes it relies on a cost–benefit analysis. When the cost of obtaining more information outweighs the benefits in additional knowledge to be gained, then it is time to stop and re-assess. This is easier to calculate with empirical and social science research. If one or two more survey forms will make no difference to the overall statistical result, then it is time to stop. With doctrinal research, it may be a matter of assessing whether all the necessary research sources have been covered and the necessary steps, particularly updating steps, have been taken. When you begin to locate the same material found elsewhere, so that you are turning up no new material in your searches, then that probably indicates that what you have is sufficient.

Be careful not to become too carried away in detail. Some research is crucial. Some details are not important in relation to the whole. Perhaps more important than this is determining whether you can address the question posed in a logical manner. If you cannot explain it in a lucid enough manner to make a novice understand the crux of the arguments, then perhaps it is still not clear in your own mind. Perhaps you have sufficient material but the thinking and synthesising phase is not complete.

Michael Lynch has described this as 'The Closed Circle Factor'; that is, when the circle of knowledge is closed. What the researcher needs to be able to do is reach a point of completion where enough information has been found regarding an area so that the references and ideas begin to be repeated, and the reports and texts are referring to sources already perused.[23]

2.10 Conclusion

This chapter aimed to investigate more closely the doctrinal research methodology classification as well as provide a number of standard techniques that can be categorised under the doctrinal methodology banner. Doctrinal research is one methodology. There are many others. You may need to consider using some of those other methods in order to provide support for conclusions tentatively drawn from your doctrinal work. This is where triangulation of methods becomes important. There is a discussion of triangulation in Chapter 5.

Further reading

Armstrong JDS and Knott CA, *Where the Law Is: An Introduction to Advanced Legal Research* (3 ed, New York: West, 2009).

Berring RC and Edinger E, *Finding the Law* (12 ed, New York: West, 2005).

Bott B, Cowley J and Falconer L, *Nemes and Coss' Effective Legal Research* (3 ed, Sydney: LexisNexis Butterworths, 2007).

Campbell E, Poh-York L and Tooher J, *Legal Research: Materials and Methods* (4 ed, Sydney: LBC, 1996).

---

23 Lynch M, 'An impossible task but everybody has to do it — Teaching legal research in law schools' (1997) 88 *Law Library Journal* 415 at 422.

Castel J and Latchman OK, *The Practical Guide to Canadian Legal Research* (2 ed, Scarborough, Ontario: Carswell, 1996).

Clinch P, *Using a Law Library* (2 ed, London: Blackstone Press, 2001).

Cook C, Creyke R, Geddes R and Hamer D, *Laying Down the Law* (7 ed, Chatswood, NSW: LexisNexis Butterworths, 2009).

Enright C and Sidorko P, *Legal Research Technique* (Sydney: Branxton Press, 2002).

Enright C, *Legal Skills* (Sydney: Branxton Press, 2006).

Farrer J, 'In pursuit of an appropriate theoretical perspective and methodology for comparative corporate governance' (2001) 13 *Australian Journal of Corporate Law* 1.

Greville M, Davidson S and Scragg R, *Legal Research and Writing in New Zealand* (3 ed, LexisNexis, 2007).

Holborn G, Butterworths Legal Research Guide (2 ed, London: Butterworths, 2001).

Jacobstein J, Mersky R and Dunn D, *Fundamentals of Legal Research* (8 ed, New York: Foundation Press, 2002).

Knowles J, Effective Legal Research (2 ed, London: Sweet and Maxwell, 2009).

Kunz C, *The Process of Legal Research* (6 ed, New York: Aspen Publishers Inc, 2004).

McConville M and Chui WH (eds), *Research Methods for Law* (Edinburgh: Edinburgh University Press, 2007).

McDowell M and Webb D, *The New Zealand Legal System: structures, process and legal theory* (4 ed, Wellington: LexisNexis, 2006).

Milne S and Tucker K, *A Practical Guide to Legal Research* (Sydney: Lawbook Co., 2008).

Pester D, Finding Legal Information (Oxford: Chandos, 2003).

Sloan A, *Basic Legal Research: Tools and Strategies* (3 ed, New York: Aspen Publishers Inc, 2003).

Thomas P and Knowles J, *Dane and Thomas' How to Use a Law Library: An Introduction to Legal Skills* (4 ed, London: Sweet & Maxwell, 2001).

Watt R, *Concise Legal Research* (6 ed, Sydney: The Federation Press, 2009).

William G, *Learning the Law* (13 ed, London: Sweet & Maxwell, 2006).

Yogis JA and Christie IM, *Legal Writing and Research Manual* (6 ed, Markham, Ontario: Butterworths, 2004).

3

Additional Legal Research Frameworks

Doctrinal research may be the primary methodology within the current legal research paradigm, but the paradigm is dynamic. At the boundaries of the existing paradigm, exciting and varied research processes have always been available. Theoretical and reform-oriented research categories were identified by the Pearce Committee. Public policy research has gained increasing sophistication and often (but not always) incorporates a legal dimension.

Theoretical research is situated within the existing legal research paradigm. It is different in that it is based in philosophy rather than praxis, but it can extend to interdisciplinary methodologies when applied to the law in action. Theoretical research encompasses and impinges on practical issues, such as the feminist view of legal education as demonstrated by surveys of law students, the economic analysis of seatbelt regulations, or the critical race theory view of the use of the death penalty in the United States taking into account statistics of government imposed deaths over the last fifty years. So there are spectrums within theoretical research stretching from pure philosophy to applied theory.

The work of the law reform commissions is also situated within traditional research paradigms. Law reform has been part of the process of incremental change for decades. However, some of its processes are not as fluid or malleable as policy and reform issues require in the present context. This is a result of its long history within a conservative legal establishment reform process. There are limitations or controls on the references it can undertake, and there are set processes or steps through which it proceeds. Law reform can be independent in suggesting outcomes, an aspect that does not always endear it to the government of the day.

On the other hand, public policy research is usually driven by the government of the day in a way that the semi-independent law reform commissions are not. Policy sections within government departments usually carry out research, and the process often begins with a number of options acceptable to the government. Sometimes the process begins with stated government policies, and departments are given the brief to investigate and implement the policies. Policy research includes a similar mixture of methodologies used by the law reform bodies.

These three frameworks and their individual but melded methodologies define the traditional boundaries of legal research.

3.1 **Theoretical research**

Theoretical research deals with the underpinnings of law — the ideas and assumptions which make up the theories upon which rules are based. Theories develop and progress within cycles. One theory is expounded, another writer adds to it and extends its application, but gradually there is a change and a new group of adherents will critique the original. This group may then put forward their own theory and the cycle will begin again. There are any number of theories about the basis and workings of the law. And it is not the case that one theory ends and another begins in a neat fashion. There may be a dominant theory prevalent amongst the establishment, or those with a predominant voice in society, at any one time. However, hangovers from previous ways of thinking remain and new ideas and theories are emerging at the same time. Some theories, such as natural law, may fall into total disrepute only to re-emerge in a different guise decades later. The Western Legal Tradition Timeline names the various theories and puts them in the context of social and political history as well as listing some of the major exponents.

It is not appropriate or possible within the walls of this text to describe, explain, critique or assess the extent of jurisprudential writing. The Further Reading list at the end of this section sets out some accessible texts which review the main legal theories. It is necessary to state strongly that anyone setting out to examine, research and think about the law should not be ignorant of the pervasive philosophical 'vibes'. Just as in the film *The Castle*, the appellants argued how basic principles regarding the importance of personal property and the rights of the individual against the State shone through the Australian Constitution, so such intrinsic and crucial philosophies are present in every aspect of law.[1] The trick is to be able to recognise the extent and effect of underlying theory in order to better critique the validity of what exists, and provide a basis for something better. An analogy has been drawn between paddling along the surface of the ocean and not considering the dangers of rocks below the waterline, and the position of a legal writer, who does not consider underlying legal theory when looking at the law in practice.[2]

Pausing with this analogy, it is interesting to think about the predominant theories as something breathed in without our awareness of their existence. Current philosophy tends to be closely linked to fashion and the events that are shaping history. One glance at the comparative timeline reinforces this view. Theory shapes history — the ideas of liberty and equality influenced revolutions, and economic agendas forced changes in the way nations structure their societies.

The foundational theory of law is natural law, whereby the law is not created by any person but by God. According to this theory, law is timeless. It exists and can be deduced or reasoned by any person. Law is not embedded in one culture. It applies to all cultures. This law is different from the regulations

---

1   See for example MacNeil P, "'It's the Constitution, it's Mabo — it's the vibe": The Common Law Imaginary Down Under — A Jurisprudential Reading of *The Castle*' (Socio-Legal Research Centre Griffith University Working Paper Series No 1).

2   Horrigan B, *Horror's Hints* (Brisbane: Queensland University of Technology Faculty of Law, 2000), 7.

created by society for its own organisation, or even religious doctrine. Many modern writers still adhere to ideas based in natural law, including John Finnis who insists that the principles of natural law are self-evident and as relevant today as they were at the time of St Thomas Aquinas. In addition, obvious links can be made between the principles of natural law and social justice and the international human rights movements in the late twentieth century.

3.1.1 *Western legal tradition timeline*[3]

Theory	Writers	Political Context	Legal Reasoning	Comparative Context
Natural Law derived from universal moral principles				
Greeks	Aristotle *The Nicomachean Ethics*[4]	City-state		
Romans	Cicero *De re publica*[5]	Republic	Roman Law	The Roman Empire
Middle Ages — Renaissance	St Thomas Aquinas 1224–1274 *Summa theologiae*[6]	Feudal system	Canon Law Magna Carta 1215	The Crusades
		Economic era of mercantile capitalism	Recourse to time-less common law principles	First Agricultural Revolution 1485 European colonisation of Americas 1492 Reformation Martin Luther 1483–1546

3 My thanks to Helen Stacy for her comments on the draft.
4 (New York: Cambridge University Press, 2000).
5 (Cambridge: Cambridge University Press, 1995).
6 Henle R (ed), (Notre Dame: University of Notre Dame Press, c1993).

Western legal tradition timeline — continued

Theory	Writers	Political Context	Legal Reasoning	Comparative Context
Seventeenth Century	Thomas Hobbes 1588–1679 *Leviathan*[7] John Locke 1632–1704 *Two Treatises of Government* (1690)[8]	English Civil Wars 1642–1651 Restoration 1660 English Revolution 1688	Declaratory Theory — judges declaring pre-existing law	Hugo Grotius 1583–1645 *De Jure Belli et Pacis* [On the Law of War and Peace] (1625) Origins of International law 1648 Based on universal laws of nature Samuel von Pufendorf 1632–1694 *De Jure Naturae et gentium* (1672)
Eighteenth Century Age of Reason	Sir William Blackstone 1723–1780 *Commentaries on the Laws of England* (1765–1769)[9]	American Revolution 1775–1783 French Revolution 1789	Beginning of rights based Liberalism US Bill of Rights and French Declaration of the Rights of Man	Blackstone's Rules for the application of law in conquered territories — 1770 Australia 'settled' not conquered
Twentieth Century Revival of Natural Law	John Finnis 1940 *Natural Law and Natural Rights* (1980)[10]	WW I 1914–1918 WW II 1939–1945	*MIEA v Teoh* (1995) 183 CLR 273 Rights of the Child	Human Rights Agreements
Positivism Legal rules created by human institutions		Beginning of economic era of industrial capitalism	Law as science No necessary connection between law and morality	Codification of laws in Europe

7   Tuck R (ed), (New York: Cambridge University Press, 1996).

8   Laslett P (ed), (London: Cambridge University Press, 1967).

9   (Abingdon, England: Professional Books, 1982).

10 (New York: Oxford University Press, 1980).

Western legal tradition timeline — continued

Theory	Writers	Political Context	Legal Reasoning	Comparative Context
Eighteenth Century Age of Reason	David Hume 1711–1776 *An Enquiry Concerning Human Understanding* (1748)[11]		Common law use of precedent. Syllogistic reasoning – law applied in a mechanical manner. Formalism	Industrial Revolution Development of contract-based societies
	Jeremy Bentham 1748–1832 *An Introduction to the Principles of Morals and Legislation* (1789)[12]	Bentham's Utilitarianism – 'greatest good for the greatest number'		
Nineteenth Century	John Austin 1790–1859 *The Province of Jurisprudence Determined* (1832)[13]	Austin's 'The existence of law is one thing; its merits or demerits another'	Law is objective and value free	
Twentieth Century	HLA Hart 1907–1992 *The Concept of Law* (1961)[14]		'Strict legalism' 1952 Owen Dixon CJ High Court *SGIC v Trigwell* (1978) 142 CLR 617	US Legal Realism 1930s Oliver Wendell Holmes
Liberalism Primacy of the individual in society		Protection of individual vis-à-vis State		
Eighteenth Century Age of Reason	Adam Smith 1723–1740, *Inquiry into the Nature and Causes of the Wealth of Nations* (1776)[15] 'classical' political economist	Importance of private property A kind of social liberalism derived from Utilitarianism	Distinction made between the public and private realm of law	Industrial Revolution 1760–1820 French Revolution International law permitting use of force in international relations

11 (La Salle, Ill: Open Court, c1988).

12 (London: Athlone P, 1970).

13 (Brookfield, Vt: Ashgate, Dartmouth, c1998).

14 (2 ed, New York: Oxford University Press, 1994).

15 Campbell R and Skinner R (eds), (Indianapolis: Liberty Classics, 1981, c1976).

Western legal tradition timeline — continued

Theory	Writers	Political Context	Legal Reasoning	Comparative Context
Nineteenth Century	John Stuart Mill 1806–1873 *On Liberty* (1859)[16]	Welfare Liberalism 1870 Mills' 'Harm to others' principle	Contracts enforced strictly. Equitable doctrines applied pedantically.	Classical Liberal Theory and Nightwatchman State UK Parliament 1832–1870
Twentieth Century	Leonard Hobhouse 1864–1929 *Liberalism* (1911)[17]		*Donoghue v Stevenson* [1932] AC 562 Neighbour Principle	Industrial regulation – Safety, Children, Wages
	Milton Friedman 1912–			Friedrich August von Hayek 1899–1992 *The Road to Serfdom* (1944) UN Charter 1945 Outlawing force in international relations
	John Keynes 1883–1946 *The End of Laissez Faire* (1926)[18] Ayn Rand 1905–1982	Rand's Individualism, Laissez faire capitalism Neo-Classical Liberalism		
	John Rawls 1921– *A Theory of Justice* (1972)[19] Robert Nozick 1938– *Anarchy, State and Eutopia* (1974)[20]		*Milirrpum v Nabalco* (1971) 17 FLR 141	US lands a craft on the Moon 1969 'Market-oriented' governments – President Ronald Reagan USA, Prime Minister Margaret Thatcher UK Privatisation Corporatisation Hilmer Reforms
	Ronald Dworkin 1931– *Taking Rights Seriously* (1977)[21]	Dworkin's Rights-based Liberalism		

16 Himmelfarb G (ed), (Harmondsworth: Penguin, 1985).

17 (rev ed, London: Oxford University Press, 1971).

18 *The Collected Writings of John Maynard Keynes* (London: Macmillan for the Royal Economic Society, 1971).

19 (Cambridge, Mass: Belknap Press of Harvard University Press, 1999).

20 (New York: Basic Books, c1974).

21 (Cambridge: Harvard University Press, c1978).

Western legal tradition timeline — continued

Theory	Writers	Political Context	Legal Reasoning	Comparative Context
Economic Analysis of Law Law should be economically efficient	In the footsteps of John Locke, Adam Smith, David Hume, Jeremy Bentham, JS Mill from the Seventeenth–Nineteenth Centuries			
Twentieth Century	Ronald Coase Coase Theorem (1959) *The firm, the market and the law* (1988)[22] Guido Calabresi The Costs of Accidents (1970)[23] Richard Posner *Economic Analysis of Law* (1992)[24]	1972 Withdrawal of Australian troops from Vietnam	US Legal Realism 1930s Julius Stone – Australian realism 1940s Chicago School; 1960 Public Choice Theory	Decolonisation Civil Rights movements Post-industrial age Self-determination in international law 1975 Human Rights Conventions
Critical Legal Studies – Critiques Liberalism; Law advantages the powerful in society	Roberto Unger The Critical Legal Studies Movement (1986)[25] Mark Tushnet *Red, white, and blue: a critical analysis of constitutional law* (1988)[26]	1989 The Berlin Wall separating East Germany from West Germany is opened.	The law is not objective, but based in liberalism. Anti-formalism in the High Court: *Mabo v Queensland (No 2)* (1992) 175 CLR 1	Growth of multinational corporations 1986 Explosion of nuclear power station at Chernobyl

22 (Chicago: University of Chicago Press, 1988).
23 (New Haven: Yale University Press, 1970).
24 (New York: Aspen Law & Business, c1998).
25 (Cambridge, Mass: Harvard University Press, 1986).
26 (Cambridge, Mass: Harvard University Press, 1988).

Western legal tradition timeline — continued

Theory	Writers	Political Context	Legal Reasoning	Comparative Context
Feminism Law advantages men in society	Carol Smart *Feminism and the power of law* (1989)[27] Carol Gilligan *In a Different Voice* (1982)[28] Catherine MacKinnon *Toward a Feminist Theory of the State* (1989)[29] Regina Graycar *The Hidden Gender of Law* (1990)[30] Margaret Davies *Asking the Law Question* (1994)[31]	1970s Equal pay for equal work in Australia Government funding for child care	Liberal feminism

Cultural feminism

Radical feminism

Justice Mary Gaudron appointed to High Court 1987 | Anti-discrimination and equity approaches

Communication and technology explosion

Globalisation

R v Lavallee [1990] 1 SCR 852 Battered Woman Syndrome |
Critical Race Theory Law advantages particular racial groups	Kimberley Crenshaw *Critical Race Theory* (1995)[32]		*Mabo v Queensland (No 2)* (1992) 175 CLR 1	
Late Twentieth Century	Larissa Behrendt[33]	*Racial Discrimination Act 1975* (Cth) *Native Title Act 1993* (Cth)	*Wik Peoples v Qld* (1996) 187 CLR 1 Pastoral leases and native title	Australian Law Reform Commission Report on the Recognition of Aboriginal Customary Laws 1986 Establishment of the Tent Embassy in Canberra
Twenty-first Century	Richard Delgado *Critical Race Theory: an introduction* (2001)[34]	The rise of the One Nation Party 1990s		

27 (London: Routledge, 1989).

28 (rev ed, Cambridge, Mass: Harvard University Press, 1993).

29 (Cambridge, Mass: Harvard University Press, 1989).

30 Graycar R and Morgan J, (2 ed, Leichhardt, NSW: Federation Press, 2002).

31 (2 ed, Sydney: Law Book Co, 2001).

32 Crenshaw K (ed), (New York: New Press, 2001).

33 'Aboriginal women and the white lies of the feminist movement: implications for Aboriginal women in rights discourse' (1) August 1993 *Australian Feminist Law Journal* 27–44.

34 Delgado R and Stefancic J, (New York: New York University Press, 2001).

Western legal tradition timeline — continued

Theory	Writers	Political Context	Legal Reasoning	Comparative Context
Post-Modernism Rejection of common experience in favour of subjectivity	Mary Joe Frug *Postmodern Legal Feminism* (1992)[35] Jean François Lyotard 'Answering the Question: What is Postmodernism?' (1984)[36]	1991 Soviet Union dissolved Emergence of Social Democrat Governments: Clinton in US, Blair in UK, Schroeder in Germany	*Masciantonio v R* (1995) 183 CLR 58 Ethnicity and the 'ordinary person'	Increasing use of the Internet Growth of global economies First Gulf War 1990–1991
Late Twentieth Century	Costas Douzinas, Ronnie Warrington and Shaun McVeigh *Postmodern Jurisprudence* (1991)[37]	Prime Minister John Howard 1996	Gleeson appointed Chief Justice 1998	
Twenty-first Century		Mandatory detention of refugees in Australia Tougher anti-terrorism legislation	*Al-Kateb v Godwin* (2004) 219 CLR 562	Terrorism September 2001 World Trade Centre attack New York Terrorist attack Bali November 2002 Second Gulf War 2003 Terrorist attacks London, Bali, India 2005
		Prime Minister Kevin Rudd 2007 (Labor)	French appointed Chief Justice 2008 *C.A.L. No 14 Pty Ltd v Motor Accidents Insurance Board; C.A.L. No 14 Pty Ltd v Scott* [2009] HCA 47 (10 November 2009) Shift to personal responsibility in negligence cases	Global Financial Crisis 2008

35 (New York: Routledge, 1992).

36 In May T (ed), *Twentieth Century Continental Philosophy* (Upper Saddle River, New Jersey: Prentice Hall, 1997).

37 (London: Routledge, 1991).

Positivism was advanced as an alternative to natural law. Positivism holds that supernatural law is not a part of law. Law deals with what the law is, rather than what the law ought to be. People created legal systems and these systems set down what the law is, and the people accepted that they would be governed by these rules. Positivism sees law as a system of rules imposed on society by a recognised supreme political or government authority. Law is differentiated from morality. It is secular regulation, made by human authority.

These views infused the common law and the development of judicial reasoning, particularly the declaratory theory of judicial reasoning, where the judges are considered oracles, declaring rather than deciding or using any personal discretion to state the law. The common law obtained its authority from its timelessness, discovered through logic and reason from previous case law. This type of decision-making led to 'slot machine justice' or formalism, where the judge treated the law as self-contained, and made no reference to any external context. This view in turn has given way to anti-formalism and the recognition that the judges do use discretion and that values from outside the system are included when decisions are made.

Thus, mainstream law in the last two centuries has become based in a secular positivist approach which values 'black letter' principles; that is, those principles and rules actually written down on the page. Aligned with this view is the dominant political ideology of liberalism. There is no one definition of liberalism. It is a concept with different manifestations and qualities, and the ideas in it are very much intertwined with ideas of formalism, positivism, rationality and increasingly the various legal critiques of the late twentieth century, such as economic analysis of law. Liberalism places emphasis on the priority of the individual, and the public/private distinction in which law, politics, and government exist in the public sphere. It should not impede on private or personal matters. It uses rationality, material proof and logic as a yardstick to predict action. It favours a benchmark of neutrality. It includes the individual's right to equality before the law, and personal liberty, economic and social freedom, and autonomy. Personal freedom can only be circumscribed in order to prevent 'harm to others'. Liberalism is usually aligned with capitalism and democratic principles. However, there are degrees of difference in the various strands of liberalism. Where *laissez faire* liberalism promotes the 'night watchman' minimalist state, welfare liberals favour more intervention by the state in the provision of health, education and industrial regulation, to protect those less well off in society.

Liberalism has spawned various critiques and associated theories. Foremost of these is the economic analysis of law, which uses economic theory to determine law's effects on society, as well as the genesis of law in economic factors. Critiquing liberalism is fashionable and the advocates of dissent have come from many directions — critical legal studies scholars reject liberal ideas of law as being neutral and objective and consider that law is a political construct with regulations formed by those with power in society. Feminist legal theory went further and said that those with power who constructed the law were male, and that the law reflects male values. Critical race theory asserts that the legal system is not objective or neutral but favours white values. Therefore, the proponents of these critiques argue that law is not necessarily objective, and that in many ways it has been formulated by 'wealthy white men' for their own benefit and in their own likeness. They also assert that the law is not a closed system, but that it exists in a wider context. This postmodern worldview encompasses the broad spectrum of society and recognises the individual subjective experience of law. It recognises that 'different people experience the world differently' and that 'differences in power have resulted in ... a monopoly on knowledge production' and too often a monopoly on law-making.[38]

Postmodernism became prominent from the mid-1980s. It emerged from ideas of modernism which signified a rational objective world governed by science.[39] Postmodernism can be described in terms of 'repeated themes' including deconstruction which is 'a practical intervention in established modes of thinking, which destabilises the stereotypes, value-judgments, and categories upon which theories are inevitably constructed'.[40] Postmodernism challenges the 'the idea of universal, abstract principles of legitimation'.[41] The movement is a reaction against modernism which was 'the attempt to find absolute grounds for knowledge, to discover abstract, transcendent principles which would be the foundation for all philosophical questioning'.[42] Postmodernism's pervasiveness in current thinking is exemplified by its supposed inroads into ideas of judicial neutrality as pointed to by the actions of the Supreme Court of Canada in *R v RDS* [1997] 3 SCR 484. As L'Heureux-Dube J has written: 'Judges should not aspire to neutrality. When judges have the opportunity to recognize inequalities in society, and then to make those inequalities legally relevant to the disputes before them in order to achieve a just result, then they should do so.'[43]

3.1.2 *Jurisprudential method*

These theories provide a smorgasbord of ideas and approaches available to enhance your research and critique of existing law. They can engender an extension of the thought boundaries, suggesting further depth and context for any research proposal. There are always theoretical underpinnings for any endeavour, and it is very challenging to attempt to identify and expose these. Even more challenging is the ability to look with other eyes at a legal scene – or to use another analogy, to see both versions of the black and white sketch. Remember the visual trick of the photo of a candlestick, which if you look hard enough becomes the profiles of two heads, or the sketch of an old woman with a long nose which, when looked at in another light, turns into a beautiful lady with a pearl necklace. These visual tricks can be echoed in new conceptual views.

---

38 Kirby S and McKenna K, *Experience/Research/Social Change* (Toronto, Ontario: Garamond Press, 1994), 26.

39 Klages M, 'Postmodernism', http://www.colorado.edu/English/courses/ENGL2012Klages/pomo.html (5/11/2009).

40 Davies M, *Asking the Law Question* (3 ed, Sydney: Lawbook Co., 2008), 327.

41 Davies M, *Asking the Law Question* (3 ed, Sydney: Lawbook Co., 2008), 335.

42 Davies M, *Asking the Law Question* (3 ed, Sydney: Lawbook Co., 2008), 328.

43 Ipp DA, 'Judicial impartiality and judicial neutrality: Is there a difference?' (2000) 19 *Australian Bar Review* 212 at 215 (quoting from 'Reflections on Judicial Independence, Impartiality and the Foundations of Equality' *CIJL Yearbook* vol vii 95 at 105).

How do you get a new take on legal fundamental theories or critique?

Having been schooled in a liberal tradition, it is sometimes difficult to change focus to bring in new ways of seeing, but the key is awareness and openness to the new. This does not necessarily mean agreement with any of these views but forewarned is fore-armed, and knowledge of potential criticisms and arguments should engender a deeper reflection and understanding of the intricacies and effects of the law.

Are there specific methodologies associated with critique of legal theory?

Within jurisprudential writing, the critique formula tends to favour a statement of the main tenets of a theory. This theory can often be sifted down into several simpler points. Having identified this skeleton, the main arguments against each of these may be isolated. The process looks something like this:

1   stating the theory with its main tenets;

2   listing the common arguments against these aspects;

3   putting forward counter-arguments; and

4   illustrating the consequences of particular points being accepted or denied.[44]

The difficulty with this method is in the assumption that theory can be categorised and boxed, when in fact theories tend to be nebulous and conflicting. They are usually expounded by groups of disparate authors who agree in some areas and disagree strongly in others so that there are many strands of thought woven into the whole. To try to reduce this to some basic platitudes can be intellectually insulting.

How does this affect the research methodology process?

There is no onus to include theory in every piece of writing or research. In fact, for most practical purposes treatment of theory is totally out of place and irrelevant — 'overt' treatment at any rate. Nor is it appropriate to look at every theory in relation to every circumstance. The trick is to be able to recognise the theoretical basis intrinsic to a practical legal problem or a view espoused in legislation or in a judgment. If you can achieve this level of analysis then you will have a broader view of the context of the issue under discussion. Armed with this knowledge, you may be able to call on the accepted arguments against this theoretical stance and, where appropriate, find a legal outcome which is backed up by a solid theoretical rationale.

Further reading

Berns S, *Concise Jurisprudence* (Sydney: The Federation Press, 1993).

Bottomley S and Parker S, *Law in Context* (2 ed, Sydney: The Federation Press, 1997).

Cuff E, Sharrock W and Francis D, *Perspectives in Sociology* (4 ed, London: Routledge, 1998).

Davies M, *Asking the Law Question* (3 ed, Sydney: Lawbook Co., 2008).

---

44 Hunter R, Ingleby R and Johnstone R (eds), *Thinking About Law: Perspectives on the History, Philosophy and Sociology of Law* (St Leonards, NSW: Allen & Unwin, 1995), 43-44.

Freeman MDA, *Lloyd's Introduction to Jurisprudence* (8 ed, London: Sweet & Maxwell, 2008).

Harris JW, *Legal Philosophies* (2 ed, London: Butterworths, 1997).

Hunter R, Ingleby R and Johnstone R (eds), *Thinking About Law* (St Leonards: Allen & Unwin, 1995).

Kelly JM, *A Short History of Western Legal Theory* (Oxford: Clarendon Press, 1992).

Leiboff M and Thomas M, *Legal Theories: Context and Practices* (Sydney: Lawbook Co., 2009).

Wacks R, *Understanding Jurisprudence* (2 ed, Oxford: Oxford University Press, 2009).

Williams C, 'Case studies and the sociology of gender' Chapter 7 in Feagin JR, Orum A and Sjoberg G (eds), *A Case for the Case Study* (Chapel Hill and London: The University of North Carolina Press, 1991).

3.2 Law reform research

> There is no cosy little world of lawyers' law in which learned men may frolic without raising socially controversial issues — I challenge anyone to identify an issue of law reform so technical that it raises no social, political or economic issue. If there is any such thing, I doubt if it would be worth doing anything about it.[45]

The modern legal context is synonymous with change. Reform research is therefore of great importance. There are numerous bodies that are involved in law reform. There are advisory councils established by government, community legal associations, ad hoc royal commissions, and special committees within the professional associations such as the State law societies and the Law Council of Australia. Academics in the university law faculties perform a law reform and policy role through their published critiques of the law. This section will concentrate on one major vehicle for change which is provided by the law reform agencies.

Law reform agencies frequently pick up issues that may not suit the existing government's priorities, but require lengthy research processes. Other avenues for reform exist, but openness and public accountability make the law reform commission methodologies more popular than the court-like procedures and secrecy followed by other formal inquiry processes, such as royal commissions, or the confidential consultation followed by government departments. Recent analysis of the Annual Reports of The Law Commission (UK) and the Australian Law Reform Commission would indicate that 'over two-thirds' of the reports of these commissions 'have been implemented or at least partially implemented'.[46]

Law reform is not a new concept in common law countries. One of the first reform committees was established by Sir Matthew Hale and sat for five years

---

45 Scarman L, *Law Reform: The New Pattern* (London: Routledge & Kegan Paul, 1968), 27-28, as quoted in Annual Report 1991 NSW Law Reform Commission at 5.

46 White B, *Consultation, Commissions and Context: A Comparative Study of the Law Commission and the Australian Law Reform Commission* (Thesis, DPhil in Law, Oxford University, Hilary 2004).

from 1652 to 1657.[47] More recently, the United Kingdom had a very active Law Revision Committee sitting from 1934 to 1939, and then in 1952 the Lord Chancellor's Law Reform Committee was established. The English Law Commission followed in 1965.[48] Commissions in Australia have largely been modelled on the English Law Commission, with the first law reform commission being established in new South Wales in 1870. The New South Wales Law Reform Commission was established in 1966 as the first permanent body taking on the role of law reform.[49] Prior to this, law reform was entrusted to ad hoc inquiries, royal commissions and, sometimes, standing committees. The Australian Law Reform Commission was established in 1975. Justice Michael Kirby, the first Chair, worked tirelessly and provided an amazing legacy of reform.

The contemporary model for law reform bodies is that of commissions within the States and at federal level, established by governments but largely independent in nature. The commissions are supposed to be neutral in their approach to topics. Continuity in staffing and budget is the norm. These organisations now usually employ full-time staff. They are likely to have a permanent library and sufficient resources to cover the release of reports and working papers. Their permanent nature, together with the fact that many are established by statute, ensure their place within the democratic process. Though law reform commissions certainly do not have a 100 per cent success rate in terms of having their reports 'acted on' by government, or indeed the judiciary, their reports are well regarded and are of significant academic value.

3.2.1 *What is law reform and what topics are likely to be covered by law reform bodies?*

William Hurlburt defines law reform as denoting 'the alteration of the law in some respect with a view to its improvement'.[50] However, there has appeared to be a demarcation line drawn in the past, so that reform issues have tended to centre on what Hurlburt has termed 'lawyer's law'. This has centred on the technical 'revamping' and updating of law, rather than 'social-policy law'.[51] Social policy law includes the 'hands off' areas of homosexuality, abortion and capital punishment.[52] It seems a reasonable response for the commissions to prefer to take a narrow view of their role and leave the wider issues to the people through Parliament.[53] The emphasis on technical aspects of law has tended to restrict the

---

47 Deech R, 'Law reform: the choice of method' (1969) XLVII *The Canadian Bar Review* 395 at 396.

48 Hurlburt W, *Law Reform Commissions in the United Kingdom, Australia and Canada* (Edmonton: Juriliber Limited, 1986), Chapter 2.

49 Ross S, *Politics of Law Reform* (Melbourne: Penguin Books Australia, 1982), 68.

50 Hurlburt W, *Law Reform Commissions in the United Kingdom, Australia and Canada* (Edmonton: Juriliber Limited, 1986), 6.

51 Hurlburt W, *Law Reform Commissions in the United Kingdom, Australia and Canada* (Edmonton: Juriliber Limited, 1986), 13.

52 Cretney S, 'The politics of law reform — A view from the inside' (1985) 48 (5) *The Modern Law Review* 493 at 495–6.

53 Sackville R, 'The role of law reform agencies in Australia' (1985) 59 *Australian Law Journal* 151 at 157.

purview of the commissions to 'a matter of patching, correction of detail and small-scale amendments'.[54] However, it is evident that in any discussion of change or legal reform or improvement, there is always likely to be winners and losers, and in this way policy can rear its head even though the issue under consideration appears neutral.

The *Law Reform Commission Act 1968* (Qld), for example, established the Queensland Law Reform Commission, and gave it similar powers as those conferred in the UK legislation in 1965. The function of the Commission is to keep under review all the law applicable to the state with a view to its systematic development and reform. In carrying out this function, the Commission receives and considers proposals for reform of the law. In particular, it undertakes work on references given to the Commission by the Attorney-General.

The Commission currently has one full-time member and a number of part-time members with support from researchers and administrative staff. The chair has 'always been a judge acting part-time' in the past, and it is presently chaired by a judge of the Supreme Court. Unexpected events can sometimes trigger a new reference, such as the disaster at the Moura coal mine, which involved the Government in a question of whether de facto partners were eligible for compensation. The information on this issue was needed as a matter of urgency within 14 days and limited the extent to which the Commission could engage in consultation. Reports of the Commission are tabled in the Parliament.

Formal law reform bodies include those agencies established under statute, organisations concerned with a review of specific areas of law, standing or select parliamentary committees, standing law reform committees established by ministers, ad hoc committees established to report on specific matters, and ad hoc inter-governmental law reform committees appointed to assist the standing committees of Attorneys-General.[55]

3.2.2   *In what form is law reform published?*

There are various types of publications, including issue papers, discussion papers, working papers, submissions, interim, final and annual reports. Many of the final reports are published in the parliamentary papers. Use the *Law Reform Digest* 1910–1980 and the supplement 1980–1985 to access information about the law reform bodies. The journal *Reform* and other journals, such as the *Admin Review*, update the Digest. Apart from these hardcopy sources, most of the law reform work from the various jurisdictions is available on the web and easily accessed through the Australian Law Reform site noted in the Checklists.

3.2.3   *How is this material used?*

In a formal sense, reform papers are used to formulate government policy for change. The reports often contain proposed drafts of new legislation, which may ultimately be enacted with minimal change. The judges, too, frequently refer to

54 Walker D, 'The Scottish Law Commission under review' (1987) 8(2) *Statute Law Review* 115.

55 Campbell E, Poh-York L and Tooher J, *Legal Research: Materials and Methods* (4 ed, Sydney: LBC Information Services, 1996), 352.

law reform reports in support of changes to the law. Take, for example, Justice Murphy's judgment in *State Government Insurance Commission v Trigwell*, where reference was made to the various reports brought down by the New Zealand, Canadian and other Australian State law reform commissions. Law reform material can be invaluable when examining an area of law because of the thorough doctrinal reviews included in the Final Reports.

However, it is also useful to be aware of the formal methodology of law reform. Formal law reform develops through several phases, and perhaps a research paper, if reform-oriented in its perspective, can aim to include at least one step of the process. A preliminary review of an area might include a comparative literature review incorporating the response of other jurisdictions to the problem, together with an assessment of how and why the changes have been successful or unsuccessful. A project might also incorporate a doctrinal argument balancing the weight to be given to public and private interests in the area. Alternatively, the paper might simply endeavour to marshal the arguments for and against change, or even suggest matters could be resolved by clearer drafting. It is quite simple to include some reform issues in a small research project.

3.2.4 *What are the usual methods pursued by the law reform commissions?*

A flowchart on the next page of the various steps might clarify the process.

The first step must always be to identify the problem.[56] This may sound quite simple, but it usually includes talking to those experiencing specific difficulties with the law and investigating the breadth of the problem including the gathering of some examples. Why is it a problem, what are the consequences, what is the law, is the law being applied correctly, has the law created the problem, has the law attempted to solve the problem, how should the law be changed? These are some of the questions that need to be addressed.

Reflection is always an important step so that the answers of those experiencing the problem can be analysed and verified. Perhaps common themes emerge. Perhaps there are workable suggestions for how the difficulties might be remedied. Perhaps the legislation itself is fine, and it is simply the implementation that is difficult. The change needed may be operational rather than legislative.

It is useful to consult with those administering the law as to their views on whether there is a difficulty and, if so, how it might be overcome. This might include the legal profession, especially representatives from the law societies, bar associations, and judges. It might also include formal representations to others in the profession, such as specialists and academics whose interests may differ from the elite in the professional bodies. After this, it might be valuable to again consult the complainants, and perhaps mediate the issues between the various parties involved in order to reach some agreement on whether there are established difficulties in the law, the way it is being applied, and how these

---

56 The ideas for this law reform methodology came from an unpublished paper on Law Reform presented by Cooper J to the Advanced Legal Research LWN048, QUT Faculty of Law Wednesday 20 October 1993.

difficulties might be remedied. Consultation might also take place with other stakeholders apart from those who are directly involved. Look to those who have some experience of or interest in the law including:

* the police or government officials and past users of the system;

* the general public who may add some general community views even though not directly affected;

* experts, such as sociologists, economists, valuers, actuaries;

* interest groups — 'interest groups can clothe the skeleton of an abstract legal problem with the flesh and blood which is necessary to enable a law reform commission to understand the problem in a way which will enable it to formulate workable proposals for law reform, and they can expose impracticalities in a commission's tentative proposals'; and[57]

* the various 'arms' of government.

If funds are available, it is sometimes possible to arrange for more extensive empirical research. This may be done by survey or by gathering available statistics, either 'off the hanger' from the Statistics Offices or by arranging special runs. This can be done by seminars, media releases, surveys and public opinion polls, interviews with the media (including participation in talk-back and public affairs programs), discussions with parliamentary committees, addresses to conferences, clubs, community organisations, industry groups, professional bodies, universities, colleges and schools, correspondence and discussion with individuals, and written submissions.[58]

It is usual for the law reform bodies to also consult sources outside their own jurisdiction including:

* gathering legislation from other States or foreign jurisdictions;

* corresponding with other law reform bodies;

* corresponding with noted experts in the field; and

* carrying out background research, looking at published source material, such as journal articles, conference papers, professional legal seminar papers and texts.

Within these other jurisdictions, it is important to find out whether there is a problem, and whether there have been any attempts at reform. If reform has not taken place, why has it not happened? Was it successful? What form did the change take and would it be compatible with the current situation? If it has not been successful, what are the reasons for this, and are they likely to be replicated in the home jurisdiction?

Having come to this point in the process, it should be possible to state the problem succinctly, and outline some cogent arguments for and against reform, together with some possible reform options. The Law Reform body will often release a discussion paper at this stage. This might take place in tandem with a public meeting or conference, or workshop to work through the various issues.

---

57 Hurlburt W, *Law Reform Commission in the United Kingdom, Australia and Canada* (Edmonton: Juriliber Limited, 1986), 337.

58 Latimer P, 'Changing the law' in Kovacs D, Heilbronn G, Latimer P, Nielsen J and Pagone T, *Introducing the Law* (5 ed, North Ryde: CCH, 1996), 213.

Law reform research process

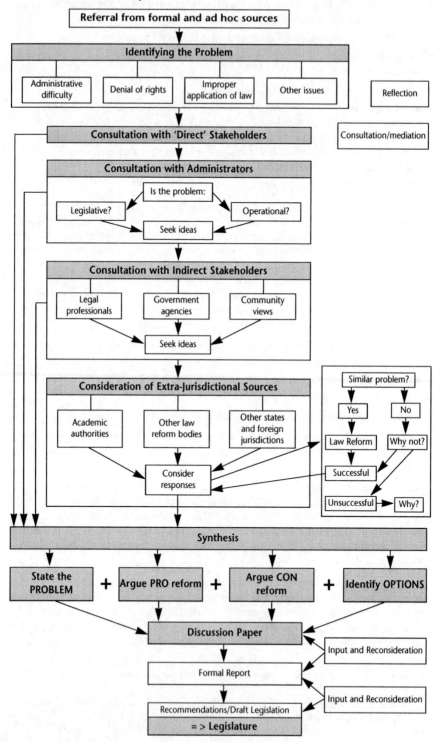

At this point, direct stakeholders may be brought into the loop and discussions regarding changes may be appropriate. Extensive consultation is always necessary and working papers may be circulated to relevant government departments and interested representative groups. After releasing the discussion paper, it is necessary to re-assess the responses from interested groups, including in that re-assessment:

* judgments as to the conflicts of public and private interests being played out and which should have more weight; and

* suggested solutions gleaned from other jurisdictions and submissions, and their viability in the current situation.

It is only at that late stage that it might be possible to release a formal report on the issue for yet more public discussion and comment, with or without a tentative draft of legislation.

Law reform commissions engage in much 'consultation', and this really can take many different forms. The consultations can be public or private, or formal or informal. Usually any consultations will be directly communicated in meetings and public discussion forums, but written documents, such as working papers, issue papers and draft reports also play a role. Responses taken to these mean that community groups have an opportunity to have their say. There are equity issues associated with this so that the process should allow the 'little person' to tell their story and participate. This process also placates the politicians by allowing the issues to go through the electorate filter, and acts as an impetus for interest groups to form and become vocal.

A useful case study of law reform methodology is recounted in David Brereton's article on the changes to the Victorian *Crimes (Rape) Act 1991*.[59] These changes occurred after the Victorian Law Reform Commission compiled a report including recommendations for legislative change and a model Bill. The process used included an amount of social science research and comparative research of rape law reform from other jurisdictions, such as Michigan in the United States. There were unusual aspects to this reference. A pressure group, the Real Rape Law Coalition, was formed as a response to the release of earlier Law Reform Commission Reports. Therefore, the report aroused a great amount of public debate and controversy. The papers included *Rape and Allied Offences: Substantive Aspects* (June 1987) and *Rape and Allied Offences: Procedure and Evidence* (June 1990). This pressure group convened public meetings to register opposition to the proposed legislation, which in turn sparked public comment in newspapers. In this instance, the Attorney-General referred the issue of rape law reform back to the Law Reform Commission, which undertook more far-reaching research. This process involved:

* collection and analysis of data from approx 150 rape prosecution files held by the Victorian Department of Public Prosecutions;

* a review of approaches to consent in other jurisdictions in Australia and overseas;

---

59 Brereton D, '"Real Rape", Law reform and the role of research: The evolution of the Victorian *Crimes (Rape) Act 1991*' (1994) 27 *Australian and New Zealand Journal of Criminology* 74.

* informal and semi-structured interviews with service providers, police, other legal system personnel, sexual assault victims and interested community groups; and

* use of a Victorian Community Council Against Violence (CCAV)-initiated complementary study of sexual assault reports made to the Victorian Police in the three years 1987_1990 using police Crime Reports and related documents.

Thus, the law reform process offers a valuable source of information for the researcher. This applies as much to what has not been implemented and strategically shelved by successive governments as to those aspects of the completed reports that have gained favour. Writing in 1982 Stan Ross commented that:

> We have seen from our profiles of the bureaucrats, judges and politicians that the law reform system is run by middle-aged, middle to upper-middle class white males. This fact in itself does not necessarily mean certain law reforms will or will not be pursued, although it can readily be argued that it frequently plays a significant role in what is and what is not pursued. Essentially, it means that significant law reform that threatens the position of those running the system will generally be opposed.[60]

Now much has changed in the interim, but it is important to note the underlying message in this statement. In any change process, there are those who will lose and those who may benefit. One of the major achievements of the law reform commissions is the emphasis on public consultation as a way of countering the influences of the status quo.

Justice Michael Kirby has written that:

> Unless there is interest and a sufficiently long attention span, anything but the simplest law reform proposal will often wait a long time until someone powerful in the parliament or the bureaucracy lifts a voice and moves the proposal forward. This is a real weakness of the system of representative and accountable democracy as we practise it. It is as bad today as it was 30 and 40 years ago. In this respect , we are not 'there'.[61]

As a researcher you should endeavour to identify the winners and losers of the reforms and changes you are promoting in order to gain a better depth of understanding and enhance your critique. If the issue is important, then your writing is one way you are empowered to promote change. In this aspect law reform is relevant to most legal research work.

Further reading

Hurlburt W, *Law Reform Commissions in the United Kingdom, Australia and Canada* (Edmonton: Juriliber Limited, 1986).

Kirby M, *Reform the Law: Essays on the Renewal of the Australian Legal System* (Melbourne: Oxford University Press, 1983).

Opeskin B and Weisbrot D (eds), *Promise of Law Reform* (Leichhardt, NSW: Federation Press, 2005).

---

60 Ross S, *Politics of Law Reform* (Melbourne: Penguin Books Australia, 1982), 242.

61 Kirby M, 'Are We There Yet?' in Opeskin B and Weisbrot D (eds), *Promise of Law Reform* (Leichhardt, NSW: Federation Press, 2005), 445.

Ross S, *Politics of Law Reform* (Melbourne: Penguin Books Australia, 1982).

Sackville R, 'The role of law reform agencies in Australia' (1985) 59 *Australian Law Journal* 151.

White B, *Consultation, Commissions and Context: A Comparative Study of the Law Commission and the Australian Law Reform Commission* (Thesis, DPhil in Law, University College, London. Hilary 2004).

3.3 Policy research

> Citizens are not government, they elect it and want to be served by it. But if they are to participate more than just via the ballot box, then they need proper access to information, meaningful consultation and opportunities to take an active part in policymaking.[62]

Public policy research is a way of studying and characterising the 'interaction between government and its clients'.[63] There has been pressure from within government and society to make the process of policy change more systematic and transparent. Of course law has been recognised as 'a sub-set of public policy', as being 'one of the ways in which policy is expressed'.[64] From a research perspective, lawyers need to be cognisant of policy research methodologies. They need to be aware of the process of researching change particularly within government.

Policy research has been described by Ann Majchrzak as the very elusive process of 'conducting research on, or analysis of, a fundamental social problem in order to provide policy makers with pragmatic, action-oriented recommendations for alleviating the problem'.[65] Policy research is directed towards providing accurate information relevant to public decisions. It is directed at fundamental and complex issues in society, such as social conditions, where there is often disagreement between those directly involved. It is action-oriented or looking for solutions.[66] Its focus is long term. However, the policy-making timeframes tend to be dominated by 'budget (generally yearly) or electoral (2–3 yearly) cycles'.[67]

The Majchrzak definition focuses on 'public' policy, with its overtones of political expediency, but also the paramount welfare of the community, the 'public good', similar to the common law concept of public policy, which brings broader social interests into the purview of judicial consideration. 'Policy' used within the parameters of judicial consideration and the adversarial system is somewhat aligned but different in its purpose. Judicial decisions come into play

---

62 Caddy J, 'Why citizens are central to good governance' *OECD Observer*, 31 October 2001, 59.

63 Hughes O, *Public Management and Administration: An Introduction* (3 ed London: Palgrave Press, 2003), 113.

64 Carney T, *Law at the Margins* (Melbourne: OUP, 1991), 112–125.

65 Majchrzak A, *Methods for Policy Research* (Beverley Hills: Sage Publications, 1984), 12.

66 Majchrzak A, *Methods for Policy Research* (Beverley Hills: Sage Publications, 1984), 12.

67 Adams D, and Hess M, 'Community in Public Policy: Fad or Foundation' (2001) 60 (2) *Australian Journal of Public Administration* 13 at 20.

further into the process when the time comes to implement government decisions. What we are concerned with primarily as lawyers is the process whereby the government's social policy is implemented through law, and what we are concerned about as legal researchers is the methodology by which the implementation of policy is achieved in government.

Who constitutes the public? In this context there is a need to ensure that any legitimate policy research method includes safeguards against confusing one smaller but vocal group interest with the general public interest. The 'silent majority' needs to be brought into the process, as well as the various organised pressure groups.

Because policy decisions are ostensibly being made for the public good, and are usually financed by public money, certain constraints become apparent. Funds may not be available for the full range of research inquiries. Trade-offs may need to be incorporated in order to ensure implementation of the decisions. Aligned incentives and disincentives may be incorporated to ensure compliance by those affected.

Strategic decisions on methodology need to be made to ensure the largest possible range of inquiries within available budgets. There are cost-benefit aspects to these decisions. If the question or policy problem to be addressed is large with potentially wide economic spin-offs, then it is rational to design bold empirical methodologies to address the issues raised. There is sense in ensuring such research is broad ranging. However, limited resources may lead to corners being cut. For example, situations may arise where consultants are employed by government and, as a cost-cutting exercise, are asked to interview and liaise with stipulated local contacts, only to find out that the contacts have been recommended to government by the organisation being assessed! Other more expensive methods, such as random samples and public discussion may lead to fairer assessments.[68]

Interdisciplinary perspectives become important to this process, and discipline bias needs to be considered in the planning of any research. Law is not a closed intellectual box, and lawyers in particular need to consider other perspectives across the whole ambit — medical, social, and scientific. Anthropologists, for example, have needed to be closely involved in native title issues, and any debate on social issues, such as consent to medical treatment, abortion and euthanasia will need to canvass the views and ways of doing of the medical professions.

Policy research occurs at the juncture between public administration and politics. In the past, politicians and those in the bureaucracy may have treated policy research with some scepticism, specifically because of the discrepancy between theory and practice. Although we can define characteristics of policy research and even a standard methodology, most politicians and administrators are devoid of this theoretical knowledge. The suspicion remains that many policy decisions are made in isolation from any real research, and that directions for change, based on anecdotal evidence, are imposed from the top. The community

---

68 Clairmont D, 'In defence of liberal models of research and policy' (1999) 41 (2) *Canadian Journal of Criminology* 151.

may only be involved at that late stage through consultation processes designed to justify and legitimise. Sometimes this consultation appears to be an afterthought, and in any case it is often driven by the strict time schedules imposed by political terms in office.

Therefore the ambit of participation is an important credibility issue. Critics have pointed out that 'People distrust having others speak for them. They want a direct say, not one filtered through elected representatives or peak lobby groups. Existing patterns of consultation are rejected as insufficient, for they assume interests can be aggregated into organisations that speak with one voice.'[69] Patrick Bishop and Glyn Davis have identified five different forms of participation, these being consultation to gauge reaction and obtain feedback, partnership through involving stakeholders directly on boards and committees, by granting standing in legal proceedings, through providing consumer choice to shape services, and by handing control of an issue to the electorate.[70] However, it would seem that the extent of participation often comes down to practical considerations — 'chosen according to the issue in hand and the political imperative of the times' — and of course the budget available.[71] A recent development in Australia is the 'citizens' forum' or 'citizens' jury'. This process brings together a small panel of 'randomly selected lay citizens' who hear from and question experts and then develop a set of recommendations.[72]

3.3.1 *Methodology for change*

Policy research methodology can be as complex as the issues it attempts to resolve. It is a creative process and needs to be tailored to the policy problem. Terry Carney identified three standard forms of policy analysis in 1991. These were the 'incremental model' where ' decision-makers consider only the close neighbours of existing policies, rather than more radical replacements', 'mixed scanning' that combines 'sustained analysis' on small parts of existing policy combined with an incremental model for the broader range of issues and thirdly, a total wide-ranging systematic analysis along the lines of a royal commission which he terms a 'synoptic' model.[73] Policy-makers can fail in regard to their methodologies, especially in the consultation process. In addition, Sophia Everett has argued that sometimes the problems presented are not amenable to a standard policy research process, but require rather 'power plays' and 'political contests' to resolve them.[74]

---

69 Bishop P and Davis G, 'Mapping Public Participation in Policy Choices' (2002) 61 (1) *Australian Journal of Public Administration* 14 at 14.

70 Bishop P and Davis G, 'Mapping Public Participation in Policy Choices' (2002) 61 (1) *Australian Journal of Public Administration* 14, and see excellent diagram at 27.

71 Bishop P and Davis G, 'Mapping Public Participation in Policy Choices' (2002) 61 (1) *Australian Journal of Public Administration* 14 at 26.

72 Hendriks C, 'Institutions of Deliberative Democratic Processes and Interest Groups: Roles, Tensions and Incentives' (2002) 61 (1) *Australian Journal of Public Administration* 64 at 65.

73 Carney T, *Law at the Margins* (Melbourne: OUP, 1991), 115.

74 Everett S, 'The Policy cycle: democratic process or Rational Paradigm Revisited?' (2003) 62 (2) *Australian Journal of Public Administration* 65 at 70.

Benchmarking and comparison often form part of the policy research process. Benchmarking consists of gathering data on other countries' or jurisdictions' programs and then analysing it:

* Why are we doing worse than others?
* What can we learn from other practice? and
* Do the policies being advertised actually work?[75]

More recently there have been moves to increase the use of social science evidence in policy formulation. In the United Kingdom, there have been various initiatives by government 'aimed at establishing mechanisms for identifying and plugging key gaps in research knowledge, improving research and evaluation methods, and promoting the use of systematic review methods to assist the process of knowledge synthesis and accumulation'.[76]

Policy research often requires input from researchers from varying backgrounds. Such collaboration calls for special effort. Some tentative guidelines have been suggested by Gabriele Bammer. These include:

> ... the ability to identify which disciplines are relevant and what it is that they might have to offer, as well as enough knowledge about each discipline to be able to have a meaningful dialogue with the experts and to be able to identify the experts with whom to have the dialogue; a good understanding of the 'cultures' of different interest groups and empathy with their concerns; a thorough understanding of the policy making process, as well as the history of the policy concerned, the key players and the political sensitivities; management, negotiation and conflict resolution skills; and the ability to integrate all aspects of the research to develop a solution to the policy problem under consideration.[77]

Peter Bridgman and Glyn Davis have identified the following stages of the Australian policy cycle:[78]

* Government identification of the issue, perhaps by public pressure and discussions or via the media.

* Policy analysis to define and assess the issue and perhaps come up with a range of possible solutions. This step includes sifting through completed law reform or other reports and published material and discussions with the authors of those. It also includes describing the status quo, describing what factors are contributing to dysfunction, and then setting up a range of alternatives with a statement of the advantages and disadvantages of each.

* Decisions on relevant policy instruments to achieve practical results. These may include a mixture of new legislation, government services, publicity, funding, or other means directed towards attaining the change.

---

75 See further Chapter Five.

76 Nutley S, 'Bridging the Policy-Research Divide: Reflections and Lessons from the United Kingdom' (2003) 10 *Canberra Bulletin of Public Administration* 19 at 20.

77 Bammer G, 'Multidisciplinary Policy Research — An Australian Experience' (1997) 15 (1) *Prometheus* 27 (Paper presented at a symposium on strategies for facilitating multidisciplinary public health policy research, School of Health Systems Sciences, La Trobe University, 23 May 1996).

78 Althaus C, Bridgman P and Davis G, *The Australian Policy Handbook* (4 ed, Crows Nest, NSW: Allen & Unwin, 2007), 32-42.

* Consultation with relevant persons from other government departments, and from outside government.
* Coordination emanating from a central agency, such as the Department of the Prime Minister and Cabinet.
* Decision-making by Cabinet following a set routine, such as those established in the relevant Cabinet Handbook.
* Implementation of the policy.
* Evaluation of the outcomes perhaps leading to another change of policy cycle.
* Evaluation objectives can be set very much earlier in the process and may include equity, cost-effectiveness and, of course, electorate acceptance.

3.3.2 Policy change cycle

Continuing policy change cycle[79]

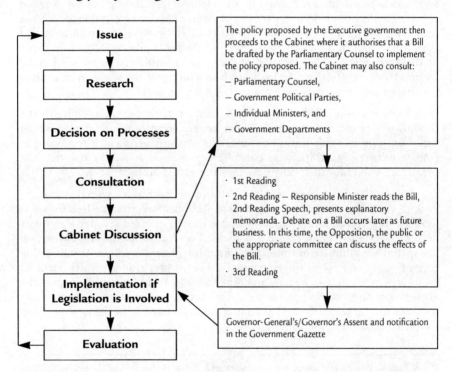

The cycle assumes that the whole process may begin again — similar to action research. As Bridgman and Davis comment, 'Policy is a wheel continually

79 See Commonwealth House of Representatives Facts Sheet No 7: http://www.aph.gov.au/house/info/infosheets/is07.pdf (5/11/2009); *The Queensland Legislation Handbook: Governing Queensland* (Brisbane: Queensland Department of the Premier and Cabinet, 2004). http://www.legislation.qld.gov.au/Leg_Info/publications/Legislation_Handbook.pdf (5/11/2009).

turning, a task never completed'.[80] Bridgman and Davis's use of the policy cycle has been critiqued[81] but the authors explain it as an attempt to set out a 'sequence of steps to turn ideas into Cabinet recommendations' which will provide structure for public servants in the 'otherwise dizzying world of policy-making'.[82] They describe their efforts as 'a pragmatic guide for the bewildered' rather than an academic theory.[83]

From this cycle, it is apparent that some steps are crucial. Most proposals for change come from within the government departments because administrators tend to pick up shortcomings in the law. Other major sources are the Cabinet, ministers and the political parties. A preliminary step must be to place the problem or issue into some type of context, identifying major associated issues from the past, present and for the future — the ambit of the area being researched. This includes identification of policy mechanisms, such as channels for the dissemination of information, possible financial measures, regulatory and control measures, buildings and facilities provision options, and administrative and tactical possibilities for action. It also includes identification of the range of opinions and values held in regard to the issues. This involves value judgments regarding the differential power structure of the various organisations and persons affected, and how to allow for this within the process. Most important of all, however, is the identification of the range of feasible recommendations to address the issue effectively, and a clear understanding of the structure or process for change and the decision points in the change process.

In conclusion, the policy research parameters can vary according to the funding source and audience for the final recommendations, and on whether the focus is on problem definition or solution. Where governments, for example, employ private organisations as consultants, there is always the risk that the consultant will tailor their advice to audience expectations.[84]

Often, the starting point is a social problem with the researcher working back to the causes, and then suggesting solutions. Policy research is forward-looking, states given values explicitly, and is usually directed at a particular user or audience. This type of research is focused on real problems and situations, and includes a summary of context and interdisciplinary overlaps. At the cutting edge of policy research is the emerging field of 'futures studies', which includes emerging issues analysis, a focus on deepening understandings of the future, the exploration and creation of new futures (social and political design) using methods such as scenarios, and 'visioning'.[85] This is likely to be the new direction for policy research in the coming years.

---

80 Althaus C, Bridgman P and Davis G, *The Australian Policy Handbook* (4 ed, Crows Nest, NSW: Allen & Unwin, 2007), 40.

81 Everett S, 'The Policy cycle: democratic process or Rational Paradigm Revisited?' (2003) 62 (2) *Australian Journal of Public Administration* 65.

82 Bridgman P and Davis G, 'What use is a Policy Cycle? Plenty, if the Aim is Clear' (2003) September 62 (3) *Australian Journal of Public Administration* 96 at 102.

83 Bridgman P and Davis G, 'What use is a Policy Cycle? Plenty, if the Aim is Clear' (2003) September 62 (3) *Australian Journal of Public Administration* 96 at 102.

84 Carney T, *Law at the Margins* (Melbourne: OUP, 1991), 117.

85 http://www.metafuture.org/index.html (5/11/2009).

Further reading

Althaus C, Bridgman P and Davis G, *The Australian Policy Handbook* (4 ed, Crows Nest, NSW: Allen & Unwin, 2007).

Bishop P and Davis G, 'Mapping Public Participation in Policy Choices' (2002) 61 (1) *Australian Journal of Public Administration* 14.

Chesterman J, 'Seeking to inspire public policy analysts' (1997) 56 (2) *Australian Journal of Public Administration* 115.

Enright C, *Studying Law* (5 ed, Sydney: Federation Press, 1995).

Everett S, 'The Policy Cycle: Democratic Process or Rational Paradigm Revisited?' (2003) 62 (2) *Australian Journal of Public Administration* 65.

Majchrzak A, *Methods for Policy Research* (Beverley Hills: Sage Publications, 1984).

Nutley S, 'Bridging the Policy-Research Divide: Reflections and Lessons from the United Kingdom' (2003) 10 *Canberra Bulletin of Public Administration* 19.

Symmons CR, 'The function and effect of public policy in contemporary common law' (1977) 51 *Australian Law Journal* 185.

4 Basic Electronic Research Techniques

This chapter overviews the basic concepts involved in undertaking doctrinal research using legal research databases. The objective is to provide several guiding principles for the novice researcher. The chapter examines how electronic research works and the advantages of using electronic techniques.

The current changing environment is very demanding for researchers. Whereas the electronic systems are becoming less 'clunky', and tend to require less technical knowledge and precise command terminology than in the past, there is now increased need for flexibility because the software updates happen more often, and complete look and feel changes are more unpredictable. The main framework factors that enhance a user's ability to search efficiently include an understanding of:

* the importance of differing database structures and how these can be used to best advantage to quickly retrieve information;
* Boolean logic and how search terms can be combined for the most efficient and specific results;
* the use of 'truncation' to ensure all different word endings are searched; and
* the use of basic search enhancement techniques for optimum results.

This chapter is sprinkled with practical examples. The aim is to inspire confidence and technical know-how in novice users. Knowledge of these generic framework techniques increases the user's overall outcomes and provides precision in the searching process.

4.1 The concept of electronic research and how it works

The changes that have taken place in electronic research represent an excellent example of a paradigm shift. Early electronic legal research systems in the late 1980s and early 1990s tended to be very expensive and their coverage of materials was limited. LexisNexis, CLIRS (later INFO-ONE) and the Commonwealth Attorney-General's SCALE database were the main players. The internet has now taken over, and substantially more Australian legal material is available, much of it without direct cost to the consumer. Electronic research has revolutionised accessibility to the law, leading to increasing speed in access, currency of materials, flexibility and enhanced information resources. Resources that had only been accessible to the profession, 'the initiated', for decades, are now available to the public without any specialised legal knowledge being required to access them. Materials previously only found on the dusty bookshelves of court libraries where there were limited entry rights, for example, family law case reports, have been placed on virtual shelves on the internet free to all to access. This alone is a revolutionary 'opening-up' of law to the general public — an important access to justice issue.

The key to efficient and successful access to this wealth of information lies in the construction of the search. The issue to bear in mind when doing an electronic search is that, for the most part, words have no meaning to the computer — they are simply groups of text arranged in certain machine-readable patterns. The rule 'Rubbish in, rubbish out' holds true in this situation. This means that if you do not construct your search thoughtfully, then the machine (the computer) will not be able to correct your mistakes. Unless it has been specially programmed to do so, the software will not recognise a word that is misspelled, or even recognise obvious synonyms. The software will not retrieve results for a search on a similar term unless you have instructed it to do so. If you ask an ill-defined question, then the retrieved list will be useless to you.

Certain words are included in the concordance or dictionary of the software, and these are searched. Common words like 'is' and 'the' are usually not in the database searchable terms concordance or thesaurus, and so can often not be searched at all. However, there is usually provision to scan for phrases. Some software allows 'natural language' searches with varying degrees of success. This means that you can type in simple questions using normal language and terminology. A less common innovation is the synonym search facility. A search for material on 'murder', for example, will result in the computer automatically searching for related terms and synonyms, such as 'homicide', 'manslaughter', 'kill', and 'killing'. However, this thesaurus feature is still not the norm, and the usual technique is to construct individual searches using specific terminology.

Most databases provide browsing facilities so that the user can consult contents lists, alphabetical subject lists or chronological lists. The user is then able to open relevant files to a depth where they can view the full text of relevant documents. The hypertext links in databases facilitate this approach. All that is necessary is to 'click' on highlighted words, titles of legislation or cases. This triggers the display of the next level, so that it is possible to 'drill down' to the full text.

Similar database search software facilities are used on the internet, so electronic research skills are readily transferable. Once the basics of searching commercial products is mastered, the search facilities on the main internet web pages will be relatively easy. However, you may find that some of the general and subject-specific internet search engines may not be as sophisticated as the commercial research products.

4.2 **Increasing benefits**

Many new researchers are seduced by the speed factor in electronic searching. Once you gain access to the resource, your response time is negligible. In the situation where you simply require references to a few journal articles on a broad topic or a specific piece of information, this may be perfect. However, if you want to gather every important piece of writing on a topic from the past ten or twenty years, then the relevance factor deteriorates.

Put briefly, electronic searching provides:

* speed in retrieval of information, especially clearly defined items, such as the full text of an Act or Bill, or a specific law report;
* access to materials not easily available in hardcopy, such as unreported decisions and press releases;
* access to very recent information, such as government reports and parliamentary material; and
* broad subject access to vast amounts of full text data rather than precisely indexed, edited and reviewed legal information.

However, there have been drawbacks to the electronic research world. Expedience has a price — sometimes a very high price where commercial systems are used. When the legal workforce was computer illiterate, except for those in the administrative, word processing and accountancy sections of the legal offices, a lack of 'technical know-how' added to the time and costs of using electronic searches. Of course, some sources are still not available electronically. And the systems do 'go down'. For those times, it is imperative to understand and be able to use the hardcopy. At times, the commercially produced legal reference tools have often been mere electronic versions mirroring the print copies. This has meant that it was very difficult to comprehend the purpose and design behind a research tool, such as an encyclopaedia, if you only saw the electronic version. Knowledge of print versions has sometimes been the key to successful electronic use. In addition, the continuous change and software development require researchers to learn to use new software searching systems on a regular basis. It is not a matter of mastering one software version and then refining the skills in using it, but rather a broader requirement to keep abreast of software refinements and adjust your basic searching methods to make best use of the changes. Thus, there are limitations to the new research framework but it is certainly constantly improving and makes legal research very much easier than it had been previously.

In the last five years, publishers have begun to increase the standardisation of software. The two main Australian providers, Thomson Reuters and Butterworths/LexisNexis, for example, while not using similar software for their legal reference sources, both offer specialised search templates for the various sources. Both these publishers are also developing closer ties with their United States counterparts, LexisNexis and Westlaw. So we now have Westlaw Australia and LexisNexis AU.

There are cultural differences in the way research materials are retrieved in Australian and US legal communities. Australian lawyers very rarely search electronically by citation but this is frequently the default search scheme for the US systems. There are also the ever-present differences in the spelling protocols between Australia and the US to contend with. For this reason, both publishers have developed specific platforms to cater for the Australian market. Legal Online, for example, is built and maintained in Australia. For comparative work, users are able to search across jurisdictions on the international databases.

4.3 A note on formats

There are several methods of gaining access to research databases. These include:

* the internet;
* fee-based online services; and
* intranets.

There are also two main formats for these databases:

* bibliographic databases; and
* full text databases.

4.3.1 *The internet*

The internet is a network of computers that provide a web of communications accessing computer databases all over the world. It is used for recreational and commercial purposes, but it is also an excellent source for legal research. The difficulty with using the internet for research is that there are, as yet, no easy 'maps'. This is because there is no real organisation or controlling body for the web. Australia's lawyers are particularly fortunate to have access to many resources on AustLII. Apart from material entered via this access point, legislation, case law and government documents are mounted on specific organisational servers, but it is a system of trial via web searching software, or word of mouth, to find the correct address.

4.3.2 *Fee-based online services*

Online subscription services require the user to have a prior arrangement with the vendor so that the full database can be accessed and searched when needed. Many online providers, for example, Thomson Reuters and LexisNexis, provide access via the publisher homepage on the internet. These subscription services were previously only available as subscription CD-ROMs.

4.3.3 *Intranets*

Intranets are secure or closed computer networks existing within companies or organisations. Materials are loaded onto computers to allow access for all users in one building or throughout several offices in a network.

In addition, there are two main formats used for electronic legal research databases — bibliographic and full text.

4.3.4 *Bibliographic databases*

Bibliographic databases contain an index of materials. These include edited details of the author, title and publishing details of articles. Sometimes the bibliographic database includes a summary or abstract of the article indexed. The main legal bibliographic databases that Australian lawyers are likely to use frequently are the journal indexes, such as AGIS (Attorney-General's Information Service) and *Index to Legal Periodicals*, and the citator CASEBASE.

4.3.5 *Full text databases*

A full text database on the other hand provides just that — the full judgment, the complete piece of legislation, or the complete journal article. The AustLII judgments databases are examples.

The information contained in a bibliographic database, such as AGIS, is thus much more limited than the information contained in a record on a full text judgments database. However, the bibliographic database is 'value added'. The information has been sifted, analysed and indexed for you. It is structured for easy searching and frequently these databases are sold with full text of the items included. Informit, the service which includes AGIS, has introduced full text with scanned images attached from 1999.

Bear in mind that the research environment is very fluid and research sources, technical formats and providers change constantly. Just as microfiche replaced microfilm and flash drives replaced CDs, new formats will emerge. Technological advances are impossible to predict or control, but the research resources lawyers need do not change, nor do the basic formats of the research sources. This is why it is so important to be aware of the main legal reference tools and when to use them, and what they contain. If you combine this with some generic electronic searching skills, you will be able to tackle the ever-changing research environment with confidence.

4.4 Overview of Australian electronic sources

All that it is possible to do here is to flag some of the main categories of legal research databases. Included are journal indexes, citators, legal encyclopaedias and current awareness publications, full text legislation, and cases. Most current legal information is now available in an electronic mode. The main journal indexes are discussed below:

* AGIS (Attorney-General's Information Service), is produced by the Attorney-General's Department Library in Canberra. It indexes Australian, New Zealand and Asia-Pacific articles from 1975, and is unusual in that it includes a summary or abstract with the article reference. Other specialised indexes are also available on AUSTROM. These include APA (Australian Public Affairs Information Service), CINCH (Australian Institute of Criminology) and FAMILY (Australian Institute of Family Studies). These are part of a larger database called Informit Search published by RMIT Publishing.

* *Index to Legal Periodicals and Books* is a United States index with international coverage, including Canada, England, Ireland, Australia and New Zealand. Although the index began in 1908, the database only covers the period from 1981. It includes monographs as well as journal articles, and is available via Wilson Web.

* The *Legal Resources Index* is another United States journal index which is available online on LexisNexis. It indexes law reviews, legal newspapers and bar association journals. However, there is also Legaltrac, available on subscription and provided on many academic library networks.

Of course, there are a host of other useful indexes. The United Kingdom *Legal Journals Index*, which has been published by Sweet and Maxwell, has now been included on the Westlaw database. Other important sources include *Index to Foreign Legal Periodicals, Hein Online, Current Contents Connect,* and the interdisciplinary journal indexes, such as *Business Source Elite* and *ProQuest Dissertations and Theses.* However, the new user is best learning to search the standard legal databases and mastering generic skills capabilities and then moving on to other variants.

The standard legal research reference sources — the legal encyclopaedias, updating services, citators and legislation annotations — remain important and are also available in electronic format. There are two main suites of materials for Australian sources. The first is LexisNexis AU (including the former Butterworths databases) which gives access to *Halsbury's Laws of Australia, Australian Current Law, ANZ Citator to UK Reports, CASEBASE,* and the unreported judgments database. The other is Legal Online from Thomson Reuters which gives access to *The Laws of Australia,* subject-specific looseleaf services, full text law reports, legal journals, current awareness services, and precedents. *The Australian Digest, Australian Legal Monthly Digest* and *Australian Case Citator* have been incorporated into FirstPoint — a searchable case citator, digest and judicial consideration source. This tool is very innovative as it is an attempt to transform what was a valuable print-based reference and research source, *The Australian Digest,* into a useable electronic format. Previously the *Digest* had been published electronically as a mirror of the old print version.

Legislative annotations have also become available within LexisNexis AU covering the federal jurisdictions, New South Wales, Victoria and Queensland. The Queensland database only includes the case annotations. Full text case law and legislation is readily available either via the internet or from the commercial providers. In fact the best source for up-to-date legislation tends to be the government sites such as the Office of the Queensland Parliamentary Counsel and the government backed ComLaw and FRLI (Federal Register of Legislative Instruments). The parliamentary websites are also excellent sources of current legislative developments and of course committee reports and debates. Both LexisNexis AU and Legal Online provide access to a range of State cases, both reported and unreported, in all jurisdictions. In addition, High Court decisions are included on ComLaw. These databases also include Federal Court, Family Court and Commonwealth Administrative Appeal Tribunal cases. The systems include decisions of the Immigration Review Tribunal, the Northern Territory Supreme Court and the Australian Capital Territory Supreme Courts. Most of this primary material is also now available free of charge on AustLII in any case.

4.5 International online services

LexisNexis is an online, full text system based in Dayton, Ohio. It was launched in 1973, although the system itself was not introduced into Australia until 1985. In late 1993, more Australian material became available with the Commonwealth SCALE databases and the Asia Pacific news services. LexisNexis uses a boutique software; that is, software the company has developed itself. It is constantly refining and changing the software to provide new features. It is more work to receive good results from LexisNexis than many of the other systems. One reason for this is the immense size of the database. A search that might work exceptionally well on a smaller database may bring a response of 500 in a retrieved list on LexisNexis. It is more efficient when used for very refined and specific searches. The LEXSEE and LEXCITE functions are particularly successful for downloading or printing particular cases or legislation from the system. The AUTOCITE and SHEPARDISING functions are excellent for judicial consideration of United States case law and the coverage includes extensive information for both federal and State jurisdictions. However, selected legal materials for Australia, the United Kingdom, the European Union and Canada are also included. It is nearly impossible to conduct any effective search of American law with the hardcopy resources generally held in Australian law libraries. There is a heavy reliance on LexisNexis and Westlaw and, more recently, the internet.

Westlaw is a United States fee-based research service that includes full text cases, statutes, administrative materials, legal periodicals and texts. The system covers United States federal and State jurisdictions. West use the key number system in their paper-based research publications. This research feature is also used in the electronic versions. Within this system, all of the cases in the West reporting system are divided into seven core categories: Persons, Property, Contracts, Torts, Crime, Remedies and Government. These categories are divided into smaller subcategories. Each final subtopic is allocated a key number. This classification system allows each specific case report to be tagged according to its subject. One case may include more than one topic and thus be given several key numbers — one for each topic. This system is used in the *American Digest* and the *American Law Reports*.

The publishers are increasingly being challenged by the free information available in Australia through AustLII. AustLII (the Australian Legal Information Institute) is the premier free legal site in Australia. AustLII was jointly established by the University of New South Wales and the University of Technology, Sydney, with funding provided by the then Commonwealth Department of Employment, Education and Training and the two universities involved, and it came online in 1995. The co-directors of AustLII are Andrew Mowbray (UTS),Graham Greenleaf (UNSW) and Philip Chung (UTS). The intellectual impetus and focus for the database has been to develop legal materials suitable for research within the Australasian community of legal scholars and teachers spanning New Zealand, Papua New Guinea and the Pacific areas. The main aim has been to make public as much legal material as possible. This initiative has been very successful and now includes over 375 individual Australian legal databases as well as providing access to international material through AsianLII, CommonLII and WorldLII. The information is arranged in hierarchical hypertext format, which allows ease of reference to layers of increasingly complex and complete data sets. The database also has its own search software, the Sino Search language, which makes provision for search languages and commands used on other legal software. In all, it is an excellent and expanding source of Australian legal materials and spectacularly easy to use in comparison with some of its commercial competitors. The citator LawCite and the full text journals in the Australasian Legal Scholarship Library are two new additions to the service. This competition is forcing the commercial publishers into increasing value-added products. For the most part, the free sources include raw data, such as unreported judgments without headnotes. It is the commercial publishers who are providing the specialised indexing services, authentication of material, and expert subject control of legal information that enhances user confidence.

4.6 **Generic search techniques**

Although the systems use different software, most databases have functions in common. The difficulty is that there are any number of different ways of signifying a specific command. Happily, all the databases have HELP screens that include general tips for searching in the particular database or as a reminder for search terminology. This characteristic is also available on the internet web pages.

4.6.1 *Overall structure of the databases*

For the most part, users do not need to know how the software within a database works, but it is useful to acknowledge at the outset that what we are dealing with is a bank of data stored in a particular way and searched via software. This is important because it underscores the mechanistic aspects of a search for specific information. Misspelling or use of the wrong command syntax can be fatal.

Specific terms in the database are stored as binary numbers. The computer can only handle information stored as numbers, so that words must be translated or coded into binary form. The letter A, for example, might be represented by 01000001, and B by 01000010, and so on. These letters from the alphabet are thus represented as 8-bit or one byte codes.[1]

Information in the database is usually held in three searchable forms. These are the print file, the postings file and the index file. The print file, usually in accession order, mirrors the record information provided in the retrieved list. However, all the actual terms included in the file are listed in the index file in alphabetical order together with the number of records in which the term is held. Many databases allow the option of searching using this thesaurus or index file. The postings file expands on the information in the index. It lists the record numbers of each time when a specific term appears in a record. It provides the location of each occurrence of a record with an indexed term.

Most of the full text databases are divided into sections or libraries. These libraries in turn are further subdivided into files and the files consist of a number of documents or records. Of course, the contents or information contained in an individual record in the database differs with each database. The basic record in a case law database is the case report itself. The basic record in a legislative database may be the whole piece of legislation or more usually one section of the act. The basic record in a news service database may be a press release.

The importance of acknowledging the structure is obvious. Once you 'log on' or gain entry to the database, you need to choose what area of the system to search or read. In the same way, when you begin to use a hardcopy encyclopaedia, you may need to decide which volume to pull from the shelf. If you do not understand how the information is arranged, you may begin looking in the wrong segment of the database. Take *Australian Current Law* as an example. This is divided into a Legislation and Caselaw Reporter. If you are not aware of this, then you may begin searching for legislative material in the case law database and not retrieve the available information. In the larger databases, such as LexisNexis, this becomes even more crucial because there is so much information

---

1   Walker DW, *Computer Based Information Systems* (3 ed, New Jersey: Prentice Hall, 1994), 311.

that efficiency demands your search is carried out in a very specific way and in a very specific data set. There is a vast difference in response to a search through all cases as against a search for cases from a particular country, in a particular State, in a specific court's jurisdiction and in a particular year.

Not all databases are segmented in similar ways. It is useful to view some comparisons of the way the various databases have divided the information.

LexisNexis is divided into jurisdictional libraries of case law, legislation and other materials. Within a jurisdiction, for example, the United States material is divided into federal and State materials. The next level of division reflects the types of materials whether case law or legislation. The next level of division will relate to the time period covered. Each group of searchable material is named a file. At the lower end of the structure is the article, which may take the form of one law report or one journal article depending on the materials.

AustLII's Sino Search allows you to select certain databases or groups of materials to search, for example, All the Legislation Databases or All the Case law Databases. Material can also be browsed by jurisdiction.

4.6.2   *Choosing search terms*

Each word in the database is potentially an indexed term and thus searchable. Often, however, databases ignore certain common words, the so-called 'stop-words', and these cannot be used as search terms. Sometimes there are words that have a specific meaning in that they constitute commands or search language; for example, the Boolean terms 'and' and 'or', or the positional command 'near'. If you wish to search for phrases containing these words, then you need to indicate that they are being used as natural words and not commands or connectors. This is often achieved by putting the word in inverted commas. A list of materials found by the search software consists of a number of retrieved articles or records in which an indexed term appears.

The database searches for a literal string of characters so that if a misspelling is included in the search, then the computer will mechanistically search through the concordance for the term and usually bring back a nil result. Some of the databases have not had adequate editing of their thesaurus, so misspellings can sometimes bring back a retrieved list!

When preparing to search databases, it is most useful to take some time to organise and prepare the search. This involves choosing the best search terms. If you are using an indexed database with defined subject headings, then one step must be to establish the most relevant subject term or heading for your search. Authorised law reports, which include headnotes, are easier to search because the editing is already available for the user. The authorised law reports are the official reports. These are approved by the court prior to publication. The authorised reports for the High Court of Australia are the *Commonwealth Law Reports*.[2]

---

2   The current authorised reports for the Australian jurisdictions are *Federal Court Reports, Administrative Law Decisions, Australian Capital Territory Reports, Northern Territory Law Reports, New South Wales Law Reports, Queensland Reports, South Australian State Reports, Tasmanian Reports, Victorian Reports*, and the *Western Australian Reports*.

You can search under the main headings used in the catchwords. Often, these have been similar to those used in *The Australian Digest* and FIRSTPOINT. Some have recognised this as the most efficient way to search such cases.[3]

However, where your text is not already indexed, the task can be more difficult. You will be dealing with the vagaries and variations of natural language. There are several methods to help identify the most appropriate words to use in your search.

The cartwheel

One such method is the cartwheel of terms. This is simply a brainstorming technique to enhance your choice of search terms. It is most beneficial in helping you to draw up a list of all the possibly relevant keywords to use in a search in a full text database. As noted previously, many of the main search databases have been compiled in the United States, and use American spelling forms. It is necessary to allow for alternative spelling when you construct your searches. This should be sufficient to cater for the 'centre'/'center' type of vocabulary difference. Sometimes terminology is different because of regional usage. In Australia, Queenslanders would often refer to 'ports' rather than 'briefcases' or 'togs' not 'bathers' or 'swimming trunks'. Jot down these synonyms when preparing the searches, especially for searches in natural language databases.

An example of a search cartwheel technique is shown below.

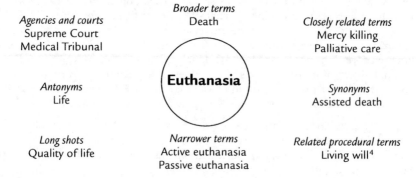

A similar result can be achieved by using analogies to identify terms. Again, the outcome you are aiming for is a list of possible search terms that will identify any possibly relevant material in your search in a database. Think about the subject of the action, and the various ways to refer to the actors. Use broader and narrower categories to tease out the possibilities. Then consider the cause of action being pursued in the particular instance and what terms might describe this. What types of remedies are being sought? What are the possible outcomes? Who is involved in the situation? How is this individual or group likely to be categorised? The following approach has been suggested as a way of analysing

---

3   Stein L, 'A methodology for computer-based retrieval of legal decisions' (1995) 69 (8) *Australian Law Journal* 650.

4   Statsky W P, *Legal Research and Writing: Some Starting Points* (14 ed, New York: West Publishing Company, 1993), 99.

facts prior to identifying legal issues raised by them. It is also an excellent way to identify likely terms for research.

Acronyms and Analogies[5]

S	Subject
CA	Cause of Action (or defence)
R	Remedy or relief sought
P	Persons involved

Consider the example of a child being hurt as a result of using a water tap that has become a conductor for electricity because of faulty electrical work on a rented house.

S	child ... or infant, youth, person electricity rented accommodation ... landlord and tenant
CA	negligence breach of contract
Defences	contributory negligence act of God statutory defence exemption clauses
R	damages in torts or contract
P	electricians contractors electricity authorities public corporations privatisation

Thus, you will be able to compile a list of terms that may be linked to provide a successful search.

Some of these terms will need to be phrases. Most search software will automatically search for phrases, but sometimes the system needs the user to stipulate that two words must appear together. So this is a point of difference in the way the searches have to be phrased.

Below is a comparative table for searching phrases:

Legal Online	place inverted commas " " around phrases
LexisNexis	automatic phrase search
AustLII	automatic phrase search but you will need to place operators or command words in double inverted commas if you want them searched as part of a phrase, eg 'life and death experience'
INFORMIT	automatic phrase search but place inverted commas " " around long phrases and those including search operators

---

5 Cook C, Creyke R, Geddes R and Holloway I, *Laying Down the Law* (5 ed, Sydney: Butterworths, 2001), 276.

4.6.3 *Searching for your terms in specific fields*

Individual documents or records are often divided into segments or fields, and searches can be conducted where terms appear in a specific field within a document; for example, the headnote or the catchwords. This is most important in full text databases, although the feature is common and at its simplest can be seen in AGIS or *Index to Legal Periodicals*. The usual fields you might encounter in a bibliographic database are author, title, journal title or source, year, volume and issue number, abstract and descriptors.

This is an example from AGIS:

TI: Evidence law and 'credibility testing' of women: a comment on the E case

AU: SHEEHY Elizabeth

SO: QUEENSLAND UNIVERSITY OF TECHNOLOGY LAW AND JUSTICE JOURNAL 2 (2) 2002: 157–174

JT: QUEENSLAND UNIVERSITY OF TECHNOLOGY LAW AND JUSTICE JOURNAL

VRF: 2

IRF: 2

PG: 157–174

PY: 2002

PD: 2002

CASE: *R v E* (1997) 96 ACrimR 489
        R v Seaboyer (1991) 2 SCR 577

SU: EVIDENCE; CHILD ABUSE; SEXUAL OFFENCES

JUR: AUSTRALIA

ABI: Yes

AB: Most testimony in court cases relies upon memory, but in the area of sexual assault prosecutions there has been an extraordinary effort to undermine the reliability of memory through 'science'. Using the NSW Court of Criminal Appeal case in E as an example, the author illustrates that the strategy of using the 'pseudo-science' of False Memory Syndrome (FMS) to discredit women's accounts of sexual violence is reliant on the 'truths' about women and rape that have been officially repudiated in law's doctrines.

IS: 1445-6230

FTI: No

DN: 20025251

Full text databases, such as reported and unreported judgments, will have a variety of fields or segments. These include case title, judgment date, judges or court, headnote and catchwords. This means that as well as being able to achieve a full text search of the database, it is possible to search for terms within segments or fields of the judgment. This often assures a better result than a full text search because specific and relevant terms are being searched only within small parts of the larger document rather than a search of the whole document. A better result is likely if a search is done within the catchwords or headnote of a document rather than in the full text because the important issues addressed in the case will be listed there. The difficulty lies in the fact that unreported decisions do not have headnotes sections. Most of the databases now have specific search templates that can be used to simplify this aspect of the search process. There are specific commands that can be used if preferred.

Below is a comparative table for field or segment searching:

Legal Online	Various fields including case name, case citation, judge surname, court, word and phrases judicially considered, etc
LexisNexis	Various segments including name, date, court, opinion, dissent eg JUDGE (Kirby)
AustLII	title (xxxx) eg title (Mabo); xxxx@title can also be used; or use the fields in the search templates
INFORMIT	terms can be searched for — in ti; in au; in ab; in abi; in de; in case; in leg; in jur — or by using the guided search form

4.6.4 *Use of logical operators and Boolean logic*

Logical operators are a way of connecting keywords to refine your search. The main Boolean operators are the terms 'AND', 'OR' and 'NOT'. The term 'Boolean' refers to the 19th century English mathematician and logician, George Boole, and this system is widely accepted so that most databases allow for Boolean terms to be used in searching.

The AND term is used where the searcher is trying to locate records containing two terms. An example might be SOLICITOR AND NEGLIGENCE.

The search would only retrieve records where both the term 'solicitor' and the term 'negligence' were used.

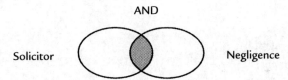

The OR term expands the retrieved list so that the search SOLICITOR OR BARRISTER would locate any articles where solicitor was mentioned and any articles where barrister was mentioned.

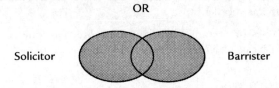

The third operator, NOT, retrieves documents where the first term is mentioned, but not articles where the second term is also mentioned. So the search SOLICITOR NOT BARRISTER would retrieve only those documents where solicitor is mentioned but not barrister.

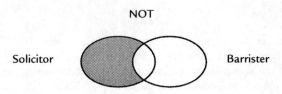

Brackets may be used to indicate which aspects of the query are to be addressed first by the computer. This is sometimes called 'forcing the order of processing'. Take a simple example of the search:

A AND B OR C
Regulation and environment or pollution

Without brackets the search would be evaluated left to right so your results would include all articles including regulation and the environment as well as articles on pollution.

If brackets were added the search would look like this:

A AND (B OR C)
Regulation and (environment or pollution)

The retrieved list would find records including regulation and either the words environment or pollution.

Often the system allows for a standard Boolean operator to be used in a phrase, but when this happens there must be some way of signifying that the word is being used other than as a command. Usually it is simply a matter of putting the term in inverted commas — 'near' death experience.

The more sophisticated softwares, such as LexisNexis, allow for many other connectors apart from these basic three, such as:

W/n
PRE/n
W/P (within paragraph)
Seg (within segment)
W/S (within sentence)
NOT W/n
ATLEAST

The operators in LexisNexis are evaluated in a certain order and brackets are used to alter that stipulated order.

This becomes important when you use more than one connector in a search. The LexisNexis order for processing requests is as follows:

1 OR
2 W/n, PRE/n, NOT W/n
3 W/S
4 W/P
5 W/SEG
6 AND
7 AND NOT

Many of the systems use Default Boolean operators, usually AND. This means that when terms to be searched are entered, then the system automatically assumes that all the terms are to be found in the one document. The software automatically includes the connector command AND between the search terms.

4.6.5   *Use of positional operators*

The positional operators are used when you are searching for words that occur in juxtaposition to your search words. Often, this simply means that you want to find documents where your first term appears close to another important term, so that the two terms are within the same paragraph, rather than one term being in the first line and the second term being in the last line of a case.

The LexisNexis terms W/# and PRE/# are positional operators in that they stipulate that terms must occur in the documents within a certain number of words or perhaps so many words before (PRE) the main term. Another common and more vague term used in other databases is NEAR. It is usually necessary to check the database settings to establish what the parameters of this term means, and the settings may be changed or adjusted to suit your requirements.

Below is a comparative table for positional operators:

Legal Online	Enter search terms within quotation marks (where n is a number) 'xxx xxx'@n. Truncation or wildcard tools (see discussion below) are not permitted inside the quotation marks, eg 'Trade Practices Act 51AC'@10
LexisNexis	W/n, W/p, W/s, PRE/n, NOT W/n
AustLII	near — within 50 words; w/n — within n words; x pre/n y — first word precedes other by less than n words[6]
INFORMIT	near (in same sentence); with (in same paragraph)

4.6.6   *Use of truncation to include plurals and alternative endings for search terms*

All systems make some provision for truncation or different endings on words. This is most useful for automatically catching plurals in your search or for finding alternative endings of words that can still be relevant to your search. Sometimes it is possible to actually choose the preferred words from a wordwheel, or to find out which words will be included in the 'root word' search. Some software makes provision for automatic plurals. It is important to be aware of such refinements because they can affect search outcomes dramatically. Most systems also allow Wild Cards to be entered to signify different spelling conventions that may affect retrieval. An example might be the word 'fertilizer' or 'fertiliser'. An asterisk or other device would be included in a search to cover the two different versions — 'fertili?er'.

In LexisNexis, the universal characters or truncation symbols are as follows:

! (the exclamation mark) for several terms

* (the asterisk) for one character within a word

Examples might be:

environment! which would capture environments, environmentally, environmental and so on

fertili*er would capture the two spellings used previously

---

6   AustLII also supports STATUS commands.

Some databases also make an automatic allowance for common plurals, that is where the plural word is established by simply adding an 's'.

Below is a comparative table for truncation:

Legal Online	* multiple	? Single	automatic basic plurals
LexisNexis	! for many	* for one in middle of word	automatic basic plurals
AustLII	* multiple	? Single	automatic basic plurals
INFORMIT	* multiple	?Single	no automatic plurals

4.6.7 *Provision for modification of searches*

The services provide ways of refining searches by looking for terms that appear in a current retrieved list. This means that you can modify or refine a previous search to identify a workable retrieved list (no more than 30 items or so). Occasionally the systems also provide for your previous individual searches to be combined to provide new search results.

Below is a comparative table for modification:

Legal Online	Use the Edit Search facility; or Locate in Result; or Recent Searches list. System retains a Research Trail.
LexisNexis	Use Modify command; the FOCUS feature or Search History
AustLII	Return to previous search in the Sino Search screen
INFORMIT	Modify previous search by using the Limit option, eg in AU; or combining a previous search with a new term eg #2 and intent; or by beginning your next search with a connector, eg and intent

4.6.8 *Retrieval*

Most systems simply acknowledge if terms are present or absent. However, some search software weights the terms as to how many times the word appears in the document, assuming that the more times the word appears, the more pertinent the article to the searcher. The newer versions of software are beginning to contain this type of facility.

Boolean searching provides a transparent process for the user in that the system usually shows the number of matching records for each term, thus allowing the searcher to make a judgment on the relevance of items retrieved. Of course, weighted searches would be preferable and some of the internet search engines, for example, Alta Vista, do have this quality. Another variation to weighted search terms would be weighted terms within a document. The ATLEAST command in LexisNexis is a variation on this idea. It aims to only retrieve documents in which the specified term appears at least a certain number of times. A search would look like this:

at least 10 (copyright w/5 internet) and Australia

This search should find articles in which the words copyright and internet appear within five words of each other and at least 10 times and Australia appears once.

LexisNexis and Legalonline have both introduced natural language searching in an effort to simplify the search process for the end user.

Below is a comparative table for retrieval:

Legal Online Display of results will vary between content types. For cases, journals and current awareness, search results are presented with the most recent items first (with content specific sort options available). For precedents and commentaries, the search results are presented in the product's alphabetical order. For the encyclopaedia, the search results are presented in order of citation.

LexisNexis ATLEAST 10(x and y) View in CITE, Key Words in Context (KWIC), Custom View or FULL format.

AustLII Items are ranked according to the number of times a term appears in a document so that those with the most matches appear first.

INFORMIT Most recent items first; use the Sort Records By to change the order of the retrieved list.

4.7 Planning electronic searches for optimum results

There are several preparatory steps involved in achieving a useful result from an electronic search and fulfilling the primary objectives in searching; that is, retrieving a useable number of records, neither too large nor too restrictive, and avoiding 'false drops' or irrelevant retrieved items.

The information available from an electronic search is often simply the same data, arranged in the same way as the hardcopy. Good search methods used for the hardcopy can carry over very well to the electronic media. Difficulties are encountered, however, when your original search methods are sloppy. With hardcopy sources, this can usually be rectified. This is not so with electronic research.

One reason for this relates to the use of natural language rather than indexed terms, especially in the full text databases. It is essential that you consider any possible variation of references to your required topic. This is where a device, such as Statsky's Cartwheel, becomes so important.

Once you have worked out possible search terms, it is then necessary to connect these terms into a workable search strategy. It is most effective to fill out such a form or strategy before logging on to an online search in particular. On a large database like LexisNexis, it is also necessary to refer to the hardcopy contents list and work out exactly which file the search is to be conducted in. The smaller your search file, the more likely that the search will bring up a reasonably sized retrieve list, and if the search has been well thought through, then there should be few false drops or irrelevant items. Sometimes the systems are menu-driven but this can waste time and money so a more efficient search strategy will include the commands to be used both to search for the items and to display and print the items, once the material is located.

So the steps to remember are:

* Decide exactly what information you need to find from the electronic search; that is, whether, for example, you require legislation. If so, do you want a consolidated statute or Acts as passed? Do you require case law, and if so do you want the unreported or reported judgment? Do you want a commentary or

encyclopaedic summary of an area? Do you require journal articles on a particular topic, either in bibliographic or summary form or full text? Do you require judicial consideration of case law or legislation? Do you require Australian or international materials?

* Choose a database which best suits your purposes. Most American legal journal indexes include the main Australian journals, but if your primary purpose is to locate Australian material then you might be better using an Australian journals index. Decide whether your requirements might be satisfied with a search on the internet in AustLII or whether you may need to use LexisNexis.

* Decide on the correct file within the database. Databases, such as LexisNexis, are so large that it is imperative to consider which part of the whole might be most useful for a specific search.

* Work out alternative terms using the Cartwheel technique or SCARP.

* Express the terms in an appropriate fashion using truncation, connectors and field searching mechanisms.

* Write out the display commands if necessary, so that you can list or browse the retrieved list.

* Check on the print commands to either print to the printer attached to your machine or to print to disk.

4.8 Conclusion

The various techniques outlined in this chapter are directed towards aiding your ability to research effectively in the electronic environment. Be prepared for constant change and renewal of the electronic resources. This is one area where you, the researcher, need to be extremely methodical in your approach. Know what information you require. Know what sources you need to access to find this data. At that point, bring the generic search techniques into play — and remember to update before signing off on your research!

Further reading

Bott B, Cowley J and Falconer L, *Nemes and Coss' Effective Legal Research* (3 ed, Sydney: LexisNexis Butterworths, 2007).

Cook C, Creyke R, Geddes R and Holloway I, *Laying Down the Law* (7 ed, Sydney: Butterworths, 2009).

Delaney S, *Electronic Legal Research: An Integrated Approach* (2 ed, New York: Delmar, 2009).

Haigh G, 'How Google is making us stupid' (2006) February *The Monthly: Australian Politics, Society and Culture* 25.

Knowles J, *Effective Legal Research* (2 ed, London: Sweet and Maxwell, 2009).

Milne S and Tucker K, *A Practical Guide to Legal Research* (Sydney: Lawbook Co., 2008).

Stein L, 'A methodology for computer-based retrieval of legal decisions' (1995) 69 *Australian Law Journal* 650.

5 Social Science Methodologies for Lawyers

> For the rational study of the law the black letter man may be the man of the present, but the man of the future is the man of statistics and the master of economics.[1]
>
> Oliver Wendell Holmes, 1897

Doctrinal research still represents the 'norm' within legal circles despite Oliver Wendell Holmes's prediction in 1897, and the historical efforts of scholars such as Karl Llewellyn and the US Realist movement proponents.[2] In the twentieth century, most operational, undergraduate and even higher degree work was based in the doctrinal mode. Perhaps this reinforces the limited capacity of law and lawyers to negotiate change or modify their paradigms. Thus, for practical purposes, and for day-to-day client matters, doctrinal research is the expected and required methodology. The busy practitioner tends to be concerned with the law 'as it is', and rarely has time to consider research that does not fit tightly within that paradigm and timeframe.

In the twenty-first century we are seeing a blurring of hard methodological boundaries. The legal profession is increasingly being pulled into a larger world. This 'world' encompasses legal and social theory, and it encompasses diverse methodologies based in the hard sciences and in the social sciences. Social science research is looking at the context in which the law operates with an aim to providing reasonably reliable data regarding human behaviour. This data can be used by lawyers to deal with the 'grey' area between the rules, their implementation and the resulting effectiveness of regulation of society. It is especially relevant to postgraduate and reform research. This view is predicated on the idea that law exists within a social framework or context, rather than in an objective doctrinal vacuum.

There are many social science methodologies and this very diversity of opportunity makes the situation for lawyers doubly difficult. If uninitiated and untrained lawyers are to step into unfamiliar territory, which methodology should they choose? The methodologies most favoured by lawyers include questionnaire surveys, interviews, focus groups, case studies, content analysis, performance measurement, and archival/historical research. This chapter presents an overview

---

1   Holmes OW, 'The path of the law' (1896–1897) 10 *Harvard Law Review* at 469 cited by Mullane G, 'Evidence of social science research: Law, practice, and options in the Family Court of Australia' (1998) 72 *Australian Law Journal* 434 at 437.

2   Tomasic R, 'Using Social Science Research Methods in the Study of Corporate Law' (1996) 3 (1) *Canberra Law Review* 24.

of social science method dealing with the differences between qualitative and quantitative research methods and the use of these types of methods for legal research. Quantitative methodologies are those methods based on a strict research design, which is developed before the research begins. They use quantitative measurement and statistical analysis; for example, through using statistical analysis of surveys. Qualitative methodologies aim to explore social relations and reality through experience; for example, through using case studies.

In the past, lawyers have been reluctant to use these methods. However, a 2001 Canadian study of legal scholarship concluded that contemporary legal academic researchers want to use empirical methodologies rather than undertaking purely doctrinal research methodologies, and in some cases the academics are using these methodologies, but their research demonstrates a lack of expertise and a need for further training in empirical methodologies.[3] A United States study into legal scholarship trends from 1982 to 1996 demonstrates that the use of empirical methods was increasing in that jurisdiction during those years.[4] The New Legal Realism movement[5] is currently a dynamic force in the United States and is leading to an increasing amount of empirical legal research being published.[6] In the United Kingdom, the 2006 Nuffield Inquiry on the current capacity of universities to carry out empirical research on how law is working in practice concluded that there was 'clear evidence of a developing crisis' because of the lack of expertise.[7] A survey of postgraduate research in Australian law schools undertaken in the early part of this decade demonstrated that only 20 per cent of all doctoral research projects could be described as purely 'doctrinal'.[8] Despite this, a 1996 survey of Family Court of Australia judges indicated that 69 per cent of the respondents considered there was 'a real need for the court to be assisted more often by reference to relevant recognised

---

3 Shanahan T, 'Legal Scholarship in Ontario's English-speaking Common Law Schools' (2006) 21 (2) *Canadian Journal of Law and Society* 25 at 36.

4 Ellickson R, 'Trends in Legal Scholarship: A Statistical Study' (2000) XXIX:I (Pt 2) *Journal of Legal Studies* 517 at 528.

5 Miles TJ and Sunstein CR, 'The New Legal Realism' *University of Chicago Law Review* 831, available at Social Science Research Network http://papers.ssrn.com/sol3/papers.cfm?abstract_id=1070283 (5/11/2009).

6 George TE, 'An Empirical Study of Empirical Legal Scholarship: The Top Law Schools' (Vanderbilt University Law School, Working Paper 05-20), 8, http://papers.ssrn.com/sol3/papers.cfm?abstract_id=775864 (5/11/2009); Chambliss E, 'When do Facts Persuade? Some Thoughts on the Market for "Empirical Legal Studies"' http://papers.ssrn.com/sol3/papers.cfm?abstract_id=1263369 (5/11/2009); ELS Blog http://www.elsblog.org/ (5/11/2009); *Journal of Empirical Legal Studies* http://www.wiley.com/bw/society.asp?ref=1740-1453 (5/11/2009); The Society for Empirical Legal Studies http://law.usc.edu/cels/sels.cfm (11/5/2009).

7 Genn H, Partington M and Wheeler S, *Law in the Real World: Improving our Understanding of How Law Works: The Nuffield Inquiry on Empirical Legal Research*, Report Summary, November 2006, 5. http://www.ucl.ac.uk/laws/socio-legal/empirical/ (5/11/2009).

8 Manderson D and Mohr R, 'From oxymoron to intersection: an epidemiology of legal research' (2003) 6 *Law Text Culture* 165 at 168. And see Manderson D, 'Law: The search for community' in Marginson S (ed), *Investing in Social Capital* (St Lucia: University of Queensland Press, 2002), 152.

research concerning human behaviour'.[9] There is therefore a growing international recognition within the 'parliament, government, businesses and NGOs', and the courts, that 'evidence-based research' has the power 'to inform the development of law, the administration of justice, and the practice of law'.[10] Thus, it seems that gradually the usefulness and importance of an interdisciplinary approach, and the use of verified data to assist within otherwise narrow legal frameworks, are being recognised more widely.

5.1 Why should lawyers consider using social science methods and empirical data?

Law does not operate in a vacuum. It operates within, and operates on, society. There is scope for the use of completed social science studies relating to law to illuminate the effects of law on society. There is room for new studies tailored to specific legal issues. There is scope for further research about legal rules and legal institutions, such as the police, in order to increase the effectiveness of groups working within society.[11] As Julius Getman has commented, 'Empirical study has the potential to illuminate the workings of the legal system, to reveal its shortcomings, problems, successes, and illusions, in a way that no amount of library research or subtle thinking can match'.[12]

Of course lawyers need to be aware of the past, of the history and previous judgments and decisions of the courts. However, they also need to be aware of current contexts, of the impact of technology, and of international concerns. For the most part, legal research requires a forward-looking agenda. For this reason, legal researchers have a responsibility to have regard not only to current thought within their own discipline, but also to be lateral in their thinking. They need to look outside the law for answers and indeed for the effect that the law is having on the world. Interdisciplinary methods are part of this extra-legal context.

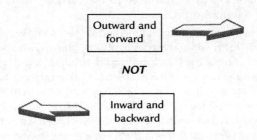

---

9   Mullane G, 'Evidence of Social Science Research: Law, Practice, and Options in the Family Court of Australia' (1998) 72 *Australian Law Journal* 434 at 455.

10   Hillyard P, 'Law's Empire: Socio-Legal Empirical Research in the Twenty-first Century' (2007) 34 (2) *Journal of Law and Society* 266 at 268.

11   Loh W, *Social Research in the Judicial Process: Cases, Readings and Text* (New York: Russell Sage Foundation, 1984), 6.

12   Getman J, 'Contributions of empirical data to legal research' (1985) 35 *Journal of Legal Education* 489.

5.1.1   *In what areas can lawyers find social science methods useful?*

Social science methodologies can be used:

* to identify the 'gaps' between law in the books and law in action;
* to increase understanding and effectiveness of the law in society;
* to increase lawyers' awareness of developments and answers from other disciplines; and
* to illustrate and contextualise the written law.[13]

Social science methods can be used to determine fact; for example, in trademark cases to establish whether there was a degree of consumer confusion in relation to the use of goods. They can be influential in terms of the making of law, by establishing the effects of certain criminal sanctions on crime rates. Much work has been done on the effectiveness or otherwise of the death penalty or mandatory sentencing in lessening crime rates and changing crime patterns. Social framework research can be used to target profiles for likely offenders in stipulated situations, or the likelihood of theft in certain suburbs.

In any case, it is often not necessary for lawyers researching the law to undertake their own social science projects. Often, the statistics are on the public record and it is simply a matter of 'thinking outside the box' in order to bring the material already publicly known into the legal arena. This is by far the easiest method of including 'hard data' in legal research; that is, by accessing published statistics gathered by other authorities.[14] Collaboration with other scholars is also an important way of filling gaps in technical knowledge.[15]

5.2   **Reasons for lawyers' reluctance to move beyond the doctrinal**

Lawyers have demonstrated a reluctance to use these other methodologies in their research for a number of reasons.

* Lawyers lack training in non-doctrinal methodologies. Most lawyers are trained to some extent in doctrinal legal research; that is, using legislation and case law to determine and critique the law. If enrolled in 'straight' law degrees, then there may be no appreciation of the existence of other methodologies apart from the recognition that quantitative or survey work can determine useable statistics. There is a paradox lying at the heart of this issue. Lawyers tend not to use empirical methods and results because they are untrained in the discipline, but in order to put time into learning the methodology, lawyers need to be able to understand the need for empirical knowledge. They also need to be certain that the results will be used within policy formulation, and perhaps within the

---

13   See generally Bottomley S, 'Corporate Law Research and the Social Sciences: A Note of Encouragement' (1996) 3 (1) *Canberra Law Review* 33.

14   Australian Social Science Data Archive http://assda.anu.edu.au/ (5/11/2009); Australian Bureau of Statistics http://www.abs.gov.au/ (5/11/2009); see also the National Library's Australian Statistics on the Internet http://www.nla.gov.au/oz/stats.html (5/11/2009).

15   Tomasic R, 'Using Social Science Research Methods in the Study of Corporate Law' (1996) 3 (1) *Canberra Law Review* 24 at 26.

dispute resolution processes.[16] Strong arguments have been put forward that it is possible to carry out valid and useful empirical research without all the training if you are aware of the pitfalls and recruit expert assistance.[17] The difficulty lies in the need for a threshold knowledge so that lawyers will at least be able to recognise when an issue is one that would successfully be plumbed using empirical techniques.

* Lawyers are used to dealing in specific cases, rather than broader aspects about the world and events affecting society generally. They want definite answers and empirical research does not usually state results in an unqualified fashion, but rather states them in terms of generalities. Therefore, they may be more suspicious of broad generalisations gleaned from statistics and survey results, and critical of deriving general observations from samples. The courtroom debate revolves around a specific client and a particular incident, not society at large. The use of statistics is limited in the operational sense. Just because the average sentence for a particular crime is two years, for example, does not mean that your client might not get four years, or even a suspended sentence. In addition, the restrictive implications in the rules of evidence place further limitations.

* Social science findings are perceived as unstable and malleable. The old adage, 'Lies, damn lies and statistics!' seems to have many exponents among the legal profession, and the perception appears to be that the outcomes from social research in particular are dependent on the way in which the results are interpreted. In fact, social scientists do not always agree. This may result from the use of different methods of collecting data, or perhaps it is simply that the questions being researched are marginally different and this is unrecognised. This apparent uncertainty reinforces lawyer bias against the findings. Modern lawyers are also aware of the critiques of claims of objectivity and neutrality as they relate to law, and duly perceive that these claims are true too of social science research. There are different schools of thought within scientific circles, and this results in differently moulded research projects and differently interpreted outcomes.

* Of course, the truth is that the outcomes need to be reliable and valid based on correct use of methodology and absence of bias. However, many lawyers perceive that they have insufficient expertise in order to judge these aspects of the studies. And some notable debacles with forensic evidence in Australian courts have reinforced these views.[18] There is a perception that the assessment of the results and claims of social science inquiries 'requires thorough understanding of the nature of social science research, including the specific nature of its methodology and the claims that science does and does not make'.[19] Perhaps if strategies can be made available to counter this lack of

---

16   Faigman DL, 'To have and have not: Assessing the value of social science to the law as science and policy' (1989) 38 *Emory Law Journal* 1005 at 1081.

17   Trubek D, 'The place of law and social science in the structure of legal education' (1985) 35 *Journal of Legal Education* 483.

18   See generally, Freckelton I, 'Judicial attitudes towards scientific evidence: The antipodean experience' (1997) 30 *UC Davis Law Review* 1137 at 1157.

19   Channels N, *Social Science Methods in the Legal Process* (New Jersey: Rowman & Allenheld, 1985), 19.

critical techniques, then lawyers may be more ready to use statistical results. Critical skills, such as the ability to 'read' statistical papers effectively, to look carefully at research reports and pick up an inadequate literature review, a lack of direction in the hypothesis, or an inappropriate or discredited methodology may be lacking. Technical failings, such as inadequate sampling techniques, bias, inaccuracies in the inferences being drawn from the statistics, and overgeneralised conclusions, might not be readily obvious to the untrained would-be user.

* There is a reluctance to research using these methods because of the time and inconvenience involved in carrying out the research, locating appropriate issues to investigate, and the possibility of 'failure' because of the uncertainty of the results. Anyone who has endeavoured to put together a short survey will be aware of the surprisingly lengthy time taken in planning the questions and second-guessing responses in order to ensure worthwhile data as the end-product for analysis. There is an extensive number of methodologies available. Time must be taken to determine the most efficient method of collecting data after actually fine-tuning the research issues being pursued. Even a small survey can require a lengthy lead-time in order to draft and redraft the survey questionnaire, ensure accurate coding of the responses, pre-testing the draft survey, producing and printing the questionnaire, selecting a valid sample, writing a covering letter, arranging return envelopes, ensuring confidentiality, numbering the responses, organising data entry and statistical analysis and representation of the data. Only after all this has been accomplished, are you in a position to reflect on and write about the results in relation to your original argument. Once the data has been gathered, it is vital to publish it reasonably quickly. Collaboration with interdisciplinary scholars and technical assistants also means additional administration. Thus, compared to doctrinal research, this type of research can be more expensive and fraught. These larger costs and lead times may make it less attractive.

There are more constraints and hurdles involved in implementing a mixed methodology rather than a straight doctrinal research project. The challenges are not insurmountable though, and increasingly this is the way of future research spurred on by the impetus to interdisciplinary perspectives and broader answers to the questions posed by global imperatives.

5.3 The role of social science in the judicial process

The use of social science in the formal legal process is another relevant consideration. In the United States, David Faigman has pointed to some 'confusion' surrounding the role of social science in the legal process, which he attributes to the lack of a standard with which to measure its relevance.[20] Louis Brandeis, in the landmark case of *Muller v Oregon*,[21] used social science research when he presented a file of evidence on the effect of long working hours to the Supreme

---

20 Faigman D, 'To have and have not: Assessing the value of social science to the law as science and policy' (1989) 38 *Emory Law Journal* 1005 at 1009.

21 *Muller v Oregon* 208 US 412 (1908).

Court. This evidence was categorised as judicial 'fact'. Since that time, a distinction has been made between adjudicative fact and legislative fact drawing largely on the writings of Kenneth Culp Davis.[22] Adjudicative facts are facts found by judges as part of litigation and these tend to be limited to the litigants in the specific dispute and are normally subject to the usual rules of evidence. Legislative facts or social facts, on the other hand, aim to define relationships in a society as a whole.[23] Other commentators have used the broader term of 'empirical facts' to encompass the categories of legislative facts, social facts, social authority and social framework amounting to 'assertions of facts about society, the world and human behaviour' which, in principle, can be tested by 'social science or empirical methodologies'.[24]

John Monahan and Laurens Walker have suggested that some social science evidence should be treated as social authority; that is, as a source of authority similar to a legal precedent rather than a source of fact, and that the normal rules of evidence might not apply to these studies.[25] This has also been referred to as 'social framework' evidence in judicial decision-making — a phrase coined by Monahan and Walker in 1987.[26] It seeks 'not so much to describe a person's mental or emotional functioning at a given time, but rather to explain the tendencies towards certain behaviour on the part of persons exposed to certain conditions or influences'.[27] This type of evidence has tended to be viewed within certain limited areas; for example, lawyers have used social science research in the domestic violence law area, specifically in regard to 'syndrome evidence'.[28]

Under the common law, judges had a 'largely unfettered' discretion to access material of this nature, so that at common law a court could 'directly rely on social science research without it being placed in evidence under the rules of

---

22 Davis K, 'An approach to problems of evidence in the administrative process' (1942) 55 *Harvard Law Review* 364.

23 Etlinger L, 'Social science research in domestic violence law: A proposal to focus on evidentiary use' (1995) *Albany Law Review* 1259 at 1263 from Bleil C, 'Evidence of Syndromes' (1990) 32 *South Texas Law Review* 37. This categorisation is accepted in the Federal Rules of Evidence in the United States.

24 Burns K and Hutchinson T, 'The impact of "empirical facts" on legal scholarship and legal research training' (2009) 43 (2) *The Law Teacher* 153 at 155, 156.

25 Monahan J and Walker L, 'Social authority: Obtaining, evaluating and establishing social science in law' (1986) 134 *University of Pennsylvania Law Review* 477 at 487; Monahan J and Walker L, 'Social Science Research in Law: A New Paradigm', in Roesch R and Gagnon N (eds), *Psychology and Law: Criminal and Civil Perspectives* (Aldershot; Burlington, VT: Ashgate, 2007).

26 Monahan J and Walker L, 'Social authority: Obtaining, evaluating and establishing social science in law' (1986) 134 *University of Pennsylvania Law Review* 477 at 487.

27 Referred to by Etlinger L, 'Social science research in domestic violence law: A proposal to focus on evidentiary use' (1995) *Albany Law Review* 1259 at 1264 from Bleil C, 'Evidence of syndromes' (1990) 32 *South Texas Law Review* 37.

28 Etlinger L, 'Social science research in domestic violence law: A proposal to focus on evidentiary use' (1995) *Albany Law Review* 1259 at 1264 from Bleil C, 'Evidence of syndromes' (1990) 32 *South Texas Law Review* 37; and for further discussion of this issue in the US context see Beiner T, 'The Impact of Science on Legal Decisions: What can Social Science Tell the Courts and Lawyers?' (2001) 24 *U Ark Little Rock L Rev* 3; *Daubert v Merrell Dow Pharmaceuticals* US S Ct on social scientific evidence admissibility standards.

evidence'.[29] Section 144 of the *Evidence Act 1995* (Cth), provides for judicial notice of matters of common knowledge.[30] Another provision, s 190 of the Act, provides for the admission of otherwise unacceptable evidence if there is consent given by both parties. Graham Mullane suggests yet other methods for accessing social science research in court proceedings, including official records and statistics, business records, or an experiment for the court.[31] In Canada, judicial notice was used in the case of *R v RDS* where a black youth was acquitted of a charge of assaulting a white police officer. The trial judge referred to the fact that 'police officers have been known to over-react when dealing with non-White groups'.[32] The judgment was upheld on appeal. 'Four justices held that the standard of impartiality requires judges to incorporate information about social context into their decisions and legitimate social knowledge is identified by looking at the knowledge of the reasonable person who is an informed and "right-minded" member of the community.'[33]

The doctrine of judicial notice has prompted some discussion in the High Court in the case of *Woods v Multi-Sport Holdings*[34] where Justices McHugh and Callinan debated the use of extra-record social scientific material in judgments.[35] In the judgment, Justice McHugh referred to a number of reports containing statistics on sporting injuries and the costs of injury, in particular figures from the Australian Bureau of Statistics National Health Survey: Injuries Australia, 1998.[36] Justice Callinan was of the opinion that this was not a legitimate course to take in that 'the parties must be given an opportunity to deal with all matters which the court regard as material'.[37] However, Callinan J did accept that Dixon J suggested in the *Australian Communist Party Case* that judges 'may refer to standard works of literature' and on that basis made oblique reference to Disraeli's purported statement: 'There are three kinds of lies: lies, damned lies and statistics.'[38] More recent studies of the use of such information in High Court negligence cases in 2003 have shown frequent use of 'social facts' including 'assumptions and statements about society, social values, and human behaviour'.[39]

---

29   Mullane G, 'Evidence of social science research: Law, practice, and options in the Family Court of Australia' (1998) 72 *Australian Law Journal* 434 at 441–442.

30   Mullane G, 'Evidence of social science research: Law, practice, and options in the Family Court of Australia' (1998) 72 *Australian Law Journal* 434 at 443–444.

31   Mullane G, 'Evidence of social science research: Law, practice, and options in the Family Court of Australia' (1998) 72 *Australian Law Journal* 434 at 452.

32   *R v RDS* [1997] 3 SCR 484.

33   Boyle C and MacCrimmon M, 'To serve the cause of justice: disciplining fact determination' (2001) 20 *Windsor YearBook of Access to Justice* 55 at 79.

34   (2002) 208 CLR 460.

35   And see the discussion of this in Burns K, 'It's just not cricket: The High Court, sport and legislative facts' (2002) 10 (3) *Torts Law Journal* 234.

36   Australian Bureau of Statistics *National Health Survey: Injuries Australia*, 1998.

37   *Woods v Multi-Sport Holdings* (2002) 186 ALR 145 at 184 [165].

38   *Woods v Multi-Sport Holdings* (2002) 186 ALR 145 at 187 [169] and footnote 138.

39   Burns K, 'The Way the World Is: Social Facts in High Court Negligence Cases' (2004) 12 (3) *Torts Law Journal* 215.

Expert evidence is another way of bringing social science evidence into the equation. There is provision for evidence to be given by an expert (ss 79 and 177) providing certain stipulated conditions are fulfilled.[40] In the famous Canadian case of *Lavallee*[41] expert evidence was led in relation to battered wives syndrome and in *R v Marquard*[42] expert evidence was used to 'explain the reasons why young victims of sexual assault often do not complain immediately'.[43] However, commentators have pointed to the difficulties of admitting expert evidence in jury trials 'as it is expensive, time-consuming, difficult or impossible to assess, may well be biased and incompetent and often simply duplicates common sense especially where there are unresolved disputes within the research area itself'.[44]

This would seem to be an area where better criteria may be required to assess this category of evidence.[45] There are, of course, ethical controls in existence within the social science profession itself, which aim to standardise methodology and criteria for judging outcomes, but these do not totally counteract the issue of scientific bias. Social science abounds in conflicting theories, so even the suggestion of having a neutral expert presenting theories on behalf of the court rather than the parties is fraught. Advisory bodies of scientists may be able to provide courts with a complete account of existing evidence, assess the soundness of the research, and provide a balanced if not 'objective' appraisal of the validity and reliability of the current social research. In any case, the final decision rests with the court to assess relevance of the issue in the specific facts of the case, and to make due allowance for an individual person's 'innate cussedness',[46] because even when research 'validly describes group behaviour, it cannot predict the behaviour of a given individual'.[47] The Australian Law Reform Commission addresses some of these issues in recent reports.[48]

There is an ever increasing volume of social and scientific data available to the courts and it is important that lawyers and judges are comfortable with the methodologies and interdisciplinary perspectives of the evidence being presented.

---

40 Mullane G, 'Evidence of social science research: Law, practice, and options in the Family Court of Australia' (1998) 72 *Australian Law Journal* 434 at 450. The conditions for admissibility are summarised in Heydon D, *Cross on Evidence* (7th Australian ed, Australia: LexisNexis, 2004), 926-927.

41 [1990] 1 SCR 852.

42 [1993] 4 SCR 223.

43 Boyle C and MacCrimmon M, 'To serve the cause of justice: disciplining fact determination' (2001) 20 *Windsor YB Access Justice* 55 at 79.

44 Boyle C and MacCrimmon M, 'To serve the cause of justice: disciplining fact determination' (2001) 20 *Windsor YB Access Justice* 55 at 80.

45 Etlinger L, 'Social science research in domestic violence law: A proposal to focus on evidentiary use' (1995) *Albany Law Review* 1259 at 1284.

46 Heinz J, 'Why study law among the TIV (or among the Los Angelenos)?' (1984–85) 79 *Northwestern University Law Review* 1269.

47 Faigman D, 'To have and have not: Assessing the value of social science to the law as science and policy' (1989) 38 *Emory Law Journal* 1005 at 1049.

48 ALRC *Experts* Adversarial Background Paper 6 (January 1999) http://www.austlii.edu.au/au/other/alrc/publications/bp/6/experts.html (5/11/2009) and see *Review of the Uniform Evidence Law* http://www.austlii.edu.au/au/other/alrc/publications/reports/102/ (5/11/2009).

Restricting legal scholarship and research training to traditional doctrinal analysis has 'obvious limitations when lawyers (and judges) are being confronted with the need for and the relevance of results of empirical and interdisciplinary scholarship.'[49] It is important that non-doctrinal methodologies and the data they produce are integrated into legal discourse.[50]

5.4 An overview of quantitative v qualitative methodologies

There are several methodologies that fall within the purview of social science research. They mainly ascribe to two very different classifications, one being qualitative research and the other quantitative. Never was the reference to 'paradigm wars' more apt than in the discussion of the rift between these two approaches to research.[51]

Quantitative research is based on a positivist tradition where the researcher is searching for 'objective' truth. In some ways it runs parallel to positivism in law. The methods are based on a belief that you can 'pin down' reality, that there is one objective reality, or in the case of law, that there is simply the 'letter of the law', and anything outside this (including contextual issues of economics, politics, social situations and gender) is irrelevant. There are four basic characteristics of a scientific approach to research. These include control of the research to limit the number of variables affecting the outcomes, exact measurement and precision so that terms are defined 'by the steps or operations used to measure them', the ability to repeat or replicate the experiment and that it results in similar outcomes, and the testing of a hypothesis through appropriate statistical methods.[52]

Qualitative research, on the other hand, has links with postmodernism, whereby the multifaceted aspects of experience are duly recognised. Qualitative research methodologies acknowledge that there is not one overriding reality, but that reality is situational and personal, and may vary between individuals and between situations. The outcomes can often not be reduced to valid statistical pictures or be generalised.

Thus, quantitative methods are often directed towards 'number-crunching' and the outcomes are statistics, whereas qualitative methods rarely have exact outcomes that can be generalised to other situations, although they may make use of statistics. Quantitative studies result in reliable information that should be easily replicated by other researchers to verify its validity, while qualitative research is peculiar to those studied and the results can very rarely be duplicated.

---

49 Burns K and Hutchinson T, 'The impact of "empirical facts" on legal scholarship and legal research training' (2009) 43 (2) *The Law Teacher* 153 at 158.

50 Burns K and Hutchinson T, 'The impact of "empirical facts" on legal scholarship and legal research training' (2009) 43 (2) *The Law Teacher* 153 at 158.

51 Wilkinson M, *Action Research: For People and Organisational Change* (3 ed, Brisbane: Merv Wilkinson, 1996), 24.

52 Burns R, *Introduction to Research Methods* (4 ed, Melbourne: Longman Cheshire, 2000), 5, 6.

5.4.1 *Quantitative research*

Quantitative research:

* refers to research based on principles of positivism; that is, a rational objective view of the situation that exists;
* views the project from the observer's viewpoint;
* deals with anonymous samples of populations or groups;
* investigates 'facts';
* uses strict research design developed before the research begins, often involving 'routine', simple questions that have previously been tested and refined;
* is research based on a stated hypothesis which is frequently 'tested' rigorously;
* uses quantitative measurements, such as statistics;
* uses the results to predict future outcomes; and
* is usually written up in an objective third person style.

5.4.2 *Qualitative research*

Qualitative research:

* refers to research methodologies based in postmodernism so that it may be idiosyncratic in its view;
* aims for an exploration of social relations and depth;
* describes reality as experienced by the respondents, by the individuals, which may not be the standard view;
* gives an insider's view of the situation;
* often investigates 'perceptions' and feelings not open to statistical compilation or comparative measurement;
* may further the research into deeper and more complex causes of statistical results;
* allows hypotheses to develop from research or during research;
* is perceived to be more open to bias because of the closeness of the relationships between the researcher and subjects;
* tends to be more difficult to ensure anonymity of subjects because of smaller numbers; and
* is often written up in a narrative or descriptive style that attempts to tell the story in the research.

This comparative list of general features of quantitative and qualitative research identifies the relevant differences in approach.

5.5 The quantitative research model and methods

A more detailed description of the usual steps involved in each type of project will make the differences clearer. Quantitative projects tend to be tightly structured along the following lines:

Step	Elements
1 Research preparation	• Selection of research topic after a review of relevant literature, preliminary discussions with those with practical experience of the issues • Reflection on general problem and possible research hypothesis • Exploration and literature review • Selection of research methodology • Consideration of timelines, funding and grants opportunities
2 Design	• Formulation of operational hypotheses, alternative hypothesis or null hypothesis • Selection of sampling procedures • Selection of methods of data collection • Selection of methods of data analysis • Arrangement of administrative procedures • Appointing and training suitable research assistants if required • Pilot study
3 Execution	• Data collection
4 Processing	• Grouping and presentation of data • Analysis and interpretation of data
5 Reporting	• Publication of findings[53]

A good deal of planning during the preparation and design phase leads to successful outcomes. In fact, the design phase is the most important part of the process and wrong decisions made at this stage tend to be difficult to overcome later.

5.5.1 *Surveys and questionnaire design*

The research method you choose must be tailored to your stated objectives. You might not have decided on a formal hypothesis but you can use a pilot study to explore the issues, perhaps starting with a basic research question. In contrast, you may want to describe a group or a specific situation. You may be interested in examining the frequency with which a phenomenon occurs, or to test a relationship between occurrences. In any case, you will need to choose a methodology that will achieve your aims.

Much research is based on simple observation, particularly in the early planning stages when basic decisions need to be made regarding the problem being researched and the behaviour of the target group. This can proceed to a more formal stage where you might have various observers noting, for example, traffic flow on a major road. Some observation research is more participatory and allows the researcher to directly experience a service and note the response

---

53   See Sarantakos S, *Social Research* (2 ed, Melbourne: Macmillan, 1998), 100.

and outcomes. You might put yourself in the place of the client or user of a service; for example, a client requiring advice from a solicitor's firm who phones and asks for basic information.

Surveys are the most popular form of quantitative research. This method is used to collect information from a large number of people. The surveys can be circulated to the whole population, as with a government census, or to a smaller segment or representative sample of the population. The objective of the survey may be to gather descriptive data regarding some issue, activity or group of people, or it may be that the survey attempts to establish opinions of particular phenomena.

Questionnaires are the most common form of data collection. They can include closed questions, which result in easy statistical summaries, or open questions, which allow for a more qualitative, lengthy and individual response.

Advantages and disadvantages of surveys

Advantages	Disadvantages
Relatively simple to draw up and administer using available web software.[54]	Time consuming to prepare and test properly.
Result in a bulk of straight information that can be analysed.	If there is something missing from the form, then it is very expensive in time and money to re-administer or 'fix' mistakes.
Good method of gathering opinion information, and useful in policy formation by the government.	Potential to be stuck with obviously inaccurate responses arising from the respondents misreading the form.
Anonymous nature of questionnaires may lead to more candid responses, but sometimes anonymity results in totally dishonest or inaccurate returns.	Responses are normally anonymous, so it is difficult to find out additional information once the survey instrument is returned.
There is an underlying assumption that each person's response is independent and equal to another person's, that is, that the responses roughly equate with one person and one vote in the political sphere.[55]	Because questionnaires result in a bank of statistics, perhaps accompanied by a number of more discursive responses, they do not provide the richness and depth of information available with other methods — some individuals have more power than others and this is not obvious from the responses.
Can be completed in the respondents' own time.	There is a tendency for those surveyed not to respond at all — questionnaires tend to have poor response rates. In addition with a web survey you have no control over the timing and context in which the response is provided.

54   For example Survey Monkey http://www.surveymonkey.com/ (5/11/2009).

55   Sjoberg G, Williams N, Vaughan T and Sjoberg A, 'The case study approach in social research' in Feagin JR, Orum O and Sjoberg G (eds), *A Case for the Case Study* (Chapel Hill and London: The University of North Carolina Press, 1991), 46.

5.5.2   *A checklist for survey research in law*

The threshold considerations

When you are making the decision to survey a group of people for specific information (for example, their relations with the police) or alternatively their responses to contemporary issues (for example, legislation of marijuana), there are various threshold issues to consider.

Is a survey the best method to obtain the information required?

Perhaps if there is published data already available this might fulfil your requirements, and thus save you and others much time and trouble. Consider whether a survey is the best method to obtain the information. Would focus groups or observation provide you with a more reliable response? Perhaps structured interviews with informed stakeholders might ensure that a more complete picture emerges? Surveys can be expensive. Once all the costs of items, such as stationery, printing, postage, follow-up letters, data entry and analysis are taken into account, it may be that other methods could be more cost-effective.

Making it easier for the respondents

In order to receive a workable number of replies, the survey must be drafted with the respondent in mind. You need to ensure that the people you are surveying know the answers to the questions being posed. Are you surveying the right people? Even if they have the information available to them, will the responses to the questions be readily available to the respondents? Will they need to consult other people or their files, or do additional calculations or does work need to be done in order to respond in the way you require? If so, the questions must be phrased so that the respondents will be willing to answer them. If you have used the ethical processes available in the university, then any aspects of con-fidentiality or incrimination will have been addressed. However, some questions may not be either of these two, and may be too personal for anyone to admit to them in paper or indeed to an interviewer. If people will not disclose the information required, then there is little use surveying them, and other methods should be considered.

Language considerations

The questions need to be phrased at an appropriate level and all technical terms or even simple timeframe questions should be defined clearly for the respondent. Have you stipulated the time coverage and frame of reference for questions precisely and reasonably; for example, restricting responses to experiences within the past three weeks? Offensive or possibly objectionable terms should be changed. For this reason, complete sentences and full words rather than abbreviations provide clarity. Ensure there is consistency in the terminology so that the same terms are used throughout the survey — one question should not refer to the 'project', for example, and the next question talk about the same concept as an 'assignment'. Questions need to be clear and meaningful — the shorter the better. This should guard against the risk that two issues are not embedded in one question, which would be difficult to quantify when the responses are received.

Internal organisation of the survey

Surveys are one of the few academic areas where the copying of previous work is encouraged. It makes good sense to use a survey form that has been previously successful because the data retrieved will be easily compared with previous results. Adjustments are always needed to deal with changed conditions and populations, but looking at previous surveys can be very rewarding. If you do use previous models, then be very careful that the purpose of the surveys is the same. Reflect on the specific objectives of the survey you are preparing and make certain that each question is linked to that purpose. Ensure that the questions are balanced so that there are a similar number of questions for each separate aspect or group of respondents.

Think about the ordering of the questions. Do the question topics flow logically? Make a decision on where to place the demographic questions, whether at the beginning or the end. Look out for any leading questions or questions displaying bias which may have the effect of skewing responses. Are there any negative questions? These tend to be confusing for respondents and may be better rephrased. Are each of the questions ordered similarly so that for example 'Yes' comes before 'No'. Make a reasoned decision as to whether open or closed questions will be more likely to provide the information you want. Often, a closed question can be routinely followed by a few lines prompting further comment.

When the responses are in, they will have to be entered, possibly by a data entry assistant so it often helps to give the survey to this person to ensure the answers can be coded clearly and entered without difficulty. It is wise to pre-empt the analysis process before the survey form is finalised to ensure that the data can be used most efficiently and follow-up questions have not been omitted.

Timing and administration

Putting a survey together can be a lengthy process, so estimate when you need to have the results for analysis and work backwards. You need to allow for a period in which the surveys can be returned, sufficient time for printing, mail-outs, pre-testing and revision, and ethical clearance.

It is quite a good idea to print the survey on coloured paper. This tags the survey as 'different' and makes it easy to identify as a separate item to be returned. The physical layout can be quite important. If you ensure clarity and an appealing layout, your respondents are more likely to spend the time on replying. State with reasonable accuracy how long it will take to do the survey and stipulate a clear return date. Some authoritative comments from the funding source or research body might improve the credentials of the survey and mark out its relevance and importance to the profession or university. Try to include an advantage for the respondent in order to encourage a reply. This advantage might simply be making sure that they are notified of the information collected through your research.

A letter outlining the purpose of the survey with a clear address for inquiries of both a substantive and ethical nature, and a return envelope will further underscore its legitimacy.[56]

---

56   See Fink A, *How to Ask a Survey Question* (Thousand Oaks: Sage, 1995 The Survey Kit No 2), 77–102 and Rossi P, Wright J and Anderson A, *Handbook of Survey Research* (New York: Academic Press, 1985).

5.5.3 *Evaluating what you read and recognising error*

As David Faigman has commented, the difficulty for lawyers intent on using social science data 'lies in distinguishing social science with a legitimate claim to objective knowledge from social science without a legitimate claim to such knowledge'.[57] This may relate to the overall conceptualisation of the research, including the methodology and techniques used, or the underlying bias within the process. Errors to be aware of are:

* overly small samples — you need at least 30 responses in order for the research to have sufficient validity — is the number of responses statistically significant;

* unrepresentative or self-selected subjects — are your respondents representative of the whole group? The subjects must be a random selection;[58]

* bias in regard to the selection of the topic, the research question, the assessment of the evidence obtained, or the interpretation of the results; and

* badly designed study that does not recognise other explanations for the phenomena, that is, 'rival hypotheses'.

There is a need to establish a complete statement of the existing evidence. This includes the 'relative coherence or inconsistency' of various parts of the evidence, an assessment of the soundness of the research underlying the various findings, relative support of the findings in the scholarly community, and the relative stability of the findings.[59]

5.6 **Qualitative research models and methods**

Qualitative research attempts to glean the insider's view of the topic, not necessarily the objective truth, but the truth as the informant perceives it.[60] This involves methods such as phenomenology, ethnography, biography and case studies. The objective of a qualitative study is to explore the topic in a deeper way than is possible when using quantitative methods. The main steps in the various qualitative methodologies are included in the following table:

---

57 Faigman DL, 'To have and have not: Assessing the value of social science to the law as science and policy' (1989) 38 *Emory Law Journal* 1005 at 1015.

58 Faigman DL, 'To have and have not: Assessing the value of social science to the law as science and policy' (1989) 38 *Emory Law Journal* 1005 at 1052.

59 Sperlich P, 'Social science evidence and the courts: Reaching beyond the adversary process' (1980) 63 *Judicature* 280–289 in Loh W, *Social Research in the Judicial Process: Cases, Readings and Text* (New York: Russell Sage Foundation, 1984), 700.

60 Burns R, *Introduction to Research Methods* (4 ed, Melbourne: Longman, Cheshire, 2000), 11.

Step	Elements
1 Research preparation	• Selection of research topic after a review of relevant literature, preliminary discussions with those with practical experience of the issues, and adequate reflection • Reflection on general problem and possible research hypothesis • Exploration and literature review • Selection of research methodology • Consideration of timelines, funding and grants opportunities
2 Design	• Apply for ethics clearance • Choice of software for data storage and analysis • Appoint and train suitable research assistants if required • Choice of participants for study
3 Execution and Reflection	• Collection of materials in natural setting (including a variety of sources such as photos, videos or film, and narratives) • Summarise data • Identify themes • Verification of data collected
4 Reporting	Publication of findings[61]

Some research methods can be used in both quantitative and qualitative research. Qualitative research interviews, for example, are less structured than their quantitative equivalent, and consist ideally of an exchange of ideas between two people on a theme. The process is not directed towards quantifying the issues being researched but rather towards providing new insights and awareness of the issue under discussion. Although the person being interviewed will be encouraged to provide concrete examples and specifics relating to the issue, these are normally fluid rather than in the situation of quantitative research where the categories are controlled and predetermined. Interview investigation has been divided into several stages, including thematising, designing, interviewing, transcribing, analysing, verifying and reporting.[62]

Case studies take a qualitative approach to an issue by looking at representative situations in more depth than would be possible in a large statistical survey. Case study methodology can be used to follow up after a more sweeping collection of data. It is crucial that the cases chosen for attention are representative. Case studies are not 'samples' in the strict sense, but examples. They are in-depth studies of a specific group or individual chosen to represent social

61   See Sarantakos S, *Social Research* (2 ed, Melbourne: Macmillan, 1998), 105.

62   Kvale S and Brinkmann S, *InterViews: Learning the Craft of Qualitative Research Interviewing* (2 ed, Los Angeles: Sage Publications, 2009), 97.

conflicts or phenomena. Case studies provide the 'reality behind appearances'.[63] They are many dimensional and, because they are more likely to be qualitative than quantitative in their methodology basis, they allow the researcher to delve further into the issues involved. They may be used to achieve greater depth of knowledge about situations that the researcher believes are 'experienced in the wider society'.[64] The case study subject can be an organisation, a family, a city, or someone occupying a certain office or role in society.

The issue of generalisation is more fraught when dealing with case studies. Unlike quantitative statistical sampling methods, the case study method is relying on a wise choice of example that can be readily accepted when attempting to draw generalised principles or conclusions from the research. For example, if you are studying law student culture in one law faculty in one university in Australia, can it be readily assumed that another Australian law faculty, even in the same State or city will have a similar, readily comparable culture, so that your findings can be generalised? One way of gaining more validity in this type of methodology may be to choose two or three representative case studies and then compare the outcomes, noting major areas of agreement and discrepancies. In this way, general theories may be broached based on the outcomes of the case study process.

Anthony Orum has pointed to the existence of three main types of case study. In the first place, anthropologists use the ethnographic method to make a detailed study of the activities of certain defined groups of people; for example, an indigenous group. In order to accomplish this research, it is usually necessary to live as a group member for some years in order to understand to any degree the subtleties within the community. The end product of this research is a type of case study. In addition, sociologists may use case studies of one person or group of people to highlight certain roles and interplays in society, such as the life history of a tramp or 'hobo'.[65] They may also use social histories of a social group in, for example, a particular geographical area as a case study in order to compare and parallel other experience elsewhere.

---

63 Sjoberg G, Williams N, Vaughan T and Sjoberg A, 'The case study approach in social research' in Feagin JR, Orum A and Sjoberg G (eds), *A Case for the Case Study* (Chapel Hill and London: The University of North Carolina Press, 1991), 39.

64 Williams C, 'Case studies and the sociology of gender' in Feagin JR, Orum A and Sjoberg G (eds), *A Case for the Case Study* (Chapel Hill and London: The University of North Carolina Press, 1991), 226.

65 Orum A, Feagin JR and Sjoberg G, 'The Nature of the Case Study' in Feagin JR, Orum A and Sjoberg G (eds), *A Case for the Case Study* (Chapel Hill and London: The University of North Carolina Press, 1991), 4–5. Reference is made in particular to Nels Anderson's *The Hobo: The Sociology of the Homeless Man* (Chicago: University of Chicago Press, 1923).

Advantages and disadvantages of case studies

Advantages	Disadvantages
It provides opportunities to verify responses by comparing a number of different approaches to resolving an issue	Lacks the statistical validity of a proper sample and objective quantitative proof
It allows the researcher to look at a particular situation in some depth	There is a risk of the Hawthorne effect being engendered, that is, people changing because they know they are being studied
It allows for a contextual rather than an artificially constructed view of experience	It may only reflect the situation through the eyes of the researcher — the data may be more reflective of the view of the beholder rather than the subject's
It allows for a contextual approach to the situation especially in regard to 'time slices' — situations can be viewed before and after major events or changes in order to document actual effects	There is more latitude for researcher bias in the actual choice of the individual or case to be examined
This method allows the researcher to delve further into inconsistent responses	The 'insider view' being presented is necessarily idiosyncratic and not as encompassing as a birds-eye external sweep of the situation
Allows for the complexities of social and political relations to be seen and for the relationships between these and the effects of one on others to become more obvious	It would be nearly impossible to replicate a case study — the researcher can only document an example of a situation — further research would almost always be deemed necessary

A modified case study approach is very possible within a legal research project. It can be combined quite well with a doctrinal study and allow for typical examples to be explored according to varied legal outcomes. These 'examples' might typify a category such as unrepresented litigants or senior partners within law firms. The narrative of one case covering the police investigation, trial transcript and appeal could constitute a legal case study.

The case study can be illustrative in that the particular study can compare practice in various organisations. It can explain the different ways a problem has been addressed. Case studies can be experimental. The study can focus on a radical solution to addressing a legal issue analysing its success or failure. Other case studies can be explanatory by seeking to explain the reasons behind a legal process.[66] Therefore, this methodology can be well utilised by legal researchers.

---

66   Clark E, 'Comparative Research in Corporate Law' Special Issue on Corporate Law Research Methods and Theory (1996) 3 (1) *Canberra Law Review* 62 at 64.

5.7 **Action research**

The scope and breadth of non-doctrinal methodologies is ever expanding. At one stage, 'non-doctrinal' may have been limited in some minds to the types of social science research typified by quantitative and qualitative research. Action research dates back to the 1930s when American Kurt Lewin promoted research linked closely to social change, and it has been gathering popularity over the last 20 years.[67] It represents itself as the fusion of the objective (quantitative) and the subjective (qualitative), so that it represents another 'paradigm' — the participatory.

Action research is, as the name suggests, the opposite of passive, and its difference lies in the fact that the research tends to take place in groups. The groups in which the research is being conducted are not subjects of the research but conduct the research with the main researcher. Action research is 'different' in regard to the power and control of the researcher. Instead of describing a situation where the researcher is questioning or observing the object of the research, the researcher in action research is actually participating on an equal power base with those involved in the process. Action research is self research rather than facilitated research by others.

Action researchers identify an issue or problem in a working environment. Their objective may be to change the environment and perhaps attempt to change practice. The action research cycle consists of reflection on the objective, planning, implementation, observation and evaluation.[68] The whole cycle is then repeated, sometimes several times. Action research tends to have very practical outcomes so that 'those affected by the planned changes have the primary responsibility for deciding on courses of action which seem likely to lead to improvement, and for evaluating the results of strategies tried out in practice'.[69] As Wilkinson comments, 'Action research is not done on someone or some group; it is done with people who can benefit from the actions, the findings and the changes that result.'[70]

Action research is therefore more than a methodology. 'It is also, most importantly, an ideology; a way of thinking about our world, our social conditions and relationships and how to improve them in terms of justice for all. It is about how to change people and organisations.'[71] For this reason, action researchers may use other methodologies to establish basic factual (empirical) knowledge about the situation. Quantitative methods, such as gathering statistics and survey data will provide background for further planning. Similarly, qualitative interviews with the people involved in the area may provide a fuller picture of the situation.

---

67 Kember D and Kelly M, *Improving Teaching through Action Research* (Campbelltown: Higher Education Research and Development Society of Australia, 1993), 2.

68 Zuber-Skerritt O (ed), *New Directions in Action Research* (London: The Falmer Press, 1996), 3.

69 Zuber-Skerritt O (ed), *New Directions in Action Research* (London: The Falmer Press, 1996), 14.

70 Wilkinson M, *Action Research: For People and Organisational Change* (3 ed, Brisbane: Merv Wilkinson, 1996), 17.

71 Wilkinson M, *Action Research: For People and Organisational Change* (3 ed, Brisbane: Merv Wilkinson, 1996), 34.

Action research is most popular within the educational arena, but little has been documented within legal education. Even within education, this methodology has its critics who claim that 'it's not scientific' in that it is not objective, generalisable, reliable, and valid.[72] However, action researchers argue that social reality, being unstable and dynamic, is not amenable to traditional scientific method in the same way as the physical world.[73] This reasoning holds doubly true of regulation of human behaviour. There appears to be immense scope for action research use within the administration of justice, criminology and legal practice. This is one of the newer frontiers within legal research.

5.8   Lawyers using non-doctrinal methods

The following examples are methodological studies which aim to illustrate a variety of successful non-doctrinal approaches that legal researchers have used to investigate and elaborate on their ideas and arguments. Legal scholarship tends to present problems that are unique and not necessarily easily investigated using standard forms of approach such as a survey or interview technique. The issue for lawyers is to find ways of benefiting from the various methodologies available 'without compromising scholarship and without being a dilettante'.[74]

5.8.1   *Comparative research*

A comparative methodology can provide an extra dimension to your research outcomes. This methodology is used in a variety of disciplines — education, political science and, of course, law. The comment has been made that 'we all teach from a comparative perspective these days'.[75] In a similar vein, it could be said that 'we all research from a comparative view these days'. The internet and improved communications and technology generally have made the world smaller. One of the few remaining limiting factors in the modern context is language. There are large slabs of important data that are inaccessible to those of us in the English speaking world by reason not of their inaccessibility but of our inability to read them. This no doubt will be one of the new frontiers for the internet — organising translations of important legal documents to enable more accessible ideas transfer. Today very few researchers would examine law in one jurisdiction without some thought as to what occurs in other jurisdictions. The comparison may not be the focus of the research but it forms part of the international legal context.

However, it is important to approach the comparison with a goal of achieving more than a mere description, or a simple chronicling of sameness and difference. Geoffrey Wilson has commented that 'Up until now the recording of information about other legal systems has been worthy of praise because of the

---

72   Stringer ET, *Action Research* (3 ed, Thousand Oaks: Sage Publications, 2007), 191.

73   Stringer ET, *Action Research* (3 ed, Thousand Oaks: Sage Publications, 2007), 193.

74   Moses I, 'Foreword' (1996) 3(1) *Canberra Law Review* 3.

75   Pendleton M, 'Non-empirical Discovery in Legal Scholarship — Choosing, Researching and Writing a Traditional Scholarly Article' in McConville M and Chui WH (eds), *Research Methods for Law* (Edinburgh: Edinburgh University Press, 2007), 166.

difficulties associated with its acquisition'.[76] It is no longer as difficult to locate the information. Wilson surmises that researchers will now be judged on 'the creative use' they make of the comparative legal information that is now available to them.[77]

The goals of the comparative method are many and include:

* learning more about our own system by comparing it to others;
* identifying solutions to specific or novel legal problems already encountered in other jurisdictions;
* looking at not only the solutions to the legal problems, but 'how the functionally equivalent need was perceived and addressed';[78]
* 'bridging differences among legal systems particularly in conflict situations';[79]
* promoting international unification in regard to transnational legal issues;
* extending theories and ideas for change beyond narrow cultural and national boundaries and thus understanding the linkages between law and other forces in societies;
* testing overarching theories; and
* encouraging countries to cooperate in addressing social issues and problems (such as juvenile crime and juvenile justice) at an international level.

Thus the advantages in comparative research are many. It can be a means of promoting harmonisation. John Farrar has paraphrased the comparative history of law approach as 'an attempt to establish a universal history of law and to measure the rhythms or natural laws of the social phenomena'.[80] Better knowledge of another nation's position is always a precursor to understanding and goodwill. Interconnectedness of laws is also vital in this era of globalisation and the prevalence of the internet which spans jurisdictional legal issues. In addition, comparative research can aid the transnational education of law students.[81] In becoming more knowledgeable about the laws of their geographical neighbours and trading partners, lawyers will be more able to practise law within a broader commercial framework. These are all important functions.

---

76 Wilson G, 'Comparative Legal Scholarship' in McConville M and Chui WH (eds), *Research Methods for Law* (Edinburgh: Edinburgh University Press, 2007), 98.

77 Wilson G, 'Comparative Legal Scholarship' in McConville M and Chui WH (eds), *Research Methods for Law* (Edinburgh: Edinburgh University Press, 2007), 98.

78 Pendleton M, 'Non-empirical Discovery in Legal Scholarship — Choosing, Researching and Writing a Traditional Scholarly Article' in McConville M and Chui WH (eds), *Research Methods for Law* (Edinburgh: Edinburgh University Press, 2007), 166.

79 Corcoran S, 'Comparative Corporate Law Research Methodology' (1996) 3 (1) *Canberra Law Review* 54 at 56.

80 Farrar J, 'In pursuit of an appropriate theoretical perspective and methodology for comparative corporate governance' (2001) 13 *Australian Journal of Corporate Law* 1.

81 Hutchinson T, *Educating the Transnational Lawyer: Globalisation and the Effects on Legal Research Skills Training* (Legal Research Communications Interest Group, Australasian Law Teachers Association Conference 2006 Victoria University of Technology, Melbourne Australia July 4-7 2006) http://www.alta.edu.au/2006_published_conference_papers.html (5/11/2009).

There are limitations to this methodology. Alan Watson has identified the risks in using comparative law such as superficiality, and getting the foreign law wrong.[82] Sometimes it is impossible to be truly systematic or indeed to find patterns of mutual development.[83] In addition, there is often some discrepancy between theory and practice of the law, and thus it is wise to check the reported law with a practitioner from the comparative jurisdiction under examination.

In addition, lawyers sometimes approach comparison with a strongly parochial view on which jurisdiction is better than the other — based largely on their own preferences and biases, rather than on the basis of recognising the value of difference and the possibility that other ways of doing could actually have an advantage over our own. Researchers need to be wary about the tendency to be ethnocentric and unaware of our own prejudices. This is good advice given the overarching prevalence of 'US triumphalism' in some areas of law.[84]

For this reason, the researcher has to choose the areas and jurisdictions for review very carefully, ensuring that there are good points of reference and overlaps for discussion. It is also important to ensure that the projects do not become too vast because of the number of jurisdictions chosen. Usually one or two jurisdictions at the most is sufficient. Otherwise the comparison can become very superficial.

The process in comparative law depends on the aspects being emphasised. There are a number of different ways of approaching the research including:

* a historical approach (for example, What mistakes and successes have already occurred? How have the systems evolved? What is the comparative history?);

* a political approach (for example, How does politics affect a nation's justice system? What are the cultural norms behind the law? What are the relative merits of the different legal institutions?);[85] or

* a descriptive approach (for example, How is the justice system of each country supposed to work, and how does it work? What are the rules?).[86]

There are standard steps in the comparative process. Firstly, the researcher must identify an issue which crosses boundaries. The topic must be in some way comparable. Some issues are not amenable to transplantation. This is extremely important. Thus, it is the 'unity of the problem' which 'warrants the possibility

---

82 Watson A, *Legal Transplants: An Approach to Comparative Law* (Scottish Academic Press, Edinburgh, 1974), 2; as quoted in Farrar J, 'In pursuit of an appropriate theoretical perspective and methodology for comparative corporate governance' (2001) 13 *Australian Journal of Corporate Law* 1 at 2.

83 Watson A, *Legal Transplants: An Approach to Comparative Law* (Scottish Academic Press, Edinburgh, 1974), 2; as quoted in Farrar J, 'In pursuit of an appropriate theoretical perspective and methodology for comparative corporate governance' (2001) 13 *Australian Journal of Corporate Law* 1 at 2.

84 Farrar J, 'In pursuit of an appropriate theoretical perspective and methodology for comparative corporate governance' (2001) 13 *Australian Journal of Corporate Law* 1 at 9.

85 Schmitthoff M, 'The Science of Comparative Law' (1939–1941) 7 *Cambridge Law Journal* 94 at 95.

86 See also Lambert E, 'Comparative Law' in Seligman E and Johnson A, *Encyclopaedia of the Social Sciences* (NY: The MacMillan Company, 1931), Volume 4.

of comparison'.[87] It is followed by a brief examination of the context or framework of the various jurisdictions in order to provide a background to the differences that have emerged. Montesquieu, the father of comparative law, pointed out the importance of examining the 'spirit of the laws' as it has developed within its cultural, political and geographical context.[88] The next step must necessarily be a brief description of the area in each jurisdiction. Only after this, is it possible to move to questions of 'difference and relationship'.[89] This in turn provides the basis for a classification or even a categorisation of the issues and sub-issues as they stand. At this stage there is the real opportunity for analysis and suggestions for reform or improvement of one or other. If major differences in approach are revealed then perhaps at this stage it might be useful to suggest ways to avoid conflict between the systems.[90] Thus there is normally a 'pure comparison' followed by 'utilisation of the results'.[91]

Corporate law is ideal for comparative treatment because of the long history of international commerce. Treating corporate law as a case study, researchers have suggested areas for legitimate comparative study (corporate theory, protection of capital, corporate distributions, minority protection, agency theory, finance theory, transaction cost theory, conflict of law theory, investor protection theory, consumer protection theory).[92] There have been other suggestions for possible comparative approaches in corporate law — historical approaches, institutional approaches (looking for example at how banks operate across jurisdictions), behavioural approaches (for example looking at levels of savings in different countries), functional approaches (looking at functions for example 'to explain some operation of corporate law by analysing its function within a wider system of economic control and regulation'), change analysis (looking at changes in systems before and after pivotal activities) and policy-centred approaches (looking for examples of best practice elsewhere).[93] The case study methodology can be usefully combined with comparative techniques.

There are 'traps' for comparative law researchers. Statistics can be problematic in the comparative context. Consider whether the data can be easily compared. Are the statistics you are comparing the same? Note for example, the difficulty in comparing court statistics and police statistics. Is the information

---

87 Schmitthoff M, 'The Science of Comparative Law' (1939–1941) 7 *Cambridge Law Journal* 94 at 96.

88 Corcoran S, 'Comparative Corporate Law Research Methodology' (1996) 3 (1) *Canberra Law Review* 54 at 58.

89 Farrar J, 'In pursuit of an appropriate theoretical perspective and methodology for comparative corporate governance' (2001) 13 *Australian Journal of Corporate Law* 1 at 5.

90 Schmitthoff M, 'The Science of Comparative Law' (1939–1941) 7 *Cambridge Law Journal* 94 at 100.

91 Schmitthoff M, 'The Science of Comparative Law' (1939–1941) 7 *Cambridge Law Journal* 94 at 96.

92 Corcoran S, 'Comparative Corporate Law Research Methodology' (1996) 3 (1) *Canberra Law Review* 54 at 60.

93 Clark E, 'Comparative Research in Corporate Law' Special Issue on Corporate Law Research Methods and Theory (1996) 3 (1) *Canberra Law Review* 62 at 64.

or data presented in a way that aids meaningful analysis?[94] Look to any differences in the 'scope or coverage of statistics', 'differences in categorisation and differences in the methods used to measure the elements used in the comparisons'.[95] Freeland argues that often comparability comes down to simply a 'matter of degree' because 'perfect comparability is unattainable'.[96]

When undertaking comparisons between jurisdictions, it is important to carefully consider the familial relationships of the chosen jurisdictions. Are these jurisdictions truly comparable? How can you determine these groupings? What characteristics make up a family? Factors to be considered include historic development, sources of law, hierarchy, legal institutions, as well as economic and political structures. England, for example, is traditionally seen as a parent of other common law systems such as Australia, Canada, and the United States. Why break the jurisdictions down into legal families? The answer is that in doing so the researcher can approach the jurisdiction with some 'rough device "pre-understanding" which is rationally constructed and epistemically has a firmer basis than reliance on one's own prejudices and possibly faulty beliefs as to the contents'.[97] These pre-perceptions will speed up the comparative process.

The University of Ottawa, Faculty of Law, Civil Law Section has prepared an excellent website that researchers can use for this purpose.[98] The site divides the world's legal systems into five separate categories — common law, civil law, customary law, Muslim law and mixed legal systems. Common law systems are derived from judge-made law and a system of precedent, though legislation is making determined inroads into this area in most jurisdictions. Civil law systems are based in the Roman tradition and favour codification. This means that the law is written down and not dependent on the rules of precedent and former case law and judgments. Customary law is less prominent in the world's legal systems but it is an important factor in some and those wishing to undertake comparative research should be highly aware of this factor. According to the classification offered: 'Custom can take on many guises, depending on whether it is rooted in wisdom born of concrete daily experience or more intellectually based on great spiritual or philosophical traditions. Be that as it may, customary law (as a system, not merely as an accessory to positive law) still plays a sometimes significant role, namely in matters of personal conduct, in a relatively high number of countries or political entities with mixed legal systems. This obviously applies to a number of African countries but is also the case, albeit under very different circumstances, as regards the law of China or India, for example.'[99] Muslim law is based in religion and on the Koran. Increasingly

---

94 Freeland B, *International Comparisons of Vocational Education and Training* (Adelaide: National Centre for Vocational Education Research, 2000), 36.

95 Freeland B, *International Comparisons of Vocational Education and Training* (Adelaide: National Centre for Vocational Education Research, 2000), 9.

96 Freeland B, *International Comparisons of Vocational Education and Training* (Adelaide: National Centre for Vocational Education Research, 2000), 10.

97 Husa J, 'Legal Families and research in comparative Law' (2001) 1 (3) *Global Jurist Advances* Article 4.

98 http://www.juriglobe.ca/eng/index.php (5/11/2009).

99 http://www.juriglobe.ca/eng/sys-juri/class-poli/droit-coutumier.php (5/11/2009).

though there are a number of hybrid systems which include aspects of various different legal traditions. These can be a mix of civil and common law such as Quebec and Louisiana, civil and customary such as China and Japan, and civil and Muslim such as Egypt and Lebanon. There can also be more complex mixes such as Vanuatu which has a mix of civil law, common law and customary law, or Malaysia which mixes common law, Muslim law and customary law.

Why is this important? Novice researchers often jump into a comparison of laws in two or three jurisdictions and ignore the basic separateness of the tenets of the jurisdictions chosen. It is obviously a clearer comparison where the legal jurisdictions chosen are in similar evolutionary stages. Thus the ease with which comparisons can be made between Canada and Australia. These two democracies are second generation children of the United Kingdom. However, if the researcher chooses Indonesia, Thailand or even Malaysia and Australia then there are more obvious differences that need to be acknowledged in order to make the comparison worthwhile. To make matters more complex, some aspects of the laws in each country might be in different stages of evolution taking into account international law. Too many student researchers will take two sections of legislation from two pieces of legislation in differing jurisdictions and expect useful outcomes and sensible conclusions. This will not occur unless the legal infrastructure has been addressed adequately. As Gutteridge commented, 'Like must be compared with like; the concepts, rules or institutions under comparison must relate to the same state of legal, political and economic development.'[100]

Some thought needs to be given to the fact that each of the jurisdictions is in flux so this makes comparative research particularly difficult. Consider, for example, the state of Iraq and the changes underway in that country. Larger scale comparative legal research seems to be very well suited to group work with international expertise being drawn from other jurisdictions. The current electronic research context is very conducive to this type of methodology. It has never been easier to locate the law and practice of other jurisdictions than now.

Further reading

Clark E, 'Comparative Research in Corporate Law', Special Issue on Corporate Law Research Methods and Theory (1996) 3 (1) *Canberra Law Review* 62.

Corcoran S, 'Comparative Corporate Law — Research Methodology', Special Issue on Corporate Law Research Methods and Theory (1996) 3 (1) *Canberra Law Review* 54.

De Cruz P, *Comparative Law in a Changing World* (2 ed, London: Routledge-Cavendish, 2007).

Farrar J, 'In pursuit of an appropriate theoretical perspective and methodology for comparative corporate governance' (2001) 13 *Australian Journal of Corporate Law* 1.

Gutteridge HC, *Comparative Law: An Introduction to the Comparative Method of Legal Study and Research* (2 ed, Cambridge: University Press, 1949).

---

100 Gutteridge HC, *Comparative Law: An Introduction to the Comparative Method of Legal Study and Research* (2 ed, Cambridge: University Press, 1949), 73.

Husa J, 'Legal Families and Research in Comparative Law' (2001) 1 (3) *Global Jurist Advances* Article 4.

Kamba W, 'Comparative Law: A Theoretical Framework' (1974) 23 *International and Comparative Law Quarterly* 485.

Mattei U and Reimann M, Introduction (1998) 46 *Australian Journal of Corporate Law* 597.

Reitz J, 'How to do comparative law' (1998) 46 *Australian Journal of Corporate Law* 617.

Rogers C, 'Gulliver's Troubled Travels, or The Conundrum of Comparative Law' (1998–1999) 67 (1) *George Washington Law Review* 149.

Schmitthoff M, 'The Science of Comparative Law' (1939–1941) 7 *Cambridge Law Journal* 94.

Smith M, 'Comparative Law and Legal Culture: A Tribute to David Allan and Mary Hiscock' (2003) 15 *Bond Law Review* 20.

University of Ottawa, World Legal Systems http://www.juriglobe.ca/eng/index.php (5/11/2009).

Van Hoecke M (ed), *Epistemology and Methodology of Comparative Law* (Oxford and Portland Oregon: Hart Publishing, 2004).

Wigmore JH, 'A New Way of Teaching Comparative Law' (1926) *Journal of the Society of Public Teachers of Law* 6.

5.8.2 *Benchmarking*

The comparative methodology has been likened to a benchmarking process. Benchmarking consists of gathering data on other countries' or jurisdictions' or institutions' programs and then analysing it with a view to changing and improving performance:

* What are each entity's programs or results or performance?
* Who are the best practitioners or entities?
* How do these differ?
* Why are we doing worse than others?
* Why are we doing better than others?
* What can we learn from other practice and performance?
* How can we implement improvements in performance?

Benchmarking involves steps very similar to other research projects including planning, collecting data and information, analysing the findings, making recommendations based in this analysis and then monitoring and reviewing the renovated performance. This process has been used widely in the university sector.[101]

---

101 Garlick S and Pryor G, *A report for the Department of Education, Science and Training* (Canberra: Department of Education, Science and Training, 2004). http://www.dest.gov.au/NR/rdonlyres/7628F14E-38D8-45AA-BDC6-2EBA32D40431/2441/benchmarking.pdf (5/11/2009).

The difference between comparison and benchmarking lies in the objectives. Comparisons tend to be theoretical and academic in approach. Benchmarking is comparison 'in the field'. It occurs more often in the world of praxis. An analogy might be made generally to the differences between policy research and law reform. One is directed to solving a particular problem and the other tends to be a review of an area. In the same way, benchmarking is practical and directed to measuring performance against others. It often has an economic aspect in that the results have a bearing on performance appraisal of an institution or program. For example, benchmarking has been used to measure performance between law firms and in this context often the focus is on financial ratios.[102] Legal comparisons are more broadly seeking to address issues and learn from others' experiences whether positive or negative in order to generally improve understanding between jurisdictions and perhaps glean insights into better ways of doing things. Both benchmarking and comparison often form part of the policy research process.

5.8.3   Citation analysis

Citation analysis is a quantitative methodology which has been borrowed from other disciplines. It can be used to measure how many times a particular researcher is cited, and which journals tend to be most influential judged by the number of times articles published in the journals are cited. In legal scholarship, citation analysis can be used to evaluate 'the influence of other disciplines (such as economics) on legal scholarship, the sources which influence judges when they draft judgments and the influence of particular articles, scholars and legal journals'.[103] Dennis Warren, for example, in 1996 undertook a particularly interesting analysis of the citations appearing in 32 Australian law journals to determine the 10 most cited law journals.[104]

There are obvious limitations to these types of broad quantity analyses. Citations are about quantity rather than quality. There is always a bias towards journals which publish more articles and more frequently, a bias towards older journals and a bias inherent in self-citation or journals which cite to their own prior published articles.

Ramsay and Stapledon attempted to counteract these limitations in their study to measure the impact of Australian law journals as compared to overseas law journals and non-law journals. The researchers restricted their examination to 13 reviews associated with Australian law schools together with the *Australian*

---

102 Beasley S and Coupland S, '2001 FMRC Legal Survey Results' (2002) Winter *Australian Law Management Journal* 5; McFadyen G, 'How to Make Your Practice FLY' (2004) August *Proctor* 23.

103 Ramsay I and Stapledon G, 'A Citation Analysis of Australian Law Journals' (1997) 21 *Melbourne University Law Review* 677.

104 Warren D, 'Australian Law Journals: An Analysis of Citation Patterns' (1996) Dec, *Australian Academic and Research Libraries* 261.

Law Journal.[105] The process of ranking law journals based on citation impact has been given a heightened level of importance because of the The Excellence in Research for Australia (ERA) Initiative.[106] The following is an example of an equation that can be used to calculate the annual impact factor (IF) of a journal:

$$IF = \frac{\text{All citations in (year) to articles in (journal) during (year − 1) + (year − 2)}}{\text{All citable articles in (journal) during (year − 1) + (year − 2)}}^{[107]}$$

This one is based on that used by the *Journal Citation Reports*. The Impact Factor uses the measure of 'the average number of times articles from the journal published in the past two years have been cited in the JCR year'. The Impact Factor is calculated 'by dividing the number of citations in the JCR year by the total number of articles published in the two previous years. An Impact Factor of 1.0 means that, *on average*, the articles published one or two years ago have been cited one time. An Impact Factor of 2.5 means that, on average, the articles published one or two years ago have been cited two and a half times.'[108]

To date there is no current list available which numerically ranks all Australian law journals based on citation impact data. The US based *Washington and Lee University Law Journal Rankings*[109] does this but draws its citation data from Westlaw, 'which features the content of only two Australian law journals (*Melbourne University Law Review, Sydney Law Review*)'.[110]

Methodologically aligned to citation analysis is jurimetrics which was founded by the Northern American 'legal realists'. Much of the work done in the field has been involved in the 'systematic and quantitative analysis of judicial decision making'.[111] In Australian legal circles, there is a form of jurimetric methodology gaining some adherents. Academics such as Russell Smyth,[112]

---

105 Ramsay I and Stapledon G, 'A Citation Analysis of Australian Law Journals' (1997) 21 *Melbourne University Law Review* 677; and see also Ramsay I and Stapledon G, 'The Influence of Commercial Law Journals: Citation Analysis' (1998) 26 *Australian Business Law Review* 298.

106 http://www.arc.gov.au/era/default.htm (5/11/2009).

107 Unwin M, 'Publication: High Impact Journals & Citation Data' (Presentation to the QUT Faculty of Law July 22, 2009) based on *Journal Citation Reports* Help http://admin-apps.isiknowledge.com.ezp01.library.qut.edu.au/JCR/help/h_impfact.htm (5/11/2009).

108 *Journal Citation Reports* Help http://admin-apps.isiknowledge.com.ezp01.library.qut.edu.au/JCR/help/h_impfact.htm (5/11/2009).

109 http://lawlib.wlu.edu/LJ/ (5/11/2009).

110 Unwin M, 'Strategies for Working with ERA' in Hutchinson T, 'Keeping research on the agenda' (2009) 3 *ALTA Newsletter* 18.

111 De Mulder R and Van Noortwijk K, 'More Science than Art: Law in the 21st century' (12th BILETA Conference The Future of Legal Education and Practice March 24th & 25th, 1997 Collingwood College, University of Durham) http://www.bileta.ac.uk/pages/Conference%20papers.aspx (5/11/2009).

112 Smyth R, 'Academic Writing and the Courts: A Quantitative Study of the Influence of Legal and Non-Legal Periodicals in the High Court' (1999) 17 (2) *University of Tasmania Law Review* 164.

Andrew Lynch,[113] Richard Haigh,[114] Patrick Keyzer,[115] and Paul von Nessen[116] have been undertaking analyses of High Court judgments and in so doing have used various empirical methodologies.[117] There have been, for example, studies on the incidence of dissent, the use of American precedent, the use of social fact evidence and the use of published journal articles in decisions. Russell Smyth examined this latter issue; that is, 'the extent to which the High Court cited legal (and non-legal) periodicals in decisions published in the *Commonwealth Law Reports* decided between 1990 and 1997'. Smyth counted all citations to legal and non-legal periodicals in the sample cases and was thus able to identify five of the most-cited journals. This was followed up by a more general study on the State Supreme Courts' citing practices, covering both case law and secondary authority, and further studies on the High Court.[118]

Some of these studies have been based on methodologies used in North American projects. Such methodologies are not always easily transferable to the Australian context. Andrew Lynch attempted 'to transparently design a quantitative methodology for the purpose of gaining greater understanding of a phenomenon of the Australian legal system, specifically the levels of dissent on the High Court of Australia'.[119] In particular, Lynch refers to the unique methodological problems in planning the dissent studies, and of the difficulties inherent in translating American methodology schemes, such as that employed by the *Harvard Law Review* for its annual statistics on the latest term of the United States Supreme Court, to the Australian context.[120] This is because of the different jurisdictional contexts of decision-making. The United States Supreme Court practice tends to be that one justice writes an opinion for the court. The Australian High Court follows the English seriatim tradition whereby each judge writes their own decision. At times in both jurisdictions, per curiam decisions, that is judgments 'given "by the Court" without identification of individual

---

113　Lynch A, 'Dissent: Towards a Methodology for Measuring Judicial Disagreement in the High Court of Australia' (2002) 24 *Sydney Law Review* 470.

114　Haigh R, '"It is Trite and Ancient Law": The High Court and the Use of the Obvious' (2000) 28 *Federal Law Review* 87.

115　Keyzer P, 'The Americanness of the Australian Constitution: The Influence of American Constitutional Jurisprudence on Australian Constitutional Jurisprudence: 1988 to 1994' (2000) 19 *Australasian Journal of American Studies* 25.

116　Von Nessen P, 'The Use of American Precedents by the High Court of Australia, 1901–1987' (1992) 14 *Adelaide Law Review* 181.

117　Lynch A, 'Dissent: Towards a Methodology for Measuring Judicial Disagreement in the High Court of Australia' (2002) 24 *Sydney Law Review* 470 (see in particular the literature review in footnote 5).

118　Smyth R, 'What do Intermediate Appellate Courts Cite? A Quantitative Study of the Citation Practice of Australian State Supreme Courts' (1999) 21 *Adelaide Law Review* 51; Smyth R, 'What do Judges Cite? An Empirical Study of the "Authority of Authority" in the Supreme Court of Victoria' (1999) 25 (1) *Monash University Law Review* 29; Smyth R, 'Other than "Accepted Sources of Law"?: A Quantitative Study of Secondary Source Citations in the High Court' (1999) 22 (1) *UNSW Law Journal* 19.

119　Lynch A, 'Dissent: Towards a Methodology for Measuring Judicial Disagreement in the High Court of Australia' (2002) 24 *Sydney Law Review* 470.

120　Lynch A, 'Dissent: Towards a Methodology for Measuring Judicial Disagreement in the High Court of Australia' (2002) 24 *Sydney Law Review* 470 at 471.

author' may also be made.[121] Lynch attempted to establish a methodology for measuring dissent that would satisfy some of the basic tenets of good empirical work; that is, that the methodology is transparent and easily replicated, so as to 'ensure accuracy and consensus in the citation of such statistics'.[122]

5.8.4 *Content analysis*

Content analysis is a little like citation analysis. Both are examining the text of judgments. Citation analysis is very quantitative in its approach. Content analysis as it has been practised in legal research has taken a primarily qualitative approach.[123] This method enables a legal scholar to collect a set of documents such as judgments, read these systematically, record 'consistent features of each one', and then draw 'inferences and meaning' from the set.[124] The sources are used as texts — 'the text becomes a focus of research in its own right rather than merely as a report of research'.[125] This method requires a reading of the cases with a subsequent coding of comments fitting within certain categories. It allows researchers to deal with a large numbers of cases, looking for broad patterns. Content analysis is considered 'perfectly suited for examining aspects of judicial method'.[126] In the United States context, this methodology has been used to analyse 'courts' reliance on social policy or social science, in contrast with more technical or formalistic doctrinal reasoning'.[127] The methodology is also able to describe more accurately the 'landscape of decided cases', and it has been referred to as the 'most precise way for documenting what appellate judges decide and how they explain their decisions'.[128]

Content analysis involves a process of reading the judgments, and coding, followed by an analysis of the results. Apart from basic coding factors such as whether there has been positive or negative treatment of the data,[129] the analysis uses specific factors identified by the researcher. An example from the Australian

---

121 Lynch A, 'Dissent: Towards a Methodology for Measuring Judicial Disagreement in the High Court of Australia' (2002) 24 *Sydney Law Review* 470 at 478.

122 Lynch A, 'Dissent: Towards a Methodology for Measuring Judicial Disagreement in the High Court of Australia' (2002) 24 *Sydney Law Review* 470 at 475.

123 Hall M and Wright R, 'Systemic Content Analysis of Judicial Opinions' (2008) 96 *California Law Review* 63.

124 Hall M and Wright R, 'Systemic Content Analysis of Judicial Opinions' (2008) 96 *California Law Review* 63 at 64.

125 Veal A, *Business Research Methods* (2 ed, South Melbourne: Pearson Addison Wesley, 2005) 13, 84.

126 Hall M and Wright R, 'Systemic Content Analysis of Judicial Opinions' (2008) 96 *California Law Review* 63 at 93.

127 Hall M and Wright R, 'Systemic Content Analysis of Judicial Opinions' (2008) 96 *California Law Review* 63 at 93.

128 Hall M and Wright R, 'Systemic Content Analysis of Judicial Opinions' (2008) 96 *California Law Review* 63 at 100.

129 Fradella H, 'A Content Analysis of Federal Judicial Views of the Social Science "Researcher's Black Arts"' (2003) 35 *Rutgers Law Journal* 103.

literature is Kylie Burns's reading of the High Court torts cases.[130] Much depends on the person reading the text so if a number of research assistants are working on the same data set then there needs to be very careful training carried out and the coding tested to ensure reliability.

5.9 Triangulation

It is important to choose the most pertinent method to facilitate your research and provide the information you need to address your hypothesis and objectives. Sometimes there is a choice of methodologies available to you. Each method might have specific advantages over others. Depending on the importance, time available and the scope of the project, it may well be that you can consider methodological triangulation.

Methodological triangulation has been defined as 'the use of more than one method or source of data in the study of a social phenomenon so that findings may be cross-checked'.[131] In this way, various methodological techniques are used to provide complementary information and together the results can provide a stronger evidence base for your hypothesis and more confidence in the results. The weakness of one method will be compensated for by the strengths of another. Interviews, surveys, participant observation, doctrinal analysis of the law as well as a review of the literature can all build a fuller picture of the issue at hand. Each technique used will address a 'different aspect' of the phenomenon as well as providing some overlap.[132] True triangulation occurs when different methods are used to investigate the same question.[133]

Methodological triangulation includes:

* Data triangulation by examining the issue at different times, in different places, at different levels (group or individual), from different points of view (management or workers);

* Researcher or Investigator triangulation by examining the issue using people from different disciplines, for example, lawyers, psychologists, social scientists, police; and

* Theory triangulation by using different theories and testing the issue through various theoretical prisms.[134]

---

130 And see the discussion of this in Burns K, 'It's just not cricket: The High Court, sport and legislative facts' (2002) 10 (3) *Torts Law Journal* 234; Burns K, 'The Way the World Is: Social Facts in High Court Negligence Cases' (2004) 12 (3) *Torts Law Journal* 215.

131 Bryman A, *Social Research Methods* (3 ed, Oxford: Oxford University Press, 2008), 700.

132 Kane E and O'Reilly-de Brun M, *Doing your own Research* (London: Marion Boyars Publishers, 2001), 108.

133 Veal AJ, *Business Research Methods: A Managerial Approach* (2 ed, Frenchs Forest: Pearson Education Australia, 2005), 40.

134 Kane E and O'Reilly-de Brun M, *Doing your own Research* (London: Marion Boyars Publishers, 2001), 110.

Triangulation Complementarity Matrix

© Dr Bill Metcalf, 2005

Parameter / Method	Time period	Intensive / Extensive	Intrusive	Theory Flexibility	Quantifiability	Cross-Cultural Applicability	Replicability	Thin / Thick Explication	Causality	Threat to Researcher
Social survey (snapshot)	once	Extensive	Modestly intrusive	Inflexible	High	Slight	High	Thin	Very low	Low
Social survey (longitudinal)	Across time into future	Extensive	Fairly intrusive	Inflexible	Very high	Slight	Limited	Fairly thin	Moderate	Low
Participant observation	Across time into future	Intensive	Very intrusive	Very flexible	Very low	Very high	Low	Very thick	Moderate	Very high
Secondary data analysis	Across, historical	Very extensive	Non-intrusive	Marginally flexible	Very high	Possible but with problems	Very high	Very thin	Very low	Nil
Semi & uns interviews	Once	Intensive	Very intrusive	Fairly flexible	Low	Fairly high	Very low	Fairly thick	Fairly low	High
Focus groups	Once	Intensive - extensive	Fairly intrusive	Fairly flexible	Fairly low	Limited	Moderately high	Fairly thick	Very low	High
Archival / historical	Across, historical	Intensive - extensive	Non-intrusive	Very flexible	Generally low	Possible	Moderate	Thick – thin	Moderate	Very low
Oral history / biography	Across, historical	Very intensive	Very intrusive	Very flexible	Nil	Slight	Very low	Very thick	Moderate	High
Case study	Across, historical and future	Intensive	Can be intrusive	Flexible	Usually low	Slight	Moderate	Thick	Moderate	Generally low
Social experiment	Once	Intensive	Very intrusive	Inflexible	High	Very slight	Very high	Fairly thin	Very high	Moderate
Content analysis	Across, historical	Extensive	Non-intrusive	Fairly inflexible	High	Slight	Very high	Very thin	Very low	Nil

Bill Metcalf has developed a Methodology Triangulation Matrix which is a good resource to assist researchers in choosing complementary methods to analyse their topic.[135] The methods suggested in this matrix are listed on the left hand column and include social surveys (snapshot), social surveys (longitudinal), participant observation, secondary data analysis, semi-structured and unstructured interviews, focus groups, archival/historical work, oral history/biography, case study, social experiment, and content analysis.

The complementary aspects appear along the top row of the matrix and include the time period under investigation, whether the method is intensive/extensive, whether the method is intrusive, the theory flexible, the extent of quantifiability of the results, cross-cultural applicability, replicability, thin/thick explication, causality and threat if any to researcher.

So take for example a survey — this would only need to be done once. It could be quite extensive, modestly intrusive in terms of the effect on the participants, theoretically inflexible, lead to highly quantifiable data, and have only a slight chance of having application across different cultures. It would be easy to replicate. It would show little in the way of the cause of the phenomenon under investigation. It would give little explanation of the reasons behind the phenomenon. An interview method on the other hand would seem to rate differently on each factor and therefore could be a useful foil or secondary methodology to use for the survey.

The various factors will be somewhat different, and of different importance, depending on the project and researcher. So one researcher may find a particular methodology 'threatening' whereas another researcher might be very comfortable with using it. The matrix is a heuristic device to help researchers decide on their optimum mix of methods — it is not a prescriptive 'one-size-suits-all' tool.

5.9.1 *Case studies of methodologies from theses*

The following examples are methodological case studies which aim to illustrate a variety of successful non-doctrinal approaches that legal researchers have used to investigate and elaborate on their ideas and arguments. Legal scholarship tends to present problems that are unique and not necessarily easily investigated using standard forms of empirical approach such as a survey or interview technique. Researchers often need to combine disparate methods in order to fully investigate their research hypotheses.

Case study one

White B, Consultation, *Commissions and Context: A Comparative Study of the Law Commission and the Australian Law Reform Commission* Thesis, DPhil in Law, Oxford University, Hilary 2004.

The methodology for this thesis covered three aspects. In the first place, it was a comparison between the Law Commission of England and Wales (Scotland

---

135 Metcalf B, 'Choosing a Research Methodology' (Griffith Graduate Research School, Griffith University, 2009).

has its own which was not considered) and the Australian Law Reform Commission. In this respect, the author adopted a comparative methodology based on Kamba's 'Comparative Law: A Theoretical Framework'[136] which included three steps — first, a description of the consultation processes of the bodies; second, identification of similarities and differences; and third, explanations of these. Secondly, a qualitative research methodology was used based on S Kvale *Interviews: An Introduction to Qualitative Research Interviewing.*[137] In particular, the seven step process described there was followed. This covered thematising, designing, interviewing, transcribing, analysing, verifying and reporting. The methodology included semi-structured interviews and document analysis. Thirdly, the thesis adopted a 'post-positivist' outlook as described in *Handbook of Qualitative Research.*[138]

The researcher began by defining the terms being used, in particular 'consultation', and distinguishing different types of consultation processes. It sets up models of consultation. The 'values' or underlying assumptions of the researcher were clarified so that claims made in the thesis could be evaluated in light of the researcher's clearly stated perspective. Sampling strategies were adopted in order to identify those to be interviewed and an interview plan prepared. The interviews were semi-structured. Transcripts were then produced for each interview relying on notes taken and recordings. Each transcript was then coded. Reflections were added by the researcher and a summary made of each interview. Two master summaries were then compiled — one for the Australian consultations and one for the United Kingdom consultations. Document analysis was undertaken too. This covered commission reports, annual reports, consultation documents and other published material. In some cases internal files and internal documents were made available to the researcher as well as the public documents. Another step in the research was attendance at commission meetings — both internal and public meetings.

Case study two

Dean G, *The Experience of Investigation for Detectives* Thesis PhD Brisbane: Faculty of Law, Queensland University of Technology (QUT) 2000.

This study focused on identifying and describing the qualitative variation in individual detectives' experiences of criminal investigation. The primary research question was 'How do detectives experience the process of a criminal investigation?' The study was undertaken within a qualitative framework. Phenomenography was chosen rather than content analysis, ethnography, phenomenology and grounded theory because of its focus on identifying and describing the qualitative variation in individuals' experiences of a particular phenomenon. The focus was on 'establishing the "ways" in which some phenomenon is experienced, how these "ways" of experiencing something are

---

136 Kamba W, 'Comparative Law: A Theoretical Framework' (1974) 23 *International and Comparative Law Quarterly* 485.

137 (Thousand Oaks: Sage Publications, 1996).

138 Lincoln Y and Guba E, 'Paradigmatic Controversies, Contradictions, and Emerging Confluences' in Denzin N and Lincoln Y (eds), *Handbook of Qualitative Research* (2 ed, Thousand Oaks: Sage Publications, 2000).

different from one another, and how these "differences" are differences in "quality".[139] Therefore, the aim was 'to capture the "critical differences" and the corresponding "qualitative differences" in how something is experienced'.[140] A phenomenographic interview was used to elicit a person's conceptions or 'way of experiencing something'.[141] In this study, the two key questions were 'What is investigation like for you?' and 'How do you know when you are doing a good investigation?'[142]

According to this method, the variation in 'ways of experiencing', which is expressed as 'conceptions' at an individual level, is 'captured at the collective level in a set of "categories of description" which represent the limited number of ways in which any phenomena can be experienced by people.'[143] After a period of becoming familiar with the content of the study's sample of interview transcripts, the next key step was 'to identify statements, utterances, expressions and so forth from the "common pool" of meanings contained in the interview transcripts, that appear to be related to various aspects of the phenomenon being researched', and these were coded accordingly.[144]

Case study three

Mackenzie G, *A Question of Balance: A Study of Judicial Methodology, Perceptions and Attitudes in Sentencing* Thesis PhD Sydney: Faculty of Law, University of New South Wales, 2001.

This thesis critically analyses the judicial decision-making process involved in sentencing criminal offenders. It in itself therefore was a study of methodology — of judicial methodology and judicial perceptions and attitudes towards sentencing. The study found that 'judges perceive the process of sentencing to be an adjudicative balancing of the relevant factors in every case, including the legal principles and the interests of all the parties, including the offender, the victim and the community'.[145]

In all, 10 Supreme Court judges and 21 District Court judges were interviewed. Open questions were used in the relatively unstructured interviews, for example:

* 'From your perspective as a judge, how do you see the sentencing process?

* How do you approach the task of sentencing?

139 Dean G, *The Experience of Investigation for Detectives* (Thesis PhD Brisbane, Australia: Queensland University of Technology (QUT) 2000), 3.

140 Dean G, *The Experience of Investigation for Detectives* (Thesis PhD Brisbane, Australia: Queensland University of Technology (QUT) 2000), 4.

141 Dean G, *The Experience of Investigation for Detectives* (Thesis PhD Brisbane, Australia: Queensland University of Technology (QUT) 2000), 17.

142 Dean G, *The Experience of Investigation for Detectives* (Thesis PhD Brisbane, Australia: Queensland University of Technology (QUT) 2000), 20.

143 Dean G, *The Experience of Investigation for Detectives* (Thesis PhD Brisbane, Australia: Queensland University of Technology (QUT) 2000), 36.

144 Dean G, *The Experience of Investigation for Detectives* (Thesis PhD Brisbane, Australia: Queensland University of Technology (QUT) 2000), 36.

145 Mackenzie G, *A Question of Balance: A Study of Judicial Methodology, Perceptions and Attitudes in Sentencing* (Thesis PhD Sydney: Faculty of Law, University of New South Wales, 2001), viii.

* How do you see your role in the process?
* What role do you think the purposes of sentencing as set out in s 9(1) of the *Penalties and Sentences Act 1992* play in the process?
* How do you make a decision concerning which of these to apply in a particular case?
* What influences you as a judge when applying the purposes under s 9(1) of the Act?
* What part do you think public opinion plays in the process, and how do you determine it?
* What role do you think the media plays in sentencing?
* What role do you think judicial discretion plays, and how important do you see this as being?'[146]

There was testing of the questions by two judges who were also involved in preliminary discussions regarding the design of the project. The final questions were included with a letter to 52 judges requesting their participation in the study. The responses to the questions were analysed and themed.

The main themes included:

1 judges and the process of sentencing — stress, workloads, procedure and the judge's role;
2 judicial discretion in sentencing — consistency, appeals, and the use of sentencing options;
3 sentencing aims and purposes — the conflicting purposes reflected in the legislation and how the judges dealt with these; and
4 law and order, public opinion, community expectations and the media.

The thesis concluded with a number of recommendations drawn from the judicial responses and an extensive literature review which included the theories of sentencing.

5.10   Conclusion

This chapter has attempted to give a broad overview of the parameters of non-doctrinal methodologies available to be used by the legal researcher. Each of the methods canvassed (and the many not included) can call for specialist knowledge and skills. The objective of this discussion was to push the door ajar. Those wanting to explore further may like to examine the reading list. The consulting units in universities provide another valuable source of information and advice on the design and analysis of research projects. Current research thinking is about considering the objective of the research and using any method which is suitable to reach an understanding of the research area.

---

146 Mackenzie G, *A Question of Balance: A Study of Judicial Methodology, Perceptions and Attitudes in Sentencing* (Thesis PhD Sydney: Faculty of Law, University of New South Wales, 2001), 122, 123.

Further reading

Allan G and Skinner C, *Handbook for Research Students in the Social Sciences* (London: Falmer Press, 1991).

Baker AJL, *Social Science Research Methods Terms* (New York: Columbia University Press, 2008).

Bryman A, *Social Research Methods* (3 ed, Oxford: Oxford University Press, 2008).

Burns R, *Introduction to Research Methods* (4 ed, Melbourne: Pearson Education, 2000).

Channels N, *Social Science Methods in the Legal Process* (New Jersey: Rowman & Allanheld, 1985).

Creswell J, *Qualitative Inquiry and Research Design: Choosing Among Five Traditions* (2 ed, Thousand Oaks, California: Sage Publications, 2007).

Crowl TK, *Fundamentals of Research: A Practical Guide for Educators and Special Educators* (Columbus, Ohio: Publishing Horizons Inc, 1986).

De Vaus DA, *Surveys in Social Research* (5 ed, St Leonards: Allen and Unwin, 2002).

Faigman D L, *Legal Alchemy: The Use and Misuse of Science in the Law* (New York: WH Freeman and Company, 1999).

Feagin J R, Orum A and Sjoberg G (eds), *A Case for the Case Study* (Chapel Hill and London: The University of North Carolina Press, 1991).

Fielding NG, Lee RM and Blank G (eds), *The SAGE Handbook of Online Research Methods* (London: SAGE, 2008).

Fink A, 'How to ask survey questions' in *The Survey Kit* (Thousand Oaks, California: Sage Publications, 1995, The Survey Kit No 2).

Fink A, 'How to design surveys' in *The Survey Kit* (2 ed, Thousand Oaks, California: Sage Publications, 2003, The Survey Kit No 5).

Gardner G, *Social Surveys for Social Planners* (rev ed, Sydney: Holt, Rinehart and Winston, 1978).

Hakel M, Sorcher M, Beer M and Moses J, *Making it Happen: Designing Research with Implementation in Mind* (Beverly Hills: Sage Publications, 1982).

Hall M and Wright R, 'Systemic Content Analysis of Judicial Opinions' (2008) 96 *California Law Review* 63.

Hutchinson T, 'Developing Legal Research Skills: Context, Framework and Practice' (2008) 32 (3) *Melbourne University Law Review* 1065.

Hutchinson T, *Educating the Transnational Lawyer: Globalisation and the Effects on Legal Research Skills Training* (Legal Research Communications Interest Group, Australasian Law Teachers Association Conference 2006 Victoria University of Technology, Melbourne Australia July 4-7 2006). http://www.alta.edu.au/2006_published_conference_papers.html (5/11/2009).

Hutchinson T and Burns K, 'The impact of "empirical facts" on legal scholarship and legal research training' (2009) 43 (2) *The Law Teacher* 153.

Hutchinson T, 'The Transnational Lawyer: GATS, Globalisation and the Effects on Legal Education' (2006) 11 *Australian and New Zealand Journal of Legal Education* 93.

Kvale S and Brinkmann S, *InterViews: Learning the Craft of Qualitative Research Interviewing* (2 ed, Los Angeles: Sage Publications, 2009).

Leighton PE, 'The case for empirical research' (1984) 18 *Law Teacher* 13.

Lynch A, 'Dissent: Towards a Methodology for Measuring Judicial Disagreement in the High Court of Australia' (2002) 24 *Sydney Law Review* 470.

McConville M and Chui WH (eds), *Research Methods for Law* (Edinburgh: Edinburgh University Press, 2007).

McNeill P, *Research Methods* (3 ed, London: Routledge, 2004).

Monahan J, *Social Science in Law: Cases and Materials* (4 ed, Westbury, New York: The Foundation Press Inc, 1998).

Monahan J and Walker L, 'Social Science Research in Law: A New Paradigm', in Roesch R and Gagnon N (eds), *Psychology and Law: Criminal and Civil Perspectives* (Aldershot; Burlington, VT: Ashgate, 2007).

Moore N, *How to Do Research: The Complete Guide to Designing and Managing Research Projects* (3 rev ed, London: Facet, 2006).

Neuman WL and Wiegand B, *Criminal Justice Research Methods* (Boston: Allyn and Bacon, 2000).

Sarantakos S, *Social Research* (2 ed, Melbourne: Macmillan Education Australia, 1998).

Saunders M, Lewis P and Thornhill A, *Research Methods for Business Students* (4 ed, Harlow, England: Pearson Education Limited, 2007).

Silverman D (ed), *Qualitative Research: Theory Method and Practice* (2 ed, London: Sage, 2004).

Stringer E, *Action Research* (3 ed, Thousand Oaks, California: Sage Publications, 2007).

Veal AJ, *Business Research Methods:A Managerial Approach* (2 ed, Frenchs Forest: Pearson Education Australia, 2005).

Walter M (ed), *Social Research Methods* (2 ed, Melbourne: Oxford University Press, 2010).

Weisberg J, Krosnick J and Brown B, *An Introduction to Survey Research, Polling and Data Analysis* (3 ed, Thousand Oaks, California: Sage, 1996).

Zuber-Skerritt O (ed), *New Directions in Action Research* (Washington, DC: Falmer Press, 1996).

6

Formulating a Research Topic

Academic writing is not an entirely fluid process. Although it is creative on some levels, it always involves planning. Planning occurs before you begin to write, but especially before you begin to research. Planning is ongoing in legal writing. You make a plan. You research further. You change and augment the ideas in your initial plan, and then you research the new points. A research and writing 'Plan' exists on two levels. First, there is the 'idea plan' — which consists of the topic you are writing about, the aspect of the main subject you intend developing, your hypothesis, and your arguments. The second plan, the 'research plan', 'hangs off' the first. Once you decide what you need, the second plan maps out how you are going to locate the relevant information — basically your research methodology.

6.1 How do you choose a topic and formulate a plan?

While freedom to choose a topic for a research project may seem an exciting prospect, the reality can prove challenging. Where do you start? Sometimes if you have been working or studying in an area for some time, then you are aware of specific difficulties with the operation of the existing law. A basic search should be sufficient to identify whether there is recently published information available about the particular topic and then you can move on from there to formulate your own project. At other times you will be required to choose a topic from an area where you may have no background knowledge whatsoever. In that situation, you will need to read broadly enough to provide yourself with a knowledge base. At an early stage in the topic formulation, it may be best to consider the issues very broadly before trying to focus on a specific point or problem. However, in order to write meaningfully about an area, you will need to identify a workable segment to investigate. The methods described below can be useful both for defining a topic and for formulating a plan.

6.2 Brainstorming

Brainstorming is the most basic method used to kick-start the process. Write down everything that seems to relate to a possible topic without being judgmental or trying to compartmentalise or censor your ideas. It is important not to edit at this stage but rather to 'strive for quantity'.[1] Once you have this material written

---

1   Adair J, *Decision Making & Problem Solving Strategies* (2 ed, London; Philadelphia: Kogan Page, 2007), 69.

down, you can then begin to assess what might 'work' or be worth pursuing. It may be that several of the separate ideas overlap. These can be sorted through so that themes will become more evident. Pull out the main points and the smaller details, perhaps reformulating half-thoughts along the way.

When you brainstorm, your list of issues tends to be centric; that is, the list represents your view of the topic. If possible, include other people's views in your emerging picture.[2] In a group situation this will happen automatically. However, if you are working alone, try to imagine the issue from the point of view of others actively involved in the problem, the stakeholders in the scenario – your client, a student, the victim of a crime, the police attending a crime scene and so on. This process should inspire you to attempt a list of the various players involved in the issue, whether it is a building dispute, environmental regulation problem or a legal conundrum, such as euthanasia. This in itself is a useful broadening process.

Brainstorming example

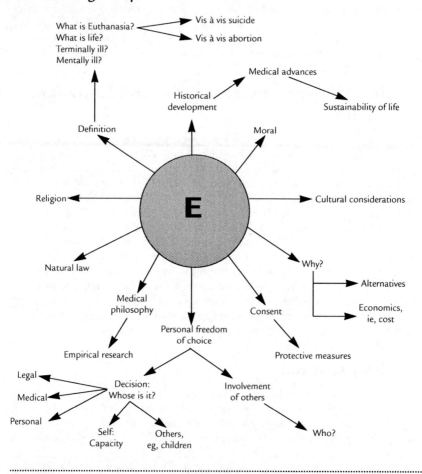

---

2   De Bono E, *Lateral Thinking* (New York: Harper & Row, 1970).

Once the brainstorm ideas are on paper, some organisation must be given to produce a paper outline. Most word processing softwares provide outliners. Consider jotting down your brainstorm issues on the outliner and then use the software facilities to reorganise and shape your document. But beware, sometimes an outliner is too mechanistic and linear in the early stages of a project.

6.3 Heuristics

Heuristics, or idea generators, are often used in problem-solving situations and can also be useful in a research setting where the real difficulty is trying to crystallise ideas in order to research and write effectively in an area. Heuristics come in different forms, but they are in essence brainstorming tricks, and include question formulas, attitudinal heuristics, and map models.

One way of building on any initial idea is to ask 'who, how, what, when, where and why' type questions. Ernest Stringer has worked out a series of questions mainly geared to change-based action research, tailored to a problem or work situation, and the incidence of worrisome events or conflict.[3] Not everything in this type of list will be relevant to your situation. The doctrinal methodology requires different questions and the results will probably be less practical, but try to tailor the prompt questions to suit the topic. The goal is to be eclectic and to think and to reflect in order to push your creativity to the outer parameters of your topic.

WHO?

Who are the stakeholders? Who is centrally involved? And who is involved but less relevant?

Who are the influential people?

Who is linked to whom? In what ways are they related?

Who is in favour of change? Who is antagonistic to change?

Who has resources?

WHAT?

What is involved in the process? Can the issues be more closely defined?

What major activities or events are relevant to the issue?

What is each person or group doing or neglecting to do?

What is each person or group aiming to achieve?

What resources are being used and by whom? What is available?

HOW?

How do events happen? What is the usual process?

How do conflicts arise?

---

3   See Stringer E, *Action Research: A Handbook for Practitioners* (2 ed, Thousand Oaks: Sage Publications, 1999), 94–95.

How do the various players interrelate?

How are decisions made?

How are resources used?

WHERE?

Where do events normally take place?

Where are the resources located?

WHEN?

When, or how often, does conflict or the event in question occur?

When is it possible to intervene?

Never neglect to ask the final question:

WHY?

Why is this particular matter important to me personally?

Why is it necessary to research and write about this issue?

Why has this issue become a problem or controversial?

Why might people want to read about it?

Aristotle is credited as suggesting one of the most useful heuristics. This method involves asking five basic questions:

What is it?

What is it like and unlike?

What caused it?

What can come of it?

What has been said about it?

This list of questions is more attuned to the physical world and may not always readily translate to legal matters. However, it can be rephrased to suit the legal context so that instead of asking 'What is it?', the question would be 'What is it defined as?'. If we take euthanasia as an example, then the issues encompassed by the term can be complex. There is, for example, passive euthanasia and active euthanasia, and it is important to clarify which of these is being discussed. It is always important to define your terms clearly.

The second question extends the concept further by introducing at the most basic level the categories of synonym and antonym. However, at a deeper level, this question resonates with the ideas of the linguist Ferdinand de Saussure. Saussure talked about the importance of difference in determining meaning. He argued that what something was, depended on its relation to other things. A table should be defined by its difference to a chair or a desk.[4] So, euthanasia can be defined by its opposite — life.

---

4   Davies M, *Asking the Law Question* (3 ed, Sydney: The Lawbook Co., 2008), 337–345.

What have been the causes of this phenomenon? Is it a recent movement? Are there instances from history? Are there analogies or relationships between euthanasia and other medical procedures? What will be the effects of the development of this? What has been said (written) about euthanasia? Aristotle held that if you answer these five questions about any topic, then you will understand it better — and you should be able to write about it more clearly.

Aristotle's Topoi[5] encompasses five main issues:

* definition (What is it?);
* comparison (What is it like and unlike?);
* relationship (What caused it?);
* testimony (What has been said about it?); and
* circumstance (What can come of it?).

The following heuristic is based on a reformulation of Aristotle's questions and is useful in getting through to the 'plain meaning' of a word or a term.[6] Used in a legal framework, the definition questions are particularly pertinent for terms like 'euthanasia' or 'consent'. However, the other queries under the various headings could be used to examine a concept, such as 'fraud'.

Definition

1 How does the dictionary define _____?

2 What earlier words did _____ come from?

3 How has the meaning of _____ changed over the years? Is its meaning different now from what it was a hundred years ago?

4 What do I mean by _____?

5 Can _____ be divided? Into what parts?

6 To what group does _____ belong? How does it differ from other things in this group?

7 Can I give some examples of _____?

8 When is _____ most often misunderstood? By whom? Why?

9 What other words have approximately the same meaning as _____? Remember, English has an incredibly rich vocabulary and no two words mean exactly the same thing, but what comes closest?

---

5 'Topoi' is a rhetorical term which in Greek translates as 'place' and in Latin as 'locus' or 'a place in the mind where the storage and retrieval of ideas take place'. Aristotle, the creator of the topoi, used the term to 'describe the place or settings of an argument' and develop rhetorical arguments.

6 Perrin T, *Better Writing for Lawyers* (Toronto: Law Society of Upper Canada, 1990), 45–47, adapted from a heuristic in Cowan G and Cowan E, *Writing* (Scott Foresman and Company, 1980), 34.

Comparison

1   What is the opposite of _____? What is it most unlike? In what ways are they different?

2   What is most like _____ while still being distinct? In what ways are they alike?

3   To what is _____ superior? What about other meanings of superior (more worthy, physically stronger, higher in rank, other meanings)? How is it superior?

4   To what is _____ inferior? What about other meanings of inferior (less worthy, under, lower in rank, other meanings)? How is it inferior?

5   To what is _____ similar? How? In what specific ways?

6   From what is _____ different? How? In what specific ways?

Relationship

1   What is the result of _____?

2   What are the purposes of _____? Why does _____ exist?

3   Why does _____ happen?

4   What causes _____?

5   What are the effects of _____?

6   What comes before _____? What comes after _____?

Testimony

1   What have I heard people say about _____?

2   What facts or statistics do I have (or can I get) about _____?

3   Have I talked to anyone about _____? What have they said?

4   Quote a parable or well-known saying about _____?

5   Do I know a poem about _____?

6   Are there any laws about _____?

7   Do I know any songs about _____?

8   Have I read any books about _____?

9   Have I seen a movie or TV show about _____?

10 Do I want to do any research about _____?

Circumstance

1   Is _____ possible or impossible?

2   What circumstances, qualities or conditions make _____ possible? Which make it impossible?

3   Even if _____ is possible, is it feasible? Why or why not?

4   When did _____ happen previously?

5   Who has done or experienced _____?

6   What can do _____ now?

7   If _____ starts, what makes it end?

8   What would it take for _____ to happen now?

9   What would prevent _____ from happening?

Obviously these questions are not directly tailored to legal issues, terms and phenomena. However, not every problem has a directly legal solution. Your issue may be based in a fundamental public policy problem and the law can be merely one facet of the resolution. Use the thought prompters to explore the extra-legal issues and to separate these from your basic concern.

6.4   De Bono's 'thinking hats'

Having categorised and defined your topic, and perhaps done some background research, try using Edward de Bono's 'Thinking Hats' heuristic.[7] The aim of this method is to encourage the examination of an issue from a variety of angles. It is particularly effective for broad social issues such as the euthanasia example we have been using. Visualise yourself wearing, one at a time, six different coloured hats. The colour of the hat you visualise yourself wearing determines the way that you think about an issue. You jot down your thoughts whilst thinking about the issue in this way, before going on to change hats and then correspondingly, the way you respond to the issue. The hats and corresponding ways of thinking are as follows:

1   *White hat:* Thinking without bias. When you wear the white hat, you attempt to expunge any bias or value judgments from your view. You become a computer and take a literal view of the world. You take a neutral, emotion-free or detached view of the situation.

2   *Red hat:* Thinking with emotion. When you put this hat on, you lay your emotions on the table. There is no need to justify your likes and dislikes. You lay bare your hunches, gut feelings and guesses based on experience.

3   *Black hat:* A negative view. The black hat gives free rein to pessimism and more critical views. This hat is usually not used first but allows for a 'devil's advocate' approach that can often be very useful and constructive when working out the details of a plan. However, de Bono warns that 'Destruction is always much easier than construction'.[8]

4   *Yellow hat:* An optimistic view. The yellow hat allows an opportunity for positive, constructive views on making things happen.

5   *Green hat:* Creativity and new ideas. The green hat forces lateral thinking or thinking 'outside the box'.

6   *Blue hat:* The big picture, pulling the issues together. The blue hat is the conductor who attempts to orchestrate, record and observe, and perhaps provides an overview of all the others.

The 'thinking hats' technique can be used by a small group to workshop an idea. Imagine eavesdropping on a conversation taking place with regard to legalisation

---

7   De Bono E, *Six Thinking Hats* (Toronto: Key Porter Books, 1985).

8   De Bono E, *Six Thinking Hats* (Toronto: Key Porter Books, 1985), 99.

of surrogacy arrangements. The white hat may suggest that this will ostensibly be perfect. It will allow children to be placed with people who really want and need their presence. The red hat might add that personally it is something that they would not wish to do unless forced by extreme circumstances. The yellow hat might add that regulations could be drawn up with stiff penalties for those breaking the rules; for example, that no payments would be made and no money must change hands. The green hat might suggest that it would be worthwhile to look at what regulations other jurisdictions have put in place, whether they are 'working' and what problems have arisen. The black hat might suggest that such arrangements are doomed because of the natural ties between parents and their children and the likelihood that legalisation will result in children being sold. The person taking the blue hat role will attempt to summarise all these issues and move the discussion forward. The blue hat could also report back on the range of issues put forward within the group's discussion. This heuristic is most valuable in gaining an insight into the range of views prompting exploration of further options and even consensus.

6.5 Mind mapping your project

A visual way of investigating the connections between ideas involves the use of concept mapping or 'mind maps'. Mind maps are a way of organising, categorising, and 'teasing out' the issues in a project. Key aspects within a concept can be graphically connected in ways that enhance understanding of the whole. This process is useful in general problem-solving, and in clarifying material that you are reading, as well as in organising or preparing written projects and presentations. This method can be fun, save time and encourage memory and learning.

Here are a few suggestions for basic mind maps:

* Identify the essence or central issue and place the word concept in the centre of your page. Perhaps represent the issue by a picture or graphic itself or surrounding it. The essence of a mind map is that you have identified a central issue from which other thoughts and ideas will emanate. If you can identify a theme or representative symbol, then you achieve a visualisation of your topic. Therefore, if you are talking about the internationalisation of Australian law, you might draw a map of Australia and then have arrows coming into the country indicating the various external influences. Countries or organisations can also be signified by mascots, such as animals, which symbolise the essence of the whole. Think of the United States as an eagle or Russia as a bear. Depending on your learning style, this type of visualisation of a concept can enhance memory and understanding.

* What are the main aspects associated with your central issue or problem? Include these keywords on the diagram or graphic with themes or major issues emanating out but connected to it.

* Other branches can be connected to the major themes with words printed on the lines. Ensure that all the lines (ideas) are connected to others. However, it is important that the inner circle, the more important aspect or aspects, is delineated clearly. This can be done through size or colour, emphasising the hierarchy of ideas.

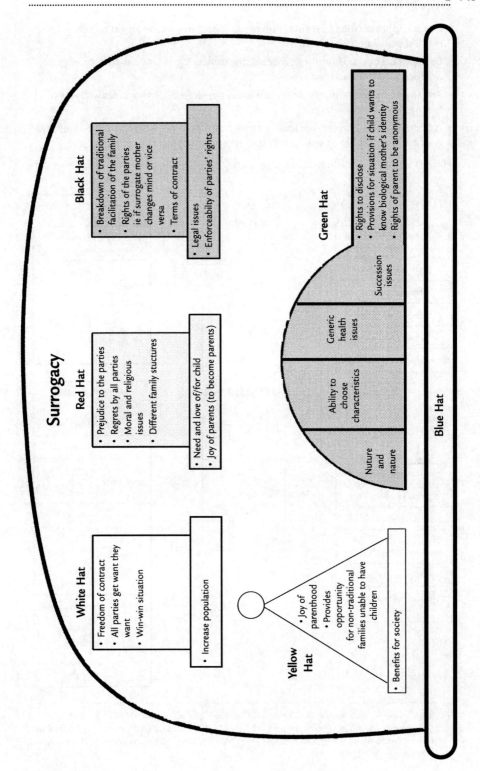

* Use one phrase (idea) per line, but be clear and do not be afraid to use hierarchy and numerical order.

* Be spontaneous and non-judgmental, try to develop your own style or imprint, and do not attempt to edit initially.

* Are any of these seemingly disparate ideas connected? Perhaps draw arrows linking these where relevant.

* Add colour and graphics including arrows and pictures where appropriate; that is where the graphic or colour will better represent your thoughts.[9]

Here is a mind map illustrating a general scan of the topic 'euthanasia':

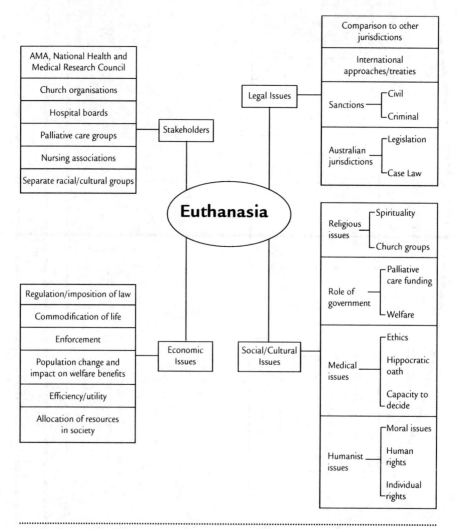

9   See Buzan T and Buzan B, *The Mind Map Book* (3 ed, London: BBC Books, 2003); Cacioppe R, *Mind Maps* (Perth: Integra, 1992), 21; Petelin R and Durham M, *The Professional Writing Guide: Writing Well and Knowing Why* (Warriewood, NSW: Business & Professional Publishing, 1998), 38.

Another example might be more graphic:

Euthanasia defined

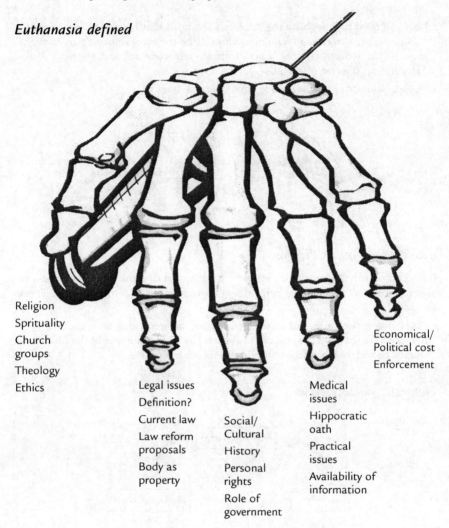

Religion
Sprituality
Church
groups
Theology
Ethics

Legal issues
Definition?
Current law
Law reform
proposals
Body as
property

Social/
Cultural
History
Personal
rights
Role of
government

Medical
issues
Hippocratic
oath
Practical
issues
Availability of
information

Economical/
Political cost
Enforcement

6.6   **Visual demonstration of ideas**

Sometimes it is enlightening to use graphics to organise your ideas, and there are various accepted methods of achieving useful visual representations. Among these are fishbone diagrams, cyclic maps, linear or numbered maps, tables, Venn diagrams, causes and effects maps, and hierarchical or relationship diagrams.

6.6.1   *Fishbone diagrams*

Another way of re-organising your initial group of brainstormed ideas is by using a 'fishbone diagram'. This method is particularly helpful when your writing is directed towards solving a problem.

* Draw a horizontal line and write the main issue or problem at the end of the line to the right.
* Next you need to categorise the potential solutions that have been identified during the brainstorming technique. This can be the most difficult part of the process. Draw diagonal lines (which form the fish skeleton) and place the categories at the end of each line.
* Include potential solutions along each diagonal line.[10]

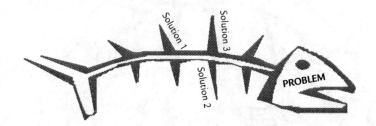

6.6.2 *Langrehr's designs*

John Langrehr has identified a series of basic visual designs that correspond to verbalised issues and can be helpful in graphically representing a topic. These include:[11]

* Cyclic maps, such as are often used to denote the lifecycle of animals, or to demonstrate the repetitive nature of events. Here is an example of the phases usually considered in discussion of domestic violence cases:

Domestic violence cycle

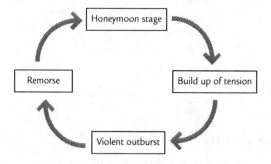

* Linear maps can present the perceived stages within a process so that a progressive development to a closure can be observed. This example relates to the Bibliographic Approach to Doctrinal Research model in Chapter Two.

---

10 Scott Fogler H and Le Blanc SE, *Strategies for Creative Problem Solving* (New Jersey: Prentice Hall PTR, 1995).

11 Langrehr J, *Become a Better Thinker* (North Brighton: Wrightbooks, 1995), 52.

Legal Research and Reasoning Model

1 Identify pertinent facts
2 Identify issues of law involved
3 Research issues
4 Analyse and synthesise facts and law
5 Come to a tentative conclusion

* Tables can be used for comparison mapping to distinguish those aspects of the concepts that may be alike and those aspects where the concepts differ.

Legal Search Engines Comparison

Database	Boolean	Narrowing	Miscellaneous
www.google.com	The default connector is AND An Advanced search includes ALL the search terms, EXACT phrase, do NOT contain the term, contain AT LEAST ONE of the words	Provision for Synonym Search (place in front of term), Domain Search, Numrange Search. For essential term place + in front	Provision for choosing language, date, domains and elimination of adult sites
www.bing.com	The default connector is AND Use quotation marks around exact phrases. Use OR for alternatives. An Advanced Search includes All of these terms, Any of these terms, This exact phrase, None of these terms	Lists of Related Searches and Search History appear on the left of the screen	To include words put + in front of it; To exclude words put – in front of it

* Comparison rings are an easy way of delineating sameness and difference. Two interleafing circles like Venn diagrams can be used to indicate overlapping issues or points of similarity between two quite separate concepts.

Forges a document   **Utters a forged document**

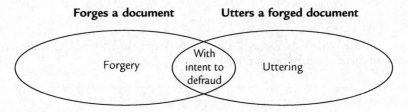

Forgery   With intent to defraud   Uttering

6.6.3   Using causes and effects mapping[12]

For this device you need to consider:

1   The core problem
2   Major antecedents to the problem
3   Other significant factors related to those antecedents
4   Major negative consequences
5   Other significant consequences

Take graffiti as an example:

1   problem — graffiti
2   antecedents — no youth leisure activities, no parental supervision, youthful
     aggression, rebellion, unchannelled talent, easy access to cheap spray paint,
     the 'theory of the commons' which suggests that people do not respect public
     property, difficulty in policing offences
3   consequences — ugly environments, community antagonism towards youth,
     conflict with youth, imprisonment and criminal records for young offenders

6.6.4   Using connections to map the scene

Various techniques may be used to break down categories into segments, to chart
relationships between people either within organisations or within communities,
or to identify forces acting on the central issue. These include hierarchical,
interacting and radial maps.

* Hierarchical maps may be used to develop the main topic into its various
  component parts.

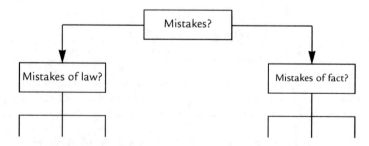

This could be used to identify the power bases and formal channels of
communication in an organisation.

---

12 Stringer E, *Action Research* (3 ed, London: Sage Publications, 2007), 115.

An aligned map could identify the informal channels of communication and aligned persons in the same organisation.

* Interacting maps can designate the characters or people who react on each other

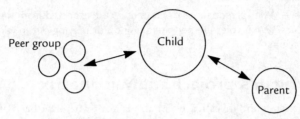

* Radial maps break down the main concept into its respective parts

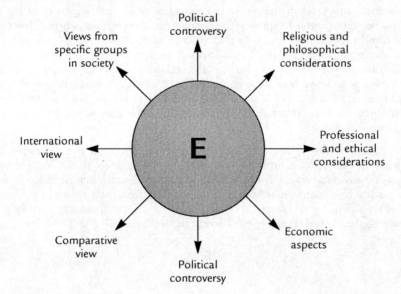

This map could as easily be used with the arrows pointing inwards to show the people or forces acting on an organisation. The example here deals once again with euthanasia, and attempts to identify various issues that might be addressed in a discussion of the topic.

6.6.5 *If you need to go further*

Sometimes you may need ways of prompting further development of the issues in the topic. Consider using the following:

* **Divisions** — Try to divide the issues logically, for example, a discussion of a book by chapter or a discussion of a book by themes.
* **History** — The chronological sequence of events or a timeline.
* **Function** — Think about what things do, their role and how they achieve the end result.

* **Process** — Think about how things work and the process involved in, for example, drafting legislation.

* **Classification** — Consider how things are related to each other. The hierarchical map could also be used for this purpose.

* **Personalities** — What personalities or characters are expected from those in stipulated roles? What roles are people taking on or playing out in various conflict situations?[13]

6.7 Horrigan's project analysis matrix

So far, the heuristics and investigative methods dealt with have been of a general nature. Bryan Horrigan has developed one method of expanding the parameters of a legal research topic in order to determine the whole area available for possible investigation.[14] Horrigan's philosophy seems to be akin to that espoused by Samuel Murumba, in that there is a recognition of the complexity of legal issues and that a surface approach to solving a problem (and to writing about a legal topic) is often too narrow, so that 'in areas of controversy or uncertainty it is necessary to take a vertical approach that cuts through different levels' of understanding.[15] Horrigan goes further, and sets out visually the various possible levels of approach to a legal issue in the matrix. While no journal article or thesis would cover all the possible issues, the idea of the matrix is to set out the possibilities so that a number of interconnecting areas may be marked out for further investigation.

There are nine separate boxes in the diagram, and each box represents a separate aspect of the main topic. The horizontal axis refers to the content of law, whether it is practical or operational in nature, 'black letter' or theoretical. The vertical axis encompasses some of the main approaches that may be taken to the law including an empirical or factual and doctrinal approach, a policy or reform approach and, at the highest level, that of critique.

---

13 Buzan T and Buzan B, *The Mind Map Book* (3 ed, London: BBC Books, 2003), 117.

14 Horrigan B, 'Black holes in black letter law: Applying legal theory and fostering critical thinking in legal practice and teaching' (Unpublished paper, Queensland University of Technology, 1999), 48–49.

15 Murumba S, 'Good legal writing: A guide for the perplexed' (1991) 17 (1) *Monash University Law Review* 93 at 96.

Horrigan's project analysis matrix[16]

		Practical/Operational Dimension	Elements of Law	Theoretical/Conceptual Dimension
Approaches to Law	Critique	How would an ideal law in a particular area work in practice and what changes in motivations, behaviour and other actions would it need?	How might the relevant law be redesigned outside its existing frame of reference to create an ideal law?	What is the best theory for explaining the relevant law, why is it best, how does it explain things best?
	Policy\Reform	What must happen in practice to accommodate incremental changes or developments in the relevant law?	How might the relevant law be changed, reformed or developed within its existing frame of reference?	How might the theories explaining the relevant law be improved within their own frames of reference or in their application to the relevant law?
	Empirical/ Doctrinal	What happens in practice in light of the relevant law?	What is the relevant law?	What theories explain the relevant law and how do they apply to it?
		Practical/Operational Dimension	Elements of Law	Theoretical/Conceptual Dimension

← **Content of Law** →

Horrigan has explained each sector in the matrix in this way, taking the example of the law of negligence to illustrate its use:[17]

Quadrant 1

> 'What happens in practice in light of the relevant law?'
>
> Example: 'How do the elements of the law of negligence apply to a particular client's situation?'

Quadrant 2

> 'What is the relevant law, and what are its elements?'
>
> Example: 'What are the elements of the law of negligence?'

Quadrant 3

> 'What theories explain the relevant law and how do they apply to it?'[18]

---

16 Horrigan B, 'Black holes in black letter law: Applying legal theory and fostering critical thinking in legal practice and Teaching' (Unpublished paper, Queensland University of Technology, 1999), Annexure II.

17 Horrigan B, 'Black holes in black letter law: Applying legal theory and fostering critical thinking in legal practice and Teaching' (Unpublished paper, Queensland University of Technology, 1999), 54–55.

18 Horrigan B, 'Black holes in black letter law: Applying legal theory and fostering critical thinking in legal practice and teaching' (Unpublished paper, Queensland University of Technology, 1999), 48–49.

Example: 'What theories explain the development of the law of negligence and the rationales underlying its rules?'

These quadrants represent the law as it is written and practised, and the current theories or philosophies behind this situation.

Quadrant 4

'What must happen in practice to accommodate incremental changes or developments in the relevant law?'

Example: 'What changes must clients implement in practice to accommodate new changes in negligence law?'

Quadrant 5

'How might the relevant law be changed, reformed or developed within its existing frame of reference?'

Example: 'What are the values and policy considerations which inform the development of particular areas of negligence law by law-making judges and legislators?'

Quadrant 6

'How might the theories explaining the relevant law be improved within their own frames of reference or in their application to the relevant law?'[19]

Example: 'How might both negligence law and theories about it be incrementally improved in light of each other's evolution and insights?'

These quadrants represent the issues that might arise in a context of reform or 'incremental' change.

Quadrant 7

'How would an ideal law in a particular area work in practice and what changes in motivations, behaviour and other actions would it need?'

Example: 'How might the fundamental assumptions and actions of key players in this area of law be critically analysed and changed?'

Quadrant 8

'How might the relevant law be redesigned outside its existing frame of reference to create an ideal law?'

Example: 'How might the elements of negligence law be critically analysed from a theoretical perspective?'

Quadrant 9

'What is the best theory for explaining the relevant law, why is it best, and how does it explain things best?'[20]

Example: 'Is negligence law fair and just as well as value-ridden, and what is the "best" theory of negligence law?'

---

19 Horrigan B, 'Black holes in black letter law: Applying legal theory and fostering critical thinking in legal practice and teaching' (Unpublished paper, Queensland University of Technology, 1999), 48–49.

20 Horrigan B, 'Black holes in black letter law: Applying legal theory and fostering critical thinking in legal practice and teaching' (Unpublished paper, Queensland University of Technology, 1999).

These highest quadrants are pushing the boundaries of what is in existence, and examine how practice might be redesigned to make the law work better, or how the law itself might be improved by being reframed, and whether there may be change on more than an incremental level — what is termed the 'best theory' to explain the law.

6.8 Conclusion

This chapter has taken a wide view of the various ways of organising and teasing out issues in a problem or an issue. Most of these have been from a generalist viewpoint so some manipulation is required to lever them into a specific legal framework. Many of these types of 'idea expansion tools' are also problem-based. These may not be specifically applicable when the actual problem is not clear. Visual learners will find the graphics particularly useful to clarify the relationships and interconnections between aspects of the topics. Horrigan's matrix is the only one of these heuristics specifically geared to the legal researcher. Treat the ideas in this chapter as devices to be used for their purpose and differently according to the situation being addressed.

Further reading

Adair J, *Decision Making & Problem Solving Strategies* (2 ed, London; Philadelphia: Kogan Page, 2007).

Buzan T and Buzan B, *The Mind Map Book* (rev ed, London: BBC Active, 2006).

Cacioppe R, *Mind Maps* (Perth: Integra, 1992).

Cryer P, *The Research Student's Guide to Success* (3 ed, Maidenhead, Berkshire: Open University Press, 2006).

De Bono E, *Lateral Thinking* (New York: Harper & Row, 1970).

Flower L, *Problem Solving Strategies for Writing* (4 ed, San Diego: Harcourt Brace Jovanovich, 1993).

Horrigan B, 'Black holes in black letter law: Applying legal theory and fostering critical thinking in legal practice and teaching' (Unpublished paper, Queensland University of Technology, 1999).

Langrehr J, *Become a Better Thinker* (North Brighton: Wrightbooks, 1995).

Perrin T, *Better Writing for Lawyers* (Toronto: Law Society of Upper Canada, 1990).

Petelin R and Durham M, *The Professional Writing Guide: Writing Well and Knowing Why* (Warriewood, NSW: Business & Professional Publishing, 1998).

Scott Fogler H and Le Blanc SE, *Strategies for Creative Problem Solving* (New Jersey: Prentice Hall PTR, 1995).

7

Refining the Topic and Thesis

In the last chapter, we discussed ways of problem-solving and exploring a new topic. The methods discussed there were of a general nature, except for Bryan Horrigan's matrix analysis which brings a specifically legal perspective to the process. The matrix echoes many of the ideas contained in Samuel Murumba's thoughtful essay on 'Good Legal Writing'.[1] In particular, it highlights the importance of higher-level thinking and critical analysis of the issues. It also emphasises the idea that law exists on several levels. Murumba represents these levels as:

* the operational or practical level experiences by the practitioner and the client;

* the legal doctrinal level where the judge balances competing legal interests; and

* critique, the level of the reformer, the social analyst and the theorist which involves higher level analysis.

Murumba argues that stimulating writing provides at least a hint of the enormous mass of complexity of ideas sitting below the surface of the law.[2] To ignore this is akin to a swimmer diving into a muddy pool full of hidden rocks.

Having delineated the likely parameters of a research topic, the next step in the writing process is to complete a proposal. In taking this step, it is important to stand back and critique your ideas through reflection on your personal conceptual framework. Sometimes the critical reflection may be addressed through a formal or informal presentation and defence.

This chapter deals with the drafting of a clear proposal, including the steps in this process — developing the topic, ensuring originality, formulating the objectives and hypothesis, and choosing a meaningful title. It investigates the planning issues that arise in larger research projects, including presenting and defending your decisions regarding methodology. The chapter also addresses the identification of the various conceptual frameworks lying behind your research topic. These varying personal, legal and theoretical frameworks affect the decisions you make on the direction or focus of your project. As well as the proposal, the chapter includes suggestions on writing a succinct abstract for your work, keeping a research diary, the literature review and deciding on a structure for your thesis.

---

1   Murumba S, 'Good legal writing: A guide for the perplexed' (1991) 17 (1) *Monash University Law Review* 93.

2   Murumba S, 'Good legal writing: A guide for the perplexed' (1991) 17 (1) *Monash University Law Review* 93 at 95.

7.1 Developing and refining the topic

Having mapped out a topic area that excites your interest and having explored the boundaries of the issues involved, the next step is to isolate a specific part of the whole. One of the usual ways of identifying a researchable issue is through experience. Perhaps you have observed a particular inadequacy in the workings of the legal system. Perhaps your experience of frustration reflects difficulties in rules affecting specific groups. Sometimes it is useful to test theory against reality; for example, aspects of the economic analysis of law might be tested against third party liability insurance legislation. Sometimes it is feasible to replicate an existing study in order to test the results within a different geographic region, or within a different legal jurisdiction. For example, a study in Western Australia may identify that certain categories of offenders are given harsher sentences. You may conduct research to investigate if this is also the case in Queensland. If you do not possess this experience then you need to develop strategies that will assist you to develop 'the kind of intense familiarity with a topic that you need so as to recognize a useful research question when you see one'![3] What are some activities that might help this process? Some suggestions are to teach in the area, attend conferences and write conference presentations, join writing groups, and make contacts with people who are working in the area.

Before you commit yourself to the topic, canvass the following basic requirements. If the research issue fulfils these criteria, then it is less likely to contain 'fatal flaws'. The issues canvassed here are useful considerations for any research you are undertaking. The responses will of course vary. Topicality may be an extremely important consideration when you are planning a journal article within a six-month timeframe. As the timeframe expands, the pendulum swings more towards saying something different or placing a 'new skin' on a broader area. Context and purpose determine the weighting to be given to these factors.

7.1.1 Is the research area 'resource-rich'?[4]

There are times when a project appears very promising. It may be an area where there is proven need for more research. On closer inspection, however, it may become obvious that it is not achievable as a short-term non-funded project. This may be because of a need for extended periods of travel. This may be because of a scarcity of secondary resources. A student interested in writing about law in Papua New Guinea or other South Pacific areas may establish that the libraries (or even internet) collections they have access to in Australia are insufficient for their purposes. They may find that the relevant primary materials are available, but there is little writing or commentary by other scholars. For an undergraduate project, or even for a postgraduate coursework paper, this can be extremely limiting. It may be more efficient and acceptable to choose a topic that is 'resource-rich', as long as there is some scope for a new viewpoint, or for augmenting an existing debate.

---

3   Campbell JP, Daft RL and Hulin CL, *What to Study: Generating and Developing Research Questions* (Beverly Hills: Sage, 1982), 118.

4   Questions adapted from a list for supervisors by Moses I, 'Research training in Australian Universities — Undergraduate and Graduate Studies', in Zuber-Skerritt O (ed), *Starting Research Supervision and Training* (St Lucia: University of Queensland Tertiary Education Institute, 1992), 17.

7.1.2 *Will the project 'work' given your stated parameters?*

Ingrid Moses speaks of this factor in terms of 'feasibility'.[5] This is sometimes a question of resources and timelines, but often it centres on methodologies. What appears a 'good idea' may be difficult to write about because the evidence is intangible, or perhaps you do not possess the necessary skills to carry out interdisciplinary research, and the timeframes do not allow for 'skilling-up'. Maybe the dominant paradigms at work in the discipline mean that new method-ologies will not be easily accepted. Action research, for example, might appear fascinating and sensible in the context in which you are researching, but it may not be the best choice in your discipline. Law examiners are used to doctrinal work, and may be hesitant to accept more avant garde methodologies. Perhaps it might be better to save this for a post-doctoral paper!

7.1.3 *Will the project be achievable within your stipulated timeframe?*

Timelines will be in issue when you come to write the proposal. However, long before that step, it may be obvious that a project is unsuitable for your time limitations. A longitudinal study requiring extensive funding and ethics approval cannot be accomplished within a year. A pilot project or feasibility study may be possible. Similarly, doctrinal research in District Court case law is time consuming and costly. If you have two weeks and no budget — forget it!

7.1.4 *Will the writing augment existing work? Is this a significant study in that the area of law requires further research?*

Your topic should be objectively worthwhile to others. The best test for this requirement is if you locate research stating the need for further study in a specific area. Research should be developed and disseminated to others. If there is definitely no audience for your work then there is little point in going ahead. So saying, you may find that once published there are others who share your interests. Perhaps if your research is entirely historical with no possible relevance to current matters, there is cause for concern. If your research deals with legislation that is changing in any case, what is the point? It all depends on the perspective from which you approach the particular topic. It is important that it is linked to other work and has relevance to someone besides you! You need to be assured that you are contributing in a small way to knowledge in the field. This point underscores the importance of the literature review. Take an example of an article on the use of a new web resource as a tool in teaching and assessing a particular legal topic or skill. There may be no published articles on this topic. However, there will be a mammoth amount of literature on assessment in tertiary education, assessment in the law degree and more specifically on assessing legal skills. Your novel approach will need to be embedded in and build on the work and research already available.

---

5   Questions adapted from a list for supervisors by Moses I, 'Research training in Australian Universities — Undergraduate and Graduate Studies', in Zuber-Skerritt O (ed), *Starting Research Supervision and Training* (St Lucia: University of Queensland Tertiary Education Institute, 1992), 17.

7.1.5   *Does the area involve unresolved issues?*

The balance between finding a topic that has been developed sufficiently to allow for further investigation and one where knowledge is for all purposes complete within present boundaries (or paradigms), is a difficult one. It is sometimes in this area that a supervisor can help. Having chosen an area of study, you might ask whether there is a problem 'to be investigated', and does the paper attempt to solve this problem?

7.1.6   *Does the topic have enough scope (or too much scope) for your research goal?*

This will differ depending on whether you are writing a PhD thesis or a coursework paper. It would seem better to take one aspect of the whole and look at it in some depth rather than skimming a subject without really connecting with the topic. There is always opportunity for a conclusion stating the unanswered questions for further research. There are always opportunities to choose an important topic and then examine the issue from various perspectives; for example, the issue of supervision can be examined from the view of the student, or from the view of the supervisor, or from the view of the academic institution.

7.1.7   *Does your academic background fit the topic chosen?*

This is not absolutely necessary. You may wish to launch into another area entirely. However, your path will be easier if you can approach the topic in some way that uses your past work experience or research. If you are choosing a new (to you) and exciting field, then you will be more reliant on the supervisor for direction to problematical or unresolved areas of study. You will need to allocate more time and you may need to enrol in additional coursework.

7.1.8   *Have you read broadly enough 'around' the topic?*

Context is all! Before jumping in to one small issue, it is vital to know where it fits in to the whole. Background reading provides the backdrop for the smaller issues. Sometimes one whole area can seem especially rich for further work, but the difficulty lies in locating a specific research question. It is at this point that the supervisor may help with some directions for further reading. However, remember the story of the PhD student who spent several years reading in an area, only to decide that everything had been said! Once you have a broad knowledge of the area, your proposal is vital in guiding your further reading. The key is purposeful or directed study. Read published research in the area, including previous doctoral dissertations, and make certain you are aware of the 'state of play' in the field. You may find that other researchers have prior work in the area or are researching the same or other aspects of the topic. Just because others have examined an issue, does not mean it is barred from further discussion. Of course, you may seek to disagree with prior research. However, you must acknowledge its existence within the context of your literature review.

7.1.9 *Does your topic coincide with the research strengths of the faculty?*

Law schools tend to have research strengths, which are usually indicated by the existence of research centres and research concentrations. These may exist within a faculty or across a range of faculties within a university. They may be multi-disciplinary or interdisciplinary. Ascertain the research strengths of your faculty by examining the research centres and their publication records. The names of the research programs are likely to be broad; for example, Citizenship, Government and Identity. You will need to investigate the specific research agendas underlying these. The purpose of research groups and centres is to identify like-minded researchers and thus increase the likelihood of joint grant applications, ensure PhD and graduate supervision opportunities, and research funding. You are more likely to gain the support and access to collegiality necessary to sustain extended effort if you surround yourself with like-minded researchers.

7.1.10 *Do you have access to a supervisor with the knowledge of the area you want to work in and knowledge of what work has been done?*

By the time you complete a PhD, you will probably know more about a specific topic than your supervisor. However, it is important to have guidance at the beginning of your work. Whether you are considering a term paper, a coursework masters paper or a full-blown thesis, it is necessary to ensure that there is an academic in the faculty available to supervise. The supervisor will have an important role in terms of helping you to define your research question, choose a methodology, identify research sources and pertinent conferences to attend, recommend writing examples, and generally act as your research mentor and keep you 'on-track' for your completion. Therefore choosing a supervisor is an important task. Keep your topic options open until you have identified a supervisor who is available and compatible for your needs. Then you will need to ensure that your supervision needs will be met by that supervisor and that the supervisor will be on campus or accessible for the life of your project. Do some research. Find out how many successful completions the supervisor has had. How many current students are being supervised by this academic? If possible, try to meet with some of those students. Think carefully and determine what your needs are in a supervisor and then perhaps have a preliminary meeting with the supervisor and see if you have matching styles. It might be wise to look over a supervision checklist such as the one reproduced here and take it along to your initial meeting with your prospective supervisor. You may then glean an idea of your individual approaches to learning and the style of supervision you are likely to encounter.

If you are undertaking a major project, you may have the option of having both a principal supervisor and an associate supervisor. The associate supervisor might have special expertise in specific methodologies that you need to use or, at least, a different skill set or approach to that of your principal supervisor. Ideally, a joint supervision process is of great benefit. One supervisor, for example, may take a 'big picture' or global approach, and the other may take a more pedantic, detailed approach to what you are writing. This can be an excellent way of ensuring all your needs are met.

Role perception rating scale[6]

Topic/Course of study

1.	It is a supervisor's responsibility to select a promising topic.	1 2 3 4 5	It is a student's responsibility to select a promising topic.
2.	In the end, it is up to a supervisor to decide which theoretical frame of reference is most appropriate.	1 2 3 4 5	A student has a right to choose the theoretical standpoint even if it conflicts with that of the supervisor.
3.	A supervisor should direct a student in the development of an appropriate program of research and study.	1 2 3 4 5	A student should be able to work out a schedule and research program appropriate to his/her needs.
4.	A supervisor should ensure that a student has access to all necessary facilities.	1 2 3 4 5	Ultimately, a student must find the necessary facilities to complete his/her research.

Contact/Involvement

5.	Staff–student relationships are purely professional and personal relationships should not develop.	1 2 3 4 5	Close personal relationships are essential for successful supervision.
6.	A supervisor should initiate frequent meetings with a student.	1 2 3 4 5	A student should initiate meetings.
7.	A supervisor should check constantly that a student is on track and working consistently.	1 2 3 4 5	Students should have the opportunity to find their own way without having to account for how they spend their time.
8.	A supervisor should terminate the candidature if he/she thinks a student will not succeed.	1 2 3 4 5	A supervisor should support the student regardless of his/her opinion of a student's capability.

6   Laske S and Zuber-Skerritt O, 'Frameworks for Postgraduate Research and supervision: An Overview' Appendix 2.1 in Zuber-Skerritt O (ed), *Frameworks for Postgraduate Education* (Lismore: Southern Cross University Press, 1996), 30.

The thesis

9. A supervisor should ensure that the thesis is finished not much later than the minimum period.	1 2 3 4 5	As long as a student works steadily he/she can take as long as he/she needs to finish the work.
10. A supervisor has direct responsibility for the methodology and content of the thesis.	1 2 3 4 5	A student has total responsibility for ensuring that the methodology and content are appropriate to the discipline.
11. A supervisor should assist in the actual writing of the thesis if the student has difficulties, and should ensure that the presentation is flawless.	1 2 3 4 5	A student must take full responsibility for the presentation of the thesis, including grammar and spelling.
12. A supervisor should insist on seeing drafts of every section of the thesis in order to review them in a timely fashion.	1 2 3 4 5	It is up to a student to ask for constructive criticism from a supervisor.

Source: Ingrid Moses, Centre for Learning and Teaching, University of Technology Sydney.

The current higher education context is geared to maximum efficiency. For this reason, it is best if both student and supervisor are fully aware of any differences in work styles or conflicting commitments early in the process.

7.1.11 *What are the likely outcomes?*

Think carefully about where the research may lead you. It is strategic to decide where you want to go, and then decide how to get there rather than hack a swathe through the jungle into a swamp. It is most important in the current tertiary education research climate to consider the practical outcomes of your research. How does this topic relate to industry, government or the community? What are the likely benefits? Is the research area capable of further extensions into larger projects, or perhaps provide an opportunity to work with those from different disciplines?

7.1.12 *Is the area likely to sustain your interest?*

Passion is all in research. The life of the mind, and the discovery of new ideas have an element of passion. For you to complete a long project, there must be an impetus to do so. Possibly the passion forcing you on pertains to the outcome of receiving a degree, but it will be easier to complete if you retain your sense of discovery and passion for knowledge. This intellectual stimulus translates to the reader through your writing. Writing (and the research that is part of it) has a pre-ordained purpose of your choosing. You need an objective and a purpose and some message. Unless you are enriched and fascinated by the ideas you are pursuing, it will be difficult to convince your readers that your message is important.

7.2 **What about originality?**

Many law students are concerned about the degree of originality required in their research projects, especially at postgraduate level. It seems much easier for a science student to discover new facts through experiment, or work out new combinations and theories from existing facts, than for a law student to come up with a wholly original argument about law. After all, in a largely doctrinal study, the lawyers' raw materials are written down already — in the legislation and case law.

For this reason, it is timely to remind yourself that there really is nothing new under the sun. Scholarship thrives on the use of what other scholars have done. We all depend on others to some extent for what we do and achieve, and how we conceive legal realities. So saying, it is possible to delve deeper and expand on what exists already, to re-read and re-interpret existing sources, and thus to say something new, or at least to put it in a different way. Knowing the boundaries of the existing commentary in the literature, new researchers can write about the law at the edges, or how it may develop in the future. They can synthesise two seemingly unrelated areas and suggest overarching principles evident in both. They can pick up new legislation and case law and discuss how this changes or melds with existing principle. They may be able to 'borrow' ideas from current social philosophy or economic theory and apply it in a legal framework. Initiatives from other jurisdictions may be translated into the Australian or State framework to find more workable solutions to domestic issues. Technology and globalisation have improved research access to foreign law, making comparison, infusion and analogy more possible. International law impinges on local law on an ever-increasing scale, and it may be possible to examine this evolving globalised scene. All that is required is that the completed thesis or master's paper would need to contribute to knowledge in the area.

Sometimes empirical methodologies from the social sciences can be translated to law. However, this is more difficult because of the technical methodological requirements necessary at an interdisciplinary level in order to gain acceptance and authoritative status for the work. Nevertheless, basic empirical work is certainly not beyond trained lawyers, given sufficient adherence to accepted norms and cross-disciplinary supervision. Estelle Phillips[7] has summarised her communication with supervisors and students by setting out the following suggestions for originality in the PhD process. All of these issues seem to be encompassed in the concept of originality:

- Saying something nobody has said before ...
- Carrying out empirical work that hasn't been done before ...
- Making a synthesis that hasn't been made before ...
- Using already known material but with a new interpretation ...
- Trying out something in this country that has previously only been done in other countries ...

---

7   Phillips E, 'The PHD — Assessing quality at different stages of its development' in Zuber-Skerritt O (ed), *Starting Research Supervision and Training* (Brisbane: Tertiary Education Institute, University of Queensland, 1992), 128–130. See also Cryer P, *The Research Student's Guide to Success* (3 ed, New York: Open University Press, 2006), Chapter 19.

- Taking a particular technique and applying it in a new area ...
- Bringing new evidence to bear on an old issue ...
- Being cross-disciplinary and using different methodologies ...
- Taking someone else's ideas and reinterpreting them in a way no one else has ...
- Looking at areas that people in your discipline haven't looked at before ...
- Adding to knowledge in a way that hasn't previously been done before ...
- Looking at existing knowledge and testing it out ...
- Playing with words. Putting things together in ways that others haven't bothered to do ...

Originality is linked to creativity. It includes an element of critical insight. It often involves a rethinking of what has been done previously. It is something nebulous, but different to what has come before. It is also aligned with quality and thoroughness in progressing the research, so that if these aspects are attended to diligently then there will be little difficulty achieving a requisite standard of originality and a significant contribution to knowledge in the area under investigation.

7.3 What should you include in the research proposal?

There are several reasons for not completing research projects on time. Two of these can be resolved by a good proposal. Students often make a slow start, particularly in the area of problem formulation and in the literature survey. There is also a temptation to be distracted from the main focus of the research project; for example, by reading texts unrelated to the topic.[8] This too can be countered by adherence to a focused guide.

Before you become too advanced in your project, you need to write a proposal. This is usually required for a postgraduate enrolment acceptance in any case, and serves to indicate your degree of familiarity with the main sources of law and commentary as well as your personal organisation and methodology. The discipline of a proposal forces you to set out a scant literature review, including the skeleton of authority and commentary being drawn on. The proposal encourages you to verbalise your objectives and incipient hypothesis. It forces you to contextualise what you are attempting, perhaps acknowledging the extent of your existing involvement in the research area and how this will affect your methodology. This is where you set out what needs to be done, when each step is likely to be accomplished, and how you plan to complete by the due date.

The proposal is a most valuable document for you, the researcher, because it forces you to plan your project. This is an opportunity to put your thoughts down and tease out the issues involved. You may find that having written a proposal, you throw the project away and start again — but if this happens, you have still saved time. Going through each step will answer all those questions

---

8   Zuber-Skerritt O and Knight N, 'Problem definition and thesis writing' in Zuber-Skerritt O (ed), *Starting Research Supervision and Training* (Brisbane: Tertiary Education Institute, University of Queensland, 1992), 191.

about viability and timeframes and having something worthwhile to say. Once you have written the proposal, you have delineated the parameters of your project by outlining your overall objectives and methodologies. With a large project, you will find that the proposal will form the skeleton or backbone of your thoughts and, when there is a question of the direction or whether a specific aspect should be expanded or more narrowly defined, it will become crucial. It will set the ambit and direction, as well as including your hypothesis or underlying focus of the whole.

Thus, the proposal is your guide during the progress of your writing. When an interesting sidetrack appears, reference to the proposal will signal whether the issue fits within the overall scheme. The proposal will give you the discipline you need to 'kill off your precious babies' as one writer has so poignantly termed the process.[9] Thus, new lines of thought can be identified as pivotal to the project or simply 'future project' material. The proposal should be detailed enough to indicate whether a certain aspect should be included or if an issue, although interesting, is actually off-point or tangential to the whole.

The proposal is the way you convince others to believe in you and your ideas and your ability to write these down and expound on them in an authoritative manner within a timeframe. It demonstrates your competence. If you can write a lucid proposal, then the chances of you writing a longer paper increase. The proposal is evidence of your threshold knowledge, and it proves your ability to conceptualise and write about the topic. As well as being a vehicle to aid planning and give structure to the project, the proposal shows that you have investigated the topic fully enough to be convinced of its viability. This means that you should be able to convince others of its worth. This persuasive quality is especially important if you are likely to need external funding. Apart from clearly defined pilot studies, money is not normally available in order to examine if a topic is feasible. Grants are not available for background literature searches. In order to apply for scholarships and grants, you need to explain aspects of your proposed writing — clear objectives, a logical methodology and, overall, a do-able project within the time limits — all components of the proposal.

7.3.1 *What is your research background and what is the context in which you are situating your work?*

There are some standard components you need to include in your proposal. To begin with, the topic needs to be put in context and some legal and personal background included where relevant. Proposals usually have to be submitted to faculty committees in order to gain endorsement for the course of study. There will be a range of expertise and knowledge in the group, so it is important to put the study into context. For example, it would make sense to include the fact that you were employed in the research section of the fire brigade and that the department was funding your project. This could impact on the range of questions that are being addressed within the project and the statistical/empirical information available to you, thus explaining any limitations in the design.

---

9   Behrendt L, 'Writing about law: A research workshop' (Australian National University 14–15 February 2000).

Apart from your personal context, it might be useful to try to situate your topic within the broader epistemological framework. This represents the 'hoe marks' in the field you have fenced off for cultivation and excavation. At some stage you will need to complete a literature review of the whole area, including current legislation, recent case law and authoritative commentary. This is the precursor to the finished product. It serves to demonstrate that you are aware of some of the main literature, even if you have not had an opportunity to read it all. This gives credence to your design and ensures sufficient research is available for you to enhance and extend. Detail or summarise the research unearthed to date and assess its relevance to your research objectives and hypothesis. Is it dated? Has the context changed? Has it been in some way questioned or discredited? How effective were previous studies? Were there any flaws in the previous work done in the area or any obvious limitations? How are you evaluating previous research in terms of your topic and any 'objective' criteria? What is the impact of previous research on your topic?

Depending on the purpose of the proposal, it may be worth considering any queries you have in regard to the project at this stage. This step may be a private one. However, if you can at least flag obvious uncertainties in the project and then try to deal with the likely outcomes in regard to these issues, then you may be better able to silence critics.

7.3.2   *Research objectives?*

Your main research objective should be stated. The objective might be, for example, to examine legal regulation of water use by farmers to determine its effectiveness judged on international environmental ethics. Therefore, you intend to determine what law exists and the tenor of any international regulations and treaties which exist. The objective is a broad statement of what you have set out to examine, together with some specific questions or sub-goals that you hope to answer along the way. Your objectives tend to be global and directed to the issues you intend traversing in your research.

7.3.3   *What about a hypothesis?*

Broad objectives and even the more specific goals that you set for yourself within the parameter of the research project are not the same as the hypothesis. In terms of a hypothesis, simply hoping to find something 'along the way' is also not sufficient. A general interest in reading and writing about an area may be part and parcel of your personal objectives, but the hypothesis is the glimmer of an idea, a 'hunch' about what it is you will find at the end of the journey, an argument which you will follow through to a conclusion.

Working out a hypothesis is usually the most difficult aspect of the proposal. This is partly due to the nature of the legal inquiry and the fact that most examples of hypotheses will be based on empirical studies. The hypothesis will determine and be determined by your research methodology — whether doctrinal or otherwise. If you are using social science methodologies, a hypothesis can be a very precise statement which asserts a relationship between concepts or ideas, and then makes a prediction about the nature of a relationship between two variables.

You may find it easier to begin with a research question. A research question aims to describe what is, rather than test for an explanation. In this way, it is more akin to basic research in that you are attempting to define an area and outline its characteristics. Having done this, it may be possible to then analyse relationships between the area and other factors.

Often a doctrinal project will not have variables to consider or even prior results of research to hang off, so the 'hypothesis' used may simply be a working idea of what the outcome of the study might be. The final hypothesis, which reflects the findings of the research, may be different. Think about your hypothesis as a tentative proposition or even simply a research question to guide your examination of the law.

However, the hypothesis needs to be set out as clearly as you can at an early stage of the project. You need to frame a viable argument, a 'guiding idea' which will direct your reading (and thinking and writing).[10] The propositions you are advancing are likely to be tentative and provide possible explanations only. At such an early stage, it is likely to be no more than a 'gut' feeling, but it will be based on prior reading and knowledge achieved through reviewing the literature. It is your aim to pull the issues down to their narrowest terms.[11]

7.3.4 *What is the appropriate methodology and how do you plan to achieve your objectives?*

Once you have outlined your project, you will be able to establish the most appropriate methodology for attaining worthwhile results. Often this will include a doctrinal or historical research base, limited largely to library research — locating the primary and secondary materials of the law. Use may also be made of published statistics. Often, case studies can be included to enhance and explain the issues inherent in the problem being investigated. Your research can take aspects of quantitative or qualitative research. Remember, however, that your method of collecting data must be aligned with the overall objects and goals of your project, and your hypothesis.

7.3.5 *A meaningful title*

A title is not usually necessary for an undergraduate assignment. However, any extended writing needs a succinct statement of its content. Sometimes titles include an eye-catcher as well as an explanatory subtitle, for example, 'Getting What You Came For: The Smart Student's Guide to Earning a Master's or a PhD'.[12] A thesis needs an extremely short pithy working title so that every time someone asks you what you are doing your PhD on, the question can be answered in one sentence. Sometimes the 'colon title' can become very hackneyed

---

10 Crowl T, *Fundamentals of Research: A Practical Guide for Educators and Special Educators* (Columbus, Ohio: Publishing Horizons Inc, 1986), 84.

11 Crowl T, *Fundamentals of Research: A Practical Guide for Educators and Special Educators* (Columbus, Ohio: Publishing Horizons Inc, 1986), 84.

12 Peters R, *Getting What You Came For: The Smart Student's Guide to Earning a Master's or a PhD* (rev ed, New York: Noonday Press, 1997).

— but the catchy phrase can often be a way of attracting your readers. It is important to 'sell' your work. What is the point of writing up research if nobody reads it! In addition, the colon fits two purposes — it invokes/sparks interest but at the same time it can deliver sufficient information to truly inform the incipient reader of what is to come (while making sure that the indexer or cataloguer does not put the item under the incorrect subject heading in the database or library).

The title is usually the last step in the proposal. However, it is no less important. Especially when you are involved in a long project, you will need to be able to explain succinctly to your close friends, parents and partners exactly what it is you are doing locked away in your office all night. For this reason, and also to crystallise your ideas, try to compose a two-minute story on what it is you are researching. Write it down and try it out on the next person who asks. Then try to crystallise it further, ensuring all the while that the title is truly reflective of the essence of your writing. Remember that when the examiner comes to look at your thesis the title is the first thing that is read. It must reflect the years of work, the content and the outcomes well.

7.3.6 *Publication of your research?*

If you have something to say and you want people to read it, then it pays to be pragmatic. Note the details regarding your plans to publish your work. Examine all of the reputable journals in the subject area giving preference to those that are refereed; that is, those which publish articles that have gone through the process of external assessment by a reviewer, usually anonymous, who is independent of the journal's editorial board. Look at the preferred method-ologies used in the articles, the depth of analysis and the writing style exhibited.[13] Check the editorial comments for information about word limits, citation styles and publication schedules. Subject specific lists are in *Ulrich's International Periodicals Directory* and elsewhere on the web.[14]

Think carefully about where you wish to publish. A professional journal may result in practical outcomes and enhance the impact of your research, but it is less likely to enthuse the academic promotions committee. However, it may enhance your local standing and reputation, ensure your research has an 'impact' factor, and if you are working within a firm of solicitors, for example, it may delight the managing partner. If you intend for your ideas and research to really influence others and the development of the law, including the judges, then refereed journals are the best option. Think about which titles the judges are likely to read and aim for these. On the other hand, international journals may impress promotions committees, but the local bar or the judges will not necessarily read them. Interdisciplinary journals may lack sufficient credibility within legal circles, so it may be wise again to only submit to refereed law

---

13 Gottlieb N and MacKay G, 'The process of writing and publishing' in Zuber-Skerritt O and Pinchen S, *Third Manual for Conducting Workshops on Postgraduate Supervision* (Nathan: Griffith Institute for Higher Education, 1995), 185.

14 *Ulrich's International Periodicals Directory* http://www.ulrichsweb.com/ulrichsweb/ (5/11/2009). Australian Government Australian Research Council *ERA PCE and HCA journal lists* http://www.arc.gov.au/era/journal_list.htm (5/11/2009).

publications. Even within the legal discipline itself, if you publish in an area that is outside your specific subject speciality; for example, an article by a criminal lawyer dealing with both negligence and criminal law and published in a torts journal, then it is likely you will miss the criminal law audience.

Journal publications and books are not the only means of disseminating your work. Consider putting up your hand for an in-house seminar or training session, or at least provide a report to your work group if it is relevant to current interests. Conferences are another way of taking your research and ideas to a wider audience. This may include large conferences where papers are refereed, but it might also include less formal specialist professional meetings. Several websites include lists of upcoming conferences.[15] At the very least, photocopy your paper and send it to another interested person working in the area, or include it on your institution's ePrints Archive.

7.3.7 *Timelines or scheme of work?*

Finally, it is important to ensure completion, and for this purpose you need a work scheme with important dates clearly set out. The timeline forms part of the proposal. The timeline set targets as to when you should have completed segments of research and have submitted drafts to your supervisor, as well as reminding you of other commitments and expected downtimes during the process. Obviously, a work scheme and timeline is most important to an extended project rather than an assignment that needs to be completed in a very short timeframe. However, the benefits will be apparent at both ends of the spectrum.

Obviously writing a PhD (or any large research project) is a major undertaking and it is arduous. It is important to make sure that you do not waste time. You can accomplish this through planning carefully. Detail the steps involved from the initial stages right up to completion. Read the higher degree rules, if applicable, and take note of the major milestones. Transfer those to your personal timetable. Include any major dates that are immutable; for example, the dates that scholarship applications close, or the date for final confirmation of enrolment. Include your vacation dates or any time periods when you are likely to be busy at work.

There is an example of a Project Timeline matrix which can be tailored to suit your project schedule, and your own needs, at the end of this Chapter (see page 194).

---

15 Law Council of Australia http://www.lawcouncil.asn.au/conferences/events-and-conferences.cfm http://www.conferencealerts.com/ (5/11/2009).

Example of Doctor of Juridical Science Schedule: 18–48 months Full-Time / 36–96 months Part-Time

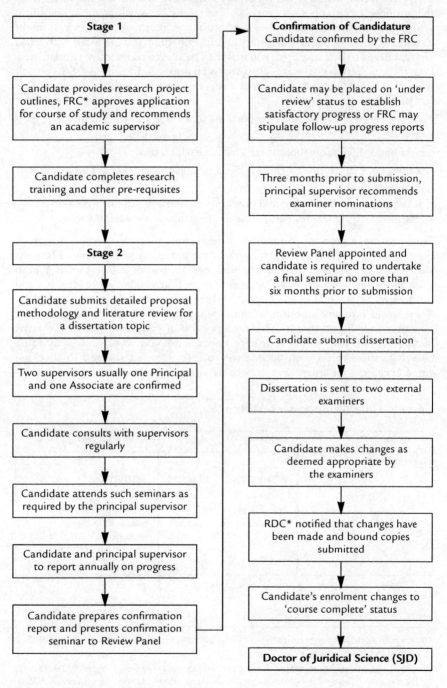

Stage 1	Confirmation of Candidature
	Candidate confirmed by the FRC

Candidate provides research project outlines, FRC* approves application for course of study and recommends an academic supervisor

Candidate may be placed on 'under review' status to establish satisfactory progress or FRC may stipulate follow-up progress reports

Candidate completes research training and other pre-requisites

Three months prior to submission, principal supervisor recommends examiner nominations

Stage 2

Review Panel appointed and candidate is required to undertake a final seminar no more than six months prior to submission

Candidate submits detailed proposal methodology and literature review for a dissertation topic

Candidate submits dissertation

Two supervisors usually one Principal and one Associate are confirmed

Dissertation is sent to two external examiners

Candidate consults with supervisors regularly

Candidate makes changes as deemed appropriate by the examiners

Candidate attends such seminars as required by the principal supervisor

RDC* notified that changes have been made and bound copies submitted

Candidate and principal supervisor to report annually on progress

Candidate's enrolment changes to 'course complete' status

Candidate prepares confirmation report and presents confirmation seminar to Review Panel

Doctor of Juridical Science (SJD)

*RDC – Research Degrees Committee

*FRC – Faculty Research Committee

This Timeline is tailored to your individual project. It is the big picture. It is at this point too that you should give some thought to your work schedule. The accepted wisdom is that writers are more productive in short bursts. This means that an hour or two on a very regular, if not daily basis will be more helpful to a successful outcome than 'binge' writing. Think about what times you might be able to block out for writing on your daily schedule. Having listed each small job that needs to be completed, you will then be able to realistically estimate how long the total process will take. 'Realistic' is an important word here. Set yourself monthly and weekly goals and use the supervision relationship effectively. This can include:

* making the next steps explicit for both the supervisor and student at each meeting;
* including a discussion about these goals at each meeting;
* sending your supervisor an email bulletin detailing what you have accomplished each week; and
* documenting the discussion and outcomes so that you gradually develop a 'paper trail'. Include a review process on the goals set for each meeting.[16]

Time becomes a precious commodity during a long project, especially if most of the research is being undertaken in part-time mode. Stephen Covey's Matrix is a useful tool to use in order to work out where most time is being spent, and to work out where your time can be organised so that you are more effective and productive. Segment II in the matrix is where most activities should take place. Try to avoid excessive amounts of time spent in Segments III and IV. Email can take over your life so that a substantial portion of your time becomes reactive, in that you are responding to others' needs above your own, and in so doing allowing others to set your agenda for you. Try to limit yourself to checking email once or twice a day. Do not become an email junkie!

Covey's Time Management Matrix[17]

	URGENT	NOT URGENT
IMPORTANT	I ACTIVITIES: Crises Pressing problems Deadline-driven projects	II ACTIVITIES: Prevention, production capability activities, relationship building, recognising new opportunities, planning, recreation

16 Yeatman A, 'Making supervision relationships accountable: graduate student logs' (1995) 2 *Australian Universities' Review* 9.

17 The Time Management Matrix from Covey S, *The Seven Habits of Highly Effective People: Restoring the Character Ethic* (Melbourne: The Business Library, Information Australia, 1989), 151.

	URGENT	NOT URGENT
NOT IMPORTANT	III	IV
	ACTIVITIES:	ACTIVITIES:
	Interruptions, some calls, some mail, some reports, some meetings, proximate, pressing matters, popular activities	Trivia, busy work, some mail, some phone calls, time wasters, pleasant activities

There are a number of guides available to assist you in general time planning for study and research purposes. Walter Pauk and John Fiore provide excellent planning tools for students, together with basic principles of time management such as working in one hour productive blocks, and overestimating (even doubling) projected completion times rather than underestimating how long your research project will take.[18] There are other ways of ensuring progress too. Join a research support group and talk to other students about how long they took to complete the various stages. A 'collaborative cohort' such as this has been found to help research students develop 'a greater breadth of knowledge and a variety of skills including research skills and generic skills through sharing and interaction with fellow students about their research experiences within a collaborative framework. The research also showed that the quality of dissertation and the completion rate of students were enhanced.'[19]

7.3.8 *Budgeting*

Sometimes the methodology requires that extra funding sources are located. This will usually mean a grant application. The application will normally require you to set out your research proposal in some detail. A detailed statement of the methodology will also be required. However, even a straight doctrinal study may require a small budget, along with researcher time. The budget might include a way of rewarding another person for taking some of your normal workload so that you can complete the project. Stipulate any travel or costs involved and how you intend to cover these. Travel may be required to attend relevant conferences and workshops in order to interact with other scholars and glean new ideas and trends in your area, or to access materials held in interstate libraries and not otherwise accessible through interlibrary loan or the internet.

---

18 Pauk W and Fiore J, *Succeed in College!* (Boston: Houghton Mifflin Company, 2000), Chapter 1.

19 Burnett C, 'The supervision of doctoral dissertations using a collaborative cohort model' (1999) 39 (1) *Counselor Education and Supervision* 46–51 as cited in Zhao F, 'Enhancing the Effectiveness of Research and Research Supervision Through Reflective Practice' UltiBASE http://pandora.nla.gov.au/pan/10088/20040811/ultibase.rmit.edu.au/Archives/articles. htm#jul03 (5/11/2009).

Here is an example of a Budget for a Small Project:

Tasks	Details	Costs ($)
Project Manager	5 hours	300
1) Requirements and design specifications 2) Focus group sessions 3) Analysis and report	Academic staff teaching release for three staff for two hours each including one original hour and one repeat hour = 13 weeks x 1 hour ($76.80 per original hour) and 13 weeks x 1 hour ($51.20 per repeat hour) + 14% on costs.	1897.00 x 3 = 5700.00
Graphic designer Programmer Instructional designer	Graphic designer to do artwork 10 hours ($60 per hour) Programmer to customise site 8 hours = $480 Instructional design to assist in the overall design of the modules to maximise learning and teaching effectiveness	2 hours 600.00 480.00 600.00
Catering	For focus group sessions	100.00
Research assistant	Research assistant to update and assist compilation, collating evaluation, and prepare manuscripts (to check footnotes and ensure correct citation styles for differing journals, and to aid in preparation of PowerPoint for presentations HEW3 Step 6 (casual) x 40 hours ($19.12 + 14% on costs)	964.04
Consumables	Stationery and photocopying	120.00
	Total:	**$ 8864.04**

* Staffing costs will need to include costs or administrative costs which are normally set at a specific percentage by your institution:

Tutoring:
$76 80 per original hour, $51.20 per repeat hour + 14% on costs.

Graphic designer,
Programmer and
Instructional designer: $60 per hour + 14% on costs

Research assistant: $19.12 + 14% on costs

As well as providing an outline of the actual hours and budget required, it is usual to also be required to provide a justification for the amount requested. This would usually include more detail about the role of each assistant and perhaps the reasons why other methods might not be used.

7.4 Critiquing your own proposal

There are a few obvious traps for new players when they come to write out their research plans or proposals. One of the most common is the temptation to vagueness and a 'broad brush' approach, which can result in a total lack of specificity or engagement with the topic. This often occurs because the topic is too broad and unfocused. Having chosen an area of law to investigate, do some basic reading and talk to prospective supervisors. Try to identify the holes in the work that has been done to date — the questions that have not been asked or answered, new cases, new legislation, or changed economic or philosophical contexts. At least put forward some 'gut reactions' to your reading. Your arguments and thesis can change. Nothing is immutable. However, you need to delve far enough into the area so that your proposal is more than platitudes and more than an extended background introduction to a whole chunk of law. Carve out your small area of concern and talk about this. In the end product, the final paper, you will need to come to a conclusion on the issue you have researched. In the early stages, in your proposal, your conclusion might be quite different, but at least it is a starting point, and without this your project will not have sufficient direction and cohesion to achieve its objectives.

A strictly historical view may have its place in a history of law unit, but the point of history is the ability to learn from others' mistakes. Good proposals are forward-looking. Although well versed in what has come before and the status quo, good research has an eye to the future. It is useful to assess situations in the light of current and future developments. Roman criminal law may be a fascinating study, but perhaps there may be some room for relating or comparing the origins of the civil law to common law developments in a specific area. Current relevance is all, because without this, your writing will not hold interest for others.

Be clear (or at least honest) about your inherent 'slant' on the topic. If you always act for the insurers in litigation, at least acknowledge to yourself that there is another side of the coin apart from the one you are used to arguing so vociferously — and then decide where the audience and topic coincides. Or, if you find it impossible to make this mind-switch, determine to write a piece for your primary audience, in this example, the insurers. Argue their case honestly and uncategorically. Put it upfront! Often, the clues to writer bias are evident to the reader in any case through an incompatibility between a value-laden title and a claim to neutrality. Language provides another clue — emotive words chosen for one side or the other in the debate. However, should we place the reader in the role of investigative critique detective unnecessarily? Having a partisan view on a topic is not necessarily 'bad', however, hiding partisan beliefs under a claim to neutrality is hardly intellectually honest.

This is where thinking about the conceptual framework for your work becomes so important. Sometimes we need to act as detective on ourselves. Some writers may only realise they have a personal framework or view of the world well into their writing career, when it becomes apparent that all their work is 'themed' or connected. This is not necessarily because they have written several pieces on a category of law, contract or international law, but because all their work relates to, for example, individual rights or women's rights in relation to the substantive law. Perhaps such theming is a gradual development related to exposure to reading and research. However, sometimes the views are more reflective of your personal theoretical underpinning derived from inculcated family and societal values. These can be Marxist, feminist, pragmatic economic rationalist, or religious-based humanitarianism. Wherever possible, you owe your reader the courtesy of personal contemplation and acknowledgment of your intellectual underpinnings.

What factors constitute success within your personal or legal worldview? What is your framework for evaluation? What criteria are you using to judge the outcome? Is there an existing mechanism against which to measure success, or are you needing to devise such a mechanism? If your underlying thesis depends on such evaluations, then establishing the means of judging these is of paramount importance.

If you have not 'dealt with' intellectual paradigm issues, then it is easier to fall into the evaluation traps. These consist of bald statements about whether something is 'good', 'bad', or 'successful', without addressing how you intend to assess or evaluate the issues in order to attach such a label. In your project, you need to provide evidence to establish your view. Provide the arguments backed up by reasons, evidence and examples.

Ethical clearance is required in circumstances where the proposal methodology uses human subjects. When you are planning your methodology, you need to give careful consideration to whether there is a need to take the methodology through the Ethics Committee at your university. If the human subjects can be in any way identified, or the information might be to their detriment if it were to be given to other sections of the community, then you should be on alert. It may be worth checking the guidelines and due dates for submission to the committees, and at least filling out a preliminary assessment form, working this into the early stages of your timeline.

Description of the status quo is important, but most lawyers will be looking for more. Empirical research is another thing. There it may be worthwhile to describe a state of being and provide a snapshot of a community. It is seen as a first step to further comparison and analysis. Lawyers may need a description of a new piece of legislation or a recent case, but ultimately they may also be looking for a critical awareness of how this innovation will impact on their practice or an understanding of the cross-sections between the new and the past. Pure description in doctrinal work can be very boring and reflect a limited perspective of the legal process.

Examples make for interesting reading. Everyone likes to be told anecdotes and stories. This is an effective means for explaining points to your reader and can serve to pull a topic down to a manageable size. Apart from isolated examples, good use may be made of case studies. Case studies provide useful information in situations where there is insufficient time, resources or expertise to conduct full non-doctrinal research using surveys or experiments. A case study, if well chosen as typical of its ilk, can provide a microcosm of the problems or advantages of the situation you are researching. It is important to choose representative subjects for careful examination. Sometimes a typical subject from several categories might be examined and then used as a comparison between the groups. Obviously, the results will have no statistical validity, but the data can be used as a pilot for a larger scale program of research.

Legal researchers can use specific reported law reports as case studies of particular situations that may arise. Perhaps situations that have not yet happened may be examined to demonstrate that the law does not work given certain circumstances, that there are loopholes in the law in the area. Pieces of legislation can be used as a case study. Even representative individuals may be interviewed in a case study methodology. Such people would need to have been chosen using standard criteria as being representative of their class.

Another major error in drafting a proposal is a superficial treatment of timeframes and work patterns. This is indicative of the researcher not really thinking through and understanding the steps to be taken during the research and writing process. Allocate sufficient time in the early stages working out your plan. Otherwise you will not make the deadlines, and your proposal will encompass too much work (and words) for the time available.

7.5 Writing a summary or abstract

On many occasions you will be called upon to write an abstract briefly summarising your research. The abstract is not simply the first paragraph of your report. An abstract is a separate writing genre and must be crafted with care. It is a summary of your main points. It is a condensed or abridged version of the whole.

An abstract will probably be required if you propose to present a paper at a research conference, when you submit an article to a refereed journal, when you submit a postgraduate thesis, for grant applications and in fact for any public presentations. The abstract is often the first part of your work that your potential audience will read. The abstract will determine whether your reader will bother to read on! Probably more people will read your abstract than read the full paper.

When you are filling out forms, you are usually given a very strict word limit for the summary or abstract — normally 150-200 words. What do you include? The abstract needs to concisely state the research problem or hypothesis, the description or crucial aspects of the research including a brief indication of the methodology, the results, and a conclusion. You might include a definite statistical research outcome. If space permits then you might include a little background or context but there is usually more space provided for these aspects in other parts of the application form or in the body of the article. You do not need to use citations or referencing in the abstract, and it is standard practice to use active rather than passive tense. Do not include abbreviations.

Your project needs a meaningful title and the abstract should be reflective of the title of the project. The abstract does not include information not contained in the main work. Use meaningful words and delete the extraneous information. Ask yourself what the main points are in each section or chapter of your paper, and then try to summarise each section in one sentence.[20] This will be an additional way to check that you have structured your paper and that the argument flows in a logical manner.

The questions you might address include:

* 'Why did you do this study or project.
* What did you do, and how?
* What did you find?
* What do your findings mean?'[21]

These same questions can be phrased differently and this explanation might be more helpful to you depending on your project:

* 'Why would another researcher be interested in this research?'
* 'What are the most important aspects of the research?' What do you want to make sure the reader knows about your research?
* 'What information will the reader have to have in order to understand the most important aspects?'[22]

Basically you need to communicate the motivation behind your research, the statement of the problem, the approach you took to solving it, your results and the conclusion setting out any implications of this research.[23]

Abstracts are also a research tool in themselves so either embedded in the summary or additional to it you should include some key words and phrases. The abstract plays a role as an indexing tool. It needs to provide sufficient information so that prospective readers will know whether the whole paper will be relevant to their work.

7.6 Presenting your research to your peers

Having drafted your proposed topic and outlined your methodology, start talking about it! Choose a trusted colleague, prospective supervisor, friend or relation as a sounding board for ideas. Having to answer their questions and being made to fill in the blanks will give you ideas to augment your own. It is also an excellent way of flagging weaknesses that may not have been apparent to

20 Laflen A, *Getting Started with your Report: Abstract* (OWL at Purdue University) http://owl. english.purdue.edu/archive/oldfiles/angela/originalfiles/e%20abstract.html (5/11/2009).

21 Procter M, *The Abstract* http://www.writing.utoronto.ca/advice/specific-types-of-writing/ abstract (5/11/2009).

22 Based on Laflen A, *Getting Started with your Report: Abstract* (OWL at Purdue University) http://owl.english.purdue.edu/archive/oldfiles/angela/originalfiles/e%20abstract.html (5/11/2009).

23 Koopman P, *How to Write an Abstract* (Carnegie Mellon Univ, 1997) http://www.ece.cmu. edu/~koopman/essays/abstract.html (5/11/2009); See also Kamler B and Thomson P, 'Abstract art or the politics of getting read' (Australian Association for Research in Education Annual Conference, Brisbane, December 1-4, 2002) http://www.aare.edu.au/ index.htm (5/11/2009).

you when you were developing the topic. Sometimes researchers are given an opportunity to take part in a presentation of work in progress. This not only allows you to test an embryonic research hypothesis to a group of peers but also to defend and clarify the direction and range of your proposal. It presents an ideal opportunity for students to receive an expanded range of views and responses to their work. Another option is to present your paper at a conference or workshop.

Take this opportunity to try to crystallise your ideas and summarise the progress you have made. The presentation is usually much more than simply a monologue. Often, there will be questions arising that you may not fully have addressed (or even considered) in your proposal. Be prepared to defend your stance on all fronts, including methodology and underlying hypothesis. Your conceptual framework may even be put in issue. Treat this presentation as a type of 'progress report'.[24]

When preparing the presentation, endeavour to address three principal aspects of the project:

1   What is your main argument or hypothesis? Explain the central issue of your paper.
2   So what? Why is this worth spending time on? Tell the group about the background to the topic including any previous research on the issue.
3   How are you intending to structure your project? This is your research plan. Having decided on the issues, where are you going from here?

Presentations of work in progress presuppose that your work is incomplete and that you may not have found or read everything on the topic. In a larger project it might be as well to endeavour to push one aspect or segment of the thesis closer to completion so that you can demonstrate some expertise even if only in a very small area. This is quite separate from the oral examination or viva. The main concern at this stage of the research is to ensure that you are addressing some pertinent questions, and that the topic is cohesive. No doubt a presentation such as this will bring together a range of expertise within the audience, and it should be expected that useful suggestions for contacts with other researchers and other aligned projects would be made. Expect that some contrary views may be aired. However, it is likely that you may have more specific knowledge than the group generally in regard to your topic, so be prepared to explain the decisions you have made, perhaps simply because of the vagaries of the area you are researching compared to other areas. Look upon this as an opportunity for you to ensure that your project is not based on unfounded assumptions, conforms to basic research requirements (such as any ethics committee scrutiny), and is at a comparable depth and scope as other postgraduate projects. It should also become obvious if the topic is 'overworked'. This is part of the topic evaluation process, so be prepared to change direction if need be after this point.

You will gain most from the presentation of your ideas to the group if you facilitate their grasp of the issues being raised in the research. This will not occur if you simply read out your proposal outline. Hand out the written abstract

---

24   Ray M and Cox B, *Beyond the Basics: A Text for Advanced Legal Writing* (2 ed, St Paul: West Publishing Company, 2003), 408.

beforehand. Make sure your introduction and conclusion are clear, and your ideas are expressed in an easily understood manner. Try to provide a background to the legal area and then home in on the main issues, and even address specific aspects of the research that are providing some concern. Overheads may be useful, or perhaps a diagram on a whiteboard. Powerpoints and graphics can enliven debate. Have a clear idea of the timeframe you have been given and practise your presentation so that it 'fits' within the time. Your ideas will not be clear if you have not had time to finish your presentation properly because you have had to rush to finish! Regard this exercise as an opportunity to gain some constructive insights from a group of peers that should help the development of your ideas, or perhaps firm up certain decisions you have already made regarding the direction of the research. This is your opportunity to defend any obvious criticisms and challenge basic assumptions about your line of reasoning. Try to anticipate the questions that may be asked and rehearse the answers. Be your own harshest critic.

Here is an example of a research presentation criteria sheet. This contains the major issue which you can use as a guide to prepare and self-assess your work.

Research Presentation Criteria Sheet

CONTENT AND ANALYSIS:

Was there sufficient history/background/evidence of research?

Is it clear why this issue is important and worthy of study?

Was there a clear statement of the central question or problem? (Hypothesis?)

What methodologies are being employed and are they well designed?

Was there evidence of higher-level thinking, analysis and critique, moving beyond description of the issues involved?

Was there an appreciation of the advantages and disadvantages of any proposed solutions?

Was there an integration of title, hypothesis, and methodology?

What are the strengths and weaknesses of this topic?

PRESENTATION:

Was there sufficient introduction to the topic and a form of summary at the end?

Were the issues presented in a clear manner?

Was the presentation interesting and did it stimulate audience involvement?

OVERALL COMMENT:

Needless to say, the tenor of these sessions should be informative and interesting and be approached in a friendly atmosphere ensuring cooperation and investigation of new knowledge.

Some postgraduate students prefer to join smaller support groups to encourage research progress by reading each other's material, sharing research tips and so on.[25] Both researchers and higher degree research students can benefit from 'writing groups' which operate in a similar fashion. These groups can be instrumental in encouraging researchers to diarise and track their research, emphasising that writing is best seen as a 'starting point, rather than an endpoint', of the research process.[26] Certainly such groups seem a sensible development because it is too easy for academic research schedules to 'lose out' to the more pressing imperatives of teaching, service, administration and marking agendas. In the end, it is really up to the individual to follow their own inclination; however, research can be quite an isolating endeavour and sometimes it is good to talk as well as write and think. Reading your own writing can also be useful but not as stimulating as engaging in a dialogue. Certainly higher degree students do benefit from group work and presenting their work to others.

7.7 The literature review[27]

Undertaking and writing up a comprehensive literature review is a critically important aspect of writing a dissertation. Literature reviews are a necessity, but the trick is to make them intrinsically relevant to the argument being pursued and much more than a description of published research. The review can deteriorate into a summary of one study after another without careful analysis of the issues. The review must include discussion of all the most relevant and important research that has been published. This includes the most current issues and progress that has taken place between your first visit to the library and first internet searches, to the month before you hand the completed paper to be assessed, examined or refereed. The individual pieces must be themed and linked in a meaningful way, otherwise the review can become very boring to write and to read. Accuracy and a focused but critical synthesis of ideas from your reading are vital.[28]

25 Burnett C, 'The supervision of doctoral dissertations using a collaborative cohort model' (1999) 39 (1) *Counselor Education and Supervision* 46–51 as cited in Zhao F, 'Enhancing the Effectiveness of Research and Research Supervision Through Reflective Practice' UltiBASE http://pandora.nla.gov.au/pan/10088/20040811/ultibase.rmit.edu.au/Archives/articles. htm#jul03 (5/11/2009).

26 Lee A and Boud D, 'Writing groups, change and academic identity: research development as local practice' (2003) 28 (2) *Studies in Higher Education* 187; See also Cuthbert D, 'Disciplining writing: the case for multi-disciplinary writing groups to support writing for publication by higher degree research candidates in the humanities, arts and social sciences' (2009) 28(2) *Higher Education Research & Development* 137.

27 Hutchinson T and Cuffe N, 'Legal Research Project Management: Skills Extension for Upper Level Law Students' (2004) 38 (2) *The Law Teacher* 159.

28 Bruce C, 'A reflective approach to reviewing the literature' in Zuber-Skerritt O and Pinchen S, *Third Manual for Conducting Workshops on Postgraduate Supervision 1995* (Griffith University 1995), 162.

What is the purpose behind the literature review? The literature review demonstrates that you have developed a full professional grasp of your research area and you know what others have done in the area. The aim is to reflect on readings you have undertaken and to record those thoughts. The literature review provides justification for your research. It places your research in context. It does more than simply summarise what you have read. It aims to synthesise, analyse and critique the state of current knowledge and research in your stated area. The literature review is also a good way to identify gaps in the literature into which your work might fit. The literature review is certainly not written simply to justify your point of view, and remember to 'avoid the trap of developing a thesis supported from the literature'.[29] Your thesis should amount to more than simply taking a position or intellectual stance on a topic and then using the literature to support that view.

The literature review is developed gradually. Use it as the beginning of your writing stage. Every time you locate a relevant piece of literature, ensure you note the full and correct bibliographical details, the keywords, subject heading, and then write some brief notes on the relevance of this item to your research topic. This journal or database entry will encapsulate your reflection on the readings you have undertaken. If you record your thoughts fully at that point then it will be easy to synthesise these when you come to pull your literature review together.

You may find that a version of the Cornell Note Taking Method is helpful when you are preparing the literature review. The method was originally developed to aid United States college students in taking lecture notes. With this method you divide your page into two columns. Your regular notes are placed in the right hand column. The left hand column is the review column and is normally completed during your reflective phase. You place keywords, page references and main ideas that relate to the longer descriptions in that left hand column.[30] This is an aid to the active reading process which was introduced in Chapter One.

Pat Cryer provides a useful game plan for evaluating the secondary literature you encounter. The questions she suggests provide criteria to help you evaluate and critique what you are reading, especially studies that use empirical methodologies. The questions include:

* How do they use terms like 'research area', 'topic', 'theme', 'focus', 'hypothesis' and 'problem'?
* How do they use research methodologies?
* How do they demonstrate academic argument, academic discourse and scholarship?
* How do they use literature?
* What is their claim for original work?
* What is their claim for significant work?

---

29 Tannoch-Bland J, 'Developing your research question' (Griffith Graduate Research School, Griffith University, 2007).

30 Pauk W and Fiore JP, *Succeed in College!* (Boston: Houghton Mifflin, 2000). http://lsc.sas. cornell.edu/Sidebars/Study_Skills_Resources/cornellsystem.pdf (5/11/2009).

* What is the claim for the reliability of their work?
* What is the claim for the validity of their work?
* What is their research paradigm?[31]

As you work through the literature, there are differing considerations depending on the types of material you encounter. In a legal doctrinal study, there are two main types of 'literature'. Firstly there are the commentaries or secondary material for example texts, government reports and journal articles. As you review each commentary, you need to be mindful of threshold criteria such as the item's currency and the authority of the author, journal or publisher. Here are some prompts for the secondary materials you will encounter:

Commentary reflections
* Summarise the key points of the item read. What is the author saying?
* What is your initial response to what you have read?
* What assumptions is the author making? Do you agree with the underlying assumptions?
* Are the interests of particular groups being promoted in this article?
* What authority does the writer have in this subject area? What weight should you attach to their arguments?
* Did the author make any specific recommendations?
* Expand on your response if you can by referring to basic principles and other reading on the issue.
* How will these ideas relate or fit with your project framework?

Secondly there are the primary materials including case law, legislation, and treaties. Here are some prompts for each genre of the primary materials:

Case law reflections
* What is the principle or ratio of this case?
* In what jurisdiction did the case originate? Has the decision been appealed?
* What is the precedent value of this case?
* How does this case affect the existing law on the topic?
* What are the implications from this case for the future of the law in the area?
* Does this case typify a trend that can or cannot be traced in other jurisdictions?
* Are there any articles published that analyse the case?

Treaty reflections
* When was this treaty signed?
* When was the treaty ratified in pertinent jurisdictions?
* Has the acceptance rate from other states/jurisdictions been high?
* Has the treaty been legislated into force in Australia?

---

31 Adapted from Cryer P, *The Research Student's Guide to Success* (3 ed, New York: Open University Press, 2006), Chapter 8.

Legislation reflections

* When was this legislation passed?
* What was the political context and policy framework surrounding its implementation? (For this, look at the Bills that introduced the legislation and the explanatory notes accompanying the Bills).
* Has the Act been updated regularly?
* Are the regulations important to your project?
* How 'successful' has the legislation been in achieving the government's stated intentions? Have there been any evaluations carried out on the legislation?
* What are the most contentious sections of the Act?
* Are there any articles published that analyse the Act/the pertinent sections of the Act?
* Are there any law reform or policy reports on the legislation?

A major difficulty in writing the literature review is determining how to organise and summarise all these different materials, and sometimes concept maps are quite useful for this purpose.

The next step is to break your reading up into topics and deal with each separately. You will need an overall reflection for each topic area in order to start drawing the connections and underlying themes. Finally you will need to place all the materials you have read together and examine and analyse them in relation to your hypothesis.

Overall reflections on commentary readings

* Do the secondary commentary readings present contrary or similar viewpoints? How can these views be reconciled?

Overall reflections on primary material

* Are the views presented in the case law consistent? Which categories of the topic are exceptions to the general rules? Are there separate lines of reasoning among the judges on the topic? How can these views be reconciled?
* What is the relevance, if any, of the approaches of different jurisdictions?
* Is there a close correlation between the legislation and the case law?
* Is there a close correlation between the treaties and the legislation?

Overall reflections to thesis development research process

Some issues you may like to think about are:

* What unexplored areas are apparent in the secondary literature?
* What unanswered questions arise from the literature?
* What areas are being suggested for further research?
* What problematic issues have not been the subject of judicial determination, legislative intervention or international agreement?
* What changes have been made to your topic to accommodate the literature?
* Has the literature review affected your topic viability? How have you dealt with this?

The key to a successful literature review lies in its brevity and your ability to synthesise, distil and critique the important issues. This is an area where brevity aids clarity. Pull together all the commentaries that are supporting a basic line of thought. Summarise the main thrust of what is being put forward by all the authors noting variations. Place this material into a broader context noting the consequences, gaps and likely future directions in the area. The literature review is the basis for your research, but it is also one of the most difficult aspects to present competently.

7.8 Keeping a research diary

Apart from writing your formal thesis draft, and your literature review, you will also find it useful to keep a research progress diary — the parallel story. This is a place to include what you have done, your 'To Do' list for each week or day, as well as your ideas to add to or improve your project. This is a way of keeping track of your research methodology and process. This is where you store your various plans, results, and conclusions pertaining to the methodology.

This diary includes research trivia such as a table of electronic filename changes. If your draft thesis has several sections and many versions of each, this note is your main indication of which file is the latest version and where backups have been saved on various home and work computers. Of course, file backups are a real necessity when using computers. Portability is a real issue. The journal needs to be able to travel easily — to the beach, to work, to home, to the hairdresser. Robert Peters suggests that students should document daily progress on their thesis. This means that the thesis is constantly uppermost in your mind, for obviously much time is wasted in picking up research once it is laid down — even for a short time.[32]

This diary is a reflective journal, so that any new ideas are scribbled in here until you have an opportunity to transfer them to your main work. Any 'thinking time' moments can be recorded in the form of mind maps and memory-joggers for follow-up issues. The research diary is a place to set out any self-reflection on your topic, and your own explanation for and justification of developments in the research topic. If you decide to change course and include something not mooted in your original proposal, this is the place to note the change and what prompted it. Similarly, it is useful when you decide to delete entire sections from the main body of writing because of a need to tailor your work or because you have allowed yourself to follow a tangent that cannot realistically fit within the whole. Therefore, when your supervisor suggests, for example, that perhaps the line of research you have been involved with for the last six weeks is peripheral to the main objective of your work, you will note this in the diary. Note why you are not developing this point in your thesis. It may be that later events will make this aspect important, or perhaps it can be developed as a separate piece of scholarship. This journal note should give you sufficient information for the occasion when you go back to the earmarked material for ideas for your next writing project.

---

32 Peters R, *Getting What You Came For: The Smart Student's Guide to Earning a Master's or a PhD* (rev ed, New York: Noonday Press, 1997), 127.

Ideally, you may discover that portions of the research progress diary can be quickly translated into your first draft. Your notes will clearly identify particular developments to your research strategy beyond the initial proposal in light of critical analysis and implementation of strategies to improve the project. This may be very pertinent to explaining to your reader why you have only dealt with certain aspects of a topic, or why your conclusions are framed in a certain style.

Every step of your research methodology should be noted in the diary. Outline the list of research sources checked with an indication of headings used and outcomes. Of course, if your thesis is based on a non-doctrinal model this explanation of research methodology will also appear in the body of the thesis.

The research progress diary should include any feedback from either your supervisor's written comments or changes suggested during the defence, and explain how you have developed your proposal to reflect these, or even why you have retained the original course. Having pursued a more complete literature review and read more widely, it may become apparent that the topic is too large or perhaps too restrictive in its outlook. This is where the development phase really commences. Often it is only when you begin to put your thoughts down on paper that the gaps in the argument become apparent. It is often at this stage that you realise that more research is needed, or that a certain line of argument lacks credibility. Sometimes the changes are a result of developments in the law, or lack of expected reform, or a change in government policy. The diary fulfils many functions including tracking details of what needs to be done, what has been completed, file names, pertinent addresses and contacts, key research terms and, most importantly, ideas and reflections on progress and improvements.

7.9 Conceptual frameworks

As noted previously, we all work within structures — physical, mental and socio-legal. In order to deal honestly with those structures in our writing, it is useful to make some preliminary attempts to assess the directions and roots for our intellectual development. This processing of nebulous internal and external elements may be referred to as a conceptual framework. The framework is one of the six 'threshold concepts' which tend to provide major challenges for research students.[33] The conceptual framework has at least three aspects — personal, legal and philosophical — and these do tend to overlap. It is useful to critically reflect on your framework, and to explicitly identify the basis of your beliefs. Critical reflective practice enables you to see your 'strengths and weaknesses in knowledge, skills, attitudes and behaviour' in the research process and to make 'conscious improvement'.[34] The idea is not novel. It dates

---

33 Margaret Kiley and Gina Wisker from their research 'Threshold concepts in research education and evidence of threshold crossing' (2009) 28 (4) *Higher Education Research & Development* 431 noted major challenges arising from students trying to identify the central argument or 'so what' factor (435), pertinent theory (436), methodological framework (436), aspect of originality (437), and providing analysis rather than description (438).

34 Zhao F, 'Enhancing the Effectiveness of Research and Research Supervision Through Reflective Practice' UltiBASE, 9. http://pandora.nla.gov.au/pan/10088/20040811/ultibase.rmit.edu.au/Archives/articles.htm#jul03 (5/11//2009).

back to John Dewey in 1916 who thought that a 'moral individual' would treat professional actions as experimental and 'reflect upon the actions and their consequences'.[35]

On one level, the conceptual framework constitutes a personal version of a legal paradigm. It is in all likelihood the source of our interest in the topic – a personal experience perhaps emanating from dealings with a government department over the finances of a relative may prompt a closer look at the legal framework in the area. Our framework and ways of seeing are determined by experience, so that a person who has spent twenty years in the armed forces, or the police, or as a social worker in a remote community, will have a perspective on the law framed by that experience. Awareness of situations that have developed can lead to insight and direction. All of this ensures the researcher's involvement in the topic.

Thus, your personal framework includes your own previous work experience in an area, individual time limitations, cultural perspectives and research purposes. For example, a person writing about the European Union legal system who may have no prior knowledge or experience in European civil legal systems, and who is unable to read or converse in any European languages, will necessarily devise a different type of project to someone who has worked within that system. The former person will have an outsider's view. The person actually working within the EU government framework would have an insider's view. An English lawyer who is endeavouring to come to terms with changes brought about because of the United Kingdom's unfolding legal relationship with the EU will have yet other perspectives to bring to the topic.

Of course, your personal conceptual framework is not as simple as this. It also relates to your philosophical views on law, society and politics. Perhaps this is something that you prefer not to reveal, but intrinsically your writing will reveal it to an observant reader. The conceptual framework includes all this conceptual baggage: a mix of assumptions, experiences, values and beliefs held by the researcher about the topic/question. The conceptual baggage is often the source of the interest in the topic and the angle taken by the researcher. Awareness of conceptual baggage, which inevitably exists in any researcher, can provide insight about choice of topic and direction. It can alert a researcher to potential biases. At the same time, conceptual baggage can highlight the strengths and priorities that the researcher is bringing into a project. Instead of pretending it is not there (objectivity), acknowledging conceptual baggage ensures that the researcher is there in the research (subjectively). This process is one step towards developing scholarship, while at the same time avoiding advocacy, no matter how 'well dressed'.[36]

---

35 Zhao F, 'Enhancing the Effectiveness of Research and Research Supervision Through Reflective Practice' UltiBASE, 2. http://pandora.nla.gov.au/pan/10088/20040811/ ultibase.rmit.edu.au/Archives/articles.htm#jul03 (5/11//2009). And see also Schon D, The Reflective Practitioner: How Professionals Think in Action (US: Basic Books, 1983).

36 Bettel Dawson T, 'Legal research in a social science setting: The problem of method' (1992) 14 (3) Dalhousie Law Journal 445 at 454.

The legal framework is even more crucial because it positions your research within the work of other scholars and published knowledge. Legal frameworks are multifarious — they can include methodological or interdisciplinary perspectives. Projects based in environmental law provide an excellent example of the need for recognition of legal frameworks. These frameworks are based in international agreements regarding the preservation of natural resources and regulations aimed at limiting degradation of the natural environment. International treaties and agreements have ensured that these principles have been infused into federal and State legislation. Addressing a small segment of that legislation without acknowledging the context is a one-dimensional approach to the area. Examining the law without somehow encompassing the interdisciplinary, scientific and other bodies of relevant knowledge is artificial.

Even a strictly doctrinal methodology examining how a specific line of case law extends or changes a principle of law prompts questions of how the common law may have developed in a particular context. The impetus for changed legislation no doubt came from particular government or social policies prevalent at the time. Wartime legislation may situate surviving regulations within a certain paradigm that needs recognition before it can be changed. Economic rationalism, for example, has its own paradigm, and such a prevalent government policy will determine a particular legislative outcome in the current climate.

Another major aspect of your conceptual framework relates to your theoretical philosophical approach. Your initial stance on an issue will likely be directed by whether you espouse feminism, liberalism, or postmodernism. Perhaps further research will moderate your approach, or, on the other hand, it may intensify your outlook. Most legal material is written in the third person. However, this in itself can be a statement of belief in the myth of objective 'truth' in law. Legal writing is presented on this basis; that is, that law exists without a wider context and can be examined by itself in a social vacuum. The ignoring of the context is a framework statement.

Your research may have a particular theoretical underpinning, such as positivism, Marxism or liberalism. The operating legal paradigm may be reflected in your philosophical view of law, your research methodology, the prior development and history of regulation and research in the area or the perspective demanded by those commissioning the research. What is the benefit in identifying this framework? The answer lies in being able to make connections and building on other work, which in addition means that analogies and parallels can be drawn between similar areas. Your framework will identify basic assumptions underlying the study and perhaps prompt you to justify these. Your framework affects the questions you ask (or do not ask at all), the methodology, and the context of your work. In addition, a discussion of conceptual frameworks benefits the reader. Readers do not have to delve beneath a charade of objective truth to weed out bias. They can identify where your particular view 'sits' in relation to other material.

Therefore the identification of your conceptual framework may not form part of the final draft of your paper. Reflecting on the conceptual framework is a threshold process. It enables you to position yourself intellectually in relation to your topic.

7.10 Structuring the final paper

Every topic tends to have its own internal 'logic'. The mystery lies in establishing this. When the proposal is being prepared, the main focus is on establishing the issues at the heart of the topic. Later, an outline of chapters or sections will probably unfold. A list of headings with a summary of your reasoned progression of the topic will result.

With extended projects, it may be necessary to focus on only one or two chapters at a time, while only sketching out a working outline for the remainder. Do not neglect to adhere to any university or faculty guidelines published in the official handbooks. These will give you some indication of the types of tables required and layout of any extra thesis components including lists of legislation and cases. Be sure to pinpoint the 'Significant' sources and list these in your bibliography. Remember to list the 'books and articles that have been used in a thesis, not those that might have been used'.[37] So a project layout would include the following:

> Title Page
>
> Acknowledgments
>
> Sources Statement
>
> Summary
>
> Table of Contents
>
> List of Charts
>
> List of Tables
>
> Chapters and Body of Thesis
>
> Bibliography
>
> Appendices
>
> Data Sheets[38]

7.10.1 *But what of the actual layout of the chapters?*

Often, the layout of the chapters is defined by the topic. Most theses will need a background or introductory chapter including a statement of the hypothesis and the theoretical context, possibly followed by a literature review and then a methodology if appropriate. The opening segment of the thesis should set out clearly the significance of what is being done. The 'middle' of the thesis will include ideas, information and evidence selected for its relevance to the research questions and hypothesis. The 'end' or conclusion will summarise the study overall, point up any limitations in your study or areas in need of further research, as well as highlighting any necessary conclusions or implications. The conclusion will include your statement on whether or not you have proven your hypothesis.

---

37 Watson G, *Writing a Thesis: A Quick Guide to Long Essays and Dissertations* (Harlow: Longman Group UK, 1987), 96.

38 See also the relevant segments in Campbell E and Kewley G, *Presentation of Legal Theses* (3 ed, Clayton, Victoria: Faculty of Law Monash University, 1996).

Many of the articles and books available on writing up research at postgraduate level provide formulas and arrangements more suited to the scientific fields and empirical research. The normal formula for a quantitative study would include:

Title
* Summary or abstract
* Introduction including background, relevant previous studies, problem being investigated and hypothesis to be tested
* Methodology including selection of sample, tests used, design, data analysis
* Results
* Discussion[39]

Qualitative studies may include similar features, although allowance needs to be made for the individual design. Comparative or chronological studies will need to be presented differently to a study that seeks to build a theory over a number of chapters. More descriptive studies might have a random structure, describing various aspects of the case in hand.[40]

Research is more than a literature review. It is a synthesis of the various issues connected to your objective linked into an argument or thesis. Somewhere in the explanation of this story it will be necessary to target several basic aspects. These questions have been summarised by various commentators. They include:

1 What did you do? How did you do it?

  This covers the purpose or object of your project, that is, what you set out to do and the methods you used or how you went about it.

2 What came of it? What was the result of your project? What did you discover?

3 Why? What was the rationale for taking this view? Why did you as researcher take this approach to the research question?

4 So what? How can you interpret what it is that has been found? What conclusions follow from these results?

5 What now? What do you think ought to be done about the situation? What are your recommendations? What still remains to be resolved or followed up? Where does this information lead the topic?[41]

---

39 Burns R, *Introduction to Research Methods* (4 ed, Melbourne: Longman Cheshire, 2000), Chapter 22.

40 Burns R, *Introduction to Research Methods* (4 ed, Melbourne: Longman Cheshire, 2000), Chapter 28. Burns lists linear-analytic, comparative, chronological, theory building, suspense, case analysis, micro-ethnological, macro-ethnological and unsequenced structures as some of the choices.

41 See Buzzard RB, 'Notes on report writing' (1972) 46 *Occupational Psychology* 201 as reported in Gardner G, *Social Surveys for Social Planners* (rev ed, Sydney: Holt Rinehart and Winston, 1978), 136; Nightingale P, 'Initiation into research through writing' in Zuber-Skerritt O (ed), *Starting Research — Supervision and Training* (Brisbane: The Tertiary Education Institute, University of Queensland, 1992), 175.

When the time comes to edit the final draft, then there may be some need to rearrange issues so that the 'why' is very prominent — in fact comes first. There appears to be plenty of advice on what to include in a social research report, such as the following list:

Minimum items to include in a social research report

1   By whom, for whom, and with what financial backing the research was undertaken.

2   The objects of the research.

3   The time at which the field work was undertaken and its duration.

4   The universe which was the subject of the research, including basic demographic details.

5   The details of any samples taken which should include the size of the sample — the sample fraction, the method of sampling and the number of completed interviews related to the number of planned interviews.

6   Descriptions of the methods of data collection, whether from documents, observation, or interview and the type of each used.

7   Details of the staff employed and their supervision

8   A copy of any questionnaires, schedules, or interview guides used.

9   The facts found, including those contrary to the hypotheses.

10 Where data is presented in the form of percentages or other indices, tables should include the number of cases on which these were based.

11 The relation of the evidence collected to comparable information collected in other studies.

12 As appropriate, the implications of the findings for previously stated theoretical propositions and/or for action.[42]

Legal doctrinal theses are, however, more fluid. Much depends on the topic itself. Be sure to explain the legal background and introduce the law appropriately. Placing the law in some type of context is useful, but there is not normally the same requirement to provide a detailed account of your electronic and other library research methodology within the substantive doctrinal paper. The reader is more interested in outcomes and answers rather than the history of the journey.

7.11   Conclusion

This Chapter covers some of the most important steps in organising research projects. These milestones include narrowing your topic, writing a research proposal, formulating a research timeline in order to ensure completion, presenting and defending your ideas to others, determining your conceptual framework, developing your ideas through a reflective research diary, writing your literature review and then structuring your research paper. Research is hard

---

42   Stacey M, *Methods of Social Research* (Oxford: Pergamon Press, 1969) as reported in Gardner G, *Social Surveys for Social Planners* (rev ed, Sydney: Holt Rinehart and Winston, 1978), 141.

work. Planning is an important step in ensuring completion. Your research proposal is a paramount planning vehicle for your research. Unpack every statement and objective you write in the proposal. Think about what information will be necessary to carry out your objectives and whether you have really covered every step in the methodology in sufficient detail. Constantly challenge your process and ideas, and seek out other opportunities for others to add to your critical reflective framework. Research is an active not a passive process.

Further reading

Bell J, *Doing Your Research Project: A Guide for First-Time Researchers in Education and Social Science* (4 ed, Philadelphia: Open University Press, 2005).

Campbell JP, Daft RL and Hulin CL, *What to Study: Generating and Developing Research Questions* (Beverly Hills: Sage, 1982).

Cennamo K, 'Survivors guide to graduate research' (1992) 37 (1) *Tech Trends* 15.

Covey S, *The 7 Habits of Highly Effective People* (Melbourne: The Business Library, 1989).

Cryer P, *The Research Student's Guide to Success* (3 ed, Maidenhead, Berkshire: Open University Press, 2006).

Davis G, *Writing the Doctoral Dissertation: A Systematic Approach* (2 ed, Hauppauge: Barrons, 1997).

Eisner C and Vicinus M (eds), *Originality, Imitation and Plagiarism: Teaching Writing in the Digital Age* (Ann Arbor: The University of Michigan Press and The University of Michigan Library, 2008.

Graves N and Varma V, *Working for a Doctorate: A Guide for the Humanities and Social Sciences* (London: Routledge, 1997).

Kiley M and Wisker G, 'Threshold concepts in research education and evidence of threshold crossing' (2009) 28 (4) *Higher Education Research & Development* 431.

Loughnan A and Shackel R, 'The Travails of Postgraduate Research in Law' (2009) 19 *Legal Education Review* 99.

Madsen D, *Successful Dissertations and Theses: A Guide to Graduate Student Research from Proposal to Completion* (2 ed, San Francisco: Jossey-Bass, 1992).

Mahony D, *The Student Guide to Preparing, Writing and Presenting Assignments: The World of Ideas and the World of Text* (3 ed, Brisbane: Queensland University of Technology, 2001).

May, 'Planning Time' in Graves and Varma VP (eds), *Working for a doctorate: a guide for the humanities and social sciences* (London: Routledge, 1997) pp 59-75.

Moore N, *How to do Research: A Practical Guide to Designing and Managing Research Projects* (3 rev, London: Facet, 2006).

Murray R, *How to Write a Thesis* (Maidenhead: Open University Press, 2006).

Pauk W and Fiore J, *Succeed in College!* (Boston: Houghton Mifflin Company, 2000).

Peters R, *Getting What You Came For: The Smart Student's Guide to Earning a Master's or a PhD* (rev ed, New York: Noonday Press, 1997).

Phillips EM and Pugh DS, *How to get a PhD: A Handbook for Students and their Supervisors* (4 ed, Maidenhead: Open University Press, 2005).

Ruestam KE & Newton RR, *Surviving your Dissertation: A Comprehensive Guide to Content and Process* (3 ed, Los Angeles: SAGE Publications, 2007).

Salmon P, *Achieving a PhD* (Staffordshire: Trentham Books, 1992).

Schön DA, *Reflective Practitioner: How Professionals Think in Action* (2 ed, Aldershot: Arena, 1995).

Schweitzer R and Elphinstone L, *How to Get a Research Degree* (Allen & Unwin, 1998).

Watson G, *Writing a Thesis: A Guide to Long Essays and Dissertations* (Harlow: Longman Group UK, 1987).

Zuber-Skerritt O (ed), *Manual for Conducting Workshops on Postgraduate Supervision* (St Lucia: University of Queensland, Tertiary Education Institute, 1992).

Zuber-Skerritt O (ed), *Starting Research — Supervision and Training* (St Lucia: University of Queensland, Tertiary Education Institute, 1992).

Zuber-Skerritt O and Pinchen S, *Third Manual for Conducting Workshops on Postgraduate Supervision* (Nathan: Griffith Institute for Higher Education, 1995).

Research Project Timeline Example

Year 2010	January		February		March		April		May		June	
Fortnight	1	2	1	2	1	2	1	2	1	2	1	2
Activity												
Major commitments			Grandfather's 80th party				Getting married			International conference presentation		Public Presentation
Vacations	Family holiday						Easter holiday					
Meet with potential supervisors to discuss topic and supervisor expectations		xx										
Clarify main deadlines and Target Dates		xx										
Finalise working hypothesis	xxxx	xx	xxxxxxxx	xx	xx	xx						
Begin organised literature review		xx	xxxxxxxx	xx	xx	xx		xx	xx		xx	xxxxxx
Investigate research methodologies		xx	xxxxxxxx	xx	xx	xx		xx				
Decide on citation style		xx										
Set up EndNote research database or personal research tracking system			xxxxxxxx	xx	xx	xx						
Determine budget requirements		xx	xxxxxxxx	xx	xx	xx		xx	xx			
Finalise proposal					xx	xx		xx	xx			
Organise ethics clearance					xx	xx		xx	xx		xx	xxxxxx
Set up series of meeting dates and agree on writing schedule with supervisors			xxxxxxx									
Start writing			xxxxxx	xx	xx	xx		xx	xx		xx	xxxxxx

8 Legal Writing Basics

Given the variety of roles that law graduates fill in society today, there is not one particular formula that can be used to produce polished legal writing for every occasion. However, some general principles remain important whatever the context. In light of the nebulous nature of 'good' legal writing, this chapter aims to provide the reader with a basic awareness of the context and the variety of tools that can be used to develop their writing skills. It is important that lawyers use an arsenal of reading, writing and communication devices to promote clear understanding for their readers.

One of the most difficult aspects of writing is to be able to find our unique 'voice' — a style that is personal and effective. Every person has a unique writing style and particular methods may suit some more than others. The ideas presented in this chapter are not meant to represent a benchmark against which to 'judge' writing. Rather, they are suggested as useful guides that can be considered, incorporated, or modified by a writer in the process of developing their 'voice'.

Legal writing can be approached at several different levels. This chapter incorporates a revision of some of the very basic issues that you need to consider in your written work, whatever the academic level. The main difference between undergraduate and postgraduate writing lies in the expectations of your readers and examiners. This expectation is often based on the increased originality and depth of analysis required from upper level students, rather than a specifically 'different' writing style.

Thus, this chapter reviews trends in legal writing including the Plain English movement, and revisits much of the accumulated wisdom about academic writing. The chapter then considers the difficulties and the strategies to be used in completing a first draft. Although this is not a grammar text, there is some consideration of a few basic writing rules, particularly in regard to acknowledging sources.

8.1 What are the current trends in legal writing?

People often experience difficulty understanding legal writing. Every profession and trade has its own jargon or terminology specific to its subject matter. In the library world, for example, acronyms are rife. Terms such as OPAC (online public access catalogue), and the use of abbreviations for standard pieces of legislation, such as the *Family Law Act 1975* (FLA), often provide difficulties for the uninitiated if they are not explained.

Some argue that legal language is a product of privilege and suggest that it bolsters an economic elite. They argue that legal language promotes discrimination in that, 'the idea of a special and separate legal language remote from common speech is the product of a society in which only a very limited class of "legally competent" people can read the texts of that language'.[1] The lawyer's well-intentioned attempt at clarity, by the use of precise terminology and repetition, often leads to confusion for the lay reader. In addition, legal terminology is peppered with obscure Law French, and Latin terms. This can provide special challenges for those who speak English as a second language.

The reasons for these style difficulties are often historical. Wordiness, for example, has often been a major cause of complaint. Apparently, the origins of this habit lie in a court-devised system of fees for preparing and filing documents. This used to be based on the number of pages in each document, so that the longer the document the greater the fee.[2] The modern context accepts that law should be inclusive and accessible to everybody. Lawyers retain a special role in society as 'communicators' of the law, so it is important that legal writing facilitates understanding for every level of audience.

8.2 **Continual development**

The history of legal language, and legalese, can be tracked to 1066 when William, Duke of Normandy, arrived in England and fought and killed the English king Harold. The Normans subjugated the English and installed themselves as the new aristocracy. William never learnt how to speak English. The language of the invaders was Norman French, and this gradually became the language spoken in the courts. This is the origin of much of today's legal jargon. Interestingly, Sir William Blackstone used to refer to Norman Law French as a 'badge of slavery'.[3] Later, Norman French merged with Middle English, but in 1731 it was still necessary for the English Parliament to enact legislation to ensure that all court documents 'shall be in the English tongue only and not in Latin or French'.[4] Many legal terms still survive from Norman Law French. These include: appeal, arrest, defendant, plaintiff, suit, verdict, demurrer, indictment, lien, replevin, tenant, and tort. Even the bailiff's cries of 'Oyez, oyez' or 'Hear ye, Hear ye' are derived from Law French.

The feudal system that operated after the Norman Conquest is also responsible for a number of legal terms, especially those associated with property ownership. These include fee simple absolute, fee simple conditional, fee simple defeasible, and fee tail. In these examples, the French influence is also detectible with the positioning of nouns so that they precede the adjectives.

---

1   Goodrich P, 'The role of linguistics in legal analysis' (1984) 47 *The Modern Law Review* 523 at 534.

2   Asprey M, *Plain Language for Lawyers* (3 ed, Sydney: The Federation Press), 32.

3   Neumann RK, *Legal Reasoning and Legal Writing* (4 ed, Boston: Little Brown), 4.

4   *Records in English Act 1731*, 4 Geo 11 ch 26.

Some legal terms may be incomprehensible to non-lawyers. Therefore, when you use pure law terms,[5] legal slang,[6] legal maxims,[7] Law Latin[8] and old English terms[9] in your writing, you need to ensure the person you are addressing is aware of their meaning.[10] The rule should be — if in doubt, leave it out! Use an alternative term or, if necessary, include a simple explanation. Similarly, if terms are used in their 'legal' sense rather than their common language meaning, then this too must be made clear.[11] A word such as 'consideration', for example, has a natural language meaning of 'care', or it can mean the price of a bargain or, on another level, it can refer to the doctrine of consideration within contract law.

Of course, some legal terms have more than one legal meaning. This can produce additional confusion. The term 'common law', for example, has at least three meanings depending on its context. It can be used in comparative legal systems to differentiate the English legal tradition from the European civil law traditions. It can be used to contrast legislative systems and the system of law based on precedent. It can also refer to the difference between Chancery or Equity based law, and the law developed in the common law courts in England.

8.3 What is plain legal language?

An emphasis on the importance of plain legal language has been developing since the 1970s. In 1976, the NRMA (National Roads and Motorists Association) introduced its plain English car insurance policy in Australia. In 1983, an international organisation of lawyers devoted to the use of plain legal language called 'Clarity' was formed.[12] The Centre for Plain Legal Language was established in Sydney in 1990. Similar steps have taken place in other common law jurisdictions including the United States and the United Kingdom.

Using plain legal language is about making the law user-friendly. The plain legal language movement has gained momentum as a reaction to criticisms that legal language is inaccessible. There are several basic ideas behind the movement. While recognising that a legal document must be technically correct and accurate, the principle is that it remains intelligible to its primary audience. This means that the average client is able to read and understand a contract, and that the public can understand basic legislation. The words used, the tone and the layout are all important in achieving readability. The tone of the document should be appropriate for the intended audience. Often, in legal writing, an 'objective tone' is adopted. However, readers may perceive such a tone as pompous and impersonal. Readability is not restricted to the words used.

---

5 Eg 'joint tenancy' and 'tenancy in common'.

6 Eg 'without prejudice'.

7 Eg 'caveat emptor'.

8 Eg 'ex parte'.

9 Eg 'therein', 'herewith'.

10 Mellinkoff D, *The Language of the Law* (Boston: Little Brown, 1963).

11 Riley A, 'The meaning of words in English legal texts: Mastering the vocabulary of the law — a legal task' (1996) *Law Teachers Journal* 68 at 71.

12 Kirby M, Review of Mailhot L and Carnwath J, *Decisions, Decisions ... A Handbook for Judicial Writing* (Quebec: Les Editions Yvon Blais Inc, 1998).

Legal language, like all language, is constructed or based on certain premises and assumptions. Feminists might say it is a gendered construct in that it reflects a dominant male worldview. Critical legal scholars might argue that language is constructed on liberal ideals and the overarching importance of concepts, such as property. Many would argue that the use of plain legal language enables the assumptions sitting behind accepted legal terminology to be 'unpacked'. To some this will feel dangerous, whilst to others it will come as a welcome relief.

The plain English movement is not yet totally accepted by the legal profession. One of the reasons given is the risk of losing precision. But often, opposition is tacit because of the amount of time (and money) involved in revising documents that have apparently been working successfully for years.

8.4   How do you best convey the message?

The most important part of the writing process is to be clear about what it is you have to say and whom you want to say it to. This determines the organisation and presentation of your thoughts.

8.4.1   *What is the purpose of your writing?*

In order to convey your message by the most effective means, you need to consider the purpose for which you are writing. There are an endless number of reasons for writing. You must consider yours. Are you trying to persuade someone else to your line of belief, or are you merely canvassing the possibilities, weighing up the advantages and disadvantages of pursuing a particular course of action? Are you writing to provide information to another person? Are you writing to prove to another that you have the skills required to investigate and research legal topics at the required level? Is your purpose to exhibit the degree of analytical and higher level thinking skills expected from postgraduate law students? Is your purpose to demonstrate knowledge, or to impart knowledge to another? Indeed, you may have several purposes for your writing and you can aim to prepare a document that will best fit all of them. However, in order to write well, the purpose needs to be clear — both to yourself and to the reader.

Once you have decided on the purpose of your writing, this needs to be reflected in the style and organisation of the document. If the reader is looking for a clear answer, provide it straight away — at the beginning. If the reader wants the arguments teased out, then state them clearly, and canvass the whole debate from both sides. If you are trying to convince a reader of a particular course of action, acknowledge any difficulties with your approach and suggest ways of overcoming these. If the reader wants information, set it out clearly, rather than obscuring the main points.

8.4.2   *Who is your intended audience?*

Another important aspect of writing is to make sure that you are connecting with your audience. The same is true of any form of communication. To achieve this 'connection', the message must be of intrinsic worth to the reader. They must want to know about the topic. With academic articles, it may be that you can 'pull in' readers because of the quality of your writing or a 'pithy' abstract. While skimming a journal, a reader may pause at an article, but they will only read the whole message if the style of writing is palatable, and the message is in some way made important to them. Sometimes, of course, the 'need to know' can eclipse everything else. All of us have had to read judgments where this has been the case! You must read the material. You must make some sense of what you are reading. Therefore, you persevere. However, normally if the reader finds the means of communication unsatisfactory, then they will simply look elsewhere for the information. Obvious difficulties result from this situation. A lawyer, for example, may think they have given information to their client, whereas the message has not been conveyed or properly understood — perhaps it has not even been read!

The most difficult part of the writing process is to identify your audience needs. In order to pitch the message correctly, you need to identify your audience and then identify the level of information they require. One way of filling this lacuna might be to write down the names of three or four potential readers and then direct your writing to that group in the first instance.

In a practical situation, when a lawyer is dealing with a single client, the issue is relatively non-existent. You know who you are communicating with and their level of knowledge of the topic, and probably also know a little of their educational background and language skills. Your letters are attuned to the recipient's needs. If you are dealing with a large corporation, this can be less clear. The recipient may be one of a group of people at various levels of administration, who may read it for different meanings. It is useful to take a moment and at least consider your potential readers and the extent of their knowledge. What role is your reader likely to play in the organisation? What will they be interested in finding out from you? What constraints are placed on them? What are their main concerns or fears? Consider all the different aspects that can affect understanding, including the recipient's age, native language, education and reading level, familiarity with subject matter, familiarity with legal language, attitude, physical or other problems, and any individual concerns that have been indicated to you.[13]

In an academic setting, whether in a coursework or undergraduate situation, you also need to think about the reader and their requirements. The audience will be the examiner. Expectations and standards can differ according to the level of the group of students, and the examiner. Sometimes it is unclear who will be marking a paper. It may be the case with a research paper that any one of a number of examiners in a teaching team will read your work. For this reason, the criteria must be given extra attention. These will have been set out clearly and all members of a teaching team will be marking your work according to these criteria.

With higher degree research work, the issue becomes murkier. Principally, you are writing for your supervisor or unit coordinator. The rules and criteria for the degree will be readily available in the unit outline or on the university

---

13 Charrow V and Erhardt M, *Clear and Effective Legal Writing* (3 ed, Gaithersburg: Aspen Law and Business, 2001), 105.

website. For a PhD there is usually a requirement that the thesis should make a 'substantial and original contribution to knowledge'. There has been some research carried out on the examination process for PhDs in Australia.[14] Gerry Mullins and Margaret Kiley determined that examiners reading a thesis considered these points:

8 'How would they have tackled the problem set out in the abstract and the title?

9 What questions would they like answers to?

10 Do the conclusions follow on from the introduction?

11 How well does the candidate explain what he/she is doing?

12 Is the bibliography up to date and substantial enough?

13 Are the results worthwhile?

14 How much work has actually been done?

15 What is the intellectual depth and rigour of the thesis?

16 Is this actually 'research' — is there an argument?'[15]

Their interviews with examiners also allowed them to formulate a list of the aspects of an 'outstanding thesis' and those for a 'poor thesis'. An outstanding thesis is categorised as being:

8 "an artistic endeavour where the student is designing the work and there is elegance of design, of the synthesis, and executions";

9 Creativity;

10 Design — where it all fits together;

11 Elegant;

12 A well-sculpted piece of work.[16]

A poor thesis on the other hand demonstrated:

8 Lack of coherence;

9 Lack of understanding of the theory;

10 Lack of confidence;

11 Researching the wrong problem;

12 Mixed or confused theoretical and methodological perspectives;

13 Work that is not original;

14 Not being able to explain at the end of the thesis what had actually been argued in the thesis.[17]

When the thesis is sent to external examiners, there are other concerns. It may be that there is a limited pool of experts in your field. Your thesis may need to

---

14 Mullins G and Kiley M, ' "It's a PhD, not a Nobel Prize": how experienced examiners assess research theses' (2002) 27 (4) *Studies in Higher Education* 369.

15 Mullins G and Kiley M, ' "It's a PhD, not a Nobel Prize": how experienced examiners assess research theses' (2002) 27 (4) *Studies in Higher Education* 369 at 377.

16 Mullins G and Kiley M, ' "It's a PhD, not a Nobel Prize": how experienced examiners assess research theses' (2002) 27 (4) *Studies in Higher Education* 369 at 379.

17 Mullins G and Kiley M, ' "It's a PhD, not a Nobel Prize": how experienced examiners assess research theses' (2002) 27 (4) *Studies in Higher Education* 369 at 378-379.

conform or allow for the dominant paradigms or worldviews of that limited group of prospective examiners for your thesis. If you are contemplating a post-modern view on a traditional legal area, then you may need to write to counter possible theoretical scepticism. Although your research endeavours cannot be totally constrained by this fact, the potential reader should be considered at all times — even when you are choosing your thesis and methodology.

The style and tone of your writing must correspond to the needs of your potential readers. After all, 'different readers have different needs'.[18] However, most readers require some 'scene setting' when confronting legal areas. This issue can be easily overlooked. If you have been reading and thinking about a specific piece of legislation or line of case law for some days (or weeks), and then begin writing a first draft, you tend to be thinking about specifics. It is usually necessary to put the reader into context on the topic. You need background to your story. This may be achieved by including the sections of legislation you are critiquing or the passages or line of authority under review. As one commentator has stated, 'Whether your essay is understandable should not be dependent on the expertise of your readers'.[19] Put your reader in the picture just as you would if they were a new person joining a group conversation.

8.4.3   *How do you organise your work?*

The content of your work depends partly on your purpose for writing. The content and purpose determine organisation. A historical or chronological survey of the law regarding married women's property rights may be relevant to a legal history assignment, although quite out of place in an office memo. An economic analysis of the legal changes brought about by third party insurance may have its place in a freewheeling journal article, but may be quite out of place in a problem-based undergraduate student exercise. Once you are clear regarding the purpose and appropriate content, you need to consider organisation.

Basic documents can conform to certain accepted formulas. The issue of layout and proper use of white space is inherent in the formulas. Headings at the top of an office memo stating the author, the intended recipient, the date and topic under discussion, are a prime example of the necessity of stating the context in a visual and clear manner. Email messages (the modern equivalent of in-house memos in 'paperless' offices) conform to a similar layout. The three writing forms commonly taught at law school are legal essays, casenotes and research memos. Each of these conforms to a legal writing genre. Each of these has a specific layout. Having determined the best way of conveying the message, the appropriate physical packaging or format, you then have to address the internal logic of what is being said. This is an entirely separate exercise.

---

18   Ray MB and Ramsfield J, *Beyond the Basics: A Text for Advanced Legal Writing* (2 ed, St Paul: West Publishing, 2003), 408.

19   Castel J and Latchman O, *The Practical Guide to Canadian Legal Research* (2 ed, Ontario: Carswell, 1996), 146.

8.4.4 *Legal essays*

Part of the process of putting your reader in the picture is to define and justify your parameters. For time or word limit reasons, you may have decided to limit your discussion to only some of the issues possible within the topic. Explain and justify what you intend dealing with and what you are leaving out. However, do ensure that the issue 'left alone' is not the core or pivot to the whole discussion. This may leave the whole paper pointless. Similarly, if there is only one difficult area on the legal horizon in the topic, one controversial issue that holds enough depth for discussion, then it once again would seem pointless to avoid it entirely on the basis that it is too hard.

Define any difficult concepts or terms at the beginning. The words may seem obvious, but different writers define their issues slightly differently. So it is worthwhile setting the record straight and putting your reader totally 'in the picture'. If you are discussing legal theory, it is quite probable that some of your readers will not be familiar with your frame of reference. Similarly, if you are writing for practitioners in a niche market, it is still worthwhile outlining any special conditions applying in the industry that may require particular forms of legal regulation or control.

You may have been given a specific question to address. If this is the case, ensure that you direct the organisation of your writing to answering the question. The following list of directive words frequently used in examination and essay questions is mainly based on a list compiled by Raymond Wacks for the use of jurisprudence students.[20]

Analyse	Show the essence of something, by breaking it down into its component parts and examining each part in detail. (What are the main features of the topic? Describe them and explain why they are significant.)
Argue	Present the case for and/or against a particular proposition or theory, and evaluate the arguments.
Compare	Look for similarities between propositions, theories, and situations.
Contrast	Look for differences between propositions, theories, and situations.
Criticise	Give your judgment about the merit of theories or opinions about the truth of facts, and support your judgment by a discussion of the evidence.
Define	Set down the precise meaning of a term or phrase. Show that the distinctions implied in the definition are necessary. (Sometimes it is helpful to add some examples of each of the defining features.)
Describe	Give a detailed account.
Discuss	Investigate or examine by argument, sift and debate, giving reasons for and against.

---

20 Wacks R, *Jurisprudence* (5 ed London: Blackstone Press, 1999), 19–20 and Seely J, *The Oxford Guide to Writing and Speaking* (Oxford: OUP, 1998), 73–74.

Enumerate	List or specify and describe.
Evaluate	Make an appraisal of the worth of something, in the light of its apparent truth or utility; include your personal opinion.
Examine	Present in depth and investigate the implications.
Explain	Make plain, interpret and account for in detail.
Illustrate	Explain and make clear by the use of concrete examples, or by the use of a figure or diagram.
Interpret	Bring out the meaning of, and make clear and explicit; usually giving also your own judgment.
Justify	Show adequate grounds for decisions or conclusions.
Narrate	Tell the story, possibly of the major events leading to a conclusion.
Outline	Give the main features or general principles of a subject.
Prove	Demonstrate truth or falsity by presenting evidence.
Relate	Narrate/show how things are connected to each other, and to what extent they are alike or affect each other.
Review	Make a survey, examining the subject critically.
State	Specify fully and clearly.
Summarise	Give a concise account of the chief points or substance of a matter, omitting details and examples.
Trace	Identify and describe the development or history of a topic from some point or origin.

Often, working out what is being asked of you is the main key to progress.

Questions often encompass the relationship between two or three different aspects. All issues need to be dealt with in order to fully address the problem posed. This can involve some deeper understanding and critique rather than mere description of the area under discussion. It might be useful to complete a mindmap to clarify your thoughts. Sometimes you may also need to illustrate your answer with examples. If you choose to take a themed response in your answer, limit your choice of examples to one or two areas.

8.4.5 *Casenotes*

Different concerns come to the fore when you are attempting to write a casenote. The most important aspect lies in your choice of a case to review. You will need to locate a case that develops the law in a certain area or perhaps one that is in some way contentious. Often, the cases that prompt the need for a casenote are obscure or lengthy. The busy reader wants to be able to use your writing to clarify the focus of the case, perhaps before even attempting to read the whole report. For that reason, just as you state your limitations in a legal essay or article, in a casenote it is necessary to outline the specific issues in the case that will principally be discussed. You may, for example, acknowledge that there were evidentiary matters discussed in an appeal, but turn your main attention to a substantive criminal law issue that includes a new interpretation of an important topic. In any case, you will need to include basic information on the history of the proceedings, the facts, and outline the reasoning of the majority. Perhaps you might also attempt to answer one of the following questions:

1 How does this case affect the existing law on the topic?

2 What are the implications from this case for the future of the law in the area?

3 Does this case typify a trend that can or cannot be traced in other jurisdictions?[21]

The ability to write concise casenotes will be invaluable in later projects, especially at the postgraduate level, where a line of cases may form part of a general literature review and context chapter.

8.4.6 *Office research memos*

Many undergraduate research courses include a research memorandum as part of the assessment for the unit. Office memos require different types of skills to those used in writing an academic essay. The memo is normally written for a specific purpose related to a client matter. However, many legal offices keep their research memos on file or on a research database for use by others in the future. The research memo is often indexed and dated so that researchers working in a similar area at a later time will be able to appreciate the parameters of the analysis before them and ideally save time by being able to simply update from the last research carried out.

The memo's structure is determined by its use. The memo heading sets out the recipient, who wrote it, the date and the client matter. Sometimes catchwords are included at the top of the document to aid database entry. A memo is a business tool so the writing is concise, with clear and meaningful headings to aid the reader in skimming the page. In a research memo, the issue and answer is stated at the beginning, followed then by the background and reasoning on which it is based.

In a more complex matter, the memo might begin by providing a statement of the assignment, then the legal issues being addressed, followed by the specific fact situation presented by the client matter, an analysis of the law and a suggested line of action, recommendations and conclusion. If there are several issues, then the memo layout will need to reflect this. William Statsky has suggested the following outline, but it is only a guide and perhaps if there are too many issues, they should be grouped then treated separately.

Statement of assignment

Summary of issues and conclusions
    Issue 1 and conclusion
    Issue 2 and conclusion
    Issue 3 and conclusion

---

21 Based on Castel J and Latchman O, *The Practical Guide to Canadian Legal Research* (2 ed, Ontario: Carswell, 1996), 148.

Facts

Analysis
      Issue 1
      Issue 2
      Issue 3

Conclusion[22]

Remember that an internal memo is written in order that someone else can make a decision, usually along the lines of whether a particular client has a case based on the current state of the law. For this to happen, all the relevant information needs to be set out clearly. The strengths and weaknesses of both sides of the case need to be highlighted, and all the possible arguments identified. Normally, there would be no place for legal history, unless it has a direct bearing on the case in hand. Nor will the partner in a busy law firm be interested in legal theory, statistics or sociology. This is a very practical and time-scripted exercise. The reader will only want to know what the law is now. Case history is an entirely different matter. Jacqueline Castel poses the questions for such a memo along these lines:

> 3. is the law which supports or goes against your client's case binding or persuasive?
> 4. Can the facts of your case be distinguished from those in the case law? If so, how?
> 5. Will a court be likely to accept these distinctions as valid? Why or why not?[23]

Come to a reasoned evaluation and provide recommendations for action using the facts of the case you are discussing. The conclusion, based on a reasoned analysis of the law and the facts, is important. That is what is usually read first — the 'bottom line'. As Lucy Katz has commented, 'a good conclusion performs four functions: summation, evaluation, prediction, and recommendation'.[24]

When the time comes and you are researching your thesis or master's paper, these simple genres are the building blocks of your literature review. If you start writing full casenotes as soon as you begin reading material for your academic paper, then the next issue of writing the first draft becomes much less problematic in a doctrinal methodology model.

8.5   How do you complete a first draft?

The answer to this question is to start writing as soon as you start reading. Most people find that it is best to begin the writing phase as early as possible in the research process. While you are reading, begin to succinctly write down not only

---

22 Statsky WP, *Legal Research and Writing: Some Starting Points* (5 ed, St Paul: West Legal Studies, 1999), 298.

23 Castel J and Latchman O, *The Practical Guide to Canadian Legal Research* (2 ed, Ontario: Carswell, 1996), 152.

24 Katz L, *Winning Words: A Guide to Persuasive Writing for Lawyers* (New York: Law & Business Inc, 1986), 118 and see Chapter 3 generally.

an outline of the facts but also your thoughts or critical analysis of how this 'fits' into your argument or hypothesis. Summarise as you go along. This is the drafting stage. The first stage in the initial writing process includes the sketching out of your ideas and arguments into a whole piece, building on your initial proposal. This involves the process of trying to translate thoughts and hunches into clear words and connected prose. Very few writers would start at the beginning and work through each chapter or section in a linear fashion. Some areas will unfold more easily than others. The first draft does not need to be perfect. That will come later — once there is a whole skeleton of ideas expressed in prose. It is only when the document is substantially correct that further careful editing and the often extended process of tidying up the document for final submission takes place.

Everyone has an individual way of approaching the writing process. Very few researchers positively enjoy writing. In fact, the most common response is procrastination ...

The best idea is to start — and then edit. In order to start, it is necessary to break the whole project down into 'bite-size' pieces and then attack boldly. There are various methods. Some authors concentrate on putting down their main arguments and thoughts on paper, and then expanding and refining from that point — expanding, re-arranging, sorting and rephrasing. This is what George Watson refers to as 'rubbishing it out'.[25]

Others start out with a notional contents list, fleshing the ideas out as much as possible. They simply research and read under those topics, writing notes and summarising as they progress through the material in an ordered fashion. When their reading is becoming circular, they print out, review and reflect on the ideas already on paper in order to achieve a first draft.

Another approach is to write segments as the reading is completed, so that there is no one final step of 'writing'. The writing occurs as part of the research process.

Experienced authors also suggest the following to 'oil the wheels':

* Before you rise from your desk, make a note of the next step in the process, and make it a relatively easy task.

* Set yourself a schedule of so many words per day and keep a record of whether this has been achieved. Keep to a regular schedule of writing because otherwise valuable time will be lost in picking up the threads if there is too long a break between writing blocks. Get into the 'writing rhythm' that bests suits your personality and lifestyle and reward yourself for your achievements along the way. Measure your output. Once a goal is achieved, give yourself a present.

* As with all large endeavours in life, it is necessary to try to break the large project into small tasks. Decide what needs to be done and try to do a little every time you sit down to write. Otherwise you risk becoming overwhelmed by the enormity of the task.[26]

---

25 Watson G, *Writing a Thesis: A Quick Guide to Long Essays and Dissertations* (Harlow: Longman Group UK, 1987), 40.

26 Watson G, *Writing a Thesis: A Quick Guide to Long Essays and Dissertations* (Harlow: Longman Group UK, 1987), 41.

* Visualise what the end product will be — and work backwards in regard to the writing needed to produce this.

* If you are having trouble clarifying an issue use subterfuge — write yourself (or an understanding friend) an email explaining the links and argument as well as possible. Peggy Nightingale has suggested the WIRMI message.[27] WIRMI stands for 'What I really mean is ...' In this way you can use your writing as the 'engine' of your thinking.[28]

* Sometimes documents just have to be written — not always because of anger — but because a voice has to speak out. Outrage can be a great spur to the writer. If your topic can inspire you with some emotion, then half the battle has been won. Practitioners may find this an excellent spur to research. Working in an area, it is sometimes extremely clear that everyone seems to be getting it wrong! Perhaps all the local professionals are following an interpretation more relevant to an old form of recently amended legislation. Perhaps a new system is incomplete in regard to the outcomes expected because of a step being missed in a process.

* Consider keeping a log of how much writing you are doing. This will at least alert you to the fact that you are spending more time making coffee and answering emails than powering through your first draft. The research journal is a vital part of your writing. In it, you can jot down stray thoughts to follow up later, or cites you come across when completing other work. Here, also, you can track the file name changes or chapter segment movements, as well as the large conceptual leaps that occur all too infrequently.

* Ask a friend or colleague or supervisor to read your work. Often, this is a way of generating the 'intellectual energy' needed to focus the discussion. Writing can be a very lonely business and often the simple exercise of talking about what you are doing can reveal new insights into the topic. This is an important function that a research assistant might perform. Ask the assistant to read the draft, checking for any obvious gaps in the flow of the argument. Perhaps you might also ask for a list of up to 10 arguments they can come up with against the position you have taken on the topic. Ask that person to point out anything that they cannot understand or writing that seems unclear. Sometimes a simple self-reflection can help here too. Ask yourself 'What have I achieved in this? What have I not achieved so well?'[29]

* Publicise your plans. Although you may find it tiring to explain your work to others, the constant summarising and fielding of questions will provide encouragement (even if it is simply to complete so the questions will cease!).

---

27 Nightingale P, 'Initiation into research through writing' in Zuber-Skerritt O, *Starting Research — Supervision and Training* (Brisbane: The Tertiary Education Institute, University of Queensland, 1992), 176.

28 Murray R, *How to Write a Thesis* (Buckingham (England); Philadelphia: Open University Press, 2002).

29 Adapted from Yeatman A, 'Making supervision relationships accountable: graduate student logs' (1995) 2 *Australian Universities' Review* 11.

* Join a research support group. Use these meetings to find out useful peer information about the processes in your university. How long have other students at your university taken to complete their projects? Talk about your progress with your peers. This can provide a great impetus to action.

* Submit your research to scrutiny through presenting a conference paper. This will give you a precise deadline and there is nothing quite like the knowledge that you are going to be standing in front of your peers to focus your mind on the task at hand. You need to ensure that the topic of the paper is within your original thesis though, so you are not taken too far off track in regard to your main project.

The main issue to bear in mind is that in order to write it is necessary to 'start'. So the first draft is vital, although you need not begin the first draft with the introduction. It is preferable to start with a segment that interests you at the time, than to sit at your desk waiting for that perfect first sentence to leap into your mind. Of course, the first sentence to a short piece may be vital. That is where you draw the reader into your topic. However, it pays to be reasonably kind to yourself. Be flexible. Do the heavy 'thinking' aspects of your work when you are fresh, and tackle more mundane tasks when you are feeling jaded, rather than sticking to an immutable plan.

While it is important to research and collect all the recent relevant materials, it is also necessary to synthesise the material collected. Take direct quotes and paraphrase the results of others' writing, but while doing this try to meld the information into your thesis. Decide whether you are going to include your research results directly into your first draft, or have a separate research notes document from which you can cut and paste relevant material. Most writers agree to the need for quiet thinking time before trying to write. Reflection time is when the issues become clearer and the words begin to make sense.

A regular writing schedule can certainly aid the writing process. Choose a regular time and place that suits your needs, whether it is from midnight to 4 am at the kitchen table or in the Sheraton coffee shop every lunch hour. Successful authors will suggest that there is a need to trick yourself into being productive, so that writing becomes a pleasurable experience, perhaps because of the quietness and tranquillity of your surroundings, or because of the personal rewards you allow yourself when your personal target has been completed.

8.6 Polishing, rewriting and revising the first draft

Having produced a first draft, the rewriting stage becomes easier. The gaps in the progression of your ideas will become obvious, as will the inadequacies of organisation and progression of topics. Mary Ray and Barbara Cox have produced the following Checklist to use in reviewing your own work. Pretend you have been requested to referee your own work. What comments would you deliver to the author?

Editing your own material is not pleasant. By the time you come to the final stages, you tend to be heartily sick of the research topic and there is a temptation to sign off too quickly. Having researched and read everything on the topic, processed the information, outlined an argument and written it down, it sometimes becomes stale. Often, the material has already gone through many reincarnations — drafts and redrafts.

However, editing is important. If you have time, put the material down for at least a week before you try to edit it. Editing ensures that what you have written down is what you wanted to say. These are the final touches that will ensure your document looks polished. Sometimes it helps if you read it several times, looking for different things each time. Here are some points to check.

CHECKLIST FOR REWRITING

1 Content and ideas

  (a) Is the law right?

  (b) Have I included all the relevant issues?

  (c) Have I included all the relevant research?

  (d) Have I updated all the research?

  (e) Have I included all the necessary background information?

  (f) Have I eliminated those points that I found while doing my research but do not add to the document?

2 Large-scale organisation

  (a) Do I have logical organisation?

  (b) Have I provided an overview so that the reader can understand how my paper progresses from introduction to conclusion?

  (c) Have I put threshold issues first?

  (d) Have I given the answer first and then the explanation?

  (e) If writing persuasively, have I organised the issues in the most persuasive order, putting the strongest first, the second strongest last, and the weakest in the middle, unless logical organisation precludes doing this?

  (f) Can any legal reader follow my logic?

  (g) Can the intended reader follow my logic?

  (h) Have I used positions of emphasis well?[30]

First, look at the footnotes. Are the references complete? Are all the page numbers and spot references there? Are there sections in the text that warrant extra footnotes? Do they conform to accepted cite formats — or the style guide that has been set for you to use? Are they self-explanatory? Are there any dead-end references where you might have referred to a previous footnote in an earlier draft, and then moved text without changing the footnote? Are the fonts the correct size and style? This is fairly mechanical but can be a very time-consuming business.

---

30 Ray MB and Ramsfield J, *Beyond the Basics: A Text for Advanced Legal Writing* (2 ed, St Paul: West Publishing, 2003), 417–418.

Next, read the paper again for grammatical errors. Check the tense of the verbs and that these agree with the subjects. Look out for spelling and punctuation errors. Is your language precise? Use the word-processing software underlining alerts to help check spelling and grammar errors. Perhaps try reading the paper aloud. Do the words flow?

Now look at the technical structure of your writing. Make certain the sentences are not too long, and that paragraphs include at least three sentences. Is there a main idea developed in each paragraph? Are there sufficient headings and subheadings? Are there plenty of linking words between sections to enhance the flow of ideas? Ensure there is a clear introduction and conclusion.

Finally, read the paper again, but this time to check the logical flow of your argument or thesis. Have you stated your points clearly? Sometimes, at this point it becomes apparent that the progression of your thoughts and the intricacies of argument would be unclear to a reader. Perhaps you need to contextualise the issues more clearly at the beginning. If possible, have someone else read the draft. It does not really matter whether or not they know about the topic. For most purposes, any reader will be able to pick out flaws and shortfalls in the logical development of the discussion.

A more detailed Checklist looking more towards form and language appears in another of Ray's texts:

CHECKLIST FOR REVISING

1 **Accuracy**

No amount of readability will replace accuracy, so make sure you check first for the content of each legal point. Ask yourself the following questions.

(a) Is the content accurately stated. Could any points be misinterpreted because of ambiguity?

(b) Are irrelevant facts or other irrelevant information excluded?

(c) Are terms of art used correctly?

(d) Are key terms used correctly?

(e) Are paraphrases accurate?

(f) Are names of parties and their status correct?

(g) Are the citations accurate? Are pinpoint cites used for specific propositions, rules, holdings, quotes? Are case names spelled accurately? Are page numbers and years accurate?

2 **Small-scale organisation**

(a) Are paragraphs internally logical?

(b) Are there topic sentences that give the overall message of each of the paragraphs, usually at the beginning of the paragraphs?

(c) Are there clear and precise transitions between paragraphs?

(d) Are there strong transitions between sentences?

3 **Readability**

   (a) Are subjects and verbs close together?

   (b) Is there more active voice than passive voice?

   (c) Are sentences free of nominalisation?

   (d) Are unnecessary modifiers eliminated, such as clearly and obviously?

   (e) Are sentences overly long?

   (f) Are lists clearly structured?

   (g) Are unnecessary prepositional phrases eliminated?

   (h) Is the text generally concise?

4 **Style**

   (a) Is style consistently objective or persuasive, depending upon the purpose of the text?

   (b) Is the tone and level of formality appropriate and consistent?[31]

8.7 Style and grammar

By this stage, most students and particularly most postgraduate law students have spent several years studying English expression, grammar and creative writing or business communication. Some of the platitudes have already been known and forgotten. Good advice has been heard and ignored — avoid legalese, be concise, get to the point, and especially use active voice.

8.7.1 *Paragraph construction, punctuation, spelling and grammar*

* Make efficient use of the white space, and ensure the layout of the writing, formatting, font size, and placement on the page enhance the document's readability.

* Use a full correct cite for cases and legislation at the beginning of the document and then consider shortening the references. *John v Smith, Roper, Jeffreys and Keys* might be referred to simply as John's Case. However, beware of the overuse of acronyms, especially when referring to various pieces of legislation. These can become very confusing for the reader.

* Read through your document. Edit and tighten the language so that unnecessary words are removed.

* Make certain your sentences (and words) are clear and unambiguous in what they say. Be concise and use one word instead of several if it does not alter the meaning, for example

      Take into consideration   Consider

      Come to the conclusion   Conclude[32]

---

31 Ray MB and Ramsfield J, *Beyond the Basics: A Text for Advanced Legal Writing* (2 ed, St Paul: West Publishing, 2003), 417–419.

32 Adler M, *Clarity for Lawyers: The Use of Plain English in Writing* (London: The Law Society, 1990), 51.

* Use a dictionary and thesaurus to extend your vocabulary and vary terminology and nuances in the language used.

* Use the right words. The words 'effect' and 'affect' are ones that are often misspelled and confused in my experience. Another is the phrase 'just deserts' in referencing to principles of sentencing. Perhaps you are aware of your own personal spelling 'bugbears'. Be conscious of your own spelling and grammar weaknesses, and try to check for them specifically.

> effect (noun) means result
>
> effect (verb) to cause
>
> affect (verb) to influence[33]

* Use the right prepositions, for example:

> emigrate **from**
>
> immigrate **to**
>
> hint **at**[34]

* Refer the words 'this' or 'that' to a noun so that there is no confusion in your writing, for example, 'This' is wrong'! What exactly is wrong?

* Use the same word at the beginning of a list like this one!

* Use positive statements rather than negative ones.

* Use the correct tense.

* Use shorter sentences.

* Use linking words between the paragraphs and between different sections of the document so that your argument flows through the document.

* Use an introduction and a conclusion to the whole document and to sections or chapters within the document.

* Use the appropriate voice rather than always choosing the 'objective' third person. Lawyers tend not to use the first person pronoun 'I'. Sometimes it is most appropriate, for example, in a narrative. On no account, use the 'querist', a quaint term that used to appear frequently in barrister's briefs.

* Use active voice by preference. Sometimes it is appropriate to use passive voice; for example, when a writer has reason to focus on the 'receiver of action'. Ronald Goldfarb points out that this can be a way of suppressing information and gives the example 'Mary was sued' — which does not disclose who sued her.[35] The statement 'John sued Mary' tells a slightly different story. The active style tends to be a personal style; simple, easy to read, informative and specific, clear and precise, direct, with short sentences. The passive style, on the other hand, is an official style; ponderous, heavy to read, evasive and vague, ambiguous, indirect, with long sentences.[36]

---

33 Smith R, *The Literate Lawyer: Legal Writing and Oral Advocacy* (2 ed, Butterworths Legal Publishers, 1991). See a list of common mistakes in Chapter 11 'The Right (or Wrong) Word' 43-68; See also the list of commonly confused words in Rylance P, *Legal Writing and Drafting* (London: Blackstone Press, 1994), 61-62.

34 Smith R, *The Literate Lawyer: Legal Writing and Oral Advocacy* (2 ed, Butterworths Legal Publishers, 1991). See Appendix A 181/182 for several common examples.

35 Goldfarb R and Raymond J, *Clear Understandings: A Guide to Legal Writing* (New York: Random House, 1982), 14.

36 Rylance P, *Legal Writing & Drafting* (London: Blackstone Press Limited, 1994), 7.

8.7.2 *Gender neutral language*

In the early twentieth century, the law was 'gendered' to the point that women were not considered to be 'persons' under the legislation providing for admission to practice in some Australian jurisdictions. Paradoxically, in that context, much legal writing was also written in terms of the masculine gender only. The masculine was generally assumed to include the feminine. In the twenty-first century, gender neutral language is the norm. Here are some suggestions for avoiding awkward phrasing:

* Try to avoid gender-specific titles, such as chairman, policeman — instead use chair, police officer.
* Use the noun instead of the pronoun — 'the student' instead of 'he' or 'she'.
* Try to avoid s/he.
* Use a plural instead of singular phrase — 'their books' rather than 'his books'.
* Use an anonymous article rather than a gendered possessive — 'the' car rather than 'his' car.
* Use second person — 'You' must go to your chambers, rather than the barrister must go to 'his' chambers.

More generally, it is important to avoid sexist stereotyping of people in your writing. Remember the story about the surgeon who was actually the patient's mother but nobody ever realises it? It is very easy to slip into a gendered mode — but this can be extremely offputting for your readers.

8.7.3 *When to use quotes*

When it comes to using quotes, it pays to remember Ronald Goldfarb's rule, 'use other people's written work incidentally and deftly'.[37] Jeffrey Williams recounts being cured of over-quoting by comments that came back to him on a philosophy paper he had written on Aristotle —'You have Aristotle almost letter perfect, although I don't know if I should give the grade to you or to Aristotle'.[38] Your writing should not be a pastiche of quotes. Try to limit the length of your quotes, and only use someone else's words when they say something better than you can, or when the words put an idea totally succinctly. Only include small pieces from others' work, and only those small parts that are truly worth quoting because they say something in a pithy way, or because they encapsulate an idea well.

So this leads to some basic rules to bear in mind when you are using others' material:

* Make sure that there is more of your commentary in your work than quotes from others' writing — even one quarter of the total is too much.
* Never begin a paragraph with a quote.

---

37 Goldfarb R and Raymond J, *Clear Understandings: A Guide to Legal Writing* (New York: Random House, 1982), Chapter 7.
38 Williams J, 'Alchemy in the Academy' (*The Australian* Higher Education Wednesday October 17 2007), 36.

* Always introduce a quote and explain its importance to the reader and where it fits into your discussion.
* Never end a paragraph abruptly with a quote — explain how this adds to the points you are trying to make.

8.7.4 How do you acknowledge sources?

Part of the skill of academic writing lies in being able to adhere to a citation guide. There are various aspects that arise in relation to acknowledging others' intellectual input in your writing. Most legal writing includes reference to primary materials and these are usually cited in the footnotes. These need to be referenced correctly.

There are now several Australian citation guides available and an Australian legal citation standard will eventually emanate from this group — a Bluebook[39] degree of acceptance by Australian law faculties. The frontrunner at present is the *Australian Guide to Legal Citation*. It is worthwhile to have some choice though, and even in the United States *The Bluebook* is facing competition from the *American Legal Writing Directors' Manual*.[40]

The Australian guides include the following:

* *Australian Guide to Legal Citation* (2 ed, Melbourne: Melbourne University Law Review Association, 2002).
* Campbell E and Fox R, *Students' Guide to Legal Writing and Law Exams* (3 ed, Sydney: The Federation Press, 2010).
* Fong C, *Australian Legal Citation — A Guide* (St Leonards: Prospect Media, 1997).
* Rozenberg P, *Australian Guide to Uniform Legal Citation* (2 ed, Sydney: LBC Information Services, 2003).
* Stuhmcke A, *Legal Referencing* (3 ed, Sydney: Butterworths, 2005).

Remember, too, the standard guides that were the only resources available prior to the new rash of offerings:

* Australian Government Information Management Office, *Style Manual for Authors, Editors and Printers* (6 ed, Brisbane: John Wiley and Sons, 2002).
* Campbell E and Kewley G, *Presentation of Legal Theses* (3 ed, Clayton, Victoria: Faculty of Law, Monash University, 1996).

Some of the noteworthy international offerings include:

* Columbia Law Review, Harvard Law Review Association, The University of Pennsylvania Law Review, *The Bluebook: A Uniform System of Citation* (18 ed, Cambridge, Mass: Harvard Law Review Association, 2005).
* Dickerson D, *ALWD Citation Manual: A Professional System of Citation* (3 ed, New York: Aspen Publishers Inc, 2006).
* French D, *How to Cite Legal Authorities* (London: Blackstone Press Limited, 1996).

---

39 Columbia Law Review, Harvard Law Review Association, The University of Pennsylvania Law Review, *The Bluebook: A Uniform System of Citation* (18 ed, Cambridge, Mass: Harvard Law Review Association, 2005).

40 Dickerson D, *ALWD Citation Manual: A Professional System of Citation* (3 ed, New York: Aspen Publishers Inc, 2006).

The current emphasis is on citations becoming vendor (and medium) neutral.[41] Many of the Australian courts have adopted medium neutral styles. The High Court of Australia has commenced the use of paragraph numbers in court judgments based on the following format:

> *Smith v Jones* [1998] HCA 99 at 17 covering the parties, the year of the decision, the Court abbreviation, the judgment number issued by the court, and an applicable paragraph number or pinpoint reference. This citation format is to operate in conjunction with the traditional methods.[42]

Medium neutral citation will make finding alternative cites for a document much easier, as a standard citation will allow the user to search for the item using one of the legal search engines available on the web. These rules will work alongside the older formats. The accepted citation rules such as citing to the authorised reports where these are available and proper use of the square and round brackets will remain important.[43]

Transience is a major concern with electronic citations. The website 'address' may be transient or may change over time. Often, material is only placed on a bulletin board for a limited time in any case. There is also the issue of 'invisible revisability' to contend with. This applies when articles are edited over time by the author, which makes it important that those citing include the date that they accessed the article. The best solution is to give the reader as much information as possible about your source, which can be an article on a home-page or government site, a reported or unreported case, legislation, messages from a discussion list or newsgroup, personal email, or online service documents. In this environment, the old caution that a reader should be able to locate the material 10 years hence using no more than the cite before them sounds excessively optimistic, no matter how particular you might be in this regard.[44]

Therefore, you need to approach the task of choosing your citation style guide with some very basic criteria in mind. Some of these are:

---

41 In 'The impact of the Internet on legal bibliography' in (1998) 46 *American Journal of Comparative Law* 665, Peter Maggs differentiates between medium neutral cites that are not linked to a specific volume and year of a published report, and public domain cites relating to material that is copyright free (where the copyright does not reside in a specific publisher).

42 Australian Law Reform Commission, *Technology — What it means for Federal Dispute Resolution* (Issues Paper No 23 Chapter 4 Technology in Legal Practice and Legal Publishing, Sydney: ALRC, 1998) http://www.austlii.edu.au/au/other/alrc/publications/issues/23/04.html#Head-20 (5/11/2009). For Canada: *A Neutral Citation Standard for Case Law* http://www.lexum.umontreal.ca/ccc-ccr/neutr/neutr.jur_en.html (5/11/2009). Kennedy B, 'Cultural Considerations Behind Neutral Citations for the International Legal Community' (2000) 3 *Journal of Information Law & Technology* http://www2.warwick.ac.uk/fac/soc/law/elj/jilt/2000_3/kennedy/ (5/11/2009).

43 Square bracket rule — Use round brackets around the year the case was handed down when the volumes of cases are numbered. Use square brackets when the year is essential to locating the volume on the shelf.

44 Internet archives are accessible since the launch of *The Internet Archive* http://www.archive.org/index.php (5/11/2009).

* Accessibility — Look for a cite guide that is simple and accessible to use. Citation is a sideline interest rather than a substantive concern, so you do not want to waste time looking for information. If you are looking for a cite point, then it is preferable to have access to the rules source quickly and specifically. An excellent detailed index and an accessible layout will be of most importance to the cite style user.

* Completeness — Most people will turn to the guide for the really 'thorny' issues, so too many follow-up references to more complete guides or separate guides for other jurisdictions are extremely frustrating. In addition, completeness of the actual record cited aids the reader. Cites should include all the necessary information so that the reader can assess the authority cited in terms of author, date, edition, publisher and jurisdiction of publication. A cite style that neglects to advise publication jurisdiction may be insufficient for some needs, unless there are fuller references in the Bibliography.

* Efficiency — Many students type their own materials — or pay for someone else's time to do so. Unnecessary punctuation adds time and cost to the finished product, so it would seem that the modern conventions should be used to omit brackets, commas, full stops and unnecessary punctuation.

* Reference to prior notes — A confusing aspect in using footnote references lies in the use of the Latin tags, such as 'supra', 'op cit' and 'loc cit'. Even 'See Above' can lead to a futile tracking through previous pages. It is wasteful to repeat heavily used cites in full, but a clear method for referring to prior notes is paramount. Perhaps in the era of 'cut and paste' technology, repetition has merit.

* New electronic formats — Provision must be made for citation from all sources, such as internet websites, email discussion lists, online subscriptions, and personal interviews.

* Historical style foundation — The modern world thrives on choice but, even so, many writers prefer to use the citation style they have become accustomed to rather than learn an altogether different way of doing things. After all, it really does not matter to the reader what order the various elements of the cite appear in — as long as all the details are present and correct, and providing there is some internal consistency in the document. There may be a natural inclination to use the style you have used in the past. Of course, it is more efficient for you, as a researcher, to learn a particular style and use it in all writing than use a variety of styles.

* Interdisciplinary work — The social science rules using in-text references have been scorned by lawyers; however, many interdisciplinary journals now use this method as a matter of course. Your guide should include a basic guide about the 'other' way of doing things.

* Legal eccentricities — Legal research sources are 'different', especially in regard to the rules governing case names and legislation, so be sure you choose a specifically legal style guide rather than a general guide, so that the intricacies of the various legal materials are covered fully.[45]

---

45 Specialist manuals are also available. See Haxton N, *A Manual on Law Reporting* (Sydney: The Federation Press, 1991).

* Examples — Cite rules are tedious and confusing if they are not accompanied by many examples. Look for a guide with plenty of examples. This also clarifies any inadequacies in the explanations.

* Quick guides — Many times a researcher will reach for the guide to check on a small point; for example, whether to include a full stop or a comma or double quotation marks, bearing in mind that any unnecessary punctuation should have been eliminated. A 'Quick Basic Guide' in the front or back of the volume is most useful for these times.

Lawyers and law students are taught to question and analyse, and so it seems absurd to present a detailed and intricate set of legal citation rules without also presenting an explanation of the underlying rationale. A complete guide will address this issue and include information and examples on how and where to use citation, and also why. The 'why' is to facilitate further understanding, critique and research by the reader and also serves to aid the writer to avoid plagiarism.

Citation relates to acknowledging published ideas. This issue was discussed in Chapter One. There are a few standard rules to abide by:

* If direct words are taken from other written work, put them in inverted quotations and footnote the spot reference.

* If ideas from elsewhere are paraphrased and used, footnote this use.

* If other researchers work on a project, ensure their contribution is acknowledged accordingly.[46]

And remember that there are new software tools now available to aid in reference checking.[47] These allow searches using large pieces of text. Such search engines can be used to locate the most recent editions of a document on the web. They can also be used to check for plagiarised material.[48]

8.8 Conclusion

This chapter concludes the substantive part of the text. This book has covered the changing context of legal research, doctrinal and non-doctrinal methodologies, including the associated areas of theoretical, reform-oriented and policy research, basic electronic research techniques, formulating research proposals and the final tips on writing. This is a vast canvas to cover and no doubt many areas of interest might have warranted further coverage. Perhaps they might be picked up for more detailed examination in the future. Hopefully this material will inform and enhance the success of your research endeavours!

---

46 An example of a case of alleged academic plagiarism is contained in the case of *Re La Trobe University; Ex parte Wild* [1987] VR 447 where it was held at 455 that 'plagiarism committed entirely as a result of carelessness or negligence might be held to amount to gross misconduct in a professor although there was no moral culpability in the plagiarism at all'.

47 See for example Turnitin http://www.turnitin.com/static/home.html (5/11/2009).

48 There are several sites available on plagiarism, for example, Stoerger S, 'Plagiarism' http://www.web-miner.com/plagiarism (5/11/2009). See Chapter One for a fuller discussion of research ethics and plagiarism.

Further reading

Asprey M, *Plain Language for Lawyers* (3 ed, Sydney: The Federation Press, 2003).

Brogan M and Spencer D, *Surviving Law School* (2 ed, South Melbourne, Vic: Oxford University Press, 2008).

Buranen L and Roy A (eds), *Perspectives on Plagiarism and Intellectual Property in a Postmodern World* (Albany: State University of New York Press, 1999).

Cremmins E, *The Art of Abstracting* (Philadelphia: ISI Press, 1982).

Edwards L, *Legal Writing, Process Analysis and Organisation* (3 ed, New York: Aspen Law and Business, 2002).

Elphinstone L and Schweitzer R, *How to Get a Research Degree: A Survival Guide* (Sydney: Allen & Unwin, 1998).

Evans D, *How to Write a Better Thesis or Report* (2 ed, Melbourne: Melbourne University Press, 2002).

Fairbairn G and Fairbairn S, *Writing Your Abstract: A Guide for would-be conference presenters* (Salisbury: APS, 2002).

Garner B, *The Elements of Legal Style* (2 ed, New York: Oxford University Press, 2002).

Goldberg N, *Writing Down the Bones* (Boston: Shambhala, 1986).

Hairston M, *Successful Writing* (5 ed, New York: Norton, 2003).

Jewinski E and Jewinski J, *How to Write an Executive Summary* (Ottawa: University of Ottawa Press, 1990).

Katz L, *Winning Words: A Guide to Persuasive Writing for Lawyers* (New York: Law & Business Inc Harcourt Brace Jovanovich, 1986).

Lewis G, *Critical Communication* (Sydney: Prentice-Hall, 1994).

Macdonald R and Clark-Dickson, *Clear and Precise: Writing Skills for Today's Lawyers* (2 ed, Pyrmont: Thomson, 2005).

Meehan M and Tulloch G, *Grammar for Lawyers* (2 ed, Chatswood, NSW: Butterworths, 2007).

Murray R, *How to write a Thesis* (2 ed, Maidenhead; New York: Open University Press, 2006).

Murumba S, 'Good legal writing: A guide for the perplexed' (1991) 17 (1) *Monash University Law Review* 93.

Neumann R, *Legal Reasoning and Legal Writing: Structure, Strategy and Style* (4 ed, New York: Aspen Publishers Inc, 2001).

Oates LC and Enquist A, *The Legal Writing Handbook: Analysis, Research, and Writing* (4 ed, New York: Aspen Publishers, 2006).

Osland D, *Writing in Australia: A Composition Course for Tertiary Students* (Sydney: Harcourt Brace Janovich, 1991).

Perrin T, *Better Writing for Lawyers* (Toronto: Law Society of Upper Canada, 1990).

Petelin R and Durham M, *The Professional Writing Guide: Writing Well and Knowing Why* (Warriewood, NSW: Business Professional Publishing, 1998).

Preece RA, *Starting Research: An Introduction to Academic Research and Dissertation Writing* (London: Printer Publishers, 1994).

Rylance P, *Legal Writing and Drafting* (London: Blackstone Press Limited, 1994).

Samuelson P, 'Good legal writing: Of Orwell and window panes' (1984) 46 *University of Pittsburg Law Review* 149.

Schultz N and Siricol L, *Legal Writing and Other Lawyering Skills* (4 ed, New York: Matthew Bender, 2004).

Seely J, *The Oxford Guide to Writing and Speaking* (Oxford: Oxford University Press, 1998).

Shapo H, *Writing and Analysis in the Law* (4 ed, New York: Foundation Press, 1999).

Stark S, *Writing to Win: The Legal Writer* (New York: Doubleday, 2000).

Zuber-Skerritt O (ed), *Starting Research: Supervision and Training* (Brisbane: The Tertiary Education Institute, University of Queensland, 1992).

PART II

Checklists for Locating and Validating the Law

Part II — Table of Contents

1 General — *How Do You Find* 227
  1.1 Abbreviations Lists? 227
  1.2 The Meaning of Particular Legal Words and Phrases? 230
  1.3 Law Reform Publications? 233
  1.4 Books on a Particular Topic? 234
  1.5 Theses? 239
  1.6 Journal Articles on Specific Subjects/Cases/Legislation? 241
  1.7 International Treaties and Conventions? 244
  1.8 Comparative Law? 250
  1.9 Alert Services? 252
  1.10 Conferences? 253
  1.11 Citation Style Guides? 254
  1.12 Archival Material on the Internet? 256
  1.13 Journal Rankings? 258
  1.14 Personal Citation Data? 258

2 Australia — *How Do You Find* 261
  2.1 An Introduction to the Jurisdiction? 261
  2.2 A Broad Picture of Australian Law? 263
  2.3 Parliamentary Publications? 264
  2.4 Bills? 270
  2.5 Explanatory Material about Bills? 273
  2.6 A Subject Index to Legislation? 277
  2.7 The Commencement Date of Legislation? 277
  2.8 Commonwealth Legislation in Full Text? 280
  2.9 Updates for Legislation? 282
  2.10 A Subject Index to Delegated Legislation? 285
  2.11 Full Text of Delegated Legislation? 286
  2.12 A Subject Index to Cases? 288
  2.13 Full Text of Commonwealth Cases? 289
  2.14 Cases that have been Judicially Considered? 294
  2.15 Cases that have Dealt with Specific Legislative Sections? 296

3   **Australian Capital Territory — *How Do You Find*** 301
     3.1   An Introduction to the Jurisdiction?. 301
     3.2   Parliamentary Publications? 301
     3.3   Bills? 303
     3.4   Explanatory Material about Bills? 303
     3.5   A Subject Index to Legislation? 304
     3.6   The Commencement Date of Legislation? 304
     3.7   Australian Capital Territory Legislation in Full Text? 305
     3.8   Updates for Legislation? 305
     3.9   A Subject Index to Delegated Legislation? 306
     3.10   Full Text of Delegated Legislation?. 306
     3.11   A Subject Index to Cases? 306
     3.12   Full Text of Australian Capital Territory Cases? 307
     3.13   Cases that have been Judicially Considered?. 307
     3.14   Cases that have Dealt with Specific Legislative Sections? 308

4   **New South Wales — *How Do You Find*** 309
     4.1   An Introduction to the Jurisdiction?. 309
     4.2   Parliamentary Publications? 309
     4.3   Bills? 311
     4.4   Explanatory Material About Bills? 311
     4.5   A Subject Index to Legislation? 312
     4.6   The Commencement Date of Legislation? 312
     4.7   New South Wales Legislation in Full Text? 313
     4.8   Updates for Legislation? 314
     4.9   Subject Index to Delegated Legislation? 314
     4.10   Full Text of Delegated Legislation?. 315
     4.11   A Subject Index to Cases? 316
     4.12   Full Text of New South Wales Cases?. 316
     4.13   Cases that have been Judicially Considered?. 319
     4.14   Cases that have Dealt with Specific Legislative Sections? 319

5   **Northern Territory — *How Do You Find*** 321
     5.1   An Introduction to the Jurisdiction?. 321
     5.2   Parliamentary Publications? 321
     5.3   Bills? 322
     5.4   Explanatory Material about Bills? 323
     5.5   A Subject Index to Legislation? 323
     5.6   The Commencement Date of Legislation? 323
     5.7   Northern Territory Legislation in Full Text?. 324
     5.8   Updates for Legislation? 325
     5.9   A Subject Index to Delegated Legislation? 325
     5.10   Full Text of Delegated Legislation?. 325
     5.11   A Subject Index to Cases? 326
     5.12   Full Text of Northern Territory Cases? 326
     5.13   Cases that have been Judicially Considered?. 327
     5.14   Cases that have Dealt with Specific Legislative Sections? 327

6 Queensland — *How Do You Find* 329
   6.1   An Introduction to the Jurisdiction?. 329
   6.2   Parliamentary Publications? 329
   6.3   Bills? 332
   6.4   Explanatory Material about Bills? 333
   6.5   A Subject Index to Legislation? 334
   6.6   The Commencement Date of Legislation? 334
   6.7   Queensland Legislation in Full Text? 335
   6.8   Updates for Legislation? 338
   6.9   A Subject Index to Delegated Legislation? 338
   6.10   Full Text of Delegated Legislation?. 339
   6.11   A Subject Index to Cases? 340
   6.12   Full Text of Queensland Cases? 341
   6.13   Cases that have been Judicially Considered?. 344
   6.14   Cases that have Dealt with Specific Legislative Sections? 344

7 South Australia — *How Do You Find* 347
   7.1   An Introduction to the Jurisdiction?. 347
   7.2   Parliamentary Publications? 347
   7.3   Bills? 349
   7.4   Explanatory Material About Bills? 350
   7.5   A Subject Index to Legislation? 351
   7.6   The Commencement Date of Legislation? 352
   7.7   South Australian Legislation in Full Text?. 353
   7.8   Updates for Legislation? 353
   7.9   A Subject Index to Delegated Legislation? 354
   7.10   Full Text of Delegated Legislation?. 355
   7.11   A Subject Index to Cases? 355
   7.12   Full Text of South Australian Cases? 356
   7.13   Cases that have been Judicially Considered?. 357
   7.14   Cases that have Dealt with Specific Legislative Sections? 357

8 Tasmania — *How Do You Find* 359
   8.1   An Introduction to the Jurisdiction?. 359
   8.2   Parliamentary Publications? 359
   8.3   Bills? 361
   8.4   Explanatory Notes about Bills? 361
   8.5   A Subject Index to Legislation? 361
   8.6   The Commencement Date of Legislation? 362
   8.7   Tasmanian Legislation in Full Text? 362
   8.8   Updates for Legislation? 363
   8.9   A Subject Index to Delegated Legislation? 363
   8.10   Full Text of Delegated Legislation?. 363
   8.11   A Subject Index to Cases? 364
   8.12   Full Text of Tasmanian Cases?. 365
   8.13   Cases that have been Judicially Considered?. 365
   8.14   Cases that have Dealt with Specific Legislative Sections? 366

9   **Victoria — *How Do You Find*** 367
    9.1   An Introduction to the Jurisdiction?. 367
    9.2   Parliamentary Publications? 367
    9.3   Bills? 368
    9.4   Explanatory Material about Bills? 369
    9.5   A Subject Index to Legislation? 369
    9.6   The Commencement Date of Legislation? 370
    9.7   Victorian Legislation in Full Text?. 371
    9.8   Updates for Legislation? 372
    9.9   A Subject Index to Delegated Legislation? 373
    9.10   Full Text of Delegated Legislation?. 374
    9.11   A Subject Index to Cases? 375
    9.12   Full Text of Victorian Cases? 376
    9.13   Cases that have been Judicially Considered?. 376
    9.14   Cases that have Dealt with Specific Legislative Sections? 377

10 **Western Australia — *How Do You Find*** 379
    10.1   An Introduction to the Jurisdiction?. 379
    10.2   Parliamentary Publications? 379
    10.3   Bills? 381
    10.4   Explanatory Material about Bills? 381
    10.5   A Subject Index to Legislation? 381
    10.6   The Commencement Date of Legislation? 382
    10.7   Western Australian Legislation in Full Text? 383
    10.8   Updates for Legislation? 383
    10.9   A Subject Index to Delegated Legislation? 384
    10.10   Full Text of Delegated Legislation?. 384
    10.11   A Subject Index to Cases? 385
    10.12   Full Text of Western Australian Cases?. 385
    10.13   Cases that have been Judicially Considered?. 386
    10.14   Cases that have Dealt with Specific Legislative Sections? 386

11 **England — *How Do You Find*** 387
    11.1   An Introduction to the Jurisdiction?. 387
    11.2   A Broad Picture of English Law? 389
    11.3   Parliamentary Publications? 389
    11.4   Bills? 394
    11.5   Explanatory Material about Bills? 396
    11.6   A Subject Index to Legislation? 397
    11.7   The Commencement Date for Legislation?. 398
    11.8   English Legislation in Full Text? 400
    11.9   Updates for Legislation? 401
    11.10   A Subject Index to Delegated Legislation? 402
    11.11   Full Text of Delegated Legislation?. 402
    11.12   A Subject Index to Cases? 403
    11.13   Full Text of English Cases?. 404
    11.14   Cases that have been Judicially Considered?. 407
    11.15   Cases that have Dealt with Specific Legislative Sections? 408

12 Canada — *How Do You Find* 409
   12.1   An Introduction to the Jurisdiction?. 409
   12.2   A Broad Picture of the Law? 411
   12.3   Parliamentary Publications? 411
   12.4   Bills? 417
   12.5   Explanatory Material about Bills? 418
   12.6   A Subject Index to Legislation? 419
   12.7   Commencement Date of Legislation?. 420
   12.8   Canadian Legislation in Full Text? 421
   12.9   Updates for Legislation? 423
   12.10 A Subject Index to Delegated Legislation? 424
   12.11 Full Text of Delegated Legislation?. 424
   12.12 A Subject Index to Cases? 426
   12.13 Full Text of Canadian Cases?. 426
   12.14 General Caselaw? 429
   12.15 Cases that have been Judicially Considered?. 429
   12.16 Cases that have Dealt with Specific Legislative Sections? 430

13 United States — *How Do You Find*. 431
   13.1   An Introduction to the Jurisdiction?. 431
   13.2   A Broad Picture of the Law? 434
   13.3   Congressional Publications? 435
   13.4   Bills? 439
   13.5   Explanatory Material about Bills? 440
   13.6   A Subject Index to Legislation? 442
   13.7   The Commencement Date of Legislation? 443
   13.8   United States Legislation in Full Text? 444
   13.9   Updates for Legislation? 445
   13.10 A Subject Index to Delegated Legislation? 446
   13.11 Full Text of Delegated Legislation?. 447
   13.12 A Subject Index to Cases? 449
   13.13 Full Text of United States Cases? 451
   13.14 Cases that have been Judicially Considered?. 456
   13.15 Cases that have Dealt with Specific Legislative Sections? 457

14 European Union Law — *How Do You Find* 459
   14.1   An Introduction to the Jurisdiction?. 459
   14.2   A Broad Picture of European Union Law? 461
   14.3   European Community Publications? 462
   14.4   Bills? 469
   14.5   Explanatory Material about Bills? 471
   14.6   A Subject Index to Legislation? 472
   14.7   The Commencement Date of Legislation? 473
   14.8   Legislation in Full Text?. 473
   14.9   Updates for Legislation? 475
   14.10 Subject Index to Delegated Legislation?. 476
   14.11 A Subject Index to Cases? 477
   14.12 Full Text of European Union Cases?. 478
   14.13 Cases that have been Judicially Considered?. 480
   14.14 Cases that have Dealt with Specific Legislative Sections? 481
   14.15 Dictionaries and Directories? 481
   14.16 Journal Articles and Commentary? 482

15 New Zealand — *How Do You Find* 483

    15.1   An Introduction to the Jurisdiction? 483

    15.2   A Broad Picture of New Zealand Law? 484

    15.3   Parliamentary Publications? 484

    15.4   Bills? 486

    15.5   Explanatory Material about Bills? 488

    15.6   A Subject Index to Legislation? 488

    15.7   Commencement Date for Legislation? 488

    15.8   New Zealand Legislation in Full Text? 489

    15.9   Updates for Legislation? 489

    15.10 A Subject Index to Delegated Legislation? 490

    15.11 Full Text of Delegated Legislation? 490

    15.12 A Subject Index to Cases? 491

    15.13 Full Text of New Zealand Cases? 491

    15.14 Cases that have been Judicially Considered? 493

    15.15 Cases that have Dealt with Specific Legislative Sections? 493

    15.16 Journal Articles and Commentary? 494

16 India — *How Do You Find* 497

    16.1   An Introduction to the Jurisdiction? 497

    16.2   A Broad Picture of Indian Law? 498

    16.3   Parliamentary Publications? 498

    16.4   Bills? 500

    16.5   Explanatory Material about Bills? 501

    16.6   A Subject Index to Legislation? 501

    16.7   Commencement Dates for Legislation? 502

    16.8   Indian Legislation in Full Text? 502

    16.9   Updates for Legislation? 503

    16.10 Full Text of Delegated Legislation? 503

    16.11 Full Text of Indian Cases? 503

    16.12 Cases that have Dealt with Specific Legislative Sections? 506

    16.13 Journal Articles and Commentary? 506

1

General —
How Do You Find

1.1 **Abbreviations lists?**

Research tool	What information will it give me?	Tips on use
Fong C and Edwards A, *Australian and New Zealand Legal Abbreviations* Sydney: Australian Law Librarians' Group, 1995	Includes many non-Australian law journals and a number of non-law journals of relevance to the legal profession.	This work supplements Raistrick and Bieber. Publishers preferred citations used where available.
Legal Online FirstPoint (Thomson Reuters) • http://legalonline. thomson.com.au/	Useful for abbreviations of Australian and international law reports and journals.	Open FirstPoint and then click on the Help hypertext at the top right hand of screen. Choose FirstPoint Table of Abbreviations. Search by Abbreviation.
CaseBase LexisNexis AU • http://www.lexisnexis. com	CaseBase Case Citator abbreviations for law reports and journal articles.	On the lower part of the LexisNexisAU Home screen, choose Quick Sources > Cases/ Legislation and click on CaseBase Cases and Journal Articles. When the CaseBase search screen opens, look to the right under Related Links and choose the Abbreviations link.
Cardiff Index to Legal Abbreviations • http://www.legalabbrevs. cardiff.ac.uk/	Useful for abbreviations of English legal publications — mainly law reports and periodicals.	Search by Title or Abbreviation. The software is not case sensitive and there is no need to use precise punctuation.

Research tool	What information will it give me?	Tips on use
The Digest: Annotated British, Commonwealth and European Cases Green Band ed, London: Butterworths, 1981– • 90 volumes updated by reissues, Annual Cumulative Supplement and Digest Quarterly Survey • Not available electronically	Volume I and the latest supplement have a list of report abbreviations in the front. Useful for very recent Commonwealth cases.	See the table of 'Reports included in this work and their abbreviations'.
Halsbury's Laws of England 5 ed, London: LexisNexis, 2008– • Paper version (56 volumes) • Updated by Cumulative Supplement, Monthly Current Service and Annual Abridgement and reissue volumes • Halsbury's Laws Direct http://www.lexisnexis. co.uk	Volume I and the supplementary updates list the reports contained in the service and their abbreviations. Generally, at the beginning of an entry on a topic, the word or phrase is defined with reference to case law and legislation.	See the table 'List of Reports etc, used in this work'.
Kavass I and Prince MM (eds), *World Dictionary of Legal Abbreviations* Buffalo, New York: WS Hein, 1991–	Extensive coverage of Australia, Canada, the UK, New Zealand and the UN. US abbreviations are not covered. *Bieber's Dictionary of Legal Abbreviations* should be consulted as a companion publication. Appendix A includes historic abbreviations and Appendix B lists abbreviations by subject.	Four volumes looseleaf service. This is not designed as a legal citation guide and many different abbreviations are listed for some entries. Abbreviations are divided under different country sections. Order sequence from Preface is &, a, A, A-Z, a, ab xyz, abc de, C de pref, C deont.
Noble's Revised International Guide to the Law Reports 2002 ed. Compiled and edited by Scott Noble Ontario: Nicol Island Publishing, 2002	This abbreviations listing includes both common law and civil law reports series.	The Guide is organised alphabetically by abbreviation and includes the reports series title, jurisdiction, years, volume numbers and comments for each listing.

Research tool	What information will it give me?	Tips on use
Olsson,LT, *AIJA Guide to Uniform Production of Judgments* 2 ed., Melbourne: AIJA, 1999 • http://www.aija.org.au/ online/judguide.htm	Medium neutral citation guidelines. Abbreviations for courts and catchword headings and general style guide.	This lists court title abbreviations.
Prince MM, *Prince's Bieber's Dictionary of Legal Abbreviations* 6 ed, Buffalo, New York: WS Hein, 2009	Contains the precise meanings of abbreviations and acronyms used in the US. Includes Forward and Reverse dictionary listings.	This is designed to be a companion to *The Bluebook* and all citations and abbreviations are from or derived from *The Bluebook* rules.
Prince MM, *Prince's Bieber Dictionary of Legal Citations: Reference Guide for Attorneys, Legal Secretaries, Paralegals and Law Students.* 6 ed., Buffalo, New York: WS Hein, 2001	Contains abbreviations and examples of citations.	Contains a copy of the latest edition of *The Bluebook* in the back.
Raistrick D, *Index to Legal Citations and Abbreviations* 3 ed, London: Sweet & Maxwell, 2008	An English publication, in its second edition. Entries cover legal sources from the US, UK, Ireland, the Commonwealth, Africa, Asia, South America and Europe. Approximately 25,000 listings of legal abbreviations and acronyms, including commonly used alternative forms.	This index reflects usage, rather than being a guide to correct form; however, publishers' official cites are included. The list uses a word-by-word approach, with single letters first then groups or part words. Order of entries after preface is a, A, A B C, A b c, ABC, Abc.

1.2 The meaning of particular legal words and phrases?

Research tool	What information will it give me?	Tips on use
The Australian Digest and *Australian Legal Monthly Digest* (ALMD) Legal Online FirstPoint (Thomson Reuters) • The Australian Digest in third edition, looseleaf commenced in 1988 replaced second edition, paper version only now available of ALMD though information is provided electronically through FirstPoint Legal Online • http://legalonline. thomson.com.au/	ALMD in hardcopy comprises two booklets: (1) Digest of Law and (2) Cumulative Tables. The Digest contains summaries of reported cases, legislation and recent articles, notes, books, etc. Cases are categorised by subject as used in *The Australian Digest* plus five other topics. Includes words, phrases and maxims containing judicial consideration of their meaning.	Hard copy: Consult the table in the How to Use section of *The Australian Digest*, and then update using the annual cumulations and the monthly updates. Electronically: Use the Words and Phrases Judicially Considered template on FirstPoint.
Australian Legal Words and Phrases Sydney: Butterworths, 1993– • Three bound volumes reissued when necessary with supplements updated annually • In LexisNexis AU • http://www.lexisnexis. com	Indexes words and phrases defined in Australian legislation or interpreted and considered in judgments of the superior courts from 1900 to date. Companion to *Butterworths Encyclopaedic Australian Legal Dictionary*.	Choose Australian Legal Words and Phrases as the Source on the Search template. The actual definition is not noted, but the cases and legislation interpreting the word or phrase are cited. The order of entries is 1, 123, 1 abc, A, Abc. Updated by *Australian Current Law — Reporter*.
Encyclopaedic Australian Legal Dictionary Sydney: Butterworths, 1997– • In LexisNexis AU • http://www.lexisnexis. com	Contains approximately 20,000 terms presented in an Australian context within Australian statutory and judicial authority including summaries of important High Court cases and select biographies.	Hyperlinks to *Australian Legal Words and Phrases*, and contextual statements. Arranged in alphabetical order not ignoring spaces, numbers apostrophes. Enter the term you are searching for in the pop-up bar.

Research tool	What information will it give me?	Tips on use
Burton W, *Burton's Legal Thesaurus* 3 ed, New York: Macmillan Library Reference, 1998	A US publication, this book is designed to give alternatives (not necessarily exact synonyms) for complex legal jargon and is useful in plain English drafting. Includes strictly legal words and more common words regularly used by lawyers.	Contains a main entry with short definition, parts of speech, synonyms, associated legal concepts, and foreign phrases and translations. Index entries assist in locating synonyms.
Duhaime's Law Dictionary • http://www.duhaime.org	A Canadian legal dictionary designed for the general public by Lloyd Duhaime.	This site has no search function but some cross-referencing links are contained in the body of the work, which is accessed through alpha-links.
Dukelow D, *The Dictionary of Canadian Law* 3 ed, Scarborough, Ont: Carswell, 2004	Designed as a Canadian common law dictionary, it is based primarily on cases but includes references to Statutes, Regulations and legal textbooks.	Frequency of use is the criteria for selection. Most definitions are verbatim, but some have been rewritten to remove sexual and racial bias. Entries include the main word in bold, upper case letters, followed by a functional label, etymology, definition, citation of authority, and cross-references.
Everybody's Legal Dictionary • http://www.nolo.com/lawcenter/dictionary/wordindex.cfm	Nolo's 'Shark Talk' Dictionary provides plain English access to legal jargon. Includes over 1000 legal terms.	Browse by topic or search the dictionary.
Findlaw Dictionary • http://dictionary.lp.findlaw.com	Online version of the *Merriam-Webster's Dictionary of Law*.	Searching is by word. With multiple results, select the appropriate entry. html format only.
Free Online Law Dictionaries • http://www.lawdictionaries.com	Includes links to free internet resources and is organised according to topic; for example, General, Commercial, Crime, Human Rights, Family ADR, International Law.	The site includes a translation tool and a thesaurus. There are also links to dictionaries of slang.

Research tool	What information will it give me?	Tips on use
Halsbury's Laws of England 5 ed, London: LexisNexis, 2008– • Paper version (56 volumes) • Updated by the Cumulative Supplement, Monthly Current Service and Annual Abridgement and reissue volumes • LexisNexis UK and Halsbury's Laws Direct http://www.lexisnexis. co.uk	Generally, at the beginning of an entry on a topic, the word or phrase is defined with reference to case law and legislation.	Consult the consolidated index for the word listed alphabetically, then use the volume and paragraph reference to find the definition provided.
The 'Lectric Law Library's Legal Lexicon's Lyceum • http://www.lectlaw.com/ def.htm	A law dictionary that provides thousands of definitions and explanations of legal terms, phrases and concepts.	Browse by selecting the beginning letter, and then select the relevant entry. html format only.
Osborn's Concise Law Dictionary 11 ed, London: Sweet & Maxwell/Thomson Reuters, 2009	Contains a dictionary of law, and a section on law reports, journals and their abbreviations.	This dictionary gives definitions, not only for English maxims, but also Latin maxims. The length of entries depends on the complexity of the topic area defined.
Stroud's Judicial Dictionary of Words and Phrases 7 ed, London: Sweet & Maxwell, 2006 • Cumulative supplements issued to update	This multi-volume set with cumulative supplements aims to include a reference to most English cases involving interpretation of language by the Court. Some interpretations include words used in repealed legislation.	There has been a reduction in the older cases and Scottish, Irish and Commonwealth material. If a word has a special or long meaning, then only a reference to the law report is given. Words in capitals indicate there is a main reference within the alphabetical list in the dictionary.

Research tool	What information will it give me?	Tips on use
Words and Phrases Legally Defined 4 ed, Edinburgh: LexisNexis, 2007– • Cumulative supplements issued annually • LexisNexis UK and Halsbury's Laws Direct http://www.lexisnexis.co.uk/	An English publication but international in coverage with extracts from the House of Lords, Privy Council, superior courts of Australia, Canada, New Zealand, some jurisdictions in the US and South Africa. Now includes statutory definitions.	Main third edition volumes updated by supplements. Designed as a companion to *Halsbury's Laws of England* and includes extracts where applicable. Definitions grouped under main subject headings.

1.3 Law reform publications?

Research tool	What information will it give me?	Tips on use
Australian Law Reform Commission site • http://www.alrc.gov.au/	Links to other Australian and international commissions. Reports and Recommendations of the ALRC, Report Summaries, Draft Recommendation Papers, Background Papers, Discussion Papers, Issue Papers, Introductory Pamphlets and Reform Papers.	Browse the current index under the Publications heading or choose to search both the ALRC and AustLII sites by clicking on the microscope symbol.
Law Reform Digest Vol 1, 1910–1980 Vol 2, 1980–1985 Canberra: Australian Government Publishing Service	Covers Australia, New Zealand, Fiji and Papua New Guinea. Lists reports by subject, giving information on law reform bodies and summaries of findings.	The subject matter is based on the Australian Digest subject headings with a General Index. References are to each report series number. There is a topic list for reports, a list of reports by agency and another for legislation based on law reform reports. Cross-referencing used throughout.

1.4 **Books on a particular topic?**

Research tool	What information will it give me?	Tips on use
National Library of Australia • http://www.nla.gov.au and catalogue at http://catalogue.nla.gov.au/cgi-bin/Pwebrecon.cgi?DB=local&PAGE=First	The National Library holds books and serials, electronic collections, films and videos, government information, manuscripts, maps, microforms, newspapers, pictures and rare books.	Use the Basic or Advanced Search templates or the Geospatial Search facilities for the map collection.

Useful bibliographies

Research tool	What information will it give me?	Tips on use
The Australian National Bibliographic Database • http://www.nla.gov.au/libraries/resource/nbd.html	The National Bibliographic Database (or NBD) has been compiled since 1981 and hosted by the National Library of Australia. Records the collections of over 1,000 Australian libraries and is accessible via the Libraries Australia service for subscribers (formerly known as Kinetica and ABN, or the Australian Bibliographic Network) and Trove.	It is possible to use the ANBD to discover the existence of a particular item (through a search by subject, author or other terms) and to determine which libraries have holdings. The ANBD is searchable on a fee-for-service basis and can currently be searched through a library's Libraries Australia account. It is available to the general public via the National Library's Integrated Discovery Service Trove.

Research tool	What information will it give me?	Tips on use
Castles A, *Annotated Bibliography of Printed Materials on Australian Law 1788–1900* Sydney: Law Book Company, 1994	Contains a selected coverage of collections from many Australian libraries. Includes some Australian and British Parliamentary Papers and Royal Commissions, and overseas material if of significant relevance to Australia. Omissions from this work include single pamphlet copies of statutory material, individual copies of British legislation dealing with Australia, and general periodical literature and newspaper discussion.	The material is arranged alphabetically by title of the publication with a table of cases, table of law reports and table of statutes at the end.
Bowker's Global Books in Print RR Bowker Company • http://www. globalbooksinprint.com	Provides online searching of the American, Canadian and Britsh Books in print family of databases simultaneously. Complete bibliographical citations of English-language books, audiobooks and videos are included, as well as selected reviews, information on award winners and bestsellers. Access to a comprehensive database of over 165,000 publishers, distributors, wholesalers and book agents is also available. Includes: Books in print; Whitaker's books in print (British books in print); Books out-of-print; Children's books in print; Forthcoming books; Bowker's publishers authority database; Bowker's complete video directory; and Words on cassette.	Provides publication and ordering information on books and other monographic materials. This service is primarily used by library staff and academics and researchers wanting to obtain the latest publications by purchase or the Library's Document Delivery service.

Research tool	What information will it give me?	Tips on use
Index of Conference Proceedings The British Library Document Supply Centre • http://catalogue.bl.uk/	*Index of Conference Proceedings* lists conference proceedings newly acquired by the British Library and available for loan or document supply. The British Library acquires the proceedings of all significant conferences held worldwide regardless of subject or language and currently holds the proceedings of over 450,000 conferences.	
International Legal Books in Print: An Annotated Bibliography London: Bowker-Saur, 1990–	The companion to *Bowker's Law Books and Serials in Print*. This title aims to include non-US legal titles published in English.	The list contains an Author/Title and Subject Index. Journal titles include ISSN, price and frequency. A thesaurus file provides cross-references between synonyms and actual subject headings.
Law Books and Serials in Print: A Multimedia Sourcebook New York: RR Bowker, 1984–, annual.	The series now indexes books, serials, audio cassettes, video cassettes, online databases, software and microform, with annotations for listed titles. The brief annotations provide information on contents, coverage, appropriate audience and focus of the titles. Serial entries include frequency, Dewey number, and publisher's name and address.	Generally uses the Library of Congress legal subject headings and is updated by quarterly cumulative supplements. This is a US publication and the companion publication for international materials is *International Legal Books in Print*.
Law Books Published Dobbs Ferry, New York: Glanville Publications, 1976–	Contains listings of books published by the publishers in the Directory. Indexes mostly American Literature, with only three Australian publishers (Butterworths, Lawbook Co and Federation Press).	Index published twice per year with the second part cumulative of that year. Indexes by author, title, subject, publisher and series.

Research tool	What information will it give me?	Tips on use
Logan E and Winterton J (eds), *Information Sources in Law* 2 ed, London: Bowker-Saur, 1997	This UK title aims to provide starting points for legal research from many different jurisdictions. It covers books and periodicals, electronic media, reports of departments and bulletin boards. The aim of the guide is to reduce the time required for searching jurisdictions throughout the world. Includes general sources, mostly European States. Regional experts have written chapters on each country.	Consult the contents for the appropriate jurisdiction. Includes an introduction to the legal system, legislation, codes and commentaries, treaties, law reports, government documents and other current information sources.
OCLC WorldCat (OCLC Online Union Catalog) • WorldCat • On OCLC First Search by subscription http://newfirstsearch.oclc.org/	Database contains bibliographic records of items catalogued by OCLC member libraries.	Web-based search software provides basic, advanced and expert searching levels. Choose WorldCat database before searching. Multiple database searches available.
Raistrick D, *Lawyers Law Books: A Practical Index to Legal Literature* London: Bowker-Saur, 1997	UK legal literature primarily, but contains some reference to foreign literature, particularly EU and international law. General law reports titles such as the *Law Reports* and general journal titles such as the *Law Quarterly Review* are not included. Includes an alphabetical list of UK and Irish Reports and a table of regnal years.	The main work is divided into (1) Encyclopaedia and Periodicals and (2) Texts. Areas with extensive listings are subdivided. There is an author index at the back.
Ulrich's International Periodicals Directory • Annual hardcopy volume • Electronic Service using Citrix ICA Client Software • http://www.ulrichsweb.com/ulrichsweb/	A directory of over 195,000 active (and dead) periodicals, irregular series and annuals. Gives information on title, publisher, price, editors, whether indexed and where, availability, title changes and a brief description of the work. Also includes information on whether the journal is refereed.	Includes the ability to search and browse by keyword, subject, and title. Use the Browse Index and Subject Option for faster results.

Publishers, catalogues of recent publications

Research tool	What information will it give me?	Tips on use
Bowker • http://www.bowker.co.uk	List of all new titles, a downloadable electronic catalogue in pdf format, and the option of searching the catalogue online.	Browsing only. Take the product link, then follow the link to the full catalogue.
Butterworths • http://www.lexisnexis.com.au/aus/default.asp	Free guide to the complete Butterworths publications.	Information may be accessed using the subject index or the search engine. The subject indexes refer to publication, with more details if you follow through the links on each publication.
CCH/Kluwers Law Stream • http://www.cch.com.au/default.asp?bhcp=1	Complete catalogue of CCH products divided into specific areas.	Take the online store link then select the area from the sidebar for a specific area or use the general search function.
The Federation Press • http://www.federationpress.com.au	A complete catalogue of all Federation Press publications able to be searched or browsed by either Author, Subject, Title, ISBN, ISSN, Series or Journal.	By selecting one of the search options from the scrolling sidebar another more specific range of options is presented.
Hein • http://www.wshein.com	A complete catalogue of Hein publishing searchable by ISBN, Title, Hein Item Number and Author. Capable of being browsed by Subject, Series and Catalogue Type.	Is very useful for identifying journals or broad topical books.
Lawbook Co • http://www.lawbookco.com.au	A catalogue of all Thomson Lawbook Co material, including some international resources from publishers like Thomson, ATP, CPD, Westlaw, Brookers and Sweet & Maxwell.	The browse function is best for finding topical books, but it is necessary to use the subject index.
Oceana • http://www.oceanalaw.com	Excellent source of international legal sources with most countries in the world covered.	The database can be searched by country or subject.

Research tool	What information will it give me?	Tips on use
Oxford University Press • http://www.oup.com/ • http://ukcatalogue.oup.com/	This is a department of the University of Oxford. The website includes the history and structure of the publisher. There is an archive of work with links to separate jurisdictions and catalogues.	The main site includes information for authors. The catalogue is on the separate site.
Palgrave Macmillan • http://www.palgrave macmillan.com.au/	A catalogue of resources on a variety of subjects.	Search the site or browse under subject on the left-hand column.
Sweet & Maxwell • http://www.sweetand maxwell.co.uk/index.html	A catalogue of English resources.	Search or browse the catalogue either by subject, publisher or product.
Thomson Reuters • http://www. thomsonreuters.com	A catalogue of primarily American resources. However, it does include entries for publications from Europe, Asia-Pacific and Latin America.	On the sidebar, select the topic of interest and then select the publication required.

1.5 Theses?

See Nash V (ed), *Monash University Theses 1961–1986; Naguwean JW, A Catalogue of Theses Submitted at the University of Papua New Guinea 1970–1990, Union List of Higher Degree Theses in Australian University Libraries 1966–1991*. Useful links to worldwide digitised access programs at http://info.library.unsw.edu.au/skills/services/postthesis.html and see the National Library of Australia's list http://www.nla.gov.au/pathways/jnls/newsite/browse/socsci.html#Theses

Research tool	What information will it give me?	Tips on use
Dissertation Abstracts Ann Arbour, Mich: UMI • On ProQuest Dissertations and Theses http://www.proquest.com/en-US/products/dissertations/individuals.shtml	Dissertations Abstracts Online has a selective coverage of masters, theses and dissertations from Canada, Great Britain, and Europe held in North American institutions. Includes dissertations since 1861 and theses from 1962 with full text access to titles published 1997 on. Includes abstracts since 1980 and thesis abstracts since 1981.	Web based search software provides basic, advanced and expert searching levels. Choose the Dissertations database before searching. Multiple database searches are available. Subscription service.

Research tool	What information will it give me?	Tips on use
Australian Digital Theses Program (ADT) • http://adt.caul.edu.au	The project is led by the University of NSW in association with the Council of Australian University Librarians (CAUL) and has the support of other universities in Australia. The aim is to provide digital copies of the theses produced by postgraduates at Australian Universities.	The theses are presented in pdf format. Search by institution, field and keyword. An advanced search template is available.
The British Library Document Supply Centre • http://www.bl.uk/ reshelp/findhelprestype/ theses/hrrtheses/ theses.html	The British Thesis Service provides access to doctoral theses awarded by British universities since the early 1970s, and also US and Canadian doctoral theses.	British theses — purchase or borrow through the British Thesis Service, the UK and International Loan Service or the Urgent Action Service. US and Canadian theses are distributed by UMI (Bell & Howell) — available only to UK registered customers on loan.
Index to Theses accepted for Higher Degrees by the Universities of Great Britain and Ireland London: Aslib, 1950– • http://www.theses.com	Includes over 464,000 theses from 1716. The database only includes abstracts.	Only subscribers may search on the website.
Canadian Collections — Theses • http://www.collections canada.ca/thesescanada/ index-e.html	Theses Canada publishes masters theses and doctoral dissertations through our current service provider, UMI Dissertations Publishing. By 2002, there were over 220,000 theses and dissertations in the collection. Approximately 10,000 more are added to the collection annually. Full text electronic versions of Canadian theses and dissertations are available in pdf format for those theses published from the beginning of 1998 to 31 August 2002.	You can locate a specific thesis in the National Library of Canada's collection by clicking either on Search or Advanced Search. Further information on searching can be found by clicking on Search Help.

1.6 **Journal articles on specific subjects/cases/ legislation?**

Research tool	What information will it give me?	Tips on use
AGIS Attorney General's Information Service Part of the Informit e-Library developed by RMIT Publishing. Informit e-Library provides access to full content from a range of Australasian journals, monographs and books, conference proceedings, research papers and reference materials. • Available through Informit http://www.informit.com.au/	The library contains several law-related databases, including: Australian Federal Police Digest; Attorney General's Information Service (AGIS), produced by Lionel Murphy Library, Attorney General's Department; Australian Public Affairs Information Service (APAIS); The Australian Criminology Database and FAMILY: Australian Family and Society Abstracts — Produced by the Australian Institute of Family Studies.	AGIS is a particularly useful Australian legal journals index because of its substantial listings dating from 1975, and because of the abstracts or summaries provided with all articles. Since 1999, many articles have been available in full text. A Guided Search form is available. Informit Search Quick Tips are available at the bottom of the search screen.
The Australian Digest 3 ed Lawbook Co • Paper version only but information incorporated into the Legal Online FirstPoint database http://www.legalonline.thomson.com.au/	Provides short summaries of all significant cases from the beginning of law reporting in Australia in 1825. Cases are arranged into titles. The purpose of the Digest is to comprehensively record developments in case law. Under the main titles, cases are further classified under an established structure. Contains a Table of Cases, Table of Statutes, General Index, List of Abbreviations and a List of Titles.	Each segment within a title is given a square bracket number. This number is the common reference point for everything dealt with in that paragraph. To identify the relevant paragraph, use the General Index or the List of Titles. Consult the Key and Research Guide volume as a starting point. Journal articles citations are listed after the case citations.

Research tool	What information will it give me?	Tips on use
CASEBASE • LexisNexis AU http://www.lexisnexis.com.au/	Over 650,000 cases from the 56 major Australian reporting series, New Zealand Reports, UK authorised reports, the Weekly Law Reports, Lloyd's Reports and more than 80 journals, as well as unreported judgments. Journal articles are included as well as judicial consideration or history.	Casebase can be searched by Primary Case, Citation, Judge, Court, Statute, Words/Phrases and Catchwords. If the search query has multiple results, then you need to select the appropriate case. Check the Scope Coverage under the Help heading for the date of the latest entries in the database. There is also a very valuable list of journal abbreviations under this heading.
Index to Legal Periodicals and Books New York: HW Wilson Co, 1908– • Paper version • On WilsonWeb http://www.hwwilson.com/	Indexes over 789 legal journals, yearbooks, books, university publications, law reviews and government publications from the US, UK, Canada, Australia and New Zealand. Limited Australian coverage. Subject entries are arranged with articles first, followed by books. Cases are listed under both the plaintiff and defendant's name. An *Index to Legal Periodicals Retrospective: 1918–1981* and a full text database are also now available electronically.	Articles are indexed by Subject and Author or Title. Articles must be two ordinary pages or one folio page to be included. The index uses American terminology and subject headings. Electronic searching available using either a Basic or Advanced search template. Ability to Browse Subject Headings and Thesaurus.
Legal Journals Index Sweet and Maxwell • Paper version 1986– • Westlaw http://www.westlaw.com/	This index contains abstracts of journal articles from UK and EU journals or covering topics relevant to these jurisdictions. Over 430 English language journals are indexed.	The references are divided into 11 separate fields including title, author, source, abstract, significant legislation or cases and key-words. Search using the Westlaw templates and connectors.
Legal Journals on the Web • http://lawweb.usc.edu/library/resources/journals.cfm	US site providing links to electronic journals.	Search by categories such as Commercial Law Journals or Foreign Law Journals. Codes: Full text (F), Abstracts (A), Table of Contents (T), Subscription Information (S).

Research tool	What information will it give me?	Tips on use
LegalTrac Foster City, California Information Access Company, 1980– • On Searchbank http://www.galegroup.com/	Indexes approximately 900 legal publications, including most US law reviews, US legal newspapers, and law publications. Several law E-journals are included in full text. Law related articles from over 1000 business and general interest periodicals.	An extensive user manual is included with the database. Adobe Acrobat is required to view full text. Brief Search Tips also provide basic instruction on viewing and saving articles. Search by Subject Guide, Relevance, Keyword and Journal. A reasonably simple search template is provided.
OCLC Articles First, PapersFirst, and Proceedings • On OCLC First Search by subscription http://newfirstsearch.oclc.org/	Databases contain indexes of articles from the contents of journals, indexes of papers presented at conferences, and an index of worldwide conference proceedings.	Web-based search software provides basic, advanced and expert searching levels. Multiple database searches available. Multiple language searching available.
Canadian Legal Literature Scarborough, Ont: Carswell • Available on Quicklaw http://www.lexisnexis.ca/ql/en/sales/academic/edu.html#howpassword	It includes articles, case comments, books, essays from edited collections, government publications, theses, CLE and lay guides. The index covers all Canadian legal material, both English and French, common law and civil law.	To update further, use *Canadian Current Law — Legal Literature*. • three volumes to 1984 • two volumes to 1986 • 1987, 1988 and 1989 in bound volumes • 1989 onwards — looseleaf supplement, cumulating quarterly
Index to New Zealand Legal Writing vol 1 Auckland: Legal Research, 1954–1981 *Index to New Zealand Legal Writing and Cases* vol 2 1982–1987 Index New Zealand (INNZ) Foundation, 1987– • http://tepuna.natlib.govt.nz/	The two-volume hardcopy index was specifically directed to New Zealand law. INNZ, on the other hand, covers a range of topics, including law. It is similar to the Australian Public Affairs Information Service (APAIS) and uses those subject headings. It is an abstracting service covering newspapers, books, reports, theses, casenotes and other publications about New Zealand as well as the South Pacific.	No author index in volume 1. Subject index divided into Part 1 with books, articles, unpublished theses and dissertations, and Part 2 with casenotes. In volume 2, this division was discontinued with theses being printed in italics only, the coverage of casenotes was expanded, and the index was extended to reports of cases. By subscription.

Research tool	What information will it give me?	Tips on use
Index to Periodical Articles Related to Law Dobbs Ferry, New York: Glanville Publications, Hardcopy cumulation 1958–1988	Includes over 2500 journals not indexed by *Current Law, Index to Legal Periodicals,* and *Index to Foreign Periodicals*. The focus is on legal articles published in non-law journals, thus providing more accessible inter-disciplinary material	This is a selective index with only research level journal articles included. It is issued quarterly with cumulations.
The Criminal Justice Periodical Index (CJPI) Ann Arbor, Mich: Bell & Howell Information and Learning • On Proquest Direct http://www.il.proquest.com/	Offers complete access for 45 criminal justice journals, and abstracts for the remaining titles. It also contains citations from 1972 and full text from 1992.	Three user guide features are included with the package — the Quick Start Guide, Quick Reference Guide, Help Contents and Search by Word Guide.
NCJRS Abstracts Database and *NCJRS Virtual Library — Full text publications* • http://www.ncjrs.org/search.htm	The National Criminal Justice Reference Service database coverage is from 1970. It is located within the National Institute of Justice which is in the US Department of Justice. Contains summaries of 170,000 publications, including US Federal, State, and local government reports; books; research reports; journal articles; and unpublished research.	Search by author, title, subject or NCJ accession number. Phrases need to be enclosed in quotation marks when searching. Searches can be limited according to date. Boolean, concept and pattern searching all available. Use the asterisk to find alternate word endings in your searches. It is possible to display the retrieved list alphabetically, by date or by number. Proximity searching also available.

1.7 International treaties and conventions?

There are a number of excellent international law Research Pathfinders available on the web, including:

• The University of Minnesota Law Library 'Researching Treaty Sources' http://www.law.umn.edu/library/tools/pathfinders/treaties.htm

• The American Society of International Law's 'ASIL Guide to Electronic Resources for International Law' http://www.asil.org/treaty1.cfm

Research tool	What information will it give me?	Tips on use
United Nations Treaty Series New York: United Nations Publications, 1946– • Paper version • http://untreaty.un.org	A collection of treaties and agreements registered or filed and recorded with the UN Secretariat since 1946. The UN Homepage also includes a collection of photographs taken at signature ceremonies and a list of titles of multilateral treaties in all official languages — Arabic, Chinese, English, French, Russian and Spanish.	The UNTS has a publication lag-time and is only up to date to March 2003. Importantly, there is a Limited Publication Policy.
Multilateral Treaties Deposited with the Secretary General and Status of Multilateral Treaties Deposited with the Secretary General • http://untreaty.un.org	Texts of treaties lodged but not yet published in the United Nations Treaty Series. The companion status list includes information that states have signed, ratified, acceded or lodged declarations, reservations or objections to instruments.	Mainly has recent treaties but also contains some variations of treaties if not registered in the UNTS.

Australia

Research tool	What information will it give me?	Tips on use
Australian Department of Foreign Affairs and Trade, *Australian Treaty Series* 1948– Electronic version 1901– • http://www.austlii. edu.au/au/other/dfat	The Australian Treaty Series contains the full text of treaties to which Australia is a party in annual sequence. Since the 1996 reforms of the treaty-making processes, a National Interest Analysis is published for each new treaty proposed. These and a link to the Parliamentary Joint Standing Committee on Treaties website are included on the AustLII site.	See generally, Australia and International Treaty Making Information Kit in the Australian Treaties Library on AustLII. The extremely useful Introduction to Treaty Terminology and Implementation Procedures is included in the List Introduction.

Research tool	What information will it give me?	Tips on use
Australian Department of Foreign Affairs and Trade, *Select Documents on International Affairs 1966–* • http://www.austlii. edu.au/au/other/dfat	Publishes text of multilateral treaties and conventions in which Australia participated in the preparation, but to which Australia did not become a party. From 1966, treaties were published in this series prior to their ratification.	The documents have been given an individual number since 1963. There is one issue each year. The whole collection is available on AustLII, listed by year, and easily accessed by hypertext. A subject search is available through the Australian Treaty List, as well as by general AustLII search capabilities.
Australian Department of Foreign Affairs and Trade, *Australian Treaties not yet in force* • http://www.austlii. edu.au/au/other/dfat/	It contains notes of treaties signed but not yet in force in Australia. Mainly one or two treaties are listed for each year. There are no individual chronological numbers assigned for the early years. Documents are relocated to the ATS or Select Documents when finalised.	Selective years from 1983 on available on AustLII. Full text accessible by hypertext.
Australian Department of Foreign Affairs and Trade, *Australian Treaty List* • Last hardcopy printed ATS 1999 No 38, see subsequent Annual updates ATS No 1 • Electronic version • On AustLII database using Sino software http://www.austlii. edu.au/au/other/dfat	The Australian Treaty List indexes all treaties to which Australia is a party as well as including references to prospective treaties (from Australian Treaties not yet in Force), and treaties to which Australia is not a party and which were previously only listed in Select Documents on International Affairs. Hardcopy updates to List printed in Foreign Affairs and Trade Record.	Monthly updates to the list are loaded on AustLII. A Subject Index and Supplementary Keyword Index are also included on the AustLII site.
Department of Foreign Affairs, Annual Reports, 1993– • http://www.dfat.gov.au/ publications/	Includes an appendix listing treaty action taken by Australia.	Reports in pdf or html format.

Treaty finding aids

Research tool	What information will it give me?	Tips on use
International Legal Materials American Society of International Law, 1962– • Published bi-monthly • http://www.asil.org/resources/ilm.html	Reproduces the final texts of international agreements and recent ICJ decisions. The publication covers private and public international law issues.	Useful for current international materials for all jurisdictions. Cumulative indexes available 1962–1969; 1970–1979; 1980–1989. Use the latest cumulative index and then update with indexes in the back of the annual volumes. Website includes current Table of Contents.
Bowman M and Harris D, *Multilateral Treaties Index and Current Status* London: Butterworths, 1984– • Annual supplements	The main index includes a Chronological list of treaties and a list of other multilateral treaties. Michael Bowman is the Director of the University of Nottingham Treaty Centre, which publishes the index supplements. They cover the period from 30 June 1983 to 1994. Provides short summaries of essential facts regarding main multilateral treaties and notes on other multilateral treaties. This series was discontinued with the 11th cumulation.	The easiest method of accessing the information contained in the work is to use the Subject Index. The supplements are in two parts, Part A contains the full entries for treaties, and Part B consists of new status and other information for treaties in the main volume. The supplement includes Additional Notes regarding constitutional changes and a Subject and Word Index.
Rohn P, *World Treaty Index* Santa Barbara, Calif: ABC-Clio Information Services, 1900–1980	The second edition of the Index was published in 1984 and since this time substantial work has been done on the publication of a new edition. The Human Rights Education and Research network now administers the database. For further information, see: http://depts.washington.edu/hrights/Treaty/history.html Sources include the League of Nations Treaty Series, United Nations Treaty Series, and National Treaty collections.	• Volume 1 Treaty Profiles • Volume 2 Main Entry Section 1900–1959 • Volume 3 Main Entry Section 1960–1980 (The main entry section indexes by chronological order according to date of signature) • Volume 4 Party Index (alphabetical order) • Volume 5 Keyword Index (keyword in context)

Research tool	What information will it give me?	Tips on use
United States Treaty Series 1776–1990 Buffalo, New York: WS Hein & Co, 1991– Updated by Current Treaty Index, issued twice per year	*The United States Treaty Series* consolidates US Treaty actions until 1990 and the *Current Treaty Index* (compiled by Igor I. Kavass and Adolf Sprudzs Buffalo, NY:W.S. Hein & Co., 1982–1999) contains update information on current actions by the US on treaties and agreements. The CTI includes slip agreements published in the Treaties and Other International Acts Series (TIAS), and those not yet published (identified by letters KAV).	The United States Treaty Index has a subject, chronological and country index. The CTI features a Numerical Index, Chronological Index, Country Index, Subject Index, and Geographical Subject Index. There are conversion tables for the TIAS and KAV numbers. Not all information contained in the supplements is current. To access agreements between Australia and the US, it is best to consult the Country Index, which contains lists of Bilateral and Multilateral US agreements.

International judicial decisions

Research tool	What information will it give me?	Tips on use
International Court of Justice Reports: Reports of Judgments Advisory Opinions and Orders • Paper version 1946– • Electronic version 1946– • http://www.icj-cij.org	This source contains all contentious cases and advisory opinions referred to the Court. They contain full case overviews or summaries of judgments and orders.	There is a list of decisions, but the search function tag must be used for searching. See the World Court Reports for decisions of the Court of International Justice.
International Law Reports London: Butterworths, 1919–	Aims to provide cases on public (not private) international law from all international tribunals and national courts. Full coverage is not given to all jurisdictions, nor are all human rights decisions covered. The European Court of Human Rights, the Inter-American Court of Human Rights and 'views' of the UN Committee on Human Rights are included. Arbitral awards between states involving international law are included.	Consolidated Index and Consolidated Tables of Cases and Treaties: • Volumes 1–80 • Volumes 81–100 A Digest of Cases is included at the beginning of each volume.

Yearbooks

Research tool	What information will it give me?	Tips on use
Australian Year Book of International Law Sydney: Butterworths, 1969– • Electronic version available from Hein-on-line 1965-2006	Published by the Centre for International and Public Law at ANU, this annual contains articles, book reviews, pertinent cases and legislation, and the official record of treaty actions by Australia in the year of publication. It is supplemented by *The Australian International Law News*. Many countries publish equivalents, including Canada and Britain.	Use the Annual Index and the Table of Cases to access the information contained in the yearbook. The Australian Practice in International Law summarises all executive and legislative dealings in international law or involvement in many countries. The treaty action details treaties that came into force in Australia in the current and the previous year in numerical Australian Treaty Series Number, Bilateral Agreements by country.
Recueil des Cours Dordrecht: Nijhoff, 1923– • Paper version, 1923–	Collected lectures of the Hague Academy of international law with sections on public international law, international community, international relations, and private international law.	A table of appendices that gives pointers to supplementary information.

Encyclopaedias

Research tool	What information will it give me?	Tips on use
Encyclopedia of Public International Law Amsterdam: North Holland Pub Co, 1992 • Published under the auspices of the Max Planck Institute for Comparative Law http://www.mpepil.com	The original encyclopaedia was in 12 volumes on particular subject areas. It has been reprinted in a consolidated library edition.	The initial articles were published gradually so every article is marked with a date at the foot of the entry to identify currency. The consolidated edition will include an index volume.

Bibliographies

Research tool	What information will it give me?	Tips on use
Szladits' Bibliography on Foreign and Comparative Law Dobbs Ferry, New York: Published for the Parker School of Foreign and Comparative Law by Oceana Publications 1790–	This bibliography includes books and articles in English language on both common law and non-common law systems. Casenotes and book reviews are generally excluded and US material is limited to the comparative aspect of the study of American Law. The bibliography deals with both public and private law.	The bibliography arranges entries under 12 headings, including General, Foreign and Comparative, Private, Commercial, Labor and Social, Criminal, Procedure, Public, International Organizations and Conflicts. Many abbreviations are used and these can be checked in the full list at the front of volume 1.

1.8 Comparative law?

Research tool	What information will it give me?	Tips on use
Martindale-Hubbell Law Digest New York: Martindale Hubbell, 1931– • On Lexis http://www. lexisnexis.com	Contains excellent overviews of law from all US state jurisdictions and most international jurisdictions. It also reproduces, in full, the US Uniform Acts and selected international conventions. There is a separate digest for European Communities Law. Part of the 27 volume Law Directory.	The Domestic Law Digests include 53 jurisdictions — the 50 states and the District of Columbia, Puerto Rico, and the Virgin Islands. Information is listed under topics (listed in the Topical Index) and standard subheadings, and is revised annually. Part II covers the US Federal Copyright, Patent and Trademark Laws; Part III covers the Federal Courts; Part 1V Uniform Acts and Model Laws; Part V Professional Conduct Rules; Part VI International Digests; and Part VII International Conventions.

Research tool	What information will it give me?	Tips on use
International Encyclopedia of Comparative Law New York:1973–	This encyclopaedia has numerous volumes with reports on national legal systems, and subject areas, such as property and trust, contracts and torts in those countries. There are no updates.	Volume One provides a series of reports on the legal systems of every country in the world. The remaining volumes are arranged by legal topics. The set does not contain an index of material and the volumes come in multiple parts.
Modern Legal Systems Cyclopedia Buffalo, New York: WS Hein, 1984– • Paper version updated as required	A looseleaf service containing 10 volumes plus supplements covering all regions, including North America, Pacific Basin, Europe, and the Middle East. The content includes governmental systems, substantive and procedural law.	Extensive source for a basis into the legal system of a particular country. The supplements are not always incorporated into the main work and are published separately. The North America volume extends to 1A. There is an index published separately.
Reynolds T, *Foreign Law: Current Sources of Codes and Legislation in Jurisdictions of the World* Littleton, Colo: FB Rothman, 1989– • Paper version supplements annually	Volume 1 covers the Western Hemisphere, volume 2 Europe and volume 3 Africa, Asia and Australasia. Contains information on the general system of law in a country and contains references to materials published on subject areas within that country.	Within each volume the countries are listed alphabetically. It then gives a history and general introduction and reference lists. It cites mainly primary resources and few secondary sources, unless extremely useful.
Constitutions of the countries of the world *Constitutions of dependencies and territories* Oceana Law Online, Dobbs Ferry, NY: Oceana Publications. • http://www.oceanalaw.com/	Constitutions for over 188 countries in English translations and also 170 dependencies. The database contains current and historical data.	You can browse by country or search the database using a basic search template. There are helpful search explanations available if you click on the Help tab at the top of the screen. Recent amendments and updates appear under the What's New! tab.

1.9 **Alert services**

A list of alerting services can be found at http://www.newcastle.edu.au/services/ library/guides/alerting/index.html

Research tool	What information will it give me?	Tips on use
Anstat/Lawlex • http://www.lawlex.com. au/modules.php?name= Content&pa=showpage& pid=21	Automatically generates an email when one of the following events occurs: new Bills, assents, proclamations, new Regulations, amendments and repeals.	Every Alert has a brief abstract summary with links back to the amending legislation and a tabulated summary of amendments by section.
CCH Daily Email Alerts • http://www.cch.com	CCH Daily Email Alerts is a week day alert service to keep you up-to-date with all the current events in the legal and commercial world. Topics covered include General Commercial; Tax and Accounting; Business Management; Financial Planning; Industry and Employment; Occupational Health and Safety; and Superannuation.	It is a subscription-based service that delivers to your email direct links to information on the latest developments in the area. There is a free subscription on the web page.
ComLaw • http://www.comlaw. gov.au/	Provides notification of all new data or, by selecting databases, allows access to individual collections, such as High Court cases or new Commonwealth consolidations of legislation.	You can select certain databases to be informed of changes. To subscribe, click on the 'Notify me when' and follow the instructions on the page.
Findlaw • http://www.findlaw.com. au/emaillists/register.asp	A variety of newsletter subscriptions is available, including: Newsletters; Daily Opinion Summaries; Subject Area, Legislation and Case law Alerts. Full text legislation and the last 30 days case law available from the site.	Choose Email Alert Service from the Homepage and choose relevant items to be sent to you.

Research tool	What information will it give me?	Tips on use
Legal Express • http://www.lexisnexis. com.au/aus/products/ upfront	Legal Express is a free legal news alert service, which can be emailed to you each business day. It contains a list of legal news headlines, short casenotes and a 'Word of the day', extracted from the *Butterworths Encyclopaedic Australian Legal Dictionary*.	Delivers either text or html outlines of recent developments in case law free of charge. Greater details are in the subscription service.
Legal Info-Online • http://www.law foundation.net.au/ media/ebulletin/	Provides announcements of new developments and sites for Australian law. This is produced by the Online Legal Access Project.	A free service, with subscriptions available at the site. Archives are also available for viewing.
Legal Scholarship Network Journals (LSN) • http://www.ssrn.com/	The Social Science Research Network provides subscriptions to networks and journals. A mix of fee-based and free services available.	Once subscribed, users receive regular Professional Announcements and Job Listings and abstracts of scholarly papers.

1.10 Conferences

Research tool	What information will it give me?	Tips on use
All Conferences.com • http://www. allconferences.com/ Government/Law/	Directory focusing on conferences, conventions, trade shows, exhibits, workshops, events and business meetings.	Browse by subject or use the advanced search facility and search by title, city, country, date, category or keyword.
Australian Institute of Criminology • http://www.aic.gov.au/ conferences/#cc	Lists conferences and seminars being held by the Australian Institute of Criminology as well as noting other conferences on criminal law, justice and criminology issues. Links to previous conference websites and papers and also to forthcoming meetings.	Browse by date and topic.

Research tool	What information will it give me?	Tips on use
Australian Institute of Family Studies • http://www.aifs.gov.au/ institute/conf/confmenu. html	Lists conferences and seminars being held by the Australian Institute of Family Studies as well as noting other conferences on family research, policy and related areas. Links to previous conference websites and papers and also to forthcoming meetings.	Browse by date and topic.
Conference Alerts: Academic and Professional Conferences Australia • http://www.conference alerts.com/australia.htm	Hyperlinked general listings of conferences on all subjects in Australia.	Browse according to date or Australian city. Links also to international events. Searchable by topic.
Law Council of Australia • http://www.lawcouncil. asn.au/conferences/law-council-events.cfm	Lists conferences, training programs and events being held throughout Australia by law societies and commercial providers.	Search by Section and Date.
Practising Law Institute • http://www.pli.edu/ product/seminars.asp	Lists programs by title, date, location, interest area and price.	Sort by clicking on column heading. Also possible to view programs on a calendar. Mainly United States locations.

1.11 Citation style guides

Research tool	What information will it give me?	Tips on use
The Bluebook: A Uniform System of Citation 18 ed, Cambridge, Mass: Harvard Law Review Association, 2005	Provides general principles and rules of legal citations for the US. It contains tables of abbreviations to reports in the US, and many foreign juris-dictions, as well as inter-governmental bodies like the UN. It also contains abbreviations for court names, documents and US and foreign periodicals.	In the Tables and Abbreviations section, it is arranged first by US jurisdictions, then foreign jurisdictions, and then information on case names, court names, explanatory phrases, judges, officials, and periodicals (American and foreign).

Research tool	What information will it give me?	Tips on use
Dickerson D, *ALWD Citation Manual: A Professional System of Citation* 3 ed New York: Aspen Publishers Inc, 2006	Part Seven consists of various appendices, including one on court-specific formats and another that lists commonly used abbreviations.	Update via the Association of Legal Writing Directors homepage: http://www.alwd.org Here you will find expanded appendices and reviews, information about adoptions, and a list of frequently asked questions.
Melbourne University Law Review *Australian Guide to Legal Citation* 2 ed Melbourne: Faculty of Law, University of Melbourne, 2002 • http://mulr.law.unimelb. edu.au/	The manual has chapters on various types of formats; for example, journal articles, books, legislation and case law. The main common law jurisdictions are treated separately and international materials are also dealt with separately. There is an abbreviation list in the back for law reports series. A read-only pdf version of the citation manual is available online	The citation recommends the use of 'above', 'below' and 'ibid' but not 'id' for subsequent references, and brackets for publication details. There is a Quick Reference in the back. This citation style does not include the place of publication for books but does include the author's full first name.
Rozenberg, P, *Australian Guide to Uniform Legal Citation* 2 ed, Pyrmont, NSW: Lawbook Co., 2003	The concise text includes general principles of referencing and citation, general style rules, footnoting rules and the main component is the citation guide. The 11 Appendices cover abbreviations for case reports, company names, councils, court identifiers, court names, honours, journals, judicial and other legal terms, jurisdictions, legislation and parts of a publication.	The footnoting rules are clearly set out. This is the area where differences in style become more acute. This manual recommends the use of 'id' and 'ibid' in conjunction with 'Above' for references earlier in the document. It also recommends brackets for publisher's details in the footnotes and in the Bibliography.

Research tool	What information will it give me?	Tips on use
Stuhmcke A, *Legal Referencing* 3 ed, Sydney: Butterworths, 2005	The text begins with a chapter on the fundamentals of legal referencing and writing. The various genres of writing are then addressed separately beginning with case law, legislation, texts, journals and so on. There is a separate chapter on electronic citation. There is also a chapter for students on referencing in exams and a segment on judging when you need to reference in writing so as to avoid plagiarism.	The format recommended does not include bracketing of publisher's details. The chapter on repeat citations for footnotes outlines a number of alternate methods but recommends the simple 'Note x' method.

1.12 Archival material on the internet?

Research tool	What information will it give me?	Tips on use
The Internet Archive • http://www.archive.org/index.php	The Internet Archive is building a 'digital library of Internet sites and other cultural artifacts in digital form'. The Wayback Machine allows users to enter an old URL and visit the website as it existed previously. This site has been built since 1996 using automated web-crawling software and requests for inclusion. The site notes that the 'Internet Archive Wayback Machine contains almost 2 petabytes of data and is currently growing at a rate of 20 terabytes per month'. It includes only publicly accessible websites and does not include email or chat. The site incorporates text, audio, moving images, software and Open Education materials. Website owners can ask that their site be excluded from the archive.	You can search by using the URL or the names of the site and it is possible to specify a date range. A full text search engine is under development. Some sites are incomplete.

Research tool	What information will it give me?	Tips on use
The Avalon Projects — Documents in Law, History and Diplomacy Lillian Goldman Law Library, Yale Law School • http://avalon.law.yale.edu/default.asp	An extensive historical document collection in full text from ancient times to the present.	Basic but effective search function available on site. Main access through Browse facility.
Pandora: Australia's Web Archive • http://pandora.nla.gov.au/ 'PANDORA is a growing collection of Australian online publications, established initially by the National Library of Australia in 1996, and now built in collaboration with nine other Australian libraries and cultural collecting organisations. The name, PANDORA, is an acronym that encapsulates the archive's mission: Preserving and Accessing Networked Documentary Resources of Australia.'	The archive includes 23,120 titles. Topics covered include Arts, Business & Economy, Defence, Education, Environment, Government & Law, Health, History, Humanities, Indigenous Australians, Industry & Technology, Media, People & Culture, Politics, Sciences, Society & Social Issues, Sports & Recreation, and Tourism & Travel. See Koerbin P, 'The Australian web domain harvests: a preliminary quantitative analysis of the archive data': http://pandora.nla.gov.au/documents/auscrawls.pdf (5/11/2009).	All archived titles are catalogued and a record is included in the National Bibliographic Database (Libraries Australia), as well as in participants' online catalogues. Access is provided via hotlinks in the catalogue record. Access is also provided via a search facility and subject and title lists on the PANDORA Home Page. Search services, such as Yahoo! and Google, index the archive down to the level of individual titles, but not the contents of the titles.

1.13 **Journal rankings?**

Research tool	What information will it give me?	Tips on use
ERA list of law journals • http://www.arc.gov.au/era/journal_list.htm	The Humanities and Creative Arts (HCA) and Physical, Chemical and Earth Sciences (PCE) journal lists were released in 2009 for the purposes of a preliminary ERA trial. The full list is due for release in 2010. The trial lists included ERA ID, Rank (rank assigned to the journal), Title (journal title), Indexed, FoR/s (the field of research code/s associated with the journal), FoR name/s (the field of research names/s associated with the journal), ISSN/s (primary, other and previous ISSNs of the journal). The HCA journal list includes multidisciplinary science journals.	The lists are formulated in Excel and include two formats — 'Unique journals with all associated FoR codes in one record' and 'Complete journals broken down on a discipline (FoR code) basis (duplicate Journals if the journal is assigned to more than 1 FoR)'.
Washington and Lee University Law Journal Rankings • http://lawlib.wlu.edu/LJ/	This list includes information on citation-based rankings including approximately 100 Australian law journals. Most Australian publications are ranked lower than those published in North America and the United Kingdom.	Choose the check boxes to tailor the list to your specifications. Choose according to country, refereed/non-refereed, subject, title ranking, impact factor, non-ranked, and online. For ranking methodology, see http://lawlib.wlu.edu/LJ/method.asp.

1.14 **Personal citation data?**

As well as the listed tools, Australian legal scholars can search most full text databases for references to their names and/or works — for example, AGIS Plus Text will search across the full-text of pdf articles. LexisNexis AU, Legal Online, CCH Australia (IntelliConnect), Lexis.com and Westlaw all include journal articles, commentary, encyclopaedias and judgments, and these can be searched. Parliamentary websites will search full-text of the Hansard and Committees databases. Other international full-text sources, such as BAILII, CanLII and NZLII are also searchable. See Unwin M, 'Strategies for Working with ERA' (2009) 3 *ALTA Newsletter* 18, 19.

Research tool	What information will it give me?	Tips on use
ISI Web of Knowledge Philadelphia, Pa: Institute for Scientific Information, Thomson Scientific. • http://wokinfo.com/ products_tools/ multidisciplinary/ webofscience/citmap/	Authors can view citations to their journal articles. Very few Australian legal titles are indexed. Includes Science Citation Index 1992-, Social Sciences Citation Index (SSCI) — 1992-, and Arts & Humanities Citation Index (A&HCI) — 1992-	The Cited Reference search template locates articles that cite a person's work.
Scopus Elsevier • http://www.elsevier. com/wps/find/ electronicproduct description.cws_home/ 704746/ description	Authors can view citations to their journal articles. Very few Australian legal titles are indexed.	Search templates include Basic, Author, Affiliation, and Advanced. Full Boolean searching is available in the Advanced search template.
LawCite • http://www.austlii.edu. au/LawCite/	A free citator resource. Allows authors of Australian law articles to view a list of other articles in the database that cite their article. In addition, a full text search of Austlii will cover journal articles, judgments, law reform publications and explanatory notes on the database. A search on a specific case will bring up a list of journal articles on that case. Those held on Austlii will be hyperlinked to the full text. The entry for the case will include legislation and sections cited; cases and articles cited, including citation, court, jurisdiction with flag mnemonic, date and citation index; cases referring to this case; and journal articles referring to this case.	Choose the LawCite option from the front page of Austlii to open the search template. Options to search under include Citation, Parties, Court, Jurisdiction, Article title, Author, Year, Cases Considered, and Legislation Considered. LawCite does not provide a digest or catchwords so you cannot search for cases on topic. See also LawCite Help: http://www. austlii.edu.au/LawCite/ doc/overview.html
Social Sciences Research Network (SSRN) • http://www.ssrn.com/	Citation data gathering feature currently in development.	

Research tool	What information will it give me?	Tips on use
Harzing's Publish or Perish used in connection with Google Scholar • http://www.harzing.com/pop.htm	Searches for citations from journals and other publication types, including books and other scholarly web documents.	This is a free software that works with Google Scholar. Searches on authors will bring up a complete list of articles with the search term. There will be a list of citations shown for each separate article by the author. The software allows you to access each article where it is available in full text to print or download.
Hein Online • http://heinonline.org/	Contains some Australian law journals. Also offers citation information. The most recent issues of journals often not on the database.	Search on author's name. Choose the Articles that cite this document at the top of the page showing each article. This will take you to subsequent citations of the main article using Hein's Scholar Check.

2

Australia —
How Do You Find

2.1 **An introduction to the jurisdiction?**

The Australian Commonwealth Government entry point is http://www.australia.gov.au/

See, generally, Commonwealth Government homepage at http://www.aph.gov.au/parl.htm for information on the Parliament, the Constitution and Government.

The main Constitutional and founding documents are available at http://www.foundingdocs.gov.au

Further historical and current facts regarding the Australian Government and parliament are available from the Australian Parliamentary Library homepage at http://www.aph.gov.au/library/

The Australian Federation Full Text Database, containing the full text of the debates and conventions of the 1890s leading up to Federation, is available at http://setis.library.usyd.edu.au/oztexts/fed.html

Note that the Australian Government Bookshop Network closed on 17 October 2003. It is necessary to use the Publications Register to find out about the continued availability of publications that were stocked by the Bookshop Network http://www.publications.gov.au/

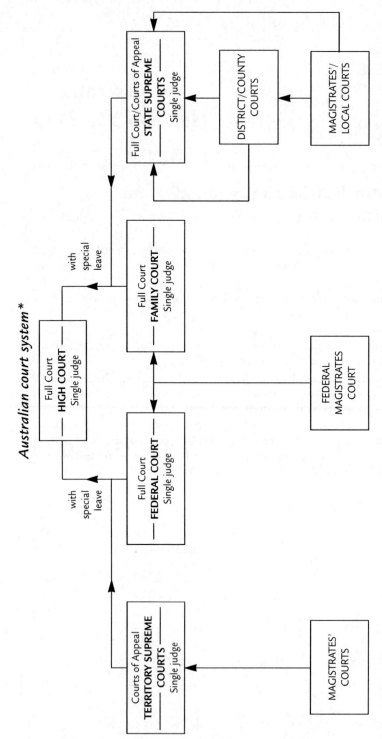

Australian court system *

* This Figure shows the principal Australian courts. In addition, there are various specialist courts, plus numerous State and federal tribunals. This also shows the main avenues of appeal in simplified form. The system of appeals is complex and there are many jurisdictional variations. The structure of appeals is further complicated by the vesting of federal jurisdiction in State courts. In some federal matters, an appeal may lie from a State court to a court in the federal hierarchy. For a more detailed examination, see Crawford J and Opeskin B, *Australian Courts of Law* (4th ed, Oxford University Press, 2004).

2.2 A broad picture of Australian law?

Research tool	What information will it give me?	Tips on use
The Laws of Australia Legal Online • Paper version (Updated using supplements and the *Australian Legal Monthly Digest*) • http://legalonline. thomson.com.au/	This encyclopaedia provides a clear and concise statement of principles. It is arranged by topic, with subject specialists authoring different areas. Topics are broken down by Title and Subtitle. Each paragraph contains a proposition of law with supporting authority from case and statute law. The service includes a Table of Cases, Table of Legislation and an Index.	Check the volume containing a cumulative topic index to locate the relevant Volume, Title, Subtitle and paragraph number. To update, use the blue pages at the end of each Subtitle under the same paragraph numbers. To update from that point, use the 'Laws of Australia – Australian Digest Cross References' table in the latest issue of *Australian Legal Monthly Digest*. This is available on subscription from Legal Online. Use the Browse facility in the online version or the search templates.
Halsbury's Laws of Australia Butterworths • Paper version updated using *Australian Current Law* • LexisNexis AU at http://www.lexisnexis.com	This encyclopaedia contains a narrative statement of the law by subject area and covering all nine jurisdictions. Generally there are concise statements of principles, including full footnotes listing relevant legislation. Differences between jurisdictions are noted.	Volume 29 contains a Topical Index which refers the reader to the relevant Volume, Title and paragraph number. The currency date is at the beginning of the title. *Halsbury's Laws of Australia* is updated by the Cumulative Tables in *Australian Current Law Reporter*. The electronic version of this and the updates in *Australian Current Law* are available via LEXISNEXIS AU. There are Browse and Search facilities available.

Research tool	What information will it give me?	Tips on use
IntelliConnect • http://intelliconnect. wkasiapacific.com/	CCH databases for legal materials arranged by subject. This includes all the looseleaf series incorporating annotated legislation.	Click on Browse to see all subscription titles listed, or search in the Google-like single search box at the top, then use the options on the left to filter your results. The online video demos are useful: http://www.cch.com.au/au/intelliconnect/MinisitePages/Flash/presentation.html

2.3 **Parliamentary publications?**

See generally, the Australian Parliament homepage at http://www.aph.gov.au/

Information on the Parliamentary System, Executive Government, Separation of Powers, Federal Judicature, the Commonwealth Parliament, Governor-General, the Senate, and the House of Representatives can be found at http://www.aph.gov.au/parl.htm

The Senate homepage is at http://www.aph.gov.au/senate/index.htm

An electronic version of Odgers' Australian Senate Practice (11 ed), edited by Harry Evans is available at http://www.aph.gov.au/senate/pubs/odgers/index.htm

See also, Senate Briefs at http://www.aph.gov.au/Senate/pubs/briefs/index.htm including papers on:

1 Electing Australia's Senators
2 The Opening of Parliament
3 Women in the Senate
4 Senate Committees
5 Consideration of Estimates by the Senate's Legislation Committees
6 The President of the Senate
7 Disagreement between the Houses
8 The Senate and Legislation
9 The Origins of the Senate
10 The Role of the Senate
11 Parliamentary Privilege
12 Questions
13 Rights and Responsibilities of Witnesses before Senate Committees
14 Ministers in the Senate

Full Search and browse facilities are available at http://search.aph.gov.au/search/ParlInfo.ASP or choose 'Search' from the Research Tool.

Research tool	What information will it give me?	Tips on use
Parliament homepage. Parliament of Australia Search Page • http://parlinfoweb.aph.gov.au/piweb/	This website includes a list of all searchable parliamentary information. Users can search documents from the House of Representatives, the Senate, legislation, procedure, committees, the Parliamentary Library, the Constitution and related documents, including the 1890 Conventions.	Search expressions include AND, OR and NOT. When searching for phrases, use quotation marks around the phrase. * can be used for wildcard searches.

Parliamentary records

Research tool	What information will it give me?	Tips on use
Parliamentary Hansard for the Senate and House of Representatives • Paper version • http://www.aph.gov.au/hansard/index.htm	This site provides access to the Senate Hansard, House of Representatives Hansard, and Senate, House of Representatives and Joint Committee transcripts.	Use the Parliament Search page to search the Hansard. To browse the Hansard, select the required format under Senate, House of Representatives or committees. The formats available are pdf and html.
House of Representatives Votes and Proceedings • Paper version • http://www.aph.gov.au/house/pubs/index.htm	The official record of business of the House of Representatives.	Use the Parliament Search page to search the Votes and Proceedings. To browse the Votes and Proceedings, select the required format — pdf or html.
Journals of the Senate • Paper version • http://www.aph.gov.au/Senate/pubs/index.htm	The official records and minutes of the Senate. This is the most authoritative source of Senate activities. It records motions, resolutions, progress of legislation, references to committees, documents lodged and all actions taken by the Senate.	Use the Parliament Search page to search the Journal. To browse the Journal, select the link. The available format is pdf.

Parliamentary committee reports

Research tool	What information will it give me?	Tips on use
Committees Reports House of Representative Committees • Paper version • http://www.aph.gov.au/house/committee/index.htm Senate — Standing and Select Committees • Paper version • http://www.aph.gov.au/senate/committee/index.htm Joint — Statutory and Standing Committees • Paper version • http://www.aph.gov.au/house/committee/index.htm	Lists the titles of all committees of the current parliament with links to the committee homepage with information on the committee and full text copies of many reports from the committee. The index pages gives links to documents listing all the reports, committee Hansards and other committee information.	To search the Committee pages, the parliament search page is used. To browse the Committee reports, select the required committee from http://www.aph.gov.au/commitee.htm and follow the links. Most of the committee reports are in pdf format. Both the House and Senate have registers of reports. The Senate version is up to date and the House version runs until 1996.

Parliamentary committee reports index

Research tool	What information will it give me?	Tips on use
House of Representatives Register of Committee Reports • Paper version • http://www.aph.gov.au/house/committee/info/curr_inq.htm	Register of Reports from Committees of the House of Representatives and Joint Committees 1970-1996. Includes a description of the report, the Parliamentary Paper No, the date tabled, the date of the government's response.	Available in pdf format. Choose 'Publications' from House of Representatives Page and then 'Index to papers presented to Parliament' from the listing. For more recent reports either search using the general parliament search page or browse the appropriate committee.
Consolidated Register of Senate Committee Reports • Paper version • http://www.aph.gov.au/senate/committee/register/report/index.htm	The register of Senate Committee Reports and subsequent annual supplements list reports tabled since 1970.	All documents are in pdf format. At http://www.aph.gov.au/senate/committee/register/report/index.htm there is a: • Chronological Listing of Reports • Chronological Listing by Committee • Chronological Listing by Subject Matter.

Other parliamentary publications

Research tool	What information will it give me?	Tips on use
Papers on Parliament • Paper version • http://www.aph.gov.au/Senate/pubs/pops/index.htm	Published by the Research Section of the Procedure Office of the Department of the Senate. These generally include the texts of the lunchtime lecture series and papers written by senators and academics since 1988.	Choose 'Senate' from the Parliament of Australia homepage and then 'Publications'. Available in pdf format.
Index to Papers Presented to Parliament • Paper version • http://www.aph.gov.au/house/pubs/index.htm	38th Parliament 1996– An index to papers presented in both Houses, and published twice per year. It contains an alphabetical subject index.	It gives page references to Journals and Votes and Proceedings. Available in pdf format. Choose 'Publications' from House of Representatives Page and then 'Index to papers presented to Parliament' from the listing.
The Senate Daily Summary • Paper version • http://www.aph.gov.au/senate/index.htm	Issued by the Senate Procedure Office, this is a summary of the business covered in the day's sittings, including progress of Bills, Committee information, including membership and reports tabled, information on delegated legislation, petitions and notices of motion. The current Daily Summary is available along with previous issues 2000–. The official record is contained in the *Journals of the Senate.*	Choose 'Senate' from the parliament of Australia homepage. These are available in both html and pdf formats.
Senate Notice Paper • Paper version • http://www.aph.gov.au/senate/work/notice/index.htm	The Notice Paper is the complete list of all business before the Senate for the entire session.	Choose 'Senate' from the Parliament of Australia homepage and then 'Publications'. Scroll down list to 'Notice Papers'. Senate Notice Papers are listed by year and month. Three years of Notice Papers are available in pdf format.

Research tool	What information will it give me?	Tips on use
Senate Order of Business (the Red) • Paper version • http://www.aph.gov.au/ senate/work/red/red.pdf	The Senate Red lists business being dealt with by the Senate for the current day only. This is only a guide.	Choose 'Senate' from the Parliament of Australia homepage and 'The Senate at Work'. Available in html and pdf formats.
Annual Report, Department of the Senate • Paper version • http://www.aph.gov.au/ senate/dept/	Report on the activities of the senate in the past year. It also includes a 'list of Senators and details of ministerial representation; a calendar of, and statistics concerning, sitting days; list of committees on which senators serve; statistics on petitions, questions, and legislation; overseas visits by Senators; financial statements, staffing statistics; lists of Senate publications, seminars, lectures, exhibitions, and addresses and publications by Senate officers'(Senate Information Guide http://www.aph.gov.au/ senate/inf_gd.htm# Annual). Published annually, usually in September.	Choose 'Senate' from the Parliament of Australia homepage and then 'Administration'. This file can be downloaded. Enhanced browse facilities are also provided.
Senate List of Public Meetings and Hearings • Paper version • http://www.aph.gov.au/ senate/committee/ hearings/hear.htm	Published weekly, it provides contacts, dates, times, and the venue of Senate Committee Public Meetings and Hearings, as well as information about the inquiries, the bills, involvement in the inquiries and transcripts.	Choose 'Senate' from the Parliament of Australia homepage and 'Committees'.
Senate Business of Committees • Paper version • http://www.aph.gov.au/ senate/committee/ red.htm	Issued as a guide to the day's proceedings with members involved, and notes start and finish times. Includes Canberra and interstate hearings.	Choose 'Senate' from the Parliament of Australia homepage and 'Committees'.

Research tool	What information will it give me?	Tips on use
House of Representatives Daily Program • Paper version • http://www.aph.gov.au/house/work/index.htm	This is a proposed program for the day's sitting published prior to the House meeting. Subject to change.	Available in Word and pdf format. Choose 'The House at Work' from House of Representatives Page and then 'Documents of the House'.
House of Representatives Notice Paper • Paper version • http://www.aph.gov.au/house/info/notpaper/index.htm	Provides a list of all business to be discussed in the sitting. Previous years available 1998-.	Choose 'The House at Work' from House of Representatives Page and then 'Documents of the House'. Available in pdf format.
House of Representatives Disallowable Instruments List • Paper version • http://www.aph.gov.au/house/info/disallow/disallow.pdf	An informal listing of tabled instruments for which disallowance motions may be moved (published for each sitting).	Available in pdf format. Choose 'Publications' from House of Representatives Page and then 'Index to papers presented to Parliament' from the listing.
House of Representatives Work of the Session • Paper version • http://www.aph.gov.au/house/pubs/wots/index.htm	36th Parliament 1990-Summary of the sitting, including statistics, progress of Bills, committee activity, motions, matters of public importance discussed, lists of papers and petitions.	Available in pdf format. Choose 'Publications' from House of Representatives Page and then 'Work of the Session' from the listing.

Parliamentary Royal Commissions

Research tool	What information will it give me?	Tips on use
Parliamentary Library's List of Royal Commissions and Commissions of Inquiry, 1902-2001 • http://www.aph.gov.au/library/intguide/law/royalcommissions.htm • Also available through the National Library's GovPubs Guide to Legal and Parliamentary Resources http://www.nla.gov.au/govpubs/	This was previously published as an appendix to a parliamentary library research paper. It is now available as an Internet law guide.	The list of Royal Commissions is listed among the additional resources in the National Library's GovPubs for Parliamentary Papers. Select either Search or Browse Web Publications, then the appropriate drop-down menus.

2.4 **Bills?**

BillsNet

Research tool	What information will it give me?	Tips on use
Current Bills • by Title • by Portfolio • by Private Member • Bills Net http://www.aph.gov.au/bills/index.htm#billsnet	Full text of Bills. Lists in alphabetical order the short title of the Bill, portfolio or private member. The information included may be: text of the Bill; Explanatory memoranda; Bills List Entry; abstract of the Bill; Bills Digest; Second Reading Speeches; proposed amendments and a schedule of amendments. Old Bills (those from previous parliaments and those that did not become law) are listed separately. There are also lists available of draft legislation not yet introduced into the House available through the BillsNet page.	Most of the documents contained are either in html or pdf format. To search, use the Parliamentary search page.
Senate Daily Bills Update • Bills Net http://www.aph.gov.au/bills/index.htm#billsnet	Contains information on Bills under consideration by the Senate. Information includes date of introduction, reporting dates and stage reached in the Senate.	Ensure the most current update is used. The format is pdf. It is arranged alphabetically in three sections: Government Bill; Private Senator's Bills and Private Member's Bills.
Senate Bills List • Bills Net http://www.aph.gov.au/bills/index.htm#billsnet	Contains information on all Bills introduced to the House or the Senate. The information available includes a summary of the Bill, House and Senate information, the date of assent and the Act number.	Ensure that the most current update is used. The format is pdf. The summary includes information on the purpose of the legislation and some detail if it is amending other legislation.

Research tool	What information will it give me?	Tips on use
Bills Digest • http://www.aph.gov.au/library/pubs/bd/index.htm	Contains information on the passage and history of the Bill, purpose, background, its main provisions, concluding comments, endnotes, and contact officer details. The Digest is prepared before the debate, so it does not contain information regarding amendments. Available 1990–.	Select relevant year to view list of Bills titles. Option of browsing in alphabetical order or by numerical list. To search, use the general Parliament search page. Available in both pdf and html format.

Other sources

Research tool	What information will it give me?	Tips on use
ComLaw • http://www.comlaw.gov.au/	The Attorney-General's Department's ComLaw legislative repository system became available online on 1 January 2005. This replaces SCALEplus. It contains: Commonwealth primary legislation, as well as other ancillary documents and information, in electronic form, and the Federal Register of Legislative Instruments (FRLI) which was established on 1 January 2005 under the *Legislative Instruments Act 2003* as the authoritative source for legislative instruments and compilations of legislative instruments. The intention is to hold only databases of the legislation of the Commonwealth and non self-governing Territories (and related material such as Bills, explanatory memoranda/statements, tables, indexes and other finding aids) on the system. Full text of Commonwealth Bills before Parliament since 1996 is available. Select 'Browse all Data' and then select the Bills database.	This Bills database can be searched or browsed. Search by word or phrase (using Boolean operators) or date. Browse by year and alphabetical order. The format is html.

Research tool	What information will it give me?	Tips on use
LawLex via Anstat • http://www.anstat. com.au	Full text linked database. Subject index of principal legislation. Commonwealth, New South Wales, Queensland and Victoria included.	Search legislation from the Anstat Legislation homepage. Introduces LawLex with searches available by keyword and jurisdiction. Free Bills link available onsite. Otherwise restricted to premium, subscription searches.
Federal Statutes Annotations Butterworths • Paper version (updated with a six monthly cumulative supplement) • LexisNexis AU at http:// www.lexisnexis.com	Designed to give users current information on legislation and case law relating to legislation. Includes assent and reprint information, current status of legislation, amending legislation, related Acts, Regulations made and relevant books and articles.	The Table of Bills lists all Bills placed before the House. An * denotes a Bill that has been assented to. The Act number is printed at the end of the entry. To update, consult *Australian Current Law* or use the electronic version and the updates in *Australian Current Law* via LEXISNEXIS AU.
Australian Current Law Butterworths • Paper version • LexisNexis AU at http:// www.lexisnexis.com	*Australian Current Law* contains two parts — 'Reporter' and 'Legislation'. The Reporter contains a digest of all judgments received from the High Court, Federal Court, Supreme Courts, and selected decisions from the House of Lords, Family Court and other courts and tribunals. Legislation contains information on all legislative developments for all Australian jurisdictions.	The Cumulative Table of Parliamentary Bills (contained in Legislation) lists all Bills received. Bills with an * have been assented to, and the Bills assented to since last edition are in bold. There is a cumulative table produced every three months. The electronic version of *Australian Current Law* is available via LEXISNEXIS AU. The Legislative and Caselaw segments have been divided for searching. Choose Cases, Legislation or commentary from the headings on the homepage.

Research tool	What information will it give me?	Tips on use
Australian Legal Monthly Digest (ALMD) Legal Online FirstPoint (Thomson Reuters) • Paper version only now available of ALMD, though information is provided electronically through FirstPoint • http://www.legalonline. thomson.com.au/	ALMD in hardcopy comprises two booklets: (1) Digest of Law and (2) Cumulative Tables. The Digest contains summaries of reported cases, legislation and recent articles, notes, books, etc. Cases are categorised by subject as used in the *Australian Digest* plus five other topics.	The Table of Bills lists all Bills introduced in the Commonwealth, State and Territories. Includes Bills received in the current year. * means list for the first time, + indicates there is Explanatory memoranda and [] means a Bill is being restored. Choose from the Research heading on Legal Online FirstPoint.

2.5 Explanatory material about Bills?

Explanatory memorandums are supplementary explanations of new legislation prepared by the Minister and the government department from which the Bill emanates. Other extrinsic materials are parliamentary debates, executive materials, commission and committee reports and international agreements. Explanatory memoranda came to real prominence with the passing of s 15AB of the *Acts Interpretation Act 1901* (Cth), which was inserted into the principal Act by s 7 of the *Acts Interpretation Act Amendment Act 1984* (Cth). This legislation and that enacted in the states and territories alters the common law rules as to the use of extrinsic materials. One result has been that since 1985, the dates of the Minister's second reading speech in the House of Representatives and the Senate has been noted at the end of each Commonwealth Act.

Research tool	What information will it give me?	Tips on use
Index to Explanatory Memoranda 1901–1982 • http://www.aph.gov.au/ library/intguide/law/ auslaw.htm# commonwealth	This index lists all items identified as Explanatory Memoranda or as Comparative Memoranda from 1901 to the end of 1982. From 1982, the provision of Explanatory Memoranda has been standard practice for government Bills introduced into the Commonwealth Parliament.	Browse the index alphabetically or by date.

BillsNet

Research tool	What information will it give me?	Tips on use
Current Bills • by Title • by Portfolio • by Private Member Old Bills • by Title • http://www.aph.gov.au/bills/index.htm#billsnet See also the Summary about the Bills in the Bills Digest http://www.aph.gov.au/library/pubs/bd/index.htm. This extensive background information has no legal status. The Second Reading Speech is also useful and appears in Hansard http://www.aph.gov.au/hansard/index.htm	Full text of memoranda. Lists in alphabetical order the short title of the Bill, portfolio or private member. The information included may be text of the Bill; Explanatory memoranda; Bills List Entry; Abstract of the Bill; Bills Digest; Second Reading Speeches; proposed amendments and a schedule of amendments.	Most of the documents contained are either in html or pdf format. To search, use the Parliamentary Search page. Browse by selecting the format then by scrolling alphabetically.

Other full text sources

Research tool	What information will it give me?	Tips on use
ComLaw • http://www.comlaw.gov.au/	The Attorney-General's Department's ComLaw legislative repository system became available online on 1 January 2005. This replaces SCALEplus. It contains: Commonwealth primary legislation, as well as other ancillary documents and information, in electronic form, and the Federal Register of Legislative Instruments (FRLI) which was established on 1 January 2005 under the *Legislative Instruments Act 2003* as the authoritative source for legislative instruments and compilations of legislative instruments. The intention is to hold only databases of the legislation of the Commonwealth and non self-governing Territories (and related material such as Bills, explanatory memoranda/statements, tables, indexes and other finding aids) on the system. Full text of Explanatory Memoranda or Explanatory Statements for Bills before Parliament since 1998 is available. The Explanatory Memoranda are in the Attachments to the Bills so you need to access the Bill as a first step.	This database can be searched or browsed. Search by word or phrase (using Boolean operators) or date. Browse by year and alphabetical order. The format is html, pdf and rtf.

Research tool	What information will it give me?	Tips on use
LawLex via Anstat 1999– • http://www.anstat.com.au	Victorian-based full text linked database. Subject index of principal legislation, includes Commonwealth, New South Wales, Queensland and Victoria.	Search legislation from the Anstat Legislation homepage. Introduces LawLex with searches available by keyword and jurisdiction. Explanatory Memoranda are accessed by locating the Bill first. Free explanatory memorandum link available where material on other free site.

Committees' reports regarding bills

Research tool	What information will it give me?	Tips on use
House of Representative Committees • Paper version • http://www.aph.gov.au/house/committee/index.htm Senate — Standing and Select • Paper version • http://www.aph.gov.au/senate/committee/index.htm Joint — Statutory and Standing • Paper version • http://www.aph.gov.au/house/committee/index.htm	Reports of dealings with Bills in committees. Lists the titles of all committees of the current Parliament with links to the committee homepage with information on the committee and full text copies of many reports from that committee. The index pages give links to documents listing all the reports, committee Hansards and other committee information.	Use the Parliament search page to search the Committee pages. To browse the current Committee work, select the required committee from http://www.aph.gov.au/committee/inquiries_comm.htm and follow the links in that committee. Most of the committee reports are in pdf format. Both the House and Senate have registers of reports. The Senate version http://www.aph.gov.au/senate/committee/register/report/index.htm covers 1970–2004 and the House version runs to 1996, and then 1998–.

Additional indexed information

Research tool	What information will it give me?	Tips on use
Australian Legal Monthly Digest (ALMD) Legal Online FirstPoint (Thomson Reuters) • Paper version only now available of ALMD, though information is provided electronically through FirstPoint • http://www.legalonline. thomson.com.au/	ALMD in hardcopy comprises two booklets: (1) Digest of Law and (2) Cumulative Tables. The Digest contains summaries of reported cases, legislation and recent articles, notes, books, etc. Cases are categorised by subject as used in the *Australian Digest* plus five other topics.	The Table of Bills lists all Bills introduced in the Commonwealth, States and Territories. Includes Bills received in the current year. * means list for the first time, + indicates there is Explanatory memoranda and [] means a Bill is being restored. Choose from the Research heading on Legal Online FirstPoint.

2.6 A subject index to legislation?

The full text legislation databases can also be utilised for this purpose. See 2.8 Commonwealth legislation in full text.

Research tool	What information will it give me?	Tips on use
Wicks Subject Index to Commonwealth Legislation Sydney: Lawbook Co, 1989– • Paper version published annually	There are two indexes: • Acts of the Parliament of the Commonwealth of Australia • Regulations made under those Acts The purpose is to set out the short title of Acts that deal with a specific subject.	The subject index for Commonwealth legislation is arranged by broad subject titles, then subtitles with references to legislation. Also contains cross-references to other subject topics.
LawLex via Anstat • http://www.anstat. com.au	It includes a subject index of principal legislation from the Commonwealth, New South Wales, Queensland and Victoria.	Choose search legislation from the Anstat Legislation homepage. Introduces LawLex with searches available by keyword and jurisdiction.

2.7 The commencement date of legislation?

Commencement date rules are set out in the interpretation legislation for each Australian jurisdiction. See the *Acts Interpretation Act 1901* (Cth) for the rules governing the commencement of Commonwealth Acts.

The full text legislation databases can also be utilised for this purpose. See 2.8 Commonwealth legislation in full text.

Notification of Royal Assent has been through the weekly Government Notices Gazette. However, this has changed to notice via the Special Gazettes. The acts are published on Comlaw within two or three days.

Research tool	What information will it give me?	Tips on use
ComLaw • http://www.comlaw.gov.au/	The Attorney-General's Department's ComLaw legislative repository system became available online on 1 January 2005. This replaces SCALEplus. It contains: Commonwealth primary legislation, as well as other ancillary documents and infor-mation, in electronic form, and the Federal Register of Legislative Instruments (FRLI) which was estab-lished on 1 January 2005 under the *Legislative Instruments Act 2003* as the authoritative source for legislative instruments and compilations of legislative instruments. The intention is to hold only databases of the legislation of the Commonwealth and non self-governing Territories (and related material such as Bills, explanatory memoranda/statements, tables, indexes and other finding aids) on the system. Full text of Explanatory Memoranda or Explanatory Statements for Bills before Parliament since 1998 is available. The Explanatory Memoranda are in the Attachments to the Bills so you need to access the Bill as a first step. The Commonwealth Acts Tables contain references to: (1) Acts assented to during the relevant year and (2) Acts amended or repealed by Acts assented to during the relevant year. Information includes proclamations, gazette references, assent and commencement dates.	Choose 'Legislation Tables' in the left-hand column then the 'Table of Commonwealth Acts' for the relevant year. There is a document covering 1901–2000. Documents are in rich text format. This earlier database cannot be searched, only downloaded.

Research tool	What information will it give me?	Tips on use
Federal Statutes Annotations Butterworths; LexisNexis AU • Paper version (updated with a six monthly cumulative supplement) • LexisNexis AU at http://www.lexisnexis.com	Index designed to give users current information on legislation and case law relating to legislation. Includes assent and reprint information, current status of legislation, amending legislation, related Acts, Regulations made, and relevant books and articles. The Constitution is listed first.	Browse or search the database. The annotations section gives the date of assent and the date when the legislation becomes operational. For amendments after the last reprint, details of the actual commencement dates are included. To update, consult *Australian Current Law* on LexisNexis AU.
Commonwealth Statutes Annotations Lawbook Co • Paper version only	Index designed to update the 1973 Consolidation of Acts, pamphlets, reprints and Acts passed by the Commonwealth Parliament. Contains information on last reprint, amendments since that reprint, the dates of parliamentary debates, cases on the Act generally, articles, cases on specific sections and Regulation information, including last reprint, amendments and cases on the Regulations.	The annotations table sets out amending legislation to the principal Act since the last reprint. The information includes the short title, year, number, assent date, commencement date and information on amending provision. Consult *ALMD* and *ALMD Advance* to update.
Australian Current Law Butterworths • Paper version • LexisNexis AU at http://www.lexisnexis.com	*Australian Current Law* contains two parts — 'Reporter' and 'Legislation'. The Legislation volume contains information on all legislative developments for all Australian jurisdictions. This is searched or browsed separately from the caselaw in the current arrangement on LexisNexis AU	Can be used as the updating service for the *Federal Statutes Annotation*. Use the Cumulative Table of Acts Passed and Table of Acts Amended (in the Legislation section). It gives information on the issue and subject number. Using the issue and subject number, go to that issue and subject legislation table. Commencement and amendment details are listed.

Research tool	What information will it give me?	Tips on use
Australian Legal Monthly Digest (ALMD) Legal Online FirstPoint (Thomson Reuters) • Paper version only now available of ALMD, though information is provided electronically through FirstPoint • http://www.legalonline. thomson.com.au/	ALMD in hardcopy comprises two booklets: (1) Digest of Law and (2) Cumulative Tables. The Digest contains summaries of reported cases, legislation and recent articles, notes, books, etc. Cases are categorised by subject as used in the *Australian Digest* plus five other topics.	Use the Cumulative Table of Acts Passed, Amended, Repealed or Proclaimed to commence and the appropriate jurisdiction. Use the paragraph number(s) in the relevant Digest of Law booklet. The details in the relevant paragraph include commencement and amendment details. Choose from the Research heading on Legal Online FirstPoint.

2.8 Commonwealth legislation in full text?

Research tool	What information will it give me?	Tips on use
ComLaw • http://www.comlaw. gov.au/	The Attorney-General's Department has developed a new legislative repository to replace SCALEplus. The new system became available online in January 2005. It contains: Commonwealth primary legislation, as well as other ancillary documents and information, in electronic form, and the Federal Register of Legislative Instruments (FRLI) which was established on 1 January 2005 under the Legislative Instruments Act 2003 as the authoritative source for legislative instruments and compilations of legislative instruments. The intention is to hold only databases of the legislation of the Commonwealth and non self-governing Territories (and related material such as Bills, explanatory memoranda/ statements, tables, indexes and other finding aids) on the system. Contains up-to-date copies of all Commonwealth Acts with the exception of Appropriation and Supply Acts.	Information given for the Act compilations include : Number, Brief Description, Date Published, Prepared Date, Incorporating Amendments to, Effective Date, Administering Portfolio, and Office Preparing. Legislation; can be accessed with Browse or by Standard, Advanced or Guided searches. Acts as passed and compilations or reprints are separated.

Research tool	What information will it give me?	Tips on use
Westlaw Australia • http://au.westlaw.com	Commonwealth Acts, Subordinate Legislation and Tables.	Select Expert or Advanced Search forms. Browse Acts alphabetically. Currency information links to subordinate legislation provided.
AustLII • http://www.austlii.edu.au	Commonwealth Consolidated Databases contains consolidated copies of all Commonwealth of Australia Acts with the exception of Appropriation and Supply Acts. The Commonwealth Numbered Acts database contains the Constitution of Australia, all Commonwealth Acts consolidated in 1973 and all subsequent Commonwealth Acts published since 1973. Austlii has launched a Point-in-Time legislation facility which can be used to check an Act or section of an Act as it was at any day in the past, for those years covered by the system — note that at the moment you can only search as far back as 2002 but it will be possible to go back further as earlier versions of the legislation become available in electronic format. It is available for NSW, Qld and SA at present but is progressively being applied to all other Australian jurisdictions including the Commonwealth. AustLII has an Update Table for its Legislation. The dates are those on which AustLII last updated the relevant legislation database and do not necessarily indicate the currency of the legislation in the databases.	Browse Acts in alphabetical order or use the search tools by entering a search query. Select the Recent Updates databases for information on consolidated legislation, which is either new or has been updated in the last 28 days. The date above does not mean that all Acts are consolidated as at that date, but rather this is the date that data was most recently received. The material can be viewed in html format or downloaded in text format.

Research tool	What information will it give me?	Tips on use
LawLex via Anstat • http://www.anstat.com.au	Full text linked database. Subject index of principal legislation, including Commonwealth, New South Wales, Queensland and Victoria.	Search legislation from the Anstat Legislation homepage. Introduces LawLex with searches available by keyword and jurisdiction.
LexisNexis AU • http://www.lexisnexis.com	LawNow Commonwealth legislation.	Choose Legislation from the Home Page and then choose to search or browse. Use the information symbol for an explanation of contents and coverage.

2.9 Updates for legislation?

Australian legislation is generally printed in pamphlet form after assent. These are cumulated in bound volumes at the end of the year. Reprinted Acts, including amendments, are then issued either in bound volume form or by publishing pamphlet reprints.

The full text legislation databases can also be utilised for this purpose.

Research tool	What information will it give me?	Tips on use
Commonwealth Statutes Annotations Sydney: Lawbook Co, 1989– • Paper version only	The *Commonwealth Statutes Annotations* is designed to update the 1973 Consolidation of Acts, pamphlets, reprints and Acts passed by the Commonwealth Parliament. Contains information on last reprint, amendments since that reprint, the dates of parliamentary debates, cases on the Act generally, articles and cases on specific sections and regulation information, including last reprint, amendments since and cases on the Regulations.	The Annotations table sets out amending legislation to the principal Act since the last reprint. The information includes the short title, year, number, assent date, commencement date and information on amending provision. Alphabetical table of Acts passed, amended, repealed or proclaimed to commence can be found at the Table of Bills. The Annotations section lists Regulations made under the parent Act. It gives the short title, statutory rule number, reprint information and amendments since last reprint. To update, consult the ALMD and *ALMD Advance*.

Research tool	What information will it give me?	Tips on use
Australian Legal Monthly Digest (ALMD) Legal Online FirstPoint (Thomson Reuters) • Paper version only now available of ALMD, though information is provided electronically through FirstPoint • http://www.legalonline. thomson.com.au/	ALMD in hardcopy comprises two booklets: (1) Digest of Law and (2) Cumulative Tables. The Digest contains summaries of reported cases, legislation and recent articles, notes, books, etc. Cases are categorised by subject as used in the *Australian Digest* plus five other topics.	Use the Cumulative Table of Acts Passed, Amended, Repealed or Proclaimed to commence and the appropriate jurisdiction. Use the paragraph number(s) in the relevant Digest of Law booklet. The details in the relevant paragraph include commencement and amendment details. Updated by *ALMD Advance*. See also the *Daily Digest* on the Lawbook Co homepage for notes on recent legislative changes. Choose from the Research heading on Legal Online FirstPoint.
Federal Statutes Annotations Butterworths • Paper version (updated with a six monthly cumulative supplement) • LexisNexis AU at http://lexisnexis.com	Designed to give users current information on legislation and case law relating to legislation. Includes assent and reprint information, current status of legislation, amending legislation, related Acts, Regulations made and relevant books and articles. Updated bimonthly.	The annotation section gives details of amending legislation since the date of last reprint. Details include Act number and year, whether the amendments are fully operational and provisions that have been amended but are not yet operational. The general annotation includes reference to Regulations made under the parent Act. Sets out details of the latest reprint and any amending details since the latest reprint. To update, consult *Australian Current Law*.

Research tool	What information will it give me?	Tips on use
Australian Current Law — Legislation Butterworths • Paper version (published monthly) • LexisNexis AU at http://lexisnexis.com	*Australian Current Law* contains two parts: (1) Reporter and (2) Legislation. The Legislation contains information on all legislative developments for all Australian jurisdictions.	The updating tool for *Federal Statutes Annotations*. Use the Cumulative Table of Acts Passed and Table of Acts Amended (Legislation part) which gives information on the issue and subject number. Using the issue and subject number, go to that issue and subject legislation table. Commencement and amendment details are listed.
Commonwealth Table of Acts ComLaw • Paper version • http://www.comlaw. gov.au/ The Attorney-General's Department's ComLaw legislative repository system became available online on 1 January 2005. This replaces SCALEplus. It contains: Commonwealth primary legislation as well as other ancillary documents and information, in electronic form, and the Federal Register of Legislative Instruments (FRLI) which was established on 1 January 2005 under the *Legislative Instruments Act 2003* as the authoritative source for legislative instruments and compilations of legislative instruments. The intention is to hold only databases of the legislation of the Commonwealth and non self-governing Territories (and related material such as Bills, explanatory memoranda/ statements, tables, indexes and other finding aids) on the system.	The Commonwealth Acts Tables in Legislation Tools contains references to: (1) Acts assented to during the relevant year and (2) Acts amended or repealed by Acts assented to during the relevant year. Information includes proclamations, gazette references, assent and commencement dates.	Choose 'Legislation Tools' in the left-hand column. Since 1993, you can choose the relevant year. There is a document covering 1901–1995. Documents are in rich text format. This database cannot be searched, only downloaded.

2.10 A subject index to delegated legislation?

The Statutory Rules were published as a separate series 1901–. These include Regulations, rules, by-laws and guidelines. Statutory Rules are issued in pamphlet form with an annual bound volume. There is a current pamphlet reprint series and an earlier bound reprint 1901–1956.

The full text legislation databases can also be utilised for this purpose. See 2.7 The commencement date of legislation?

Research tool	What information will it give me?	Tips on use
Wicks Subject Index to Commonwealth Legislation Sydney: Lawbook Co, 1989–	There are two indexes: (1) Acts of the Parliament of the Commonwealth of Australia and (2) Regulations made under those Acts. The purpose is to set out the Regulations which deal with a specific subject	Where the short titles do not agree with those found for the parent Act in the main subject index, 'see' references are included. The reference given is to the original Act or latest amendments. (Earlier amendments are normally set out at the end of each set of amending Regulations.)
Australian Government Gazettes Online Attorney-General's Department • http://www.ag.gov.au/ govgazette	Government Notices (GN) from 3/7/02, Special Notices (s) from 1/7/02, Periodic Notices (P) from 1/7/02. These Gazettes contain a wide variety of legislative information including: Date of Royal Assent for Acts of Parliament; Notification of the making of Statutory Rules; The notification (and occasional full text) of several forms of delegated legislation and instruments made under Acts such as determinations, rules, declarations, notices, and orders; and Notification and publication of Letters Patent. Indexes are available for specific time periods.	The Government Gazette is published each Wednesday. A Gazettes Referral Page gives access to gazettes published by individual departments. These include the Public Service Gazette, Commonwealth Purchasing and Disposals Gazette, Business Gazette, Australian Securities and Investments Commission (ASIC) Gazette, Tariff Concessions Gazette, Chemicals Gazette and National Registration Authority (NRA) Gazette. The Gazettes are published in pdf and also some are in html format.

Research tool	What information will it give me?	Tips on use
LawLex via Anstat • http://www.anstat. com.au	Free title search on Australian legislation, including Commonwealth, New South Wales, Queensland and Victoria subject indexes.	Search legislation from the Anstat Legislation homepage. Introduces LawLex with searches available by keyword and jurisdiction.
Explanatory Statements to Commonwealth Statutory Rules 1982–1990 • Microfilm National Library of Australia	Available online on ComLaw 1991–	Use the call number mfm N 563, or Amicus Record 27181954 for the National Library.

2.11 Full text of delegated legislation?

Legislative instruments are written instruments that are made in the exercise of power delegated by the Parliament. Examples include regulations, ordinances, determinations or other written instruments that determine the law. The *Legislative Instruments Act 2003* establishes an electronic Federal Register of Legislative Instruments which will be accessible via Comlaw. It will also include up-to-date compilations, showing the text of legislative instruments as currently in force following amendments. It also provides that instruments will need to be tabled before Parliament and the vast majority will be subject to Parliamentary scrutiny, and that legislative instruments will sunset after 10 years, ensuring that instruments will be regularly reviewed and updated and will only remain operative if they continue to be relevant.

See *Delegated Legislation Monitor: Disallowable Instruments of Delegated Legislation Tabled in the Senate* Published by Canberra Senate Procedure Office, 1990–. This is a list of disallowed delegated legislation. Lists all delegated legislation with date made, date tabled and brief summaries. Published weekly with annual reprint.

http://www.aph.gov.au/senate/committee/regord_ctte/mon2005/index.htm

Research tool	What information will it give me?	Tips on use
AustLII • http://www.austlii. edu.au	Commonwealth Consolidated Regulations contains selected Commonwealth Statutory Rules passed since 1989 and subsequently amended. They are an electronic equivalent of the pasted up paper copies of those Statutory Rules. The Commonwealth Numbered Regulations contains the Numbered Rules and Regulations of the Commonwealth of Australia.	Browse Acts in alphabetical order or use the search tools by entering a search query Select 'Recent Documents' for Regulations which are new or have been updated by the Commonwealth Attorney-General's Department. Entries on this page are kept for 28 days.

Research tool	What information will it give me?	Tips on use
Federal Register of Legislative Instruments • http://www.frli.gov.au/ • http://www.comlaw.gov.au/ available also via ComLaw	The Attorney-General's Department's ComLaw legislative repository system became available online on 1 January 2005. This replaces SCALEplus. It contains: Commonwealth primary legislation, as well as other ancillary documents and information, in electronic form, and the Federal Register of Legislative Instruments (FRLI) which was established on 1 January 2005 under the *Legislative Instruments Act 2003* as the authoritative source for legislative instruments and compilations of legislative instruments. The intention is to hold only databases of the legislation of the Commonwealth and non self-governing Territories (and related material such as Bills, explanatory memoranda/statements, tables, indexes and other finding aids) on the system.	Choose FRLI in the left-hand column then Search or Browse the database. There are also Standard, Advanced and Guided Search options provided. Authorised versions of legislative instruments and compilations are provided in pdf format and include the FRLI logo.
Westlaw Australia • http://au.westlaw.com	Commonwealth Acts Regulations from 1901.	Select Expert or Advanced Search forms. Browse Acts alphabetically. Currency information links to subordinate legislation provided.

2.12 **A subject index to cases?**

Research tool	What information will it give me?	Tips on use
The Australian Digest Legal Online FirstPoint (Thomson Reuters) • Paper version — Third edition, looseleaf commenced in 1988 replaced second • http://www.legalonline. thomson.com.au/	Provides short summaries of all significant cases from the beginning of law reporting in Australia in 1825. Cases are arranged into titles. The purpose of The Digest is to comprehensively record developments in case law. Under the main titles, cases are further classified under an established structure. Contains a Table of Cases, Table of Statutes, General Index, List of Abbreviations and a List of Titles.	Each segment within a title is given a square bracket number. This number is the common reference point for all dealt with in that paragraph. To identify the relevant paragraph, use the General Index or the List of Titles. Consult the Key and Research Guide Volume as a starting point. Choose from the Research heading on Legal Online FirstPoint.
Australian Legal Monthly Digest (ALMD) Legal Online FirstPoint (Thomson Reuters) • Paper version only now available of ALMD, though information is provided electronically through FirstPoint • http://www.legalonline. thomson.com.au/	ALMD in hardcopy comprises two booklets: (1) Digest of Law and (2) Cumulative Tables. The Digest contains summaries of reported cases, legislation and recent articles, notes, books, etc. Cases are categorised by subject as used in the *Australian Digest* plus five other topics.	Use the General Index and select the appropriate subject Title. Identify any relevant topics within the title, noting paragraph numbers. Refer to that paragraph number in the Digests of Law for case details. Update using *ALMD Advance*. Choose from the Research heading on Legal Online FirstPoint.

Research tool	What information will it give me?	Tips on use
Australian Current Law —Reporter Butterworths • Paper version (published fortnightly) • LexisNexis AU at http://www.lexisnexis.com	*Australian Current Law* contains two parts (1) Reporter and (2) Legislation. Reporter contains digest of all judgments received from the High Court, Federal Court, Supreme Courts, and selected decisions from the House of Lords, Family Court and other courts and tribunals. Legislation contains information on all legislative developments for all Australian jurisdictions.	Each case is digested according to subject. If the case is on more than one subject, then it is referenced in each. All case digests contain the case name, court, judge/s, date, case no, pages and date received. Use the cumulative Index to identify the subject and the subheading. Use the citation to find the case description. Choose Cases or Legislation Tab at top of LEXISNEXIS screen. Choose to Browse the contents by opening the database using the plus symbols. Choose to search using the customised search template — by topic, case type, case name, citation, judgment date, catchwords/summary, jurisdiction, court, judge, quantum or sentencing.

2.13 **Full text of Commonwealth cases?**

The *Commonwealth Law Reports* (CLR) are the authorised reports for the High Court and the *Federal Court Reports* (FCR) are the authorised reports for the Federal Court. Often High Court cases are reported in several report series. The citation for the authorised report series should be used first and in preference to other series, eg *Mabo v Queensland (No 2)* (1992) 175 CLR 1; (1992) 107 ALR 1; (1997) 66 ALJR 408; (1992) EOC 92-443; BC9202681.

Research tool	What information will it give me?	Tips on use
AustLII • http://www.austlii.edu.au	• High Court of Australia Decisions 1903– • Transcripts of High Court Cases 1994– • Family Court of Australia Decisions 1977– • Federal Court of Australia Full Court Decisions 2002– • Federal Magistrates Court of Australia 2000– • Federal Magistrates Court of Australia – Family Law Decisions 2000– • Australian Competition Tribunal Decisions 1997– • Australian Designs Offices Decisions 1983– • Australian Patent Offices Decisions 1981– • Australian Takeovers Panel Decisions 2000– • Australian Trade Marks Offices Decisions 1991– • Copyright Tribunal Decisions 1997– • Defence Force Discipline Appeal Tribunal Decisions 1999– • Federal Privacy Commissioner of Australia Cases 2002– • Migration Review Tribunal Decisions 1999– • Industrial Relations Court of Australia Decisions 1994– • Administrative Appeals Tribunal Decisions 1976– • Immigration Review Tribunal 1990– • Australian Industrial Relations Commission 1988– • National Native Title Tribunal Decisions 1994– • Refugee Review Tribunal Decisions 1993– • Human Rights and Equal Opportunity Commission Decisions 1985–	The case law databases on these systems can be used as a Digest. A broad topic is much better searched in hardcopy. A small or obscure point may be picked up more easily using electronic searching. The cases do not contain headnotes, catchwords or parts of the hearing details, which are subject to Lawbook Co copyright. The High Court has provided catchwords for decisions since 1996.

Research tool	What information will it give me?	Tips on use
LexisNexis AU • http://www.lexisnexis.com	• High Court of Australia September 1989– • Federal Court of Australia May 1994 • Administrative Law Decisions • Australian Consumer Credit Reports • Australian Corporation Law Reports (ACSR and ACLR) • Australian Law Reports • Intellectual Property Reports • Family Law Reports • Motor Vehicle Reports	Choose Cases and then Search or Browse.
Westlaw Australia • http://au.westlaw.com	• Commonwealth Law Reports volume 1– • Federal Court Cases 1984– • Federal Court Reports 1984– • Federal Law Reports volume 1, 1956– • Australian Criminal Law Reports volume 1, 1979– • Australian Tax Reports volume 1, 1970 • Local Government and Environment Reports volume 1, 1956 • Australian Corporations Law Cases • Australian Financial Services Cases • Australian Trade Practices Cases • High Court of Australia Unreported Judgments 1 July 2000– • Federal Court of Australia Unreported Judgments includes all Federal Court of Australia cases decided since September 1999 which have not been published in the Federal Court Reports	The Default search is by citation. Find by Title also available.

Research tool	What information will it give me?	Tips on use
Legal Online • http://www.legalonline. thomson.com.au/	• Commonwealth Law Reports volume 1– • Federal Court Reports 1984– • Federal Law Reports volume 1, 1956– • Industrial Reports • Australian Bankruptcy Cases • Local Government and Environmental Reports • High Court of Australia unreported 1976– • Federal Court of Australia unreported 1977– • Federal Magistrates Court unreported 2000– • Industrial Relations Court of Australia unreported 1995– • Family Court of Australia unreported 1995– • Administrative Appeals Reports • Australian Tax Reports	Search specific databases by ticking the appropriate box.

Research tool	What information will it give me?	Tips on use
Federal Court of Australia eSearch • http://www.fedcourt. gov.au/ecourt/ecourt_ esearch_slide.html	Includes records of cases in New South Wales, Victoria, South Australia, Tasmania, ACT and N.T. The facility also includes information on cases in the Federal Magistrates Court's federal law jurisdiction. The information you can obtain through eSearch includes: name of each participant in the case; file number; date the case commenced; type of application eg, migration, trade practices; type of each document filed in the case and the date on which it was filed; past and future hearing dates; current status of the case; and, where available, text of Orders made. The database is updated in real time and includes all cases that have commenced since 1 January 1984.	When using the service, please note the new file prefixes for all States eg 'VID' instead of 'V', for Federal Court cases in Victoria, and 'MLG' for Federal Magistrates Court cases, in Victoria.

2.14 **Cases that have been judicially considered?**

The full text databases can also be utilised for this purpose.

Research tool	What information will it give me?	Tips on use
Australian Case Citator Legal Online FirstPoint (Thomson Reuters) • Paper version Legal Online • http://www.legalonline.thomson.com.au/	An alphabetical listing of all reported cases with full references to all series in which cases have been reported since 1825, containing references to all subsequent cases in which a reported case has been judicially considered. Reference is also made to journal articles and notes in which a reported case has been discussed.	Cases are listed alphabetically. Find the name of the case, under which are the names of cases and articles that cite that case. The record gives the full citation, history of the listed case, references to journal articles, and references to cases judicially considering the listed case. Only cases usefully considering the case are recorded. This citator is now accessible electronically via Westlaw Australia. Use KeyCite by citation or title of case.
Australian and New Zealand Citator to UK Reports Butterworths • Paper version • LexisNexis AU at http://www.lexisnexis.com	Alphabetical listing of UK decisions cited in Australia and New Zealand courts. Some other foreign law jurisdiction cases are included from Canada, the US and Europe.	This is a selected database which only includes decisions discussed in later cases. The cross-referencing numerical code allows that more than one case deals with that point of law or contrasts cases. The code number for each case in main volume also allows for cross-checking with the supplement. Search by subject, primary case name, citation or references to cases.

Research tool	What information will it give me?	Tips on use
LawCite • http://www.austlii. edu.au/LawCite/	A free citator resource. Allows authors of Australian law articles to view a list of other articles in the database that cite their article. In addition, a full text search of Austlii will also cover journal articles, judgments, law reform publications, and explanatory notes on the database. A search on a specific case will bring up a list of journal articles on that case. Those held on Austlii will be hyperlinked to the full text. The entry for the case will include legislation and sections cited; cases and articles cited including citation, court, jurisdiction with flag mnemonic, date and citation index; cases referring to this case; and journal articles referring to this case.	Choose the LawCite option from the front page of Austlii to open the search template. Options to search under include Citation, Parties, Court, Jurisdiction, Article title, Author, Year, Cases Considered, and Legislation Considered. LawCite does not provide a digest or catchwords so you cannot search for cases on topic. See also LawCite Help: http://www.austlii.edu.au/LawCite/doc/overview.html
CaseBase Butterworths • LexisNexis AU at http://www.lexisnexis.com	Over 650,000 cases from 56 Australian reporting series, New Zealand Reports, UK authorised reports, the Weekly Law Reports, Lloyd's reports and more than 80 journals.	CaseBase can be searched by Browse or search by Primary Case or article name, citation, judgment date, jurisdiction, court, judge, reference to legislation, words/phrases and catchwords/summary. If the search query has multiple results, then you need to select the appropriate case. Abbreviations for journals and reports used in CaseBase are listed under the Abbreviations heading on the right of the screen. The signal appearing next to the primary case name indicates whether the decision has received positive, negative, cautionary or neutral treatment in subsequent judgments.

Research tool	What information will it give me?	Tips on use
Australian Current Law — Reporter Butterworths • Paper version • LexisNexis AU at http:// www.lexisnexis.com	*Australian Current Law* contains two parts: (1) Reporter and (2) Legislation. The Reporter contains digest of all judgments received from the High Court, Federal Court, Supreme Courts, and selected decisions from the House of Lords, Family Court and other courts and tribunals.	See Table of Cases judicially considered in each issue. This table is not cumulative, but it is consolidated every six months. Cases are listed alphabetically and give citations for ACL Digest. Use that citation to find the details of the case considering the authority. ACL Reporter can be searched separately on the electronic database. Choose Cases or Legislation Tab at top of LEXISNEXIS AU screen. Choose to Browse the contents by opening the database using the plus symbols. Choose to search using the customised search template by topic, case type, case name, citation, judgment date, catchwords/summary, jurisdiction, court, judge, quantum or sentencing.

2.15 Cases that have dealt with specific legislative sections?

The full text databases can also be utilised for this purpose. See 2.13 Full Text of Commonwealth Cases?

Research tool	What information will it give me?	Tips on use
Federal Statutes Annotations Butterworths • Paper version • LexisNexis AU at http:// www.lexisnexis.com	Designed to give users current information on legislation and case law relating to legislation. It includes assent and reprint information, current status of legislation, amending legislation, related Acts, Regulations made and relevant books and articles.	The annotation section sets out leading case authorities to sections of the Act and to Regulations and rules made under the Act. To update, consult *Australian Current Law*. Use Browse or subject search or Legislation title, section regulation or rule number, and references to cases.

Research tool	What information will it give me?	Tips on use
Commonwealth Statutes Annotations Lawbook Co • Paper version only	The *Commonwealth Statutes Annotations* is designed to update the 1973 Consolidation of Acts, pamphlets, reprints and Acts passed by the Commonwealth Parliament. It contains information on last reprint, amendments since that reprint, the dates of parliamentary debates, cases on the Act generally, articles, cases on specific sections and regulation information, including last reprint, amendments since and cases on the Regulations.	The Act, in general and specific sections, is annotated with cases since 1967. The most authoritative decisions are used. To update, use the Australian Case Citator. For additional cases, see the ALMD Table of Legislation Judicially Considered.
LawCite • http://www.austlii. edu.au/LawCite/	A free citator resource. Allows authors of Australian law articles to view a list of other articles in the database that cite their article. In addition, a full text search of Austlii will also cover journal articles, judgments, law reform publications, and explanatory notes on the database. A search on a specific case will bring up a list of journal articles on that case. Those held on Austlii will be hyperlinked to the full text. The entry for the case will include legislation and sections cited; cases and articles cited including citation, court, jurisdiction with flag mnemonic, date and citation index; cases referring to this case; and journal articles referring to this case.	Choose the LawCite option from the front page of Austlii to open the search template. Options to search under include Citation, Parties, Court, Jurisdiction, Article title, Author, Year, Cases Considered, and Legislation Considered. LawCite does not provide a digest or catchwords so you cannot search for cases on topic. See also LawCite Help: http://www.austlii.edu.au/ LawCite/doc/overview. html

Research tool	What information will it give me?	Tips on use
Australian Current Law — Legislation Butterworths • Paper version • LexisNexis AU at http://www.lexisnexis.com	*Australian Current Law* contains two parts: (1) Reporter and (2) Legislation. The Reporter contains digest of all judgments received from the High Court, Federal Court, Supreme Courts, and selected decisions from the House of Lords, Family Court and other courts and tribunals.	Legislation contains information on all legislative developments for all Australian jurisdictions. ACL Legislation can be searched separately on the electronic database. Choose Cases or Legislation Tab at top of LEXISNEXIS AU screen. See Table of Legislation Judicially Considered in each issue. This table is not cumulative, but it is consolidated every six months. Legislation is listed by jurisdiction and then alphabetically. The ACL citation is listed beside the appropriate section. Use this to find the case details in the ACL Digest.
Australian Legal Monthly Digest (ALMD) Legal Online FirstPoint (Thomson Reuters) • Paper version only now available of ALMD, though information is provided electronically through FirstPoint Legal Online • http://www.legalonline.thomson.com.au/	ALMD in hardcopy comprises two booklets: (1) Digest of Law and (2) Cumulative Tables. The Digest contains summaries of reported cases, legislation and recent articles, notes, books, etc. Cases are categorised by subject as used in the *Australian Digest* plus five other topics.	Use the Cumulative Table of Acts Passed, Amended, Repealed or Proclaimed to commence and the appropriate jurisdiction. Use the paragraph number(s) in the relevant Digest of Law booklet. The details in the relevant paragraph include commencement and amendment details. Choose from the Research heading on Lawbook Online. Browse the latest issue or search in the ALMD Legislation search template. Choose Legislation Judicially Considered. Choose from the Research heading on Legal Online FirstPoint.

Research tool	What information will it give me?	Tips on use
CaseBase Butterworths • LexisNexis AU at http:// www.lexisnexis.com	Over 650,000 cases from 56 Australian reporting series, New Zealand Reports, UK authorised reports, the Weekly Law Reports, Lloyd's reports and more than 80 journals.	CaseBase can be searched by Browse or search by Primary Case or article name, citation, judgment date, jurisdiction, court, judge, reference to legislation, words/phrases and catchwords/summary. If the search query has multiple results, then you need to select the appropriate case. Abbreviations for journals and reports used in CaseBase are listed under the Abbreviations heading on the right of the screen. The signal appearing next to the primary case name indicates whether the decision has received positive, negative, cautionary or neutral treatment in subsequent judgments.

3

Australian Capital Territory
— *How Do You Find*

3.1 **An introduction to the jurisdiction?**

See generally, Government homepage at http://www.act.gov.au/accesspoint?
uniqueSessionToken=vkqutgtfq1-3976574938226366598&action=menuHome

Fact Sheets are available at http://www.parliament.act.gov.au/education/
fact-sheets.asp, including 'A brief history of self-government in the ACT', 'Self-
Government — Setting the Scene', 'Government in the ACT', 'Spheres of
government', 'Members of the Legislative Assembly', 'Electing Members of the
Legislative Assembly', 'The Chamber', 'Legislation', 'The Budget Process',
'Hansard', 'What is a Petition?' and 'Committees'.

For an overview of ACT law, see http://www.dpa.act.gov.au/ag/Reports/
Other/History/History.html

3.2 **Parliamentary publications?**

Hansard

Research tool	What information will it give me?	Tips on use
Hansard 1995– • http://www.hansard. act.gov.au/start.htm	The official record of the legislative assembly speeches and debates, Hansard is published as soon as practicable after each sitting week.	By clicking on Sittings (html format), you can view tables of contents and conduct more detailed page-by-page searches, including context searches. This format also has direct links to the Subject and Speech indexes. Transcripts prior to 1995 can be downloaded as an entire day in pdf format.

Index to the Hansard

Research tool	What information will it give me?	Tips on use
Index to the Hansard 1995– • http://www.hansard.act.gov.au/start.htm	Contains an alphabetical index to speeches by Year of Sittings, members and subjects. There is a subject index for each year.	The indexes are for each year, and listings are in alphabetical order. Searching is by free text, with html or pdf formats available.

Committee reports

Research tool	What information will it give me?	Tips on use
Committee Office • http://www.parliament.act.gov.au/committees/index.asp?category=standing&assembly=7	Contains links to Committees and a listing of reports.	Reports are available. Follow through to each committee page and click on the automatic search function.

Other parliamentary publications

Research tool	What information will it give me?	Tips on use
Notice Papers For current and previous Assembly • http://www.legassembly.act.gov.au/assembly-business/index.asp?Category=2&assembly=7	Daily Program for each sitting day and the Orders of the day.	Listings are by time period. There is a draft index for Papers in Pdf format for the 3rd–6th assemblies at http://www.parliament.act.gov.au/downloads/minutes-of-proceedings/Papers_Sixth_Assembly.pdf
Minutes of Proceedings 1992– • http://www.parliament.act.gov.au/assembly-business/index.asp?Category=1&assembly=7	Official record of the motions and transactions of the Legislative Assembly.	Listings are by time period. There is a draft index for Minutes in pdf format for the 3rd–6th assemblies. Pdf format available.

Research tool	What information will it give me?	Tips on use
Bills List • http://www.parliament.act.gov.au/assembly-business/bills-list.asp	The Bills before the Assembly for each Assembly from the 2nd Assembly, with type of Bill; eg, Private Member's Bill, date introduced and the Bills passed. Full text is only available on ACT Legislation Register.	The List is in pdf format. Select the Assembly and browse for information on the relevant Bill.
Summary of Bills • http://www.parliament.act.gov.au/assembly-business/summary.asp	A summary of each bill before the Assembly. The 3rd–6th assemblies are available in pdf format.	The summaries are in alphabetical order.

3.3 Bills?

Research tool	What information will it give me?	Tips on use
ACT Legislation Register • http://www.legislation.act.gov.au/b/default.asp	Contains a Full Text of Bills before the Legislative Assembly. Information includes date of introduction, reporting dates and stage reached in the Assembly.	There is a series of lists including an alphabetical list of Current Bills, an annual listing of bills by year from 1991, bills passed and awaiting notification, bills negatived or discharged by year from 1992. Always check that the instrument has not been disallowed. Text or pdf format available.

3.4 Explanatory material about bills?

Research tool	What information will it give me?	Tips on use
ACT Legislation Register • http://www.legislation.act.gov.au/es/default.asp	Contains a full text of available Explanatory Memoranda for Bills before the Legislative Assembly. Information includes date of introduction, reporting dates and stage reached in the Assembly.	Listings are alphabetical by bill title. Pdf format available.

3.5 A subject index to legislation?

Research tool	What information will it give me?	Tips on use
ACT Legislation Register Acts • http://www.legislation.act.gov.au/a/default.asp	Contains Current, As Notified, and Repealed legislation.	Use the Search facility to access relevant legislation. The Advanced Search form allows a search by category of legislation, current, future or historical version, and pdf or rtf format.

3.6 The commencement date of legislation?

Commencement date rules are set out in the interpretation legislation for each Australian jurisdiction. See the *Interpretation Act 1967* (ACT) for the rules governing the commencement of Australian Capital Territory legislation.

Research tool	What information will it give me?	Tips on use
Laws of the Australian Capital Territory • Paper version with a quarterly update	Acts and Ordinances as passed in hardcover volumes and reprint series. There is also an Acts and Ordinances Reprint series. Contains information on the dates of assent and commencement, amendment details and Acts passed but not yet in force. Consult the most recent annual volume, then use the pink quarterly update.	Otherwise, consult the updating information contained in the reprint series.
ACT Legislation Register Notifications of Commencement Notices 2001– • http://www.legislation.act.gov.au/notify.asp	The ACT Legislation Register is established by the *Legislation Act 2001*. The Act commenced on 12 September 2001. Provides information on notification date, authorising law, name of Act, year and Act number.	Hyperlinks to pdf or rtf version of commencement notice.

3.7 Australian Capital Territory legislation in full text?

The authorised version is published by the Government Printer.

Research tool	What information will it give me?	Tips on use
ACT Legislation Register Acts • http://www.legislation.act.gov.au/a/default.asp	The ACT Legislation Register is established by the *Legislation Act 2001*. The Act commenced on 12 September 2001. Contains the full text of Current Acts, Acts as Notified and Repealed Acts.	Use hyperlinks to access the full text of the legislation in pdf (authorised) or rtf (non-authorised) versions.
AustLII • http://www.austlii.edu.au	Current consolidated legislation and ordinances. Numbered Acts and ordinances.	Listing is alphabetical by title.

3.8 Updates for legislation?

See Checklist 2 Australia for general sources.

Research tool	What information will it give me?	Tips on use
Laws of the Australian Capital Territory Tables 1911–1999 • http://www.legislation.act.gov.au/	The Primary Laws — Alphabetical Table lists amendments to Acts, Ordinances, Subordinate Laws and Regulations since 1911.	The table lists the most recent reprint and then any amendments since that date. Click on 'Legislation update' on the dark blue band on the homepage; you will find listed electronic versions of the tables for the years 2000 to date.
Laws of the Australian Capital Territory Canberra: Government Printer • Paper version with a quarterly update	Acts and Ordinances as passed in hardcover volumes and reprint series. There is also an Acts and Ordinances Reprint series. Contains information on the dates of assent and commencement, amendment details and Acts passed but not yet in force.	Consult the most recent annual volume, then use the pink quarterly update. Otherwise, consult the updating information contained in the reprint series.

Research tool	What information will it give me?	Tips on use
ACT Legislation Register • http://www.legislation. act.gov.au/updates/ Finding_Leg.asp	Yearly legislation updates (including Acts and Delegated Legislation) from 2000 in pdf or rtf format.	The updates have alphabetical and chronological tables for ease of searching.

3.9 A subject index to delegated legislation?

Research tool	What information will it give me?	Tips on use
ACT Legislation Register Subordinate Laws • http://www.legislation. act.gov.au/sl/default.asp	Contains Current, As Notified, and Repealed Subordinate legislation.	Use the Search facility to access relevant subordinate legislation. The Advanced Search form allows a search by category of legislation, current or historical version in pdf or rtf format.

3.10 Full text of delegated legislation?

Research tool	What information will it give me?	Tips on use
ACT Legislation Register Subordinate Laws • http://www.legislation. act.gov.au/sl/default.asp	The ACT Legislation Register is established by the *Legislation Act 2001*. The Act commenced on 12 September 2001. Contains Current, As Made, and Repealed Subordinate legislation.	Use hyperlinks to access the full text of the subordinate legislation in pdf (authorised) or rtf (non-authorised) versions.
AustLII • http://www.austlii. edu.au	Contains current Consolidated Regulations 1979– as well as Numbered Regulations.	This is not the official or authorised version. This is accessed on the ACT Legislation Register. A date of last update is displayed clearly. There is an alphabetical listing and provision for searching.

3.11 A subject index to cases?

See Checklist 2 Australia for general sources.

3.12 Full text of Australian Capital Territory cases?

The authorised reports of the ACT are the *Australian Capital Territory Reports*, which are included in the *Australian Law Reports* (ALR).

Research tool	What information will it give me?	Tips on use
The Supreme Court of the ACT • http://www.courts.act.gov.au/supreme/content/judgments.asp?textonly=no	Supreme Court of the Australian Capital Territory Decisions 2002– ACT Court of Appeal Decisions 2002–	Browse alphabetically or free text search. html only.
AustLII • http://www.austlii.edu.au	Supreme Court of the Australian Capital Territory Decisions 1986– Administrative Appeals Tribunal of the ACT Decisions 1996– Residential Tenancies Tribunal of the ACT Decisions 1998– ACT Court of Appeal Decisions 2002–	Browse alphabetically or search by Act name or individual word. html only.
Westlaw Australia • http://au.westlaw.com	Australian Capital Territory Unreported Judgments September 1999–	Find by citation or title. KeyCite citator facilities available. Full text search template available.
Legal Online • http://legalonline.thomson.com.au/	• Supreme Court of the ACT unreporteds 1995–	Search specific databases by ticking the appropriate box.
LexisNexisAU • http://lexisnexis.com	Australian Law Reports Unreported Judgments – ACT 1995–	Updated daily. Subscription required.

3.13 Cases that have been judicially considered?

See Checklist 2 Australia for general sources.

3.14 Cases that have dealt with specific legislative sections?

Research tool	What information will it give me?	Tips on use
Australian Law Reports Consolidated Index Tables — Vols 1–200 (as at May 2005). Cumulative supplements exist for volumes past 200.	Includes 'Table of Statutes Judicially Considered' and denotes ACT and NT reports.	If there is no consolidated index or cumulative supplement, then check each volume.

New South Wales —
How Do You Find

4.1 **An introduction to the jurisdiction?**

See generally, New South Wales Government homepage http://www.nsw.gov.au and see also http://www.parliament.nsw.gov.au/prod/web/common.nsf/key/ ResourcesSystem for a description of the Courts, Parliament and system of government in New South Wales.

4.2 **Parliamentary publications?**

Hansard

Research tool	What information will it give me?	Tips on use
NSW Legislative Council NSW Legislative Assembly 1991– • http://www.parliament. nsw.gov.au/prod/web/co mmon.nsf/V3HHBHome	Hansard transcripts are the official record of the proceedings of the Parliament. They are not a strict verbatim record, but rather a literate, accurate and verified record.	The Hansard is accessible in many ways — by Date, by Subject, by Member, by Bill Name, by House of Parliament, in Full Text Transcript and by searching the Hansard. Available in html format and download in pdf.

Committee reports

Research tool	What information will it give me?	Tips on use
Committee Reports Assembly, Council, Joint September 1999– ; also selected reports from 1991. • http://www.parliament.nsw.gov.au/prod/parlment/Committee.nsf/V3ListReports	The Parliamentary committees' reports give detailed consideration to issues of concern to the House, including proposed laws and policies.	The Committee reports can be browsed or searched. Browsing is by committee name and, for Current Parliament, by Date, Title, Committee, Inquiry, Awaiting Government Response. For Past Parliaments (pre 2003), by Date, Title, Committee, and Inquiry. To search, use the link on the Committee homepage. Individual committees' contact details are provided under the Committee Profiles and historical records of committees are available under the Archives link.

Other parliamentary publications

Research tool	What information will it give me?	Tips on use
House Papers NSW Legislative Council NSW Legislative Assembly 1991– • http://www.parliament.nsw.gov.au/prod/web/common.nsf/V3HHBHome	The House papers contain procedural information concerning issues before Parliament. This includes the Daily Program, Notices of Motion, Minutes, Questions and Answers, and Statutory Rules.	Choose either 'Legislative Council' or 'Legislative Assembly' and then the category of document required (All, Notices, Minutes, Questions, Statutory Rules). Documents are available for download as Word or pdf. To search, use the link on the House Papers homepage.

4.3 **Bills?**

Research tool	What information will it give me?	Tips on use
Bills Homepage – NSW Parliament • http://www.parliament. nsw.gov.au/prod/ parlment/nswbills.nsf/ V3BillsHome	This database provides full text of the Bills and explanatory notes, and status of the Bills, with all pertinent dates, including dates introduced in both houses, First, Second and Third Readings, Amendment dates, and Assent dates. The Bills List provides information about the passage of Bills through the Parliament, together with an explanatory note, the current version of each Bill, as well as Hansard references.	This database can be searched or browsed. To search, use the link on the Bills homepage. Browsing is either alphabetically by session, government or private Bills, or by status, such as withdrawn, negatived, Legislative Assembly or Council, or Bills receiving assent. Bills and other information are available pdf format, with Explanatory Memoranda in html format.

4.4 **Explanatory material about Bills?**

Research tool	What information will it give me?	Tips on use
Explanatory Notes • http://www.parliament. nsw.gov.au/prod/ parlment/nswbills.nsf/ V3BillsHome	Explanatory notes are attached to the Bills website. The Bills database provides full text of the Bill and explanatory notes, as well as status of the Bill with all pertinent dates including dates introduced in both houses, First, Second and Third Readings, amend-ment dates and assent dates. The Bills List provides information about the passage of Bills through the Parliament, together with the explanatory note, the current version of each Bill, as well as Hansard references.	This database can be searched or browsed. To search, use the link on the Bills homepage. Browsing is either alphabetically by session, government or private, or by status like withdrawn, negatived, Legislative Assembly or Council or Bills receiving assent. Bills and other information are available in pdf format and Explanatory Memoranda in html format.

Research tool	What information will it give me?	Tips on use
LawLex via Anstat • http://research.lawlex.com.au/	Free title search on Australian legislation, which includes all Australian jurisdictions.	Searches available by keyword, year, number and jurisdiction. Free Explanatory Memorandum link available where material is on other free site.

4.5 A subject index to legislation?

Research tool	What information will it give me?	Tips on use
New South Wales Statutes Annotations LexisNexis AU • Paper version • http://www.lexisnexis.com	Information on assent, commencement, reprint, repeal, name changes, amendments, Regulations made and relevant books and articles. Specific sections of each Act are annotated where an amendment has been made to that section or where a relevant case has been decided with respect to that section.	Use the Index to identify legislation relevant to a subject. *Australian Current Law* should be used to update *New South Wales Statutes Annotations*.
New South Wales Statutes Annotations and References Lawbook Co • Paper version – looseleaf service updated monthly	Provides case law, articles and annotations for statutes from 1824 to the present date. Also includes cross-references to related legislation for each statute.	Use *Wicks Subject Index to the Acts and Regulations NSW*.
LawLex via Anstat • http://research.lawlex.com.au/	Subject index of principal legislation from all Australian jurisdictions.	Searches available by keyword, year, number and jurisdiction.

4.6 The commencement date of legislation?

Commencement date rules are set out in the interpretation legislation for each Australian jurisdiction. See the *Interpretation Act 1987* (NSW) for the rules governing the commencement of New South Wales legislation.

Information about the commencement dates of Acts can also be obtained from the Weekly Acts Tables, Chronological List, located under NSW Legislation on the Parliamentary Counsel website. See http://www.legislation.nsw.gov.au/ for commencement information under Historical Notes for each Act.

Research tool	What information will it give me?	Tips on use
New South Wales Statutes Annotations LexisNexis AU • Paper version – issued annually with supplements issued quarterly • http://www.lexisnexis. com	Information on assent, commencement, reprint, repeal, name changes, amendments, Regulations made and relevant books and articles. Specific sections of each Act are annotated where an amendment has been made to that section or where a relevant case has been decided with respect to that section.	Look under the relevant Act, then consult the section outlining the legislative history of the Act. It sets out original commencement dates of amending Legislation. Update using *Australian Current Law*.

4.7 New South Wales legislation in full text?

The only authorised version of legislation is that produced by the NSW Government Printer.

Research tool	What information will it give me?	Tips on use
Legislation Pamphlets Series • Paper version	Contains the most recent authorised reprint.	Consult the blue page at the back of each reprint for amending legislation since the last reprint.
Parliamentary Counsel's Office website • http://www.legislation. nsw.gov.au/maintop/ scanact/inforce/NONE/0	Full Text of New South Wales legislation in html format. Listed by In Force, As Made and then alphabetical by title.	No pdf format available. Individual sections can be accessed or select Whole Instrument for full text.
Austlii • http://www.austlii. edu.au	This database contains consolidated Acts and delegated legislation of New South Wales as provided by the NSW Parliamentary Counsel's Office.	Browse Acts in alpha-betical order or use the search tools by entering a search query. Select the Recent Updates databases for information on consolidated legislation, which is either new or has been updated in the last 28 days. The date above does not mean that all Acts are consolidated as at that date, but rather this is the date that data was most recently received. The material can be viewed in html format or downloaded in text format. Unauthorised version.

Research tool	What information will it give me?	Tips on use
LawLex via Anstat 1999– • http://research.lawlex.com.au/	Subject index of principal legislation from all Australian jurisdictions.	Searches available by keyword, year, number and jurisdiction.

4.8 Updates for legislation?

Research tool	What information will it give me?	Tips on use
New South Wales Legislation in Force Sydney: Parliamentary Counsel's Office • http://www.legislation.nsw.gov.au	Gives details of the Acts and Instruments In Force on a monthly basis, including amendments. Update available in pdf format.	Click on the relevant link to update.
Legislation Pamphlets Series	Contains the most recent authorised reprint.	Consult the blue page at the back of each reprint for amending legislation since the last reprint.
New South Wales Statutes Annotations LexisNexis AU • Paper version – issued annually with supplements issued quarterly • http://www.lexisnexis.com	Information on assent, commencement, reprint, repeal, name changes, amendments, Regulations made and relevant books and articles. Specific sections of each Act are annotated where an amendment has been made to that section or where a relevant case has been decided with respect to that section.	Look under the relevant Act, and then consult the section outlining the legislative history of the Act. It sets out original commencement dates and commencement dates of amending legislation. Update using *Australian Current Law*.

4.9 Subject index to delegated legislation?

Research tool	What information will it give me?	Tips on use
New South Wales Statutes Annotations LexisNexis AU • Paper version – issued annually with supplements issued quarterly • http://www.lexisnexis.com	Information on assent, commencement, reprint, repeal, name changes, amendments, Regulations made and relevant books and articles. Specific sections of each Act are annotated where an amendment has been made to that section or where a relevant case has been decided with respect to that section.	Use the Index to identify legislation relevant to a subject. *Australian Current Law* should be used to update.

Research tool	What information will it give me?	Tips on use
New South Wales Statutes Annotations and References Lawbook Co • Paper version — looseleaf service updated monthly	Provides case law and articles annotations for statutes from 1824 to the present date. It also includes cross-references to related legislation for each statute.	Use *Wicks Subject Index to the Acts and Regulations of NSW*.
LawLex via Anstat 1999– • http://research.lawlex. com.au/	Subject index of principal legislation from all Australian jurisdictions.	Searches available by keyword, year, number and jurisdiction.

4.10 **Full text of delegated legislation?**

Research tool	What information will it give me?	Tips on use
NSW Consolidated Regulations	Regulations are required by law to be published here. Annual volumes and a looseleaf reprint service are also available.	
AustLII • http://www.austlii. edu.au	This database contains consolidated Acts and delegated legislation of New South Wales as provided by the NSW Parliamentary Counsel's Office.	This database can be searched or browsed. Browsing is alphabetical and searching can be by Act name or word. Available in html format. Browse Acts in alphabetical order or use the search tools by entering a search query. Select the Recent Updates databases for information on consolidated legislation, which is either new or has been updated in the last 28 days. The date above does not mean that all Acts are consolidated as at that date, but rather this is the date that data was most recently received. The material can be viewed in html format or downloaded in text format.

Research tool	What information will it give me?	Tips on use
Regulations in Force (Principal regulations, rules, by-laws etc) • http://www.legislation.nsw.gov.au/maintop/scanact/inforce/NONE/0	An alphabetical list of Regulations in Force.	Click on first letter of title to browse. Available in html format only.
LawLex via Anstat 1999– • http://research.lawlex.com.au/	Subject index of principal legislation from all Australian jurisdictions.	Searches available by keyword, year, number and jurisdiction.

4.11 A subject index to cases?

See Checklist 2 Australia for general sources.

4.12 Full text of New South Wales cases?

The authorised law reports are: 1863–1879 *Supreme Court Reports*; 1880–1889 *Law Reports New South Wales*; 1900–1970 *State Reports New South Wales*; 1971 onwards *New South Wales Law Reports*.

Research tool	What information will it give me?	Tips on use
Caselaw NSW • http://www.lawlink.nsw. gov.au/lawlink/caselaw/ ll_caselaw.nsf/pages/ cl_index	Decisions of the following: Administrative Decisions Tribunal (1999–2005) Compensation Court (2001–2003) Court of Appeal (1999–2005) Court of Criminal Appeal (1999–2005) Drug Court (1999–2005) Dust Diseases Tribunal (2001–2005) Fair Trading Tribunal (1999–2002) Industrial Relations Commission (2000–2005) Land and Environment Court (1999–2005) Local Court (2002–2005) Medical Tribunal (1999–2005) Supreme Court (1999–2005) Victim Compensation Tribunal – appeals (1999–2005) Judgments and decisions pre 1999.	Click on the link to the relevant Court or Tribunal, then browse by year or use the search function. The database also has an Advanced Search option with fields such as parties, judge, legislation cited and Boolean operators.

Research tool	What information will it give me?	Tips on use
AustLII • http://www.austlii.edu.au	Supreme Court of New South Wales Decisions 1995– Supreme Court of New South Wales — Court of Appeal Decisions 1999– Supreme Court of New South Wales — Court of Criminal Appeal Decisions 1999– Compensation Court of New South Wales Decisions 1985– Drug Court of New South Wales Decisions 1999– Land and Environment Court of New South Wales Decisions 1988– Administrative Decisions Tribunal of New South Wales 1999– Community Services Appeals Tribunal of New South Wales Decisions 1998– Dust Diseases Tribunal of New South Wales Decisions 1989– Industrial Commission of New South Wales Decisions 1985– Residential Tenancies Tribunal of New South Wales Decisions 1986– Strata Schemes Board of New South Wales Decisions 1997–	The case law databases on these systems can be used as a Digest. A broad topic is much better searched in hardcopy. A small or obscure point may be picked up more easily using electronic searching. The cases do not contain headnotes, catchwords or parts of the hearing details, which are subject to Lawbook Co copyright. Page numbers (where present) have been inserted by SCALE. The Court has provided catchwords for decisions since 1996.
Westlaw Australia • http://au.westlaw.com	Unreported judgments Supreme Court 1999–	Select Keycite or Quick Search mode.
Legal Online • http://legalonline.thomson.com.au/	Supreme Court of New South Wales unreported decisions 1995– Court of Appeal for New South Wales unreported decisions 1995– Court of Criminal Appeal for New South Wales 1995–	Search specific databases by ticking the appropriate box.

Research tool	What information will it give me?	Tips on use
LexisNexisAU • http://www.lexisnexis.com	*New South Wales Law Reports*. Contains reported decisions from 1901 and unreported decisions from 1984.	Contains New South Wales Supreme Court decisions. This database can be searched or browsed. Search terms are extremely wide, including case name, citation, and keyword. Browsing is by year and then case number.

4.13 Cases that have been judicially considered?

See Checklist 2 Australia for general sources.

4.14 Cases that have dealt with specific legislative sections?

See Checklist 2 Australia for general sources.

Research tool	What information will it give me?	Tips on use
Caselaw NSW • http://www.lawlink.nsw.gov.au/lawlink/caselaw/ll_caselaw.nsf/pages/cl_index	Decisions of the following: Administrative Decisions Tribunal (1999–2005) Compensation Court (2001–2003) Court of Appeal (1999–2005) Court of Criminal Appeal (1999–2005) Drug Court (1999–2005) Dust Diseases Tribunal (2001–2005) Fair Trading Tribunal (1999–2002) Industrial Relations Commission (2000–2005) Land and Environment Court (1999–2005) Local Court (2002–2005) Medical Tribunal (1999–2005) Supreme Court (1999–2005) Victim Compensation Tribunal – appeals (1999–2005) Judgments and decisions pre 1999.	Click on the link to the relevant Court or Tribunal, then browse by year or use the search function. The database also has an Advanced Search option with fields such as parties, judge, legislation cited and Boolean operators.

Research tool	What information will it give me?	Tips on use
New South Wales Statutes Annotations LexisNexis AU • Paper version — issued annually with supplements issued quarterly • http://www.lexisnexis. com	Information on assent, commencement, reprint, repeal, name changes, amendments, Regulations made and relevant books and articles. Specific sections of each Act are annotated where an amendment has been made to that section, or where a relevant case has been decided with respect to that section.	Look under the title of the main Act and then use the Annotations section. *Australian Current Law* should be used to update *New South Wales Statutes Annotations*.
New South Wales Statutes Annotations and References Lawbook Co • Paper version — looseleaf service updated monthly	Provides case law and articles annotations for statutes from 1824 to the present date. Also includes cross-references to related legislation for each statute.	Use *Wicks Subject Index to the Acts and Regulations NSW*.
NSW Law Reports Index 1971–1984, 1985–1993, 1992–2001 and 2000–2003	All references to legislation that has been judicially considered in reported decisions.	See the table for Statutes, Rules, etc, Judicially Considered.
NSW Judgments Bulletin Sydney: Legal Bulletin Service, 1984–	Digests recent information — discontinued.	Look at the table of Statutes, Rules, etc, cited.

5

Northern Territory —
How Do You Find

5.1 **An introduction to the jurisdiction?**

See generally, the Legislative Assembly's Publications page http://www.nt.gov.au/lant/pub/pub.shtml and http://www.nt.gov.au/lant/pub/ip2.shtml 'A Brief History of Administration' for information on the establishment of the Northern Territory Government and Legislative Assembly, and the legislative history of the development of the Government.

The Northern Territory Government homepage http://www.nt.gov.au provides the entry point for information on the various agencies and departments of the Northern Territory Government.

5.2 **Parliamentary publications?**

Hansard

Research tool	What information will it give me?	Tips on use
Parliamentary Record 1990– • http://www.nt.gov.au/lant/hansard/hansard.shtml	The Parliamentary Record database represents an electronic version of the Historical record of the proceedings of the Northern Territory Legislative Assembly. It contains the Debates, Minutes of the proceedings, Questions and Answers, Members' speeches and Parliamentary Summary.	The Daily Hansard contains the most recent day only. Select the appropriate Assembly (eg Sixth) from the Hansard homepage. The Debates Record can then be browsed by date, by topic, including debates on Bills, Minutes of the day, and then questions and answers. Searching is by a full free text search using Lotus Notes. Results can be arranged by relevance or date. In html format only. Enhanced Search function available since Ninth Assembly only.

Indexes to the Hansard

Research tool	What information will it give me?	Tips on use
Index to the Parliamentary Record 1990– • http://www.nt.gov.au/ lant/hansard/hansard. shtml	There are indexes to debates, member's speeches and questions. The index to debates contains links to speeches, adjournments, messages, explanations and tabled papers. The tabled papers section contains committee reports.	The Daily Hansard provides the most recent day only. Select the appropriate timeframe from the Hansard homepage. Browsing is by date, then alphabetically by the type of record, such as Bill introduction, adjournment, or address in reply. Searching is by a full free text search using Lotus Notes. Results can be arranged by relevance or date. Html format only. Enhanced Search function available since Ninth Assembly only.

Committee reports

Research tool	What information will it give me?	Tips on use
Committee Reports • http://www.nt.gov.au/ lant/parliament/ committees/comm/ comm.shtml	Full text of reports.	Listed by title. Available in pdf.

5.3 Bills?

See Checklist 2 Australia for general sources.

Research tool	What information will it give me?	Tips on use
Register of Legislation 1995– • http://www.dcm.nt.gov. au/strong_service_ delivery/supporting_ government/register_of_ legislation	Contains details of Bills under consideration by the Legislative Assembly, and any resulting Acts. There are the dates of introduction, first, second and third reading, assent, commencement and the Gazette number. Includes text of Bills, Acts and second reading speeches.	Text is only available for more recent Bills. Use the All Records to find information pertinent to an Act in force. The Bills by session (in reverse chronological order), by sponsor (alphabetically) and current (by Act amending or uncategorised) if new legislation. Html format only.

5.4 Explanatory material about Bills?

Explanatory notes are generally not available online. However, it can be of use to search the Northern Territory homepage at http://www.nt.gov.au/ as some departments have selected explanatory notes on the web.

5.5 A subject index to legislation?

Research tool	What information will it give me?	Tips on use
Lawlex via Anstat • http://www.anstat.com.au	Alphabetical subject index of all Northern Territory legislation and regulations.	Browse alphabetically or search using keywords, year, number, and type: Act, regulation, bill.

5.6 The commencement date of legislation?

An Act assented to by the Administrator comes into operation on the day on which that assent is declared. An Act reserved for the Governor-General comes into operation on the day upon which notification that the Governor-General has assented to the Act is published in the Gazette.

Research tool	What information will it give me?	Tips on use
Northern Territory History of Legislation 1995– • http://www.dcm.nt.gov.au/strong_service_delivery/supporting_government/northern_territory_legislation_history_database	Contains historical consolidations of Acts and subordinate legislation, first alphabetically and then by date.	Use the alphabetical table to find the most recent consolidation of the legislation or Regulation, then see the information at the top of the page for amending legislation and its commencement. In Html format only.
Register of Legislation 1995– • http://www.dcm.nt.gov.au/strong_service_delivery/supporting_government/register_of_legislation	Contains details of Bills under consideration by the Legislative Assembly and any resulting Acts. There are the dates of introduction, first, second and third reading, assent, commencement and the Gazette number. Includes text of Bills, Acts and second reading speeches.	Text is only available for more recent Bills. Use the All Records to find information pertinent to an Act in force. Find the Bills by session (in reverse chronological order), by sponsor (alphabetically) and current (by Act amending or uncategorised) if new legislation. In html format only.

Research tool	What information will it give me?	Tips on use
Laws of the Northern Territory of Australia Canberra: Commonwealth Government Printer, 1948– • Paper version	Acts and ordinances as passed in hardcover volumes and reprint series. There is also an Acts and Ordinances Reprint series. It contains information on the dates of assent and commencement, amendment details and Acts passed since 1911.	Consult the most recent annual volume, then use the blue quarterly update. Otherwise, consult the updating information contained in the reprint series.

5.7 Northern Territory legislation in full text?

The Government Printer publishes the official authoritative version of the Acts and Regulations (together with subsequent amendments).

Research tool	What information will it give me?	Tips on use
Current Northern Territory Legislation Database • http://www.dcm.nt.gov. au/strong_service_ delivery/supporting_ government/current_ northern_territory_ legislation_database	This database contains all the current consolidated Acts, Regulations, and By-Laws of the Northern Territory. Amendments that have been made that have not commenced are not included until they are in force.	Can be viewed alphabetically, by type, by controlling agency or by parent Act and subordinate legislation. In Word, pdf and html format.
AustLII • http://www.austlii. edu.au	Contains Consolidated Acts and Regulations of the Northern Territory.	Data provided from Northern Territory Parliamentary Counsel database.
Northern Territory Acts by year 1995– • http://notes.nt.gov.au/ dcm/legislat/Acts.nsf/ 84c76a0f7bf3fb7269256 49e001c03bb?OpenView	Contains information on Acts as passed since 1995. Information includes Act No, Title, Assent, and commencement dates.	Acts are listed by year, then alphabetically. Click on the side arrows. Searching is by a full free text search. Results can be arranged by relevance or date. In html format only.

Research tool	What information will it give me?	Tips on use
Laws of the Northern Territory of Australia Canberra: Commonwealth Government Printer, 1948– • Paper version	Acts and ordinances as passed in hardcover volumes and reprint series. There is also an Acts and Ordinances Reprint series. Contains information on the dates of assent and commencement, amendment details and Acts passed since 1911.	Consult the most recent annual volume, then use the blue quarterly update. Otherwise, consult the updating information contained in the reprint series.

5.8 Updates for legislation?

See Checklist 2 Australia for general sources.

Research tool	What information will it give me?	Tips on use
Laws of the Northern Territory of Australia Canberra: Commonwealth Government Printer, 1948– • Paper version	Acts and ordinances as passed in hardcover volumes and reprint series. There is also an Acts and Ordinances Reprint series. Contains information on the dates of assent and commencement, amendment details and Acts passed since 1911.	Consult the most recent annual volume, then use the blue quarterly update. Otherwise consult the updating information contained in the reprint series.

5.9 A subject index to delegated legislation?

There is no subject guide to delegated legislation in the Northern Territory. See Checklist 2 Australia for general sources.

5.10 Full text of delegated legislation?

Research tool	What information will it give me?	Tips on use
Current Northern Territory Legislation Database • http://www.dcm.nt.gov. au/strong_service_ delivery/supporting_ government/current_ northern_territory_ legislation_database	This database contains all the current consolidated Acts, Regulations, and By-Laws of the Northern Territory. Amendments that have been made but have not commenced are not included until they are in force.	Can be viewed alphabetically, by type, by controlling agency or by parent Act and subordinate legislation. In Word, pdf or html format.

Research tool	What information will it give me?	Tips on use
AustLII • http://www.austlii.edu.au	Contains Consolidated Acts and Regulations of the Northern Territory.	Data provided from Northern Territory Parliamentary Counsel database.
Laws of the Northern Territory of Australia Canberra: Commonwealth Government Printer, 1948–	Regulations are also published here.	Looseleaf reprint since 1979, and individual issues with annual volumes. Chronological and alphabetical lists.

5.11 A subject index to cases?

See Checklist 2 Australia for general sources.

5.12 Full text of Northern Territory cases?

The authorised Law reports of the Northern Territory are the *Northern Territory Reports* (NTR), contained in the *Australian Law Reports* (ALR).

The Northern Territory Law Reports (NTLR), from 1992 are in paper version only.

Research tool	What information will it give me?	Tips on use
AustLII • http://www.austlii.edu.au	Supreme Court of the Northern Territory Decisions 1986– Supreme Court of the Northern Territory – Court of Appeal Decisions 2000– Supreme Court of the Northern Territory – Court of Criminal Appeal Decisions 2000– Anti-Discrimination Commission Decisions 1995–	The case law databases on these systems can be used as a Digest. A broad topic is much better searched in hardcopy. A small or obscure point may be picked up more easily using electronic searching. The cases do not contain headnotes, catchwords or parts of the hearing details, which are subject to Lawbook Co copyright. Page numbers (where present) have been inserted by SCALE. The Court has provided catchwords for decisions since 1996.
LexisNexis AU • http://www.lexisnexis.com	Northern Territory Reports Unreported Judgments from NT Supreme Court 1995–	Reported judgments may be found in Casebase and unreported judgments in the Unreported Judgments search function.

Research tool	What information will it give me?	Tips on use
Westlaw Australia • http://www.westlaw.com.au	Unreported Judgments from September 1999. Supreme Court of the Northern Territory (Full Bench only). This includes cases from the Supreme Court of the Northern Territory (Full Bench only), the Northern Territory Court of Appeal and the Court of Criminal Appeal of the Northern Territory.	Search by citation, title, catchwords.
Legal Online • http://legalonline.thomson.com.au/	Supreme Court of the Northern Territory 1995– Court of Criminal Appeal of the Northern Territory 1995–	Search specific databases by ticking the appropriate box.

5.13 **Cases that have been judicially considered?**

See Checklist 2 Australia for general sources.

5.14 **Cases that have dealt with specific legislative sections?**

See Checklist 2 Australia for general sources.

Research tool	What information will it give me?	Tips on use
Queensland and Northern Territories Judgments Bulletin Sydney: Legal Bulletin Service vol 1, 1987–1999	Digested recent decisions – discontinued.	Look at table of Statutes, Rules, etc, cited.

Queensland —
How Do You Find

6.1 **An introduction to the jurisdiction?**

Queensland has a unicameral system.

An overview of the Queensland legal system can be found at http://www.parliament.qld.gov.au/view/education/education.asp?area=overview&LIndex=0&SubArea=overview

This page contains an excellent glossary of terms used in Queensland and Australian Parliamentary Legislative and Financial processes.

An overview of the court system in Queensland can be found at http://www.courts.qld.gov.au/98.htm

For current and historical information on Parliament and members, see http://www.parliament.qld.gov.au/view/historical/historical.asp?area=committees&LIndex=0&SubArea=committees

6.2 **Parliamentary publications?**

Hansard

Research tool	What information will it give me?	Tips on use
Parliamentary Debates/Hansard 1990– • General Information on the Hansard can be found at http://www.parliament.qld.gov.au/view/legislativeAssembly/legislativeAssembly.asp?area=hansard&LIndex=3&SubArea=hansard • Search mechanism is at http://parlinfo.parliament.qld.gov.au/ISYSHanSimp.htm	The Hansard provides transcripts of the debates of the Parliament, ministerial conferences and evidence given before parliamentary committees and commissions of inquiry for members of Parliament, committee secretariats, Government departments and other clients. The information contained in Hansard includes: • The second reading speech made by the Minister who introduced the Bill • The second reading debate • Debate on the Bill in Committee of the Whole House (including the text of any amendments moved).	To search the Hansard, first select the year, then type the word or phrase and click OK to submit. For complex queries use AND, OR, BUT operators before submitting. Requiring the word to be within one paragraph or a string of words can narrow the search. If undertaking a broad search, the results may be numerous. If searching for the second reading speech, narrow the results by using past or current master Bill registry.

Committee reports

Research tool	What information will it give me?	Tips on use
Parliamentary Committee Reports • General Information on the Committee System is at http://www.parliament.qld.gov.au/view/committees/committees.asp?area=introduction&LIndex=0&SubArea=introduction#subnav • Search mechanism is at http://parlinfo.parliament.qld.gov.au/ISYSComSimp.htm	This site will gives information on each committee, their current investigations, and completed committee reports. The committees in Queensland are the: • Legal, Constitutional and Administrative Review Committee • Members' Ethics and Parliamentary Privileges Committee • Standing Orders Committee • Travelsafe Committee • Scrutiny of Legislation Committee • Public Accounts Committee • Public Works Committee • Parliamentary Criminal Justice Committee • Estimates Committees • Select Committee on Procedural Review • Select Committee on Parliamentary Entitlements	Unless trying to access a specific committee report, it is better to use the search mechanism. When searching, it is useful to select the relevant committee. Therefore, a general understanding of the role and functions of each of the committees will make the process of access to relevant information faster and easier.

Other parliamentary publications

Research tool	What information will it give me?	Tips on use
Votes and Proceedings of the Legislative Assembly • General Information about Votes and Proceedings at http://www.parliament.qld.gov.au/view/legislativeAssembly/legislativeAssembly.asp?area=tableOffice&LIndex=4&SubArea=VP&Bindex=0&nav=VP • Search mechanism using ISYS http://parlinfo.parliament.qld.gov.au/ISYSToSimp.htm	This is the official record of the Legislative Assembly, akin to minutes of a meeting. The Votes and Proceedings gives information about the progress of Bills through the Legislative Assembly along with the text of any amendment moved, and whether it is agreed to and the date of assent. It also gives information about the progress of subordinate legislation, including the tabling of the subordinate legislation and the text of any motion of disallowance moved and its outcome.	The Votes and Proceedings are published each day. For a simple search, type in the word or phrase. Do not press 'enter' because it will start a compound search build. Compound searches can use AND, OR, BUT and NOT, or within paragraphs or within a certain number of words. The results first contain the sitting date and then the page number. The page can be viewed in html or pdf format.

6.3 **Bills?**

For further information on procedure, see http://www.legislation.qld.gov.au/Bills.htm

See Checklist 2 Australia for general resources.

Research tool	What information will it give me?	Tips on use
Bills — Legislation Homepage 1992– • http://www.legislation.qld.gov.au/Bill_Pages/bills_home.htm	This database contains current full text electronic copies of Bills and the explanatory notes if available since 1992. They are listed according to parliamentary session in which they were introduced. The Bills database also provides the following information: • The short title of the Bill (An asterisk (*) indicates a private member's Bill) • Explanatory memorandum of the Bill (where available) • The name of the Member introducing the Bill • The date of the introduction of the Bill • The date of enactment if relevant	The 'What's New' page also provides information on the most recent Bills introduced into Parliament. The 'search' page allows Bills to be searched by name rather than by year of introduction. Documents can be downloaded in pdf format.
Current Master Bills Registry • http://www.parliament.qld.gov.au/view/legislativeassembly/legislation.asp	A guide to legislation currently before, and passed by, the Queensland Legislative Assembly.	Available only in pdf format. To search for a word, use the Ctrl + F function.
Current Bills Information Paper • http://www.parliament.qld.gov.au/view/legislativeAssembly/legislativeAssembly.asp?area=tableOffice&LIndex=14&SubArea=tabled&nav=tabled	The information contained in this document consists of extracts from the Explanatory notes (where available) accompanying Bills on their introduction to the House. Bills and Explanatory notes (1992 to 2000) are available on the Internet at http://www.legislation.qld.gov.au/Bills.htm	Available in pdf or unformatted html. To search for a word, use the Ctrl + F function.

Research tool	What information will it give me?	Tips on use
LawLex via Anstat 1999– • http://www.anstat.com.au	Free title search on legislation. Subject index of legislation, regulations and bills.	Search legislation from the Anstat Legislation homepage. Introduces LawLex with searches available by keyword and jurisdiction. Free Explanatory memorandum link available where material on other free site.

6.4 Explanatory material about Bills?

The explanatory notes are usually only available for Public Bills, not Private Members' Bills http://www.legislation.qld.gov.au/Bills.htm

The notes aim to summarise and explain the provisions of the proposed legislation. The ways in which the notes may be used to interpret the legislation are set out in s 14B of the *Acts Interpretation Act 1954* (Qld).

Research tool	What information will it give me?	Tips on use
Bills – Legislation Homepage • http://www.legislation.qld.gov.au/Bill_Pages/bills_home.htm	All Public Bills are issued with an explanation of the operation of the proposed law since 1990. The OQPC website alphabetically lists Bills introduced during the relevant parliamentary year and session. It provides links to download Explanatory memoranda. The page also gives the date, status of the Bill and the name of the person introducing the Bill.	The Acrobat Reader icon in the EXP column indicates that an explanatory note is available for that Bill. Clicking on the icon displays the explanatory note (in pdf format).

6.5 **A subject index to legislation?**

See Checklist 2 Australia for more general information.

Research tool	What information will it give me?	Tips on use
Queensland Legislation Annotations — Current Legislation Brisbane: Government Printer, 1996– • Paper version with six monthly consolidations and weekly cumulating supplement. • http://www.legislation. qld.gov.au/Leg_info/ anno_current.htm	Table 4 is a brief subject guide to Queensland Legislation.	Look up the likely subject area, noting the Acts that are listed.
LawLex via Anstat 1999– • http://www.anstat. com.au	Alphabetical subject index of all Queensland legislation and regulations.	Browse alphabetically or search using keywords, year, number, and type: Act, regulation, bill.

6.6 **The commencement date of legislation?**

Commencement date rules are set out in the interpretation legislation for each Australian jurisdiction. See the *Acts Interpretation Act 1954* (Qld) for the rules governing the commencement of Queensland legislation.

See Checklist 2 Australia for general information.

Research tool	What information will it give me?	Tips on use
Queensland Legislation Annotations — Current Legislation Brisbane: Government Printer • Paper version with six monthly consolidations and weekly cumulating supplement • http://www.legislation. qld.gov.au/Leg_info/ anno_current.htm	Table 1 contains details of assent and commencement, including proclamations. Also lists provisions not yet in force.	Look under the alphabetical title of the Act, and then see the details under the relevant Act. Consult the Consolidated volume then use the weekly supplement.

Research tool	What information will it give me?	Tips on use
Queensland Legal Indices — Queensland Legislation Service • Paper version — Consolidated Volume (1 July 1987–31 December 1998) and looseleaf service updated fortnightly • http://qli.sclqld.org.au/	Use the Queensland Legislation service to locate parliamentary Bills, legislation enacted, amended, repealed, reprinted and judicially considered. Includes commencement or proclamation and assent dates.	Acts are listed alphabetically. Under each Act the commencement or proclamation date is set out for the principal Act and any amendments. Consult the consolidation and then the yearly cumulations for a complete listing.
Bills Update • http://www.parliament.qld.gov.au/view/legislativeAssembly/legislativeAssembly.asp?area=tableOffice&LIndex=14&SubArea=tabled&nav=tabled	Provides a guide to legislation currently before the Assembly.	Table stipulates commencement: A — Date of assent B — By Proclamation C — See Act for details Commencement dates in Endnotes of latest reprint.

6.7 Queensland legislation in full text?

Users should note that the electronic versions of legislation (including endnotes) are not recognised as the official or authorised version of legislation. The official or authorised versions of Queensland legislation can be found in hardcopy versions printed by the Queensland Government Printer — GOPRINT.

Research tool	What information will it give me?	Tips on use
Office of the Queensland Parliamentary Counsel • http://www.legislation.qld.gov.au/OQPChome.htm	• Electronic reprints (current and superseded) • Acts as passed since 1991 There are links to repealed legislation and text of earlier reprints. The purpose is to update legislation as soon as possible. Authorised reprints are numbered consecutively. If an electronic version of a reprint is not yet authorised, then it is given a roman letter, for example, 1A or 1B.	Queensland Electronic Reprints are presented in alphabetical order. Acts passed are presented by the year in which the Act was passed. The current reprint can be download in pdf format.

Research tool	What information will it give me?	Tips on use
AustLII • http://www.austlii.edu.au	Current Consolidated Acts. Queensland Acts (Point-in-Time) Queensland Consolidated Regulations AustlII has launched a Point-in-Time legislation facility which can be used to check an Act or section of an Act as it was at any day in the past, for those years covered by the system; note that at the moment you can only search as far back as 2002, but it will be possible to go back further as earlier versions of the legislation become available in electronic format. It is available for NSW, Qld and SA at present but is progressively being applied to all other Australian jurisdictions including the Commonwealth. AustLII has an Update Table for its Legislation. The dates are those on which AustLII last updated the relevant legislation database and do not necessarily indicate the currency of the legislation in the databases.	Choose Queensland from the homepage, and then search the Acts database. Browse Acts in alphabetical order or use the search tools by entering a search query. Select the Recent Updates databases for information on consolidated legislation, which is either new or has been updated in the last 28 days. The date above does not mean that all Acts are consolidated as at that date, but rather this is the date that data was most recently received. The material can be viewed in html format or downloaded in text format.

Research tool	What information will it give me?	Tips on use
Queensland Historical Legal Collection • http://ozcase.library.qut.edu.au/qhlc/	The 'aim is to provide a cross-sectoral collaboration between Universities, Government Departments and Private Law firms in South East Queensland'. The site includes easy access to law library catalogues, special collections and legal research guides. The Queensland Historical Legal collection includes: Applicable commencement legislation 1793–1867 (for Queensland); Applicable lands legislation 1833–1910 (for Queensland); Chief Law Officers (Queensland); Criminal Code 1899 Queensland – preparatory and extrinsic materials; Letters Patent establishing the boundaries of Queensland (includes Proclamations, Legislative Assembly resolutions, maps etc); Public Acts of Queensland 1828–1936; Local Personal and Private Acts of Queensland 1828–1936; Queensland Government Gazettes 1859–1890 (information only).	Main access through the browse facility, but basic search also available.

6.8 **Updates for legislation?**

See Checklist 2 Australia for general sources.

Research tool	What information will it give me?	Tips on use
Queensland Legislation Annotations — Current Legislation Brisbane: Government Printer • Paper version with six monthly consolidations and weekly cumulating supplement. • http://www.legislation. qld.gov.au/Leg_info/ anno_current.htm	Table 1 contains details of amending legislation of principal Acts. It also lists details of amendments since the last authorised reprint.	Look under the alphabetical title of the Act, then see the details under the relevant Act. Consult the Consolidated volume, then use the weekly supplement.
Queensland Legal Indices — Queensland Legislation Service, Queensland Supreme Court • Paper version — Consolidated Volume (1 July 1987-31 December 1998) and looseleaf service updated fortnightly • http://qli.sclqld.org.au/	Use the Queensland Legislation service to locate parliamentary Bills, legislation enacted, amended, repealed, reprinted and judicially considered. Includes commencement or proclamation and assent dates.	Acts are listed alphabetically. Under each Act the commencement or proclamation date is set out for the principal Act and any amendments. Consult the consolidation and then the yearly cumulations for a complete listing.

6.9 **A subject index to delegated legislation?**

In Queensland, there are a wide range of Statutory Instrument opinions following Part 2 of the *Statutory Instruments Act 1992* (Qld). The *Statutory Instruments Act 1992* (Qld) modifies the rules of statutory interpretation.

Research tool	What information will it give me?	Tips on use
Queensland Legislation Annotations — Current Legislation Brisbane: Government Printer • Paper version with six monthly consolidations and weekly cumulating supplement. • http://www.legislation. qld.gov.au/Leg_info/ anno_current.htm	Table 4 is a brief subject guide to Queensland legislation.	Look up the likely subject area, noting the Acts that are listed. Go to Table 1, look under the Acts noted and see subordinate legislation made under that Act.

6.10 **Full text of delegated legislation?**

Research tool	What information will it give me?	Tips on use
Queensland Statutory Instruments Reprint	Covers 1952 to June 1991. Replaced by *Queensland Subordinate Legislation*.	This series includes reprints of the statutory rules as they appear in the Gazette. Each volume includes a Cumulative Index. Only those categories of material noted in the *Statutory Instruments Reprint Act 1952* (Qld) are reprinted. Not everything published in the Gazette is found here.
Subordinate Legislation • http://www.legislation. qld.gov.au/Legislation. htm	• Subordinate Legislation as made 1991– • Current Consolidated Subordinate Legislation There are links to repealed legislation and text of earlier reprints. The purpose is to update legislation as soon as possible. Authorised reprints are numbered consecutively. If an electronic version of a reprint is not yet authorised, then it is given a roman letter, for example, 1A or 1B.	Queensland Electronic Reprints of Subordinate Legislation are listed under the parent Act. Subordinate Legislation as passed is presented by the year in which it was passed. The current reprint can be downloaded in pdf format.
AustLII • http://www.austlii. edu.au	Queensland Current Consolidated Regulations	Choose Queensland from the homepage, and then search the Acts database. Browse Acts in alphabetical order or use the search tools by entering a search query. Select 'Recent Changes' for Regulations which are new or have been updated by the Commonwealth Attorney-General's Department. Entries on this page are kept for 28 days.

6.11 **A subject index to cases?**

See Checklist 2 Australia for general sources.

Research tool	What information will it give me?	Tips on use
Queensland Legal Indices — Queensland Legislation Service, Queensland Supreme Court • Paper version — Consolidated Volume (1 July 1987– 31 December 1998) and looseleaf service updated fortnightly • http://qli.sclqld.org.au/	Subject index of Supreme Court and Court of Appeal judgments. Each judgment is catchworded with cases and statutes cited by that judgment. It only gives a brief description of the case.	The pink pages are the updating service and the white pages are the permanent supplement. Cases are listed by subject. Consult the consolidation and then the yearly cumulations for a complete listing.

6.12 **Full text of Queensland cases?**

The authorised reports of Queensland are the *State Reports* (1902–1957) and then the *Queensland Reports* (1958–).

Research tool	What information will it give me?	Tips on use
Queensland Courts Homepage 2000– • http://www.courts.qld.gov.au	It provides judgments from January 2000 onwards. Extempore judgments are not included in this service, except in the Supreme Court: Court of Appeal Division. Judgments and decisions of the following Courts and Tribunals can be accessed: • Supreme Court – Trial Division • Supreme Court – Court of Appeal • District Court • Mental Health Court • Planning and Environment Court • Health Practitioners Tribunal • Legal Practice Tribunal • Medical Assessment Tribunal • Registrar's Notes • Sentencing Remarks • Supreme Court: Court of Appeal Summary Notes • Judicial Committee Judgments are listed in citation number order, not necessarily reflecting chronological order.	Judgments can be accessed via the various court and tribunal indexes or through the search facility. The search facility does not search the full text of the judgments, but only encompasses the headnote of each judgment. Catchwords are included in the headnote when provided on the cover sheet. Judgments on this site are available in pdf.

Research tool	What information will it give me?	Tips on use
AustLII • http://www.austlii.edu.au	• Supreme Court of Queensland — Court of Appeal Decisions 1994– • Supreme Court of Queensland Decisions 1994– • Queensland District Court Decisions 1999– • Queensland Industrial Court Decisions 1999– • Queensland Planning and Environment Court Decisions 1999– • Anti-Discrimination Tribunal Queensland 1992– • Queensland Building Tribunal 1994– • Queensland Body Corporate and Community Management Commissioner — Adjudicators Orders 2000– • Queensland Commercial and Consumer Tribunal 2003– • Queensland Guardianship and Administration Tribunal Decisions 2000– • Queensland Industrial Relations Commission Decisions 1999– • Queensland Information Commissioner Decisions 1993– • Queensland Liquor Appeals Tribunal Decisions 1994– • Queensland Property Agents and Motor Dealers Tribunal 2001–	The case law databases on these systems can be used as a Digest. A broad topic is much better searched in hardcopy. A small or obscure point may be picked up more easily using electronic searching. The cases do not contain headnotes, catchwords or parts of the hearing details, which are subject to Lawbook Co copyright. Page numbers (where present) have been inserted by SCALE. The Court has provided catchwords for decisions since 1996.

Research tool	What information will it give me?	Tips on use
LexisNexis AU • http://www.lexisnexis.com	• Unreported Judgments • Queensland Crown Lands Law Reports • Queensland Land Court Reports • Queensland Planning and Environmental Law Reports • Queensland Reports	The database can be browsed using the content page or searched by case name, year, individual word and jurisdiction.
Westlaw Australia • http://www.westlaw.com.au	Unreported Judgments from September 1999. Contains Unreported Judgments of the Supreme Court of Queensland (Full Bench only) and the Queensland Court of Appeal.	Search by citation, title, catchwords.
Legal Online • http://legalonline.thomson.com.au/	Supreme Court of Queensland, 1995– Queensland Court of Appeal,1995–	Search specific databases by ticking the appropriate box.

6.13 **Cases that have been judicially considered?**

See Checklist 2 Australia for general sources.

Research tool	What information will it give me?	Tips on use
Queensland Legal Indices — Queensland Current Case Citator, Queensland Supreme Court • Paper version — Consolidated Volume (1 July 1987– 31 December 1998) and looseleaf service updated fortnightly • http://qli.sclqld.org.au/	Lists by first party name, all judgments that are catchworded and cases that are included in catchworded judgments. Includes: • Anti-Discrimination Tribunal • Court of Appeal • Court of Criminal Appeal • District Court • District Court Ruling • Freedom of Information Tribunal • Full Court • High Court • Industrial Commission • Industrial Court • Industrial Registrar • Local Government Court • Medical Assessment Tribunal • Medical Health Tribunal • Planning and Environment Court • Supreme Court	Look up the case name in the alphabetical list. The cases cited have either been considered, distinguished, followed, allowed or applied. Consult the consolidation then the yearly cumulations for a complete listing.

6.14 **Cases that have dealt with specific legislative sections?**

See Checklist 2 Australia for general sources.

Research tool	What information will it give me?	Tips on use
LexisNexis AU • http://www.lexisnexis.com	In the Cases database, it will give the full text link of all cases that have dealt with the specific legislative section.	To search reported cases for consideration of legislation, use the References to Legislation field. To search unreported cases, use the Search Terms field.

Research tool	What information will it give me?	Tips on use
Queensland Legal Indices — Queensland Legislation Service, Queensland Supreme Court • Paper version — Consolidated Volume (1 July 1987– 31 December 1998) and looseleaf service updated fortnightly • http://qli.sclqld.org.au/	Use the Queensland Legislation service to locate parliamentary Bills, legislation enacted, amended, repealed, reprinted and judicially considered. Includes commencement or proclamation and assent dates.	Find the Act in the alphabetical list and see the cited section for cases judicially considering statutes and statutory instruments. Consult the consolidation and then the yearly cumulations for a complete listing.
Queensland Reports Brisbane: Incorporated Council of Law Reporting for the State of Queensland	Lists cases that refer to specific legislative sections.	Consolidated Indexes from 1860, 'Table of Statutes and Subordinate Legislation Judicially Considered'.
Queensland and Northern Territory Judgments Bulletin Sydney: Legal Bulletin Service vol 1, 1987–1999	Digested recent decisions — discontinued.	Table of Statutes, Rules, etc Cited.

South Australia — *How Do You Find*

7.1 **An introduction to the jurisdiction?**

See generally, the South Australian Government homepage at http://www.sa.gov.au/

For information on the Parliament, see http://www.parliament.sa.gov.au

For information on the courts system, see http://www.courts.sa.gov.au/

The Law Foundation of SA Incorporated has an online version of the Law Handbook which provides a plain English overview of the law in South Australia. See http://www.lawhandbook.sa.gov.au

7.2 **Parliamentary publications?**

See, generally, the South Australian Parliament homepage, in particular articles on 'How a Bill becomes Law', 'Financial Procedure' and 'Proceedings of Parliament' at http://www.parliament.sa.gov.au/aboutparliament

There are also articles about the Legislative Council at http://www.parliament.sa.gov.au/aboutparliament/howparliamentworks/houseofassembly.htm and the House of Assembly at http://www.parliament.sa.gov.au/aboutparliament/howparliamentworks/legislativecouncil.htm

Hansard

Research tool	What information will it give me?	Tips on use
Hansard (Debates) in the House of Assembly, Legislative Council and Parliamentary Committees 1993– • http://www.parliament.sa.gov.au/Hansard	Transcripts of debates in the Houses of Parliament and Committees.	First select the appropriate House, then search by menu-assisted search, by date or keywords. Results are available in html or pdf formats.

Hansard indexes

Research tool	What information will it give me?	Tips on use
Hansard Indexes • http://www.parliament.sa.gov.au/Hansard	House of Assembly Index to Questions and Speeches House of Assembly Index to Subjects Legislative Council Index to Questions and Speeches Legislative Council Index to Subjects	The Indices are in pdf format which can be searched using Ctrl + F function in Adobe Acrobat.

Other parliamentary publications

Research tool	What information will it give me?	Tips on use
Business of the House of Assembly • http://www.parliament.sa.gov.au/HouseOfAssembly/Businessoftheassembly/Programs	The Agenda, including Daily and Weekly programs, and the Notice Paper; Records and Papers and Standing Orders. Notices of motions to be moved (including motions for the introduction of Bills), Orders of the Day, Unanswered Questions on Notice, answers to previous Questions on Notice, Subordinate Legislation, Index to Bills which have been introduced in the Assembly or received from the Legislative Council.	Latest version only. Available in html format only.
Business of the Legislative Council • http://www.parliament.sa.gov.au/LegislativeCouncil/Businessofthecouncil/Businessofthecouncil.htm	Notice Paper, Subordinate Legislation able to be disallowed, Questions on Notice, Index to Parliamentary Papers, Index to Bills and Acts, the Minutes of Proceedings, Statistical Summaries and Standing Orders.	Latest version only. Available in html format only.

Research tool	What information will it give me?	Tips on use
Digest of the House of Assembly 1997–1998 — • http://www.parliament.sa.gov.au/HouseofAssembly/BusinessoftheAssembly/RecordsandPapers/Digest.htm	Includes lists and information on members, summary of session, business analysis, question analysis, Bill statistics, synopsis of legislation, Bills which did not pass into law, motions and resolutions, petitions, subordinate legislation, printed parliamentary papers, parliamentary staff and so on.	Available under 'Records and Papers' on House of Assembly homepage. 1997–2000 available in html. 2000–2003 available in pdf.

7.3 Bills?

Research tool	What information will it give me?	Tips on use
House of Assembly and Legislative Council Bills • http://www.legislation.sa.gov.au/browseBills.aspx	The full text of all versions of Bills before the House of Assembly and the Legislative Council.	Searching is available by using keywords. Browse by parliamentary session.
Index to Bills for House of Assembly and Legislative Council • http://www.parliament.sa.gov.au/BillsMotions/HouseofAssemblyIndextoBills.htm • http://www.parliament.sa.gov.au/BillsMotions/LegislativeCouncilIndextoBills.htm	Contains Index to Bills that have been introduced in the Assembly or received from the Legislative Council.	Browse by parliamentary session. Searching is available by using keywords.

Research tool	What information will it give me?	Tips on use
House of Assembly Notice Paper • http://www.parliament. sa.gov.au/ HouseofAssembly/ BusinessoftheAssembly/ Programs/ NoticePaper.htm	Bills being discussed on day listed at top of document.	Information on the progress of the Bills is provided via the use of symbols, the meaning of which is indicated at the bottom of the list, for example: # Received from Legislative Council ♣ Restored in the Legislative Council ♦ Restored in the House of Assembly § Discharged in the House of Assembly Φ Withdrawn in the House of Assembly ♠ Cognate Bill * Passed both Houses but not yet assented to Ω Negatived in House of Assembly Available in html format only.

7.4 Explanatory material about Bills?

Explanatory memoranda are not available online for South Australia. See the Parliamentary site for explanatory material such as second reading speeches and legislation synopses.

7.5 A subject index to legislation?

Research tool	What information will it give me?	Tips on use
Index of South Australian Legislation • http://www.legislation. sa.gov.au/Web/ Information/ Fortnightly%20index/ Annual%20index2008. pdf	There is a pdf alphabetical index containing the consolidated information for all Acts of the South Australian Parliament that are currently in force and Acts that have been repealed or have expired since 31 December 1975. This information includes the commencement date of the legislation. It is currently consolidated as at the end of 2002. It is updated. The *2004 Index of South Australian Legislation* (published separately and as part of the 2004 annual volume of *South Australian Statutes*) includes: • a list of Acts and the Minister to whom each Act is committed • a list of Ministers who have been incorporated • a list of administrative units of the Public Service • a list of councils.	The update is published fortnightly on a cumulative basis. Entries made since the previous issue of the update are underlined. The update is prepared by the Office of Parliamentary Counsel. Use the Ctrl + F function to find the particular Act.

7.6 **The commencement date of legislation?**

Commencement date rules are set out in the interpretation legislation for each Australian jurisdiction. See the *Acts Interpretation Acts 1915* (SA) for the rules governing the commencement of South Australian legislation.

Research tool	What information will it give me?	Tips on use
Index of South Australian Legislation • http://www.legislation.sa.gov.au/Web/Information/Fortnightly%20index/Annual%20index2008.pdf	There is a pdf alphabetical index containing the consolidated information for all Acts of the South Australian Parliament that are currently in force and Acts that have been repealed or have expired since 31 December 1975. This information includes the commencement date of the legislation. It is currently consolidated as at the end of 2002.	Use the Ctrl + F function to find the particular Act.
South Australian Government Gazette • Paper version • Latest at http://www.governmentgazette.sa.gov.au	Published by the South Australian Attorney General. Includes date of assent, and notice and commencement dates.	See the beginning of each Gazette for commencement dates of Acts as passed.
Legislation – South Australian Parliament Homepage • http://www.legislation.sa.gov.au/advsearch.aspx	The Acts and Regulations of the Government of South Australia; includes commencement/assent dates of Acts and amending Acts.	Search South Australian legislation on this site by menu-assisted search, or a plain English query. There are also alphabetical listings of all the Acts and Regulations.

7.7 **South Australian legislation in full text?**

The electronic versions of legislation on http://www.parliament.sa.gov.au/dbsearch/legsearch.htm are not recognised as the South Australian official or authorised versions of legislation. You must not rely on these versions. For official purposes, you must refer to the South Australian legislation published by authority of the South Australian Attorney-General.

Research tool	What information will it give me?	Tips on use
Legislation – South Australian Parliament Homepage • http://www.legislation.sa.gov.au/advSearch.aspx	The Acts and Regulations of the Government of South Australia.	Search South Australian legislation on this site by menu-assisted search, or a plain English query. There are also alphabetical listings of all the Acts and Regulations.
AustLII • http://www.austlii.edu.au	This database contains the South Australian consolidated Acts.	Browse alphabetically or search by Act name or individual word. In html format only.

7.8 **Updates for legislation?**

Research tool	What information will it give me?	Tips on use
South Australian Statutes Index 1975– • Paper version updated fortnightly – South Australian Legislation Update Online at parliament • http://www.legislation.sa.gov.au/Web/Information/Fortnightly%20index/fornightly%20index.pdf	Contained in the annual publication of the statutes as passed in the calendar year. Use this service to update from the last authorised reprint. Contains case annotations from 1975 onwards.	See the Index of South Australian Legislation at the end of annual volume. This includes information on the commencement dates of Acts and Regulations and amendments with Gazette references. The online version is a Pdf, search by using the Ctrl + F keys.

7.9 **A subject index to delegated legislation?**

Research tool	What information will it give me?	Tips on use
Index of South Australian Legislation • http://www.legislation.sa.gov.au/Web/Information/Fortnightly%20index/Annual%20index2008.pdf	There is a pdf alphabetical index containing the consolidated information for all Acts of the South Australian Parliament that are currently in force and Acts that have been repealed or have expired since 31 December 1975. Regulations are listed under the Act name. This information includes the commencement date of the legislation. It is currently consolidated as at the end of 2002. It is updated. The *2004 Index of South Australian Legislation* (published separately and as part of the 2004 annual volume of *South Australian Statutes*) includes: • a list of Acts and the Minister to whom each Act is committed • a list of Ministers who have been incorporated • a list of administrative units of the Public Service • a list of councils. The update is published fortnightly on a cumulative basis. Entries made since the previous issue of the update are underlined. The update is prepared by the Office of Parliamentary Counsel.	Use the Ctrl + F function to find the particular Act.

7.10 **Full text of delegated legislation?**

Research tool	What information will it give me?	Tips on use
Legislation — South Australian Parliament Homepage • http://www.legislation. sa.gov.au/advsearch.aspx	Full text of the Regulations of the Government of South Australia.	Search in South Australian legislation on this site by using a menu-assisted search or a plain English query. There are also alphabetical listings of all the Acts and Regulations with links to the full text.
AustLII • http://www.austlii. edu.au	This database contains the South Australian Acts consolidated regulations.	Browse alphabetically or search by Act name or individual word. In html format only.

7.11 **A subject index to cases?**

See Checklist 2 Australia for general sources.

7.12 **Full text of South Australian cases?**

The authorised reports series is the *South Australian State Reports* since 1921.

Research tool	What information will it give me?	Tips on use
AustLII • http://www.austlii. edu.au	• Supreme Court of South Australia Decisions 1989– • District Court of South Australia Decisions 1997– • South Australian Industrial Relations Court Decisions 1992– • Environment Resources and Development Court of South Australia Decisions 1997– • South Australian Industrial Relations Commission Decisions 1991– • South Australian Residential Tenancies Tribunal Decisions 1997– • South Australian WorkCover Levy Review Panel Decisions 2000– • South Australian Workers Compensation Appeal Tribunal Decisions 1991– • South Australian Workers Compensation Tribunal Decisions 1996–	Browse alphabetically or by recent cases. Search by case name or individual word. In html format only.
LexisNexis AU • http://www.lexisnexis. com	Unreported Judgments will provide all South Australian Supreme Court judgments since January 1987–	The database can be browsed using the content page or searched by case name, year, individual word and jurisdiction.
Legal Online • http://legalonline. thomson.com.au/	South Australian State Reports Supreme Court of South Australia 1995–	Select database for searching using template provided.

Research tool	What information will it give me?	Tips on use
Westlaw Australia • http://westlaw.com.au	South Australian State Reports and South Australian Unreported Judgments. Contains officially reported documents from the South Australian Supreme Court from volume 1, 1971. Unreported Judgments of the Supreme Court of South Australia (Full Bench only). This includes cases from the Supreme Court of South Australia (Full Bench only) and the Court of Criminal Appeal for South Australia. From September 1999.	Search by keyword or citation.

7.13 Cases that have been judicially considered?

No specific South Australian resources. See Checklist 2 Australia for general sources.

7.14 Cases that have dealt with specific legislative sections?

Research tool	What information will it give me?	Tips on use
Index of South Australian Legislation • http://www.legislation.sa.gov.au/Web/Information/Fortnightly%20index/Annual%20index2008.pdf	Information on reported cases citing legislative sections.	Choose legislation from alphabetical listings by title. Cases cited under sections and following legislative amendments.
South Australian Statutes Index 1975– • Paper version updated fortnightly — South Australian Legislation Update • http://www.legislation.sa.gov.au/Web/Information/Fortnightly%20index/fornightly%20index.pdf	Contained in the annual publication of statutes as passed in the calendar year. Use this service to update from the last authorised reprint. Contains case annotations from 1975 onwards.	See the Index of South Australian Legislation at the end of the annual volume. This includes information on the commencement dates of Acts and Regulations and amendments with Gazette references. The online version is a pdf, search by using the Ctrl + F keys.

Research tool	What information will it give me?	Tips on use
South Australian Statutes 1837–1975 *South Australian Statutes* 1976–1989 Adelaide: Government Printer	Lists cases that have judicially considered legislation in South Australia.	See 'Notes of Reported Cases' Table in Index V13.
South Australian and Western Australian Judgments Bulletin Sydney Legal Bulletin Service, 1988–2005	Digests recent information — discontinued.	Look at table of Statutes, rules, etc cited.
South Australian State Reports Index Melbourne: Lawbook	Information on reported cases citing legislative sections.	Look at the Statutes, Rules, etc cited.

Tasmania —
How Do You Find

8.1 **An introduction to the jurisdiction?**

For general information on the Tasmanian parliamentary system, see http://www.parliament.tas.gov.au/ which includes information on the members, as well as election results. The Parliamentary Library site contains an extensive collection of Fact Sheets, including information on referendums, petitions and individual electorates.

For information on the courts system, see http://www.courts.tas.gov.au

8.2 **Parliamentary publications?**

Hansard

Research tool	What information will it give me?	Tips on use
Hansard 1992– House of Assembly — • http://www.parliament. tas.gov.au/ HansardHouse Legislative Council — • http://www.parliament. tas.gov.au/ HansardCouncil	Retrospective material is available from 1992 onwards. Printed versions of all Hansards from 1979 only. Prior to 1979, see the Mercury Reprints (1920–1978) for details of debates.	First select the required House, and then search by year, individual word and multiple Boolean search criteria. Results are available in html format only.

Committee reports

Research tool	What information will it give me?	Tips on use
Committee Reports — Legislative Council, House of Assembly and Joint · http://www.parliament. tas.gov.au/ctee/ comminte.htm	Lists names of all current and past committees with links to reports form that committee.	First select the required committee, and then select the reports if available. If not available, use the Parliamentary Papers Index to search for committee reports. This website also contains archived committees and reports information.

Other parliamentary papers

Research tool	What information will it give me?	Tips on use
Tabled Papers 1981– • http://www.parliament.tas.gov.au/LC/LCTabledPaper.htm	An index to all the papers tabled in the Tasmanian Parliament. As new papers are tabled, they are entered into the database. A program of retrospective entry is ongoing and, therefore, the index will progressively cover many of the earlier years. The database contains only tabled Parliamentary Papers, not all government documents.	'U' in number means an unprinted paper. Use Boolean terms between search terms; ie, AND, OR and NOT. Use Title in paper title field to retrieve all records.
Votes and Proceedings of the Legislative Council and House of Assembly 1992– Legislative Council – • http://www.parliament.tas.gov.au/HansardHouse House of Assembly – • http://www.parliament.tas.gov.au/HansardCouncil	The official record of proceedings of each House of the Parliament. The Votes and Proceedings records what motions were moved, how Bills were dealt with and how Members voted in divisions in the House.	First select the year, individual word and multiple Boolean search criteria. Results are available in html format only.
Notice Papers of the Legislative Council 1992– and the House of Assembly 1995– • http://www.parliament.tas.gov.au	A detailed list of motions and Bills to be considered by the House, including matters which Members intend to raise (Notices of Motion) and matters which are already under consideration (Orders of the Day).	First select the required House, put the cursor over the item so as to display the drop-down list of papers available or simply choose 'More ...'. This directs to the House of Assembly http://www.parliament.tas.gov.au/ha/House.htm or the Legislative Council http://www.parliament.tas.gov.au/lc/council.htm and then search by source type. Results are available in pdf format. There is also an Advanced Search template on the Parliament Homepage.

8.3 **Bills?**

Research tool	What information will it give me?	Tips on use
BillsWeb • http://www.parliament. tas.gov.au/bills/billsweb. htm for Bills currently before Parliament. • http://www.parliament. tas.gov.au/bills/ annualbillsweb.htm for Bills tabled in previous years.	A detailed list of Bills presently before the parliament. Includes Bill progress. Annual Register of Bills includes all Bills from 20 July 2002.	Results are available in html format only.

8.4 **Explanatory notes about Bills?**

Explanatory Notes generally not available on the Internet. Consult the Hansard 1992– for explanatory material.

8.5 **A subject index to legislation?**

Research tool	What information will it give me?	Tips on use
Indexes to the Legislation of Tasmania • Paper version • http://www.dpac.tas. gov.au/divisions/opc/ publications.html	Contains subject index and alphabetical table of statutes and regulations in force.	Look up the Act in the subject section and then consult the alphabetical listing for updating information.
Subject Index to Tasmanian legislation • http://www.dpac.tas. gov.au/divisions/opc/ publications.html	Lists the Acts and subordinate legislation and, in some cases, specific sections under each subject.	Pdf version available at this link.

8.6 **The commencement date of legislation?**

Commencement date rules are set out in the interpretation legislation for each Australian jurisdiction. See the *Acts Interpretation Act 1931* (Tas) for the rules governing the commencement of Tasmanian legislation.

See Checklist 2 Australia for general sources.

Research tool	What information will it give me?	Tips on use
Indexes to the Legislation of Tasmania • Paper version • http://www.dpac.tas.gov.au/divisions/opc/publications.html	Contains subject index and alphabetical table of statutes and regulations in force.	Look up the Act in the subject and then consult the alphabetical listing for updating information.
Table of Acts (with commencement details) made in the years 2003– • http://www.dpac.tas.gov.au/divisions/opc/publications.html	Lists the Act title, number, date of royal assent and commencement date.	Two versions are available for each year — alphabetical and numerical. Html format only.

8.7 **Tasmanian legislation in full text?**

Reference should be made to authorised versions of legislation for official purposes. Authorised versions are those printed by the Government Publisher. However, once http://www.thelaw.tas.gov.au/ has completed extensive internal and external testing, it is the Crown's intention to make the site a source of authorised legislation in accordance with the *Legislation Publication Act 1996* (Tas).

Research tool	What information will it give me?	Tips on use
Tasmanian Legislation 1997– • http://www.thelaw.tas.gov.au	Contains sessional and historical versions of Tasmanian legislation. See http://applications.dpac.tas.gov.au/opc/enact_not.html for further detailed information of database contents.	Can be browsed by selecting the first and second letter of the first word in the Act's short title. Searching is by title, number or individual word.
AustLII • http://www.austlii.edu.au	This database contains consolidated copies of all Tasmanian Acts as provided by the Department of Premier and Cabinet (Tasmania).	Browse alphabetically or search by Act name or individual word. Note currency date.

8.8 Updates for legislation?

See Checklist 2 Australia for general sources.

Research tool	What information will it give me?	Tips on use
Indexes to the Legislation of Tasmania • Paper version • http://www.dpac.tas.gov.au/divisions/opc/publications.html	Contains subject index and alphabetical table of statutes and regulations in force.	Look up the Act in the subject area, and then consult the alphabetical listing for updating information.
Table of the Acts of Parliament • http://www.dpac.tas.gov.au/divisions/opc/publications.html	List of Acts from 1826 to present, repealed Acts from 1998, Acts not yet commenced, repeals of Acts yet to commence, Acts with expiry dates. Updated monthly.	The table of Acts of Parliament sets out in either alphabetical or numerical order, the title, number, assent date and commencement dates.

8.9 A subject index to delegated legislation?

Research tool	What information will it give me?	Tips on use
Indexes to the Legislation of Tasmania • Paper version • http://www.dpac.tas.gov.au/divisions/opc/publications.html	Contains subject index and alphabetical table of statutes and regulations in force.	Look up the regulation in the subject area and then consult the alphabetical listing for the pertinent Act and any updating information.
Subject Index to Tasmanian Legislation • http://www.dpac.tas.gov.au/divisions/opc/documents/subject.pdf	Lists the Acts and Subordinate Legislation and, in some cases, specific sections under each subject.	Search using Ctrl + F function as the index is in pdf.

8.10 Full text of delegated legislation?

Research tool	What information will it give me?	Tips on use
Tasmanian Legislation 1998– • http://www.thelaw.tas.gov.au/	Contains Tasmanian Regulations from 1998. Some from previous years have also been loaded. Sessional and historical versions available.	Can be browsed by selecting the first and second letter of the first word in the Act's short title. Searching is by title, number or individual word.

8.11 **A subject index to cases?**

See Checklist 2 Australia for general sources.

Research tool	What information will it give me?	Tips on use
Tasmanian Supreme Court Judgments 1859– • Updated by the *Lillas Digest*	Digest of Cases arranged by subject.	Cases are arranged by subject title then by sub-subject alphabetically.
tasInLaw • http://www.niumedia. com/tasinlaw/	Contains several digests: *Lillas Digest* — A digest of cases of the Supreme Court of Tasmania 1897– *Bartlett Digest* — A digest of List 'B' Supreme Court decisions Supreme Court Judgments' Catchwords Index — A set of catchwords of Supreme Court judgments from 1970 onwards. The Digest contains exclusive access to over 300 unnumbered and unreported judgments *Badger's Digest* — Tasmanian decisions reported in Badger's Digest of cases decided on the Torrens Acts of Australasia *Hore's Digest* — A digest of cases decided by the Supreme Court of Tasmania between 1856 and 1896 Catchwords of decisions of the Motor Accidents Compensation Tribunal — from 1976 onwards Tasmanian (State) Reports Consolidated Index (1970–2002) —An Index to the authorised law reports of Tasmania	Fee based CD-ROM subscription. Uses Folio software.

8.12 **Full text of Tasmanian cases?**

The authorised law reports for Tasmania are *Tasmanian State Reports* (1941–1978) and the *Tasmanian Reports* (1979–).

Research tool	What information will it give me?	Tips on use
AustLII • http://www.austlii. edu.au	Supreme Court of Tasmania Decisions 1987– Resource Management and Planning Appeal Tribunal of Tasmania Decisions 1996– Anti-Discrimination Tribunal of Tasmania 2000–	Browse alphabetically or by recent cases. Searching is by case name or individual word. In html format only.
tasInLaw 1985– • http://www.niumedia. com/tasinlaw/	The judgments of the Superior Courts infobase has all Supreme Court cases from 1985, a sentencing database and tribunal decisions.	Judgments from 1999 have medium neutral paragraph binders. Access by subscription.
LexisNexis AU • http://www.lexisnexis. com	Full text of all Supreme Court of Tasmania judgments from 1985.	The database can be browsed using the content page or searched by case name, year, individual word and jurisdiction.
Westlaw Australia • http://westlaw.com.au	Unreported judgments of the Supreme Court of Tasmania (Full Bench only). This includes cases from the Supreme Court of Tasmania (Full Bench only) and the Court of Criminal Appeal for Tasmania. From September 1999–.	Search by keyword or citation.
Legal Online • http://legalonline. thomson.com.au/	Supreme Court of Tasmania 1995– Court of Criminal Appeal for Tasmania 1995–	Search specific databases by ticking the appropriate box.

8.13 **Cases that have been judicially considered?**

See Checklist 2 Australia for general sources.

8.14 Cases that have dealt with specific legislative sections?

See Checklist 2 Australia for general sources.

Research tool	What information will it give me?	Tips on use
Tasmanian Reports Hobart: Published for the Council of Law Reporting of Tasmania by Lawbook Co, 1981–	Lists all decisions that have referred to legislative provisions.	See Annual Table of Statutes Judicially Considered.
Lillas M, *Tasmanian Supreme Court Judgments: A Digest of Cases* Burnie, Tas: Lillas, 1989	Digest of Cases arranged by subject.	Consult the table of 'Statutes Judicially Considered'.

Victoria —
How Do You Find

9.1 **An introduction to the jurisdiction?**

See generally, Government homepage http://www.vic.gov.au

See further, http://www.parliament.vic.gov.au/law.html for 'How a law is made in Victoria', and information on published consolidations of statutes.

9.2 **Parliamentary publications?**

Hansard

Research tool	What information will it give me?	Tips on use
Hansard 1991– • http://tex.parliament.vic.gov.au/bin/texhtmlt?form=VicHansard.adv	Record of the Parliamentary Debates of both houses available online. Daily Hansard available approximately four hours after sitting, and the weekly Hansard is available approximately three working days after the end of the sitting week. The Daily Hansard is a 'proof' or draft document. The Revised Book replaces the draft version of Hansard and is divided by day.	The database is divided into an archive and a current session. Searches are available under Member, Activity, Year, Month, House and keyword Boolean search on text. There is an option to display one page or the entire speech. Mostly available in html format with some in pdf. There is no real index though the search function acts as such.

Committee reports

Research tool	What information will it give me?	Tips on use
Joint, Legislative Council and Legislative Assembly • http://www.parliament.vic.gov.au/committees/	These include the reports of the committees which have been established to consider proposed legislation, regulations and policies.	The appropriate committee should be selected and then the report required. Available format differs, but normally in either html or pdf.

Other parliamentary documents

Research tool	What information will it give me?	Tips on use
Parliamentary documents Victoria Parliamentary Documents Homepage • http://www.dms.dpc.vic.gov.au/domino/Web_Notes/LDMS/PubPDocs.nsf?OpenDatabase	Links to databases of parliamentary documents such as: Bills, Bills Status List, Hansard, Archive, Legislative Council — Notice Papers, Question Papers, Minutes of Proceedings, Legislative Assembly — Notice Papers, Question Papers, Votes, and Proceedings.	Browse or search using keyword in each database.

9.3 **Bills?**

Research tool	What information will it give me?	Tips on use
Bills List • http://www.dms.dpc.vic.gov.au/domino/Web_Notes/LDMS/PubPDocs.nsf?OpenDatabase	Each Bills List published includes information on Bill Title and Progress. The full text of the Bill is not included. However, the list notes Introduction Date, Date second reading moved, whether amended, the House debating Legislative Assembly (LA) or Legislative Council (LC), and also whether the Bill is awaiting assent.	Archived Lists can be found via the Archive link. Keyword search facilities available. In Word or pdf.
Victorian Government Bills Homepage • http://www.dms.dpc.vic.gov.au/domino/Web_Notes/LDMS/PubPDocs.nsf?OpenDatabase	Bills currently before the Parliament of Victoria. The changing versions of the bill are provided in full text, including 1) an Introduction print, 2) a circulation print. A Status Report is also provided.	The current Bills before Parliament are listed alphabetically and can be searched by Keyword. Bills are in pdf.
Victoria Government Gazette • Electronic version 1998– • http://www.gazette.vic.gov.au	VGG General is published each Thursday and provides information regarding Acts of Parliament and their effective date of operation.	All Victorian Government Gazettes on this site must be viewed with Adobe Acrobat Reader.

9.4 **Explanatory material about bills?**

Research tool	What information will it give me?	Tips on use
Victorian Government Bills Homepage • http://www.dms.dpc.vic.gov.au/domino/Web_Notes/LDMS/PubPDocs.nsf?OpenDatabase	Pdf version of introduction and circulation prints of explanatory memoranda for that particular Bill.	The current Bills before Parliament are listed alphabetically and can be searched by Keyword.

9.5 **A subject index to legislation?**

Research tool	What information will it give me?	Tips on use
Index to Subject Matter of Victorian Legislation Office of the Chief Parliamentary Counsel • Paper version 1999-, published annually	This index covers all unrepealed principal public acts and statutory rules including those not yet in operation. Amending legislation is only included 'when the subject matter is considered important enough to index and the relevant provisions are not yet in operation'. Any titles which are not yet in operation are printed in italics. A list of repealed acts removed from the index is included at the end.	Use the Index to identify legislation relevant to a subject. An entry will include the subject heading, any See Also references, titles of principal acts and statutory rules, and titles of any amending material with provisions not yet in force.
Victorian Statutes Annotations Butterworths • Paper version • In LexisNexisAU • http://www.lexisnexis.com	Information on assent, commencement, reprint, repeal, name changes, amendments, Regulations made and relevant books and articles. Specific sections of each Act are annotated where an amendment has been made to that section or where a relevant case has been decided with respect to that section.	Use the Index to identify legislation relevant to a subject. *Australian Current Law* should be used to update *Victorian Statutes Annotations*.

Research tool	What information will it give me?	Tips on use
LawLex via Anstat • http://www.anstat.com.au	Free title search on all Australian legislation. Subject index of principal Australian legislation. Includes all Australian jurisdictions.	Search legislation from the Anstat Legislation homepage. Introduces LawLex with searches available by keyword and jurisdiction. Can also browse the subject index alphabetically under each jurisdiction individually or collectively.

9.6 The commencement date of legislation?

Commencement date rules are set out in the interpretation legislation for each Australian jurisdiction. See the *Interpretation of Legislation Act 1984* (Vic) for the rules governing the commencement of Victorian legislation.

See Checklist 2 Australia for general sources.

Research tool	What information will it give me?	Tips on use
Victorian Statutes Annotations Lawbook Co, 1996– • Paper version	Provides a record of Acts included in the 1958 consolidation and Acts as passed since. Gives amendment information, commencement information and case citations of cases referring to legislation.	Find the relevant Act and then see the Act history to determine commencement date/s.
Victorian Statutes Annotations Butterworths • Paper version • LexisNexisAU • http://www.lexisnexis.com	Acts are listed with assent and reprint information, the current state of the Act, such as repeal or change of name, amending Acts with relevant commencement information, related Acts, Regulations made under the Act, and relevant books and articles.	The index lists in subject order legislation and delegated legislation that is related to a specific topic.

9.7 Victorian legislation in full text?

'The only authorised version of an Act or reprint is that contained in the Pamphlet Series printed by the Government Printer. The Versions system has been designed to be used in conjunction with the Reprints (authorised hardcopy) system in use in Victoria. The Version numbering system enables the user to also track existing Reprints. The first two digits of the number identify the last Reprint and the last digit identifies the Version. When a Version and a Reprint are produced at the same time, the last digit in the Version number is zero. The text of the law contained in the Version and the Reprint is the same, but the Reprint contains additional material. Up to 9 Versions may be published in between Reprints of a law.'

See http://www.dms.dpc.vic.gov.au/

Research tool	What information will it give me?	Tips on use
Victorian Statute Book 1996– • http://www.dms.dpc.vic. gov.au/Domino/ Web_Notes/LDMS/ PubStatbook.nsf? OpenDatabase	The Statute Book contains all the numbered Acts and Statutory Rules of Victoria. The full text of the Act or Statutory Rule will be displayed.	To choose an Act or Statutory Rule, click on the year it was enacted or made. You can then scroll through the alphabetical or chronological list, or enter specific search criteria.
Victorian Law Today 1997– • http://www.dms.dpc.vic. gov.au/Domino/ Web_Notes/LDMS/ PubLawToday.nsf? OpenDatabase	Contains the consolidated versions of Principal Public Acts and Principal Statutory Rules. A new consolidation is lodged when amendments are passed. It is possible to 'view the law as it is in operation today, or, by nominating a previous version of the law, view the law in effect at a particular point in time after 1 July 1997'. Not the official or authorised version.	Select the version of the Act for the period in which you are interested. 'The system will display the law as it was at that point.' Retrospective Amendments are amendments which were passed after the date that the version of the law came into operation, but which affect the law prior to that date. Keyword search facilities available.
AustLII 1996– • http://www.austlii. edu.au	Contains copies of Victorian Acts as consolidated in 1996 and subsequent Acts. Also contains copies of Victorian Consolidated Regulations as provided by Parliamentary Counsel Victoria.	Can be browsed or searched. Browse alphabetically or search by Act name or keyword.

Research tool	What information will it give me?	Tips on use
Anstat • http://www.anstat.com.au	Contains current year Acts as passed and consolidations that are on the Internet.	You will need to search for a particular word in either the Act's title or body, then accept the terms and conditions, then select the relevant Act and then select the relevant Act again.

9.8 Updates for legislation?

Research tool	What information will it give me?	Tips on use
Cumulative Acts Table Office of the Chief Parliamentary Counsel Victoria • Paper version prepared as at 1 July each year	This consists of 3 volumes. Table 1 is an alphabetical Table of Acts, Table 2 is a chronological Table of Acts, Table 3 lists unrepealed Principal Public Acts, Table 4 includes administration of acts information such as the responsible ministers, Volumes 2 and 3 have the amendment history for all current acts.	Use the last cumulative year index and update using http://www.ocpc.vic.gov.au
Victorian Statutes Annotations Butterworths • Paper version • LexisNexisAU • http://www.lexisnexis.com	Information on assent, commencement, reprint, repeal, name changes, amendments, regulations made and relevant books and articles. Specific sections of each Act are annotated where an amendment has been made to that section or where a relevant case has been decided with respect to that section.	Use the Index to identify legislation relevant to a subject. *Australian Current Law* should be used to update *Victorian Statutes Annotations*.
Victorian Statutes Annotations Lawbook Co, 1996– • Paper version only	Provides a record of Acts included in the 1958 consolidation and Acts passed since. Gives amendment information, commencement information and case citations of cases referring to legislation.	Find the relevant Act and then see the Act history to determine if there are any amendments since the last authorised reprint.

9.9 A subject index to delegated legislation?

Research tool	What information will it give me?	Tips on use
Index to Subject Matter of Victorian Legislation Office of the Chief Parliamentary Counsel • Paper version 1999-, published annually	This index covers all unrepealed principal public acts and statutory rules including those not yet in operation. Amending legislation is only included 'when the subject matter is considered important enough to index and the relevant provisions are not yet in operation'. Any titles which are not yet in operation are printed in italics. A list of repealed acts removed from the index is included at the end.	Use the Index to identify legislation relevant to a subject. An entry will include the subject heading, any See Also references, titles of principal acts and statutory rules, and titles of any amending material with provisions not yet in force.
Victorian Statutes Annotations Butterworths • Paper version • LexisNexisAU • http://www.lexisnexis.com	Information on assent, commencement, reprint, repeal, name changes, amendments, Regulations made and relevant books and articles. Specific sections of each Act are annotated where an amendment has been made to that section or where a relevant case has been decided with respect to that section.	Use the Index to identify legislation relevant to a subject. *Australian Current Law* should be used to update *Victorian Statutes Annotations*.
Victorian Statutes Annotations Lawbook Co, 1996- • Paper version only	Provides a record of Acts included in the 1958 consolidation and Acts passed since. Gives amendment information, commencement information and case citations of cases referring to legislation.	Note 'Table of Annotated Regulations' at the front of each volume. Reference is given to delegated legislation under the empowering Act in the main body of work. Reference is made to the reprint if one exists, and to any amending Regulations. There may be several different sets of Regulations listed under the one Act.

Research tool	What information will it give me?	Tips on use
LawLex via Anstat • http://www.anstat.com.au	1999– Free title search on Australian legislation. Commonwealth, New South Wales, Queensland and Victoria included.	Search legislation from the Anstat Legislation homepage. Introduces LawLex with searches available by keyword and jurisdiction.
Cumulative Statutory Rules Tables Office of the Chief Parliamentary Counsel Victoria Published annually and including law as at 1 January	Table 1 includes unrevoked Principal Statutory Rules, Table 2 contains a list of Statutory Rules under the title of their authorising act, Table 3 lists those rules expiring in the following year.	The rules in regard to the expiration are included in Subordinate Legislation Act 1994 s 5 'Automatic revocation of statutory rules' and this is included in the front of this volume. There is also the definition of the term statutory rule from s 3 of that act.

9.10 Full text of delegated legislation?

Research tool	What information will it give me?	Tips on use
Victorian Statute Book 1996– • http://www.dms.dpc.vic.gov.au/Domino/Web_Notes/LDMS/PubStatbook.nsf?OpenDatabase	The Statute Book contains all the Acts and Statutory Rules of the State of Victoria. The full text of the Act or Statutory Rule will be displayed.	To choose an Act or Statutory Rule, click on the year it was enacted or made. You can then scroll through the list or enter specific search criteria.
Victorian Law Today 1997– • http://www.dms.dpc.vic.gov.au/Domino/Web_Notes/LDMS/PubLawToday.nsf?OpenDatabase	Contains the consolidated versions of Principal Public Acts and Principal Statutory Rules. A new consolidation is lodged when amendments are passed. It is possible to 'view the law as it is in operation today' or, by nominating a previous version of the law, view the law in effect at a particular point in time after 1 July 1997'. Not the official or authorised version.	Select the version of the Act that includes the point in time you are interested in. The system will display the law as it was at that point. Retrospective Amendments are amendments which were passed after the date on which the version of the law came into operation, but which affect the law prior to that date. Keyword search facilities are available.

Research tool	What information will it give me?	Tips on use
AustLII 1996– • http://www.austlii. edu.au	Contains copies of Victorian Acts as consolidated in 1996 and subsequent Acts. Also contains copies of Victorian Consolidated Regulations as provided by Parliamentary Counsel Victoria.	Can be browsed or searched. Browse alphabetically or search by Act name or keyword.
Anstat • http://www.anstat. com.au	Contains current year Regulations as passed and consolidations that are on the Internet.	You will need to search for a particular word in either the Regulation's title or body, then accept the terms and conditions, then select the relevant Regulation, and then select relevant regulation again. Some searches free but it is generally a fee-based subscription service.

9.11 A subject index to cases?

See Checklist 2 Australia for general services.

9.12 **Full text of Victorian cases?**

The authorised Law Reports between 1875–1957 were the *Victorian Law Reports* and since then the *Victorian Reports*.

Research tool	What information will it give me?	Tips on use
AustLII 1998– • http://www.austlii. edu.au	Supreme Court of Victoria – Court of Appeal Decisions 1997–1998 Supreme Court of Victoria – Court of Appeal Decisions 1998– Supreme Court of Victoria Decisions 1998– Victorian Civil and Administrative Tribunal Decisions 1998– Victorian Domestic Building Tribunal Decisions 1996–1998 Victorian Anti-Discrimination Tribunal Decisions 1996–1998 Office of the Victorian Privacy Commissioner Case Notes 2003–	The case law databases on these systems can be used as a Digest. A broad topic is much better searched in hardcopy. A small or obscure point may be picked up more easily using electronic searching. The cases do not contain headnotes, catchwords or parts of the hearing details, which are subject to Lawbook Co copyright. Page numbers (where present) have been inserted by SCALE. The Court has provided catchwords for decisions since 1996.
LexisNexis AU • http://www.lexisnexis. com	Victorian unreported decisions since 1984 and reported decisions since 1957.	Search and browse facilities available.
Legal Online • http://legalonline. thomson.com.au/	Lawbook Co Unreported Judgments Supreme Court of Victoria 1995– Victorian Court of Appeal 1995–	Select Expert or Advanced Search forms, or use Browse mode.
Westlaw Australia • http://www.westlaw. com.au	Unreported Judgments Victorian Supreme Court (Full Bench only) 1999–	Search by citation or free text.

9.13 **Cases that have been judicially considered?**

See Checklist 2 Australia for general sources.

9.14 Cases that have dealt with specific legislative sections?

See Checklist 2 Australia for general sources.

Research tool	What information will it give me?	Tips on use
Victorian Statutes Annotations Butterworths • Paper version • LexisNexisAU • http://www.lexisnexis. com	Information on assent, commencement, reprint, repeal, name changes, amendments, Regulations made and relevant books and articles. Specific sections of each Act are annotated where an amendment has been made to that section or where a relevant case has been decided with respect to that section.	Use the Index to identify legislation relevant to a subject. *Australian Current Law* should be used to update *Victorian Statutes Annotations*.
Victorian Statutes Annotations Lawbook Co, 1996- • Paper version only	Provides a record of Acts included in the 1958 consolidation and Acts as passed since. Gives amendment information, commencement information and case citations of cases referring to legislation.	Find the relevant Act and then see the Act history to determine whether there have been any amendments since the last authorised reprint.
Victorian Law Reports – Consolidated Tables Sydney: Butterworths 1861-1996	Indexes all decisions that have referred to legislation.	See 'Table of Statutory References' in the Consolidated Tables volumes.
Victorian Judgments Bulletin Sydney: Legal Bulletin Service, 1985-	Digests recent information – discontinued.	Look at table of Statutes, rules, etc, cited.

10

Western Australia —
How Do You Find

10.1 **An introduction to the jurisdiction?**

For an introduction to the parliamentary process, see http://www.parliament. wa.gov.au/web/newwebparl.nsf/iframewebpages/About+Parliament

For a detailed table of Western Australian courts and their jurisdictions, see http://www.justice.wa.gov.au/A/aboutcourts.aspx?uid=5859-5368-0742-1499

10.2 **Parliamentary publications?**

Hansard

Research tool	What information will it give me?	Tips on use
Hansard 1997– • http://www.parliament. wa.gov.au/web/ newwebparl.nsf/ iframewebpages/ Hansard+-+Advanced+ Search	A daily proof of Hansard is produced. A corrected weekly Hansard is published on the following Tuesday. Corrected Hansards are eventually bound in hard-cover for the permanent record. See the following site for information on the production of Hansard: http://www. parliament.wa.gov.au/ web/newwebparl.nsf/ iframewebpages/ Hansard	This database can be browsed by date. There are subject indexes to Questions and Speeches and Subjects from 1999. It is also possible to search by Member, Subject, House, Proceeding or Date. It is possible to sort the retrieved list by relevance or recency.

Committee reports

Research tool	What information will it give me?	Tips on use
Parliamentary Committee Homepage 1994– • http://www.parliament. wa.gov.au/web/ newwebparl.nsf/ iframewebpages/ Committees	Contains information on past and present committees, inquiries, public hearings, government responses as well as the reports of the committees.	This site can be searched or browsed. To search, type the word in the search box at the top of the page. You can browse according to 'Reports by Name', 'Reports by Committee Name' or 'Reports published in the last six months', where the lists are alphabetical. http://www.parliament.wa .gov.au/web/newwebparl. nsf/iframewebpages/ Committees+-+Reports There is also a user guide. In pdf format only.

Other parliamentary documents

Research tool	What information will it give me?	Tips on use
Parliamentary Business • http://www.parliament. wa.gov.au/web/ newwebparl.nsf/ iframewebpages/ Parliamentary+Business +-+Chamber+Documents • http://www.parliament. wa.gov.au/web/ newwebparl.nsf/ iframewebpages/ Parliamentary+Business +-+Tabled+Papers	Contains Questions, Notice Papers, Tabled Papers (including Annual Reports), Votes and Proceedings, Supplementary Notes and Minutes of the Legislative Assembly and Legislative Council.	Can be searched using keyword, House, document type and date. Browsing is by year, month, date and then House. In pdf only. For Tabled Papers, search by selecting House and then keyword or browse by selecting House and parliamentary session. Collapse and Expand keys provide a means of viewing the complete lists of papers. Those available in electronic form are highlighted.

10.3 **Bills?**

Research tool	What information will it give me?	Tips on use
Bills — Parliament Homepage 1997– • http://www.parliament. wa.gov.au/web/ newwebparl.nsf/ iframewebpages/ Bills+-+All	Information on Bills can be found at http://www. parliament.wa.gov.au/web /newwebparl.nsf/ iframewebpages/Bills There are separate listings for All Bills, Current Bills and Private Members Bills. The alphabetical Bills Lists indicates in which House the Bill was introduced and the date of assent or present treatment. Bill details contain information since 6 March 1997, including the most current version and Explanatory memoranda.	Choose the individual Bill to access a Progress Spreadsheet showing the Progress of Bills through the Parliament, including first, second and third readings, dates to committee and assent dates. Adobe Acrobat Reader is required to download the Bills and explanatory Memoranda.

10.4 **Explanatory material about Bills?**

Research tool	What information will it give me?	Tips on use
Explanatory Memoranda accessible from the Bills Details page 1997– • http://www.parliament. wa.gov.au/web/ newwebparl.nsf/ iframewebpages/ Bills+-+All	Bill details contain information since 6 March 1997, including the most current version and Explanatory Memoranda.	Choose the individual Bill to access a Progress Spreadsheet showing the Progress of Bills through the Parliament, including first, second and third readings, dates to committee and assent dates. Adobe Acrobat Reader is required to download the Bills and explanatory Memoranda.

10.5 **A subject index to legislation?**

There is no subject index to Western Australian Legislation. Use topic or keyword searches in the full text databases.

10.6 **The commencement date of legislation?**

Commencement date rules are set out in the interpretation legislation for each Australian jurisdiction. See the *Interpretation Act 1984* (WA) for the rules governing the commencement of Western Australian legislation.

See Checklist 2 Australia for more general sources.

Research tool	What information will it give me?	Tips on use
Assent and commencement information accessible from the Bills Details page • http://www.parliament. wa.gov.au/web/ newwebparl.nsf/ iframewebpages/ Bills+-+All	Act Number, Short title, Assent Date and Commencement information for Acts in force.	Alphabetical list. Search facility available.
The Statutes of Western Australia – Index • http://www.slp.wa. gov.au/statutes/ index.nsf/pt	Lists the Acts and Regulations in force as at the currency date. Gives information on commencement date, assent and amendments.	Table 9 Part 1 shows the assent and commencement information for Acts passed since 2000 as at the date indicated at the top of the list. Part 2 shows Acts prior to 1990 that are awaiting proclamation (in whole or part). This Table is also accessible from the Parliament Current Bills Details page. The link Assent and Commencement information for Acts is available at the top of that page. It is listed by number but use Ctrl + F to search.

10.7 **Western Australian legislation in full text?**

The authorised version is the paper version, which can be purchased from the State Law Publisher. The State Law Publisher produces Acts as passed and an authorised pamphlet reprint series.

Research tool	What information will it give me?	Tips on use
State Law Publisher Western Australian Legislation and Regulations (SWANS) • http://www.slp.wa. gov.au/statutes/ swans.nsf	The State Law Australia Western Australian Legislation (SWANS) database is a compilation of the public general Acts of Western Australia that are in force, with certain exceptions. The database is based on Table One of the Index of Statutes, published by the Government Printer. This is not an official or authorised version of the legislation or Regulations.	A–Z Browse: The 'A–Z browse' facility lets you access either Statutes or Regulations by Title. Selecting a letter from the A–Z list jumps straight to Titles beginning with that letter. Use the 'Next' and 'Previous' buttons to progress through to the required title. Searching is by word, and the hit list contains the most relevant at the top.
AustLII • http://www.austlii. edu.au	Western Australia Consolidated Acts as available from the State Law Publisher.	Browse alphabetically or search by Act name or word. The currency note is on the main page of the legislation database. This may be less current than the SWANS version.

10.8 **Updates for legislation?**

See Checklist 2 Australia for general sources.

Research tool	What information will it give me?	Tips on use
The Statutes of Western Australia – Index • http://www.slp.wa. gov.au/statutes/ index.nsf/pt	Lists the Acts and Regulations in force as at the currency date. Gives information on commencement date, assent and amendments. Table 6 has separate list of Acts Affected by the latest year's legislation.	Consult this, and then use the progress of Bills database to update for the current year.

10.9 A subject index to delegated legislation?

Research tool	What information will it give me?	Tips on use
State Law Publisher Western Australian Legislation and Regulations (SWANS) • http://www.slp.wa. gov.au/statutes/ swans.nsf	The State Law Australia Western Australian Legislation (SWANS) database is a compilation of the public general Acts and Regulations of Western Australia that are in force, with certain exceptions. This is not an official or authorised version of the legislation or Regulations.	Choose Regulations and then Search Current Regulations. The 'A–Z browse' facility lets you access Regulations by Title. Selecting a letter from the A–Z list jumps straight to titles beginning with that letter. Use the 'Next' and 'Previous' buttons to progress through to the required title. Searching is by word and the hit list contains the most relevant at the top. There is also an All in One Search and Browse template.

10.10 Full text of delegated legislation?

Research tool	What information will it give me?	Tips on use
State Law Publisher Western Australian Legislation and Regulations (SWANS) • http://www.slp.wa. gov.au/statutes/ swans.nsf	The State Law Australia Western Australian Legislation (SWANS) database is a compilation of the public general Acts of Western Australia that are in force, with certain exceptions. The database is based on Table One of the Index of Statutes, published by the Government Printer. This is not an official or authorised version of the legislation or Regulations.	A–Z Browse: The 'A–Z browse' facility lets you access either Statutes or Regulations by Title. Selecting a letter from the A–Z list jumps straight to titles beginning with that letter. Use the 'Next' and 'Previous' buttons to progress through to the required title. Searching is by word and the hit list contains the most relevant at the top.
AustLII • http://www.austlii. edu.au	Western Australia Consolidated Regulations as available from the State Law Publisher.	Browse alphabetically or search by Act name or word. The currency note is on the main page of the legislation database. This may be less current than the SWANS version.

10.11 A subject index to cases?

See Checklist 2 Australia for general sources.

10.12 Full text of Western Australian cases?

Western Australia has two authorised reports series. From 1979 the *State Reports (Western Australia)* has covered the Family Court of Western Australia (State Jurisdiction), District Court and other Tribunals. The *Western Australian Reports* (formally known as *Western Australian Law Reports*) contains decisions of the Supreme Court of Western Australia.

Research tool	What information will it give me?	Tips on use
AustLII • http://www.austlii.edu.au	Supreme Court of Western Australia 1999– Supreme Court of Western Australia – Court of Appeal 1999– State Administrative Tribunal of Western Australia Decisions 2005– Criminal Injuries Compensation Assessor of Western Australia Decisions 2004– Western Australian Industrial Relations Commission Decisions 1991– Western Australian Information Commissioner Decisions 1994– Town Planning Appeal Tribunal of Western Australia Decisions 2003–2004	Browse alphabetically or by recent cases. Searching is by case name or individual word.
LexisNexis AU • http://www.lexisnexis.com	Western Australia Supreme Court Unreported Decisions since Feb 1987–	The database can be browsed using the content page or searched by case name, year, individual word and jurisdiction.
Westlaw Australia • http://au.westlaw.com	Unreported judgments from Supreme Court of Western Australia since 1994.	Search by subject, title or citation.

Research tool	What information will it give me?	Tips on use
Legal Online • http://legalonline. thomson.com.au/	Supreme Court of Western Australia 1995– Industrial Appeals Court of Western Australia 1995– Court of Criminal Appeal for Western Australia 1995–	Search specific databases by ticking the appropriate box.

10.13 Cases that have been judicially considered?

See Checklist 2 Australia for general sources.

10.14 Cases that have dealt with specific legislative sections?

See Checklist 2 Australia for general sources.

Research tool	What information will it give me?	Tips on use
State Reports (Western Australia) Sydney: Law Book Company vol 1, 1980–	Lists all decisions that have dealt with a specific legislative section.	Table of Statutes, Rules, etc, Judicially Considered in annual volumes, otherwise consolidation for 1989.
South Australian and Western Australian Judgments Bulletin Sydney: Legal Bulletin Service, 1988–2005	Digests recent information — discontinued.	Look at table of Statutes, Rules, etc cited.

11

England —
How Do You Find

11.1 **An introduction to the jurisdiction?**

For general information on the UK legal system, see UK Law Online http://www.leeds.ac.uk/law/hamlyn/toc.htm

See also, the US Library of Congress' site 'The Guide to the Law Online' for a range of links to pertinent national material http://www.loc.gov/law/guide/index.html

Other guides include Clinch P, *Using a Law Library* (2 ed, London: Blackstone Press, 2001); Holborn G, *Butterworths Legal Research Guide* (2 ed, London: Butterworths, 2001); Knowles J, *Effective Legal Research* (2 ed, London: Sweet and Maxwell, 2009); Pester D, *Finding Legal Information* (Oxford: Chandos, 2003); Thomas P and Knowles J, *Dane and Thomas' How to Use a Law Library: An Introduction to Legal Skills* (4 ed, London: Sweet & Maxwell, 2001); and William G, *Learning the Law* (13 ed, London: Sweet & Maxwell, 2006).

'In October 2009, The Supreme Court replaced the Appellate Committee of the House of Lords as the highest court in the United Kingdom. The Supreme Court's 12 Justices will maintain the highest standards set by the Appellate Committee, but will now be explicitly separate from both Government and Parliament. The Court will hear appeals on arguable points of law of the greatest public importance, for the whole of the United Kingdom in civil cases, and for England, Wales and Northern Ireland in criminal cases. Additionally, it will hear cases on devolution matters under the *Scotland Act 1998*, the *Northern Ireland Act 1988* and the *Government of Wales Act 2006*. This jurisdiction was transferred to the Supreme Court from the Judicial Committee of the Privy Council': http://www.bailii.org/uk/cases/UKSC/ (5/11/2009).

The Modern English Court System[1]

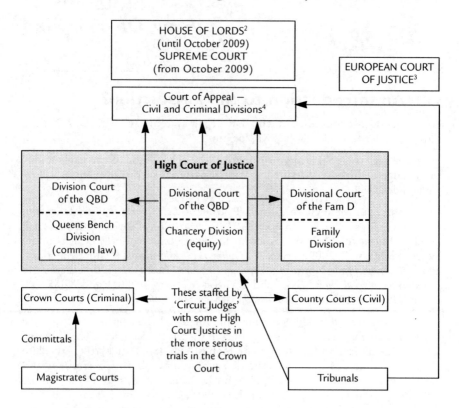

1 Adapted from Pyke J and Macadam A, LWB141 *Legal Institutions and Methods Study Guide* (Brisbane: QUT Faculty of Law 2001), p 93.

2 Ultimate appellate court in both civil and criminal matters. Appeals are heard by the Appellate Committee and its decisions are endorsed by the full House.

3 *European Community Act 1972* (UK) confers jurisdiction on UK courts to hear matters of European law. Appeals on these matters to the European Court of Justice. Campbell E, Poh-York L and Hooker J, *Research Materials and Methods* (4 ed, Sydney: LBC Information Services, 1996), p 87.

4 The Court of Appeal and the High Court of Justice are collectively referred to as the Supreme Court of Judicature.

11.2 **A broad picture of English Law?**

See generally, http://www.direct.gov.uk/Homepage/fs/en and the links to government departments and agencies, and the Office of Public Sector Information homepage http://www.opsi.gov.uk/

Research tool	What information will it give me?	Tips on use
Halsbury's Laws of England 4 ed, London: Butterworths, 1973– • Paper version (56 volumes) • Updated by Cumulative Supplement, Monthly Current Service and Annual Abridgement • Available electronically as Halsbury's Law Direct • http://www.lexisnexis.co.uk	*Halsbury's Laws of England* attempts to provide a comprehensive statement of the laws of England and Wales. This encyclopaedia contains law derived from legislation, statutory instruments and common law, and it is divided into alphabetically arranged subject titles. It contains a consolidated table of cases, a consolidated table of statutory instruments, and a consolidated index. The annual abridgement combines the monthly reviews into a consolidated issue and the cumulative supplement summarises legal developments over the parliamentary year. Two looseleaf binders contain the noter-up and monthly reviews.	*Halsbury's Laws of England* can be accessed in three ways; by Title, through the Consolidated Index or the Consolidated Table. *Halsbury's Laws of England* includes approximately 165 subject areas. Each subject is treated in sections. Consolidated Index volumes 55 and 56 combine information from all the titles and volumes 53 and 54 combine all entries from legislation tables in all volumes. Updating *Halsbury's Laws of England* is by the most recent reissue, then the cumulative supplement and then the noter-up and monthly services.

11.3 **Parliamentary publications?**

Research tool	What information will it give me?	Tips on use
United Kingdom Parliament • http://www.parliament.uk	Information on the UK Parliament, the House of Commons and the House of Lords. This site contains links to publications of each House.	The information on this site contains mainly links to other government pages that have the ability to be searched or browsed. Links are to the Houses and general information. By using the index, specific areas can be accessed more rapidly. Available in html format only.

Hansard

Research tool	What information will it give me?	Tips on use
House of Commons Hansard • http://www.parliament.uk/hansard/hansard.cfm	The last five days of the Hansard are kept with access to the record copy text since 1988. The Hansard is the official record of parliamentary proceedings, debates and activities of the House and its committees.	This site allows access to browse records of debates. The records that have not been bound have links to written answers, oral questions, debates and Westminster Hall. To search the Hansard, use the UK Parliament search page at http://www.publications.parliament.uk/cgi-bin/semaphoreserver?DB=semukparl&FILE=search
House of Lords Hansard • http://www.publications.parliament.uk/pa/ld199900/ldhansrd/pdvn/home.htm	This database contains the full uncorrected text of Lords Hansard from 10 June 1996 up to present. It is updated at 9 am the day after each sitting day.	This site can be searched or browsed. Searching is through the search site and browsing is first by date and then by subject alphabetically through the website. Available in html format only.
House of Lords Hansard – Volume Edition • http://www.publications.parliament.uk/pa/ld/ldse9900.htm	This database contains Volume Editions of the Hansard for the 1999–2000 session.	This site can be searched or browsed. Searching is through the search site and browsing is first by date, then debates or written answers, and then by subject alphabetically through the website. Available in html format only.

Indexes to the Hansard

Research tool	What information will it give me?	Tips on use
Volume Indexes to the House of Lords Parliamentary Debates • http://www.publications.parliament.uk/pa/ld/ldbvindx.htm	Contains references to the bound volumes of the Hansard. Information is categorised by subject or name of topic, speaker or committee.	The indexes use alphabetical word heading. The indexes can be browsed or searched. Browsing in html format can be by the links from http://www.publications.parliament.uk/pa/ld/ldbvindx.htm and searching through the search site. Available in html format only.

Research tool	What information will it give me?	Tips on use
Fortnightly Index • http://www.publications.parliament.uk/pa/cm/cmhansrd.htm	References to the column numbering in the daily parts and weekly edition.	The indexes use alphabetical word heading. The indexes can be browsed or searched. Browsing in html format can be by the links from http://www.publications.parliament.uk/pa/cm/cmpubns.htm and searching through the search site. Available in html format only.
Sessional Index	References the bound volumes for a whole session.	The indexes use alphabetical word heading. The indexes can be browsed or searched. Browsing in html format can be by the links from http://www.publications.parliament.uk/pa/cm/cmpubns.htm and searching through the search site. Available in html format only.
Volume Index • http://www.publications.parliament.uk/pa/cm/cmbvindx.htm	Contains references to the bound volumes of the Hansard. Information is categorised by subject or name of topic, speaker or committee.	The indexes use alphabetical word heading. The indexes can be browsed or searched. Browsing in html format can be by the links from http://www.publications.parliament.uk/pa/cm/cmpubns.htm and searching through the search site. Available in html format only.

Committee reports

Research tool	What information will it give me?	Tips on use
House of Commons — Standing Committee Debates • http://www.publications.parliament.uk/pa/cm/stand.htm	Outlines the developments of Bills in the House of Commons Standing Committee. It also gives access to the latest version of the Bill.	This site can be searched or browsed. Searching is through the search site and browsing is through the website. Available in html format only.

Research tool	What information will it give me?	Tips on use
House of Commons — Private Bill Committee Publications • http://www.publications. parliament.uk/pa/cm/ cmprbill.htm	Gives the report from the committee formed to investigate the proposed Bill and gives reasons why it is justified or not. It also recommends any changes.	This site can be searched or browsed. Searching is through the search site and browsing is through the website. Available in html format only.
House of Commons — Select Committee Publications • http://www.publications. parliament.uk/pa/cm/ cmselect.htm	This website gives access to publications (mainly reports) of committees of the House of Commons and Joint Committees by area.	This site can be searched or browsed. Searching is through the search site and browsing is through the website. Available in html format only.
Select Committee Reports • http://www.publications. parliament.uk/pa/ld/ ldselect.htm	This website gives access to reports of committees of the House of Lords and Joint Committees by area.	This site can be searched or browsed. Searching is through the search site and browsing is through the website. Available in html format only.

Other parliamentary publications

Research tool	What information will it give me?	Tips on use
House of Commons Papers • http://www.publications. parliament.uk/pa/cm/ cmhocpap.htm	Miscellaneous publications of the House of Commons, including Standing Orders.	This site can be searched or browsed. Searching is through the search site and browsing is through the website. Available in html and pdf format.
House of Commons Sessional Information Digest • http://www.parliament. the-stationery- office.co.uk/ pa/cm/cmsid.htm	The Sessional Information Digest is a cumulation of the Weekly Information Bulletin.	This site can be searched or browsed. Searching is through the search site and browsing is through the website. Available in html format only.

Research tool	What information will it give me?	Tips on use
House Business — House of Commons • http://www.parliament.the-stationeryoffice.co.uk/pa/cm/cmpubns.htm	House Business ('Vote Bundle') contains Summary Agenda and Order of Business, Future Business, Votes and Proceedings, European Community Documents, Public Bill List, List of Private Bills, Private Business, Deregulation Proposals and Draft Orders, List of Statutory Instruments, Early Day Motions, Questions for Oral or Written Answer ('The Order Book'), and deferred divisions for the next sitting day.	This site can be searched or browsed. Searching is through the search site and browsing is through the website. Available in html format only.
House of Commons and House of Lords — Weekly Information Bulletin • http://www.publications.parliament.uk/pa/cm/cmwib.htm	The Bulletin contains information on Business forthcoming in the House of Commons and House of Lords, Public Bills before Parliament, and other activities of the Parliament in the coming week. Published on a Saturday.	This site can be searched or browsed. Searching is through the search site and browsing is through the website. Available in html format only.
House of Lords — Minutes and Order Paper • http://www.publications.parliament.uk/pa/ld/ldmin.htm	This site contains a record of the most recent day's business in the House of Lords, the next judicial Business of the House of Lords, the agenda for the coming day, future business in the House, questions for written answers and Bills and instruments in progress.	This site can be searched or browsed. Searching is through the search site and browsing is through the website. Available in html format only.
Command Papers • http://www.official-documents.gov.uk	Contains brief descriptions and links to full text of white papers and green papers and other consultative documents.	This site can be searched or browsed. Available in pdf format. For older documents, a key selection of papers published before 2005 is available in the archive http://www.official-documents.gov.uk

Research tool	What information will it give me?	Tips on use
Badger Index *Current Legal Information (CLI)* • http://www.venables.co.uk/pubsweet.htm	Current Law Cases, BADGER (an index to publicly available legal information such as press releases), Legal Journals Index, Financial Journals Index, Current Law Case Citator, Current Law Legislation Citator and the Inns of Court library catalogues.	Most of this service is now also available through Westlaw and can be searched using the Westlaw commands.

11.4 Bills?

Research tool	What information will it give me?	Tips on use
Public Bills before Parliament • http://www.publications.parliament.uk/pa/pabills.htm	This site gives the full text of public Bills current before either House of Parliament. At the head of each Bill is a note of the stage the Bill has reached in its passage through Parliament. Amendments currently proposed to Bills in the House of Lords or the House of Commons can be found under each Bill. There are links to the Explanatory memoranda for each Bill.	A green marker indicates Bills in the House of Commons, and red marker those in the House of Lords. Bills which start in the House of Lords have 'HL' in their title. This site can be searched or browsed. Searching is through the search site and browsing is through the website.
Private Bills before Parliament • http://www.publications.parliament.uk/pa/privbill.htm	This site gives the full text of private Bills current before either House of Parliament. At the head of each Bill is a note of the current stage the Bill has reached in its passage through Parliament. Amendments currently proposed to Bills in the House of Lords or the House of Commons can be found separately under each Bill. There are links to the parliamentary agents and any committee reports for each Bill.	A green marker indicates Bills in the House of Commons and red marker those in the House of Lords. Bills which start in the House of Lords have 'HL' in their title. This site can be searched or browsed. Searching is through the search site and browsing is through the website.

Research tool	What information will it give me?	Tips on use
Weekly Information Bulletin • http://www.publications. parliament.uk/pa/cm/ cmwib.htm	Contains information on the status of all current Bills before either House of Parliament with information on their progress through Parliament, including the reading dates and the date of assent.	This site can be searched or browsed. Searching is first through the search site and browsing is first by the most recent date and then by selecting either pubic or private Bills through the website. Available in html format only.
Current Legal Information (CLI) • http://www.venables. co.uk/pubsweet.htm	Current Law Cases, BADGER (an index to publicly available legal information such as press releases), Legal Journals Index, Financial Journals Index, Current Law Case Citator, Current Law Legislation Citator and the Inns of Court library catalogues.	Most of this service is now also available through Westlaw and can be searched using the Westlaw commands.
Current Law Monthly Digest London: Sweet & Maxwell, 1990– • Cumulates into the annual Supplement and Year Book • Updated by the weekly updates in *Current Law Case Citator* and *Current Law Legislation Citator* on *Current Legal Information (CLI)* • http://www.venables.co. uk/pubsweet.htm and Westlaw.	A guide to developments in case law, legislation and secondary material. The information is arranged by jurisdiction then by broad subject headings. A comprehensive list of topics is at the front of each Monthly Digest. Contains a cumulative index, table of cases, current law notes, and information on Acts, Bills, Statutory Instruments and commencement dates.	The 'Progress of Bills' table lists all public Bills before Parliament in alphabetical order showing the stage reached and any provisional stages planned.
Current Law Statutes London: Sweet & Maxwell, 1948– • Cumulated into bound volumes • Updated by the *Current Law Statute Service*	This service contains full text copies of Public and Private Acts (many annotated), Commencement Orders, Statute Citators, Progress of Bills table and Legislation not yet in force.	The 'Progress of Bills' Table lists all public and private Bills pending before Parliament.

Research tool	What information will it give me?	Tips on use
Sessional Information Digest London: The Stationery Office, 1983– • http://www.publications. parliament.uk/pa/cm/ cmsid.htm	Contains information on all Bills before either House of Parliament in that parliamentary session with information on their progress through Parliament, including the reading dates and the date of assent.	This site can be searched or browsed. Searching is first through the search site and browsing is first by the most recent date and then by selecting either public or private Bills through the website. Available in html format only.
House of Commons – Public Bill List • http://www.publications. parliament.uk/pa/cm/ cmpblist/cmpblist.htm	Gives the title of the Bill, the member in charge and its progress. It contains the most recent edition only.	* indicates a Government Bill and indicates that a Bill has not yet been printed. This site can be browsed. Available in html format only.
Halsbury's Laws of England Current Review • http://www.lexisnexis. co.uk	Provides information on Bills in Progress, New Bills and Royal Assents.	Updated daily.

11.5 Explanatory material about Bills?

Research tool	What information will it give me?	Tips on use
Explanatory Notes 1999– • http://www.opsi.gov.uk/ acts.htm	The Explanatory Notes sets out the purpose, summarises the legislation, context for the operation of the legis- lation, the Act and commentary on the operation of the Act.	This site can be browsed only, although a search using the parliamentary search function may bring back information on a topic. Available in html format only.

11.6 A subject index to legislation?

Research tool	What information will it give me?	Tips on use
United Kingdom Public Acts • http://www.opsi.gov.uk/acts.htm	Contains full text of UK Public Acts since 1988 and Private Acts since 1991.	This site can be browsed, but there is also an Advanced Search template. From October 2005 onwards all legislation will be available in both html and pdf formats.
Halsbury's Statutes of England and Wales 4 ed, London: Butterworths • 50 Volumes updated by a looseleaf service, a reissue program and a Cumulative Supplement	The work is designed to provide a comprehensive, annotated record of all Acts of Parliament under 143 subject headings. The main edition or reissue of Acts includes all repeals, amendments and other changes. Each statute passed since the last reissue is in the looseleaf service.	Acts can be accessed by either name or consolidated subject index. For Acts not in the main work or reissue volumes consult the looseleaf service by either the List of Statutes booklet or the subject title list of statutes.
Index to the Statutes London: HMSO, 1235–1990	Cumulative subject index to public general statutes.	The reference in brackets after the entry is a reference to the Statutes in Force series. Although this is no longer published there is now the ongoing *Chronological table of the statutes* and there are the Chronological Tables of Local and Private Acts on the web at: http://www.opsi.gov.uk/chron-tables/chron-index.htm

11.7 The commencement date for legislation?

Research tool	What information will it give me?	Tips on use
Halsbury's Laws of England 4 ed, London: Butterworths, 1973 • Updated by Cumulative Supplement, Monthly Current Service and Annual Abridgement • Paper version (56 volumes) • http://www.lexisnexis.co.uk	*Halsbury's Laws of England* attempts to provide a comprehensive statement of the laws of England and Wales. This encyclopaedia contains law derived from legislation, statutory instruments and common law and it is divided into alphabetically arranged subject titles. It contains a consolidated table of cases, a consolidated table of statutes and statutory instruments, and a consolidated index. The Annual Abridgement combines the monthly reviews into a consolidated issue and the cumulative supplement summarises the law developments over the parliamentary year. Two looseleaf binders contain the noter-up and monthly reviews. See the Commencement of Statutes Tables in the Current Service	*Halsbury's Laws of England* can be accessed in three ways; by Title, through the Consolidated Index or the Consolidated Table. It includes approximately 165 subject areas. Each subject is treated in sections. Consolidated index volumes 55 and 56 combine information from all the titles and volumes 53 and 54 combine all entries from legislation tables in all volumes. Updating *Halsbury's Laws of England* is by the most recent reissue, then the cumulative supplement and then the noter-up service and monthly. Fee-based.
Halsbury's Statutes of England and Wales 4 ed, London: Butterworths • 50 Volumes updated by a looseleaf service, a reissue program and a Cumulative Supplement	The work is designed to provide a comprehensive, annotated record of all Acts of Parliament under 143 subject headings. The main edition or reissue of Acts includes all repeals, amendments and other changes. Each statute passed since the last reissue is in the looseleaf service.	The supplementary work to *Halsbury's Statutes of England and Wales, 'Is It In Force?'* is an alphabetical guide to the exact commencement dates of Acts of general application in England. It contains Royal Assent date, the authority for the commencement date and information on provisions not commenced.

Research tool	What information will it give me?	Tips on use
Current Law Legislation Citator London: Sweet & Maxwell, 1989– • Hardcopy updated by Current Law Statutes Service • On *Current Legal Information (CLI)* • http://www.venables. co.uk/pubsweet.htm	Details all changes to legislation (since 1989) and Statutory Instruments (since 1993). It also contains information on judicial consideration of statutes and statutory instruments and assent and commencement dates. It shows where and how statutes and statutory instruments have been amended, considered or otherwise affected through subsequent legislation.	Searching can be done by field, which includes subject, keyword, legislation and type of document. The database can also be searched by free text. The field search is easiest because it gives a list of keywords and documents. It does not contain full text. Most of this service is now also available through Westlaw and can be searched using the Westlaw commands.
Current Law Statutes London: Sweet & Maxwell • Cumulated into bound volumes and updated by the Current Law Statute Service	This service contains full text copies of Public and Private Acts (many annotated), Commencement Orders, Statute Citators, Progress of Bills table and Legislation not yet in force.	The 'Commencement Orders Table' lists in both chronological and alphabetical order, Acts that have been given a commencement date.
Current Law Monthly Digest London: Sweet & Maxwell • Cumulates into the annual supplement and year book, and is updated by the *Current Law Week.*	A guide to developments in case law, legislation and secondary material. The information is arranged by jurisdiction, then by broad subject headings. A comprehensive list of topics is at the front of each Monthly Digest. Contains a cumulative index, table of cases, current law notes, and information on Acts, Bills, Statutory Instruments and commencement dates.	The Dates of Commencement – Statutes lists in alphabetical order the commencement date for each Act and the authorising section or statutory instrument.
Is It In Force? London: Butterworths • Published annually • http://www.lexisnexis. co.uk	A guide to the Assent dates and commencement of Statutes passed since 1 January 1960. Subscribers to *Halsbury's Statutes* receive *Is It In Force?* annually as part of the subscription.	Update the hardcopy by using the looseleaf noter-up service to *Halsbury's Statutes of England and Wales.* Update this information electronically using the Daily Update service http://www. lexisnexis.co.uk/

11.8 **English legislation in full text?**

Research tool	What information will it give me?	Tips on use
United Kingdom Public Acts • http://www.opsi.gov.uk/acts.htm	Contains full text of UK Public Acts since 1988 and Private Acts since 1991. These are not the reprinted Acts including amendments.	This site can be browsed but there is also an Advanced Search template. From October 2005 onwards all legislation will be available in both html and pdf formats.
United Kingdom Legislation • http://www.bailii.org/uk/legis/num_act/	Full text of unconsolidated United Kingdom statutes from 1988- to date and the full text of primary legislation from Magna Carta 1215 and 1267 onwards.	This site can be browsed, although a search using the search function may bring back information on a topic. Available in html format only.
Current Law Statutes London: Sweet & Maxwell • Cumulated into bound volumes and updated by the Current Law Statute Service	This service contains full text copies of Public and Private Acts (many annotated), Commencement Orders, Statute Citators, Progress of Bills table and Legislation not yet in force.	Each volume covers one year. In that year all legislation as passed is in full text. There are some annotations in each year.
United Kingdom Law in Force London: Sweet & Maxwell • Westlaw http://www.westlaw.com	This service contains full text copies of consolidated statutes and statutory instruments currently in effect in the United Kingdom. Includes rules of the Supreme Court and county court rules. The statutes coverage is from 1267.	Search using the Westlaw commands.
Halsbury's Statutes of England and Wales 4 ed, London: Sweet & Maxwell • 50 volumes updated by a looseleaf service, a reissue program and a Cumulative Supplement	The work is designed to provide a comprehensive, annotated record of all Acts of Parliament under 143 subject headings. The main edition or reissue of Acts includes all repeals, amendments and other changes. Each statute passed since the last reissue is in the looseleaf service.	Acts can be accessed by either name or consolidated subject index. For Acts not in the main work or reissue volumes, consult the looseleaf service by either the List of Statutes booklet or the subject title list of statutes.

Research tool	What information will it give me?	Tips on use
UK Statutes • http://www.lexisnexis.co.uk and also http://www.lexisnexis.com	This database contains amended/reprinted text of public Acts arranged in alphabetical order.	There is a daily update available.

11.9 Updates for legislation?

Research tool	What information will it give me?	Tips on use
UK Statutes • http://www.lexisnexis.co.uk and also http://www.lexisnexis.com	This database contains amended/reprinted text of public Acts arranged in alphabetical order.	There is a daily update available.
Halsbury's Statutes of England and Wales 4 ed, London: Butterworths • 50 volumes updated by a looseleaf service and reissue program and a Cumulative Supplement	The work is designed to provide a comprehensive, annotated record of all Acts of Parliament under 143 subject headings. The main edition or reissue of Acts includes all repeals, amendments and other changes. Each statute passed since the last reissue is in the looseleaf service.	To update legislation since the last reissue, use the cumulative supplement and noter-up service. The supplement follows the format of the main issues. The noter-up is a preview of the upcoming cumulative supplement. The supplement lists any relevant Acts passed since the last reissue. Fee-based.
Current Law Legislation Citator London: Sweet & Maxwell, 1989– • Hardcopy updated by Current Law Statutes Service • On *Current Legal Information (CLI)* • http://www.venables.co.uk/pubsweet.htm	Details all changes to legislation (since 1989) and Statutory Instruments (since 1993). It also contains information on judicial consideration of statutes and statutory instruments and assent and commencement dates. It shows where and how statutes and statutory instruments have been amended, considered or otherwise affected through subsequent legislation.	Searching can be done by field, which includes subject, keyword, legislation and type of document. The database can also be searched by free text. The field search is easiest because it gives a list of keywords and documents. It does not contain full text. Most of this service is now also available through Westlaw and can be searched using the Westlaw commands.

11.10 **A subject index to delegated legislation?**

Research tool	What information will it give me?	Tips on use
Statutory Instruments 1987– • http://www.opsi.gov.uk/stat.htm	Full text of all Statutory Instruments made since 1987.	This site can be browsed, although a search using the search function may bring back information on a topic. Available in html format only. There is an Advanced Search template.
Halsbury's Statutory Instruments London: Butterworths, 1992– • 22 volumes updated with reissues, Annual Cumulative Supplements and the Monthly Survey	There are 99 alphabetical subject titles each containing a number of subject headings depending on the area. It also contains a Chronological List of Instruments, Table of Instruments No Longer in Operation, Table of Statutes, Commencement dates.	The Annual Consolidated Index covers the whole of the main work and the Annual Supplements. The index will give details of the relevant volume.
United Kingdom Statutory Instruments • http://www.bailii.org/uk/legis/num_reg/	Selected documents from 1987 and full text from 2002.	Browse by year or document title. Full Boolean search facility available using AustLII software.

11.11 **Full text of delegated legislation?**

Research tool	What information will it give me?	Tips on use
Statutory Instruments 1987– • http://www.opsi.gov.uk/stat.htm	Full text of all Statutory Instruments made since 1987. This site also contains Explanatory Memorandum from June 2004. These provide information about policy objective and policy implications.	This site can be browsed, although a search using the search function may bring back information on a topic. Available in html format only. There is an Advanced Search template.
Halsbury's Statutory Instruments London: Butterworths, 1979– • 22 volumes updated with reissues, Annual Cumulative Supplements and Monthly Survey	There are 99 alphabetical subject titles, each containing a number of subject headings depending on the area. It also contains a Chronological List of Instruments, Table of Instruments no Longer in Operation, Table of Statutes, Commencement dates.	There are five main ways of accessing Statutory information: by subject, by number, by title, by enabling power and appropriate title. The easiest is to consult the consolidated Annual Index. To update, use the two-part looseleaf service and the Annual Cumulative Supplement.

Research tool	What information will it give me?	Tips on use
UK Statutory Instruments • http://www.lexisnexis.co.uk and also http://www.lexisnexis.com	This database contains amended/reprinted text of statutory instruments arranged in alphabetical order.	There is a daily update available.
United Kingdom Law in Force London: Sweet & Maxwell • Westlaw http://www.westlaw.com	This service contains full text copies of consolidated statutes and statutory instruments currently in effect in the United Kingdom. Includes rules of the Supreme Court and county court rules. The statutory instruments coverage is from 1948.	Search using the Westlaw commands.
United Kingdom Satutory Instruments • http://www.bailii.org/uk/legis/num_reg/	Selected documents from 1987 and full text from 2002.	Browse by year or document title. Full Boolean search facility available using AustLII software.

11.12 A subject index to cases?

Research tool	What information will it give me?	Tips on use
Current Law Cases London: Sweet & Maxwell, 1947– • On *Current Legal Information (CLI)* • http://www.venables.co.uk/pubsweet.htm	Digests over 100 commercial law series reports both main and specialist, and some transcripts of unreported judgments. Judgments are from all courts and some tribunals.	Searching can be done by field, which includes subject, keyword, case, legislation and type of document. The database can also be searched by free text. The field search is easiest because it gives a list of keywords and documents. It does not contain full text. This database is now also available through Westlaw and can be searched using Westlaw commands.

Research tool	What information will it give me?	Tips on use
The Digest: Annotated British, Commonwealth and European Cases London: Butterworths, 1981– • 90 volumes updated by reissues, Annual Cumulative Supplement and Digest Quarterly Survey • Not available electronically	Digests cases from over 1000 report series from medieval times to the present. Covers the case law of England and Wales and many of Australia, Canada, Ireland, New Zealand and other Commonwealth countries.	Each title has a table of contents which breaks down the title into subject areas. The Digest's Annual Index also may be consulted. To update, consult the supplement and quarterly survey.

11.13 **Full text of English cases?**

Official Law Report Series:

    Year Books to 1535

    Nominate Reports 1530–1865

    Law Report Series 1865– (authorised)

Others:

    All England Law Reports 1936–

    Weekly Law Reports 1953– (Published by Incorporated Council of Law Reporting, volumes 2 and 3 will eventually be published in the Law Report Series.)

Research tool	What information will it give me?	Tips on use
Lawfinder • http://www.infolaw. co.uk/lawfinder/	General links to decisions online. Fee-based.	
Smith Bernal • http://www. smithbernal.com	Casetrack available free of charge to some users. Found under link called WordWave Websites at top right hand corner of the Homepage.	Full text search facilities. Browse facilities (by date and case name) also available.
House of Lords Judgments • http://www.publications. parliament.uk/pa/ ld199697/ldjudgmt/ ldjudgmt.htm	The full text of all opinions of the House of Lords since 14 November 1996.	This page cannot be searched only browsed by the case name listed in date of judgment.

Research tool	What information will it give me?	Tips on use
Courts Service • http://www.hmcourts-service.gov.uk/	Decisions from: Chancery Division Commercial Court Companies Court Court of Appeal – Civil Division Court of Appeal – Criminal Division Court of Appeal – Civil Division Courts Martial Appeal Court Divisional Court Divisional Court – Crown Office High Court of Justice Patents Court Queen's Bench – Divisional Court Queen's Bench Division Queens Bench Division – Divisional Court Restrictive Practices Court Supreme Court Costs Officer Technology and Construction Court	Can be searched by free word, keyword, parties, court or date. Browsing is in an expandable format based on one of the search.
UK Caselaw • http://www.lexisnexis.co.uk and see http://www.lexisnexis.com	The Law Reports and All England Law Reports and All England Reprints Extensions are available. There are reported cases from 1558 from 30 series of law reports, tax cases from 1875 and unreported cases and transcripts from 1980. Daily updates.	Search facilities and subject access. Links between databases. Fee-based.

Research tool	What information will it give me?	Tips on use
BAILII • http://www.bailii.org	Extensive full text case law from England and Wales, Privy Council decisions; United Kingdom House of Lords decisions; United Kingdom Supreme Court; Upper Tribunal (Administrative Appeals Chamber); Upper Tribunal (Finance and Tax); Upper Tribunal (Lands Chamber); First-tier Tribunal (Health Education and Social Care Chamber); First-tier Tribunal (Tax); United Kingdom Competition Appeals Tribunal; Nominet UK Dispute Resolution Service; Special Immigrations Appeals Commission; United Kingdom Employment Appeal Tribunal; United Kingdom Financial Services and Markets Tribunals Decisions; United Kingdom Asylum and Immigration Tribunal; United Kingdom Information Tribunal including the National Security Appeals Panel; United Kingdom Special Commissioners of Income Tax Decisions; UK Social Security and Child Support Commissioners' decisions; and United Kingdom VAT & Duties Tribunals decisions.	Browse by year or decision title. Full Boolean search facility available using same software as AustLII.
English Reports 1220–1873 • http://www.commonlii.org/int/cases/EngR/	The Commonwealth Legal Information Institute (CommonLII) 'aims to provide ... core legal information from all Commonwealth countries'. 'CommonLII will assist the development of a genuinely international common law'.	Browse by year or decision title. Full Boolean search facility available using AustLII software.

11.14 Cases that have been judicially considered?

Research tool	What information will it give me?	Tips on use
Current Law Case Citator London: Sweet & Maxwell, 1947– • On *Current Legal Information (CLI)* • http://www.venables. co.uk/pubsweet.htm	A comprehensive guide to case law since 1947, the database consists of a list of citations and abstracts for each case reported in the UK Law Report Series. Each citation identifies whether a case has been affirmed, approved, considered, disproved, distinguished, followed, not applied, not followed, overruled and reversed.	Searching can be done by field, which includes subject, keyword, case, legislation and type of document. The database can also be searched by free text. The field search is easiest because it gives a list of keywords and documents. It does not contain full text. This database is also now available through Westlaw and can be searched using Westlaw commands.
The Digest: Annotated British, Commonwealth and European Cases London: Butterworths, 1981– • 90 volumes updated by reissues, Annual Cumulative Supplement and Digest Quarterly Survey • Not available electronically	Digests cases from over 1000 report series from medieval times to the present. Covers the case law of England and Wales and many of Australia, Canada, Ireland, New Zealand and other Commonwealth countries.	Find the original case authority and then consult the references at the end of each entry, which outlines whether that case has been applied, approved, considered, distinguished, doubted, explained, extended, not followed or overruled.

11.15 Cases that have dealt with specific legislative sections?

Research tool	What information will it give me?	Tips on use
Halsbury's Statutes of England and Wales 4 ed, London: Butterworths • 50 volumes updated by a looseleaf service and reissue program and a Cumulative supplement	The work is designed to provide a comprehensive, annotated record of all Acts of Parliament under 143 main subject headings. The main edition or reissue of Acts includes all repeals, amendments and other changes. Each statute passed since the last reissue is in the looseleaf service.	To update legislation and annotations since the last reissue, use the cumulative supplement and noter-up service. The supplement follows the format of the main issues. The noter-up is a preview of the upcoming cumulative supplement. The supplement lists any relevant Acts passed since the last reissue.
Current Law Legislation Citator London: Sweet & Maxwell, 1947– • Hardcopy updated by Current Law Statutes Service • On *Current Legal Information (CLI)* • http://www.venables.co.uk/pubsweet.htm	Details all changes to legislation (since 1989) and Statutory Instruments (since 1993). It also contains information on judicial consideration of Statutes and Statutory Instruments, and Assent and Commencement dates.	Searching can be done by field, which includes subject, keyword, case, legislation and type of document. The database can also be searched by free text. The field search is easiest because it gives a list of keywords and documents. Does not contain full text. For the paper version go to the appropriate Act listed. This database is now also available through Westlaw and can be searched using the Westlaw commands.

Canada —
How Do You Find

12.1 **An introduction to the jurisdiction?**

As a federation, Canada has a parliamentary form of government comparable to Australia. There are ten provinces and two territories. There are two houses of parliament at the Federal level:

1 the Senate; and

2 an elected House of Commons.

Each province or state has a unicameral provincial parliament, usually called the Legislature.

The Constitution is defined within the *Constitution Act 1982* (Can), which is Schedule B to the *Canada Act 1982*, and individual rights and freedoms are protected by the Canadian Charter of Rights and Freedoms.

The Supreme Court of Canada has nine members, including one Chief Justice and eight 'puisne' (or 'ranked after') judges. Three judges come from Quebec, three from Ontario, two from Western Canada and one from the Atlantic Provinces. Federal Cabinet appoints the judges. The Court sits in Ottawa and hears appeals from the appeal courts in the provinces and territories and from the Federal Court of Appeal. The Supreme Court is the final court of appeal for both federal and provincial courts in all areas — civil, criminal and constitutional.

Until 1949, the Judicial Committee of the Privy Council was the final court of appeal from the Supreme Court of Canada. Appeals to the Privy Council were abolished in 1947, therefore the Supreme Court's decisions are final.

The Federal Court of Canada was established in 1971 as the successor to the Exchequer Court of Canada, which had been created in 1875. It has two divisions — the Federal Court of Appeal and the Trial Division. The Federal Court's jurisdiction includes actions by and against the Crown, maritime law, intellectual property law (patents, copyright, trademarks and industrial designs), appeals from the Tax Court of Canada and citizenship and immigration appeals.

The provinces have their own courts divided into trial and appeal divisions. These courts mainly deal with minor civil matters and criminal cases. Quebec has a civil law system.

See the US Library of Congress site 'The Guide to the Law Online' for a range of links to pertinent national material at http://www.loc.gov/law/guide/index.html

Basic Court Hierarchy

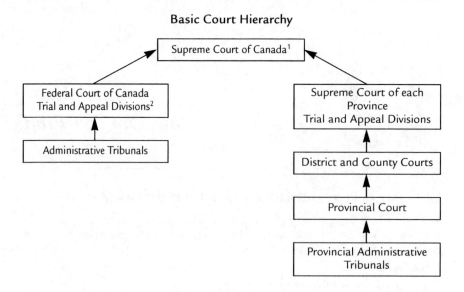

Court decisions from the more populous provinces such as Ontario and British Columbia carry more weight than those decisions from the smaller provinces.

General information on the Canadian Parliament is available from the Parliamentary Internet site. Access the site map at http://www.parl.gc.ca/common/sitemap.asp?Language=E&Parl=50&Sess=1 for an overview.

See also the Department of Justice site http://www.justice.gc.ca/eng/index.html which contains links under the heading Canadian Justice System to Canada's System of Justice, Dean R and Sandell H's *Canada's Court System, Laws of Canada, and A Guide to the Making of Federal Acts and Regulations* http://www.justice.gc.ca/eng/index.html

The University of Minnesota Law Library has a research guide titled *Researching the Law of Canada* at http://local.law.umn.edu/library/pathfinders/canadalaw98.html

In addition, see generally:

Access to Justice Network http://www.acjnet.org which is sponsored by the Department of Justice in Canada, the Legal Studies Program at the University of Alberta, the University of Montreal and Web Networks and provides links to legislation, parliamentary material, legal directories and legal information for schools.

American Law Sources On-line http://www.lawsource.com/also/index.htm#[Canada] which provides links to sources of law for Canada, the US and Mexico.

---

1   Comprises Chief Justice and eight judges. It is a court of *general* jurisdiction.

2   Comprises 25 judges including a Chief Justice, an Associate Chief Justice and nine judges of the Court of Appeal.

Canadian Legal Network http://www.canlaw.net/canlaw which aims to provide an 'index of Canadian content websites with primary focus given to Canadian law and its supporting industry'. Topics covered include the government, courts, police and corrections, bailiffs, law schools and law libraries, law societies, legal aid, legal classifieds and more.

Duhaime's Canadian Legal Information Centre http://www.wwlia.org/ca-home.htm which includes links to subject specific legal material, plain language articles on legislation and a legal dictionary.

The Continuing Legal Education Society of BC — Legal Links, including links for the profession, experts, consultants, practice tools, and the media http://www.cle.bc.ca

Jurist Canada is a legal information network directed at law teachers. The emphasis is on university programs, conferences, and current scholarship. See http://jurist.law.utoronto.ca/

Many of the Canadian sources are available on subscription services, including LexisNexis: http://www.lexisnexis.com; Westlaw/ Carswell: http://home.westlawecarswell.com; Westlaw International: http://www.westlawinternational.com/; Quicklaw: http://www.quicklaw.com; and BestCase: http://www.canadalawbook.ca

See generally, Castel J and Latchman O K, *The Practical Guide to Canadian Legal Research* (2 ed, Scarborough, Ontario: Carswell, 1996); and Yogis J A and Christie I M, *Legal Writing and Research Manual* (6 ed, Markham, Ontario: Butterworths, 2004).

12.2 A broad picture of the law?

Research tool	What information will it give me?	Tips on use
Canadian Encyclopaedic Digest • http://www.westlaw international.com/	This provides a digest of the law of Ontario and the four western provinces, including 'provincial, federal and common law'. Includes a very succinct sentence or two with a statement of the law followed by extensive case and legislation references.	The references are cross-linked to the Canadian Abridgement. Browse and search facilities are available. The Currency Note for each title is accessible from the browse screen.

12.3 Parliamentary publications?

See information about Parliament at http://www.parl.gc.ca/common/Aboutparl. asp?Language=E&Parl=50&Ses=2 and especially the Precis of Procedure http://www.parl.gc.ca/information/about/process/house/precis/titpg-e.htm

Pages are available in French and English.

Parliamentary debates and journals

Research tool	What information will it give me?	Tips on use
Debates of the House of Commons 1997– • http://www2.parl.gc.ca/housechamberbusiness/ChamberSittings.aspx?View=H&Language=E&Mode=1&Parl=50&Ses=2	The printed verbatim record of the proceedings in the House of Commons is published after each sitting. The daily debates records are called 'blues'. The debates can be accessed in three different ways — as a 'Complete Hansard' with one day in a html file, in '5 Minute' segments so readers access a series of small files or by FTP of the whole file. The 'Oral Questions' file allows access to Question Period as one complete file. Consult the User Guide available at the Hansard site.	Choose date from Calendar hypertext links on the main page. To access non-current sessional information, click on the relevant session or parliament. To search, use the Parliamentary Business and Publications Search Engine at the top of the Chamber Business homepage.
Debates of the Senate 1997– • http://www.parl.gc.ca/common/Chamber_Senate_Debates.asp?Language=E&Parl=50&Ses=2	The printed verbatim record of the proceedings in the House of Commons is published after each sitting. The daily debates records are called 'blues'. The debates are available in several formats — as a 'Complete Hansard' with one day in a html file or by FTP of the whole file.	Choose the date from the Calendar hypertext links on the main page. To access non-current sessional information, click on the relevant session or parliament. To search, use the Parliamentary Business and Publications Search Engine at the top of the Chamber Business homepage.
Journals of the House of Commons of Canada 1997– • http://www2.parl.gc.ca/housechamberbusiness/ChamberSittings.aspx?View=J&Language=E&Parl=50&Ses=2	The official record of the decisions and transactions of the House of Commons for each sitting day. In html format only.	Choose date from Calendar hypertext links on the main page. To access non-current sessional information, click on the relevant session or parliament. To search, use the Parliamentary Business and Publications Search Engine at the top of the Chamber Business homepage.

Research tool	What information will it give me?	Tips on use
Journals of the Senate of Canada 1997– • http://www.parl.gc.ca/ common/Chamber_ Senate_Journals.asp? Language=E&Parl= 50&Ses=2	The official record of the decisions and transactions of the Senate for each sitting day. In html format only.	Choose date from the Calendar hypertext links on the main page. To search, use the Parliamentary Business and Publications Search Engine at the top of the Chamber Business homepage. To access non-current sessional information, click on the relevant session or parliament.

Index to the debates and journals

Research tool	What information will it give me?	Tips on use
Index to the Journals of the House of Commons 1997– • http://www2.parl.gc.ca/ housechamberbusiness/ ChamberSittings.aspx? View=J&Language=E& Mode=1&Parl=50&Ses=2 User Guide • http://www2.parl.gc.ca/ housechamberbusiness/ ChamberPublication IndexSearchFAQ.aspx? View=G&Language=E	The Journals Index is subject-based and includes references to every item that is tabled and introduced into the House of Commons. The Journals Subject Index is prepared by the Parliamentary Publications Directorate Index and Reference Service.	To use the Index, select the relevant alphabetical range. Click on the page number that will open the relevant issue. To access non-current sessional information, click on the relevant session or parliament. To search, use the Parliamentary Business and Publications Search Engine at the top of the Chamber Business homepage.
Index to the Debates of the House of Commons • http://www2.parl.gc.ca/ housechamberbusiness/ ChamberPublication IndexSearch.aspx?View= H&arpiD=1&arpiJ= 0&Language=E&Mode= 1&Parl=50&Ses=2 User Guide • http://www2.parl.gc.ca/ housechamberbusiness/ ChamberPublication IndexSearchFAQ.aspx? View=G&Language=E	This is a subject index to comments by Members of Parliament. The index uses a subject breakdown by parliamentary member. The Hansard Subject Index is prepared by the Parliamentary Publications Directorate Index and Reference Service.	To use the Index, select the relevant alphabetical range. Click on the page number that will open the relevant issue. Html format links only. To search, use the Parliamentary Business and Publications Search Engine at the top of the Chamber Business homepage. To access non-current sessional information, click on the relevant session or parliament.

Committee reports

Research tool	What information will it give me?	Tips on use
House of Commons Committee Reports • http://www2.parl.gc.ca/ CommitteeBusiness/ ReportsResponses.aspx? Language=E&Mode= 1&Parl=40&Ses=2	Lists all reports for the current parliament from House of Commons committees. In html format only. Arranged by Committee area.	To search, use the Parliamentary Business and Publications Search Engine at the top of the Chamber Business home-page. To access non-current sessional information, click on the relevant session or parliament.
Senate Committee Reports • http://www.parl.gc.ca/ 40/2/parlbus/commbus/ senate/com-E/rep-E.htm	Lists all reports for the current parliament from Senate committees. In html format only.	To search, use the Parliamentary Business and Publications Search Engine at the top of the Chamber Business home-page. To access non-current sessional information, click on the relevant session or parliament.
Joint Committee Reports • http://www2.parl.gc.ca/ CommitteeBusiness/ ReportsResponses.aspx? Language=E&Mode= 1&Parl=40&Ses= 2&CmteInst=joint	Lists all reports for the current parliament from joint committees. In html format only.	To search, use the Parliamentary Business and Publications Search Engine at the top of the Chamber Business home-page. To access non-current sessional information, click on the relevant session or parliament.

Other parliamentary publications

Research tool	What information will it give me?	Tips on use
Index to Status of House Business House of Commons 1997– • http://www2.parl.gc.ca/content/hoc/house/402/status/index/index-E.htm?Language=E&Mode=1&Parl=40&Ses=2	This is in three parts: PART I — Bills, Government Bills, Private Bills, Private Members' and Public Bills. Information for each Bill includes name of Member introducing Bill, title, dates of 1st, 2nd and 3rd reading, committee referrals, when passed in Senate, and assent. PART II — includes Motions (Supply, Ways and Means, Government Business), and Motions by Private Members. PART III — Written Questions by Private Members.	Bills are numbered C for Commons and S for the Senate and then sequentially, eg C-1. Symbols used are: R — Recommended by the Governor General * — Referred to Committee before second reading 1 — Requires Oral Answer 2 — Response requested within 45 days There is a Subject index available in a separate file. To access non-current sessional information, click on the relevant session or parliament. To search, use the Parliamentary Business and Publications Search Engine at the top of the Chamber Business homepage.

Research tool	What information will it give me?	Tips on use
Progress of Legislation 1997– • http://www2.parl.gc.ca/ senatebills/Bills Government.aspx? Language=E&Mode= 1&Parl=40&Ses=2	Tracks the progress of all government, public and private Bills introduced into the Senate by Bill number. In a table format and updated weekly. Html format only, eg http:// www.parl.gc.ca/40/2/ parlbus/chambus/senate/ deb-E/prog-E.htm? Language=E&Mode= 1&Parl=40&Ses=2	To access non-current sessional information, click on the relevant session or parliament. To search, use the Parliamentary Business and Publications Search Engine at the top of the Chamber Business homepage.
Order Paper and Notice Paper House of Commons 1997– • http://www2.parl.gc.ca/ housechamberbusiness/ ChamberSittings.aspx? Language=E&Mode= 1&Parl=40&Ses= 1&View=N	The Order Paper is the official agenda of the House of Commons for that day. The Notice Paper outlines all notices of Bills, motions and questions. It includes Private Members' Business, Weekly Review of Business, and reports the Stage of Bills by Bill number.	French and English on same page in two columns. Business is grouped and presented in order. To access non-current sessional information, click on the relevant session or parliament. To search, use the Parliamentary Business and Publications Search Engine at the top of the Chamber Business homepage.
Order Paper and Notice Paper of the Senate • http://www.parl.gc.ca/ common/Chamber_ Senate_Debates.asp? Language=E	The Order Paper is the official agenda of the Senate for that day. The Notice Paper outlines all notices of Bills, motions and questions. Includes Private Members' Business, Weekly Review of Business, and Reports the Stage of Bills by Bill number. See eg http:// www.parl.gc.ca/40/2/ parlbus/chambus/senate/ orderpaper/ord-e.htm	French and English on same page in two columns. Business is grouped and presented in order. To access non-current sessional information, click on the relevant session or parliament. To search, use the Parliamentary Business and Publications Search Engine at the top of the Chamber Business homepage.

12.4 **Bills?**

Research tool	What information will it give me?	Tips on use
Canadian Current Law — Legislation Toronto: Thomson Carswell • Paper version	Summarises recent legislative activity in the Canadian and provincial parliaments. Includes Progress of Bills, Statutes Amended, Repealed Legislation or Proclaimed in Force and Regulations.	Monthly publication with annual cumulation. Consult the Progress of Bills Table and Proclaimed in Force to determine most recent changes to the law.
Canada Statute Citator — Weekly Bulletin Service Canada Law Book Co • Paper version — Five volume looseleaf service updated quarterly	Provides information on the progress of all government Bills as they pass through their various stages in the House of Commons and the Senate and includes information on proclamations, bringing legislation into force as well as amendments made to existing Acts by the new Bills.	Consult the looseleaf service, then each weekly bulletin since the last update. Excludes the *Income Tax Act, Divorce Act, Young Offenders Act* and the Criminal Code.
Bills • http://www.parl.gc.ca/ common/bills.asp? Language=E&Parl= 50&Ses=2	This site gives links to all Bills introduced, including Government Bills, Private Member's Public Bills, Private Bills, Private Senator's Public Bills and Legislative Summaries. There are also links to the Progress of Legislation and Status of House Business publications. The electronic version is not the authorised copy of the Bill. Reference must be made to the hardcopy official version.	The letter 'S' denotes government Bills first introduced in the Senate. The letter 'C' denotes government Bills first introduced in the House of Commons. Browse Bills on the site by choosing Senate or House of Commons, then government or non-government Bills, then relevant Bill number. In order to find a Bill by subject, use the Hansard Index, and then see the User's Guide if further information is required. To access non-current sessional information, click on the relevant session or parliament. To search, use the Parliamentary Business and Publications Search Engine at the top of the Chamber Business homepage.

12.5 **Explanatory material about Bills?**

Research tool	What information will it give me?	Tips on use
Legislative Summaries • http://www.parl.gc.ca/common/library_prb.asp?Language=E	Prepared by the Parliamentary Research Branch to provide an explanatory document for most government Bills. Some exceptions are taxation measures, omnibus or brief legislation.	The virtual Library is arranged by subject, with documents arranged alphabetically within each subject area. Many legislative summaries are provided for recent Bills. To search, use the Parliamentary Business and Publications Search Engine at the top of the Chamber Business homepage.
Senate Government Bills • http://www2.parl.gc.ca/senatebills/BillsGovernment.aspx?Language=E&Mode=1&Parl=50&Ses=1	This Table includes references to a Legislative Summary prepared by the Parliamentary Research Branch of the Library of Parliament. There is a summary at the beginning of each Bill.	The Table provides links to First Reading, text as passed by the Senate and at Assent. The Legislative Summary describes the Bill as of the date shown at the beginning of the document.
House of Commons Bills • http://www.parl.gc.ca/common/Bills_House_Government.asp?Language=E&Parl=50&Ses=2	This Table includes references to a Legislative Summary prepared by the Parliamentary Research Branch of the Library of Parliament. There is a summary at the beginning of each Bill.	The Table provides links to First Reading, text as passed by the Senate and at Assent. The Legislative Summary describes the Bill as of the date shown at the beginning of the document.

12.6 A subject index to legislation?

The Justice Laws are moving to a new website to conform to the Government of Canada's Common Look and Feel Standards for the internet (CLF 2.0). This process is ongoing and therefore some of the following URLs will change (6/1/2010).

Research tool	What information will it give me?	Tips on use
Department of Justice Canada, Consolidated Statutes and Regulations • http://laws.justice.gc.ca/en/index.html	The ability to browse and search consolidated Acts and Regulations using focused search engines. The date under the title of the Act is the consolidation date.	Search Templates are provided for advanced search queries. Choose from the following search template options: Assisted Search, Extended Search, Specialised Search, Search Consolidated Statutes, Search Consolidated Regulations, Search the Annual Statutes of Canada, Search the Index of Statutory Instruments, Search the Table of Public Statutes and Search the Table of Private Statutes.
Department of Justice Canada, Consolidated Statutes and Regulations, Access by Subject • http://laws.justice.gc.ca/en/BrowseRegTitle	Access by Title provides an alphabetical listing, whereas the subject entry provides broad subject areas that can be further refined using easy search templates provided on the page.	Select the area of interest, then use the search function provided to search that specific subject. In html format only.
Department of Justice Canada, Table of Public Statutes • http://laws.justice.gc.ca/en/publaw/index.html	This table provides an alphabetical listing of all the consolidated Public Statutes (1907–31 August 1998). It includes a chronological listing of amendments, repealed Acts, years of enactment and responsible ministers.	The Revised Statutes cite is included in the heading. The French title appears under the Act. Individual section amendments are listed. CIF refers to 'coming into force' date. Search Templates are provided for advanced search queries. Choose from the search template options.
Department of Justice Canada, Table of Private Statutes • http://laws.justice.gc.ca/en/privlaw/index.html	This table provides an alphabetical listing of all the consolidated Private Statutes (1867–31 December 1997). Acts dealing with divorces have been omitted. Acts are listed under 12 major headings.	Search templates are provided for advanced search queries. Choose from the search template options.

12.7 **Commencement date of legislation?**

'Royal Assent is given to a Bill when it has been passed in exactly the same form by both Houses; it is at this stage that a Bill becomes law. The Bill comes into force on the day of Assent, unless otherwise provided in the Bill itself. Provision is sometimes made for coming into force on a certain day or a day fixed by order of the Governor in Council, and parts of Bills may be brought into force at different times.'

House of Commons Precis of Procedure:
http://www.parl.gc.ca/information/about/process/house/precis/titpg-e.htm

Research tool	What information will it give me?	Tips on use
Canada Gazette Part III 1998– • http://canadagazette.gc.ca/index-e.html	Published as soon as is reasonably practicable after the Royal Assent. Part III contains the most recent Public Acts of Parliament and their enactment proclamations.	Available only in pdf format. Generally, online is only the unofficial bilingual version. The first section prints in full text of statutes according to Act number, then corrections to Acts and then proclamation dates and dates of coming into force.
Statutes of Canada – Table of Proclamation and Orders in Council relating to the coming into force of Acts	The table sets out the date that the legislation comes into force and includes references to the Canada Gazette Part II.	Refer to the table of 'Proclamations' in the latest annual volume. This gives a date in force and a Canada Gazette reference. The cumulative 'Table of Public Statutes' in the same volume has this information.
Canada Statute Citator and Weekly Bulletin Service Canada Law Book Co • Paper version – Five volume looseleaf service updated quarterly	Provides information on the progress of all government Bills as they pass through their various stages in the House of Commons and the Senate. It includes information on proclamations, bringing legislation into force as well as amendments made to existing Acts by the new Bills. As well, pertinent cases are digested and inserted under the appropriate Act and section.	All amendments to Acts are listed, and when a section is replaced it is set out in bold-face type. Proclamations and Orders in Council are included where they affect an Act listed in the Canada Statute Citator. Consult the looseleaf service, then each weekly bulletin since the last update. Excludes the *Income Tax Act, Divorce Act, Young Offenders Act* and the Criminal Code.

Research tool	What information will it give me?	Tips on use
Canadian Current Law — Legislation Toronto: Thomson Carswell • Paper version	Summarises recent legislative activity in the Canadian and provincial parliaments. Includes Progress of Bills, Statutes Amended, Repealed Legislation or Proclaimed in Force and Regulations.	Monthly publication with annual cumulation. Consult the Progress of Bills Table and Proclaimed in Force to determine most recent changes to the law.

12.8 Canadian legislation in full text?

Federal legislation is published in French and English. On enactment, the Bills are included in The Canada Gazette Part III. They are then published in the Revised Statues of Canada 1985 — supplementary volumes are published for subsequent years.

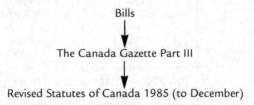

Bills

↓

The Canada Gazette Part III

↓

Revised Statutes of Canada 1985 (to December)

The statutes and sections are renumbered with each reprint. References to the revised Statutes are presumed to include subsequent amendments. The legislative history is given after each section and refers back to the previous revision and amendments.

For all purposes of interpreting and applying the law, users should consult the Acts as passed by Parliament. These are published in the 'Assented to' Acts service, Part III of the Canada Gazette and the annual Statutes of Canada, and Regulations, as registered by the Clerk of the Privy Council and published in Part II of the Canada Gazette.

Research tool	What information will it give me?	Tips on use
Consolidated Statutes of Canada Department of Justice Canada • http://laws.justice.gc.ca/ en/index.html	Legislation available by text file or compressed text file, in French or English with Regulations. Complete documents available to download and an indication of the size of the file are provided. The currency date is also provided. Repealed Acts are listed separately and provide date of repeal.	Access to Statutes — classified by title order, eg 'Canada Labour Code' will appear under 'C' Access to Statutes — classified by chapter number, eg, 'Canada Labour Code' will appear under 'L', according to its alphanumerical code, L-2

Research tool	What information will it give me?	Tips on use
Consolidated Statutes of Canada • http://www.lexisnexis.com	The Consolidated Statutes of Canada is the up-to-date consolidation of Canadian federal statutes arranged alphabetically according to statute name. This consolidation includes the 1985 revision together with the 4 supplements to the RSC 1985 and annual sessional volumes.	Choose Legal Excluding US as source in which to search, then Canada Case Law.
Canada Gazette — Part III • http://canadagazette.gc.ca/index-e.html	The Canada Gazette is the official newspaper of the Government of Canada since 1841. The Canada Gazette is published under the authority of the Statutory Instruments Act. The Canada Gazette consists of three parts: Part III contains the most recent Public Acts of Parliament and their enactment proclamations.	Each issue of the Canada Gazette, Part III is in a separate single pdf file with a table of contents and an index containing bookmarks and hyper-links. The Internet version of the Canada Gazette, Part III begins in January 1998 with volume 132. The list will give you access to the issues in a reverse chronological order, most recent issue being first.
CanLII 1995– • http://www.canlii.org	Contains Consolidated Statutes of Canada in Alphabetical List, Consolidated Regulations of Canada in Alphabetical List and Annual Statutes of Canada by year.	The databases can be searched using Sino software or browsed either alphabetically or by year. Available in html format only.
Annual Statutes 1995– • http://laws.justice.gc.ca/en/BrowseAnnual	The Annual Statutes of Canada contain the text of the Acts of Parliament (other than appropriation Acts and private Acts) which received royal assent in a given calendar year. The Bill reference is given with each Act and the Acts are filed in Chapters.	The Acts are in html format and there is an additional search template provided for each.

12.9 Updates for legislation?

Research tool	What information will it give me?	Tips on use
Table of Public Statutes • Paper version contained at the end of the Annual Statutes • http://laws.justice.gc.ca/en/BrowseRegTitle	The Table of Public Statutes is a reference document which provides useful historical information on the Acts comprising the consolidated statutes, including a chronological listing of amendments, repealed Acts, years of enactment and responsible ministers.	This database can be searched or browsed. Searching is any word and browsing is alphabetically by title as listed at the bottom of the page.
Table of Private Statutes • http://laws.justice.gc.ca/en/privlaw/index.html	The Table of Private Acts is a historical index showing all private Acts of Canada, other than those Acts that deal with divorces, that have been enacted since 1867 and that appear in the Statutes of Canada from 1867–31 December 1997. Each Act is listed alphabetically in accordance with its subject matter.	This database can be searched or browsed. Searching is by any word and browsing is by the list of subjects at the bottom of the page.
Canada Statute Citator and Weekly Bulletin Service Canada Law Book Co • Paper version — Five volume looseleaf service updated quarterly	It provides information on the progress of all government Bills as they pass through their various stages in the House of Commons and the Senate. It includes information on proclamations bringing legislation into force as well as amendments made to existing Acts by the new Bills. Excludes the *Income Tax Act, Divorce Act, Young Offenders Act* and the Criminal Code.	All amendments to Acts are listed, and when a section is replaced it is set out in bold-face type. Proclamations and Orders in Council are included where they affect an Act listed in the Canada Statute Citator. Consult the looseleaf service then each weekly bulletin since the last update.
Canadian Current Law — Legislation Toronto: Thomson Carswell • Paper version	Summarises recent legislative activity in the Canadian and provincial parliaments. Includes Progress of Bills, Statutes Amended, Repealed Legislation or Proclaimed in Force and Regulations.	Monthly publication with annual cumulation. Consult the Progress of Bills Table and Proclaimed in Force to determine most recent changes to the law. Also consult the Amended Legislation and Repealed Legislation Table to update legislation.

12.10 A subject index to delegated legislation?

Research tool	What information will it give me?	Tips on use
Department of Justice Canada, Consolidated Statutes and Regulations, Access by Subject • http://laws.justice.gc.ca/ en/subject/index.html	Access by Title provides an alphabetical listing, whereas the subject entry provides broad subject areas that can be further refined using easy search templates provided on the page.	Select the area of interest, then use the search function provided to search that specific subject. In html format only.
Consolidated Index of Statutory Instruments • http://laws.justice.gc.ca/ en/index/index.html	The Consolidated Index of Statutory Instruments table provides a reference to Regulations, statutory instruments (other than Regulations), and other documents that were in force at any time in the current calendar year. For instruments published in the Canada Gazette Part II which have ceased to be in force in any previous year, reference should be made to the Consolidated Index of Statutory Instruments of 31 December of the year in question.	Documents are listed alphabetically under the title of the enabling statute rather than the SI title. Details of amendments are indicated.

12.11 Full text of delegated legislation?

Research tool	What information will it give me?	Tips on use
Canada Gazette Part II 1998– • http://canadagazette. gc.ca/index-e.html	Published every second Wednesday, Canada Gazette, Part II contains regulations as defined in the Statutory Instruments Act, and certain other classes of statutory instruments.	The non-official ASCII or pdf versions are available. Prints in full all Regulations made. The Index lists the date on which the changes will take place.
Consolidated Regulations of Canada, 1978 • Paper version — 19 volumes with two updated in the Canadian Gazette — Part II Cumulative Index	Contains the Regulations as in force on 15 August 1979.	See the most recent quarterly cumulative index and bi-weekly Part II of Canada Gazette, and Canadian Current Law — Legislation.

Research tool	What information will it give me?	Tips on use
Consolidated Regulations • http://laws.justice.gc.ca/ en/index.html	Contains Federal Statutory Orders and Regulations in full text. Selected Regulations from the provinces are also available.	Use either the search function or browse by the index, subject area or by the parent Act. In html format only.
Consolidated Regulations of Canada • http://www.lexisnexis. com	The Consolidated Regulations of Canada is an online version of the 1978 revision together with all subsequent regulations (SOR or SI) from the year 1979 through the present. New regulations and amendments to existing regulations are integrated into this consolidation as they come into force.	Choose Legal Excluding US as source in which to search, then Canada Case Law.
Canada Regulations Index • Paper version – monthly consolidated index	Provides direct access to all Canadian Regulations and statutory instruments currently in force. Consolidated Regulations of Canada. All amendments made since 1978 are noted in the Canada Regulations Index together with the particular issue of the Canada Gazette in which the full text of the amendment can be found.	The specific Regulations can be found by locating the particular citation number in the Canada Regulations Index and looking up the full text of the Regulation or statutory instrument in the 1978 and subsequent issues of the Canada Gazette. Internal headings of Regulations indicate where Regulations have been amended, specific sections amended are indicated.
CanLII 1995– • http://www.canlii.org	Contains Consolidated Statutes of Canada in alphabetical list, Consolidated Regulations of Canada in alphabetical list and Annual Statutes of Canada by year.	The databases can be search using Sino software or browsed either alphabetically or by year. Available in html format only.
Canadian Current Law – Legislation Toronto: Thomson Carswell • Paper version	Summarises recent legislative activity in the Canadian and provincial parliaments. Includes Progress of Bills, Statutes Amended, Repealed Legislation or Proclaimed in Force and Regulations.	Monthly publication with annual cumulation. The Regulations Table is arranged alphabetically according to the empowering statute and amendments are shown.

12.12 **A subject index to cases?**

Research tool	What information will it give me?	Tips on use
Canadian Abridgment Revised 2 ed, Carswell • Paper version – 80 main volumes (reissued when necessary) with annual cumulative updates. Monthly updating is through *Canadian Current Law* – Case Digests • CD-ROM with integrated updates quarterly	A digest of reported decisions of Canadian Courts and tribunals since early 1800s. Since 1987, many unreported decisions have been digested. Includes Table of Cases, Words and Phrases, and General Index.	Consult the Key and Research Guide or Quick Reference Guide on how to use. The Digest contains a Table of Classification which outlines the contents of each topic. The two ways of accessing information are through the Key or the General Index which is a consolidation of the Classification Tables.
All Canadian Digests • http://www.lexisnexis. com	Digests or summaries of Canadian court decisions from 1976 from publications such as the All-Canada Weekly Summaries.	Choose Legal Excluding US as source in which to search, then Canada Case Law.

12.13 **Full text of Canadian cases?**

The Supreme Court's decisions are published in English and French in its official reports, the *Canada Supreme Court Reports*. All written and oral judgments and reasons for judgment are printed in their entirety along with a summary of the reasons. The first case reported, published in 1877, was for an appeal heard in 1876 from the Supreme Court of Judicature of Prince Edward Island. Originally numbered in series from 1 to 64, the Reports have been identified since 1923 by their year of publication. In 1975, the printed reports went from one to two volumes per year, and since 1990, three or four volumes have been published annually, each consisting of six to eight parts issued periodically, and containing indexes and a table of cases cited.

The Federal Court decisions are selected for eventual publication in the official reports series whether in full text or as digests. Prior to their publication in the *Canada Federal Court Reports*, these cases undergo a thorough editorial process. This includes: copy editing and reference verification by Legal Research Editors; legal editing (the preparation of captions, headnotes, lists of cases, statutes and authors judicially considered as well as translation accuracy confirmation) done by members of the legal profession, and proofreading by Editorial Assistants.

The unofficial reports include the *National Reporter* which reports all judgments of the Supreme Court of Canada and the Federal Court of Appeal and some cases from the Federal Court Trial Division (1974–). Case headnotes are given subject and topic numbers which are also indexed in 10 year digests of cases within the series. The *Dominion Law Reports* covers cases decided by both federal and provincial courts. The *Atlantic Provinces Reports* covers New Brunswick, Newfoundland, Nova Scotia and Prince Edward Island. The other provincial series are the *Ontario Reports* and the *Alberta Law Reports*. The *Western Weekly Reports* cover Alberta, Saskatchewan, Manitoba and British Columbia.

Supreme Court

Research tool	What information will it give me?	Tips on use
Supreme Court of Canada 1985– • http://www.lexum. umontreal.ca/cscscc/en/ index.html The Supreme Court cases are also available at The Canadian Legal Information Institute site • http://www.canlii.org/ index_en.html	Judgments are published in the Official Reports: Canada Supreme Court Reports (SCR). This series contains cases from the Supreme Court of Canada 1876– Decisions in English and French 1970–	Select relevant year and volume number. Use the 'search by concept' tool – select topic heading of the case being searched (for example, Aboriginal Law). Full text search and Field Search in Judgments also available.

Federal Court

Research tool	What information will it give me?	Tips on use
CanLII • http://www.canlii.org	This collection includes decisions handed down by the Federal Court of Canada with selected cases since 1981. Recent years are complete.	The databases can be searched using Sino software or browsed either alphabetically or by year. Available in html format only.

Research tool	What information will it give me?	Tips on use
Federal Court of Canada Reports Office of the Commissioner for Federal Judicial Affairs 1993– • http://reports.fja.gc.ca/eng	Judgments are published in the Canada Federal Court Reports. The Federal Court of Canada was established in 1971 as the successor to the Exchequer Court of Canada which had been created in 1875. It reports cases from the Federal Court of Appeal and selected cases from the Federal Court trial Division 1971–. In 2003 the two divisions of the Federal Court became a separate court of appeal, with a 'Federal Court of Appeal', and a trial court, the 'Federal Court'. To reflect these legislative changes, the Federal Court Reports, the official reports of the two courts was continued under the name 'Federal Court Reports' commencing with 2004, Volume 1. The citation was changed to 'FCR'.	As a case is published in the Federal Court Reports, that version will replace the raw decision previously available. Each raw decision will bear the identifier R or D so that readers may know whether the case has been selected for full text or digest format publication.

Provincial courts

Research tool	What information will it give me?	Tips on use
British Columbia Court of Appeal 1996– • http://www.courts.gov.bc.ca/Court_of_Appeal/index.aspx	Reasons for judgments Note – The official version of the Court of Appeal reasons for judgment is the signed original in the court file. In the event that there is a question about the content of a judgment (contained on this site) the original of the judgment in the court file takes precedence.	Select year of judgment or search the Reasons for Judgments Database.

Research tool	What information will it give me?	Tips on use
British Columbia Supreme Court 1996– • http://www.courts.gov.bc.ca/supreme_court/index.aspx	BC Supreme Court Reasons for Judgments Note — The official version of the Supreme Court reasons for judgment is the signed original in the court file.	Select year of judgment or search the Reasons for Judgments Database.
Ontario Courts • http://www.ontariocourts.on.ca/decisions/index.cfm	Judgments from the Court of Appeal for Ontario.	Use the Search Tips link to access a list of Boolean commands.

12.14 General caselaw

Research tool	What information will it give me?	Tips on use
BestCase • http://www.canadalawbook.ca/OnlinePublications.html	This contains Canadian caselaw from publisher Canada Law Book, including full text cases — for example, Canadian Criminal Cases, Dominion Law Reports, Labour Arbitration Cases as well as the All-Canada Weekly Summaries and the Weekly Criminal Bulletin.	It has a browsable classification scheme and indices. You can browse and search across the full text, and it also has a NoteUp function. The four main search templates provided are: Boolean, Caselaw, Index, and Advanced Custom.

12.15 Cases that have been judicially considered?

Research tool	What information will it give me?	Tips on use
Canadian Case Citations Toronto: Carswell, 1867– • Paper version — 22 main volumes updated with annual cumulative supplements and Quarterly/Monthly updates • CD-ROM updated quarterly • http://www.ontariocourts.on.ca/	Case histories of reported cases since 1867 and some unreported decisions since 1987. The *Case Citations* indicate whether that case has been affirmed, reversed, followed, distinguished, overruled or considered in a subsequent cases.	Consult the Canadian Abridgement Quick Reference Guide for an overview of use. Generally look up the case in the hardcover books, then consult the cumulative supplements and then the Quarterly/Monthly Supplements.

12.16 Cases that have dealt with specific legislative sections?

Research tool	What information will it give me?	Tips on use
Canada Statute Citator and Weekly Bulletin Service Canada Law Book Co • Paper version — Five volume looseleaf service updated quarterly	Provides information on the progress of all government Bills as they pass through their various stages in the House of Commons and the Senate and includes information on proclamations, bringing legislation into force as well as amendments made to existing Acts by the new Bills. As well, pertinent cases under the legislation are digested and inserted under the appropriate Act and section.	All amendments to Acts are listed and when a section is replaced, it is set out in bold-face type. Proclamations and Orders in Council are included where they affect an Act listed in the Canada Statute Citator. Consult the looseleaf service then each weekly bulletin since the last update. Excludes the *Income Tax Act, Divorce Act, Young Offenders Act* and the Criminal Code.
Canadian Citations: Statutes Judicially Considered and Rules Judicially Considered • Paper version — 19 volumes with annual cumulative supplements and Quarterly/Monthly Supplements • CD-ROM with integrated quarterly update	Reports the judicial consideration of Statutes since 1867 and rules since 1986. Alphabetically lists the legislation/rules and cases that have discussed that section of statute. It also notes amending legislation so the correct version of the section is being referred to.	See the Canadian Abridgement Quick Reference Guide on how to use. The series has undergone a name change in its publication history. Therefore, to search, first consult *Statutes Judicially Considered* annual supplements until 1987, and then *Canadian Citations*, which includes *Statutes Judicially Considered* and *Rules Judicially Considered* for the given jurisdiction.

CHECKLIST
13

United States —
How Do You Find

13.1 **An introduction to the jurisdiction?**

See generally, American Law Sources On-line http://www.lawsource.com/ also/index.htm which provides links to sources of law for Canada, the US and Mexico. This includes links to the North American Commission for Environmental Cooperation *Introduction to the US Legal System* http://www.cec. org/pubs_info_resources/law_treat_agree/summary_enviro_law/publication/us01. cfm?varlan=english and 'How US Courts Work' in (1999) 4(2) September *An Electronic Journal of the US Information Agency* http://usinfo.org/mirror/ usinfo.state.gov/journals/itdhr/0999/ijde/ijde0999.htm

See, American Legal Resource Guide http://www.ilrg.com/ a categorised index of legal websites with the emphasis on United States sources. Search the site or use the annotated index of contents.

The World Wide Web Virtual Law Library http://vlib.org/Law based at Indiana University School of Law Bloomington. It provides a searchable collection of law related websites.The Georgetown Law Library has a page titled 'Free and Low Cost Legal Research' which includes an edited tabulation of the 'best' free websites for US materials.

Most of the US sources are available in full text on both LEXIS and Westlaw. The free LEXIS/NEXIS website at http://lexisone.com is useful for global case searching.

See also the US Library of Congress site, 'The Guide to the Law Online', for a range of links to pertinent national and international material: http://www. loc.gov/law/guide/index.html. Standard US texts are Jacobstein J, Mersky R and Dunn D, *Fundamentals of Legal Research* (8 ed, New York: Foundation Press, 2002), Berring R C and Edinger E, *Finding the Law* (12 ed, West, 2005) and Armstrong J D S and Knott C A, *Where the Law Is: An Introduction to Advanced Legal Research* (3 ed, New York: West 2009).

For Australian researchers, see generally Watt R, *Concise Legal Research* (6 ed, Sydney: The Federation Press, 2009).

Jurisdiction of the US Supreme Court

Article 111 Constitution

Section 1. The judicial Power of the United States, shall be vested in one supreme Court, and in such inferior Courts as the Congress may from time to time ordain and establish. The Judges, both of the supreme and inferior Courts, shall hold their Offices during good behaviour, and shall, at stated times, receive for their services, a compensation, which shall not be diminished during their continuance in office.

Section 2. [1] The judicial power shall extend to all Cases, in Law and Equity, arising under this Constitution, the Laws of the United States, and Treaties made, or which shall be made, under their authority

• to all cases affecting ambassadors, other public ministers and consuls
• to all cases of admiralty and maritime jurisdiction
• to controversies to which the United States shall be a party
• to controversies between two or more states
• between a state and citizens of another state
• between citizens of different states
• between citizens of the same state claiming lands under grants of different states, and between a state, or the citizens thereof, and foreign states, citizens or subjects.

[2] In all cases affecting Ambassadors, other public ministers and consuls, and those in which a state shall be a party, the Supreme Court shall have original jurisdiction. In all the other cases before mentioned, the supreme court shall have appellate jurisdiction, both as to law and fact, with such exceptions, and under such Regulations as the Congress shall make.

Like Australia, the US is a federation with both State and Federal courts. The US federal courts have limited jurisdiction, whereas the state courts have general jurisdiction. Federal court jurisdiction then extends to hearing cases on substantive points of law arising under the Constitution, treaties and federal statutes. These courts also deal with cases concerning the federal government or federal officers or agencies. Finally, the federal courts hear conflicts or diversity cases arising where there are conflicts involving citizens of different states or foreign states.

Federal Jurisdiction	State Constitution
US Constitution	State Constitution
Federal legislation	State Legislation
Treaties	Criminal Law
Admiralty Jurisdiction	Torts
Where parties include the US, Ambassadors, Public Ministers, Consuls, States, Citizens of different states, Foreign States, amounts in excess of $75,000	Property Law
	Domestic Relations (Family)
	Contract Law
	Non-exclusive grants of federal jurisdiction

The Supreme Court hears appeals from decisions of the US Courts of Appeals, from the highest appeal court of each state when a federal question of law is involved, and sometimes directly from the federal district courts. The Court can also act as a trial court. The Supreme Court has the power of judicial review, which encompasses the authority to invalidate legislation or executive actions that may conflict with the Constitution. This authority was confirmed in the 1803 case of *Marbury v Madison*.

Federal Courts	State Courts[1]

Supreme Court
 	
United States Reports (official) 489 US 202
 	
US Supreme Court Reports, Lawyers' Edition (Lawyers Cooperative)
 	
100 L Ed 2d 401
 	
Supreme Court Reporter (West)
 	
104 S Ct 104
	State Supreme Courts
	
	The names of the courts vary between states. They are called either Courts of Appeal or Supreme Courts.
	
	Individual State reporters
	
	National Reporter Series (West)
	
	published according to geographic region, for example,
	
	  • Atlantic
	  • North Eastern
	  • Pacific
	  • North Western
	  • South Western
	  • South Eastern
	
	Also California Reporter Cal Rptr.
	
	New York Supplement NYS.

Appellate Courts known as the Circuit Courts Federal Reporter (West) F Reporter 460 F 2d 201 (2d Cir 1982) There are 13 Circuit Courts, 11 numbered circuits, which hear appeals from the Federal District Courts (First Circuit, Second Circuit). The other two are the Court of Appeals from the District of Columbia (DC) District Court and Federal and Administrative agencies, and the Court of Appeals for the Federal Circuit hears appeals from specialised subject courts.	State Courts of Appeal in some states only. Some states only have two levels of courts.
Federal Trial Courts These are known as the US District Courts and named after the geographic area they cover Federal Supplement (West) 203 F Supp 200 Procedural rules decisions for the federal district courts published in Federal Rules Decisions (FRD)	State Trial Courts County District Probate or special courts Justice of the Peace Municipal (local courts)[2]

1 Al Coco, *Finding the Law: A Workbook on Legal Research for Laypersons* (Rockville: Government Institutes, 1986).

2 Names of the state courts differ. Some state trial courts are called Supreme Courts, while others are called Courts of Common Pleas.

13.2 **A broad picture of the law?**

Research tool	What information will it give me?	Tips on use
Corpus Juris Secundum St Paul, Minn: West, 1962– • 162 volume paper version (updated annually by a cumulative supplement) • http://www.westlaw.com	Statements as to law in the US derived from legislation and case law. It is designed to give a summary of the general law, key definitions and the exceptions to the general rule. Provides complete citations and histories of cases with key number reference to West's Digest System.	Searching CJS can be done by: • General Index • Article Index for each article • Detailed topic and section analysis • Table of Statutes, Rules and Regulations Cited • Table of Corresponding Section.
American Jurisprudence 2 ed, St Paul, Minn: West, 1962– • 140 volume paper version (updated annually by cumulative supplement) • http://www.westlaw.com • http://www.lexisnexis.com	Contains approximately 425 articles on federal and state law listed alphabetically and designed to give a concise statement of the general law. It includes citations of cases, legislation, articles and other publications and to West's Key numbers.	Searching American Jurisprudence can be by: • Article Index • Article Outline • Table of Statutes and Rules Cited • Table of Parallel references.
Restatement of the Law • Paper version covering 20 restatements fields of Law • http://www.westlaw.com covering 14 restatements • http://www.lexisnexis.com	Not an encyclopaedia. Designed to outline the principles of common law operating in a majority of the 50 American states. Contains definitions, basic principles and then commentary on specific areas within that topic.	Restatements can be searched by index at the end of each volume. It does not contain an article outline or general index. It does contain a Table of Cases, Statutes, Parallel tables and references to ALR and West Digest number system.

13.3 **Congressional publications?**

Congressional Record

Research tool	What information will it give me?	Tips on use
Thomas US Congress on the Internet • http://thomas.loc.gov	Not the official record of legislative actions and debates of the US Congress, but the most commonly used as it contains more detail than the Journals of the House and Senate (official record). There are two versions of the Congressional Record published, a daily and a permanent. The permanent edition has the same information as the daily but rearranged so it is a continuous account of proceedings. The Daily Record contains four sections: • Proceedings of the House • Proceedings of the Senate • Extension of Remarks • Daily Digest of activity. The Congressional Record (permanent) presents a complete and correct rendition of all activities in the Congress.	There are two ways to search the Congressional Record on Thomas. There is simple searching using a word or phrase or the 'InQuery' link which use relevance ranking. Browsing is by date and section or word selected. Documents are in html format with links on the page to GPO Access for pdf file.

Research tool	What information will it give me?	Tips on use
US Government Printing Office Access • http://www.access.gpo.gov Volume 140, 1994–	*GPO Access* is a service of the US Government Printing Office that provides free electronic access to Federal Government information. This site is the official, published version and the information retrieved from *GPO Access* can be used without restriction, unless specifically noted. Access the Congressional Record via the A–Z Resource List.	To get to the page, you need to take the link to GPO Access, then the link to legislative and then Congressional Record. Browse the daily records or conduct a Simple Search by volumes and subject (1994–). Advanced Searches by volume, section, date, bill number and page, including Boolean search capabilities also available (1995–). Phrases must be placed in inverted commas. When using operators (AND, OR, NOT and ADJ) they must be in capitals Documents are available in ASCII and pdf files.
Cornell University Law School Legal Information Institute • http://www.law.cornell.edu/	The Legal Information Institute (LII) is a research and electronic publishing activity of the Cornell Law School, founded in 1992 by co-directors Thomas R Bruce and Peter W Martin. Its work is supported by the National Center for Automated Information Research, sponsors, and the Keck Foundation through grants and funded joint studies. The Institute publishes electronic versions of core materials in numerous areas of the law.	The site links with the GPO Access service so searching is as set out on that page.

Congressional Record Index

Research tool	What information will it give me?	Tips on use
Thomas US Congress on the Internet • http://thomas.loc.gov	The Congressional Record Index lists the proceedings and debates by subject terms as published in the Congressional Record. This contains information and references to amendments, problem analysis, articles and editorials, Bills and legislation, excerpts, letters, motions, remarks in the House and Senate, reports from committees, statements, testimonies and texts relied upon. This has two versions, one for the daily record and one for the permanent record.	This site enables searching or browsing of the daily record indexes. Searching is only by word or phrase. The database can be browsed by either Major Topic or complete listings. Documents are in html format with links on the page to GPO Access for pdf file.
US Government Printing Office Access 1983– • http://www.gpoaccess. gov/cri/index.html	The Congressional Record Index lists the proceedings and debates by subject terms as published in the Congressional Record. This contains information and references to amendments, problem analysis, articles and editorials, Bills and legislation, excerpts, letters, motions, remarks in the House and Senate, reports from committees, statements, testimonies and texts relied upon. This has two versions, one for the daily record and one for the permanent record.	This allows searching and browsing of the permanent record index. To get to the page, you need to take the link to GPO Access, then the link to Legislative, and then Congressional Record Index. When searching for a phrase, it must be in quotation marks. When using operators (AND, OR, NOT and ADJ) they must be in capitals.

Congressional Committee reports

Research tool	What information will it give me?	Tips on use
Thomas US Congress on the Internet • http://thomas.loc.gov	When a Bill is introduced into either of the Houses of Congress, it is referred to a committee responsible for that jurisdiction. A committee report summarises the scope and purpose of the Bill, reasons for approving the legislation, the committee findings, recommendations, costs involved and changes to existing law outlined. This is designed to reveal the legislative intent. Sometime reports are not linked to a piece of legislation, but are designed for a background on a public policy issue.	From the Thomas homepage, select the Committee Reports. Committee Reports can be searched by word/phrase, report Number, Bill number, committee and date. The index can be browsed House, Senate, Conference and Joint or by words in the database, with links to the GPO ACCESS site for pdf file.
Congressional Committee Prints 1997– US Government Printing Office Access • http://www.gpoaccess.gov/cprints/index.html	When a Bill is introduced into either of the Houses of Congress, it is referred to a committee responsible for that jurisdiction. A committee report summarises the scope and purpose of the Bill, reasons for approving the legislation, the committee findings, recommendations, costs involved and changes to existing law outlined. Some basic varieties of committee prints include: draft reports and Bills, directories, statistical materials, investigative reports, historical reports, situational studies, confidential staff reports, hearings, and legislative analyses.	This site can be searched only. When searching for a phrase, use quotation marks. When using operators (AND, OR, NOT and ADJ), use capitals. Available in downloadable pdf and text files.

13.4 **Bills?**

Research tool	What information will it give me?	Tips on use
Full text of bills and resolutions 1989– Thomas US Congress on the Internet • http://thomas.loc.gov	Contains the text of Bills and resolutions as introduced and as amended into Congress.	Multiple version of the same Bill may be returned with the amendments added. Select the most current version. To update the Bill, check Bill Summary and Status. In html format with links to GPO Access for pdf format.
Summary and status information about bills and resolutions 1973– Thomas US Congress on the Internet • http://thomas.loc.gov	The goal of this source is full information about Federal legislation. The information contained in this source includes links to text of the Bills, purpose or description of the Bill, floor action, public law number and commencement date, companion Bills, a summary or digest of the most recent version of the Bill, committee information, amendment information and a link to a subject database.	The database can be searched by: • Word/phrase • Subject • Bill/amendment number • Legislative stage • Committee and • Date of introduction. When searching by word or phrase, results are by concentration of the particular word or phrase searched. It is also possible to browse this source by: • Public Law Number • Legislation Introduced to Congress. Documents are in html format.
US Code Congressional and Administrative News 1941– • http://www.lexis.com	A commercial publication which publishes newly enacted public laws. The 'Legislative History' Table 4 gives the Bill No and dates of Consideration and Passage. See also Table 5 'Bills and Joint Resolutions Enacted' and Table 9 'Major Bills Enacted'.	It is issued monthly in paperbound pamphlets; at the end of each congressional session, these are cumulated into a hardbound multi-volume annual set.

Research tool	What information will it give me?	Tips on use
Congressional Bills 1993– US Government Printing Office Access • http://www.gpoaccess. gov/bills/index.html	Contains the text of Bills and resolutions introduced into the Congress by the congressional period.	This site allows searches only. When searching for a phrase, use quotation marks. When using operators (AND, OR, NOT and ADJ), use capitals. Available in downloadable pdf and text files.

13.5 Explanatory material about Bills?

Research tool	What information will it give me?	Tips on use
Bill Summary and Status 1973– Thomas US Congress on the Internet • http://thomas.loc.gov	The goal of this source is full information about Federal legislation. The information contained in this source includes links to text of the Bills, purpose or description of the Bill, floor action, public law number and commencement date, companion Bills, a summary or digest of the most recent version of the Bill, committee information, amendment information and a link to a subject database.	The database can be searched by: • Word/phrase • Subject • Bill/amendment number • Legislative stage • Committee • Date of introduction. When searching by word or phrase, results are by concentration of the particular word or phrase searched. It is also possible to browse this source by: • Public Law Number • Legislation Introduced to Congress.

Congressional Record

Research tool	What information will it give me?	Tips on use
Thomas US Congress on the Internet • http://thomas.loc.gov	Not the official record of legislative actions and debates of the US Congress, but the most commonly used as it contains more detail than the Journals of the House and Senate (official record). There are two versions of the Congressional Record published, a daily and a permanent edition. The permanent edition has the same information as the daily, but rearranged so it is a continuous account of proceedings. The Daily Record contains four sections: • Proceedings of the House • Proceedings of the Senate • Extension of Remarks • Daily Digest of activity. The Congressional Record (permanent) presents a complete and correct rendition of all activities in the Congress.	There are two ways to search the Congressional Record on Thomas. There is simple searching using a word or phrase or the InQuery link, which uses relevance ranking. Browsing is by date and section or word selected. Documents are in html format with links on the page to GPO Access for pdf file.
Congressional Record 1995– US Government Printing Office Access • http://www.gpoaccess. gov/crecord/index.html	Full text of record as pdf file. 1994 database also available with limited search fields.	The Congressional Record comes under legislative resources. Use browse or search facilities. When searching for a phrase, use quotation marks. When using operators (AND, OR, NOT and ADJ), use capitals.

13.6 **A subject index to legislation?**

Research tool	What information will it give me?	Tips on use
Summary and Status Information about Bills and Resolutions 1973– Thomas US Congress on the Internet • http://thomas.loc.gov/ home/search.html	The goal of this source is full information about Federal legislation. The information contained in this source includes links to text of the Bills, purpose or description of the Bill, floor action, public law number and commencement date, companion Bills, a summary or digest of the most recent version of the Bill, committee information, amendment information and a link to a subject database.	The database can be searched by: • Word/phrase • Subject • Bill/amendment number • Legislative stage • Committee • Date of introduction. When searching by word or phrase, results are by concentration of the particular word or phrase searched. It is also possible to browse this source by: • Public Law Number • Legislation Introduced to Congress.

United States Code subject index

Research tool	What information will it give me?	Tips on use
US Code • paper version • http://uscode.house.gov • http://www4.law.cornell. edu/uscode/ • http://www.westlaw.com • http://www.lexis.com • http://www.gpoaccess. gov/uscode/index.html	The United States Code is the consolidated and codified general and permanent laws of the US by subject. There are 50 subject titles in the series. Each of those titles has a sub-index, which can be used to browse the law contained in that title.	The topics contained in the Code are extremely broad. This is not normally useful for specific searches of legislation as many subjects are contained in multiple titles. The search function can act as a subject guide.

13.7 **The commencement date of legislation?**

Research tool	What information will it give me?	Tips on use
United States Statutes-at-Large	The *Statutes-at-Large* is a chronological arrangement of the laws enacted in each session of Congress. Though indexed, the laws are not arranged by subject matter nor is there an indication of how they affect previously enacted laws.	To find law as it currently stands, arranged by subject matter, consult the latest edition of the US Code. Look for Approval date at the end of the Act.
US Code Congressional and Administrative News 1941– • http://www.westlaw.com • http://www.lexis.com	A commercial publication publishing newly enacted public laws. The 'Legislative History' Table 4 gives the Bill No and dates of Consideration and Passage. See also Table 5 'Bills and Joint Resolutions Enacted' and Table 9 'Major Bills Enacted'.	It is issued monthly in paperbound pamphlets. At the end of each congressional session, these are cumulated into a hardbound multi-volume annual set.
Summary and Status Information about Bills and Resolutions 1973– Thomas US Congress on the Internet • http://thomas.loc.gov	The goal of this source is full information about Federal legislation. The information contained in this source includes links to text of the Bills, purpose or description of the Bill, floor action, public law number and commencement date, companion Bills, a summary or digest of the most recent version of the Bill, committee information, amendment information and a link to a subject database.	The database can be searched by: • Word/phrase • Subject • Bill/amendment number • Legislative stage • Committee • Date of introduction. When searching by word or phrase, results are by concentration of the particular word or phrase searched. It is also possible to browse this source by: • Public Law Number • Legislation Introduced to Congress.

13.8 **United States legislation in full text?**

Federal public laws are published as Slip Laws. After each two-year session of Congress, the slip laws are bound together as the Statutes at Large (Stat). These are the sessional laws.

United States Code (USC)

Research tool	What information will it give me?	Tips on use
Office of the Law Revision Council • http://uscode.house.gov	Some titles in the USC are enacted into positive law and are legal evidence of the law contained while for others they are only prima facie evidence of the laws contained in that title. The legislation is arranged by topic or subject rather than by year and date, so having a reference to a year when legislation was enacted with the name of the Act is not necessarily sufficient information to locate the legislation. On the electronic versions, the database contains a date up to which the USC is accurate. Many of the databases will give access to amendments sections that have not been incorporated. The GPO Access and paper versions require manual updating for the current year. Paper version (published every six years and updated annually with supplements).	This database can be searched by word or phrase and section of the Code. The Code can be viewed in html format. The Code can be down-loaded in pdf format or in text file.
• http://www4.law.cornell.edu/uscode/ • http://www.westlaw.com • http://www.lexisnexis.com		This database can be searched or browsed. Searching can be by any word or phrase using Boolean operators, specific sections in US Code or title. Browsing is by title. Once to a specific section, the sidebar menu allows automatic updating.
US Government Printing Office Access • http://www.gpoaccess.gov/uscode/index.html		This database can only be searched. It is not as up to date as the Office of the Law Revision Council, as it relies on the supple-ments. The only available format is text.

General

Research tool	What information will it give me?	Tips on use
United States Code Annotated (USCA) • Paper version (updated annually with cumulative supplement and interim pamphlets) • http://www.westlaw.com	The USCA follows the USC, but inserts relevant case law construing the United States Code. It also includes Executive Orders, Proclamations and reorganisation plans affecting the USC.	The general index published annually can be used to find annotations to specific sections. Indexed are topic, descriptive, conceptual and colloquial terms.
United States Statutes-at-Large Washington: US Government Printing Office	The Statutes-at-Large are a chronological arrangement of the laws enacted in each session of Congress. Though indexed, the laws are not arranged by subject matter, nor is there an indication of how they affect previously enacted laws.	To find law as it currently stands, arranged by subject matter, consult the latest edition of the US Code. Look for Approval date at the end of the Act.

13.9 Updates for legislation?

Research tool	What information will it give me?	Tips on use
Office of the Law Revision Council • http://uscode.house.gov • http://www4.law.cornell.edu/uscode	The US House of Representatives publishes the United States Code.	There is a date either in the top right corner or lower left corner. That date indicates when amendments are incorporated up until. There is a link to amendments not included.
United States Code Annual Cumulative Supplement • Paper version issued annually	The changes to the USC since the last reprinting.	As the update is annual, it is necessary to update by using the United States Code Congressional and Administrative News.
United States Code Classification Tables • http://uscode.house.gov/classification/tables.shtml	Contains information on where recently enacted laws will appear in the USC and which sections of the USC have been amended. Contains two tables, Public Law Order and USC order.	The Public Law Order Table can be used to determine which sections of the Code a certain law amends. The USC Order Table can be used to determine which section of the code has been amended.

Research tool	What information will it give me?	Tips on use
US Code Congressional and Administrative News 1941– • http://www.westlaw.com • http://www.lexisnexis.com	A commercial publication which publishes newly enacted public laws. The 'Legislative History' Table 4 gives the Bill No and dates of Consideration and Passage. See also Table 5 'Bills and Joint Resolutions Enacted' and Table 9 'Major Bills Enacted'.	It is issued monthly in paperbound pamphlets; at the end of each congressional session, these are cumulated into a hardbound multi-volume annual set.
United States Code Annotated (USCA) Supplement Updates • Paper version • http://www.westlaw.com	The supplements update the US Code. The electronic version is updated as changes occur.	Start with the main work and use the cumulative updates.

13.10 A subject index to delegated legislation?

Code of Federal Regulations (CFR) index

Research tool	What information will it give me?	Tips on use
• Paper version (revised annually in quarterly segments) • http://www.law.cornell.edu . • http://www.gpoaccess.gov/cfr/index.html • http://www.westlaw.com • http://www.lexis.com	The CFR Index contains a subject/agency table, a table of laws and presidential documents cited as authority, a list of CFR titles, chapters, subchapters and parts.	The subject/agency index directs the user to specific parts of the FCR. The Index is listed first by subject and then by agency name. It is based on the Federal Register thesaurus. The electronic versions can search for words or phrases not contained in the thesaurus.

13.11 **Full text of delegated legislation?**

Federal Register

Research tool	What information will it give me?	Tips on use
US Government Printing Office Access • http://www.gpoaccess. gov/fr/index.html	The official daily publication for Rules, proposed Rules and federal agency organisation notices, presidential proclamations, Executive Orders, federal agency documents having general applicability and legal effect, documents required to be published by Acts of Congress and other federal agency documents of public interest. Indexes in each daily issue with annual cumulation. Amendments appear, as they are issued by the government, in the Federal Register.	Use the A–Z Resource List to locate. This database can search the FR by date, FR sections, FR volume and by subject.
National Archives and Records Administration • http://www.archives.gov/ federal_register/index. html	The official daily publication for Rules, proposed Rules and federal agency organisation notices, presidential proclamations, Executive Orders, federal agency documents having general applicability and legal effect, documents required to be published by Acts of Congress and other federal agency documents of public interest. Indexes in each daily issue with annual cumulation.	Provides access to the cumulating daily index and the annual index. They are arranged first by the agency then by category. The categories are Rules, Proposed Rules and Notices.

Code of Federal Regulations (CFR)

Research tool	What information will it give me?	Tips on use
US Government Printing Office Access • http://www.gpoaccess. gov/cfr/index.html	The CFR is a codification of the general and permanent Regulations published in the Federal Register by the Executive and its agencies. Divided into 50 titles representing broad subject areas which are then divided into chapters for each agency generally. Revision is done in stages on an annual basis, eg: Titles 1–16 by January 1 Titles 17–27 by April 1 Titles 28–41 by July 1 Titles 42–50 by October 1. The general index is revised and republished after every revision.	This database can be searched or browsed. Search by citation or by word or phrase from the GPO access site. Browse by title. The CFR can be viewed in html or downloaded in pdf format.
Cornell University Legal Information Institute • http://www4.law.cornell. edu/cfr	The CFR is a codification of the general and permanent Regulations published in the Federal Register by the Executive and its agencies. Divided into 50 titles representing broad subject areas which are then divided into chapters for each agency generally. Revision is done in stages on an annual basis, eg: Titles 1–16 by January 1 Titles 17–27 by April 1 Titles 28–41 by July 1 Titles 42–50 by October 1. The general index is revised and republished after every revision.	This database can be searched or browsed. Searching is by word or phrase using Boolean operators. Browsing is by Title and section number. The text of the CFR cannot be viewed on this database, but can be downloaded in pdf or text format.

13.12 **A subject index to cases?**

The American Digest System

Research tool	What information will it give me?	Tips on use
• Paper version • http://www.westlaw.com Century Digest 1658–1896 First Decennial Digest 1897–1906 Second Decennial Digest 1907–1916 Third Decennial Digest 1917–1926 Fourth Decennial Digest 1926–1936 Fifth Decennial Digest 1936–1946 Sixth Decennial Digest 1946–1956 Seventh Decennial Digest 1956–1966 Eighth Decennial Digest 1966–1976 Ninth Decennial Digest 1976–1986 Tenth Decennial Digest 1986–1996 General Digest 1996–	The *American Digest System* covers both federal and state decisions reported in the *National Reporter System* and other standard reports. There are seven main divisions: • persons • property • remedies • contracts • torts • crimes • government. Each division is subdivided into alphabetically arranged topics and each topic into points which are numbered and identified by a key symbol. Every case published by West is given individual treatment in the Digest. The General Digest is the updating volumes and is published annually. Update using LEXIS.	It is necessary to check all the decennial digests under the appropriate topic and the General Digest. The Digest includes a: • Descriptive-Word Index • Table of Key Numbers • Table of Cases • Table of Cases Affirmed, Reversed or Modified. The Descriptive-Word Index can be used to locate cases on the relevant topic. The Table of Key Numbers uses the key number to locate cases reported (cases reported in the NRS, in the headnote key no to the Digest System is given). The table of cases affirmed, reversed or modified gives subsequent case history. The General Digest series produces a cumulative index every 10 volumes.

American Law Reports (ALR and ALR Federal)

Research tool	What information will it give me?	Tips on use
• Available in Paper version and online from http://www.westlaw.com • ALR 1st — 175 volume 1919-1948 • ALR 2nd — 100 volumes 1949-1965 • ALR 3rd — 100 volumes 1965-1980 • ALR 4th — 90 volumes 1980-1992 • ALR 5th — currently 79 volumes 1992– • ALR Federal — currently 163 volumes 1969–	The ALR is designed to organise and analyse cases on a specific issue covering every US jurisdiction. Each article or annotation is designed to cover all of the case law relevant to a specific point of law or fact. The format and contents of the ALR has changed over the edition, but in general the articles contain: • General conclusions on the law • Facts and contentions before the Court • Courts reasoning • References to related topics.	There are six ways to find relevant annotations in the ALR Series: • Index — lists legal term or fact in alphabetical order • Digest Topic • Keycite Citator (Westlaw) • Shepard's Annotation (Westlaw) • Jurisdictional Table of Cited Statutes and Cases • Related Annotations section. There are three ways to update: • Annual cumulative supplement; • Case service Hotline • Keycite.

General

Research tool	What information will it give me?	Tips on use
Supreme Court Digest • Paper version (31 volumes updated with annual cumulative supplement.) • http://www.westlaw.com	Indexes all decisions of the US Supreme Court from the beginning of the Court to present. The book is arranged by the West Key Number system with references to Corpus Juris Secundum.	Use the Digest Topics to identify the appropriate topic. Topics are arranged alphabetically in the series. Consult the Title Index to determine the specific subject. The descriptive word index allows faster more detailed references.

Research tool	What information will it give me?	Tips on use
United States Supreme Court Digest Lawyer's Edition • Paper version • http://www.westlaw.com	Index to US Supreme Court decisions reported in United States Supreme Court Reports Lawyer's Edition volumes 1–100, United States Supreme Court Reports Lawyer's 2 ed volumes 1–111. The US Supreme Court Reports/Digest combines Lawyer's Edition reports and Lawyer's Edition Digest into one system. Included is a table of Federal Constitutional Provisions, Statutes, Court Rules and Regulations Cited and construed and an annotations history.	Topics in the Digest are represented by abbreviations which are listed in the front of the volume. To find cases, use the complete list of digest topics to find the relevant area. The digest is arranged alphabetically in the series. Go to the relevant title and check the Title Index for more specific details. To update, use the pocket annual and the website. There is no general index.

13.13 **Full text of United States cases?**

United States Supreme Court

Research tool	What information will it give me?	Tips on use
United States Reports • Paper version	These are the only official reports of the US Supreme Court.	
Supreme Court Reporter • Paper version • http://www.westlaw.com	Complete information on all case decisions issued by the Supreme Court, including memorandum decisions and dissents. Advance sheets are issued twice per month during court sessions.	In each volume there is reference to West's Key Number system, Statutes Cited, Words and Phrases Table defined by cases reported in that volume.
United States Supreme Court • http://www.supremecourtus.gov	Contains the latest slip opinions, judgments from that term, orders, in-camber applications and pdf of complete volumes since volume 502.	This database can only be browsed. This is extremely useful for current or recent opinions. All documents can be dowloaded in pdf format.

Research tool	What information will it give me?	Tips on use
Findlaw • http://www.findlaw.com	Contains all decisions reported in US Reports 150 1893– and some more historically important decisions.	This database can be searched or browsed. Browsing is by: • Volume • Year • Recent decisions. Searching is either by citation, party name or full text. Judgments are in html. Does not carry per curiam decisions or court orders, such as denials of certiorari.
USSCplus • http://www.usscplus.com	Complete coverage of Supreme Court decisions from 1907 with selected cases going back to 1793.	Cases can be downloaded for a fee in pdf. Searching is by word or phrase, subject, concept, activity, categories of individuals, opinion types and author's name.
Cornell Legal Information Institute • http://www.law.cornell.edu/lii.html	Contains Federal caselaw and legislation, selected state materials, international treaties, and links.	This database can be searched or browsed. Searching is by term, case or statute citation. Browsing is by the current month, by date, topic or party name. Judgments are in html or WordPerfect formats.
Fedworld • http://supcourt.ntis.gov/	Contains full text of US Supreme Court decisions from 1937 until 1975.	This database can be searched by case name or keyword.

United States Courts of Appeal (Circuit Courts)[3]

Research tool	What information will it give me?	Tips on use
Federal Circuit • http://www.cafc.uscourts.gov/dailylog.html (very recent opinions) • http://www.law.emory.edu/fedcircuit/ August 1995–	Decisions from the Patent, International Trade, Claims Court and Veteran's Affairs. New opinions pasted on the US Court of Appeals for the Federal Circuit for at least 90 days and then removed.	The Emory site includes a chronological list, an alphabetical list by first and second parties and a keyword search facility.
District of Columbia Circuit • http://www.cadc.uscourts.gov/internet/internet.nsf 1997– • http://www.ll.georgetown.edu/federal/judicial/cadc.cfm February 1995–	Decisions from DC Tax Court, and Federal Administrative Agencies Reviews. Possible to search full text. Opinions are in pdf formats.	The EBWilliams Law Library site includes hypertext chronological lists.
First Circuit • http://www.ca1.uscourts.gov/opinions/main.php Jan 2000– • http://www.law.emory.edu/1circuit/ November 1995–	Decisions from Maine, Massachusetts, New Hampshire, Puerto Rico, Rhode Island. Older opinions are in ASCII text format.	The Emory site includes a chronological list, an alphabetical list by first and second parties and a keyword search facility.
Second Circuit • http://www.ca2.uscourts.gov/ January 1993–	Decisions from Connecticut, New York, Vermont.	Allows searching of reported cases and summary orders. No phrase searching. * for truncation.
Third Circuit • http://www.ca3.uscourts.gov 1997– • http://vls.law.vill.edu/Locator/3/index.htm May 1994–	Decisions from Delaware, New Jersey, Pennsylvania and Virgin Islands. Villanova Law Library is the official archive for the opinions of the Third Circuit.	Decisions listed by year and month. Keyword search facilities using Google.
Fourth Circuit • http://www.law.emory.edu/4circuit/index.html January 1995–	Decisions from Maryland, North Carolina, South Carolina, Virginia, West Virginia.	The Emory site includes a chronological list, an alphabetical list by first and second parties and a keyword search facility.

---

3   See also the map of West's regional reporters in Cohen ML, Berring RC and Olsen KC, *How to Find the Law* (9 ed, St Paul, Minn: West Publishing Co, 1989), 50; Emory Law Library Federal Courts Finder map http://library.law.emory.edu/law-library/research/federal-courts-finder/

Research tool	What information will it give me?	Tips on use
Fifth Circuit • http://www.ca5. uscourts.gov/	Decisions from Louisiana, Mississippi and Texas.	Search by Date, Docket Number, Name or keyword using ISYSsoftware.
Sixth Circuit • http://www.ca6. uscourts.gov/internet/ opinions/opinions.php • http://www.law.emory. edu/6circuit/index.html January 1995–June 1999	Decisions from Kentucky, Michigan and Tennessee.	Published opinions are produced in WordPerfect and are available in pdf and html. The Emory site includes a chronological list, an alphabetical list by first and second parties and a keyword search facility.
Seventh Circuit • http://www.ca7. uscourts.gov 1991–	Decisions from Illinois, Indiana and Wisconsin. Cases available from the official court site and also the Chicago-Kent College of Law.	Search official court site by case number and name. The Chicago-Kent site offers additional search and browse facilities.
Eighth Circuit • http://www.ca8. uscourts.gov/opinions/ opinions.html 1995–	Decisions from Arkansas, Iowa, Minnesota, Missouri, Nebraska, North Dakota and South Dakota.	Search by keyword or case number, release date or party name. Reports in pdf format and catch-words provided on search.
Ninth Circuit • http://www.ca9. uscourts.gov/ 1995–	Decisions from Alaska, Arizona, California, Hawaii, Idaho, Montana, Nevada, Oregon, Washington, Guam and North Mariana Islands.	Search by date, docket number, party name and full text.
Tenth Circuit • http://www.kscourts. org/ • http://www.law.emory. edu/10circuit/index.html August 1995– October 1997	Decisions from Colorado, Kansas, New Mexico, Oklahoma, Utah, and Wyoming.	Access by party name, docket number, filing date and keyword. Download in rich text format or WordPerfect. The Emory site includes a chronological list, an alphabetical list by first and second parties and a keyword search facility.
Eleventh Circuit • http://www.ca11. uscourts.gov/opinions/ index.php May 1999– • http://www.law.emory. edu/11circuit/index.html November 1994–	Decisions from Alabama, Florida and Georgia.	The official court site provides opinions in compressed zip archive files. The Emory site includes a chronological list, an alphabetical list by first and second parties and a keyword search facility.

General

Research tool	What information will it give me?	Tips on use
Cornell Legal Information Institute • http://www.law.cornell.edu/federal/opinions.html	This database searches all Circuit Court Opinions available on the Internet. It is not maintained by Cornell, but is drawn from other services. Therefore, there is not consistency in format, date and results.	This database is only searchable. The database can be searched by word or phrase, and by statute and case citation.
Findlaw • http://www.findlaw.com/casecode/	This database contains links to all circuit court reports from 1995 onwards. All reports are viewable in html format.	This database can be searched or browsed. Searching is by docket number, party name or full text search. It can be browsed by date.

National Reporter System

Research tool	What information will it give me?	Tips on use
Supreme Court Reporter Saint Paul: West • http://www.westlaw.com	Decisions of the United States Supreme Court.	The National Reporter system. Includes West Key Number system in the headnote information. This allows cross-referencing with other cases on the same topic using *The American Digest System*.
Atlantic Reporter • http://www.westlaw.com	Decisions of the Supreme Courts in Connecticut, Delaware, Maine, Maryland, New Hampshire, New Jersey, Pennsylvania, Rhode Island and Vermont.	The National Reporter system. Includes West Key Number system in the headnote information. This allows cross-referencing with other cases on the same topic using *The American Digest System*.
Pacific Reporter • http://www.westlaw.com	Decisions of the Supreme Courts in Arizona, California, Colorado, Idaho, Kansas, Montana, Nevada, New Mexico, Oklahoma, Oregon, Utah and Washington.	

Research tool	What information will it give me?	Tips on use
Southern Reporter • http://www.westlaw.com	Decisions of the Supreme Court in Alabama, Florida, Louisiana and Mississippi.	
South Eastern Reporter • http://www.westlaw.com	Decisions of the Supreme Court in Georgia, South Carolina, North Carolina, Virginia and West Virginia.	
South Western Reporter • http://www.westlaw.com	Decisions of the Supreme Court in Arkansas, Kentucky, Missouri, Tennessee and Texas.	
North Western Reporter • http://www.westlaw.com	Decisions of the Supreme Court in Iowa, Nebraska, Michigan, Minnesota, North Dakota, and Wisconsin.	
North Eastern Reporter • http://www.westlaw.com	Decisions of the Supreme Court in Illinois, Indiana, Massachusetts, New York and Ohio.	

13.14 Cases that have been judicially considered?

See also Keycite on Westlaw http://www.westlaw.com and Auto-cite and Shepardise on LEXIS http://www.lexisnexis.com

Research tool	What information will it give me?	Tips on use
Findlaw • http://www.findlaw.com	The ability to find cases that have cited a certain case.	Retrieve the case and then use the cases citing this case link either for Supreme Court or circuit courts.

13.15 Cases that have dealt with specific legislative sections?

See KeyCite on Westlaw http://www.westlaw.com and Auto-cite and Shepardise on LEXIS http://www.lexisnexis.com

Research tool	What information will it give me?	Tips on use
Cornell • http://www.law.cornell.edu	Cases that have dealt with specific legislative sections.	Enter the citation of the legislation in the quick search. For a relevance ranking search, use the search link at top of page.
United States Code Annotated (USCA) • Paper version (updated annually with cumulative supplement and interim pamphlets) • http://www.westlaw.com	The USCA follows the USC, but inserts relevant case law construing the United States Code. It also includes Executive Orders, Proclamations and reorganisation plans affecting the USC.	The general index published annually can be used to find annotations to specific sections. Indexed are topic, descriptive, conceptual and colloquial terms. To update, check in the bound volume, in the pocket part for that volume and in any supplemental pamphlets at the end of the code.

European Union Law —
How Do You Find

14.1 **An introduction to the jurisdiction?**

Researching European Union law can be difficult for common law practitioners because this jurisdiction does not conform to accepted common law classifications. European Union history is complex and the treaties and membership in flux. Useful introductions for researchers are contained in Robert Watt's *Concise Legal Research* (6 ed Sydney: Federation Press, 2009), Chapter 9; and Peter Clinch's *Using a Law Library: A Student's Guide to Legal Research Skills* (2 ed London: Blackstone Press Ltd, 2001), Part 3. See also Harvey Matthew's *European Union Law: An Australian View* (Chatswood, NSW: LexisNexis Butterworths, 2008); Cavendish Lawcards Series, *European Union Law* (6 ed London: Routledge-Cavendish Publishing, 2009); and Johnsrud K, *Research Guide: European Union Legal Materials* (Arthur W Diamond Law Library): http://library. law.columbia.edu/guides/European_Union_Legal_Materials (5/11/2009). As the UK is part of the EU, all documentation is available in English. The EU treaties and legislation are to be found in the various series of the *Official Journal of the European Communities*. Most of the EU sources are available in full text on both LEXIS and Westlaw.

The Europa Gateway to the European Union http://europa.eu/index_ en.htm is one of the main portals to European Union Law. The Europa site has headings for institutions, documents, activities and services. It contains the following information:

* a subject guide to areas in which the EU operates; and
* links to the various organisations that comprise the EU.

While Europa is an excellent resource for recent EU materials, it lacks a comprehensive archive of older materials. See generally, the European Institutions and other bodies' page at http://europa.eu/institutions/index_en.htm for information on the EU Institutions (the European Parliament, the Council of the European Union and the European Commission).

Historical and current facts regarding the EU are available at http://europa. eu/about-eu/eu-history/index_en.htm

EUR-Lex http://eur-lex.europa.eu/en/droit_communautaire/droit_commun autaire.htm#1 contains a useful outline of processes and the players. There are links to the EU Constitution, Treaties, International agreements, Legislation in force, Preparatory acts, Case-law, and Parliamentary questions.

Access to EU Documents common to all the institutions and documents of individual institutions are available at http://europa.eu/documentation/ official-docs/index_en.htm

WebLaw — European Union Law http://www.weblaw.edu.au/weblaw/ display_page.phtml?WebLaw_Page=European+Union+Law also has various links under the following seven headings:

* Courts & tribunals and their decisions;
* Publications;
* International resources;
* Constitutional History;
* General Media & Telecommunication sites;
* Journals; and
* Treaties and Conventions.

Each link has a reference to a full record, which contains a description of the materials available on the webpage, the subjects, keywords, date of creation and coverage.

The Council of Europe has its own website. This is a separate organisation to the EU. The Parliamentary Assembly site http://assembly.coe.int/default.asp gives access to the texts adopted by the Parliamentary Assembly, its public working papers (the Documents) and the Assembly records. The link referring to 'documents' will open up a window with an individual quick search option for the adopted texts; the working documents; and the assembly records.

The European Community

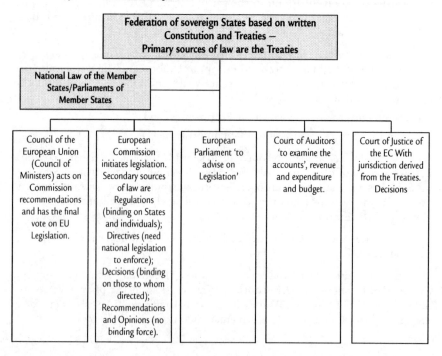

14.2 A broad picture of European Union law?

Research tool	What information will it give me?	Tips on use
Halsbury's Laws of England 4 ed, London: Butterworths, 1973– • Paper version (56 volumes) • Updated by Cumulative Supplement, Monthly Current Service and Annual Abridgement • Available electronically as Halsbury's Law Direct • http://www.lexisnexis. co.uk	*Halsbury's Laws of England* attempts to provide a comprehensive statement of the laws of England and Wales. This encyclopaedia contains law derived from legislation, statutory instruments and common law, and it is divided into alphabetically arranged subject titles. It contains a consolidated table of cases, a consolidated table of statutory instruments, and a consolidated index. The annual abridgement combines the monthly reviews into a consolidated issue and the cumulative supplement summarises legal developments over the parliamentary year. Two looseleaf binders contain the noter-up and monthly reviews. There are two volumes devoted to the European Communities (volumes 51 and 52).	*Halsbury's Laws of England* can be accessed in three ways, by Title, through the Consolidated Index or the Consolidated Table. *Halsbury's Laws of England* includes approximately 165 subject areas. Each subject is treated in sections. Consolidated Index volumes 55 and 56 combine information from all the titles and volumes 53 and 54 combine all entries from legislation tables in all volumes. Updating *Halsbury's Laws of England* is by the most recent reissue, then the cumulative supplement and then the noter-up and monthly services.
European Union Law Reporter London: Sweet & Maxwell (Previously CCH.NewLaw), 1972–	Formerly titled the *Common Market Reporter* this reprints regulations and directives. Four volumes looseleaf with various updates including the weekly Common Market Reports: Euromarket news, fortnightly amendment pages under the title Common Market Reports, and periodic supplements.	Arranged by subject; for example Transport, Environment. Contains good summaries.

Research tool	What information will it give me?	Tips on use
Encyclopedia of European Union Law KR Simmonds, London: Sweet & Maxwell, 1973–	Looseleaf publication containing a complete list, with the exception of agriculture, of the acts contained in the L series of the Official Journal of the European Communities. Three series including Volume A: United Kingdom sources; Volume B: European Community treaties; Volume C: Community secondary legislation.	Full indexes provided for complete series.

14.3 European Community publications?

The European Parliament has four main powers and duties, they are:

* supervisory function;

* participation in legislative process;

* budgetary function; and

* special powers.[1]

The Parliament has power in the legislative process, but does not have the same legislative power typically associated with a national parliament or legislative power. The Parliament has no authority to propose legislation directly, but may request the European Commission to do so and the Parliament must approve most legislation.

See generally, the European Parliament homepage at http://www.europarl. europa.eu/parliament/public/staticDisplay.do?id=146&language=en

Under the Parliament heading, click on the 'in detail' icon at the top of the page for information on the internal bodies of the Parliament, and the rules of procedure and working practices.

---

1   Cavendish Lawcards Series, *European Union Law* (6 ed London: Routledge-Cavendish Publishing, 2009) 59.

Research tool	What information will it give me?	Tips on use
European Parliament Central Historical Archives • http://www.europarl. europa.eu/parliament/ archive/staticDisplay. do?language=EN&id= 196	Historical archives from 1952 until the 4th parliamentary term (1994–1999), including: • Reports by parliamentary committees • Motions for resolutions • Questions • Minutes of parliamentary committee meetings • Minutes of plenary sittings of the European Parliament • Plenary debates.	Refer to the Documentation Service http://www.europarl. europa.eu/parliament/ archive/staticDisplay.do? language=EN&id= 193&pageRank=1
European Parliament Website • http://www.europarl.eu. int/guide/search/ default_en.htm	This website gives access to several types of parliamentary information. Users can search the public register of Documents of the European Parliament (titles only), Documents from the Legislative Observatory, Reports of the European Parliament, Parliamentary Questions, Texts adopted by Parliament and Debates of the European Parliament.	The search option called '...a non-exhaustive presentation of the different types of documents and search possibilities' contains: • a brief description of the different types of documents • sets out the year when the documents were made available on the website • sets out a list of search options for each type of document • sets out a description of when the documents are available • how to access each document.

Parliamentary records

Research tool	What information will it give me?	Tips on use
Materials from the Plenary Session of the European Parliament • http://www.europarl. europa.eu/activities/ plenary.do?language=EN	This site provides access to the Agenda, the Calendar, Reports, Motions for resolutions, Debates, Texts adopted by Parliament, Minutes, Consolidated legislative documents and joint texts approved by the Conciliation Committee.	Depending on the user's knowledge about the information to be acquired, the user can elect the way to search for a document by selecting the appropriate link under each heading. For example, a search for motions for resolutions can be made either by date, author, word(s), reference, or advanced search.
European Parliament Votes and Proceedings • http://www.europarl. europa.eu/activities/ plenary/pv.do? language=EN	The official records and minutes of the European Parliament, the results of votes and roll-call votes.	Use the search function by date if current information is required. This search/browse function takes the user to a calendar which has links to the available minutes for each sitting. To browse the Minutes or the Votes and Proceedings, select the required format pdf, or doc. An Advanced Search template is also available for searches combining date and subject.
Bulletin of European Parliament • http://www.europarl. eu.int/references/bull/ default_en.htm	Activities, calendar of meetings and post-session activities of the European Parliament. This is the most authoritative source of Senate activities. It records motions, resolutions, progress of legislation, references to committees, documents lodged and all actions taken by the Senate.	Editions are accessible from 1999–2005, in various European languages. The available format is pdf. The Activities link gives access to the editions of the Bulletin which contains a variety and general information.

Parliamentary committee reports

Research tool	What information will it give me?	Tips on use
Committee of the Regions (COR) • http://www.cor.europa.eu/pages/HomeTemplate.aspx	A consultative body, which must be consulted during the legislative process regarding laws affecting trans-European infrastructure, education, culture, environment, or employment or anything having a particular local or regional effect. The COR issues opinions at the request of other EU institutions.	
Committees Reports European Parliament (6th parliamentary term 2004-2009) • http://www.europarl.europa.eu/activities/committees.do?language=EN	Lists the titles of all committees of the current Parliament with links to each committee's home page. Each committee's home page contains information on the particular committee and full text copies of many reports of the committee. The committee's reports home page (as set out above) gives a link to the Committees of the 5th Parliamentary Term 1999-2004.	Prior to the meetings of Parliament's committees, all documents on the agenda are published on Europarl. They are accessible via the heading 'Meeting documents' for each committee. Access to these documents is at present possible only by date of committee meeting.

Parliamentary Committee reports index

Research tool	What information will it give me?	Tips on use
European Parliament – Register of Committee Reports • http://www.europarl.europa.eu/activities/committees/reports.do?language=EN	All reports adopted in committee and tabled for adoption in plenary as of 1994. After being adopted by the committee responsible and tabled with the sittings division, reports are debated in plenary. At this stage the text of the report also incorporates the opinion(s) of the committee(s) which were asked to deliver one.	The reports can be accessed through a search by: • a list of new reports, this option lists the 40 most recent reports • rapporteur • committee responsible • report number • PE number • the type of legislative procedure • keywords in title or text.

Other parliamentary publications

Research tool	What information will it give me?	Tips on use
European Parliament – Policy Department General Working Papers • http://www.europarl.eu.int/studies/default.htm	Contains all publicly available working papers produced by the Directorate-General for Research over the last five years. Older documents can be accessed by a search including the archives.	If using the search option 'Catalogue of working papers', the hit list will only give access to abstracts of the working papers. However, a search of the 'Series' will give access to full text documents, which are available in pdf and doc format. This site was not updated after 1 May 2004.
Research Papers and Documents by STOA Programme (Scientific Technologies Options Assessment) • http://www.europarl.europa.eu/stoa/default_en.htm	A publications list which contains Options Briefs and Executive Summaries, Final Studies, STOA Briefing Notes and Briefing from the EPTA Network.	Available in pdf format and in various languages. All documents are not available. Click on the desired language in order to access a particular document.
Debates of the European Parliament • http://www.europarl.europa.eu/activities/plenary/cre.do?language=EN	The texts of speeches by Members of the European Parliament in plenary sitting. Every speech appears in the language used by the speaker.	A Verbatim Report is first published on the Internet in pdf format at the same time as it is sent for printing. The Verbatim Report can be accessed by date only. A few days later, the same text appears in a html version, which is easier to read. A Verbatim Report is thereafter translated into all of the official languages and is made available on the Internet in pdf format. This is referred to as a provision translation. A final edition of the translated Debates is later published in a html version. This edition replaces the provisional, multilingual edition, as soon as the final corrections in the official language versions have been completed.

European Commission

The Commission proposes new legislation and introduces new policy initiatives. The Commission serves as the executive of the EU and enters into international agreements on behalf of the EU. In addition, the Commission is the guardian of EU policy and can initiate legal proceedings to ensure compliance with EU policy and legislation.

Research tool	What information will it give me?	Tips on use
European Commission Papers • http://europa.eu/documentation/official-docs/	Access to all documents of the Commission for example: • Green papers, which are discussion papers published by the Commission on a specific policy area • White papers, which are documents containing proposals for Community action in a specific area.	Look at the documents of individual institutions listed at the bottom of the page. Each heading will link to the listed documents.

Council of the European Union (Council of Ministers)

Research tool	What information will it give me?	Tips on use
Council of the European Union • http://ue.eu.int/cms3_fo/showPage.ASP?lang=en	Also known as the Council of Ministers and is the main decision-making body of the European Union. The Council is composed of selected ministers from each Member State and it exercises legislative power along with the European Parliament. The Council operates through committees such as the Permanent Representatives Committee (COREPER).[2] The purpose of the Council is to represent the national interest. This site gives access to: • Council policies such as foreign policy and security & defence • the European Convention • Council documents, such as Council Acts and Council Minutes.	The Search in the Register option gives access to a simple search and an advance search or to a browse facility of the latest public documents in full text (pdf format).

European Council

The European Council is different to the Council of the European Union. The European Council possesses no formal powers. It is a forum for discussions on an informal basis.

Research tool	What information will it give me?	Tips on use
European Council • http://europa.eu/european-council/index_en.htm	The page contains a limited number of materials such as, the presidency conclusions from 1993–present and transcripts of press conferences.	The site does not have a search facility.

---

2 Johnsrud K, *Research Guide: European Union Legal Materials* Arthur W Diamond Law Library http://library.law.columbia.edu/guides/European_Union_Legal_Materials (30/11/2009).

14.4 **Bills?**

Legislation in preparation

There are four sources of law in existence within the EU, they are:

* treaties (primary legislation);
* secondary legislation (regulations, directives, decisions — referred to as legally binding acts) (recommendations and opinions — referred to as non-legally binding acts);
* general principles (fundamental rights, proportionality); and
* international agreements.

For a general overview of the process and key players in EU legislation see http://eur-lex.europa.eu/en/prep/index.htm

Research tool	What information will it give me?	Tips on use
The European Convention – New Draft EU Constitution • http://europa.eu/ scadplus/constitution/ index_en.htm	Information about the draft constitution for the EU was completed on 18 July 2003. The draft was not ratified. 'At the European Council meeting on 21 and 22 June 2007, European leaders reached a compromise and agreed to convene an IGC to finalise and adopt, not a Constitution, but a reform treaty for the European Union. The final text of the treaty, drawn up by the IGC, was approved at the informal European Council in Lisbon on 18 and 19 October. The Treaty of Lisbon was signed by the Member States on 13 December 2007.' http://europa.eu/lisbon_ treaty/index_en.htm	See the earlier history of the Constitution at http://european-convention.eu.int/ bienvenue.asp?lang=EN The site's contents are current as of 31 July 2003 and remain open for consultation purposes.

Research tool	What information will it give me?	Tips on use
European Parliament's Legislation in Preparation • http://eur-lex.europa.eu/ en/prep/latest/index.htm	Full text of proposals including proposals not yet included in the directory. The 'Directory of Commissions Proposals' contains a link to a list in alphabetical order of the various proposals grouped into a particular order. Information includes Council Decision, proposal for a Council Decision and opinions.	There are four available search options; they are: search by document number; search by procedure; search by publication reference in the official journal; and search by word. If a user is intending to conduct a general search, the link to the Directory of Commission proposals is a good starting point for a browse into the various topic areas.
Celex • http://www.justis.com/ data-coverage/celex.aspx	Through the menu searching function, information on preparatory acts/documents by the Commission, the Council, the Parliament, the Economic and Social Committee and the Committee of the Regions can be found. Legislation, case law and parliamentary questions can also be accessed on this database.	Even though access to Celex is free of charge, the use of a login and password is temporarily required. Note, that Celex is no longer updated since 1 January 2005, the information past this date is available on http://eur-lex.europa.eu/ en/tools/about.htm
EUR-Lex • http://eur-lex.europa.eu/ en/index.htm	Preparatory documents, which means all documents corresponding to the various stages of the legislative or budgetary process.	By using the link 'search in preparatory acts' users are given various search options by way of tick boxes, the user is then directed to a further search window where search options by way of search terms, date or time span, author, classification headings or keywords can be inserted.

Research tool	What information will it give me?	Tips on use
COM documents • http://ec.europa.eu/ transparency/regdoc/ aidetypesdoc.cfm?CL=en	The site contains information in relation to proposals of council decisions including explanatory memorandums, council decisions and proposal for council regulations, which also includes explanatory memorandums.	Select the relevant year and relevant month to view the date and the number of each document. Available in pdf, html and doc format.
CELEX EU Law Database • http://www.lexisnexis. com	The Preparatory Acts database contains proposals, reports, notices, communications and opinions of the different EC institutions that lead up to the various directives and decisions, for example: Economic and Social Committee opinions and Council preparatory documents from 1957, however full text generally available from 1979.	Updated regularly, normally within 24–48 hours of receipt or within 1–2 weeks of the Official Journal publication date. The Source Information link contains a useful dictionary of terms used.

14.5 Explanatory material about Bills?

To gain information about the steps in the enactment of a particular legislative proposal the following sites/databases are useful.

Research tool	What information will it give me?	Tips on use
Parliamentary Questions • http://www.europarl. eu.int/QP-WEB/ home.jsp?language=en	Access to questions and responses and information about the deadline for tabling questions.	A search window is displayed when entering each expert mode or simplified mode link. A search takes you to a question, which in turn contains a link to the answer.

Research tool	What information will it give me?	Tips on use
CELEX EU Law Database • http://www.lexisnexis.com	Full text parliamentary questions and answers from 1996 and references to oral questions, submitted by European Parliament members to the Council and Commission at question time.	The source information in the database has a small dictionary, which explains the terms used in the documents. For example: addressee — to whom the question was addressed, usually the Council or Commission.
PreLex • http://ec.europa.eu/ prelex/apcnet.cfm? CL=e	Contains the documents issued at each step of the legislative and decision-making process.	The documents are searchable by a standard search, an advance search or by monitoring the decision-making process search.
OEIL — the Legislative Observatory • http://www2.europarl. eu.int/oeil/index.jsp	Provides a synopsis of legislative procedures taken in enacting legislation.	The 'procedure tracking search' and the simple search option provide a glossary, which includes hypertext links to relevant documents.
RAPID • http://europa.eu/rapid/ searchAction.do	Contains the press releases by various EU institutions.	Frequently, press releases are the quickest and easiest way to learn of new developments in EU law.

14.6 **A subject index to legislation?**

The primary legislation within the European Union is the Founding Treaties, which are published in the Official Journal of the European Communities (the OJ). The OJ publishes the text of legislation and other official acts of the European Union. It contains treaties, all four types of legislation mentioned above, (Regulations, Directives, Decisions, Recommendations and Opinions) working papers, judgments of the European Court of Justice, proposals for legislation, and other official communications between EU institutions.

Research tool	What information will it give me?	Tips on use
Official Journal of the European Communities • http://eur-lex.europa.eu/ JOIndex.do?ihmlang=en	A subject index to Treaties, Legislation in Force and Preparatory Acts as of 1 January 2005.	This is a new website, as of 1 January 2005, which incorporates the CELEX features and provides free access in 20 languages to a documentary database on EU Law. For documents dated before 31 December 2004 the CELEX website can be used http://europa.eu.int/celex/htm/celex_en.htm

14.7 **The commencement date of legislation?**

Research tool	What information will it give me?	Tips on use
EURLex Directory of Community Legislation • http://eur-lex.europa.eu/ en/legis/index.htm	Access to the Community Legislation currently in force.	The information is available in pdf format. Each piece of legislation states its commencement date.

14.8 **Legislation in full text?**

Research tool	What information will it give me?	Tips on use
Europa — Treaties • http://eur-lex.europa.eu/ en/treaties/index.htm	Official site containing the full text of EU treaties — the basic legal texts on which the European Union and the European Communities are founded. This includes the founding Treaties (original versions and later updatings), the amending Treaties, the Accession Treaties for each of the five enlargements, plus other essential documents such as the Constitution.	The Simple Search template is very comprehensive allowing searching by File Category, Document Number, Publication Reference, or General Search for keyword, author or title. Available in html and pdf.

Research tool	What information will it give me?	Tips on use
Official Journal of the European Communities • http://eur-lex.europa.eu/ JOIndex.do?ihmlang=en • The electronic version gives access to the online editions of the journal in pdf format. • The main texts are published from 1998 until present, however texts prior to 1998 can be accessed by using the search function. • Each journal edition usually contains links to issues concerning Legislation and other Information and Notices. • The Official Journal (OJ) is supplemented by Public procurement notices, which are available at http://ted.publications. eu.int/official/	Full text access to Treaties, Legislation in Force and Preparatory Acts. The OJ gives information about developments in relation to regulations, agreements, directives and decisions. It gives access to acts whose publication is obligatory and acts whose publication is not obligatory. The OJ also contains information about various other matters such as: Euro exchange rates, authorisation for State Aid, publication of vacancies and entry into force of agreements and it publishes the text of judgments. The OJ is divided into the L series (legislation), the C series (proposed or draft legislation) and the S series (supplemental material).	The electronic version of the OJ divides the access to editions into three categories: Latest Issues, Recent Issues and Access by Year. There are Browse and Search facilities, and a link to the supplement available. Prior to 1973, the OJ was not published in English. This is a new website, as of 1 January 2005, which incorporates the CELEX features and provides free access in 20 languages to a documentary database on EU Law. For documents dated before 31 December 2004 the CELEX website can be used http://europa.eu.int/celex/ htm/celex_en.htm
EUR-Lex Legislation in force • http://eur-lex.europa.eu/ en/legis/index.htm	The site contains legislation as classified according to the Directory of Community legislation, which comprises 20 chapters with divisions into further subsections as necessary. The Directory covers agreements, directives, regulations and decisions. The Directory also gives access to consolidated texts which have no legal value but which integrate a basic instrument of Community legislation with its subsequent amendments and corrections in a single text.	Selecting one of the chapters and a subsection will return a list of all titles of acts in force classified in that subsection. The format is pdf.

Research tool	What information will it give me?	Tips on use
European Union Legislation • http://www.westlaw.com	Full text of legislative acts of the Council of the European Union, the European Parliament, and the European Commission reported in the Official Journal of the European Community, L Series, including international agreements; secondary legislation such as regulations and European Coal and Steel Community (ECSC) general decisions, directives, and recommendations; and supplementary legislation (legislation resulting from agreements between member states). From 1952.	Use the Westlaw search terms and connectors. Field searches and index term and title combinations are recommended for this database.

14.9 Updates for legislation?

Research tool	What information will it give me?	Tips on use
Official Journal of the European Communities • http://eur-lex.europa.eu/ JOIndex.do?ihmlang=en	Updates for legislation.	Check the date when the page has last been updated.

Research tool	What information will it give me?	Tips on use
European Current Law London: Sweet & Maxwell	Legislation recently passed, and digests generally of legislation, cases, articles and books. Also includes cumulative updating tables of regulations in numerical order, regulations by subject, draft directives in numerical order and by subject, directives in numerical order and by subject, Commission competition decisions, Commission merger decisions, notifications received, competition cases before the ECJ and CFI and anti-dumping proceedings information. Section Two includes National Jurisdictions updates.	There is a standard list of subject headings used in *European Current Law*. The material is cumulated annually in the *European Current Law Yearbook*.

14.10 Subject index to delegated legislation?

According to Article 249 of the Treaty establishing the European Community (EC Treaty), directives are binding but the manner of their implementation is left to the discretion of the Member State. Consequently, the United Kingdom, which operates under a Common Law system, may bring an EU law into effect by using delegated legislation. Hence, any information about delegated legislation is accessible via the Member States' internal legislative sources.

14.11 A subject index to cases?

Research tool	What information will it give me?	Tips on use
Curia • http://curia.eu.int/ index.htm The official website of the European Court of Justice and Court of First Instance which consists of 25 Judges and 8 Advocates-General. The Court of Justice ensures that the law is observed in the interpretation and application of the Treaties establishing the European Communities and of the provisions laid down by the competent Community institutions. To enable it to carry out that task, the Court has wide jurisdiction to hear various types of action. The Court has competence to: • rule on applications for annulment or actions for failure to act brought by a Member State or an institution; • take actions against Member States for failure to fulfil obligations; and • provide references for a preliminary ruling and appeals against decisions of the Court of First Instance.	Full text cases since June 1997. Information about cases since 1953.	A number of the digests and subject lists are only available in French.

14.12 **Full text of European Union cases?**

Research tool	What information will it give me?	Tips on use
European Court Reports Printed (official)	This set of reports is in English from 1954 onwards. Contains the decisions of the Court of First Instance and summaries of the decision of the Court of Justice in such cases.	Text appears in the language of the case, however abstracts are provided in English as well.
Reports of Cases before the Court of Justice and the Court of First Instance (European Court Reports or ECR) • http://eur-lex.europa.eu/JURISIndex.do?ihmlang=en Also available in paper version.	An official report of cases before the European Court of Justice and Court of First Instance.	Often delayed, due to the time taken to translate the cases into the 20 official languages of the EU.
CELEX • http://www.justis.com/data-coverage/celex.aspx	The case-law file includes: • Judgments, orders and third-party proceedings concerning cases brought before it by the institutions, the Member States, or any legal or natural person against the Community institutions and the European Central Bank, on disputes between institutions, and on cases against Member States, concerning a failure to implement an obligation under the treaties. • Preliminary rulings, interpreting Community law at the request of national courts and tribunals. • Decisions in staff cases, concerning disputes between the Community and its servants. • Opinions of the Advocate General. • Opinions of the Court on agreements between the Community and non-member States or international organisations.	Even though access to Celex is free of charge, the use of a login and password is temporarily required. Note, that Celex is no longer updated since 1 January 2005, the information past this date is available on http://eur-lex.europa.eu/en/tools/about.htm The case-law documents of the European Court of Justice and Court of First Instance are located in Sector 6 of CELEX. All judgments and orders issued since the establishment of the Courts are included. Coverage of the opinions of the Advocates General is from 1965; the full texts of these are available since 1987.

Research tool	What information will it give me?	Tips on use
AustLII/WorldLII • http://www.worldlii.org/#region"europe	• Commission of the European Communities Decisions 2003– • Court of Justice of the European Communities (including Court of First Instance Decisions) 1954– • European Court of Human Rights Decisions 1960–	Cases can be found by an alphabetical or year browse.
LexisNexis EU Law Database • http://www.lexisnexis.com	This is a full-text database and includes English language decisions from the Court of Justice of the European Communities and the Court of First Instance as contained in the CELEX database. References to decisions in other languages are also included. There is a selection of European Court of Justice decisions from 1954 and Court of First Instance decisions from December 1989. Summaries and transcripts of decisions of the European Court of Human Rights from 1960, Butterworths Human Rights Cases from 1996 are also included.	Search within individual databases or combine sources to search using LexisNexis search software.
Common Market Law Reports Printed (unofficial)	This series runs from 1962 onwards. Published weekly by Sweet & Maxwell it also covers cases with an EU dimension in national courts. It appears more quickly than the European Court Reports with a full, if not official, report.	The indexes are especially useful covering subject matter, treaties and regulations judicially considered as well as cases judicially considered.

Research tool	What information will it give me?	Tips on use
European Union Cases Combined • http://www.westlaw.com	The database contains full-text decisions of the Court of Justice of the European Communities and the Court of First Instance of the European Communities reported in European Court Reports, as well as materials from the Law Reports series published by the Incorporated Council of Law Reporting for England and Wales, Lloyd's Law Reports published by LLP Reference Publishing, and the Sweet & Maxwell series of law reports on Westlaw. Also includes judgments and orders of the Court of Justice covered by the Official Journal of the European Communities, C Series.	Use the Westlaw search terms and connectors. Extensive field searching facilities.

14.13 Cases that have been judicially considered?

Research tool	What information will it give me?	Tips on use
CURIA • http://curia.europa.eu/jcms/jcms/Jo2_7083/	Annotations of judgments from 1954 to date.	Annotations by legal commentators relating to the judgments delivered by the Court of Justice, the General Court and the Civil Service Tribunal since those courts were first established. The section is divided into three parts.

14.14 Cases that have dealt with specific legislative sections?

Research tool	What information will it give me?	Tips on use
Europa • http://curia.europa.eu/jurisp/cgi-bin/form.pl?lang=en	Case law of the Court of Justice and the Court of First Instance and Notices for publication in the official journal as of 1997 to present.	The search tool contains a field option which enables the user to limit the search to cases which have considered a particular EU topic.

14.15 Dictionaries and directories?

Research tool	What information will it give me?	Tips on use
Glossary: Institutions, Policies and Enlargement of the European Union • http://europa.eu/scadplus/glossary/index_en.htm	The glossary contains about 220 terms and concepts relating to European integration and the institutions and activities of the EU.	Not a comprehensive glossary, only a selection of particular terms.
A to Z Index of European Union Websites • http://eurunion.org/infores/euindex.htm	Alphabetical list of all of the websites of the European Union's institutions and specialised agencies in Europe.	Often, the links go to the home page or area on each site where the specified information can be found, rather than to a specific page.
The European Commission – Alphabetical Index • http://europa.eu.int/comm/atoz_en.htm	Alphabetical list of selected topics within the European Union.	Often, the links go to the home page or area on each site where the specified information can be found, rather than to a specific page.

14.16 **Journal articles and commentary?**

Research tool	What information will it give me?	Tips on use
ECLAS • http://ec.europa.eu/ eclas/F	Catalogue of the European Commission Library. Contains documents on European affairs and includes the departmental collections of 20 directors general, web resources and secondary sources.	This database is an index and does not necessarily contain full-text documents. However, with the increasing availability of online electronic resources, some documents consequently contain hyperlinks (URLs) that provide single-click access to the full electronic documents.
European Journal of International Law • http://www.ejil.org/	Information concerning the relationship between international law and EU law. The Archive contains all issues published since the Journal's inception in 1990.	The recent journal numbers publishes one lead article, review essays and book reviews in full text. Other articles are available in abstracts.

15

New Zealand —
How Do You Find

15.1 An introduction to the jurisdiction?

New Zealand is a unitary, unicameral state. It only abolished appeals to the Privy Council in 2002.

For general information on the New Zealand legal system, see the New Zealand Government website, especially the section entitled: Find Information on the New Zealand legal system at http://www.justice.govt.nz/ministry/

See also the New Zealand Parliament's website at http://www.parliament.nz/en-NZ and the Ministry of Justice, especially the section entitled New Zealand Courts at http://www.justice.govt.nz/courts/ This section contains a useful overview of courts, tribunals and other authorities and the appeal processes in place at http://www.justice.govt.nz/courts/hierarchy.html

There is a useful article on New Zealand legal research by Margaret Greville 'An Introduction to New Zealand Law and Source of Legal Information' at http://www.nyulawglobal.org/globalex/new_zealand.htm

See also Greville M, Davidson S and Scragg R, *Legal Research and Writing* (2 ed Wellington: LexisNexis, 2004); and McDowell M and Webb D, *The New Zealand Legal System: Structures, Process and Legal Theory* (4 ed, LexisNexis, 2006).

15.2 A broad picture of New Zealand Law?

See generally, http://www.govt.nz/ and the A–Z of Government which contains links to government departments and agencies.

Research tool	What information will it give me?	Tips on use
The Laws of New Zealand (LONZ) Butterworths • Paper version (approximately 40 volumes), updated by loose-leaf, quarterly • http://www.lexisnexis. co.nz/products/catalog/ browse/reference&LR/ LawsofNZ.asp	An encyclopaedic coverage of the law of New Zealand following the tradition of *Halsbury's Laws of England.* The titles are presented in individual booklets. Each contains separate Contents, List of Related Topics, Table of Statutes, Table of Statutory Instruments, Table of Cases and a comprehensive index. The text is divided into parts with numbered paragraphs. A statement of the law is given with extensive footnotes provided to relevant authority.	Each booklet includes extensive cross-referencing to *Halsbury's Laws of Australia* and *Halsbury's Laws of England.* The currency date appears in the front of each main title, and at the front of the Service volume. Refer to *Butterworths Current Law* for subsequent changes.

15.3 Parliamentary publications?

Research tool	What information will it give me?	Tips on use
New Zealand Parliament • http://www.parliament. govt.nz/	Information on the New Zealand Parliament, Parliamentary Agencies and Executive Government Agencies. This site contains links to the Parliamentary Counsel Office (PCO) which is responsible for drafting and publishing most New Zealand legislation.	The information on this site contains mainly links to other government pages that have the ability to be searched or browsed. Links are to the House and Committees, politics and news and general information. This site can only be browsed. Available in html format only.

Hansard

Research tool	What information will it give me?	Tips on use
The Office of the Clerk • http://www.parliament.nz/en-NZ/PB/Debates/	This site gives access to Hansard Advances and final copies of Hansards as they become available since 2003.	The Hansard is available in two formats, a browsable html format or a pdf file. Links are to Questions for Oral Answer.
The Knowledge Basket • http://www.knowledge-basket.co.nz/kete/db/db.html	Access to Hansard archives from 1987 to present.	The site is fully searchable and browsable and is available in html and pdf format.

Indexes to the Hansard

Research tool	What information will it give me?	Tips on use
Amalgamated Indexes, Monthly Indexes and Weekly Indexes to the Parliamentary Debates (Hansard) • http://www.parliament.nz/en-NZ/PB/Debates/	Contains references to the bound volumes of the Hansard. Information is categorised by subject or name of topic, speaker or committee.	The indexes use Year, Week or Volume headings. The indexes are available in pdf format only.

Committee reports

Research tool	What information will it give me?	Tips on use
House of Representatives – Select Committees • http://www.parliament.nz/en-NZ/SC/Reports/	Outlines the Bills before the Select Committees. It also outlines other business before select committees.	This site can be searched or browsed.
House of Representatives – Constitutional Arrangements Committee • http://www.parliament.nz/en-NZ/SC/Reports/e/9/b/e9b156d30c1840eb8ffa20c6b28277de.htm	Gives access to the discussion documents which the Committee has before it. It also contains the submissions received from members of the public following an open invitation from the committee.	This site can only be browsed. Available in both pdf and html format.

Other parliamentary publications

Research tool	What information will it give me?	Tips on use
House of Representatives — Standing Orders • http://www.parliament. nz/en-NZ/PB/Reference/	Gives access to a pdf file of the standing orders as of 10 February 2004. Also gives access to miscellaneous publications of the House of Representatives, including speakers' rulings, sessional orders and other orders of continuing effects.	This site can be searched or browsed. The documents relating to the standing orders are available in pdf only.
House of Representatives — Parliamentary Papers • http://www.parliament. nz/en-NZ/PB/Presented/ Papers/	Miscellaneous publications of the House of Representatives, including reports of commissions and committees of inquiry.	This site can be searched or browsed. Browsing may be conducted by subject group or by year between 1999–present.
Beehive — Records of Cabinet • http://www.beehive. govt.nz/	Records of the Cabinet from 1993–1996 and other Parliamentary and governmental activities from a government point of view.	This site can be searched or browsed. Searching is available through an advanced search site and browsing is through the website. Another option is to search by way of selecting the relevant Minister and/or selecting the relevant portfolio.

15.4 **Bills?**

Research tool	What information will it give me?	Tips on use
Bills before Select Committees • http://www.parliament. nz/en-NZ/PB/ Legislation/Bills/	This site gives access to a summary of the titles of the bills before Select Committees. The summary includes the closing date for submissions for the bills and the dates when the reports of bills are due.	The document is only browsable and brief. For a full text access of public bills use the Knowledge Basket at http:// legislation.knowledge- basket.co.nz/gpprint/ docs/welcome.html

Research tool	What information will it give me?	Tips on use
Bills — Knowledge Basket • http://legislation. knowledge-basket. co.nz/gpprint/ docs/welcome.html	This site gives the full text of public Bills currently before the House of Representatives. The site also contains the full text of Supplementary order papers which are issued along the way of a Bill to indicate proposed amendments to a Bill which are then read into it.[1]	The Bills and the Supplementary order papers are in plain text format. The first printed version of a Bill is allocated a -1 version, after the suffix to the Bill's number (for example No 124-1). The first reprint of the Bill is allocated a -2 symbol, again after the suffix to the Bill's number (for example No 124-2). The -3 version (for example No 124-3) follows the debate in the Committee of the Whole House.[2]
Current Law — Bills • Looseleaf • http://www.lexisnexis. com.au/nz/products/ bills/default.asp	A fortnightly publication which contains Bills before Parliament, Acts of Parliament, Regulations, Rules and notes decisions of Courts and administrative tribunals.	A detailed cumulative index is published quarterly enabling *Current Law* to be used as a rapid and reliable guide to legal developments. *Current Law* uses *Laws of New Zealand* headings. Each issue includes a list of cases to be reported in *New Zealand Law Reports*.
Legislation Direct — Bills • http://www. gplegislation. co.nz/bills.shtml	List of Bills introduced from 2003 to present.	Only available for browsing and full text of public Bills are only available for a fee.
Brookers Online NZ Law Partner Legislation and Cases • http://brookersonline. co.nz/	Includes current Bills and Brookers Bills of NZ Update.	Basic Boolean search terms used including 'and', 'or', 'not'. Truncate using *. Use inverted commas around phrases. For proximity searching use 'two or more words'@7. For ordered proximity use 'two or more words'/10. Use ? to replace a single character.

1 Greville M, Davidson S and Scragg R, *Legal Research and Writing* (2 ed Wellington: LexisNexis, 2004) 42.
2 Greville M, Davidson S and Scragg R, *Legal Research and Writing* (2 ed Wellington: LexisNexis, 2004) 42.

15.5 **Explanatory material about Bills?**

Research tool	What information will it give me?	Tips on use
Bills Digests • http://www.parliament. nz/en-NZ/PubRes/ Research/BillsDigests/	Gives access to Bills Digests which explains the purpose of the Bill.	May be browsed by chronological or alpha-betical order. Available in pdf format only.

15.6 **A subject index to legislation?**

Research tool	What information will it give me?	Tips on use
Annotations to the New Zealand Statutes • Butterworths, 2 ed – Statutes • Looseleaf service, four volumes, updated monthly	Provides an account of all amendments to the New Zealand Statutes and full text of the amendments is included in alphabetical order by statute.	In order to successfully use this tool, it is recommended that: • the most recent version of an act is obtained; and • that act is read in conjunction with *Butterworths Annotations*.
Index to New Zealand Statutes • LexisNexis • Looseleaf service, published four times a year	Provides a general subject index to New Zealand statute law.	Public, Private and Local Acts are convened alphabetically in separate lists. The Acts are also available in chronological tables.

15.7 **Commencement date for legislation?**

Research tool	What information will it give me?	Tips on use
Annotations to the New Zealand Statutes • Butterworths, 2 ed – Statutes • Looseleaf service, four volumes, updated monthly	Contains information on the commencement dates of New Zealand statutes, where these dates are *not* the dates of assent. It also contains information on the amendments to New Zealand statutes.	Most New Zealand statutes come into force on the date of assent.
Butterworths Current Law • Looseleaf service and online • Eight volumes, 25 issues a year • http://www.lexisnexis. co.nz/products/catalog/ browse/reference&LR/ BW_CurrentLaw.asp	The Table of Statutes gives details of the date of Royal Assent and Date in Force of New Zealand statutes.	Published fortnightly and a detailed cumulative index is published quarterly.

15.8 New Zealand legislation in full text?

Research tool	What information will it give me?	Tips on use
Public Access to Legislation Project Unofficial • http://www.legislation.co.nz/	Contains full text access to New Zealand statutes.	This site can be browsed in alphabetical order or searched using the search function.
The Knowledge Basket • http://gpacts.knowledge-basket.co.nz/gpacts/actlists.html	Contains full text access to current New Zealand Acts.	The site can be browsed in alphabetical order. A limited search can be conducted by entering a year, this search brings a list of Acts for that year.
Reprinted Statutes of New Zealand • Official paper version	Contains reprints of individual New Zealand Acts with amendments incorporated.	Volumes 1–42 contain reprints of individual Acts bound together. From 1 November 2002 each reprinted Act is issued individually with title 'Reprinted as at …'.
Brookers Online NZ Law Partner Legislation and Cases • http://brookersonline.co.nz/	Includes Bills, statutes of NZ, Regulations, local and private statutes and unconsolidated principal and amending Acts.	Basic Boolean search terms used including 'and', 'or', 'not'. Truncate using *. Use inverted commas around phrases. For proximity searching use 'two or more words'@7. For ordered proximity use 'two or more words'/10. Use ? to replace a single character.

15.9 Updates for legislation?

Research tool	What information will it give me?	Tips on use
Table of Acts and Ordinances and Statutory Regulations in Force • http://www.pco.parliament.govt.nz/legislation/	Contains information about Acts that have been reprinted. A reprint reference is given.	The Acts are arranged by title in alphabetical order.
Progress of legislation • http://www.parliament.nz/en-NZ/PB/Debates/Progress/	Contains information about the schedule of bills.	The bills are arranged by title in alphabetical order. Only available in pdf format.

Research tool	What information will it give me?	Tips on use
Annotations to the New Zealand Statutes • Butterworths, 2 ed — Statutes • Looseleaf service, four volumes, updated monthly	Contains information about statutory amendments. Lists acts in force and acts repealed.	Acts are listed by title in alphabetical order.

15.10 A subject index to delegated legislation?

Research tool	What information will it give me?	Tips on use
Statutory Regulations • http://www.pco. parliament.govt.nz/ online-legislation/	Contains information about New Zealand Statutory Regulations.	Regulations are listed in alphabetical order. The table is current as at 1 January 2005.
Deemed Regulations • http://www.pco. parliament.govt.nz/ online-legislation/	Contains information from departments and organisations in relation to Codes, Rules and Notices.	Deemed Regulations are listed in alphabetical order. The table is current as at 30 June 2000.
Legislation Direct — Regulations • http://www. legislationdirect.co.nz/ regulations.shtml	Information about the Legislation Direct's own publication list of Regulations.	This is an up-to-date list of the Regulations, as new Regulations are added as soon as they are in print.

15.11 Full text of delegated legislation?

Research tool	What information will it give me?	Tips on use
Regulations of New Zealand • http://www.legislation. govt.nz/regulation/ browse.aspx	Gives full text access to Regulation.	The site can be browsed in alphabetical order. A limited search can be conducted by entering a year, this search brings a list of Regulations for that year.
The Knowledge Basket — Lists of Regulations • http://gpacts.knowledge- basket.co.nz/regs/ reglists.html	Gives access to the full plain text version of New Zealand Regulations.	Can be browsed by way of using an alphabetical list or by year.

15.12 A subject index to cases?

Research tool	What information will it give me?	Tips on use
Annotations to the New Zealand Statutes • Butterworths, 2 ed — Statutes • Looseleaf service, four volumes, updated monthly	Case annotations in relation to decisions that interpret statute law. Butterworths Annotations indexes these reported cases under the relevant acts and sections.	Need to know the title of the act and preferably the relevant sections in order to get easy access to the major cases decided referencing that act.
The Abridgment of New Zealand Case Law • Looseleaf, updated by cumulative supplements	Digest of case law reported in the official reports.	A consolidated Table of Cases and Index are contained in Volume 17. A list of annotated cases and a list of words and phrases judicially considered are contained in Volume 18. Cases are classified under titles with contents pages, then summaries of cases. Cases classified for more than one title are repeated. Out of date cases have catchwords only.
Butterworths Current Law • Looseleaf service and online • Eight volumes, 25 issues a year • http://www.lexisnexis. co.nz/products/catalog/ browse/reference&LR/ BW_CurrentLaw.asp	Notes current legal activity including New Zealand Court of Appeal and selected High Court decisions.	Published fortnightly and a detailed cumulative index is published quarterly.

15.13 Full text of New Zealand Cases?

Research tool	What information will it give me?	Tips on use
The New Zealand Law Reports Official • http://www.lexisnexis. co.nz/products/catalog/ browse/reference&LR/ LawsofNZ.asp	Reports cases from the Privy Council, the New Zealand Court of Appeal and the High Court (formerly the Supreme Court).	The Report is digested and indexed by its own integral series of digests and indexes and is updated by cumulative supplements.

Research tool	What information will it give me?	Tips on use
Brookers Online NZ Law Partner Legislation and Cases • http://brookersonline.co.nz/	Database includes BriefCase with access to over 42,000 full text, searchable decisions of the Supreme Court (all cases), Privy Council (all cases), Court of Appeal (all cases from 1986), and High Court (all available cases from 1986). FindCase updates the database daily.	Follow hyperlinks on main Search Screen. Basic Boolean search terms used, including 'and', 'or', 'not'. Truncate using *. Use inverted commas around phrases. For proximity searching use 'two or more words'@7. For ordered proximity use 'two or more words'/10. Use ? to replace a single character.
AustLII – New Zealand Case Law • http://www.austlii.edu.au/databases.html#nz	Decisions from: • Supreme Court of New Zealand 2004– • Court of Appeal of New Zealand 1999– • Human Rights Review Tribunal of New Zealand 2004– • New Zealand Privacy Commissioner 1996–	The site can be browsed or searched. Decisions can also be displayed in chronological order, with the most recent decision first.
Ministry of Justice – Judicial Decisions of Public Interest • http://www.justice.govt.nz/judgments/	This site provides access to the full text of selected judicial decisions from the Supreme Court, Court of Appeal and the High Court. Decisions are restricted to criminal sentences and judgments in which there may be a public interest.	The site can be browsed and the decisions are published in pdf form only. The site claims that decisions are generally made available within one day of being delivered by the Court.
Ministry of Justice – Tribunal Decisions • http://www.justice.govt.nz/tribunals/	Information about the tribunals including a brief description of their composition and work and links to individual tribunals' web pages.	In order to access the decisions follow the links at http://www.justice.govt.nz/judgments/othersources.html

15.14 Cases that have been judicially considered?

Research tool	What information will it give me?	Tips on use
The Abridgment of New Zealand Case Law • Looseleaf, updated by cumulative supplements	Digest of case law reported in the official reports.	A consolidated Table of Cases and Index are contained in Volume 17. A list of annotated cases and a list of words and phrases judicially considered are contained in Volume 18. Cases are classified under titles with contents pages, then summaries of cases. Cases classified for more than one title are repeated. Out of date cases have catchwords only.
The New Zealand Law Reports Official • http://www.lexisnexis. co.nz/products/catalog/ browse/reference&LR/ LawsofNZ.asp	Reports cases from the Privy Council, the New Zealand Court of Appeal and the High Court (formerly the Supreme Court).	The Report is digested and indexed by its own integral series of digests and indexes and is updated by cumulative supplements.

15.15 Cases that have dealt with specific legislative sections?

Research tool	What information will it give me?	Tips on use
Annotations to the New Zealand Statutes • Butterworths, 2 ed — Statutes • Looseleaf service, four volumes, updated monthly	Case annotations in relation to decisions that interpret statute law. Butterworths Annotations indexes these reported cases under the relevant acts and sections.	Need to know the title of the act and preferably the relevant sections in order to get easy access to the major cases decided referencing that act. Case annotations appear behind separate blue guide cards and are printed on blue pages.

Research tool	What information will it give me?	Tips on use
New Zealand Case Law Digest Thomson Brookers • Looseleaf, monthly updates	Summaries of reported and unreported judgments and decisions of New Zealand Courts and Tribunals.	A summary of each judgment and decision is published under a statutory or common law heading. There is a list of Cases Noted, Cases Cited, Statutes and Regulations and General Index. The Statutes and Regulations list refers to cases citing specific sections of legislation.

15.16 Journal articles and commentary?

Research tool	What information will it give me?	Tips on use
Index to New Zealand Legal Writing • Paper version	Volume 1, Part I contains information concerning books, articles and unpublished theses. Volume 1, Part II contains information about case notes. Volume 2 contains 'all cases reported in all law report series in New Zealand, where the court or tribunal included a person having District Court Judge Status or higher, and case notes, relating to the same decisions'.	The major subject areas have been divided into subcategories. It is only current to 1987.
WorldLII — New Zealand Law Journals • http://www.worldlii.org/catalog/53183.html	Links and information about electronic legal journals concerning legal matters in New Zealand.	The journals are listed in alphabetical order and the site is available in html format only.

Research tool	What information will it give me?	Tips on use
CaseBase Sydney: Butterworths, 1997– • In LexisNexis AU • http://www.lexisnexis.com	CaseBase Case Citator abbreviations for law reports and journal articles.	On the lower part of the LexisNexisAU Home screen, choose Quick Sources > Cases/Legislation and click on CaseBase Cases and Journal Articles. When the CaseBase search screen opens, look to the right under Related Links and choose the Abbreviations link. Within the search engine for 'cases', Jurisdiction and Courts can be limited to New Zealand only.

India —
How Do You Find

16.1 **An introduction to the jurisdiction?**

India is a federation of 28 States and seven centrally administered Union Territories. The Indian Parliament consists of the President and the Lower House, the Lok Sabha or House of the People, and the Upper House, the Rajya Sabha or Council of States. The Prime Minister is appointed by the President. Some states are bicameral and others unicameral. There is a federal Supreme Court and state High Courts. For further general information on this legal jurisdiction see the *Martindale-Hubbell International Law Digest* on LexisNexis. There is also a succinct section in Watt R, *Concise Legal Research* (6 ed, Sydney: The Federation Press, 2009).

Research tool	What information will it give me?	Tips on use
GLR — Online Guide to Indian Law • http://www.globallawreview.com	The guide contains various links to legal information in India, including the judiciary, information about standard legal texts, the structure of the legal profession and information about the Ministries and Departments. There are hyperlinks to the main Indian law websites including, for example, the Supreme Court of India and some of the 18 High Courts.	The site claims that the guide is always under construction and in order to ensure that each part is complete, there is occasional duplication, but each page has an indication of when it was last updated. Note: not in English.

Research tool	What information will it give me?	Tips on use
The World Factbook — India • http://www.cia.gov/cia/ publications/factbook/ geos/in.html#Govt	Contains a map, information and statistics under the following headings: • Introduction • Geography • People • Government • Economy • Communications • Transportation • Military • Transnational Issues.	The Government link contains legal information. The following symbol is a link to definitions of various concepts used on this site ▭
Law Library of Congress • http://www.loc.gov/law/ guide/india.html	The site contains useful Executive, Judicial and Legislative links and various other links to legal guides and miscellaneous materials.	This site can only be browsed. The site appears to be current.

16.2 A broad picture of Indian law?

Research tool	What information will it give me?	Tips on use
The Law Commission — Reports • http://lawcommission ofindia.nic.in/	List of Reports and access to the full text of recent Reports published by the Law Commission of India. This highlights the reform agenda for Indian law generally.	Only the most recent Reports, beginning with Report 170, are available in full text in pdf format.

16.3 Parliamentary publications?

Research tool	What information will it give me?	Tips on use
Parliament of India — Rajya Sabha • http://rajyasabha.nic.in/	Access to the Official Reports of the Parliamentary Proceedings of the Rajya Sabha, Parliamentary Business, Members, Questions, Debates, Committees, Procedures, Legislation before the House, Parliamentary Library and links to legislation and other official sites.	The site is very comprehensive, is searchable and browsable. It contains links to full text documents. Most documents appear in html format.

Research tool	What information will it give me?	Tips on use
Parliament of India — Lok Sabha • http://loksabha.nic.in/	Access to Debates, Questions, Legislation before the House, Procedures, Members and other Links.	The site is very comprehensive, is searchable and browsable. It contains links to full text documents. Most documents appear in html format.
The President of India's Website • http://presidentofindia. nic.in/welcome.html	This site links to separate pages for the Prime Minister and various government sites. There is additional information such as full text of the President's addresses to the Parliament, press releases, speeches and lectures.	The speeches are available in text format and can be listened to on the site.

Committee reports

Research tool	What information will it give me?	Tips on use
Parliamentary Committees • http://loksabha.nic.in/ (House of the People Committees) • http://rajyasabha.nic.in/ (Council of States Committees)	Contains links to the Parliamentary Committees home pages, which gives access to reports the Committees have tabled.	The site is browsable only. The Committees which do not table their Reports (and do not make them available to the public) are denoted by this symbol **.
Departmentally Related Standing Committees • http://164.100.24.208/ ls/committee/ depcomm.asp	Lists the various Committees in alpha-betical order and each Committee contains a link to its reports and list of members.	The sites are browsable only. The Reports are available in pdf format only.

Other parliamentary publications

Research tool	What information will it give me?	Tips on use
Constituent Assembly Debates on the Drafting of the Indian Constitution • http://164.100.24.208/ ls/condeb/debates.htm	Links to all of the debates in the Assembly in relation to the drafting of the Indian Constitution. The debates are dated from 9 December 1946 to 24 January 1950.	The debates are published in 12 volumes, which are listed in chronological order. Each volume is divided into the individual days when the debates took place. The site is browsable only and available in htm format.

16.4 **Bills?**

Research tool	What information will it give me?	Tips on use
Parliamentary Bills Information System • http://164.100.24.167: 8080/bills/search_form. asp	Information about the current stage of particular bills, such as the bill number and year, the short title, the type of bill, the member/minister in charge and the status.	The information about a particular bill is only available via a search. By choosing the particular Ministry to be searched, all bills relating to that topic or area are displayed.
Legislative Department • http://indiacode.nic.in	Full text access to: • Bills introduced in Rajya Sabha (Council of States) during current budget session; • Bills introduced in Lok Sabha (House of the People) during current budget session.	The site is browsable only and the full text information is available in pdf format only.
India Code Information System (INCODIS) • http://rajyasabha.nic.in/ bills-ls-rs/bills-ls-rs-main. htm	Full text of legislative bills as introduced in Rajya Sabha from 1999 to present and Lok Sabha as of 2005.	The site is browsable only by year of introduction and the format of the full text materials is pdf.
Lok Sabha — Status of Government Bills • http://parliamentofindia. nic.in/ls/bills/billsmain. htm	Full text of legislative bills as introduced in Lok Sabha from 1991 to 2002.	The site is browsable only and the available format is pdf. A link to the current Bills of Rajya Sabha is available.

16.5 Explanatory materials about Bills?

Research tool	What information will it give me?	Tips on use
Parliament of India, Rajya Sabha — Debates • http://rajyasabha.nic.in/ debate/official_debate. htm	Gives access to the full text records of the official debates of Rajya Sabha including debates concerning various Bills.	The link named 'Official Report (Proceedings)' gives access to records from 2000 to present. A search may be conducted by submitting session number and/or the time period and/or type of debate and/or key word.
Parliament of India, Rajya Sabha — Parliamentary Questions • http://164.100.24.219/ rsq/main.asp	Gives full text access to Parliamentary questions from 1990 to present, including Parliamentary questions concerning Bills.	In some instances, where the authoritative English text was not available, the Hindi text has been used.
Parliament of India, Lok Sabha — Debates (Proceedings) • http://loksabha.nic.in/	Full text access to proceedings other than questions and answers from 1991 to present.	The link titled 'Debates search' gives access to a user-friendly search template for documents from 2004 to present. The 'Debates Archive' link gives access to documents dated from 1991.
Parliament of India, Lok Sabha — Parliamentary Questions • http://loksabha.nic.in/	Full text access to Parliamentary questions raised in Lok Sabha from 2004 to present.	The link titled 'Search Questions' gives access to a user-friendly search template. The available format is plain text.

16.6 A subject index to legislation?

Research tool	What information will it give me?	Tips on use
Legislative Department • http://lawmin.nic.in/ Legis.htm	List of Central Acts in Alphabetical or Chronological order.	The site is browsable and the lists of Central Acts are displayed in htm format only. The lists are current as of 17/01/05.

16.7 Commencement dates for legislation?

Research tool	What information will it give me?	Tips on use
What's New? • http://lawmin.nic.in/ whatsnew.htm	This lists the latest acts with pdf files giving the full text. The acts note the date of commencement in Section 1.	The site is browsable only.

16.8 Indian legislation in full text?

Research tool	What information will it give me?	Tips on use
India Code Information System (INCODIS) • http://indiacode.nic.in/	Full text access to Acts as of 1834 to current. Use the Search Indiacode heading.	It appears that full text access to the Acts is only available through the search engine. The full text format is htm. By using the search option 'Act Year' users quickly gain access to full text versions of Acts for a particular year. Search by Act Year, Act Number, Section Number, Schedule Number, or 'A Word or a combination of Words appearing anywhere in the text of the Act. These words may be keywords only or even stopwords (ie, AND, OR, OF, IN etc)'.
The Indian Constitution • http://indiacode.nic.in/ coiweb/welcome.html	Access to the full text of the Constitution including updates to the 92nd Amendment Act.	The Indian Constitution has been published in parts on this site, as it is the longest document of its type, with almost 400 Articles. It has been amended on 92 occasions since 1950. The heading titled 'Index-wise access to Constitution of India' contains links to the various parts of the Constitution.
Indian legislation • http://www.commonlii. org/in/legis/num_act/	Constitution of India (CommonLII) and Indian numbered legislation based on data obtained from the India Code website.	Browse by year or legislation title. Full Boolean search facility available using AustLII software.

16.9 Updates for Legislation?

Research tool	What information will it give me?	Tips on use
Legislative Department — What's New — Latest Bills/Acts • http://lawmin.nic.in/whatsnew.htm	Gives full text access to the most recent Amendment Acts, Ordinances, Bills and Acts.	The site is browsable only, gives access to documents in pdf format and documents are available from 2003 to present.

16.10 Full text of delegated legislation?

Research tool	What information will it give me?	Tips on use
Legislative Department • http://lawmin.nic.in/ld/subord/legislation.htm	Full text access to Rules and Orders under the Constitution (Vol I) and Statutory Rules and Orders relating to Election Law (Vol II).	The site is browsable only and gives full text access in htm format.
Department of Legal Affairs • http://lawmin.nic.in/la/subord/legislation.htm	Full text access to subordinate legislation of the Department of Legal Affairs. The following four sources are available: • Appellate Tribunal for Foreign Exchange Rules • The Notaries Rules • Bar Council of India Rules • The National Legal Services Authority Rules.	The site is browsable only and gives full text access in html format.

16.11 Full text of Indian cases?

Research tool	What information will it give me?	Tips on use
Indian Law Reports (ILS) — Official Printed	Authorised report series containing High Court cases.	Even though this report series is authorised, it is often difficult to locate copies in Australian collections.

Research tool	What information will it give me?	Tips on use
All India Reporter (AIR) — Unofficial Printed	The reporter contains all of the reported cases of the Supreme Court from 1914 to present. The main series contain decisions from all the High Courts and courts of the Union Territories. The reporter also has a journal section which gives references to journal articles.	The various High Court decisions of each State are kept together and published within the series under the name of the State.
Judgement Information System (JUDIS) • http://www.judis.nic.in/	Comprehensive online case law library that contains all reportable judgments of the Supreme Court of India from 1950. It also contains case law from the following courts: • Delhi High Court • AP High Court • J & K High Court • Orissa High Court • Bombay High Court • Madras High Court • High Court of Bombay at Goa • Delhi District Court — Tis Hazari • Allahabad High Court • Allahabad HC — Lucknow Bench • Gauhati High Court • Chattisgarh High Court.	Each Court gives the user different search options in order to access case law. The format is html. The Supreme Court cases, for example, may be searched by Petitioner or Respondent's Name, Act Name, Judge Name, Text/Phrase, or Headnotes.

Research tool	What information will it give me?	Tips on use
Indian Caselaw on CommonLII • http://www.commonlii.org/resources/221.html	Supreme Court of India Decisions 1950–, High Court of Andhra Pradesh Decisions 1999–, High Court of Allahbad Decisions 1999–, High Court of Allahbad (Lucknow Bench) Decisions 2002–, High Court of Bombay Decisions 2000-2003, High Court of Bombay at Goa Decisions 2002–, High Court of Chattisgarh Decisions 2002–, High Court of Delhi Decisions 2004–, High Court of Gauhati Decisions 2003–, High Court of Jammu and Kashmir Decisions 2005–, High Court of Judicature at Patna Decisions 2003–, High Court of Kerala Decisions 2002–, High Court of Madras Decisions 2001–, High Court of Orissa Decisions 1999–, High Court of Punjab and Haryana Decisions 2000–, High Court of Rajasthan Decisions 2004–, High Court of Madhya Pradesh Decisions 2006–, High Court of Uttarakhand 2006–, District Court of Allahabad Decisions 2006–, District Court of Delhi Decisions 2003–, District Court of Kamrup Decisions 2005–, District Court of Nainital Decisions 2006–, District Court of Ranchi Decisions 2007–, Central Information Commission of India Decisions 2006–	Browse by year or legislation title. Full Boolean search facility available using AustLII software.

16.12 Cases that have dealt with specific legislative sections?

Research tool	What information will it give me?	Tips on use
Supreme Court Yearly Digest Lucknow: Eastern Book Co	This publication contains digests of the annual Supreme Court decisions arranged under topic and statute title.	The digest of cases covers cases from 1977 to present.

16.13 Journal articles and commentary?

Research tool	What information will it give me?	Tips on use
Legal Service India – Articles • http://www.legalserviceindia.com/articles/articles.html	Full text articles which have been published from 2001 to present.	Most of the articles have been given a rating out of five. The format is html and the site is browsable; however, a search option with Google is also available through the site.
Index to Indian Legal Periodicals New Delhi: The Indian Law Institute.	Indexes periodicals, including Year Books and other annual publications, pertaining to law and related fields published in India.	The materials are indexed under specific subject headings. A separate list of the cases which are being commented on is also included.
Commonlii • http://www.commonlii.org/resources/221.html	Law journal articles and other materials concerning India.	Browse by year or legislation title. Full Boolean search facility available using AustLII software.

Index

Abstract, 177–8
Acknowledging sources, 214–17
Acronyms and abbreviations, 195, 211
Action research, 10, 23, 116–17
Active progress management, 19
Active reading, 29
AGIS, 82–3, 90
Applied research, 6
Aristotle's topoi, 141
Assembling facts, 41
Audience, intended, 198–201
AustLII, 29, 83–4
    full text database, 83–4
Australian Digest database, 43, 84
Australian Standard Research
    Classification (ASRC), 6
Authorised reports, 87, 215

Background reading, 41–2, 160
Benchmarking, 123–4
    definition, 123
    policy research, 74
Bias
    conceptual framework, 187–8
    language, in, 31, 175
    scientific, 105
    writer, of, 175
Bibliographic approach to doctrinal
    research, 41–2
Bibliographic databases (BDBs), 29, 82
    AGIS, 82–3, 90
    CASEBASE, 82, 84
Bibliographical search cards, 28–9
Bibliography
    cards, 28–9
    running, 27

Biography, 112, 129–30
Black letter principles, 60
Boolean logic, 79, 91–2, 94
Brainstorming, 137–9
Broad to narrow approach, 43
Budgeting, 173–5

Card files, 28
Cartwheel of terms, 45, 88, 95–6
Case studies, 112–5
    advantages, 115
    disadvantages, 115
    methodologies, 114–5, 130–3
    use of, 168, 176–7
CASEBASE, 82, 84
Casenotes, 203–4
Cases
    case approach, 44
    citators, 42, 44
    citing, 215
    digests, 42, 44–5
    existing knowledge, using, 43–6
    headnotes, 30–1, 45
    keyword/case/legislation approach, 45
    medium neutral citation, 215
    reading, 30–1
Categorising topics, 46
Causes and effects mapping, 150
CD-ROM, 82
Centre for Plain Legal Language, 197
Changing contexts
    higher education sector, 18–21
    legal forces driving, 13–18

Checklists, using, 46–7
CINCH, 83
Citation analysis, 124–5, 127 see also
    Quantitative research
Citation guides, 214
Civil law, 121–2
Clarity, 196–7
'Closed Circle Factor', 49
Code of conduct, 25
    infringement of, 25
Common law, 12, 103, 121–2
    international agreements,
        incorporating, 13–14
    precedent, 11
Communicating, 40
Comparative common law jurisdictions,
    12, 119, 121
Comparative law, 14
Comparative research, 117–23
    advantages, 118
    aims, 118
    approaches, 119
    benchmarking, distinguished, 123
    corporate law, 120
    jurisdictions, 119, 121
    statistics, 120–1
Comparison rings, 149
Computers
    draft, organising, 185
    file backups, 185
Conceptual frameworks, 186–8
'Concordat', 17
Content anaylsis, 127
Context
    changes in, 12–21
    personal, 167
    topic, of, 160, 166–7
    work, of, 166–7
Cornell Note Taking Method, 182
Corporate law, 120
Cost-benefit analysis, 49, 72
Covey's time management matrix, 172–3
Critical race theory, 60
Critical reflective practice, 186, 192
Critical thinking, 33, 152–4
Customary law, 121
Cyclic maps, 147–8

Databases see also Electronic research;
    Electronic searches
    bibliographic, 28–9, 82–3, 90
    full text, 83
    generic search techniques, 86–95
    software, 29, 33, 86
    structure, 86–7
Dawkins Reforms, 18
De Bono's thinking hats, 143–4
Declaratory theory of judicial reasoning,
    60
Democratic principles, 60
Diary, 27, 185–6
Dictionaries, 41–2, 45
Directive words, 202–3
Doctor of Juridical Science, 171
Doctoral qualifications, 5–6
Doctrinal research
    bibliographic approach, 37, 41
    case approach, 44
    communicating, 22
    criticism, 22
    definition, 7, 36–7
    handy hints, 48
    hermeneutics, 36
    hypotheses, 23
    keyword/case/legislation approach, 45
    keyword/fact approach, 44
    law students, by, 22
    legislative approach, 44
    library based, 7, 39
    literature review, 37–8
    looseleaf approach, 45
    methodologies, 7–9, 22, 35–9
    planning, 22
    positivist model, 40–3
    practising lawyers, by, 22
    qualitative research, 27, 37
    records, 27–9
    reformist approach, 7
    sourcing information, 22, 27–8, 41–3
    standard research methods, 22, 39–40
    words and phrases approach, 45
Draft
    completing, 205–8
    editing, 208–11
    first, 205–8
    polishing, 208
    revising checklist, 208, 210
    rewriting checklist, 208–9
    writing process, approaches to, 206–8

Economic analysis of law, 60

Economic rationalism, 11

Editing draft, 208–11

Electronic citations, transience of, 215

Electronic research *see also* **Databases**
  acknowledging sources, 214–17
  Australian sources, overview, 83–4
  basic techniques, 79–80
  benefits, 80–1
  bibliographic databases, 82
  changes in, 79–81
  comparison of systems, 87, 149
  concept, 79–80
  fee-based online services, 82
  formats, 82–3
  full text databases, 83
  generic search techniques, 86–95
  internet, 82
  international online services, 84–5
  intranets, 82
  paradigm shift, 79–80
  searches *see* **Electronic searches**
  sources, 22
  structure of databases, 79, 86–7

Electronic searches *see also* **Databases**
  analogies, using, 88–9
  benefits, 80–1
  Boolean logic, 87, 91–2
  cartwheel of terms, 45, 88–9
  choosing search terms, 87–8
  generic techniques, 86–95
  logical operators, 91–2
  modification, 94
  natural language, 88
  optimum results, 95–6
  positional operators, 93
  retrieval, 94
  specific fields, 90–1
  truncation, 79, 93

Email, 172, 201, 207, 215–16

Empirical methodologies *see* **Social science methodologies**

Encyclopaedias, 41–2, 44, 47

EndNote, 29

Errors, checking for, 210

Essay writing, 202–3

Ethics, 24–7
  committees, 24, 176, 179
  ethical clearance, 24–5, 176
  misconduct, 25
  plagiarism, 24–7

research involving humans, 24, 176
  social science research, 25

Ethnography, 112, 131

Evaluation traps, 176

Examples, use of, 176–7

Existing knowledge, extending, 43–6

Experimental development, 7

Expert evidence, 105

External affairs power, 14

Fabrication of data, 24–5

Facts
  analysis, 41
  assembling, 41

Falsification of data, 24–5

FAMILY, 83

Fee based online services *see* **Electronic searches**

Feminist legal theory, 60

Final paper, structuring, 189–91

Fishbone diagrams, 147–8

Flowcharts, using, 47–8

Footnotes, 209, 214

Foreign law, 13

Foreign precedent, 13

Formalism, 60

Full text databases
  AustLII, 83–4

Fundamental research, 8

Gender neutral language, 213

Globalisation, 11, 18, 118

Government departments
  obtaining information from, 39
  policy research, 24, 39

Grammar, 211–12
  errors, checking for, 210

Grant applications, 161, 173, 177

Graphics, 146

Hardcopy sources, 22, 28–9

Heuristics, 139–43, 152, 155
  idea generators, 139

High Court
  changing composition of bench, 15–17
  Counter-Reformation, 17
  dissent studies, 126

High Court — *continued*
  jurimetric methodology, 125
  less closed view of, 12
  less formalist approach, 15
  new legalism, 17
  Reformation, 15
Higher education context, 18–21
  Bradley Report, 20
  Dawkins reforms, 18
  National Research Priorities, 20
Historical views, 138
Homosexuality
  social policy law, 64
  Tasmanian criminal sanctions, 14
Horrigan's project analysis matrix, 152–5
Hypothesis, 137

Ideas
  generators, 139–43
  mapping, 144–7
  sounding board, 178
  testing, 178–80
  visual demonstration, 147–52
Identifying legal issues, 41
Index to Legal Periodicals, 82–3
Inferences, drawing, 32
Information
  critiquing, 29–33
  gathering, 27–9
  indexing, 27–9
  note-taking, 27
  reading, 29–33
  sourcing, 41–3
  storage, 27–9
International agreements, 13–14
  common law incorporating, 14
Internationalisation, 11
Internet, 82 *see also* Electronic research
Intranets, 82 *see also* Electronic research
IRAC, 41

Judgments, 16–17, 27
Judicial notice, 104
Judicial reasoning
  declaratory theory, 60
Jurimetric methodologies, 125
Jurisprudence, 8
Jurisprudential method, 61–2

Keyword/case/legislation approach, 45
Keyword/fact approach, 44
  Knowledge, extending existing, 43–6
Kuhn, Thomas, 10

Langrehr's designs, 148–9
Language
  bias in, 31, 175, 187
  gender neutral, 213
  legal *see* Legal language
  plain legal language, 197–8
  surveys, used in, 110
Law
  modern context, 22
  several levels, existing on, 157
  traditional view of, 22
Law reform
  agencies, 63
  bodies, 64–5
  commissions, 51, 63–6
  concept, 63–4
  consultation, 63, 65, 67–71
  definition, 64–5
  history of, 51, 63–4
  methodology, 66–70
  policy research, distinguished, 124
  process, 68
  publications, 47, 65
  research, 23–4, 63–71
  technical aspects of law, 63–4
  topics covered, 64–5
  use of material, 65–6
  what is, 64–5
Law reports, 23, 28
Layout of chapters, 189–91
Legal framework, 186–8
Legal issues, identification, 41
Legal language
  economic elite, 196
  history, 196
  plain, 197–8
  premises and assumptions, 198
Legal research *see also* Doctrinal research;
    Methodologies
  amount required, 49
  broad to narrow, 43
  categorisation, 9, 46
  changing contexts, 12–21
  communication, 22
  conceptualisation, 22
  definitions of, 5–7, 20
  ethics, 24–7

Legal research — *continued*
  expanded frameworks, 23-4
  how much is enough, 49
  impact, 20-1
  knowledge, extending existing, 43-6
  law reform, 63-71
  methodology, 21-3
  paradigms, 9-11
  parameters, 7
  planning, 21-2, 27
  preparation, 35-9
  public policy, 71-7
  quality, 20-1
  recording the process, 27-9
  standard research methods, 39-40
  steps in formulating, 40-41
  what is, 5-7
  writing and, 5
Legal research frameworks *see also*
    Paradigms
  doctrinal *see* **Doctrinal research**
  expanded frameworks, 23-4
  law reform research, 23-4, 51
  policy research, 23-4
  theoretical research, 23, 51
Legal Resources Index, 83
Legal writing
  acknowledging sources, 214-17
  acronyms and abbreviations, 195-6,
    211
  active voice, 211-12
  audience, intended, 198-201
  basics, 168-219
  casenotes, 203-4
  citation guides, 214
  continual development, 196-7
  conveying message, 198-205
  current trends, 195-7
  editing draft, 208-11
  errors, checking for, 210
  essays, 202-3
  first draft, 205-11
  footnotes, 209, 214
  formulas, 201
  gender neutral language, 213
  grammar, 210-12
  intended audience, 198-201
  legal terminology, 196, 198
  office memos, 204-5
  organisation of work, 201
  paragraph construction, 211-12
  plain language, 197-8
  punctuation, 211, 216-17
  purpose, 198
  quotes, 213-14

  research and, 5
  rewriting draft, 208-11
  schedule, 206, 208
  sources, acknowledging, 214-17
  spelling, 210-12,
  style, 195-6, 201, 209, 211-17
  technical structure, 210
  wordiness, 196
Legislation
  Australian conditions, 12
  existing knowledge, 43
  history in Australia, 12
  interpretation and change, 11
  keyword/case/legislation approach, 45
  legislative approach, 44
  locating, 42
Legitimate expectation, 14
LEXISNEXIS, 79, 81-7, 89, 91-6
Liberalism, 11, 60
Library research, 39-40
Linear maps, 148
Literature reviews, 27, 181-5
Literature searches, 166
Looseleaf services, 41-2, 45

Mabo case, 14
Mapping ideas, 144-7
Maps
  hierarchical, 150-2
  interacting, 150-1
  radial, 150-1
Medium neutral citation, 215
Methodologies
  appropriateness, 168
  case studies from theses, 130-3
  comparative, 117-23
  comparing, 21-3
  definition, 21
  doctrinal, 21-2, 35-49
  jurimetric, 125
  law reform, 51, 63-71
  non-doctrinal, 23, 117-28
  policy research, 51, 71-7
  qualitative, 23, 106-7, 112-15
  quantitative, 23, 106-12
  research proposal, details in, 167-8
  social science based, 23
  standard research methods, 39-43
  testing, 23
  theoretical research, 7-8, 22-3, 51
  triangulation, 128-33

Mind mapping, 31, 144–7

Misleading ascription of authorship, 25–6

Mixed legal systems, 121

Modernism, 59, 61

Muslim law, 121

National Health and Medical Research Council, 24–6

Natural law principles, 52–4, 60

Neological seduction, 9

New legalism, 17

Non-doctrinal methodologies, 8, 23
benchmarking, 123–4
comparative research, 117–23
parameters, 97–135

Objectives, 165–7
achieving, 168
personal, 167
research, 167

Office memos, 204–5

Online research *see* Electronic research

Organisation of work, 201

Originality, 164–5

Paradigms
changing, 9
criteria, 9
critical race theory, 51
current legal research paradigm, 11
dominant, 11
economic analysis, 51
extension of, 51–2
feminist legal theory, 51
jurisprudential method, 61–2
liberalism, 11, 60
natural law, 51, 60
positivism, 11, 60–1
postmodernism, 61
shifts, 9–11
technology, impact of, 10
traditional research, 51
unifying rationale, as, 10
western legal tradition timeline, 53–9
what are, 10–11

Parallel story, writing, 185

Parameters of legal research, 7

Pearce Committee, 7–8, 51

Personal freedom, 60

PhD, 18, 22, 160–1

Phenomenology, 112, 131

Philosophical approach, 186–8

Plagiarism, 24–7, 217

Plain legal language, 197–8

Planning, 137
idea plan, 137, 144–52
research plan, 137

Policy research, 23–4, 71–7
benchmarking, 74
change cycle, 75–6
interdisciplinary perspectives, 72, 76
law reform, distinguished, 124
methodology, 73–5
public good, 71–2

Positivism, 11, 54, 60
Postmodernism, 61

Presentation of work in progress, 178–81
criteria sheet, 180

Primary material, locating, 38, 42–3, 47

Privy Council
abolition of appeals to, 12

Professional doctorate, 11, 18

Professional practice, 25

Progress, ensuring, 185–6

Public policy research, 51, 71–7

Publication of research, 169–70

Punctuation, 210–11, 216–17

Pure basic research, 6

Qualitative research, 106–7, 112–15
case studies, 113–15

Quantitative research, 106–12
citation analysis, 124–5, 127
design, 108
errors, recognising, 112
evaluation, 112
questionnaire design, 108
surveys, 108

Queensland Law Reform Commission, 65

Questionnaires, 108

Quotes, 203–4

Rationality, 60

Reading, 29–33
  active reading strategies, 29
  argument indicators, 31
  background, 41–2, 160
  bias, identifying, 31
  cases, 30–1
  critical, 33
  critiques, 32
  evaluation, 31–2
  inferences, drawing, 31–2
  topic, around, 160

Recording research process, 27–29

Reform-oriented research, 7

Research *see* **Legal research**

Research diary, 27, 185–6

Research hints, 48

Research progress presentation, 178–81

Research project
  abstract, 177–8
  steps in formulating, 40–1
  summary, 177–8

Research proposal
  budgeting, 173–4
  Covey's time management matrix,
      172–3
  critiquing, 175–7
  hypothesis, 167–8
  importance of, 165–6
  inclusions in, 165–6
  meaningful title, 168–9
  methodology, 168
  objectives, 167
  publication plans, 169–70
  research background, 166–7
  research question, 158, 168
  scheme of work, 170–2
  specificity, lack of, 175
  timelines, 159, 170–2
  title, 168–9
  traps, 175–6

Research Quality Framework, 19–20

Research techniques *see* **Electronic
      research**

Research topic
  academic background, 160
  Aristotle's topoi, 141
  brainstorming, 137–9
  causes and effects mapping, 150
  choosing, 11, 137
  context, 158, 160, 166–7
  criteria, 176–7, 180, 182–3
  De Bono's thinking hats, 143–4
  developing, 157–63
  epistemological framework, 167
  existing work, 159
  feasibility, 159
  fishbone diagrams, 147–8
  formulating, 137
  heuristics, 139–43
  Horrigan's project analysis matrix,
      152–5
  idea generators, 139–43
  interest in area, 163
  Langrehr's designs, 148–9
  likely outcomes, 163
  mapping ideas, 147–52
  mind mapping, 31, 144–7
  originality, 164–5
  parameters, 159
  personal context, 167
  planning, 137, 157, 166, 170, 172–3
  proposal *see* **Research proposal**
  reading around, 160
  refining, 157–63
  research strengths of faculty, 161
  resource-rich, 158
  scope, 160
  significance, 159
  slant on topic, 175
  supervisor's knowledge, 161
  topicality, 158
  traps, 175–6
  unresolved issues, 160
  visual demonstration of ideas, 147–52

Scheme of work, 170–3

Scientific bias, 105

Search engines, 80, 94, 149

Searches
  electronic *see* **Electronic searches**
  literature, 166

Social policy law, 64

Social research reports, 191

Social science
  expert evidence, 105
  judicial process, role in, 102–6

Social science methodologies
  action research, 116–17
  ethical issues, 25
  general, 97–9
  qualitative research, 98, 106–7, 112–15
  quantitative research, 98, 106–12
  reluctance to use, 98, 100–2
  role of social science in law, 102–6
  usefulness to lawyers, 99–100

Sources, acknowledging, 214–17

Sourcing information, 27–8, 41–3

Spelling and grammar, 210–12

Standard research methods, 39–40

Statistics, 100–2, 104, 106–7, 120–1, 126–7

Stereotyping, sexist, 213

Storage, 27–9

Strategic basic research, 6

Structuring project
layout of chapters, 189–91

Summary, 177–8

Supervisor, 161–3
access to, 162
knowledge of, 161
role perception rating scale, 162–3

Support groups, 181

Surveys
accompanying letter, 110
administration, 111
advantages, 109
appropriateness, 110
checklist, 110
design, 108
disadvantages, 109
internal organisation, 111
language considerations, 110
questionnaires, 108
threshold considerations, 110
timing, 111

Technology
impact of, 12
revolution, 12

Theoretical approach, 157, 162, 188–9, 191

Theoretical research, 7–8, 23, 51
definition, 7
methodologies, 23
paradigms, 51

Timeframe, 158–9
research proposal, 166

Timelines
example, 171
Western legal tradition, 53–9
work, for, 159, 170–3

Title, 157, 168–9

Topic *see* Research topic

Triangulation
case studies of methodologies, 130–3
complementary matrix, 129–30
definition, 128

United Nations Convention on the Rights of the Child, 14

United Nations Human Rights Committee, 14

Validation of sources, 38, 43

Visual demonstration of ideas, 147–52
causes and effects mapping, 150
fishbone diagrams, 147–8
Langrehr's designs, 148–9

Vocabulary, 212

Website addresses, 215–16

Western legal tradition timeline, 53–9

Westlaw, 81, 84–5

Words, directive, 202–3

Words and phrases approach, 45

Writing *see* Legal writing